The Definitive
Andy Griffith
Show Reference

The Definitive Andy Griffith Show Reference

*Episode-by-Episode, with
Cast and Production Biographies
and a Guide to Collectibles*

by Dale Robinson *and*
David Fernandes

McFarland & Company, Inc., Publishers
Jefferson, North Carolina, and London

LIBRARY OF CONGRESS CATALOGUING-IN-PUBLICATION DATA

Robinson, Dale, 1958–
  The definitive Andy Griffith show reference : episode-by-episode,
with cast and production biographies and a guide to collectibles /
by Dale Robinson and David Fernandes.
     p.   cm.
  Includes bibliographical references and index.

  ISBN 0-7864-2068-5 (softcover : 50# alk. paper)

  1. Andy Griffith show (Television program)   I. Fernandes, David,
1959–   . II. Title.
PN1992.77.A573R63   2004
791.45'72 — dc20   96-4042

British Library cataloguing data are available

Cover images ©2004 Photodisc and Clipart.com

Manufactured in the United States of America

*McFarland & Company, Inc., Publishers
  Box 611, Jefferson, North Carolina 28640
    www.mcfarlandpub.com*

This book is dedicated to Jack, Helen and Stan,
better known to me as my Dad, Mom and Brother.
Thank you for your never-ending patience, understanding, love and support.
Also, to Bernice and Judy Vieira,
Thank you for your kindness and a lifetime of love.
And to the memory of my Uncle Bill, whose sense of humor lives on in me.

—D.R.

and

To my family ... my parents, Glenn and Colleen, my sisters, Debbie and Rita,
my nieces, Brianna and Kristina, and my grandparents, Dorothy and Wayne Hull.
Your love and support mean everything to me.
And to the memory of my paternal grandparents, Lester and Ruth Fernandes.

—D.F.

ACKNOWLEDGMENTS

We would like to thank the following people for the encouragement, support and help during the writing of this book:

Carrie Adams, Dave Bakke, Mrs. Arlene Beebe, Karen Blaskie, L.W. Brannan, Bart Boatwright, David Britton, the Brookens Library at Sangamon State University, Gina Cagle, Fran Campbell, Ed Cannon, Kent and Diane Chapman, Pat Clarey, Mike Creech, Mrs. Leanne Dean, Charles Dowell, Donna Drummond, Eric and Diane Enz, Joyce Elliott, Bruce Evans, Rita Fenelon, Mary Ann Flynn, Everett Greenbaum, Russell Hiatt, Hoke Howell, John Hull, Michael and Linda Ippolito, Jim Leach, the Lincoln Library, Mike Magner, Dorothy and Charlie Menge, Martha Pate Morthole, Paul Mulik, Allan Newsome, Mark, Denise, Alisha and Sean Parks, Raymond Patterson, Margaret Ann Peterson, Kathy Petitte, Don and Mary Lou Read, Jim and Mary Read, Doug Schnell, James R. Schwenke, Mrs. Gloria Slavens, Brad Smith, Christy Smith, Mikel Snow, Alma and L.P. Venable, Johnny, Wilma and Gary Walker, Christy Woods and Allen Yow.

Special thanks to Diana Drummond for her patience, love and support.

And most of all, to our friend Jim Clark, thank you for your guidance, support and for all the confidence you gave to a couple of rookie writers.

TABLE OF CONTENTS

PREFACE

The life of every episode of *The Andy Griffith Show*—the quality that has sustained its popularity for nearly 30 years with enthusiastic fans nationwide — is in the details. With *The Definitive Andy Griffith Show Reference*, it is our intention to make these details available in a reference format. This book contains complete summaries for all 249 episodes of the series, as well as for the rarely seen pilot (which aired on *The Danny Thomas Show*), the first episode of "Mayberry R.F.D.," and the 1986 television reunion movie *Return to Mayberry*.

We have compiled this book because we believe that this beloved comedy series deserves to be honored with a detailed episode-by-episode guide.

We present the episodes in order of filming. (This is sometimes at odds with the order of their original air dates: for example, episode 161 was aired *before* episode 160. Today, in syndication, the episodes are usually broadcast in the order of filming.) Following the title, we note original air date, writer(s), and director. In each case, there follows a thorough summary of the episode. Next come "Cast Notes," which briefly lists regular cast members appearing and then deals in more detail with guest stars, providing short biographies and lists of credits where possible.

These notes are followed by "Episode Notes," which provides further details on such topics as characters, sets, and music in the episode. Within these notes you will also find some discussion of how certain details, such as place and character names, were apparently inspired by real places and people from Andy Griffith's childhood. Griffith was born and raised in the small town of Mount Airy, North Carolina, and it is widely acknowledged that this town often served as a model for Mayberry.

In addition to the episode summaries, this book contains extensive information on the lives and careers of the people who made *The Andy Griffith Show* possible. This information may be found following the episode summaries, in sections entitled "Regular Cast," "Producers and Directors," and "Writers." For music lovers, we have also included a biography of Earle Hagen, the man responsible for the music on the show.

The final section, an appendix titled "Collecting Memories of Mayberry," discusses series-related material available (or, sometimes, rumored to be available) for sale, such as books, video tapes, and memorabilia.

Our main objective in writing this book was to do justice to a series that has been close to our hearts since we were children. We hope we have accomplished this objective.

Dale Robinson
David Fernandes
December 1995

INTRODUCTION: ANDY LORE

There are countless ways that Americans (and viewers from other countries, too) show their love for *The Andy Griffith Show* and the mythical land of Mayberry. Most of us simply enjoy watching the show on a daily basis. Some of us purchase Mayberry memorabilia from catalogs like *The Mayberry Collection*. Thousands of us belong to The Andy Griffith Show Rerun Watchers Club, founded by (Presiding Goober) Jim Clark. Jim, with Ken Beck, wrote *The Andy Griffith Show Book*. They also compiled a Mayberry-related cookbook. T.A.G.S.R.W.C. issues the official newsletter (*The Bullet*) of *The Andy Griffith Show*. It is chock-full of information and updates on cast and crew, and on the 800 separate chapters of the club. The club has an impressive list of honorary members, such as the Bellamy Brothers, Clint Black, Roy Clark, Katie Couric, Phil Donahue, Radney Foster, Amy Grant, Lee Greenwood, Emmylou Harris, Alan Jackson, George Jones, the Judds, the Kentucky Headhunters, Lyle Lovett, Barbara and Louise Mandrell, Kathy Mattea, Charly McLain, Reba McIntire, John Prine, Marty Stuart, Randy Travis, Travis Tritt, and (last, and possibly least) Bob Uecker (just kidding, Bob...).

Some fans have created replicas of the squad car used on the series. These ambitious fans include Bill Flynn, Rodney Thomas, David Hollen, Luther Venable (who, with wife Alma, operates Mount Airy's Mayberry Motor Inn), and Bob Scheib. Mr. Scheib also built a full-size replica of Wally's Service Station, near his Bradford, Ohio, home. Since 1993, it has served as a site of an annual gathering of "Andy" fans, who flock in from all over to see it, meet other fans and mingle with such celebrities as George Lindsey, Howard Morris, Betty Lynn and Jean Carson.

Looking for a bite to eat? Try the Snappy Lunch in Mount Airy, North Carolina; the Blue Goose in Starkville, Mississippi; the Mayberry Cafe in Danville, Indiana; Brown's Diner in Nashville, Tennessee; or Dick's Hot Dog Stand in Wilson, North Carolina. For dessert, try any one of several Mayberry Ice Cream Restaurants sprinkled throughout North Carolina.

Listen to a radio or watch TNN and you may hear such tributes as Confederate Railroad's "Elvis and Andy," The Lonely Riders' "Nip It," "The Andy Griffith Show" by the Bellamy Brothers, or Joe D. Herrings' songs "Down in Mayberry" and "Ernest T. Bass." Other musicians, such as Danny Hutchins and Chuck Burns and Don Huber, also include Mayberry-related songs in their repertoires.

Interested in radio? Chances are you've heard of Larry King and Rush Limbaugh. Though vastly different in their political views, each has used themes from *The Andy Griffith Show* on his program. If you are near Cincinnati, Ohio, tune in WMOH AM, 1450 on the dial. Every Saturday morning from 10:00 A.M. to 12:00 P.M. (EST), D.J.'s Dennis Hasty and Golden Richards bring us "Good Morning, Mayberry."

Other media besides radio have honored the series. Gene Sculatti's *Catalog of Cool* included

The Andy Griffith Show. A 1989 episode of *48 Hours* on syndicated television referred to the show as an "evergreen program" because of its long-lasting popularity.

Mayberry is thoroughly ingrained in the pop culture and in the minds of both young and old. A commercial for Old Milwaukee beer featured the theme song from the show and in an episode of *Silver Spoons*, the song is whistled by a father and son on a camping trip. There have been many references to the show on other television series, such as *St. Elsewhere*, *It's Garry Shandling's Show*, and *Wiseguy*. You'll see other references in ads and comic strips, and you may hear such Andy-isms as "Nip it in the bud!" or "Citizen's Arr-ay-est!" in everyday conversation. There's even a series of Andy-related Shoebox Greeting Cards. Computer buffs who love the series can connect with one another on Prodigy and Internet. And if you wish to further your education (like Ernest T. Bass), why not enroll in a course on *The Andy Griffith Show*? Neal Brower teaches a college course on the subject!

"We've all heard of someone who has a bird that can whistle some song or another, but on a 1993 segment of *America's Funniest Home Videos*, a cockatiel from North Carolina whistled the theme from *The Andy Griffith Show* and won its family $10,000. That should keep him in bird feed the rest of his life!

Next time you're in Buena Park, California, be sure to check out the wax statues of Andy, Barney, and Gomer at the Movieland Wax Museum.

A fine place to stay, the Mayberry Motor Inn (note the area code is now 910).

Our Trips to the Mecca of Mayberry

April 1992

When we began our 800-mile journey to Andy Griffith's birthplace, Mount Airy, North Carolina, we were uncertain about what we would find there. Would the eagerly anticipated vacation be worth the long drive — or would we discover that Mount Airy is just another Anytown, U.S.A., with a population of 7,000?

As we approached the town, our doubts seemed justified. It was raining so hard that we could barely see the road, much less locate our residence for the next few days. We began to wonder just how we would explain to our family and friends back in Illinois that we managed to get lost in such a small town. Moments later, we spotted the Mayberry Motor Inn, and our spirits

Top: **Items from the Aunt Bee room on display at the Mayberry Motor Inn in Mount Airy.** *Bottom:* **The real Mount Pilot, Pilot Mountain State Park in North Carolina. It is located 14 miles from Mount Airy.**

brightened—especially when the first thing that caught our eye was Andy and Barney's squad car in the parking lot.

The owners of the Mayberry Motor Inn are Luther and Alma Venable. They have worked tirelessly to make their inn a treasure trove for fans of the series. The lobby is decorated with photos and posters of Andy Griffith, as well as other celebrities, such as country singer Donna Fargo. You may remember her hits, "The Happiest Girl in the Whole U.S.A." and "Funny Face."

Like Andy Griffith, Ms. Fargo was born in Mount Airy. Also in the lobby are numerous souvenirs of the show, such as T-shirts, fly swatters, books, and trading cards. A unique feature at the inn is the Aunt Bee Room. This lovely tribute to America's favorite aunt was decorated and furnished by Alma, with artifacts that once belonged to Aunt Bee herself, actress Frances Bavier.

The squad car we saw in the parking lot was Luther's labor of love — a 1963 Ford Galaxie, painstakingly restored to produce an exact replica of the squad car used in the series. It even has the familiar license plate JL 327 on the front, and the rarely seen DC 269 plate on the back of the car.

We took a drive around town and gazed at the many historical homes and lovely churches. The town is much larger than we imagined. Many smaller towns border Mount Airy, and we smiled as we drove through tiny Bannertown, recalling that in the series it was home to Parnell Rigsby, who lost $50.00 in episode 136, "Opie's Fortune."

Later, we returned to the inn and had a great conversation with Alma and Luther. They filled us in on the history of Mount Airy and treated us as if we were long-lost relatives. They also told us about the real Earlie Gilley, who is mentioned a few times in the series. He owns an automotive repair shop in nearby Pilot Mountain, better known as "Mount Pilot" to fans of the series. The town is located about 14 miles from Mount Airy. The mountain itself towers over the town, rising 2,421 feet above sea level, and is the center of a beautiful state park. It was used as a lookout by Confederate forces during the Civil War.

Earlie Gilley is married to the former Lorraine Beasley, who was also mentioned in the series. Lorraine is Andy Griffith's cousin. The Venables and Gilleys used to go square-dancing together.

On the next day, we visited the downtown area of Mount Airy. Main Street is lined with dozens of lovely shops, run by some of the friendliest people on earth. We met so many nice folks, including Jim Kemp, Earlie McKinnon, Dawn Miller, Paula Eubanks, and Carol Burnett, among others. No, this Carol Burnett is not the famous comedienne: she is a very kind sales clerk at the Mount Airy Art Market, where you may buy some one-of-a-kind Mayberry artwork of your favorite characters.

All of the merchants are wonderful, but there are two proprietors, who are legends in their own time: Russell Hiatt and Charles Dowell.

Mr. Hiatt was surely the inspiration for Floyd the barber. He owns and operates Floyd's City Barbershop on Main Street. The place is always full of customers and visitors, but Russell will always find the time to visit, even while he is cutting hair. He also found the time to give a couple of wide-eyed guys from Illinois some nifty souvenirs. Memorabilia from *The Andy Griffith Show* abounds in this cozy shop, while hundreds of photos of satisfied customers cover the walls. Russell is a true gentleman and a tireless worker.

Right next door to the barbershop is the Snappy Lunch, which is mentioned in episode 9, "Andy the Matchmaker." Its owner and chef, Charles Dowell, has worked there for over 50 years. Charles remembers when a youthful Andy Griffith used to patronize the restaurant, usually buying a five-cent bologna sandwich. Once seated at the restaurant, we noticed some great photos of Andy and other cast members adorning the walls. There are also some historic photos of Mount Airy.

The town was wonderful, and it was a joy to meet Luther and Alma Venable, as well as their young grandson, Mikel Snow (who loves to collect police badges and dress up in his Mayberry sheriff's uniform). Unfortunately, we had to leave all too soon. However, we vowed to return as soon as possible.

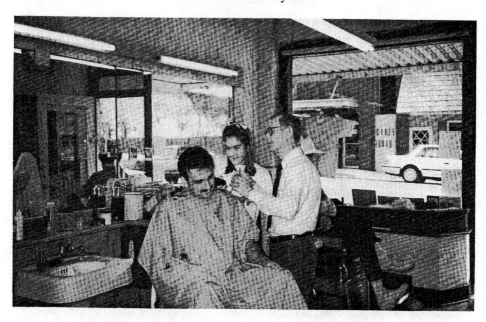

Top: The real Floyd the Barber (Russell Hiatt) teaching a newcomer the tricks of the trade. *Bottom:* Pictures of hundreds of satisfied customers and fans of *The Andy Griffith Show* grace the walls of Floyd's City Barber Shop in downtown Mount Airy, North Carolina.

May 1993

Somehow, the second trip seemed shorter than the first one. We were returning to our adopted "stompin' grounds." We easily located the Mayberry Motor Inn, and once again enjoyed seeing our friends Alma and Luther Venable.

This time, in addition to the friends we had made on our first trip, we had some specific sites we wanted to visit.

Top: Aunt Bea's Family Restaurant in Mount Airy, North Carolina. (The traditional spelling is "Bea," which actress Frances Bavier agreed with. However, the writers always spelled it "Bee." Ms. Bavier had no affiliation with the restaurant.) *Bottom:* A look inside the Aunt Bee Room at the Mayberry Motor Inn — Mount Airy, North Carolina. The room was furnished with items that once belonged to Frances Bavier, and are now owned by Alma and L.P. Venable.

First, we located the nearby White Plains Church and cemetery. At this site, we found the graves of the original Siamese twins, Chang and Eng Bunker. The famous twins toured with the circus throughout the late 1800s before they settled in Mount Airy and became farmers. Both raised large families, and some of their descendants still live in the area.

We also visited the Mount Airy Granite Quarry, which is the largest open-face granite quarry in the world. Many buildings in town and all over the country are built from the granite taken from this quarry.

Emmett's Fix-It Shop truck, owned by L.P. Venable of Mount Airy, North Carolina.

The last big item on our agenda was to locate the newly built Mayberry courthouse and Otis's jail cell. We found it at the old county courthouse in Mount Airy, which now houses Friendly Plumbing and Heating. We enjoyed our visit. The courthouse and cell were constructed with careful attention to detail. The tour is free, but drop a few coins in the bucket by the entrance when you visit. The proceeds are used to maintain this charming salute to Mayberry.

April 1994

Our third trip to the Mecca of Mayberry in as many years, was pleasing to the eye as well as the soul. Mount Airy felt more like home than ever. It was great to see the friendly faces of Luther and Alma once again. Our accommodations were, as always, comfortable and spotless.

Luther had added a blue pickup truck to his collection. The words "Emmett's Fix-It Shop" were emblazoned on its doors. It sat next to the squad car, and together they were a sight to behold! On Main Street, our first stop was Floyd's City Barber Shop, where we found Russell Hiatt. He was busy, as usual, but took the time to chat with us. While we were there, we discovered that Mount Airy had been selected as one of the top 100 communities in North Carolina. (A few months later, Mount Airy was chosen as one of the top 10 towns in America.)

We enjoyed visiting with Ms. Burnett at the Mayberry Art Market, and we stopped in at the new Visitor's Center, which is also located on Main Street. It is housed in a lovely structure, and we were warmly greeted at the front door by a nice lady named Susie Caldwell. She gave us a tour and offered us a chance to watch a brief videotape about the town. Afterwards, we viewed the Andy Griffith memorabilia room. Much of the awe-inspiring display is from the collection of Emmitt Forrest, a lifelong friend of Andy's. Mr. Forrest was the inspiration for fix-it man Emmett Clark on the series and still lives in Mount Airy. Among the items on display are comic

Top: The Mayberry Mall in Mount Airy, North Carolina. *Bottom:* Many plays and concerts in Mount Airy are presented at the Andy Griffith Playhouse.

and coloring books from the series, records, numerous autographed photos, a *MAD Magazine* version of "What It Was Was Football," letters from Andy, and much more. In separate rooms are items about the town itself. The Visitor's Center is a must-see attraction for fans of *The Andy Griffith Show*.

If you plan to visit Mount Airy, you might want to arrive near the end of September. Every year at this time, the entire town becomes "Mayberry" for a special weekend known as

Mayberry Days. This celebration features all kinds of music, games, food, and "Andy"-related activities.

Whenever you choose to visit, the town will welcome you with open arms. We suggest you reserve a room in advance at the Mayberry Motor Inn, located on Highway 52 in Mount Airy, North Carolina, 27030. The phone number is (910) 786-4109. You will be treated with true southern hospitality, and the rooms are reasonably priced.

There are many other great places to stay when you come to Mount Airy. The friendly folks at these nice lodgings will be happy to see you: the Bluvue Motel (Mount Airy's first motel!), Callaway Motel, City View Motel, Comfort Inn, the Hollows, Holly Inn Motel, and Star-Lite Motel. For those folks who want a bed and breakfast, we recommend the Pine Ridge Inn. Finally, for those who like to commune with nature (like Barney Fife in "Back to Nature") try the Blue Ridge Campground. Just follow the call of the web-footed red crested lake loon!

Our days in Mount Airy are among our most cherished experiences. We hope to return again and again. If, as Andy Griffith has said, Mayberry is a fictional town, so be it. But Mount Airy is remarkably similar. Make a visit and judge for yourself.

THE EPISODES

THE PILOT

Many television pilots go nowhere, but thanks to a tremendous effort by cast and crew, the pilot episode for *The Andy Griffith Show* was an exception. Until "Nick at Nite" picked up *The Danny Thomas Show* in the early 1990s, many devoted fans of *The Andy Griffith Show* had never seen the pilot. If you get a chance to see it sometime, don't miss the opportunity.

"Danny Meets Andy Griffith"

Pilot Episode. Air Date: 2-15-60. Writer: Arthur Stander. Director: Sheldon Leonard.

Entertainer Danny Williams and his family are returning to their home in New York after vacationing in the south. After entering the small, rural town of Mayberry, North Carolina, Danny is pulled over by the local sheriff, Andy Taylor. Andy explains that he pulled Mr. Williams over because he ignored a stop sign. The exasperated driver says that he did not stop because there was no oncoming traffic in either direction, and he points out that, oddly, there was no intersecting road. Andy informs him that, about six years ago, the town council voted to build a road. Unfortunately, they were only able to raise enough money to put up a stop sign. Danny finds this entire situation to be a farce. When he demands to see the justice of the peace in order to get out of this "tourist trap travesty," he learns that Andy is Mayberry's justice of the peace. Danny threatens to tell his story to the editor of the town's newspaper, *The Mayberry Gazette*, only to discover that *Andy* is the editor.

Next, an amazed Danny looks on as the town drunk, a man named Will Hoople, stumbles into the courthouse, announces that he is arresting himself and then locks himself in a jail cell.

This is all too much for Danny to take. He declares that he has a good reason to hurry home to New York. He is scheduled to appear on the television program *Face to Face* and be interviewed by its host, Ted Parker. Andy says that if he pays a $5 fine, he can be on his way. Danny produces a large wad of money and flaunts it in front of Andy. This prompts the lawman to raise the fine to $100 or 10 days in jail. Danny is outraged. Eventually, he says he will take the jail sentence.

Danny calls Ted Parker and explains his predicament. Mr. Parker suggests that the interview could be done as a live remote broadcast from Mayberry. He arranges for a nearby CBS affiliate to set up the necessary cameras and lights at the courthouse. Danny brags that he will be able to tell some 40 million viewers about the injustice that has been heaped onto him.

Before this occurs, Andy's young son, Opie, comes into the courthouse, crying. He is upset because his pet turtle, Wilford, has just been killed. It seems that Opie had set Wilford down on the floor of the ice cream parlor, and a customer, Mrs. Balford, accidentally stepped on him. Opie asks Andy to arrest Mrs. Balford, give her a fair trial "and then hang her." Andy explains that Opie must learn to deal with his sorrows in the same way that Andy himself dealt with the loss of Opie's mother. Andy manages to cheer his son a bit by announcing that Wilford will receive a fine burial. Afterwards, Andy will cook up some barbecued ribs and tell Opie about the tortoise and the hare.

Andy has another matter to deal with before Danny's scheduled television broadcast. He gently reminds an elderly Mayberrian named Henrietta Perkins that she has not paid her taxes for two years. The poor widow confesses her sorrowful story. When her husband, Charlie, passed away two years ago, Henrietta wanted him to look elegant while he lay in state. It seems that Charlie had been a failure in most aspects of life, but his loving widow wanted him to go out in style. She rented a full dress suit from Mr. Johnson's hand-me-down store.

However, she forgot to tell the undertaker to remove the suit from Charlie just prior to burial! Ornery Mr. Johnson penalized her by making her pay him fifty cents per day ever since. If she refused to pay, Mr. Johnson would tell the entire town and cause her great embarrassment. Because she has paid over $350 to Johnson, she has been unable to pay her taxes. Andy promises to take care of this unfair situation. He orders Mr. Johnson to refund more than $300 to Mrs. Perkins or be charged with fraud. Mr. Johnson reluctantly agrees to refund the money.

Finally, the nationwide broadcast begins. Andy stays off-camera while Danny tells the world of his plight. But when Danny comments on the "poor conditions" at the courthouse, Andy feels compelled to step forward to contradict him. When Mr. Parker asks Andy about the outrageous fine levied against Danny, Andy admits that this is a special case. He explains that he wanted Mr. Williams to "feel the weight of the law." As a wealthy entertainer adored by millions, Danny has a responsibility to set a good example, Andy explains. The usual fine of $5 or $10 would have meant nothing to him. A more substantial penalty was necessary to make him aware of the law. Andy adds that he wanted to slow Danny down a little so that he might appreciate the beautiful countryside or take the opportunity to meet people.

Danny realizes what a buffoon he has been, and he apologizes to Andy before the broadcast ends. Perhaps Andy isn't such a country bumpkin after all. However, apology or no apology, Danny still has seven days left in his jail sentence, unless he pays a $70 fine. Tightwad that he is, he chooses to stay in jail.

CAST NOTES. The regulars from *The Danny Thomas Show* who appear are **Danny Thomas** as Danny Williams, a successful New York nightclub entertainer; **Marjorie Lord** as Kathy Williams, Danny's wife; **Rusty Hamer** as Rusty Williams, Danny's son; and **Angela Cartwright** as Linda Williams, Danny's daughter. **Andy Griffith** stars as Sheriff Andy Taylor. **Ronny Howard** also stars as Opie Taylor. **Frances Bavier** appears as Henrietta Perkins. She will soon be better known as Aunt Bee Taylor. **Frank Cady** appears as the town drunk, Will Hoople. On *The Andy Griffith Show*, the character will be known as Otis Campbell (as played by Hal Smith). Mr. Cady is best known for his role as Sam Drucker on *Petticoat Junction*. **Bill Baldwin** appears as Ted Parker. **Will Wright**, who would become known to *Andy* fans as crusty Ben Weaver, appears in a similar role as the cigar-smoking Mr. Johnson. **Rance Howard**, proud father of Ron and Clint Howard, appears briefly in this episode as the

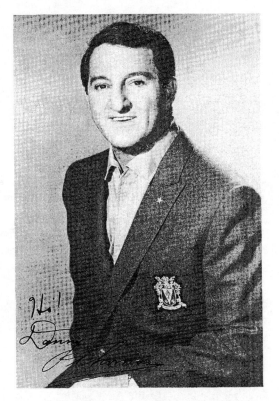

Danny Thomas—a television legend.

television director. His dialogue in the episode is, "That's it. Wrap it up."

EPISODE NOTES. 1. This episode aired as a segment of the long-running series *The Danny Thomas Show*. In syndication the series is known as "Make Room for Daddy." 2. The musical team of Herbert Spencer and Earle Hagen provided the music for this episode. Both of these men would later provide the music for *The Andy Griffith Show*. 3. Danny's nicknames for Andy include Clem, Hayseed, a Jesse James with a badge, an imitation Wyatt Earp, a backwoods racketeer with a badge, a crooked politician, an ornery and greedy critter, a southern fried politician, Simon Legree, a tyrant, a one-man Gestapo, a rube, and a hick. 4. Danny refers to Mayberry as a tourist trap and as Hicksville. 5. As one exits the courthouse, a hardware store is to the immediate left and a barber shop to the immediate right. 6. Pictures of George Washington and Ulysses S. Grant hang behind Andy's desk in the courthouse. 7. Will Hoople's father preceded him as the town drunk before he died. 8. Danny refuses to eat the fine meals that Andy serves him. Instead he asks for bread and water. 9. Sarah is the name of Mayberry's telephone operator. 10. Andy and Opie's housekeeper is

Andy's Aunt Lucy. She prepares the prisoners' meals and cleans the jail on a daily basis. She's won several shirt-washing contests at the county fair. 11. Andy implies that Danny Williams has a large nose. 12. Danny's wife and two children do not stay in Mayberry. He sends them on to New York.

COMMERCIAL. *Note: It was a fairly common practice for television shows in the 1960s to conclude their broadcasts with advertisements featuring characters and situations from the episode just aired. The* Andy Griffith Show *was no exception. We were able to view a few of the original CBS broadcasts that included such advertisements. Where possible, we have provided summaries of these ads.*

The setting is the Mayberry courthouse and Andy and Danny are standing next to an old-fashioned coffee machine that Andy uses. Andy is turning the wheels that are affixed to both sides of the odd-looking contraption. Danny observes that small-town people are "way behind when it comes to making coffee" and counsels Andy to use Instant Maxwell House instead. Danny goes to great lengths to explain this marvelous innovation. Andy listens carefully — then pulls out his own jar of Instant Maxwell House Coffee, which he had already purchased at the general store. Addressing the camera, Andy says that anyone passing through Mayberry should stop at the general store and pick up a jar of Instant Maxwell House. Danny ruefully reminds viewers to "watch out for the stop sign."

SEASON ONE

The first season of *The Andy Griffith Show* introduced us to many nice folks, such as the Taylor family, Barney Fife, and Ellie Walker. The very Southern dialect, particularly that of Andy and Barney, would be noticeably toned down by the season's end. A.C. Nielsen Co. rating for the 1960–1961 season: 27.8; rank: 4.

"The New Housekeeper"

Episode #1. Air date: 10-3-60. Writers: Jack Elinson and Charles Stewart. Director: Sheldon Leonard.

Andy and Opie's housekeeper and mother figure, Rose, is marrying Wilbur Pine and moving away. Andy's Aunt Bee is coming to live with them and raise Opie, just as she raised Andy years before. Aunt Bee is thrilled to be needed. Opie pleads for Rose to stay, but Andy explains that she is leaving for good.

Opie attempts to show Andy that Aunt Bee is not needed. In a great scene, Opie prepares some 45-minute boiled eggs for Andy, who can't help chuckling at his son's feeble attempt to keep the Taylor household all male. Andy explains to him that he will learn to love Aunt Bee as much as or even more than Rose.

When Aunt Bee arrives, Opie immediately rejects her. He tells Andy that Aunt Bee can't fish, hunt frogs, or play baseball like Rose did. These are important things for a little boy. Andy attempts to teach Aunt Bee, but she is a total washout as an angler and athlete. The situation worsens when Aunt Bee accidentally allows Opie's pet bird, Dickie, to escape from his cage. Believing that Opie will never accept her, Aunt Bee regretfully decides to leave.

Upon overhearing Aunt Bee's farewell to Andy, Opie rushes to her and begs her to stay. He reasons that Aunt Bee needs *him* to teach her the important things like fishing, hunting frogs, and playing baseball. Aunt Bee and Andy happily agree, and the foundation for *The Andy Griffith Show* is firmly established in this touching scene.

By the way, Dickie finds his way back home all by himself.

MEMORABLE SCENES. 1. Opie asking Andy's permission to run away from home. 2. "Naughty Deputy" Barney Fife arresting Emma Brand for jaywalking in the middle of Maple Street.

CAST NOTES. Regulars: **Andy Griffith, Don Knotts, Ronny Howard,** and **Frances Bavier.**

Mary Treen appears as Rose. Treen, who would also appear in the series as various townspeople, was born in St. Louis, Missouri, on March 27, 1907. Among her regular TV roles are Emily Dodger on "Willy" (1954–55) and Hilda on *The Joey Bishop Show* (1962–65). She guest-starred in several series, most notably on *The Donna Reed Show, Green Acres,* and *The Brady Bunch* (as Kay, who takes Alice's housekeeping job after she temporarily quits). Treen has appeared in more than 100 movies, including *The G-Men* (1935, with James Cagney), *It's a Wonderful Life* (1946, with Jimmy Stewart), *Paradise, Hawaiian Style* (1966, with Elvis Presley), and *The Strongest Man in the World* (1975, with Kurt Russell). In later years, Treen, working with a former vaudeville partner, entertained elder citizens at sanitariums and rest homes near her home in Balboa Beach, California.

Frank Ferguson portrays Wilbur Pine. Ferguson would also appear in many roles on the series, most notably as grocer Charlie Foley. Ferguson was born on Christmas day in 1899 and died on September 12, 1978. Among his regular television roles were Gus Broeberg on *My Friend Flicka* (1956–57) and Eli Carson on the prime-time serial *Peyton Place*

(1964–69). When the latter series became a daytime serial in 1972, he returned as Eli and continued in the role until the serial ended in 1974. He guest-starred in many series, including episodes for *Petticoat Junction, Gunsmoke, Lassie, No Time for Sergeants, Green Acres, Bonanza, The Real McCoys, Sugar Foot, The Danny Thomas Show, Leave It to Beaver, Kung Fu,* and *Maverick.* He also appeared in the 1976 made-for-television film *The Macahans* as Grandpa Macahan. Ferguson appeared in scores of motion pictures, many of them westerns. His films include *Life Begins for Andy Hardy* (1941, with Mickey Rooney), *They Died with Their Boots On* (1941, with Errol Flynn and Olivia DeHavilland), *Rhapsody in Blue* (1945, with Robert Alda), *Night and Day* (1946, with Cary Grant), *Fort Apache* (1948, with John Wayne and Henry Fonda), *The West Point Story* (1950), *Bend of the River* (1952, with Jimmy Stewart), *The Big Leaguer* (1953, with Edward G. Robinson), *Tribute to a Bad Man* (1956, with James Cagney), *The Phantom Stagecoach* (1957), *Sunrise at Campobello* (1960), *A Pocketful of Miracles* (1961, director Frank Capra's final effort), *Hush, Hush, Sweet Charlotte* (1964, with Bette Davis), and *The Great Sioux Massacre* (1965).

Cheerio Meredith appears as Emma Brand. Meredith would repeat this role during the first season. However, in the second season, she appeared as Emma Watson. The name change was never mentioned or explained. Meredith was born in 1890 and died on Christmas day, 1964. She was a regular performer on *The Ames Brothers Show* in 1955 and a regular cast member on the 1961 series *One Happy Family* as Lovey Hackett. Among the many series in which she guest-starred are *The Donna Reed Show, Bonanza, Many Happy Returns,* and *The Dick Van Dyke Show.* (In the latter, she appeared as Miss Prinder in the episode "Teacher's Petrie.") Meredith was quite active in movies, too. Among them are *The Fat Man* (1951, with Rock Hudson), *I'll Cry Tomorrow* (1955, with Susan Hayward), *I Married a Woman* (1958, with "Lonesome" George Gobel), *The Legend of Tom Dooley* (1958, starring a young Michael Landon), *The Three Stooges in Orbit* (1962), and *The Wonderful World of the Brothers Grimm* (1962).

EPISODE NOTES. 1. Andy performs the wedding ceremony between Rose and Wilbur in his role as justice of the peace. 2. Barney plays "Here Comes the Bride" (a.k.a. "The Wedding March") on harmonica during the marriage ceremony. 3. Barney refers to himself as "Reliable Barney Fife." 4. This is the only episode in which Rose and Wilbur Pine appeared and the only episode in which Andy is shown owning a pickup truck. 5. Fried chicken and watermelon are two of Opie's favorite foods, according to Andy. 6. Andy and Opie perform a duet on "The Crawdad Song." 7. During Opie's bedtime prayer, he asks God to bless the following: his pa, his bird Dickie, his lizard Oscar (who ran away), Barney Fife, his friends Jerry, Tommy, and Billy, his dog Gulliver, his white mouse, his snake, and Rose, even though she ran away and got married. 8. In April of 1993, Ron Howard revealed on the television show *Later with Bob Costas* that as a child he actually owned a pet dog named Gulliver. 9. Andy claims that he and Barney are cousins. 10. In five episodes in the series, including this one, a publicity picture of Frances Bavier (Aunt Bee) in her younger days can be seen hanging on the wall in the Taylors' home. In this episode, the picture is hanging on the wall to the right of the kitchen door. Andy and Aunt Bee pass it as they enter the kitchen after Aunt Bee first arrives. We will note the other appearances of the picture as they occur.

COMMERCIAL. Opie is in his room, looking at his pet bird, Dickie, who is in his cage. Andy walks in, drinking a cup of Sanka coffee. Opie and Andy speculate on why Dickie returned. Andy says he might have come back for the good food. He then suggests that Opie finish Dickie's next meal with a cup of Sanka. When Opie expresses surprise, Andy points out that Dickie is a "modern bird" and Sanka is a "modern coffee." Opie finally objects, reminding his pa that parakeets don't drink coffee. Andy turns to the camera and remarks that the sponsor doesn't know that. He then urges viewers to enjoy some Sanka themselves.

"The Manhunt"

Episode #2. Air date: 10-10-60. Writers: Charles Stewart and Jack Elinson. Director: Don Weis.

Opie believes his pa is the most important person in the world. He shares this thought with Andy as they fish from their patched-up boat named Gertrude. The boat promptly springs a leak, ending the fishing for the day.

Barney reports to Andy that an escaped convict named Dirksen is reportedly heading toward Mayberry. Captain Barker of the state police arrives in town with a large contingent of troopers. Barker arrogantly refuses to accept Andy and Barney's assistance in the manhunt, saying their time could be better spent chasing chicken thieves.

When the citizens of Mayberry begin questioning their public servants' lack of involvement in the case, Opie publicly defends his pa. This inspires Andy to take action, even without the support of the state police. An energetic Barney sets up a road-block and stops such citizens as a lifelong resident of Mayberry named Cal, the mayor, and even his own mother. Barney is soon ambushed by Dirksen and loses his gun to the criminal.

Captain Barker scolds Andy and Barney for their blundering and orders them to stay out of the way. Andy won't hear a word of it. He has a hunch that Dirksen may be enticed by the homemade pies Emma Brand makes daily at her lakeside cabin. Andy's hunch is right, and, through Emma, he indirectly informs Dirksen of the whereabouts of old Gertrude. Next, Andy notifies Captain Barker, who arrives at the Old Crystal Creek entrance to the lake just as Dirksen discovers the leaks in Gertrude. Barker makes an easy arrest as Dirksen swims right up to the shore to him. Andy's reputation as a lawman is preserved in the eyes of his son and the townsfolk.

CAST NOTES. Regulars: **Andy Griffith, Don Knotts, Ronny Howard,** and **Francis Bavier. Hal Smith** makes his first appearance as Otis Campbell. **Cheerio Meredith** returns as Emma Brand.

Dick Elliott appears for the first time as the mayor of Mayberry. In upcoming episodes he will be referred to as Mayor Pike. In this episode, he's simply called "Mayor." Mayor Pike's character was based on a resident of Andy Griffith's hometown, Mount Airy, North Carolina. The gentleman's name was Floyd Pike and he was a well-respected businessman. Elliott (1886–1961) made well over 60 films during his career. He was a wonderful comic actor. He guest-starred in such series as *Superman, The Rifleman,* and *I Love Lucy.* He appeared in two episodes of the latter program: first, in "Lucy Is Envious," as a man named Henry, and then as a spectator at a Cleveland Indians/New York Yankees baseball game in the episode "Lucy and Bob Hope." Elliott's unique manner of speech and his flair for comedy served him especially well in films. Among his movies: *Mr. Smith Goes to Washington* (1939, starring Jimmy Stewart and directed by Frank Capra), *Wintertime* (1943, with skater Sonja Henie), *Christmas in Connecticut* (1945, with Barbara Stanwyck), *Night Unto Night* (1949, with future United States president Ronald Reagan), *Don't Knock the Rock* (1956, with Bill Haley and His Comets and Little Richard), and *Up in Smoke* (1957).

Ken Lynch stars as Captain Barker. Lynch made a career as a character actor, portraying policemen and investigators in numerous movies and television shows. He was a regular performer on the 1949–54 series *The Plainclothesman.* His character was simply referred to as "the Lieutenant." Most viewers know him as Sergeant Grover from

television's *McCloud,* 1970–77. Lynch has appeared on countless other programs in guest-starring roles. Among the most well known: *All in the Family, The Big Valley, Bonanza, The Dick Van Dyke Show, The Fugitive, Gomer Pyle, U.S.M.C., Gunsmoke, The Honeymooners, How the West Was Won, Kung Fu, The Lucy Show, Maverick, The Munsters, The Patty Duke Show, Perry Mason, Star Trek* (as Vanderberg in "The Devil in the Dark"), *The Twilight Zone* (as Charlie in "Mr. Denton on Doomsday"), *Wagon Train,* and *The Wild Wild West.* Somehow, Lynch found the time to build an impressive movie career. Among his films: *When Willie Comes Marching Home* (1950, directed by John Ford), *Run Silent, Run Deep* (1958, with Clark Gable and Burt Lancaster), *I Married a Monster from Outer Space* (1958), *Pork Chop Hill* (1959, with Gregory Peck), *The Legend of Tom Dooley* (1959, with Michael Landon), *Anatomy of a Murder* (1959, with James Stewart and Lee Remick), *North by Northwest* (1959, starring Cary Grant and directed by Alfred Hitchcock), *Walk on the Wild Side* (1962, with Jane Fonda), *The Days of Wine and Roses* (1962, with Jack Lemmon and Lee Remick), *Dead Ringer* (1964, with Bette Davis), *Mister Buddwing* (1966, with James Garner), *Hotel* (1966, with Rod Taylor), and *Run, Simon, Run* (1970, with Burt Reynolds). The latter film is also known as *Savage Run.*

Norman Leavitt appears as Cal. Leavitt would appear as other characters in the series, most notably as Wally, the owner of Mayberry's only gas station. This dour-looking funnyman has made many television appearances in such series as *The Addams Family, The Beverly Hillbillies* (including one episode called "The Clampetts and the Dodgers," in which Coach Leo Durocher likes Jethro's pitching arm; Leavitt plays an attendant), *The Big Valley, Dennis the Menace, Desi-Lu Playhouse* (he was in three hour-long episodes of this variation of *I Love Lucy,* including an appearance as a chauffeur in the final episode, "Lucy Meets a Mustache," in 1960), *Green Acres, Gunsmoke, The Guns of Will Sonnett, Kung Fu, Lassie, The Lucy Show, Mayberry R.F.D.* (appearing in a few episodes as Mailman Felton), *Mister Ed, Rawhide, The Twilight Zone* (as Sheriff Gilchrist in "Mr. Garrity and the Graves"), *Wagon Train,* and *The Wild Wild West.* He has also appeared in several movies, including *The Harvey Girls* (1946, with Judy Garland), *Yellow Sky* (1948, with Gregory Peck), *The Inspector General* (1949, with Danny Kaye), *Harvey* (1950, with Jimmy Stewart), *Showboat* (1951), *O. Henry's Full House* (1952), *The Long, Long Trailer* (1954, with Lucille Ball and Desi Arnaz), *Friendly Persuasion* (1956, with Gary Cooper), *Jumbo* (1962, with Doris Day), *The Patsy* (1964, with Jerry Lewis), *McHale's Navy Joins the*

Air Force (1965, with Tim Conway), and *The Marriage of a Young Stockbroker* (1971).

Burt Mustin makes his first of many appearances on the series. He always portrayed a Mayberry resident with time on his hands. Mustin was born in Pittsburgh, Pennsylvania, on February 18, 1884, and died on January 28, 1977. Before he began his television and movie career at the age of 67, he was a car salesman. On television he had regular roles in many series, including *Date with the Angels* as Mr. Finley (1957–58), *Ichabod and Me* as Olaf (1961–62), *The Funny Side* with Queenie Smith as the old couple (1971), *All in the Family* as Jason Quigley (1973–76), and *Phyllis* as Arthur Lanson (1976). From 1950 to 1965 he was seen many times on *The Jack Benny Show* as the guard of Mr. Benny's bank vault. Many viewers loved him as the occasionally seen fireman Gus on *Leave It to Beaver*. His list of guest appearances is quite extensive, including *The Fugitive, Get Smart, The Lucy Show, The New Andy Griffith Show, Gomer Pyle, U.S.M.C., Mayberry R.F.D., The Beverly Hillbillies, Bewitched, The Dick Van Dyke Show, My Three Sons, The Brady Bunch, Rowan and Martin's Laugh-In, Batman,* and two very special episodes of *The Twilight Zone.* (In an episode originally aired on December 23, 1960, and titled "Night of the Meek," Mustin plays a friendly bum. Art Carney is outstanding in the lead role, as a man who is transformed, literally, into Santa Claus. In another episode titled, "Kick the Can," Mustin is seen as Mr. Carlson. The episode deals with aged citizens recapturing their youth.) Mustin's movie appearances are numerous. Here is a small sampling of his better-known films: *The Detective Story* (1951, with Kirk Douglas), *The Desperate Hours* (1955, with Humphrey Bogart), *The Thrill of It All* (1963, with Doris Day), *The Killers* (1965, with Ronald Reagan in his final film), *The Cincinnati Kid* (1965, with Steve McQueen), *Cat Ballou* (1965, with Lee Marvin), *The Reluctant Astronaut* (1967, with Don Knotts), *Speedway* (1968, with Elvis Presley), *Hail, Hero!* (1969, with a young Michael Douglas), and *The Skin Game* (1971, with James Garner and Louis Gossett, Jr.).

Lillian Culver portrays Barney's mother. This is the only episode in which viewers get to see Mrs. Fife. Her only line is "But Barney, I'm your mother!" **Mike Steen** appeared as the sergeant, **Frank Gerstle** as Dirksen, and **Frank Challee** also appears.

AWARD NOTE. This episode earned the writers, Charles Stewart and Jack Elinson, the prestigious Writer's Guild of America award, for best writing in a comedy or variety series.

EPISODE NOTES. 1. Andy catches a fish using a piece of ham as bait. 2. Otis Campbell sings in the Mayberry choir. 3. Three of Captain Barker's state troopers are named Wilson, Walters, and Porter. 4. Barney claims to have perfect 20/20 vision. 5. Emma Brand suffers from sciatica. The afflication causes pain in the back and hips. 6. Barney refers to the squad car as Unit 1. 7. Andy refers to Barney as his cousin. 8. Dirksen's mug shot number is 7458. His prison uniform number is 2604. 9. Barney accidentally shoots off his gun in its holster for the first time in this episode. 10. Andy and Barney's squad car is a Ford Galaxie. In this episode and most others, the license plate number is JL-327. 11. The music that would soon become known as Barney's theme, "The Manhunt," is played as the state police arrive in Mayberry.

"The Guitar Player"

Episode #3. Air date: 10-17-60. Writers: Jack Elinson and Charles Stewart. Director: Don Weis.

Jim Lindsey, Mayberry's resident guitar whiz, has a bad habit of playing rock 'n' roll in front of Orville Monroe's Funeral Parlor and Mortuary. Mr. Monroe takes exception to this and repeatedly forces Andy to arrest Jim for disturbing the peace. Andy knows that Jim has the talent to become famous and encourages him to pursue a career in music. Jim doesn't believe he has what it takes and cannot be budged.

Andy gets an idea when a musical group called Bobby Fleet and His Band with a Beat stops at Mayberry while on their way to a gig at the state capital. In order to get the shy guitar player and the sharp-tongued Mr. Fleet together, Andy has to trump up a few legal charges. First, he sentences Bobby and his band to spend 24 hours in jail after finding them guilty of illegal parking, insult to the dignity of his robes, and bribery. Next, Andy arrests Jim for the sole purpose of getting all the musicians together. When Jim and Bobby meet at the jail, Jim is too shy to show off his talent, so Andy coaxes him into playing by asking him to tune his guitar. While Jim is tuning, Bobby infuriates him by making one too many wisecracks about the "beautiful" sounds emanating from the instrument. As soon as Jim finishes tuning, he loses his inhibitions and gets down with some heavy duty rock 'n' roll playing that impresses Bobby Fleet. In fact, Bobby "digs" Jim so much he offers him a job with the band. Andy serves as Jim's agent and secures the young guitar player $75 to $100 per week from the somewhat reluctant Mr. Fleet.

MEMORABLE SCENE. Barney conducting the band and getting down to the sound.

CAST NOTES. Regulars: **Andy Griffith, Don Knotts, Ronny Howard** and **Frances Bavier.**

James Best stars as Jim Lindsey. He would reprise this role in episode 31, "The Guitar Player Returns." Best was born on July 26, 1926, in Croydon, Indiana. A male model in his younger days, Best has also taught acting. He has had a long career in television and on the screen. In the 1950s and early 1960s, Best appeared on many dramatic anthology programs, such as *G.E. Theater* and *Dupont Theatre.* Among his regular roles, he was Gotch on *Temple Houston* (1963–1964) and Sheriff Roscoe P. Coltrane on *The Dukes of Hazzard* (1979–1985). He has appeared as a guest star in countless series, many of them westerns. Here is an abbreviated list of shows he appeared on: *Alfred Hitchcock Presents, Amos Burke, Ben Casey, The Bob Cummings Show, Bonanza, Centennial* (the 1978 mini-series), *Combat, Dan August, Death Valley Days, Destry* (a 1964 episode, as Curly Beamer), *Enos, Flipper, The Fugitive, The Green Hornet, Gunsmoke, The Guns of Will Sonnett, Have Gun, Will Travel, Hawaiian Eye, Hawk, Hawkins, In the Heat of the Night, I Spy, Lancer, Laramie, The Mod Squad, Perry Mason, Rawhide, The Rebel, Redigo, The Rifleman, Surfside 6, The Texan, The Twilight Zone* (in three cajun-flavored episodes), *The Virginian, Wagon Train, Wanted: Dead or Alive* and *Whispering Smith.* In 1978, Best starred as the artist Walter Anderson in a PBS special called *The Islander.* Best has appeared in several movies made for TV, including *Run, Simon, Run* (1970), *Savages* (1974, as Sherrif Hamilton, with Andy Griffith). *The Runaway Barge* (1975, as "Bingo"), and *The Savage Bees* (1976). Some of the many films in which Best has appeared include *Commanche Territory* (1950), *Winchester 73* (1950), *Francis Goes to West Point* (1952, with Donald O'Connor), *The President's Lady* (1953, with Charlton Heston), *The Caine Mutiny* (1954, with Humphrey Bogart), *The Rack* (1956, with Paul Newman), *The Naked and the Dead* (1958), *The Left-Handed Gun* (1958, with Paul Newman), *Verboten!* (1959), *The Killer Shrew* (1959), *The Mountain Road* (1960, with Jimmy Stewart), *Shock Corridor* (1963), *Shenandoah* (1965, with Jimmy Stewart), *Three on a Couch* (1966), *Sounder* (1972, with Cicely Tyson), *Ode to Billy Joe* (1976, with Robby Benson), *Rolling Thunder* (1977, with William Devane), *The End* (1978, with Burt Reynolds), and *Hooper* (1978, with Burt Reynolds). In 1991, the multi-talented Best wrote, directed, and starred in the play "Hellbent for Good Times."

Henry Slate portrays Bobby Fleet. In subsequent episodes, other actors would take over this role. Mr. Slate appeared in the TV series *Adventures in Paradise* in 1960 and 1961. The name of his character was Bulldog Lovey.

Jonathan Hole makes his first appearance as Orville Monroe. Mayberry's mortician/TV repairman made a career making guest appearances on TV. He had a regular role on the 1950 series *Stud's Place* as Mr. Denby. He appeared as a guest star in a couple of pilots in the mid to late 1960s, neither of which led to a series. Other programs on which Hole has appeared include *The Addams Family, Batman, The Big Valley, Dennis the Menace, Green Acres, Kung Fu, The Lucy Show, The Man from U.N.C.L.E., Maverick, Perry Mason, Petticoat Junction,* and *Rawhide.* Many viewers may remember him in two episodes of *The Brady Bunch.* (He appeared in the episode "The Possible Dream," in which Cindy gives away Marcia's diary. In "Tell It Like It Is," he appears as photographer Willie Witherspoon. The plot involves Carol writing an article about her family.) In movies, Hole's best-known film must be director Mike Nichols' 1967 masterpiece *The Graduate,* which starred Anne Bancroft and Dustin Hoffman. In 1972, Hole made a film called *Til Death,* although it was not released until 1978.

Veteran character actor **Dub Taylor** appears as Talbot, the Mayberry postmaster. **Connie Van** also appears.

EPISODE NOTES. 1. Jim bought his new guitar pick in Winston-Salem. 2. Aunt Bee's chicken and dumplings are a favorite of Jim's. 3. Barney and Talbot, the postmaster, argue over who is going to get the best wanted posters for their respective bulletin boards. 4. Bobby Fleet calls Andy "Hiram" and "Charlie" during the episode. Andy calls Barney "Tiger." 5. Barney tells Andy that Bobby Fleet is "one of those joke crackers." 6. Bobby Fleet claims the inscription "If lost, please return to Wyatt Earp" appears on the back of Andy's badge. 7. Andy sings "New River Train" with Jim. Barney joins in on the second chorus. This is one of the numbers Rafe Hollister performs in episode 83, "Rafe Hollister Sings." 8. Barney auditions, in vain, for Bobby Fleet on harmonica by playing what will become his standard harmonica piece, "Jingle Bells." 9. Orville Monroe's Funeral Parlor and Mortuary is located next door to the barbershop. 10. It is interesting to note that Jim Lindsey gets electric guitar sounds out of an acoustic guitar with no amplifier.

"Runaway Kid"

Episode #4. Air date: 11-7-60. Writer: Arthur Stander. Director: Don Weis.

As a prank, Opie and his pals Steve and Tommy push Andy's squad car in front of a fireplug.

Ever-efficient Barney Fife writes Andy a citation for the offense. In a funny scene, Andy defends himself and convinces Barney that mischief makers were responsible for the deed. Meanwhile, Opie confides to Andy that he and his friends were the perpetrators of the practical joke. Andy warns Opie that he should never snitch on his friends, and even though he appreciates his son's honesty, he reminds him that he should never break a trust.

Later Opie befriends an eight-year-old runaway boy from nearby Eastmont, George "Tex" Foley. Tex is passing through Mayberry on his way to Texas, where he plans to become a cowboy. Andy is in a dilemma because although he promised Opie that he would not tell George's parents his whereabouts, he realizes that Mr. and Mrs. Foley must be worried sick. Andy uses some nifty child psychology on Tex to convince him to return home. The tactics work, and Andy telephones the Foleys to say that he is bringing George home. Opie feels betrayed by his father and reminds Andy that he has broken their trust. Andy explains that sometimes the rules need to be broken when a third party may get hurt. Opie understands and happily accompanies Andy and George to Eastmont.

CAST NOTES. Andy Griffith, Don Knotts, Ronny Howard, and Frances Bavier.

Pat Rosson stars as George "Tex" Foley. Rosson appeared in many shows throughout the 1960s, including Dennis the Menace. Dennis Holmes and Donald Losby appear as Opie's pals, Steve and Tommy, respectively.

EPISODE NOTES. 1. The Mayberry Theater can be seen during the scenes filmed outside the courthouse. 2. The Mayberry Hotel is located directly across the street from the courthouse. 3. George Foley was born in August. 4. Barney refers to Andy as his cousin. 5. Opie owns a pet frog. 6. Opie prepares the following culinary delights for Tex to take with him on the road: a peanut butter and sardine sandwich, a peanut butter and bologna sandwich, a peanut butter and liverwurst sandwich, and a peanut butter and peanut butter sandwich. He also sends along some sweet pickles, olives, marshmallows, and bubblegum. 7. Tex had also considered running away to Wyoming. 8. Barney is said to own an automobile in this episode. This bit of information causes a discrepancy with the premise of the storyline in episode 90, "Barney's First Car."

"Opie's Charity"

Episode #5. Air date: 11-28-60. Writer: Arthur Stander. Director: Don Weis.

Annabelle Silby is the chairperson for the Underprivileged Children's Charity Drive that is currently underway in Mayberry. She is a proud woman. Two years earlier, her husband Tom was supposedly run over by a taxicab while on a business trip in Charlottesville. Annabelle never publicly acknowledged that Tom was a heavy drinker and not quite the upstanding citizen she had him made out to be. She was simply too proud. In fact, she gave Tom the finest funeral Mayberry had ever seen.

When Annabelle informs Andy that Opie has contributed only a measly three pennies to the Underprivileged Children's Drive, Andy gets upset. After referring to his youngster as "Moneybags" and "Diamond Jim," Andy encourages Opie to give more money to such an important cause. Opie explains to his pa that he cannot contribute more money because he's planning to spend his entire savings, $2.20, on a present for his girlfriend Charlotte. Andy is not pleased with his playboy son.

Meanwhile, Andy is shocked when none other than Tom Silby shows up at the courthouse. As Tom and Andy go visit Mr. Silby's "grave," they both come to the conclusion that Annabelle was too proud to admit she couldn't hold on to her wandering husband. Tom also admits that after two years, he misses his wife. He says he has been sober for many months.

Later, Andy stops insisting that Opie should increase his donation when Aunt Bee reminds him that Opie is a fine young man and must have a good reason for his apparent stinginess. Andy reluctantly agrees. When Opie returns home, Andy tells him that he has permission to buy Charlotte's present without any further interference. Opie informs him he is buying his girlfriend a winter coat because her mother cannot afford one. An embarrassed Andy realizes what a terrific son he has.

CAST NOTES. Regulars: Andy Griffith, Ronny Howard and Frances Bavier.

Stuart Erwin appears at Tom Silby. Erwin starred in the 1950s television series The Stu Erwin Show, and in 1936 he was nominated for a best supporting actor Oscar for his work in the motion picture Pigskin Parade.

Lurene Tuttle portrays Annabelle Silby. In the 1930s Tuttle starred on radio as detective Sam Spade's secretary, Effie. She has appeared in numerous television shows throughout the years as a character actress. In her most familiar television role, she co-starred with Lloyd Nolan and Diahann Carroll as head nurse Hannah Yarby on Julia from 1968 through 1971.

EPISODE NOTES. 1. In this episode, the town of Mayberry is said to be located in Mayberry

County. The size of the county is 267 square miles. 2. Opie's classmate, Roy Pruitt, contributed the second lowest amount to the Underprivileged Children's Drive. Roy donated five cents, but he can be forgiven because he is one of the underprivileged children. 3. Andy recalls the time that a carnival man passed through Mayberry with a stuffed whale. A large crowd came to see it. 4. The mayor of Mayberry was a man named Jenkins when Tom Silby "passed away." 5. Sam Peabody is a Mayberry alderman. 6. Tom Silby was a member of the Mayberry lodge, and he sang second tenor in their chorus. 7. At Tom Silby's "funeral," his lodge brothers sang "We're Brothers Together." 8. The inscription on Tom Silby's grave reads: *RIP/THOMAS SILBY/"A FINE MAN AND A DEAR HUSBAND"/1908- 1958.* 9. Grover's Place, Cornwell's Station, Tate Warren's Store, and Banner Street are Mayberry locations mentioned in this episode. 10. Andy proclaims that Jonas Conway raises prize-winning pigs on his farm. 11. Opie gave his friend Jimmy a sock in the head for making fun of Charlotte. 12. This is the first of three episodes in which the license place number on the Mayberry squad car is not JL-327. In this episode, episode 6, "Ellie Comes to Town," and episode 9, "Andy the Matchmaker," the license plate number is DC-269. 13. Tonic with a beer chaser was one of Tom Silby's favorite drinks before he got off the booze.

"Ellie Comes to Town"

Episode #6. Air date: 10-24-60. Writers: Charles Stewart and Jack Elinson. Director: Don Weis.

Young and beautiful Elinor Walker has just arrived in Mayberry. She is a recent graduate of Bernard University, where she earned her degree in pharmacy. Ellie has come to assist her uncle, Fred Walker, at his establishment, Walker's Drugstore. Fred has been in ill health for some time, and Ellie is immediately put in charge of the pharmacy. As she is going to work on her first day, she discovers two strangers inside the closed store. Ellie alerts Barney, who promptly discovers that the "crooks" are none other than Andy and Aunt Bee. Andy explains that Fred has always allowed him to help himself. Ellie tells him she will not condone this way of doing business.

A few minutes later, she encounters her second problem of the day. This time it's hypochondriac Emma Brand. All Emma wants to do is purchase her 10-cent pills, but Ellie refuses to sell them without a doctor's prescription. Emma claims she will die without her pills, but Ellie won't budge. As a

disappointed Emma leaves, Andy remarks that she is already starting to walk crooked. The lady druggist is not winning any popularity contests in her new town.

Later, Ellie discovers through Fred that Emma's pills are made entirely out of sugar and they have a placebo effect on all of Emma's many ailments. When Ellie explains to Andy, he remarks that he had always thought that 10 cents was a small price to pay for a miracle drug.

The townsfolk accept Ellie and she settles in for her all-too-brief stay in Mayberry.

MEMORABLE SCENES. 1. Ellie and Opie making faces at each other in the drugstore window. 2. Barney attempting to recite the sheriff's rules to Andy. For the record, the sheriff's rules read as follows: "An officer of the law shall enforce the law and order without regard to personal welfare and safety."

CAST NOTES. Regulars: **Andy Griffith, Don Knotts, Ronny Howard,** and **Frances Bavier. Elinor Donahue** makes her first appearance in the series.

Cheerio Meredith returns as Emma Brand.

EPISODE NOTES. 1. The license plate number on the squad car is DC-269. It is the second of three episodes where it is not JL-327. The first one is episode 5, "Opie's Charity," and the third one is episode 9, "Andy the Matchmaker." 2. Ellie's degree in pharmacy is known as a Ph.G. Andy asks her if the initials stand for "Pharmacy Gal." 3. Fred Walker keeps the key to the drugstore above the front door. 4. An ice cream cone costs a dime at Walker's Drugstore. 5. During World War II, Andy spent some time in Paris, France. 6. Ellie drives a Ford station wagon. 7. Walker's Drugstore is located across the street from the courthouse. 8. When Ellie refuses to sell Emma her "medication," Barney recalls the court case of Wilson *vs.* Thorpe's Pharmacy. The trial took place in Mount Cory in 1952 and was concerned with the fact that Mr. Thorpe did not want to sell arsenic to Mr. Wilson. Thorpe claimed that Wilson was mentally unstable. The court ruled in favor of Mr. Wilson on Tuesday, May 4. Barney notes that Wilson was buried on Friday, May 7. 9. A discrepancy occurs in this episode over where Emma Brand lives. In episode 2, "The Manhunt," she lives in a cabin by the lake. In this episode, she is shown living in the heart of Mayberry.

"Irresistible Andy"

Episode #7. Air date: 10-31-60. Writer: David Adler. Director: Don Weis.

When Ellie accepts Andy's invitation to the upcoming church picnic and dance, he begins to wonder if she was a bit too eager in her acceptance. He stews about the subject until at last he convinces himself that Ellie is desperate to marry him. He relates this to Aunt Bee, and Opie overhears their conversation. Aunt Bee doesn't believe his theory for a minute, but Andy is convinced. In order to combat this "deadly female hunter," Andy enlists the aid of three of Mayberry's most eligible bachelors to try to woo Ellie and make her forget about him. The three bachelors are Pete Johnson, the possessor of long eyelashes; Franklin Pomeroy, who has the cutest little nose; and Charlie Beasley, who is a muscleman. Ellie is puzzled by the attention she is receiving from the three men, until Opie lets the cat out of the bag. Ellie furiously confronts Andy and randomly selects Barney Fife as her escort. Andy gives Barney a work assignment on the day of the church event in the hope that Ellie will accept his apology and be his date. After she slams her front door in his face four times, Ellie finally accepts, but she takes along Opie as a second escort.

MEMORABLE SCENE. The three bachelors (and Andy) displaying their physical assets.

CAST NOTES. Regulars: **Andy Griffith, Don Knotts, Ronny Howard, Frances Bavier,** and **Elinor Donahue.**

Harry Antrim appears as Fred Walker. Antrim was born in Chicago, Illinois, in 1895 and died in 1967. Among his television guest appearances were roles in *Dennis the Menace, Green Acres, Gunsmoke,* and *I Love Lucy.* (In the latter series, he was in episode 137, "Ricky's European Booking," as shopkeeper Mr. Feldman.) Among Antrim's movies are *Miracle on 34th Street* (1947), *Ma and Pa Kettle* (1949), *Teacher's Pet* (1958, with Doris Day and Clark Gable), and the Disney film *Monkey's Uncle* (1965).

Robert Easton portrays Pete Johnson. Easton has appeared in countless television shows and movies over the years. He also has been the dialogue coach in numerous productions. In fact Easton recently appeared and was the dialogue coach in the 1993 hit movie *The Beverly Hillbillies.*

Bill Mulliken portrays Franklin Pomeroy. **Ray Lanier** appears as Charlie Beasley.

EPISODE NOTES. 1. Jim Summers owns a meat market in Mayberry. Andy says that Jim always wins the sack race at the church picnic. 2. Ellie gives Opie a free ice cream cone. She also tells him that his pa has a nice smile. 3. When Ellie selects Barney as her escort, he had come to Walker's Drugstore to purchase foot powder. 4. The last reported pickpocket case in Mayberry was Old Man Burnett against Old Lady Burnett. 5. Andy suggests using Jeff Pritchard as a temporary deputy while Barney is taking Ellie to the picnic. 6. Bar-

ney wears his signature "salt and pepper" suit for the first time in this episode. Andy tells him that the suit makes him look like the Adolphe Menjou of Mayberry. Barney hasn't worn the suit since Clarey Dorsett's funeral, two years earlier.

"A Feud Is a Feud"

Episode #8. Air date: 12-5-60. Writer: David Adler. Director: Don Weis.

The Carters and the Wakefields have feuded for more than 87 years. When Mr. Carter's daughter, Hannah, and Jedediah Wakefield's son, Josh, decide to have Andy marry them, the ceremony is stopped at gunpoint by their fathers.

After some prodding by Aunt Bee and Opie, Andy searches for the origin of the feud. He discovers that neither family knows how or why the hostilities began. One other interesting fact is that no one on either side has ever been killed or even injured during all the years of feuding.

Andy announces that a duel to the death between the family patriarchs would settle the matter once and for all. This would also allow Josh and Hannah to get married. Privately, Andy tells the young couple that he is sure neither Mr. Carter nor Mr. Wakefield has any intention of inflicting harm and that the senseless (and victimless) feud will finally come to an end. Sure enough, Carter and Wakefield prove to be cowards as Andy attempts to officiate their duel. The two hillbillies run for their lives as soon as Andy shoots his pistol in the air to start the battle.

Later, Josh and Hannah stand up to each other's fathers and emphatically tell them to take out their shotguns and use them now, because that is the only way the wedding plans will be canceled. Andy remarks that the union of such a courageous young couple could only produce fine grandchildren for the two old codgers. Carter and Wakefield agree and, finally, consent to the marriage.

MEMORABLE SCENE. Andy's homespun version of "Romeo and Juliet." This is a rare example of Andy Griffith using material from his old nightclub routine.

CAST NOTES. Regulars: **Andy Griffith, Ronny Howard,** and **Frances Bavier.**

Arthur Hunnicut stars as Jedediah Wakefield. Hunnicut is well known as Percy Kilbride's successor in the Ma and Pa Kettle movie *The Kettles in the Ozarks* in 1956. He also appeared in numerous guest roles on television, including a memorable episode of *The Twilight Zone* called "The Hunt," written by Earl Hamner, the creator of *The Waltons.*

Chubby Johnson appears as Mr. Carter. **Tammy Windsor** portrays Hannah Carter. **Claude Johnson** appears as Josh Wakefield. In the early 1970s, Johnson portrayed police officer Norm Green on *Adam-12*.

EPISODE NOTES. 1. Andy wears a nightcap to bed. 2. This is the second and final wedding ceremony that Andy performs as justice of the peace in the series. He had previously married Rose and Wilbur Pine in episode 1, "The New Housekeeper." He will begin a wedding in episode 36, "Barney on the Rebound," but it's a trick to unmask some con artists. 3. Andy learned to speak a few words of French while he was stationed in France during WW II. 4. Aunt Bee plays the piano at the wedding ceremony that Josh and Hannah's fathers stop. 5. On September 14, 1908, Jedediah Wakefield had to be taken to the hospital after he was injured by his mule, Emmie. The scene in which this fact comes up is often omitted from syndication packages. 6. The publicity photo of a young Frances Bavier (Aunt Bee) can be seen hanging in the Taylors' home. It is on the wall to the right as they enter the kitchen.

"Andy the Matchmaker"

Episode #9. Air date: 11-14-60. Writer: Arthur Stander. Director: Don Weis.

Barney has decided to resign as deputy. He is discouraged by the absence of crime as well as a lack of respect for law enforcement in Mayberry. It seems some older boys wrote a limerick on the wall of the bank, teasing Barney for never having caught a criminal. Barney initially accuses Opie of the misdeed, but Opie is innocent because he hasn't learned how to write yet.

In order to lift Barney's spirits, Andy fakes a robbery at Walker's Drugstore. Ellie goes along with the plan, explaining to Barney that the robber was a masked man who took $24.00. Next, Andy tries to get Barney to take a shy seamstress named Miss Rosemary out on a date. Barney remarks that he has walked her to church on many Sundays but has never gotten up the nerve to ask her out.

Later, Andy is shocked to hear that Barney has arrested a man named Tracy Crawford for the "drugstore robbery." Andy then discovers that Crawford is actually wanted for five more serious crimes in Chattanooga. Everything ends well for Barney when he gets credit in the Mayberry newspaper for capturing a dangerous criminal. He is even sufficiently emboldened to ask Miss Rosemary out on a date. Needless to say, she accepts. Who wouldn't want to go out with such a respected lawman?

CAST NOTES. Regulars: **Andy Griffith, Don Knotts, Ronny Howard,** and **Elinor Donahue.**

Amzie Strickland as Miss Rosemary holds the distinction of being Barney's first girlfriend. Strickland would appear in a handful of episodes throughout the run of the series in a variety of guest roles. Her most notable role was as Otis Campbell's sister-in-law, Verlaine Campbell, in episode 63, "Deputy Otis." Strickland has had a very long career, appearing in nearly 400 series and pilots. She portrayed Beth Perce on *Full Circle* (1960–1961) and Mrs. Phillips on *The Bill Dana Show* (1963-1965). Among the hundreds of series she has guest-starred in are *Adam-12, Barnaby Jones, The Bob Newhart Show, Bonanza, Carter Country, The Danny Kaye Show, The Danny Thomas Show, The Donna Reed Show, The Doris Day Show, Dragnet, Empty Nest, F-Troop, The F.B.I., The Fugitive, Golden Girls, Happy Days, Ironside, The Jeffersons, Leave It to Beaver, The Lucy Show, The Mod Squad, My Three Sons, Mission:Impossible, The Patty Duke Show, Petticoat Junction, The Real McCoys, Sea Hunt, St. Elsewhere, That Girl, The Twilight Zone, The Untouchables, The Virginian, The Waltons,* and *Zorro.* Strickland has appeared in about one dozen made-for-television movies. Three of the most notable are *The Legend of Lizzie Borden, A Matter of Death and Life,* and *Silent Night, Lonely Night.* Among notable feature films in which she has appeared are *Man with a Gun* (1955, with Robert Mitchum), *Captain Newman, M.D.* (1963, with Gregory Peck), and *The One and Only* (1978, starring Henry Winkler and directed by Carl Reiner).

Jack Mann appears as Tracy Crawford.

EPISODE NOTES. 1. Miss Rosemary is making pies for Abigail Milkin's party during this episode. 2. When Barney is in the process of resigning, he turns in the following items to Andy: one badge, one notebook, one pencil, one gun belt, one holster, one revolver, one bullet, one whistle (with a new pea that Barney replaced), one tie clip, one tie, one cap, and one flashlight. 3. Barney states that he will seek employment as a brine tester at the local pickle factory. 4. Blueberry pie is a favorite of Andy's. 5. Andy states that the Snappy Lunch is one of his favorite eating spots. There is a real Snappy Lunch in Mount Airy, North Carolina, and it was indeed frequented by Andy Griffith in his high school days. 6. After Barney captures Tracy Crawford, he refers to himself as "Foxy Fife." 7. The license plate number for the Mayberry squad car is DC-269 for the third and final time in the series. In all the remaining episodes, the plate number will be JL-327. For the record, the two other "DC-269" episodes are 5, "Opie's Charity," and 6, "Ellie Comes to Town." 8. Tracy Crawford is actually an alias. His real name is never given. "Mr. Crawford" is about six feet tall, weighs between 165 and 170 pounds and has curly brown hair. 9. At Walker's Drugstore, a disgruntled Barney comments that he hasn't had a chance to use his fingerprint set in two years. 10. The headline in the Mayberry newspaper features a picture of Barney smiling ear to ear with a caption that states: "Deputy Sheriff Fife Cracks Walker Robbery." Under Barney's photo, a second caption reads: "Deputy Fife — Hero." The caption above the article declares: "Dangerous Criminal Captured Single-Handed Through The Clever Sleuthing Of Our Local Deputy."

"Stranger in Town"

Episode #10. Air date: 12-26-60. Writer: Arthur Stander. Director: Don Weis.

Ed Sawyer, a stranger in Mayberry, arouses the suspicions of the townsfolk when he seems to know every intimate detail of their lives. He can even distinguish between Mrs. Buntley's infant twins, Robert and William, because William has a mole on his right ear. Ed tells Jason, the Mayberry Hotel clerk, that he prefers not to stay in room 209 because that is where Wilbur Hennessey got drunk and jumped out the window. He accepts room 216 because he knows that it has recently been repainted green, even though it is not his favorite color. Later, Ed tells George Sapley that he would like to buy his service station that's for sale so he can settle down in Mayberry. Some folks start believing that Ed is a spook, an alien, or a foreign spy.

Ed goes a little too far when he tells pretty Lucy Matthews that she is a Capricorn, the valedictorian of her class, loves the color blue, likes to dance and enjoys eating hot fudge sundaes. Worse than that, he tells Andy that he is in love with Lucy but admits that he doesn't even know her.

Soon, George Sapley refuses to sell the service station to Ed, and the townspeople (led by Lucy's brother Bill) threaten to run Mr. Sawyer out of Mayberry. Luckily, Andy comes to the rescue after learning the truth about the stranger in town. Andy explains to one and all that Ed had served in the army with Mayberry native Joe Larson and had always enjoyed hearing about his buddy's hometown. After his hitch was up, Ed returned to his native New York but subscribed to the Mayberry newspaper. He studied and learned all he could and decided to adopt Mayberry as his own hometown. Ed had simply failed to approach his new neighbors correctly. After Andy's explanation, Ed is completely accepted by the people of Mayberry.

CAST NOTES. Regulars: **Andy Griffith, Don Knotts,** and **Ronny Howard.**

William Lanteau stars as Ed Sawyer. In the 1980s Lanteau portrayed Mayor Chester Wanamaker on *Newhart.*

Walter Baldwin makes his one and only appearance as Floyd the barber. **Howard McNear** would soon assume the role that made him famous as America's favorite barber.

Phil Chambers makes his first of many appearances as Jason, the clerk at the Mayberry Hotel. Chambers had a few regular roles in other television series including that of Mr. Atkinson in *The Long Hot Summer* (1965-1966). He was also in the 1957 series *The Gray Ghost* as Lt. St. Clair. Among other series in which he appeared are *Daniel Boone, Trailmaster, The Fugitive, Lassie, Kung Fu,* and *The New Andy Griffith Show.*

Sara Seegar appears as Mrs. Buntley. Seegar would appear in many subsequent episodes in a variety of roles. Many viewers may recall her as a regular on three other series: *The Red Buttons Show* (1952-1954), as a featured performer in this variety series, *Dennis the Menace* (1962-1967), as Mrs. John (Eloise) Wilson; and *Occasional Wife* (1966-1967), as Mrs. Christopher. She made a guest appearance on *The Brady Bunch* (in the episode "Everyone Can't Be George Washington" she appeared as Miss Bailey) and a few episodes of *Bewitched* (including its first Christmas episode, "A Vision of Sugar Plums," and the final episode, "The Truth, Nothing but the Truth, So Help Me Sam," which aired in 1972). Besides other television appearances, she performed in a few movies, most notably in *The Music Man* (1962), which starred the legendary Robert Preston and a young Ronny Howard.

Pat Colby portrays Bill Matthews. Colby would also appear as Jim Morgan in episode 85, "The Great Filling Station Robbery." **Marlene Willis** appears as Lucy Matthews. **William Erwin** portrays George Sapley. **George Dunn** also appears as Pete in this episode.

EPISODE NOTES. 1. Sarah, the telephone operator, enjoys taking a pinch of snuff now and then. 2. Floyd the barber enjoys pitching horseshoes, but sometimes suffers from rheumatism. 3. Pete and Edie are the names of Joe Larson's parents. 4. Old Joe MacKnight celebrated his 103rd birthday. He had given Andy his first job years ago. 5. Andy states that the three secrets of Mayberry are 1) how to make fried chicken and johnny cake; 2) how to make possum pie; and 3) how to make turnip jam. 6. Ed Sawyer was never seen or referred to again after this episode. Barney may have been right when he thought Ed was a foreign spy.

"Christmas Story"

Episode #11. Air date: 12-19-60. Writer: David Adler. Director: Bob Sweeney.

It's Christmas Eve, and Andy is filled with the spirit of the season. He allows all of the jail's prisoners to go home for the holiday, with the promise that they'll return the day after Christmas. Ben Weaver shows up and has hauled in Sam Muggins for moonshining. Ben legally sells liquor at his department store, and Sam is cutting in on his sales. Mr. Weaver—a real Scrooge when it comes to Christmas — has the evidence in hand and demands that Andy do his sworn duty. Andy not only arrests Sam, he also "arrests" Sam's wife, Bess, daughter Effie and son Billy as accessories to the crime. Then Andy, Barney, Aunt Bee, Ellie, and Opie throw a Christmas celebration at the courthouse in honor of the captive family. Ben is outraged at Andy's actions, but in order to guard against impropriety, Sheriff Taylor has deputized Aunt Bee, Ellie and even Opie.

Ben cannot believe what Andy is getting away with, but he is powerless to stop it. He can only hoist himself up on a crate outside the courthouse and secretly watch the joyous proceedings. He then commits some petty crimes for no apparent reason, but Andy refuses to arrest him since it's Christmas time. Later, Ben causes a commotion outside when he slips and falls off the crate. When Andy investigates the noise, he finds a stubborn and lonely old man who secretly wishes to celebrate Christmas with other people. Andy pretends to arrest Ben, who just happens to be bearing gifts for everyone at the courthouse. On this Christmas Eve, Ben Weaver goes to sleep in his jail cell filled (literally) with Christmas cheer.

MEMORABLE SCENES. 1. Andy and Ellie's beautiful duet on "Away in a Manger." 2. Barney in costume as a very thin Santa Claus.

CAST NOTES. Regulars: **Andy Griffith, Don Knotts, Ronny Howard, Frances Bavier,** and **Elinor Donahue.**

Will Wright turns in an outstanding performance in his first of three appearances as Ben Weaver. Wright (1891-1962), as fans of this series know, perfected the art of playing cantankerous old goats. Never settling down in any one series, he nevertheless made his mark. From 1959 through 1961, he was seen occasionally, on *Dennis the Menace* as Mr. Mercivale, the florist. On *The Dick Van Dyke Show*, he was the first actor to portray Sam Petrie, Rob's father. He appeared in *I Love Lucy, Jeff's Collie, Maverick, Mr. Ed, Pete and Gladys,* and many other programs. Wright made two appearances in the religious series *The Living Christ* (in the episodes "Escape to Egypt" and "Triumph and Defeat"). This series was made for television in the 1950s but is now available on videotape. Wright also enjoyed a long movie career. Among his films are *China Clipper* (1936, with Humphrey Bogart), *In Old Oklahoma* (aka *War of the Wildcats*; 1943, with John Wayne), *Road to Utopia* (1945, with Bob Hope and Bing Crosby), *Rhapsody in Blue* (1945), *The Walls of Jericho* (1948, with Kirk Douglas), *Whispering Smith* (1948, with Alan Ladd), *No Way Out* (1949, Sidney Poitier's first film), *Adam's Rib* (1949, with Spencer Tracy and Katharine Hepburn), *All the King's Men* (1950, with Broderick Crawford), *Dallas* (1950, with Gary Cooper), *People Will Talk* (1951, with Cary Grant), *Niagara* (1953, with Marilyn Monroe), *The Wild One* (1954, with Marlon Brando), *The Man with the Golden Arm* (1955, with Frank Sinatra), *These Wilder Years* (1956, with Jimmy Cagney), and *Cape Fear* (1962, with Gregory Peck).

Sam Edwards portrays Sam Muggins. Edwards would turn up in a few more episodes, most notably as Lester Scobie in episode 28, "Andy Forecloses." **Margaret Kerry** appears as Bess Muggins. Kerry would also return in episode 28, "Andy Forecloses," as Helen Scobie — meaning that once again, her character would be married to Sam Edwards' character. **Joy Ellison** appears as Effie Muggins. Ellison is not listed in the credits. She would return as Lester and Helen Scobie's daughter, Mary, in episode 28, "Andy Forecloses." Ellison also appeared as "Little Miss Mayberry" in episode 20, "The Beauty Pageant."

EPISODE NOTES. 1. This was the first episode directed by the most prolific director of the series, Bob Sweeney. In all, Mr. Sweeney directed 80 episodes of *The Andy Griffith Show*. 2. This is the one and only Christmas episode in the history of *The Andy Griffith Show*. 3. Jim is the name of one of the prisoners Andy releases. He was arrested for disturbing the peace. One other prisoner's name is Larry Joe. 4. Barney bought a Christmas tree for the courthouse and a smaller tree for the jail cell holding Sam Muggins and his family. 5. Ben Weaver's license plate number is BTV-663. 6. Andy and Barney receive a letter from the Hubacher brothers, whom Andy and Barney sent to state prison. Under their picture is the message, "Greetings from State Prison." In a blooper, Andy mistakenly reads the message as "Merry Christmas from State Prison." 7. Aunt Bee prepares a turkey with orange dressing for the Christmas feast. 8. Three Christmas carols were sung in this episode. Barney sadly sings a few lines of "Jingle Bells"; Andy and Ellie perform a duet on "Away in a Manger"; and everyone in the courthouse sings "Deck the

Halls." 9. Barney bought the Christmas tree lights at Smith's Hardware Store in Mayberry. 10. Ellie pays Ben Weaver's $2.00 parking ticket. 11. Barney receives a Christmas card from his girlfriend, Hilda Mae. On the inside of the card she wrote, "Merry Christmas, Barney - Parney - Poo!" Andy gives him a hard time over it. 12. Andy receives a Christmas card from an old friend named D. Floren. 13. Ben Weaver gives the following gifts: to Opie, a pair of roller skates; to Billy, a baseball mitt; to Effie, a doll; to Ellie, a bottle of perfume; and to Aunt Bee, a sewing basket. Andy, Barney, Sam, and Bess all receive wrapped gifts. Viewers never see the contents.

"Ellie for Council"

Episode #12. Air date: 12-12-60. Writers: Jack Elinson and Charles Stewart. Director: Bob Sweeney.

While on a picnic, Ellie notices an article in *The Mayberry Gazette* citing an opening on the Mayberry town council. She remarks that all of the current council seats are held by men. Against Andy's wishes, she decides to toss her hat into the ring. This decision proceeds to turn Mayberry upside down. The men are against the idea of a woman on the council, while the women believe that if Ellie is on the council, their collective voice will be heard. To force the women to retreat, Andy suggests that the men take away their spouses' credit at the local stores. Ellie retaliates by instructing the women to do no cooking, sewing, or cleaning. The resulting stalemate causes complete chaos. Upset by the turmoil, Ellie tells Andy that she was not trying to start a civil war in Mayberry. She goes on to say that she is withdrawing her name from the ballot.

Upon hearing this, Opie makes some anti-women remarks that he has overheard since Ellie launched her campaign. He tells Andy how the men beat the women. These comments make Andy realize the serious nature of the situation and how wrong he was in his thinking. He and Ellie go to her election rally at the public square, where the majority of the town's men and women are gathered in their separate camps. Andy makes a speech to the crowd that convinces the men that Ellie has every right to compete in the election. Everyone agrees, and peace is finally restored in Mayberry.

MEMORABLE SCENE. Sam confronting Barney over signing Ellie's petition.

CAST NOTES. Regulars: **Andy Griffith, Don Knotts, Ronny Howard, Frances Bavier, Elinor Donahue,** and **Hal Smith.**

Frank Ferguson returns to the series. This time he appears as Sam. **Mary Treen** also returns. She portrays Sam's unnamed wife. In episode 1, "The New Housekeeper," Ferguson and Treen portrayed a married couple named Wilbur and Rose Pine. Rose was Andy and Opie's original housekeeper.

Dorothy Neumann appears for the first time as Otis Campbell's wife. Neumann, who was a founder of the Turnabout Theater in Los Angeles in the 1940s, had regular roles in the following television series: *Fibber McGee and Molly* (1959-1960) as Mrs. La Trivia; *Hank* (1965-1966) as Miss Mittleman; and *Mona McLuskey* as Agatha Kincaid. She has guest-starred in many of television's most popular series, including *The Addams Family, Bewitched, Bonanza, F-Troop, Gunsmoke, Lassie, Mannix, Perry Mason, The Dick Van Dyke Show, Tales from the Crypt* and *The Twilight Zone.* Among the numerous films she's appeared in are *Molly and Me* (1945), *Sorry, Wrong Number* (1948, starring Barbara Stanwyck), *The Snake Pit* (1948), *The Day the Earth Stood Still* (1951, with Frances Bavier), *Mr. Belvedere Rings the Bell* (1951), *The Long, Long Trailer* (1958), *Gigi* (1958), *The Thrill of It All* (1963, starring Doris Day), *The Greatest Story Ever Told* (1965), *The Shakiest Gun in the West* (1968, starring Don Knotts), *Private Parts* (1972), *Missouri Breaks* (1976), and *Things Are Tough All Over* (1982). Sadly, Neumann passed away on May 20, 1994. She was 80 years old.

Florence MacMichael appears for the first time as Barney's first steady girlfriend, Hilda Mae. MacMichael (now Florence McCoy) began her career doing radio and Broadway shows. On television, she became a regular on *My Three Sons*, as Mrs. Florence Pearson, from 1960 to 1961. Then came the role of Winnie Kirkwood on *Mr. Ed* from 1963 to 1965. She has guest-starred in several series, including *Alfred Hitchcock Presents, Bachelor Father, Dennis the Menace* and *Alcoa Premier.* In the latter, she appeared in the 1961 production of "Delbert, Texas," as Ruth Willoughby. She has appeared in several movies, including *Young and Willing* (1943, with William Holden), *Woman Obsessed* (1959, with Susan Hayward), *The Children's Hour* (1962, with Audrey Hepburn and Shirley MacLaine), *The Horse in the Gray Flannel Suit* (1968), and *Welcome Home, Solder Boys* (1972, with Joe Don Baker).

Forrest Lewis also appears for the first time in this episode. He would go on to make numerous appearances in the series. The talented actor was born in 1900 and died on June 2, 1977. He specialized in small but hilarious roles. He had a few regular television roles, including Mr. Mack on *Sandy Strong* (1950-1951), druggist Mr. Peavey on *The Great Gildersleeve* (1955-1956), and Mr. Colby on *Ichabod and Me* (1961-1962). He appeared as a guest star in many popular television shows. These include *Dennis the Menace*, *F-Troop*, *The Munsters*, *The New Andy Griffith Show* and *Peter Gunn*. He also made two appearances on the classic series *The Dick Van Dyke Show*. (He was Mac, the night watchman, in the episode, "Obnoxious, Offensive, Egomaniac, Etc…" and was featured in another episode, "The Great Petrie Fortune," as Mr. Harlow, a numismatist, hired by Rob to examine some old coins.)

EPISODE NOTES. 1. Otis is in jail for hitting his mother-in-law in the mouth with a leg of lamb. He admits to Andy that he was actually aiming at his wife. 2. Barney escorts Hilda Mae to the picnic. 3. Barney's signature on Ellie's petition is the first of 100 she needs to compete in the election. Barney claims that she persuaded him to sign it by calling him "Honey," "Sugar," and "Cream Puff." The men of Mayberry nickname him "Turncoat." 4. Andy proceeds to burn rice and scrambled eggs after Aunt Bee refuses to cook. 5. Otis takes away his wife's credit at Davis's store in Mayberry. 6. At Ellie's rally, the women of Mayberry hold the following signs: "Ellie, Ellie, Ellie," "Ellie Means Equal Representation," "We Wives Want Ellie," "A Fair Deal for the Fair Sex — Ellie for Council," "We Want Ellie," and "Mayberry Needs Ellie." 7. This episode was filmed over 30 years ago, yet it remains a refreshing example of the fight for equality. This was rare on a television show in 1960.

"Mayberry Goes Hollywood"

Episode #13. Air date: 1-2-61. Writers: Benedict Freedman and John Fenton Murray. Director: Bob Sweeney.

Mayberry's relaxed atmosphere and natural beauty create the ideal setting that Hollywood movie producer Mr. Harmon is looking for. He plans to use the scenic town as the backdrop for his new movie. The town council, consisting of Andy, Mayor Pike, Floyd, and Orville Monroe (Ellie must have lost her bid for a council seat in episode 12) agrees with the idea, and Mr. Harmon heads back to Hollywood to gather up his equipment and film crew. During his absence, every citizen, with the sole exception of Andy, catches "Hollywood Fever." For instance, the Mayberry Cafe becomes "The Cinemascope Cafe," Phoebe's Beauty Shop becomes "Phoebe's Beauty Salon," the Mayberry Funeral Home becomes "Hollywood Funerals," and Floyd's Barbershop becomes "Colby's Tonsorial Parlor," featuring Cary Grant haircuts. Barney sports a new uniform that makes him look like Smokey the Bear. Aunt Bee and Opie catch the fever and buy new

clothes that would look out of place even in Hollywood. To make matters worse, Mayor Pike organizes the following welcoming celebration for Mr. Harmon's return: A greeting by the Mayberry Drum and Bugle Corps; three ladies presenting Mr. Harmon with three homemade pies; Mayor Pike's daughter, Juanita, singing "Flow Gently Sweet Afton"; and the chopping down of the old oak tree in the center of town. Andy cannot believe (or control) what is happening around him.

When Mr. Harmon arrives, he is startled by the ceremony and the transformation of the peaceful little town. He scolds everyone present for changing their appearance, and he particularly chastises Mayor Pike for wanting to chop down the oak tree. This tirade brings everyone back to reality, and Mr. Harmon is able to proceed with filming the real Mayberry.

CAST NOTES. Regulars: **Andy Griffith**, **Don Knotts**, **Ronny Howard**, and **Frances Bavier**. **Howard McNear** makes his first appearance as Floyd the barber. This is the only episode in which Floyd's surname is Colby, not Lawson. **Dick Elliott** returns as the mayor. This is the first episode where he is referred to as Mayor Pike. **Jonathan Hole** returns as Orville Monroe.

Dan Frazier stars as Mr. Harmon. Frazier is best known as Telly Savalas's boss, Frank McNeil, on *Kojak*.

Josie Lloyd appears as Juanita Pike. Lloyd would later appear in other roles throughout the series, most notably as Goober's girlfriend, Lydia Crosswaithe. In the 1965-1966 series *The Long Hot Summer*, Lloyd had the regular role of Agnes. Among her guest appearances, she can be seen in *The Farmer's Daughter* (in the episode entitled "Stag at Bay"). She also appeared on *Alfred Hitchcock Presents*. Lloyd is the daughter of actor and director Norman Lloyd, who was famous in the 1980s for his portrayal of Dr. Auschlander on *St. Elsewhere*.

EPISODE NOTES. 1. Orville Monroe, Mayberry's mortician and television repairman, refers to Mayor Pike as "our fat little mayor." 2. Aunt Bee's favorite movie actor is Rock Hudson. 3. As a youngster, Floyd practiced barbering on alley cats. 4. When Mr. Harmon returns, the headline of *The Mayberry Gazette* states: "Hollywood Comes to Mayberry." The article under the headline is "Local Citizens To Be In Movies." 5. Mayberrian Gordon Bellfield once traveled to Hollywood and stood on Gary Cooper's lawn. Gordon and his friends were asked to leave by Mr. Cooper's maid. 6. Effie Bartlett loves to watch wrestling on television. 7. Mr. Harmon claims to be a good friend of one of Barney's favorite actors, Gabby Hayes. 8. Andy and Barney accidentally lock themselves in cell #1.

Barney will proceed to lock himself in the same cell two more times during this episode. 9. While Andy and Barney are fixing up cell #1, there is a calendar on the wall with a picture of Ron Howard's younger brother, Clint. He is standing with a dog. Clint would later appear in the series as the little peanut butter and jelly sandwich-eating cowboy, Leon.

"The Horse Trader"

Episode #14. Air date: 1-9-61. Writers: Jack Elinson and Charles Stewart. Director: Bob Sweeney.

Opie wants satisfaction. He traded a perfectly good cap pistol to a friend named Tommy Farrell in exchange for "licorice seeds." Opie soon discovers how worthless the seeds are. He tells Andy that he plans to sell the seeds to Jerry Parker for a pair of roller skates. Andy reminds his son of the golden rule, "Do unto others as you would have them do unto you." This convinces Opie to cancel the trade.

Later, the town council (with the sole exception of Barney) votes to get rid of the old town cannon and replace it with a plaque donated by a successful ex-Mayberrian named Milford Phillips. The cannon has become an eyesore since its muzzle was broken during the last Fourth of July celebration when some folks attempted to fire the old relic. Mayor Pike and the council put Andy and Barney in charge of selling it. They have no luck until they meet an out-of-town antique dealer named Ralph Mason at Walker's Drugstore. In order to unload the cannon, Andy tells Mr. Mason that it fired the first shot of the Civil War and that Teddy Roosevelt used it when he charged up San Juan Hill. He even points out the initials T.R. on the cannon and swears they belong to Teddy himself. Barney and Opie can't believe what they are seeing. It is common knowledge that the initials belong to a Mayberrian named Tracy Ruppert.

Mr. Mason agrees to buy the cannon for $175.00. Meanwhile, Opie, having witnessed Andy's brand of "horse trading," carries out his original plan of selling the licorice seeds to Jerry Parker for the roller skates. Andy scolds his son for making an unfair trade, but Opie reminds him of the tactics he used when the cannon was sold.

To clear the air, father and son mutually decide to correct their misdeeds. Opie gives the skates back, and Andy tells Mr. Mason the truth about the worthless cannon. Andy proceeds to sell him the cannon for $20.00. Ellie and Barney are both relieved that Andy chose the honest way of doing business.

The episode ends on a funny note when Mr. Mason sells the cannon to Milford Phillips in an out-of-town transaction. Then Mr. Phillips decides on donating the cannon, rather than the plaque, to his old hometown. It is also discovered that Ralph Mason used Andy's remarks to sell the cannon to Mr. Phillips.

CAST NOTES. Regulars: **Andy Griffith, Don Knotts, Ronny Howard,** and **Elinor Donahue. Dick Elliott** returns as Mayor Pike.

Casey Adams stars as Ralph Mason. Adams has appeared in numerous television and movie roles. He was the original Ward Cleaver in the pilot episode of *Leave It to Beaver.* (The pilot entitled "It's a Small World," aired in April of 1957. Hugh Beaumont was selected to portray Mr. Cleaver for the actual series.) Casey Adams's real name is Max Showalter, and from time to time he is credited on screen by that name. He is also a gifted songwriter. It is believed that he wrote the first television musical, *Time for Love,* which aired on NBC in 1939.

Pearl Cooper and **Spec O'Donnell** also appear in this episode.

EPISODE NOTES. 1. Charlie Ross, Mayberry's junkman, agrees to take the cannon off Andy and Barney's hands, if they pay him $15.00. 2. At Walker's Drugstore, Ralph Mason buys a tin of pipe tobacco. He also buys an old copper wash boiler for $5.00. Ellie had been using the wash boiler to display hand soap. 3. Barney is mad at the Postal Service because they installed a postage stamp machine in the Mayberry post office. Barney claims that he doesn't like the U.S. government endorsing slot machines. 4. At Walker's Drugstore, a copy of *TV Guide* magazine, featuring Lucille Ball on the cover, can be seen in the magazine rack. 5. Barney drinks four root beer floats as a substitute for alcohol when he gets upset at Andy's dishonest trading practices. He winds up with a bellyache. 6. When Opie completes the trade with Jerry Parker for the roller skates, he also gives Jerry one of Andy's broken cuff links. He claims it was from a uniform worn by George Washington. 7. In this episode, Barney is a member of the Mayberry town council, yet in the two previous episodes, he wasn't a member. 8. Why did Opie want Jerry Parker's roller skates so badly? Three shows earlier, in episode 11, "Christmas Story," Ben Weaver gave him a pair of roller skates as a Christmas present. He must have worn them out in a hurry.

"Those Gossipin' Men"

Episode #15. Air date: 1-16-61. Writers: Charles Stewart and Jack Elinson. Director: Bob Sweeney.

Andy pokes fun at Aunt Bee and her two friends Emma Brand and Clara Lindsey for making a mountain out of a molehill through idle gossiping. Barney had cut his trigger finger while taking his gun apart, and Andy went to get some medicine to treat it at Walker's Drugstore. Aunt Bee, Emma, and Clara were in the drugstore at the time, and one by one, they relayed the story to some of their other friends. The story kept gaining momentum until poor Barney was pronounced dead of a gunshot wound!

Andy brags to Aunt Bee that a man would never gossip and cause such a stir. This prompts Aunt Bee to retaliate. She hints to Andy that traveling shoe salesman Wilbur Finch may not be what he seems. Why would a salesman from the Manhattan Shoe Company of New York City be wasting his time in the tiny town of Mayberry? Andy takes the bait, and a short time later, he and Barney convince most of the male population in Mayberry that Mr. Finch must be a talent scout for a popular amateur television talent show, "The Manhattan Show Time," which just happens to be sponsored by the Manhattan Shoe Company. The men are convinced that Mr. Finch is traveling under the guise of a shoe salesman so as not to give away his real profession.

One by one, all of the men go to Mr. Finch's room and display their various musical abilities, while playing along with Mr. Finch's "game" by purchasing large amounts of shoes. Some of the men even take their children to play music and sing for Mr. Finch. They also buy shoes. Mr. Finch is puzzled as to why he is being serenaded, but he is happy to be selling shoes at a record pace.

Aunt Bee, Emma, and Clara get the last laugh when "those gossipin' men" discover that Wilbur Finch *was* merely a shoe salesman, and in a few days the bills for all the newly purchased shoes arrive. This time, poor Andy takes the blame for his idle gossiping.

CAST NOTES. Regulars: **Andy Griffith, Don Knotts, Ronny Howard, Frances Bavier,** and **Howard McNear. Harry Antrim** returns as Fred Walker. **Cheerio Meredith** returns as Emma Brand. **Jonathan Hole** returns for his final appearance as Orville Monroe. **Phil Chambers** returns as Jason, the clerk at the Mayberry Hotel.

Mary Treen makes her third appearance, in her third role (Clara Lindsey). Her previous roles were in episodes 1 and 12.

Jack Finch stars as Wilbur Finch.

Sara Seegar also appears in this episode.

EPISODE NOTES. 1. A copy of *TV Guide* featuring Lucille Ball on the cover, which first appeared in episode 14, "The Horse Trader," appears once again on the magazine rack at Walker's Drugstore.

2. Rose Blake, a friend of Aunt Bee's went to Raleigh to buy a new set of false teeth. She told her friends she went there to visit her sister. 3. Another friend of Aunt Bee's, Millie Parsons, recently dyed her hair blond. She had been a brunette for years. 4. Emma Brand claims to be in her forties. 5. According to Barney, New York City is 900 miles from Mayberry. 6. Floyd the barber's son, Norman, auditions on the saxophone. He plays a selection from *Saxomania*. 7. Effie Monroe, Orville's daughter, auditions on the accordion. 8. Barney's shoe size is 7 1/2B. His feet are ticklish. 9. A mailbox is located directly in front of Walker's Drugstore. 10. Barney auditions on the harmonica. He offers to play "I'm Just a Vagabond Lover," "Animal Crackers" and "Finiculi, Finicula." He wears his salt and pepper suit to the audition. 11. The Baxters of Mayberry have their "No Trespassing" sign stolen by trespassers during this episode. 12. Mr. Finch reports to his boss, Mr. Simmons in New York, that he sold 67 pairs of shoes during his one-day stay in Mayberry. 13. In a scene not shown, Andy auditions on the guitar and orders three pairs of shoes from Wilbur Finch.

"Andy Saves Barney's Morale"

Episode #16. Air date: 2-20-61. Writer: David Adler. Director: Bob Sweeney.

Andy is called to nearby Centerville to testify at a trial. He reluctantly puts Barney in charge for the short time he's gone. When Andy returns, he discovers that his overzealous deputy has arrested nearly everybody in Mayberry. Among those arrested are Aunt Bee, who was in violation of Code 421, unlawful assemblage and inciting a riot; Mayor Pike, for violation of Code 439, vagrancy and loitering; and Jud Fletcher, who was found guilty of violating Code 721-8, disturbing the peace.

Andy immediately drops all the charges, and Barney soon becomes the butt of everyone's jokes. Barney's girlfriend, Hilda Mae, confides to Andy that the folks around town are just joking, but as Andy and Hilda Mae both know, Barney cannot stand to be made fun of.

Andy ponders the situation and comes up with a plan. He tells everyone in town that he can't keep a deputy who is not respected by the community. One by one, all those who had been arrested by Barney return to the courthouse and demand to be locked up. They remind Andy that a crime is a crime and that Deputy Fife was only doing his job. Thus Andy is able to save Barney's morale.

CAST NOTES. Regulars: **Andy Griffith, Don**

Knotts, Ronny Howard, Frances Bavier, Howard McNear, and Hal Smith. Dick Elliott returns as Mayor Pike. Florence MacMichael appears for the final time as Hilda Mae.

Burt Mustin portrays Jud Fletcher. George Dunn appears as Pete. Joseph (Joe) Hamilton portrays Chester Jones. Hamilton would go on to appear in numerous episodes in the series, usually as a town loafer.

EPISODE NOTES. 1. Jud Fletcher is 74 years old, and he was accused of throwing a checkerboard and checkers at Chester Jones. He is also accused of yelling, "Chester Jones, you're a two-faced cheatin' liar." 2. On a variety of charges, Barney also arrested the following folks: Miss Johnson, a schoolteacher; Franklin, a banker; Charlie, a councilman; Otis Campbell, the town drunk; Chester Jones, a loafer; a woman named Nellie; two men named Tom and Harry; and a lady named Miss Mary. 3. Andy tells Nellie that she is wearing a pretty dress. 4. During the episode, Barney is referred to as "Sherlock Jones," "Wild Bill Fife," and "Wyatt Earp." 5. The Mayberry Hotel serves breakfast from 8:00 A.M. to 9:30 A.M.; lunch from 12:30 P.M. to 2:30 P.M.; and dinner is at 7:00 P.M. only. 6. Barney wears his salt and pepper suit while on his date with Hilda Mae. 7. Andy keeps an extra set of the squad car's keys in his top desk drawer at the courthouse. 8. When Barney is considering resigning, he turns over the following items to Andy: one cap, one badge, one revolver, one bullet, and one gunbelt. 9. Barney's theme, "The Manhunt," is played for him for the first time in the series at the conclusion of the episode. It had been played as background music only in episode 2, "The Manhunt." 10. When Barney arrests Aunt Bee, he exclaims, "There will be no favoritism in Barney Fife's administration." 11. When Barney realized that he was wrong to arrest everybody, he spoke these words of wisdom: "Once bit, best forgit"; Once burnt is a lesson learnt'"; and "One mistake, a better cake." 12. In a continuity blooper, Chester Jones appears in two places at the same time. This occurs when Andy drops in on Jud and Chester, who are in the middle of a game of checkers. Andy announces that he is going to replace Barney. Next, Andy goes immediately to Floyd's Barbershop with the same announcement. There at Floyd's, acting as if he has not heard the message previously, is Chester Jones.

"Alcohol and Old Lace"

Episode #17. Air date: 1-30-61. Writers: Charles Stewart and Jack Elinson. Director: Gene Reynolds.

Andy and Barney are in the process of destroying all of the illegal stills in and around Mayberry. To their surprise, two spinster sisters, Clarabelle and Jennifer Morrison, give correct information as to the whereabouts of Ben Sewell's still in Cowsill Flat and Rube Sloane's still at Furnace Creek. The sisters neglect to tell Andy they are operating their own still in the hothouse of their otherwise legitimate flower shop. The good-hearted sisters intend for their "special elixir" to be used only for holidays, celebrations, and special occasions. Unfortunately, some folks, like Otis Campbell, take advantage of the sisters' naivete.

Later, Opie inadvertently stumbles upon the Morrison's still. He doesn't realize what the contraption is, and at the courthouse, he tells Andy that he saw a flower-making machine. When Andy asks him about it, the youngster describes a still to a tee. Otis slumps down in his cell in sorrow. Andy and Barney go to the flower shop, and Barney relishes taking a big ax and going POW! POW! POW! on the still. Andy realizes that the sisters didn't believe they were doing anything illegal, so he doesn't arrest them.

The sisters then turn to making homemade preserves, but they use the same jars that contained the moonshine, and Barney proceeds to get gassed while eating a piece of toast.

CAST NOTES. Regulars: **Andy Griffith, Don Knotts, Ronny Howard, Hal Smith** and **Howard McNear.**

Gladys Hurlbut stars as Clarabelle Morrison, and **Charity Grace** co-stars as Jennifer Morrison.

Jack Prince appears as Ben Sewell. Prince would appear in future episodes, mainly as Rafe Hollister. Prince was born John Upchurch on January 19, 1920, in Shreveport, Louisiana. By the early 1940s, he had taken the name Prince, his mother's maiden name. In 1942, he served the U.S. Army in France, where he formed a band called "The Chowhounds." After the war he took a job as vocalist for Shep Field's band. A couple of years later, he landed the role of Nicely Nicely Johnson in a national tour of *Guys and Dolls*. In 1955, he took his first and only regular role on television as a vocalist on *The Johnny Carson Jello Hour*. Later, actor and dancer Ray Bolger brought Jack Prince to Las Vegas, where the talented vocalist had a band called "The Prince and His Paupers." From there, Prince went to New York and worked with jazz legend Charlie Parker. He also played Marryin' Sam in *Li'l Abner* on Broadway for three years. He met Andy Griffith in 1960 when they appeared together in the Broadway version of *Destry Rides Again*. Jack played Wash, while Andy had the lead role. Later, Andy heard Jack play with the Charlie Teagarden Band in Las Vegas and invited the vocalist to appear on

The Andy Griffith Show. Jack took him up on his offer, appearing a half-dozen times. From 1963 to 1964, he played with the Harry James Band. Later on, he held jobs in Florida and Las Vegas, not slowing down until the early 1980s. In September of 1991, Jack thrilled viewers of TNN's *Nashville Now* by appearing on "Mayberry Night" and reprising "Lonesome Road." He performed again before large audiences at Opryland in Nashville, Tennessee, along with other alumni from *The Andy Griffith Show.* Multi-talented Jack Prince passed away in 1994.

Thom Carney portrays Rube Sloane.

EPISODE NOTES. 1. Andy states that any type of alcohol is illegal in the county of Mayberry, yet in episode 11, "Christmas Story," Ben Weaver legally sells spirits at Weaver's Department Store. 2. Barney originally thought that Ben Sewell's still was located at Hawk's Point. 3. Ben Sewell lives on Hash Road near Cowsill Flat. He is a potato farmer and moonshiner. 4. Jennifer Morrison loves the smell of witch hazel on a man. Her sister, Clarabelle, claims Jennifer is "boy crazy." 5. Otis tells the Morrison sisters that he needs their elixir so he can celebrate the day Sir Walter Raleigh landed in Virginia. Lars Hanson gets his elixir by telling the sisters he is celebrating Mohammed's birthday. (The sisters always thought Lars was a Lutheran.) One other customer told the sisters that he needed the elixir for Panama Canal Day. 6. Rube Sloane believed that either Les Peterson or Frank Watson told Andy the whereabouts of his still. 7. The sisters sell the elixir for $4.00 a jar. 8. Miss Johnson is the name of Opie's first grade teacher. 9. Andy suggests deputizing non-drinkers Orville Monroe and Reverend Aiken to assist in wiping out the moonshiners. 10. Andy and Barney believe that a still may be located at Fancy Gap. (Fancy Gap is a real town in Virginia, a few miles north of Mount Airy, North Carolina.) 11. Andy sings the Woody Guthrie song "Goin' Down That Road Feeling Bad."

COMMERCIAL. When this episode originally aired, Andy and Opie appeared in ads for Post Cereal. The first one came right after the theme song. In it, Andy and Opie are seen getting out of their rowboat and walking towards the camera, and then off screen. The commercial announcer, unseen, reminds viewers that *The Andy Griffith Show* is "brought to you by Post, the cereals that happen to be just a little bit better." At this point, Andy is heard singing a Post Cereal jingle, with Opie joining in toward the end.

After the episode, but before the closing theme, another ad ran. It began with Clarabelle (holding a covered basket) and Jennifer Morrison greeting Andy as he leaves Floyd's Barbershop. Clarabelle

announces, as though it is a great secret, what Leonard Beasley is selling at his grocery store. It turns out to be Post Sugar Crisp. Andy explains that there's nothing wrong with selling this cereal with "controlled sweetness." (That is, the sugar-coated cereal has "less sugar than young'uns would put on themselves.") It can be bought in any amount and eaten anytime. Relieved, Clarabelle reveals the contents of her basket — several boxes of Post Cereal. Andy looks at the camera and encourages viewers to try Post Sugar Crisp. At the very end of the ad after wishing viewers goodnight, Andy is heard singing the Post Cereal song.

"Andy the Marriage Counselor"

Episode #18. Air date: 2-10-61. Writer: David Adler. Director: Gene Reynolds.

Andy and Barney are repeatedly called upon to break up the domestic fighting between Fred and Jennie Boone. The Boones are newcomers to Mayberry and live a few houses down from the Taylors. Fred and Jennie get along fine with everyone except each other. An exasperated Andy gives the combative couple an ultimatum. Either they can attend his daily counseling sessions, or they can go to jail. The Boones choose the former, and Andy is proud of himself when his personal counseling appears to be working.

However, while Fred and Jennie treat each other well, they vent their frustrations on everyone else. When Fred punches his friend Cliff in the nose and dumps a pitcher of water on another friend named Gil during their weekly game of hearts, Andy realizes his plan is failing. Aunt Bee suggests that bickering with each other may be the only way Fred and Jennie know how to express their love for one another. Andy agrees and states that "what looks like rasslin' to one, is dancin' to another." He instigates an argument between the Boones, and everything returns to normal.

CAST NOTES. Regulars: **Andy Griffith, Don Knotts, Ronny Howard,** and **Frances Bavier.**

Veteran television and movie actor **Jesse White** stars as Fred Boone. White has appeared in such movies as *Harvey* (1950, with James Stewart) and the 1956 classic *The Bad Seed.* He also co-starred with Don Knotts in the 1967 feature film *The Reluctant Astronaut.* On television, White portrayed show-biz agent Jesse Leads on *The Danny Thomas Show.* He is best known as the lonely Maytag repairman in television commercials during the 1960s and 1970s.

Claudia Bryar co-stars as Jennie Boone. Bryar

would go on to appear in many television roles, including some return visits to Mayberry. She portrayed Mary Barrett in the 1970s television series *The Manhunter*.

Norman Leavitt appears as Gil. Leavitt would later assume the role of Wally, the filling station owner in Mayberry. **Forrest Lewis** returns to the series. In this episode, he portrays Cliff. **Tim Stevenson** appears as Billy.

EPISODE NOTES. 1. Barney is reading the book *The Art of Judo* by Professor Matzamota. He also practices judo, unsuccessfully of course, on Andy. 2. Opie and his pal Billy love to fight with each other while playing cowboys and indians and cops and robbers. Andy gives them each a nickel every time they play nicely with each other. This doesn't last long, though, because the boys think that playing nicely is boring. 3. Andy gives Fred and Jennie some sweet cider for successfully graduating from his counseling sessions. 4. The publicity photo of a younger Frances Bavier (Aunt Bee) is shown once again. In this episode, it can be seen on the back wall when Cliff and Gil go to Andy's house to complain about Fred's temper.

COMMERCIAL. During the original CBS network broadcast of "Andy the Marriage Counselor," an advertisement for Sanka aired at the conclusion of the episode. It began with Andy sitting at his desk at the courthouse. Barney walks in with Fred and Jennie Boone and explains they were disturbing the peace again. As Andy pours four cups of coffee, Fred complains loudly about the coffee Jennie serves, and Jennie fires back insults. Andy shushes them and hands Fred a cup of coffee, explaining that it's Sanka brand. After Andy extols the virtues of Sanka, Fred and Jennie resume their fighting. Andy manages to squeeze in a few more good words about Sanka, in the "new economy five-ounce jar," and bids viewers goodnight over Fred and Jennie's bickering.

"Mayberry on Record"

Episode #19. Air date: 2-13-61. Writers: John Fenton Murray and Benedict Freedman. Director: Gene Reynolds.

Mr. Maxwell, a New York City record promoter, wants to record a folk music album in Mayberry. Andy and his musician friends perform "Flop-Eared Mule" and "The Crawdad Song" for the project. The non-musical folks, such as Barney, Ellie, Floyd, and some others, convince Mr. Maxwell to allow them to invest $40.00 each in the venture. Mr. Maxwell claims he will make 25 cents

per album sold and the investors will earn 3 cents each. Andy warns the investors they should not have been so eager, because Mr. Maxwell may be a con man.

Andy believes his theory is correct when he discovers that Mr. Maxwell has suddenly left town. He tells the investors their money is gone for good. Everyone believes him, with the sole exception of Ellie. She truly believes Mr. Maxwell is an honest man.

Everyone but Ellie is surprised when Mr. Maxwell returns from National Records in Richmond, announcing he has sold the album, "Music from Mayberry." He presents an advance check for $5000.00 to the stunned investors.

MEMORABLE SCENE. Barney "diversifying" while reading *The Wall Street Journal.*

CAST NOTES. Regulars: **Andy Griffith, Don Knotts, Ronny Howard, Elinor Donahue,** and **Howard McNear.**

Hugh Marlowe stars as Mr. Maxwell. Marlowe portrayed Ellery Queen on television during the 1950s and is best known for his role of Jim Mathews on the daytime soap *Another World*, which he held from 1969 until his death in 1982.

The real-life bluegrass group **The Country Boys** performs with Andy on songs for the album. **George Dunn** and **William Erwin** appear as unnamed Mayberry investors in the episode.

EPISODE NOTES. 1. Andy demonstrates to Barney how easy it is to be taken in by a con man when he agrees to sell him a buffalo head nickel with the buffalo facing the wrong way for $75.00. 2. During the episode, Barney refers to himself as "Barney Sucker" and "Ol' Eagle-Eye Barney." 3. Andy orders a sundae at Walker's Drugstore but lets Opie eat it. 4. While in Mayberry, Mr. Maxwell records an instrumental by The Country Boys. He also records an unnamed fiddler and jew's harp player. 5. Barney offers to play "Que Sera Sera," on harmonica for Mr. Maxwell. Fortunately, the offer is declined. 6. Andy sings "Cripple Creek" while sweeping the floor of the courthouse. 7. This episode is a rare example of Andy showing poor judgment in the character of another person.

"The Beauty Contest"

Episode #20. Air date: 1-23-61. Writers: Jack Elinson and Charles Stewart. Director: Bob Sweeney.

It's Founder's Day in Mayberry, and the town council wants to close the festivities with something new. The day will consist of the traditional booth sales, street dance, pie-eating contest, white elephant sales, free watermelons and the Founder's Day play, followed by the new event: a beauty contest.

A reluctant Sheriff Taylor is chosen by the town council (including Ellie — in this episode, unlike episode 13, she appears to have won the election covered in episode 12) to be the sole judge of the beauty contest. Ellie gets mad at Andy when he assures her that she didn't need to nominate him, because he would have chosen her to win the contest anyway. Ellie, as it happens, had no plans of entering the contest.

Soon, Andy is besieged by potential beauty queens trying to win the judge's favor. The candidates for Miss Mayberry include Floyd Lawson's niece, Virginia Lee; Mayor Pike's third daughter, "the lovely, beauteous and tempestuous" Josephine; Henrietta Swanson's 19-year-old daughter, Darlene; Sam Lindsey's daughter, Barbara Sue; and Opie's own nomination, classmate Mary Wiggins.

The big moment arrives, and everyone is surprised when Ellie is secretly nominated by Aunt Bee. Andy is in a pickle, but he makes a great escape. Everyone is stunned when he selects the coordinator of the play and the beauty contest, Erma Bishop. Andy reasons that the elderly Miss Bishop is the only logical choice because real beauty is on the inside and no one approaches this quality quite like Erma Bishop. Miss Bishop proudly wears the crown and robe, while Floyd sings, "Hail to Thee, Miss Mayberry," a song he wrote specifically for the contest. Later, Andy chooses Mary Wiggins as "Miss Mayberry, Jr." She also gets serenaded by the singing barber.

CAST NOTES. Regulars: **Andy Griffith, Ronny Howard, Frances Bavier, Howard McNear,** and **Elinor Donahue. Dick Elliott** returns as Mayor Pike.

Frank Ferguson appears as Sam Lindsey. **Josie Lloyd** portrays Josephine Pike. In episode 13, "Mayberry Goes Hollywood," she appeared as Juanita Pike. **Lillian Bronson** appears as Erma Bishop. **Elvia Allman** portrays Henrietta Swanson. Allman is best known as Granny's nemesis, Elverna Bradshaw, on *The Beverly Hillbillies.* **Joy Ellison** is unbilled in the credits, but she portrays Mary Wiggins. **Gail Lucas** as Barbara Sue Lindsey and **Yvonne Adrian** as Darlene Swanson also appear.

EPISODE NOTES. 1. In this episode, the Mayberry town council consists of Mayor Pike, Ellie, Floyd, Andy, and Sam Lindsey. 2. For many years, the climax of the Founder's Day celebration consisted of Mayor Pike's wife singing opera while riding a horse. Everyone, including Mayor Pike is thankful for the change. 3. Darlene Swanson was voted "young lady most likely to become charming"

at Miss Wellington's School for Girls in Raleigh. 4. In order to influence Andy, Barbara Sue Lindsey personally delivers a bag of peat moss from her daddy's store to the judge's home. 5. At the beauty contest, Barbara Sue Lindsey is contestant #5, Josephine Pike is #6, and Ellie is #7. 6. A man named Tom worked on the pageant and also provided refreshments. 7. Floyd runs an ad in the Founder's Day program that reads, "Compliments Of Floyd's Tonsorial Parlor, The Best Clip Joint In Town." 8. In the annual play, Floyd portrays the founder of the town, John Mayberry. 9. Erma Bishop made all of the costumes for the Founder's Day play.

"Andy and the Gentleman Crook"

Episode #21. Air date: 2-27-61. Writers: Ben Gershman and Leo Solomon. Director: Bob Sweeney.

Barney gets excited when Andy informs him that the infamous "gentleman crook," Dan Caldwell, will be staying at the Mayberry jail for a few days before being sent on to Atlanta. In order to make Caldwell feel more comfortable, Barney puts a picture of a boat on the ocean in cell #1 to remind Caldwell of his old cell at Alcatraz. When Gentleman Dan arrives, Barney treats him like an honored guest. He gives him a television, stereo, and books, among other items in his cell. Barney goes so far as to get Caldwell's autograph, even though he claims it's for a friend.

Gentleman Dan's charming ways soon win over Aunt Bee and Opie as well. Soon, both Barney and Opie refer to the crook as "Uncle Dan." They listen to Caldwell's exciting stories about the Kansas City Million Dollar Heist, the Toledo Payroll Caper, and numerous yarns about "Baby Face" Nelson and John Dillinger. Andy is the only one who doesn't trust the convicted forger, swindler, and confidence man.

During a game of gin rummy inside his cell, Caldwell steals Barney's pistol. At that moment, Aunt Bee, Opie, and Andy arrive at the courthouse. Andy believes the gun is empty, since he had scolded Barney just the day before for accidentally shooting off the weapon inside the courthouse. Caldwell thinks Andy is bluffing until he attempts to fire the gun with no luck. Andy confidently takes the pistol away, aims it in the air, and is shocked when he fires a bullet through the roof. It seems Barney had put a bullet back in the gun and it luckily misfired when Caldwell tried to use it.

MEMORABLE SCENE. Andy's homespun version of "Jack and the Beanstalk," as told to Opie and Barney. This fairy tale can be heard, complete with a 100-piece orchestra conducted by Earle Hagen, on the 1961 Capitol Records album, "Songs, Themes and Laughs from the Andy Griffith Show."

CASE NOTES. Regulars: **Andy Griffith, Don Knotts, Ronny Howard, Frances Bavier,** and **Hal Smith.**

Veteran character actor **Dan Tobin** stars as Dan Caldwell. Tobin appeared as Kerwin Tobin in *I Married Joan*, Oliver Sheppard in *My Favorite Husband*, and Terrance Clay in *Perry Mason*, among other television roles.

Mike Steen portrays the police sergeant.

EPISODE NOTES. 1. Besides shooting off his gun in the courthouse, Barney lost two other bullets in the laundry. 2. Barney says he'll be called "Porky" if he keeps eating Aunt Bee's meals. 3. Aunt Bee's rhubarb pie won the blue ribbon at the county fair. 4. One time the boiler in the Mayberry courthouse ruptured and flooded the floor. 5. Dan Caldwell's patented line is "On my word as a gentleman." Andy gets upset when he overhears Opie repeating this phrase. 6. Dan Caldwell smokes cigars that are custom-made in Tampa. 7. Andy attempts to tell Opie the story of "Jack and the Princess that Couldn't Laugh," but Opie would rather hear one of Gentleman Dan's crime stories. 8. Dan Caldwell committed crimes in Bowling Green, Kentucky, and Jacksonville, Florida.

"Cyrano Andy"

Episode #22. Air date: 3-6-61. Writers: Jack Elinson and Charles Stewart. Director: Bob Sweeney.

Barney confides to Andy how strong his feelings are for Thelma Lou. Barney believes that she is "the cat's." He cares for her so much that he even sees her face in his eggs when he eats breakfast. Andy urges his lovestruck deputy to let Thelma Lou know how he feels, but Barney doesn't believe he can properly express his feelings face to face.

Without Barney's knowledge, Andy visits Thelma Lou and tells her about the situation with Barney. In an attempt to release Barney's feelings through jealousy and anger, Thelma Lou tells Barney that Andy came to visit her and wants to date her. Barney initially wants to fight Andy until he hears the explanation of what actually happened.

In an attempt to retaliate, Barney tells Andy that he can steal Ellie away from him. Andy finds this humorous. In order to properly woo Ellie, Barney has Floyd the barber give him the works: shave, haircut, witch hazel, eau de cologne and toilet water. In a hilarious scene, Barney fails in his seduction of Ellie.

Next, Ellie and Andy mutually decide to "come on strong" to Barney and Thelma Lou, respectively. They hope such aggressiveness will frighten them into each other's arms. The trick works, and soon Barney and Thelma Lou truly begin their days of courting.

MEMORABLE SCENE. When Andy keeps interrupting Barney trying to make out with Thelma Lou.

CAST NOTES. Regulars: **Andy Griffith, Don Knotts, Ronny Howard** and **Elinor Donahue.** **Betty Lynn** makes her first appearance in the series as Thelma Lou. She was never given a last name.

EPISODE NOTES. 1. Barney's telephone number is given as 431. 2. Barney hums "Beautiful Dreamer" while Andy is kidding him about Thelma Lou. 3. Andy, Ellie, Barney, and Thelma Lou sing, "Seeing Nellie Home" and "Liza Jane." 4. Opie is thrilled when he beats Andy at a game of checkers. 5. Andy nicknames Barney "Casanova." He refers to Ellie as "Ellie Mae." 6. Barney learned how to be romantic by watching Rock Hudson movies. 7. Barney wears his salt and pepper suit on his dates with Thelma Lou. 8. Once again, the issue of *TV Guide* featuring Lucille Ball on the cover can be seen on the magazine rack at Walker's Drugstore. For the record, the two other episodes showing this same *TV Guide* are 14, "The Horse Trader" and 15, "Those Gossipin' Men."

"Andy and Opie, Housekeepers"

Episode #23. Air date: 3-13-61. Writer: David Adler. Director: Bob Sweeney.

Aunt Bee is mad at Andy and Opie for being so sloppy around the house. She is further upset when she receives a telephone call from her cousin Edgar in Mt. Pilot. It seems that Edgar's wife, Maude, has been stricken with a case of bursitis and Edgar needs Bee's assistance. Aunt Bee reluctantly leaves for Mt. Pilot, all the while worrying about the welfare of Andy and Opie and what condition her immaculate house will be in upon her return.

Indeed, the Taylor men prove to be inept housekeepers. In no time at all, the place is a mess. When Aunt Bee phones home, she tells Andy that Maude has improved and she'll be returning home earlier than expected. Andy and Opie roll up their sleeves and completely clean the house. After they are finished, Opie comments that they did a great job and that Aunt Bee will see how well they got along without her. This makes Andy realize that the house needs to be messed up in order to make Aunt Bee feel needed. Andy and Opie purposely mess up the just-cleaned house. Then, exhausted, they leave to pick up Aunt Bee at the bus station. Meanwhile, a well-meaning neighbor, Bertha Edwards, sees the condition of the house and takes it upon herself to clean it up.

Upon arriving home, Aunt Bee is sad (and Andy and Opie are shocked) to see how nice the house looks. Peace is restored, however, when Andy and Opie mess up the house behind Aunt Bee's back, and she catches them trying to clean up the artificial mess.

CASE NOTES. Regulars: **Andy Griffith, Ronny Howard,** and **Frances Bavier.**

Hope Summers makes her first appearance in the series as Bertha Edwards. In future episodes, she will be referred to as Bertha Johnson and ultimately as Clara Edwards. **Rory Stevens** appears as Opie's schoolmate Jimmy.

EPISODE NOTES. 1. Andy has to repair the stop sign that got knocked over on Spring Street. 2. Opie and Jimmy use Opie's bed as a trampoline. 3. Opie has a bad habit of sticking half-eaten peanut butter and jelly sandwiches and apples under his pillow. 4. The publicity photo of Frances Bavier (Aunt Bee) turns up again. This time it can be seen hanging on the wall in the Taylors' home near the front door as Aunt Bee is getting ready to leave. 5. Throughout the eight-year run of *The Andy Griffith Show*, numerous references were made to Mount Pilot. The real Mount Pilot is actually Pilot Mountain, North Carolina, located about 14 miles south of Mount Airy on Highway 52.

"The New Doctor"

Episode #24. Air date: 3-27-61. Writers: Charles Stewart and Jack Elinson. Director: Bob Sweeney.

Doctor Robert Benson is the new doctor in Mayberry. He is young, handsome and single. He is also spending most of his time with Ellie Walker at the drugstore. Aunt Bee and Barney try to convince Andy that he will lose Ellie to the physician. At first Andy seems unconcerned, but they finally get through to him, and he rushes to Ellie's house and asks her to go to the upcoming church social. She accepts, and all seems fine until Ellie insists that Dr. Benson accompany them. A disenchanted Andy reluctantly agrees.

Barney decides to do some undercover work to learn more about Dr. Benson's intentions. He goes to the doctor's office under the guise of wanting a complete physical. Barney asks a few questions, but he completely forgets his mission when Dr. Benson tells him that he has low blood pressure.

Later, Barney snoops on Ellie and Dr. Benson and hears them discussing marriage plans. He nearly gets run over by a car as he rushes back to Andy with the big news. Andy immediately confronts the couple at the drugstore and makes a hasty proposal of marriage to Ellie. It is then Sheriff Taylor discovers that the marriage plans were for Dr. Benson and his fiancee, who is arriving in Mayberry in just a few days. A smiling Ellie politely refuses Andy's forced proposal. Andy is relieved, but very embarrassed.

MEMORABLE SCENE. Barney spying on Dr. Benson and Ellie at Walker's Drugstore.

CAST NOTES. Regulars: **Andy Griffith, Don Knotts, Ronny Howard, Frances Bavier,** and **Elinor Donahue.**

George Nader appears as Dr. Robert Benson. In the late 1950s, Nader starred on television as super-sleuth Ellery Queen in *The Adventures of Ellery Queen.* He also appeared on many other television shows and in numerous movies, mostly in Europe, during the 1960s.

EPISODE NOTES. 1. Three of Mayberry's previous doctors were Old Doc Carruthers, Old Doc Green and Old Doc Mackenzie. 2. Aunt Bee makes refreshments for the church social. 3. A four-piece orchestra is scheduled to perform at the church social. 4. Barney's "Manhunt" theme is played as he is spying on Dr. Benson and Ellie and also near the end of the episode. 5. Andy and Barney drink soda pop at Walker's Drugstore. Andy prefers his in a bottle, while Barney likes his in a glass. 6. Sundaes cost 10 cents at Walker's Drugstore. 7. Dr. Benson says that Mayberrian Harvey Willick is a hypochondriac. 8. Barney accidentally locks himself in a cell as Andy goes to confront Dr. Benson and Ellie. 9. Dr. Benson and Ellie patch up Opie after he falls and skins his elbow. 10. The following sign appears on the front window of Orville Monroe's funeral parlor: "Everything In Time Of Need."

"A Plaque for Mayberry"

Episode #25. Air date: 4-3-61. Writers: Leo Solomon and Ben Gershman. Director: Bob Sweeney.

Mrs. Harriett Wicks and Mrs. Bixby of the Women's Historical Society are trying to locate the last living descendant of Revolutionary War hero Nathan Tibbs. The ladies have discovered that the person they are seeking lives in Mayberry. The society is planning a gala celebration to reveal and honor the descendant, who will receive a commemorative plaque.

Barney does some researching and convinces

himself that he is the one. He even writes and practices an acceptance speech for the big occasion. However, to the surprise of everyone, the descendant turns out to be none other than the town drunk, Otis Campbell.

Mayor Pike implores Andy to find a suitable replacement for Otis, fearing that he will show up drunk at the award ceremony and embarrass the entire town. Andy will hear nothing of it, and his faith in Otis is rewarded when the descendant of Nathan Tibbs comes through with an excellent (and sober) acceptance speech. Otis proudly donates the plaque to the town of Mayberry.

CAST NOTES. Regulars: **Andy Griffith, Don Knotts, Ronny Howard,** and **Hal Smith. Dick Elliott** returns as Mayor Pike. **Burt Mustin** returns as Jud. **Dorothy Neumann** returns as Otis Campbell's wife, Rita.

Joseph Hamilton and **Joseph Crehan** also appear in this episode.

Isabel Randolph appears as Mrs. Bixby, and **Carol Veazie** portrays Mrs. Harriett Wicks. These actresses have something in common. In *The Dick Van Dyke Show* (which was also produced by Danny Thomas), Randolph and Veazie portrayed Rob and Laura Petrie's mothers from time to time. Randolph portrayed Laura's mother in the episode "What's in a Middle Name?" (In this episode, Ritchie Petrie wants to know why his middle name is Rosebud.) Veazie portrayed Rob's mother in the episode "Empress Carlotta's Necklace." In that same episode, Will Wright (Mayberry's grouchy Ben Weaver) appeared as Rob's father. The guest-star similarities in *The Andy Griffith Show* and *The Dick Van Dyke Show* are easy to spot because both programs are now seen in syndication.

EPISODE NOTES. 1. Barney gives Otis an endurance test to make sure he is fit to go out in public after one of his binges. Andy witnesses the test and calls it "The Barney Fife Peter Piper Nose Pinching Test for Drunks." The test consists of reciting the Peter Piper tongue twister, touching one's fingers together with both eyes closed, and hopping on one foot. 2. In this episode, Barney's middle name is Oliver. 3. Mayor Pike brags that his daughter can sing the following tunes: "Yankee Doodle," "Jimmy Crack Corn," and "Flow Gently Sweet Afton." The mayor neglects to say which of his three daughters is such a good singer, but a good bet is Juanita, who sang "Flow Gently Sweet Afton" to Hollywood movie producer Mr. Harmon in episode 13, "Mayberry Goes Hollywood." 4. Barney's research shows that he is a descendant of Duncan Phyfe. He somehow comes to the conclusion that Duncan was a carpenter. Andy reminds Barney that their last names are spelled differently. 5.

Barney tells Andy that all Fifes (and Phyfes) are sensitive people. 6. Nathan Tibbs had a wife name Anna. 7. In a rare scene, Andy wears a tie with his sheriff's uniform to the award ceremony. 8. What did Nathan Tibbs do to make him a Revolutionary War hero? It was said that he ran eight miles through the snow to set the Mayberry bridge on fire. This act turned back the enemy and allowed George Washington and his troops to capture an entire regiment.

"The Inspector"

Episode #26. Air date: 4-10-61. Writers: Jack Elinson and Charles Stewart. Director: Bob Sweeney.

Andy learns that the state police inspector is on his way to Mayberry to conduct a full inspection of the Mayberry jail and courthouse. Barney is upset by the news, but Andy assures him that the inspector, Sam Allen, is an old hunting and fishing buddy.

Andy is surprised to learn that Sam has been replaced by Ralph Case. Mr. Case is all business and is appalled by Andy and Barney's lack of proper procedure and discipline. He compares their law enforcement tactics to those of the Katzenjammer Kids. Mr. Case telephones his boss, Mr. Brady, at the state capitol and tells him that the condition of the jail may warrant Andy and Barney's dismissal. Andy ignores the threats, but Barney is a nervous wreck.

Meanwhile, Andy has to deal with a local bootlegger named Luke Rainer. Luke is shooting at strangers from his cabin, fearing they are federal agents. Ralph Case accompanies Andy and Barney to Luke's cabin. As they arrive, Luke greets them with some fireworks from his shotgun. Mr. Case wants to radio the state police and use tear gas in order to flush Luke out of the cabin. Andy tells him none of that is needed. He proceeds to walk up to Luke's door amid a steady blast of gunfire. Mr. Case believes Andy is a goner, but Barney sheepishly says Andy knows what he's doing.

As all this action is going on, Mr. Brady arrives on the scene and witnesses Andy arresting Luke without receiving a scratch. Both Ralph Case and Mr. Brady are impressed with Andy's courage and the common-sense approach he used to end the confrontation. Mr. Case decides to stop the dismissal proceedings.

MEMORABLE SCENE. Barney playing checkers against himself at the beginning of the episode. He also enjoys playing parcheesi and casino by himself.

CAST NOTES. Regulars: **Andy Griffith, Don Knotts, Ronny Howard,** and **Hal Smith.**

Tod Andrews stars as Ralph Case. Andrews also appeared as Mr. Franklin in episode 249, "A Girl for Goober." He appeared in numerous television and movie roles in the 1950s and 1960s. In the early part of his career, he was known by the name Michael Ames.

Jack Prince, later to be known as Rafe Hollister, portrays Luke Rainer. **Willis Bouchey** appears as Mr. Brady. **Ray Lanier** portrays Sam.

EPISODE NOTES. 1. Otis Campbell celebrates his birthday during this episode. Andy plans a big celebration, complete with a birthday cake. Otis sings, "For I'm a Jolly Good Fellow" to himself. 2. Barney accidentally shoots off his gun in the courthouse. Mr. Case is not impressed. 3. Opie brings Andy a polka dot tie and his fishing hat (complete with hooks) in an honest attempt to make his pa look more official in the eyes of Mr. Case. 4. Andy and Barney inadvertently lock themselves in cell #1. A disgusted Ralph Case releases them. 5. Andy explains to Mr. Case that he used to subscribe to *The Police Gazette* but had to cut it out when Barney joined the force. It had a lot of girlie pictures and Barney's never been married. 6. Barney uses the police bull horn at picnics for races and other games. 7. Barney's "Manhunt" theme is played as Andy, Barney, and Ralph Case arrive at Luke Rainer's cabin. 8. The chairs in the jail cells at the Mayberry courthouse are adorned with Aunt Bee's handmade doilies. This really seems to anger Ralph Case. 9. Andy and Barney receive a package from the Hubacher brothers. (Their last communication from these brothers, who still reside in state prison, was in episode 11, "Christmas Story.") Andy receives a wallet and Barney gets a leather bookmark. The letter says that Elmer Hubacher had been out on parole but ended up back in prison.

"Ellie Saves a Female"

Episode #27. Air date: 4-17-61. Writer: David Adler. Director: Bob Sweeney.

A young woman named Frances (Frankie) Flint is the only child of Farmer Flint. Thus, she is his only farmhand to pitch in with the daily chores. Frankie is not allowed to use such items as nail polish and perfume, because her father says the farm is their number one priority and she doesn't have time to mess with such things. Ellie feels sorry for Frankie and puts together a care package consisting of nail polish, lipstick, hand lotion, and powder. She convinces Andy to take her to the Flint farm to deliver the goods. Old Man Flint (no first name was given) throws Ellie and Andy off his farm

and doesn't allow Frankie to keep the samples. He explains that Frankie doesn't have the need for such things.

Ellie gets mad at Andy for not standing up to Flint, but he explains that the man is her father, so it is his decision to make. Barney overhears the conversation and, without Andy's knowledge, tells Ellie he can convince Old Man Flint to let Frankie keep the cosmetics. Barney visits Flint by himself and gets tossed out as well, but he sneaks back and locates Frankie and sneaks her back into town under his custody. Ellie does a complete makeover on Miss Flint, who turns out to be a beautiful woman. Andy and Ellie take her back to the farm, where her own father doesn't even recognize her. Mr. Flint admits she is pretty, but he tells her to put her work clothes back on, because the farm cannot function without her help.

Andy gets an idea when Flint mentions that his neighbor, Mr. Jenkins, has sons who are built-in farmhands. When Andy takes Frankie over to let the Jenkins boys get a good look at their "new neighbor," they are instantly entranced. Old Man Flint recognizes Andy's plan and reasons that if Frankie marries one of the Jenkins boys, he will not be losing a fair farmhand of a daughter, he will be gaining an experienced and better farmhand as a son-in-law.

MEMORABLE SCENE. When Ellie sprays "Midnight Madness" perfume on Andy, Opie says he smells like a gardenia blossom. In a rare turn-of-the-tables scene, Barney unmercifully teases Andy about the "lovely fragrance" he's sporting.

CAST NOTES. Regulars: **Andy Griffith, Don Knotts, Ronny Howard,** and **Elinor Donahue.**

Edris March stars as Frances (Frankie) Flint.

R.G. Armstrong co-stars as Old Man Flint. Armstrong has appeared in countless television and movie roles over the years. On the silver screen, he can be seen in such movies as *Ride the High Country* (1962), *The Great White Hope* (1970), and *Heaven Can Wait* (1978).

Bob McQuain also appears.

EPISODE NOTES. 1. Frankie samples Frosted Cherry-Cherry Bon-Bon nail polish and Midnight Madness perfume at Walker's Drugstore. 2. Ellie sells the following powders at the drugstore: Tempting Touch, Shimmering Rose, and Twilight Blush. Andy jokingly says Twilight Blush fits his complexion better than the other two. 3. Andy refers to makeup as "female war paint." 4. Andy refers to Barney as "Tiger" during the episode. 5. Frankie buys chewing tobacco for her father at Walker's Drugstore. A pouch costs 20 cents. 6. Andy gives Opie a nickel to buy a candy bar at the drugstore.

"Andy Forecloses"

Episode #28. Air date: 4-24-61. Writers: Leo Solomon and Ben Gershman. Director: Bob Sweeney.

Lester Scobey, wife Helen and young daughter Mary rent a house from mean-spirited Ben Weaver. When Lester cannot come up with his monthly rent of $52.50, Ben demands in no uncertain terms that Andy serve an eviction order on the family. This is one sheriff duty Andy can do without. He visits the Scobeys and quizzes Lester about locating a job in order to pay the rent. Lester explains that he recently lost his job, and although he has checked with the local mill and the Mayberry Furniture Factory, neither place is hiring at this time. He has been able to do some odd jobs around town, and Helen has taken in some ironing, but nothing can be found on a permanent basis. Alas, the well-meaning but down-on-their-luck family has fallen behind in their rent.

Andy and Barney vow to help the Scobeys after Andy discovers that Ben Weaver wants to use the property as a warehouse for his department store. To make matters worse, Ben orders Andy to serve the foreclosure notice immediately, threatening him with removal from office if he refuses. Ben also informs Andy that the Scobeys owe the entire balance of their rent, a whopping $780.00, because they have not abided by the payment clause in their contract.

Andy decides to use some stall tactics before foreclosing, in order to help the family raise the money. With the help of Aunt Bee, Andy and Barney put on a "Save the Scobey House Fund" rummage sale. It helps, but the debt is simply too great.

When all seems lost, Andy decides to use some reverse psychology. Declaring that the Scobeys have had enough time, he proceeds to take a stunned Ben Weaver into the Scobey home, where he demands that the family vacate the premises. Seeing eviction firsthand, Ben has a change of heart. Andy's reassuring wink of the eye explains to Lester and Helen that his plan has succeeded. Ben even hires Lester to work at his department store in order to help pay the rent.

MEMORABLE SCENE. At the rummage sale, Barney attempts to sell a "slightly used" suit jacket, imported all the way from Richmond, to a man named Bill.

CAST NOTES. Regulars: **Andy Griffith, Don Knotts, Ronny Howard,** and **Frances Bavier. Will Wright** returns as the memorable miser, Ben Weaver.

In this episode, **Sam Edwards** portrays Lester Scobey, **Margaret Kerry** is Helen, and **Joy Ellison**

appears as Mary. In episode 11, "Christmas Story," these actors portrayed the Muggins family.

Bob McQuain appears as Bill. **Jack Prince** and **Hope Summers** also appear.

EPISODE NOTES. 1. Barney and his mother do not like people to touch their hats. 2. Barney's never-seen girl on the side, Juanita Beasley, is introduced in this episode. She works as a waitress at the Junction Cafe. Her telephone number is 142R. 3. The stall tactics used by Andy to hold off the foreclosure are (1) neglecting to tell Ben about the $2.00 registration fee for a foreclosure notice, and (2) stealing Lester's glasses so he cannot read or understand the terms of the foreclosure notice. 4. A family named Wilson donates a lawnmower to the rummage sale. 5. Aunt Bee and her friends in the ladies auxiliary once had a rummage sale that raised enough money to buy the school a new public address system. 6. Despite their differences, Andy and Ben Weaver enjoy going fishing together. 7. It took Ben Weaver exactly 17 episodes to turn into a grouch again. At the end of episode 11, "Christmas Story," he had changed into a kind old man. 8. In this episode, Lester Scobey tries in vain to get a job at the Mayberry Furniture Factory. Andy Griffith's father, Carl, was employed at the furniture factory in Mount Airy for many years.

"Quiet Sam"

Episode #29. Air date: 5-1-61. Writers: Jim Fritzell and Everett Greenbaum. Director: Bob Sweeney.

Barney is suspicious of a new farmer in Mayberry named Sam Becker. Sam rarely talks to anyone, he's always in a hurry, and no one knows anything about his past. Barney becomes more suspicious when he sees Sam buy the following items at Walker's Drugstore: large quantities of absorbent cotton, antiseptics, vitamins, tranquilizers, and swab sticks. When Sam is seen farming at night, Barney tells Andy that he may be growing marijuana! Andy replies that he sees nothing wrong with Sam's behavior, or his farming methods.

Late one night, Andy is called to the Becker farm and discovers that Sam's wife, Lily, is about to have a baby. This explains Barney's earlier discovery. When Andy attempts to phone Barney, he gets cut off by one of Lily's false alarms. Barney believes Andy's in trouble, so he heads to Sam's farm, after instructing Floyd the barber to enlist a couple of fellows named Nate and Clarence to form a posse and trail behind him to the Becker farm.

When Barney barges into Sam's house, he

discovers the real nature of the situation. Old Doc Winters, Mayberry's only doctor, is out of town, so Andy is asked to deliver the baby. A worried Barney reminds Andy that in the spring of 1938, he froze while dissecting a grasshopper in Miss Webster's biology class. In order to keep both Sam and Barney calm, Andy coaxes them into trading some old stories from their days in the military. In no time at all, Andy interrupts army story number 17 by showing Sam his new son. About that time, Floyd and his "posse" arrive and Barney has some explaining to do. By the way, the eight-pound, nine-ounce boy is named Andy.

CAST NOTES. Regulars: **Andy Griffith, Don Knotts, Ronny Howard, Frances Bavier, Howard McNear,** and **Hal Smith.**

William Schallert, a television and movie veteran, stars as Sam Becker. Schallert starred as Patty Duke's dad, Martin Lane, in the 1960s sitcom *The Patty Duke Show.* He was also Dobie Gillis' English teacher, Mr. Leander Pomfritt, on *The Many Loves of Dobie Gillis.* Schallert's other television roles are too numerous to mention. On the big screen, he has appeared in a variety of roles, including a cock-eyed judge in Steve Martin's first feature, *The Jerk* (1978).

The bluegrass group **The Country Boys** returns in this episode. Andy joins them on "She'll Be Comin' Round the Mountain." They are unbilled in the credits. Their other appearance was in episode 19, "Mayberry on Record."

EPISODE NOTES. 1. Sam and Lily Becker's house is known as the old Birch farm. 2. Lily Becker is never seen in the episode. 3. Four-year-old Nat Pike told Opie that a penny that's been hit by lightning is worth six cents. Andy gives Opie two pennies to try out Nat's theory. It is not mentioned whether Nat Pike is related to Mayor Pike. 4. Otis Campbell is scared to death of thunderstorms. 5. Sam Becker cuts his own hair. 6. Floyd Lawson's wife, Melba, has a pretty heavy walking stick which she uses to prop up their cellar door. 7. Barney's "Manhunt" theme is played as he departs to Sam's house. 8. Sam Becker drives an old pickup truck with the license plate number F-57975. 9. During the war, Barney served in the army. He was second in command of over 3,000 books at the PX library on Staten Island, but he'd rather not talk about it. 10. Sam Becker is a veteran of the Korean War. 11. This is the first episode written by the team of Jim Fritzell and Everett Greenbaum, the most prolific writers on *The Andy Griffith Show* and the favorites of many viewers.

"Barney Gets His Man"

Episode #30. Air date: 5-8-61. Writers: Leo Solomon and Ben Gershman. Director: Bob Sweeney.

While writing a littering citation to a seemingly harmless stranger, Barney inadvertently aids in the capture of an escaped convict named Eddie Brooke. Eddie is supposed to be serving a twenty-year prison sentence in Atlanta. Brooke vows revenge against Barney as he is taken into custody by state police sergeants Johnson and Miller.

Mayberry hails Barney as a hero, and he begins to believe it himself. He starts referring to himself as "Barney the Bulkhead." He brags about using "the old body block" in subduing Brooke. Barney also states that capturing dangerous criminals is "the deadly game" and he's "in it for keeps."

Unfortunately, Brooke quickly escapes from custody, and Captain Ardell of the state police tells Andy that Brooke was seen headed toward Mayberry. All of a sudden, "Barney the Bulkhead" turns into quivering jelly. Somehow, however, he musters up the courage to accompany Andy on the manhunt, along with Sergeants Johnson and Miller. The trail leads to an abandoned barn in Thatcher's Woods, just three miles from the Mayberry courthouse. Once inside the barn, Andy spots Brooke in a hayloft and cleverly sets up the action so Barney can make the arrest. Deputy Fife's self-confidence is restored and he is a hero once again, even though he admits he was so nervous that he swallowed his gum while capturing Brooke.

CAST NOTES. Regulars: **Andy Griffith, Don Knotts, Ronny Howard, Frances Bavier,** and **Betty Lynn.**

Barney Phillips portrays Eddie Brooke. **Bob McQuain** appears as Sergeant Johnson and **Mike Steen** portrays Sergeant Miller. **Burt Mustin, Joseph Hamilton,** and **Norman Leavitt** all appear in this episode.

EPISODE NOTES. 1. The following businesses in Mayberry are shown in this episode: the Coffee Shop, Mort's Clothing Store and the Fleur De Lis Beauty Salon. 2. Barney's "Manhunt" theme is played throughout the episode. 3. A rare camera angle, from the ground up, is used to make Barney appear much taller after he captures Eddie Brooke for the first time. 4. Andy refers to Barney as "Tiger Fife." 5. Barney refers to Mayberry as "the Gateway to Danger." 6. Andy, Aunt Bee, Thelma Lou, and Sergeants Johnson and Miller throw a surprise party in honor of Barney. They all join in and sing the line, "What's the Matter with Barney, He's All Right." 7. Barney claims to have 20/20 eyesight.

"The Guitar Player Returns"

Episode #31. Air date: 5-15-61. Writers: Charles Stewart and Jack Elinson. Director: Bob Sweeney.

Mayberry's own Jim Lindsey returns to town, an apparent success in the world of music. Since having a big hit record ("Rock 'n' Roll Rosie from Raleigh"), Jim is driving a bright red Mercedes SL convertible, has three new guitars and sports a fancy "set of threads." He's given a hero's welcome, complete with a parade featuring the Mayberry Drum and Bugle Corps. As grand marshal, Barney Fife escorts Jim from the courthouse to the Mayberry Hotel (five doors down). A big sign proclaims, "Welcome Home, Jim." Mayor Pike's plan of having his daughter sing, "Flow Gently Sweet Afton" was, fortunately, canceled.

Later, Jim tells Andy that he left Bobby Fleet's band because he was the main attraction and he believed more success would follow as a solo artist. Andy has his doubts about Jim's prosperity when he discovers unpaid bills at the Mayberry Hotel, Walker's Drugstore, and Floyd's Barbershop. Jim even borrowed ten dollars from Barney and has yet to pay it back.

Without Jim's knowledge, Andy contacts Bobby Fleet and asks him to come to Mayberry. At the courthouse, Bobby explains that Jim left the band after an argument, and other than "Rosie," his solo career has been a total washout. He goes on to say that he would love to have Jim back in the band but figures Jim is too proud and stubborn to ask on his own. Andy takes matters into his own hands by "arresting" Jim for vagrancy, in order to set up a meeting at the courthouse with Bobby. The meeting goes well, and Bobby agrees to pay Jim's $75.00 bail. Mr. Fleet regains his guitar player and gives Jim a substantial raise to boot.

CAST NOTES. Regulars: **Andy Griffith, Don Knotts, Ronny Howard, Frances Bavier,** and **Howard McNear. James Best** returns for his final appearance as Jim Lindsey. Sadly, this episode also marks the final appearance of **Elinor Donahue** in her role of Ellie Walker. **Dick Elliott** returns as Mayor Pike. **Phil Chambers** returns as Jason, the clerk at the Mayberry Hotel.

In this episode, **Herb Ellis** portrays Bobby Fleet. In 1952 Ellis played Joe Friday's partner, Frank Smith, on *Dragnet*. For the record, in episode 3, "The Guitar Player," Henry Slate portrayed Bobby Fleet.

Thomas B. Henry appears as the "repo man."

EPISODE NOTES. 1. Jim stays in room 22 at the Mayberry Hotel. 2. Aunt Bee calls Jim Lindsey "Jimmy." She also prepares him two of his favorite dishes, fried chicken and cornbread. 3. Andy sings and plays the guitar with Jim on "The Midnight Special." 4. Barney wears his salt and pepper suit to dinner at the Taylors. 5. During the episode, Jim performs four unnamed instrumentals on guitar. 6. Jim's Mercedes is financed by the Mid-Mountain Finance Company. 7. Barney enjoys an ice cream soda at Walker's Drugstore in this episode. 8. Barney brags that he can play the following tunes on the harmonica: "I'm Just a Vagabond Lover," "Roll Out the Barrel," "Mairzy Doats," and "Tiptoe Through the Tulips." 9. Two men named Charlie and Ralph are members of the Mayberry Drum and Bugle Corps. A man named Kester quit the corps because the other band members refused to practice at his house.

"Bringing Up Opie"

Episode #32. Air date: 5-22-61. Writers: Jack Elinson and Charles Stewart. Director: Bob Sweeney.

When Opie handcuffs his classmate Ralph Baker to a flag pole and starts using salty language, Aunt Bee lays down the law, forbidding him to go to the courthouse after school. She believes the jailhouse setting has been a bad influence on the boy and his time could be better spent at home. So, from now on, Opie must leave school everyday at 3:00 P.M. and go straight home. No more lessons in the fast draw from Barney; no tacking the new wanted posters to the bulletin board for Andy; and no more listening to any of Andy's slightly fractured fairy tales, such as "Beauty and the Beast" and "King Arthur and the Knights of the Round Table." Instead, he goes home, eats milk and cookies, and does chores for Aunt Bee. She even has him plant two rows of spinach in the garden. Yech!

At the courthouse, Andy, Barney, and Otis all miss the youngster. They ask Aunt Bee to reconsider, but she won't budge an inch. Otis claims he was the worst influence on Opie, but Andy and Barney disagree.

Soon, Opie becomes so bored at home that one day he decides to kick a can all the way out of town. He goes up to the entrance of the condemned Johnson mine, where he barely escapes disaster when a cave-in occurs. He then meets a young boy and trades the can for some apples. After eating seven of the apples and one bit of an eighth, he falls fast asleep in the back of a truck heading to nearby Elm City. Later, a man named Fred notifies a frantic Andy and Aunt Bee of Opie's whereabouts. After Opie is scolded for running away from home, Aunt

Bee realizes how important it is for the young man to spend time with his father. To the joy of everyone, she reinstates Opie's courthouse visits.

CAST NOTES. Regulars: **Andy Griffith, Don Knotts, Ronny Howard, Frances Bavier,** and **Hal Smith.**

Mike Brent appears as the unnamed boy who traded the apples for the can.

EPISODE NOTES. 1. Otis is arrested for violation of Ordinance 502, intoxicated in a public place. The fine is $2.00 or 24 hours in jail. Otis opts for the 24 hours. 2. Opie handcuffed Ralph Baker to the flag pole while playing cops and robbers at school. Opie said Ralph had resisted arrest. Barney had secretly given Opie the handcuffs, but had instructed him not to use them on people. 3 Two warning signs outside the entrance to the Johnson mine proclaim: "Dangerous Condemned Mine" and "Trespassing Forbidden." 4. It is not mentioned in the episode, but the man named Fred who notified Andy of Opie's whereabouts must have been the driver of the Elm City Delivery Service truck in which Opie fell asleep. 5. Barney disputes Andy's version of "King Arthur and the Knights of the Round Table." 6. Under normal circumstances, Opie's favorite dessert is apple pie. 7. Special mention must be given to the outstanding background music supplied by Earle Hagen and his crew during the "kick the can" sequence.

SEASON TWO

In this season, many wonderful episodes highlight relationships among the characters of Andy, Opie, Barney, and Aunt Bee. A.C. Nielson Co. rating for the 1961-1962 season: 27.0; rank: 7.

"Barney's Replacement"

Episode #33. Air date: 10-9-61. Writers: Jack Elinson and Charles Stewart. Director: Bob Sweeney.

First of all, Andy doesn't care for the way Barney updates the bulletin board. Next, Andy picks on his deputy for not repairing a broken stop sign. Later, Andy admonishes Barney for bumping into a parked vehicle with the squad car. To make matters worse, Andy's friend Ralph Baker of the state's attorney's office sends a lawyer named Bob Rogers to Mayberry to learn law enforcement procedures from Andy. Barney believes this is the last straw. He tells Thelma Lou that Andy is dissatisfied with his work as a deputy and that Bob Rogers is going to replace him.

Barney's assumption appears to be coming true when Bob uses the "law officer's manual" to come up with a more efficient bulletin board. He also devises a statistical chart that predicts crimes. From this chart, Bob predicts that during the current month, there will be twelve traffic violations, three breaking-and-enterings, one wife-beating and one case of vagrancy in Mayberry. Barney scoffs at this, especially the wife-beating prediction, until a call comes in saying Ed Simpkins just beat up his wife. To Barney's dismay, Andy assigns Rogers to the case.

Barney can take no more, so he resigns as Mayberry's deputy. Andy tries to talk him out of it, but Barney has had it. He takes a job selling Miracle Sweep vacuum cleaners. Unfortunately, both of his potential customers, Clara Johnson and Emma Brand, say he looks nice in his salt and pepper suit, but they are not in need of a vacuum cleaner.

Later, Bob Rogers sees Barney attempting to sell the vacuum cleaners and tells Andy his ex-deputy is violating Code 304, the Green River Ordinance, which requires door-to-door salesmen to have a permit to sell their wares. Bob arrests Barney for the violation. Furious, Barney tells Deputy Rogers in no uncertain terms, "There is more to sheriffin' than books and charts." Both Andy and Bob agree, and in no time at all, Barney is back in uniform as the one and only deputy of Mayberry. No one could be happier than Andy.

CAST NOTES. Regulars: **Andy Griffith, Don Knotts, Ronny Howard,** and **Betty Lynn. Cheerio Meredith** returns as Emma Brand. **Hope Summers** appears as Clara Johnson.

Mark Miller stars as Bob Rogers. Miller is best known as Jim Nash in the 1960s television show *Please Don't Eat the Daisies.*

EPISODE NOTES. 1. Andy observes that Barney weighs about 100 pounds, and 50 of it is proud." 2. Bob Rogers' license plate number on his car is the popular DC-269. 3. Barney's "Manhunt" theme is played when he plans his resignation and at the end of the episode. 4. In this episode, Barney tells Andy that he plans to marry Thelma Lou. 5. Barney keeps his citation book under his police hat. 6. Andy instructs Bob Rogers to tell Ralph Baker, his boss, to come to Mayberry so they can go frog-gigging. 7. It is not stated whether Andy's state's attorney friend, Ralph Baker, is related to the little boy that Opie handcuffed to the flag pole in episode 32, "Bringing Up Opie." That youngster's name was also Ralph Baker. 8. According to Bob Rogers, the Green River Ordinance was inspired by a case that occurred in 1924 in a town called Green River, or as Rogers says "Green Wiver." This mispronunciation went unnoticed.

"Opie and the Bully"

Episode #34. Air date: 10-2-61. Writer: David Adler. Director: Bob Sweeney.

Seven-year-old Opie is being threatened on a daily basis by a tough schoolboy named Sheldon. Every morning, Sheldon makes Opie give him his milk money (a nickel) or he will pulverize him, knock his block off, give him the old 1-2 and jump on him. Needless to say, Opie keeps his mouth shut. However, Andy begins to suspect a problem when Opie borrows a nickel from Aunt Bee after he's already been given milk money. On another day, the youngster borrowed a nickel from Barney after he'd received his milk allotment for the day.

When Andy tells Barney about the mystery, Deputy Fife can't resist following Opie to school the next morning. In a hilarious scene, Barney uses all of his spying and undercover tactics to witness the extortion. He reports the happenings to Andy. Andy realizes Opie must fight back, but he runs into a problem in explaining how or why to the boy.

Finally, while fishing with Opie at their favorite spot, Andy takes advantage of the situation by concocting a story about how he once had to defend this particular fishing hole from a bully named Hodie Snitch. He tells his son that when Hodie Snitch slugged him, he laughed in his face and tore into him like a "windmill in a tornado." This inspires Opie to end the extortion, once and for all.

The next morning, Opie leaves a clean set of clothes with Andy at the courthouse, just in case the ones he's wearing happen to get messed up before school. Andy and Barney nervously await the outcome of Opie's showdown. The tension ends when Opie rushes through the door, proudly sporting a black eye. More importantly, he still has his milk money, plus all the money he'd borrowed! He tells his pa that he tore into Sheldon like a "windmill in a tornado" and when he was punched by Sheldon, he laughed in the bully's face. A joyful Opie turns down Barney's offer of applying a steak to the black eye. Opie would prefer to sport his medal of courage for a week or two.

CAST NOTES. Regulars: **Andy Griffith, Don Knotts, Ronny Howard,** and **Frances Bavier.**

Terry Dickinson appears as Sheldon. Could his name been inspired by executive producer Sheldon Leonard? Mr. Leonard appeared in countless television and movie roles as a tough guy.

EPISODE NOTES. 1. Andy's quote of the day, as told to Opie: "Millions for charity, but not one penny for tribute." This quote was used in a slightly different variation in episode 196, "Goober Makes History." In that episode, Howard Sprague gave

credit to Charles Cotesworth Pinckney for the origin of that phrase. Charles Cotesworth Pinckney (1746-1825) was a Revolutionary War soldier, statesman, and lawyer. He was born in South Carolina and appointed in 1796 as the U.S. minister to France. The slogan "Millions for defense, but not one cent for tribute" is often credited to him. Actually, the phrase was said as a toast by Robert Goodloe Harper, at a dinner for John Marshall in 1798. What Pinckney said (to French agents demanding money before negotiations) was, "It is No! No! Not a sixpence!" 2. Aunt Bee fixes Opie a sandwich and a piece of apple pie for his school lunch. 3. While spying on Opie Barney tore a hole in a newspaper that a man was reading. The newspaper was the *Press Herald.*

"Andy and the Woman Speeder"

Episode #35. Air date: 10-16-61. Writers: Charles Stewart and Jack Elinson. Director: Bob Sweeney.

While fishing, Andy, Opie, Barney, and Floyd witness Elizabeth Crowley (a magazine reporter from Washington, D.C.) going 70 mph in a 45 mph zone. Ms. Crowley tells Sheriff Taylor she will not return the following week for her court date. She then asks to see the justice of the peace and is surprised to see that Andy holds this post as well. He fines her $10.00 for speeding and $20.00 more for contempt. When she won't be quiet, he ultimately fines her an extra $30.00 for "insulting the dignity of his robe." Andy calms down and finally settles on a total of $25.00. The stubborn lady still refuses to pay, so Andy places her in jail.

Ms. Crowley may be stubborn, but she is certainly not dumb. Soon, she starts putting the charm on everyone she comes in contact with. She tells Barney that he bears an amazing resemblance to Frank Sinatra. She praises Floyd's prowess with hair, gives Opie a baseball signed by the New York Yankees, and even wraps Aunt Bee around her finger. Mayor Pike is also taken in by her charms and decides to hold a special "mayor's court," rather than make Ms. Crowley wait for the traveling judge, who won't arrive in Mayberry for another week. At the trial, Barney, Floyd, and Opie prove to be reluctant witnesses to the crime. Mayor Pike dismisses the case, and Andy expresses his displeasure with everyone, especially Barney.

As Ms. Crowley is leaving, she sees the error of her ways and the turmoil created. She proceeds to speed in full view of Andy and Barney. When they stop her, she happily pleads guilty and pays her fine of $10.00 *and* the original fine of $25.00. She tells

Andy and Barney that she has acted unethically and may now leave Mayberry with a clear conscience. Andy wholeheartedly agrees and approves.

CAST NOTES. Regulars: **Andy Griffith, Don Knotts, Ronny Howard, Frances Bavier,** and **Howard McNear. Dick Elliott** returns as Mayor Pike.

Jean Hagen stars as Elizabeth Crowley. Hagen is fondly remembered as Danny Thomas's wife, Margaret Williams, on The Danny Thomas Show."

EPISODE NOTES. 1. Elizabeth Crowley drives a Ford Thunderbird. Her license plate number is JR-4128. 2. Floyd Lawson caught three trout and two perch while fishing. Barney caught a frog. 3. Ms. Crowley represented herself at mayor's court. This is the only episode in which Mayor Pike served as a judge or held a mayor's court. 4. Mayberry has an attorney named Rafe Peterson, who also sells aluminum siding. Another Mayberry attorney, Clarence Polk, umpires baseball games. 5. Aunt Bee serves as Elizabeth Crowley's matron while she is in jail. Aunt Bee asks Barney to bring Ms. Crowley some nail polish and eau de cologne. 6. Barney imitates Frank Sinatra by singing the first lines of "One More for My Baby (and One More for the Road)." 7. Elizabeth Crowley calls Andy "Jesse James" when he imposes the fines. 8. This episode has a storyline similar to the pilot episode of The Andy Griffith Show. The pilot was aired on The Danny Thomas Show. In that episode, Marjorie Lord appeared as Danny's wife, Kathy Williams.

"Barney on the Rebound"

Episode #36. Air date: 10-30-61. Writers: Charles Stewart and Jack Elinson. Director: Bob Sweeney.

Barney is instantly attracted to Melissa Stevens, a pretty newcomer to Mayberry. He goes so far as to give her a police escort from the courthouse to the post office, which is just across the street. Melissa and her father, George, have moved to Mayberry from Savannah, where he had operated a cotton mill. They're living at the old Pierson house on Post Road. When Thelma Lou sees how Barney acts around Melissa, she gets mad and tells him that he's a free man.

After Barney's second dinner date with Melissa and George at their home, Melissa claims Barney proposed marriage to her. Of course he didn't, but that doesn't stop Melissa from reporting the "proposal" to the *Mayberry Merry-Go-Round* newspaper. After the paper publishes the alleged proposal, Barney tells Thelma Lou the true story and begs her forgiveness. She believes him and decides to take

him back. Next, Barney attempts to break all ties with Melissa, but this results in her filing a breach of contract suit with Andy at the courthouse.

Andy senses that George and Melissa are con artists who are out to make an easy buck in an out-of-court settlement. At the breach of contract hearing, Andy surprises Melissa, George, and especially Barney when he assumes his role of justice of the peace and begins a wedding ceremony. The wedding and the lawsuit come to an abrupt stop when Melissa and George admit they are married to each other. In fact, Melissa's name is actually Gladys. Andy tells them to leave town or face criminal charges. The couple decide to leave Mayberry and never come back. Andy tells Barney he hopes he learned his lesson.

MEMORABLE SCENE. Barney and Thelma Lou making out at the end of the episode.

CAST NOTES. Regulars: **Andy Griffith, Don Knotts, Ronny Howard, Frances Bavier** and **Betty Lynn.**

Noted actor **Jackie Coogan** appears as George Stevens. Coogan is well known for his television role of Uncle Fester on The Addams Family from 1964 through 1966. He was also one of the most noted child stars in the history of the movies. Coogan appeared in such silent movie classics as Peck's Bad Boy, Oliver Twist, and The Kid (with Charlie Chaplin). He also appeared in countless television and movie roles through the 1970s.

Beverly Tyler stars as Melissa (Gladys) Sevens.

EPISODE NOTES. 1. Barney first meets Melissa after she has illegally parked her car. Her license plate number is VT-772. 2. Melissa claims to have attended junior college in Savannah for two years. 3. George Stevens smokes a pipe. 4. Barney's "Manhunt" theme is played as he gives Melissa a police escort from the courthouse to the post office. 5. Barney tells George and Melissa that he would like to be a private detective, or work for J. Edgar Hoover at the F.B.I. 6. Barney offers to play the following songs on harmonica for George and Melissa Stevens: "Kitten on the Keys," "Roses of Piccardy" and "Finiculi Finicula." He ends up playing "Jingle Bells." 7. After Barney apologizes to Thelma Lou, he refers to himself as "Level-Headed Barney Fife."

"The Perfect Female"

Episode #37. Air date: 11-27-61. Writers: Jack Elinson and Charles Stewart. Director: Bob Sweeney.

Karen Moore, Thelma Lou's cousin from Arkansas, is vacationing in Mayberry. Barney and Thelma Lou decide to play cupid and introduce her to Andy. In the past, this type of setup has been unsuccessful, but this time the two hit it off. To Barney and Thelma Lou's surprise, Andy invites Karen to go with him on a date — shooting crows at Finnegan Flats, just outside Mayberry. On the date, Andy has a poor day shooting, and in order not to hurt his feelings, Karen doesn't mention she is the skeet shooting champion of Arkansas.

When Barney quizzes Andy about the date, he makes a flippant remark, saying he likes Karen but wants to date her some more in order to see if she "measures up" to his standards. Of course, Barney cannot keep his mouth shut. He tells Karen what Andy said, and she gets infuriated. Barney neglects to tell Andy that he spilled the beans.

By a strange twist of fate, Andy invites Karen to watch him at a skeet shooting contest, in which he is heavily favored to win. Much to everyone's surprise, especially Andy's, Karen enters the contest as his competition. Karen proceeds to hit all 25 targets, while Andy nets only 23. As Karen receives her first-place trophy, she lets Andy know in no uncertain terms that she doesn't like feeling she has to "measure up" to his standards.

Despite Barney's advice, Andy sees something special in Karen and pursues a relationship. This may have been a good match, but it is the only episode in which Karen appeared or was ever referred to.

CAST NOTES. Regulars: **Andy Griffith, Don Knotts, Ronny Howard, Frances Bavier,** and **Betty Lynn.**

Gail Davis stars as Karen Moore. Davis appeared in numerous Gene Autry westerns in the 1950s and starred on television as the title character in *Annie Oakley* from 1953 through 1956. This role may have inspired the producers of *The Andy Griffith Show* to have Ms. Davis portray another shooting expert.

Alfred Hopson appears as the judge of the skeet shooting contest.

EPISODE NOTES. 1. Barney and Thelma Lou introduce Andy to Karen at a prearranged meeting. The place was the Mayberry Coffee Shop, at 3:00 P.M. Barney takes two helpings of sugar in his coffee. 2. Barney had once set up Andy on a blind date with a girl named Melinda Keefer from Detroit. Andy said Melinda had fat knees and talked too much. One other time, Barney introduced Andy to a girl who Andy said looked like Benjamin Franklin. 3. Barney refers to himself as "Subtle Barney Fife." 4. Andy's favorite pie is gooseberry. 5. Andy and Karen sing a duet on the tune "Sourwood Mountain." 6. Both Andy and Karen enjoy reading mystery stories.

"Aunt Bee's Brief Encounter"

Episode #38. Air date: 12-4-61. Writers: Leo Solomon and Ben Gershman. Director: Bob Sweeney.

Aunt Bee has a kind heart and finds it difficult to turn down door-to-door salesmen or anyone who's looking for work. One day, a handyman named Henry Wheeler stops by, and Aunt Bee hires him to spray her roses. Soon, she is charmed by Mr. Wheeler and convinces Andy to let him stay to paint the front porch and repair the roof. In no time at all, Aunt Bee and Mr. Wheeler start dating, and Andy is stuck doing all the repair work. He doesn't mind, because he's pleased to see Aunt Bee happy. Mr. Wheeler takes her to the movies, they eat ice cream sodas, she shows him around Mayberry, and they go on picnics.

Things are going fine until Andy introduces Mr. Wheeler to George Bricker, the Mayberry mailman. George wonders out loud how a handyman could have such soft hands. This arouses Andy's suspicions, so he telephones Sheriff Mitchell in Mount Pilot, where Mr. Wheeler had told Aunt Bee and Andy he'd recently done some work. Sheriff Mitchell tells Andy that Henry ("Goldbrick") Wheeler is a ladies' man who is not on the up-and-up. He did the same thing in Mount Pilot that he's currently doing in Mayberry. While in Mount Pilot, "Goldbrick" dated Mary Grady while her brother Bill did all the chores. Sheriff Mitchell went on to say that when Wheeler gets tired of one place, he simply moves on without notice, leaving a trail of broken hearts and unfinished work.

In order to spare Aunt Bee's feelings, Andy quietly threatens Mr. Wheeler with a shotgun, and "Goldbrick" leaves in a big hurry. Later, a second handyman named Mr. Murray shows up, but this time Aunt Bee catches herself and tells him that no work is needed.

CAST NOTES. Regulars: **Andy Griffith, Ronny Howard,** and **Frances Bavier. Edgar Buchanan** stars as Henry (Goldbrick) Wheeler. Buchanan is well known for his television role of Uncle Joe Carson, on the 1960s classic *Petticoat Junction."* He also appeared in over 100 movies, including *Benji* in 1974. In that movie he was reunited with Frances Bavier.

Doodles Weaver appears as George Bricker, the mailman. For an in-depth view of Weaver's career, see the Cast Notes section on episode 102, "A Black Day for Mayberry."

George Cisar portrays Sheriff Mitchell. In future episodes, Cisar would portray Cyrus Tankersley. He would also appear, occasionally, on *Mayberry R.F.D.*

in the same role. Cisar had regular roles in a couple of television series, including *Stand By for Crime* (1949) in which he portrayed Sergeant Kramer, and *Dennis the Menace* (1963-1965) in which he played Sergeant Theodore Mooney. He made guest appearances in such series as *The Addams Family, The Beverly Hillbillies, The Double Life of Henry Phyfe, Lassie, Leave It to Beaver, Many Happy Returns, Perry Mason,* and *Room for One More.* Cisar appeared in many movies, including *Call Northside 777* (1948, with Jimmy Stewart), *Don't Knock the Rock* (1956, with Bill Haley and His Comets and Little Richard), *Jailhouse Rock* (1952, with Elvis Presley), *Viva Las Vegas* (1964, with Elvis Presley), and *tick... tick...tick...* (1970).

Sherwood Keith appears as Mr. Murray.

EPISODE NOTES. 1. Mr. Wheeler charges Aunt Bee $1.60 to spray her roses. He compliments her on the Peabody rose she grew. 2. "Goldbrick" claims to suffer from a touch of lumbago, even though roofing is his specialty. 3. When Aunt Bee was 18 years old, her family moved to Peoria. She was quite skinny in those days. 4. Aunt Bee serves chicken and corn on the cob to Mr. Wheeler. She also makes sure he gets plenty of fresh lemonade. 5. Mr. Wheeler claims to have once owned and operated a hardware store, but says he gave it up when the pressure got to him. 6. Breakfast is served promptly at 7:00 A.M. at the Taylor house. 7. Mr. Wheeler's license plate number on his truck is the familiar DC-269, while Mr. Murray's license plate number is the equally familiar VT-772. 8. A hardware store in Mayberry is referred to, but not shown in the episode. 9. The advertisement on Mr. Wheeler's truck states: "Henry Wheeler, Gardening, Carpentry, Painting." "A Job Well Done Means A Satisfied Customer." 10. While Andy is threatening Mr. Wheeler with a shotgun, he refers to him as "Uncle Henry." 11. Mr. Wheeler tells Andy that clouds are like women: They're beautiful, but no one appreciates them. 12. The publicity photo of Frances Bavier (Aunt Bee), depicting the actress in her younger days, appears for the final time in the series. It is hanging on the wall in the Taylors' living room. At one point, it is directly behind Henry Wheeler.

"Mayberry Goes Bankrupt"

Episode #39. Air date: 10-23-61. Writers: Jack Elinson and Charles Stewart. Director: Bob Sweeney.

The Mayberry town council forces Andy to serve an order of eviction on a kindly old gentle-man named Frank Myers. Frank has not been able to pay his taxes for some time, and the council has run out of patience. The council also states that Frank's run-down shack is an eyesore and makes the town of Mayberry look bad. His house is the first home seen by travelers who enter Mayberry from the north.

Andy asks Frank if there is any way he can raise the needed tax money, but Frank explains that his profession of making berries for women's hats has been very slow of late. Next, Andy invites Frank to stay at his home, with Aunt Bee and Opie, until he can locate a new home. Frank brings a strongbox with him containing many valuables that he could possibly sell. His "valuables" include a medallion from the 1906 World's Fair in St. Louis; a spoon featuring the skyline of Milwaukee, Wisconsin; a genuine whalebone napkin ring; a buttonhook used for old-time boots that had buttons on them; and a red, white and blue sleeve guard. Then, Frank pulls out a $100.00 savings bond, issued in 1861 by the town of Mayberry. He explains that his great-grandfather had given him the bond when he was a youngster. The bond earns 8 1/2 percent interest, compounded annually. Andy, Mayor Pike, Mayberry treasurer Harlan Fergus, and especially Frank are astounded to discover the town owes Frank the sum of $349,119.27.

The debt is simply too large to be paid, so Frank agrees to allow the members of the council to completely refurbish his home. Everything is fine until Frank tells Mayor Pike about a portrait given to him by the same great-grandfather who gave him the bond. The portrait is of Frank's great-grandfather posing with Confederate general Robert E. Lee. It is then the town council verifies the bond was issued by the Confederate government and is totally worthless today. Just as the council starts to turn on poor Frank, Andy comforts them with the thought that they have helped a friend in need and created a "showplace" which will encourage strangers to visit Mayberry, the charming garden spot of North Carolina.

CAST NOTES. Regulars: **Andy Griffith, Don Knotts, Ronny Howard** and **Frances Bavier. Dick Elliott** returns as Mayor Pike.

Andy Clyde turns in a great performance as Frank Myers. In the 1920s Clyde starred in numerous two-reel comedies produced by Mack Sennett. In the 1940s, he was Hopalong Cassidy's sidekick, "California," in western movies. In later years, Clyde appeared on television as Timmy's elderly friend Cully on *Lassie.* He also was George Mac-Michael on *The Real McCoys.*

Warren Parker makes his first appearance in the series as bank president and town treasurer Harlan Fergus. In later episodes, his name in the show will

Buddy Ebsen stars as Dave Browne in "Opie's Hobo Friend."

be changed to Mr. Meldrim. Parker had a regular role in the 1948-1949 television series *The Growing Paynes*. He has guest-starred in such television series as *The Fugitive, The Munsters,* and *The Twilight Zone.* He has appeared in many movies, including *Too Soon to Love* (1960, with Jack Nicholson), *The Sound of Music* (1965, with Julie Andrews), and *If He Hollers, Let Him Go!* (1968).

Jason Johnson and **Phil Chambers** appear as Mayberry councilmen. **Hal Torey** portrays an out-of-town visitor.

EPISODE NOTES. 1. Frank Myers has a pet chicken named Hazel. He also has fifty boxes of different berries for women's hats. 2. When Frank thought he was rich, he smoked a big cigar and planned to buy the following items from a mail order catalog: an air conditioner, a stove, a color television, and a stereo phonograph. 3. Aunt Bee wears eyeglasses when she sews. 4. Frank's great-grandfather also gave him a personal letter he had received from the president of the Confederacy, Jefferson Davis. 5. The visitors passing through Mayberry thought they were in Elm City. 6. Frank's medallion is from the "1906 World's Fair in St. Louis," but that World's Fair occurred in 1904. 7. It is more than a coincidence that when this episode was produced and aired, Frank E. Myers was the name of the production manager of *The Andy Griffith Show*.

"Opie's Hobo Friend"

Episode #40. Air date: 11-13-61. Writer: Harvey Bullock. Director: Bob Sweeney.

While fishing, Andy and Opie bump into a shrewd vagabond named Dave Browne. Opie is soon impressed by "Mr. Dave," who does magic tricks and talks to the fish in Meyers Lake. Barney, however, is not impressed by Browne and arrests him for violating Code #63, vagrancy and loitering.

In order to keep Barney off his back, Andy hires Mr. Dave to do some hedge-trimming at his house, but the hobo would rather go fishing with Opie. As Dave Browne tells his young friend "The most perfect day to start any job — tomorrow." Soon, Mr. Dave teaches Opie the art of irresponsibility and encourages him to cheat, procrastinate, and play hooky.

When Barney hauls in Opie after catching him skipping school, Andy pays Mr. Dave a visit. He explains the situation and orders him to leave town. Browne tells Andy that when he departs all of Andy's troubles with Opie will be over. Andy disagrees, stating that Opie thinks so much of Mr. Dave that his troubles are just beginning.

In order to amend the damage done, Mr. Dave allows Barney to see him making off with a ladies' pocketbook. It just so happens the pocketbook belongs to Aunt Bee. Barney arrests him for purse-snatching, and when Opie sees what his hero has done, he wants nothing more to do with him. A thankful Andy releases Mr. Dave when he sees that the "stolen" pocketbook was one that Aunt Bee had thrown in the trash some time ago.

CAST NOTES. Regulars: **Andy Griffith, Don Knotts, Ronny Howard,** and **Frances Bavier.**

Buddy Ebsen turns in an outstanding performance as Dave Browne. Mr. Ebsen is best known for his portrayal of Jed Clampett on *The Beverly Hillbillies* and for his other famous television role of *Barnaby Jones.* Ebsen also was the first choice to pay the tin woodsman in the 1939 classic *The Wizard of Oz,* but he had to leave the movie when the makeup he was forced to wear got into his lungs and he nearly died. He was replaced by Jack Haley.

EPISODE NOTES. 1. Barney suspects that Mr. Dave may be Al Capone himself, hiding out in Mayberry. 2. Barney remarks that he has "baby blue" eyes. 3. Mr. Dave gives Opie his homemade "Gollywobbler Super Fish Catcher." It's a device that is supposed to attract fish. He also shows Opie how to get free gumballs from a machine by using magic. He taps the machine twice, says "tuscarora," and (with the help of a metal wire) gets all the free gumballs his heart desires. 4. Barney refers to Dave

Browne as "Pete the Tramp." 5. Mr. Dave steals and eats the sandwiches Aunt Bee had sent with Andy and Opie on their fishing trip. He also steals a chicken from Jesse Pearson and an apple pie from Mrs. Tillman. 6. Dave Browne claims to be part Indian. 7. Barney reads a book titled *Magic*, in order to perform magic tricks. After he messes up one of the tricks, he storms out of the courthouse in a huff because Opie performed the same trick perfectly. 8. The train stops for water in Mayberry at 3:45 P.M. daily. This is the train that Mr. Dave catches at the end of the episode.

"Crime-Free Mayberry"

Episode #41. Air date: 11-20-61. Writer: Paul Henning. Director: Bob Sweeney.

F.B.I. Special Agent Fred Jenkins comes to Mayberry to present an award to Andy and Barney for achieving the lowest crime rate in the country. A gala award ceremony is planned for the following evening. While Andy credits the good people of Mayberry for the award, Barney, Floyd, and Mayor Pike prefer to bask in the glory. In fact, Mayor Pike commissions Ray Watson to make medals for Andy and Barney. Andy thinks the idea is silly, while Barney tells Ray he'd like to have his birthstone, a ruby, attached to his medal. Floyd starts giving tours of the courthouse (for two bits a head), to the anger and dismay of Andy. Barney writes two songs about himself and Andy. Even Aunt Bee gets caught up in the act, by heading up the newly formed "Greater Mayberry Historical Society and Tourist Bureau, Ltd." When Andy see Aunt Bee showing pictures of him as a youngster, he agrees the organization is definitely limited.

Later, an Intercontinental News photographer named Joe Layton shows up and takes a picture of Andy shaking hands with Fred Jenkins. Layton and Jenkins are actually con men who plan to rob the Mayberry bank during the award ceremony. At the ceremony, as Mr. Jenkins makes a stirring speech about crimefighting, Andy notices Joe Layton slipping out the back door. It takes Layton 15 minutes to break into the bank vault. He is shocked to see Andy sitting in a chair inside the vault with waiting handcuffs. Andy explains to the crook that the vault hasn't been opened for 15 years because the combination was lost. A back door was built and has been used ever since. Later, Andy explains to a dejected Barney that he knew the men were crooks because a special agent of the F.B.I. would never allow his picture to be taken and published.

MEMORABLE SCENE. Andy's fishing story

to Raleigh newspaper reporter Margaret Williamson.

CAST NOTES. Regulars: **Andy Griffith, Don Knotts, Frances Bavier, Howard McNear,** and **Hal Smith. Dick Elliott** returns as Mayor Pike.

Edmon Ryan stars as Fred Jenkins. **George Petrie** appears as Joe Layton. **Elizabeth Talbot-Martin** portrays Margaret Williamson. **Stanley Farrar** appears as Ray Watson.

EPISODE NOTES. 1. Margaret Williamson's column in the Raleigh newspaper is called, "Meandering with Margaret." 2. Floyd's tour group consisted of folks from a New Orleans–bound bus. He refers to Andy as "Dead-Eye Andy," while Barney refers to himself as "Fast Gun Fife." Barney claims that his fast draw has never been successfully photographed. In the presence of the tour group, Otis confesses to Barney that he committed a murder. He killed off a pint! 3. Andy sings "John Henry" to Otis and offers to sing "The Wreck of the Old 97" to Barney. 4 Barney is envious of the new state policy facility that recently opened in Mount Pilot. 5. Andy greets a man named Jeff on the street in front of the courthouse. 6. This is the only episode written by Paul Henning, the creator of *The Beverly Hillbillies.*

"The Clubmen"

Episode #42. Air date: 12-11-61. Writers: Fred S. Fox and Iz Elinson. Director: Bob Sweeney.

Andy's fishing buddy Roger Courtney invites Andy and Barney to present themselves for membership at the prestigious and exclusive Esquire Club in Raleigh. Barney is ecstatic and plans to put his best foot forward by studying up on the stock market and "rich men's" games, such as golf. He brags to Floyd, Jud, Aunt Bee, and Opie how the club is seeking him out for membership. He chomps on a big cigar in order to look like "the Esquire type." On the other hand, Andy couldn't care less about joining.

The Esquire Club meets on Thursdays at 8:00 P.M. and on the big night, Andy and Barney arrive right on time. Roger Courtney introduces them to Esquire members Cliff Britton, Tom Wilson, Jim Baker, John Danby, and George Bronson. Barney looks sharp in his salt and pepper suit, but he proceeds to make a fool of himself by making dumb remarks about golf scores and the stock market. The coup de grace occurs when the hapless deputy says that baked Alaska came into being after Alaska was admitted to the Union. Needless to say, the Esquire members are not impressed with Barney.

A few days pass, and Barney is fit to be tied because he and Andy have yet to hear if they've been accepted. Roger Courtney and Tom Wilson show up at the courthouse while Barney is patrolling the school crossing. They tell Andy that he as been accepted, but Barney was rejected. Andy politely refuses the membership, and Roger and Tom leave on good terms.

Barney sees the two depart and immediately quizzes Andy. Andy tells him that the club accepted only one of them. Barney assumes that Andy was not accepted and proceeds to write a letter to the Esquire Club, canceling his membership. He states that the members are snobs and he wants no part of their club. Andy doesn't have the heart to tell Barney the truth.

Later, the president of the Tomahawk Club, Opie Taylor, admits Andy and Barney into his organization.

MEMORABLE SCENE. Andy catching Barney napping without his shoes and socks on.

CAST NOTES. Regulars: **Andy Griffith, Don Knotts, Ronny Howard, Frances Bavier,** and **Howard McNear. Burt Mustin** returns as Jud.

George Neise stars as Roger Courtney. **Ross Elliott** appears as Tom Wilson. Elliott portrayed Sheriff Abbott on *The Virginian* from 1967 through 1970. **Bob McQuain** appears as Jim Baker. **Brad Olson** also appears.

EPISODE NOTES. 1. Andy caught a mess of trout while fishing with Roger Courtney. 2. The members of the Mayberry Lodge have met on Friday nights for the past six years. 3. Floyd Lawson says that Raleigh has a five-chair barbershop. That's big! Floyd remarks that someday he would like to open up a barbershop in Raleigh. 4. Barney complains that Floyd always asks him how much money he sends his mother every month and when is he going to get married. 5. Barney repairs a broken stop sign on Elm Street. 6. Andy leaves the keys to the courthouse with Floyd when he and Barney go to Raleigh. 7. Marie Simms telephones Aunt Bee while Barney is anxiously waiting to hear from the Esquire Club. Barney calls Marie "the biggest blabbermouth in town." 8. To be initiated into Opie's Tomahawk Club, new members must put on an Indian headdress, raise a tomahawk in the right hand, and say, "As a Tomahawk, I solemnly swear to be fair and square at all times." 9. In this episode, it is implied that the city of Raleigh is rather close to Mayberry. Remember, Andy and Barney planned to attend meetings every Thursday evening. The real-life town of Mount Airy, N.C., is 142 miles from Raleigh.

"The Pickle Story"

Episode #43. Air date: 12-18-61. Writer: Harvey Bullock. Director: Bob Sweeney.

Aunt Bee is a great cook, but her homemade pickles are simply awful. Barney refers to them as "kerosene cucumbers." (When she offers him one, he responds, "I'll smoke it, I mean, I'll eat it later.") She has recently made eight quarts for Andy, Barney, and Opie, and the men are having a hard time facing the world, knowing there are eight quarts of Aunt Bee's pickles with their names on the jars. When Aunt Bee comments that her pickles are not disappearing fast, the men decide to secretly replace the kerosene cucumbers with store-bought pickles. In a funny scene, Barney sneaks Aunt Bee's pickles out of the Taylor house right under Aunt Bee's nose by stuffing the jars in a suitcase and telling her he is going to visit a cousin she doesn't know. Next, Barney gives the nearly toxic pickles to out-of-towners passing through Mayberry, as a safe driving award. Later, Barney tells Andy that Aunt Bee's pickles are scattered from Oregon to Nova Scotia. Andy refers to this deception as "Operation Pickle Switch."

When Aunt Bee notices how the boys gobbled up *her* pickles, she decides to enter the pickle contest at the county fair. At first, Andy and Barney think it would be funny to see store-bought pickles win the contest, but a problem soon arises. Clara Johnson has won the pickle contest for the past eleven years, and every year she puts her heart and soul in an effort to improve her entry. Clara is a lonely widow and takes great pride in showing Andy her scrapbook filled with the eleven blue ribbons. When Andy samples her delicious pickles (with extra allspice), he realizes how important the contest is to Clara and how horrible he would feel if the store-bought pickles won first prize. So, to the dismay of Barney and Opie, Andy forces himself and them to eat up all the store-bought pickles, so Aunt Bee will have to prepare a new batch for the contest.

The three Mayberry men bravely gulp down the eight quarts of store-bought pickles. Aunt Bee prepares her new batch just in time for the county fair. At the contest, everyone, including Aunt Bee, is thrilled to watch Clara Johnson walk off with her twelfth consecutive blue ribbon. Meanwhile, the judges of the pickle contest immediately go to the water fountain and attempt to wash the smell of kerosene off their hands.

Later, Andy and Barney discover that Aunt Bee's newly made homemade marmalade (16 full quarts!) tastes and smells like ammonia. For the sake of the judges, we hope there isn't an upcoming marmalade contest.

CAST NOTES. Regulars: **Andy Griffith, Don Knotts, Ronny Howard,** and **Frances Bavier. Hope Summers** appears as Clara Johnson.

Lee Krieger appears as the out-of-town motorist from Portland, Oregon. **Stanley Farrar** and **Warren Parker** appear as the judges of the pickle contest.

EPISODE NOTES. 1. On the *Andy Griffith Silver Anniversary Special,* aired on October 3, 1985, on WTBS, Don Knotts selected "The Pickle Story" as his favorite episode. 2. Andy and Barney sing a duet on "Tell My Darling Mother I'll Be There." 3. A fly lands on one of Aunt Bee's pickles and *dies.* 4. Clara Johnson tells Aunt Bee that her pickles are pleasant and nice, but they need the following: a not-so-heavy brine, an extra sprig of parsley, fresher vinegar, younger cucumbers that need to be drained better, and fresher spices. Also, the vinegar needs to be boiled for a few more seconds. 5. On her second batch of pickles, Aunt Bee borrows some cucumbers from Mrs. Treadmarr. 6. The preacher's wife also entered the pickle contest. Her jar was number 10 on the judges' table. Aunt Bee's jar was number 11 and Clara's was number 4. 7. Barney picks up Andy for work every morning at 8:00 sharp. 8. The music playing while Andy, Barney, and Opie gulp down the eight quarts of pickles deserves special notice for how well it fits the scene.

"Sheriff Barney"

Episode #44. Air date: 12-25-61. Writers: Leo Solomon and Ben Gershman. Director: Bob Sweeney.

The *Mayberry Gazette* runs a picture of Andy and Barney on the front page, honoring the two men's work in keeping Mayberry's crime rate the lowest in the state. The caption read, "Mayberry Sheriff Best In State." Mayor Purdy and Councilman Dobbs of the nearby town of Greendale are impressed with Andy and Barney's reputation as lawmen. In fact, Mayberry has had the lowest crime rate in the state for the third consecutive year. Sheriff Maloney of Greendale is leaving prior to the end of his term, and Purdy and Dobbs decide they want Barney to replace him. The two Greendale officials meet with Andy and tell him of their plan.

When Andy tells Barney the news, he is ecstatic, but Andy isn't. He tells Barney that sheriff work is very different from deputy's work and Barney simply lacks the experience needed for the job. In order to prove his point, Andy makes Barney the sheriff of Mayberry for one day, while Andy assumes the role of deputy.

Barney's first act as sheriff is to try to discover from Otis Campbell the whereabouts of bootlegger Rafe Hollister's still. Barney attempts to probe Otis's subconscious mind while he is asleep, through hypnotism. Otis doesn't let on that he's wide awake. After Barney "probes" Otis for a while, he discovers the directions lead to 411 Elm Street in Mayberry — Barney's address. Andy and Otis get a good laugh at Sheriff Barney's means of interrogation, which Andy calls, "The Barney Fife Subconscious Prober Primer."

Next, Barney attempts to solve a dispute between two farmers, Huey Welch and a man named Osgood. Osgood has built a fence that blocks the sun from reaching Welch's laying hens. The two argue so violently that Barney locks them up and starts examining law books to find a similar case. Andy appears and settles the problem in seconds by suggesting that Osgood replace the solid fence with chicken wire, which would allow the rays of the sun to reach the hens. Osgood and Welch agree and proceed to ridicule Barney about his qualifications. A dejected Barney decides not to be the high sheriff of Greendale. He walks down the street, kicking cans and feeling sorry for himself.

As soon as Barney leaves the courthouse, none other than Rafe Hollister shows up and turns himself in to Andy on the bootlegging charge. Andy decides to strike a deal with Mr. Hollister. He tells Rafe that if he goes out and finds Barney and allows the deputy to arrest him, he will make sure that Aunt Bee will prepare him chicken and dumplings and sweet'tater pie. Rafe can't pass up this deal, so Barney is able to "capture" Mayberry's most wanted fugitive. A now confident Barney Fife telephones Mayor Purdy in Greendale and explains he cannot be his sheriff because his services are needed in Mayberry.

CAST NOTES. Regulars: **Andy Griffith, Don Knotts, Ronny Howard, Howard McNear,** and **Hal Smith.**

Dabbs Greer appears as Councilman Dobbs. **Ralph Dumke** portrays Mayor Purdy. **Jack Prince** appears for the first time as Rafe Hollister. (Prince had appeared in a few previous episodes, most notably as another bootlegger, Luke Rainer, in episode 26, "The Inspector.") **Orville Sherman, Frank Warren, Paul Bryar, Joseph Hamilton** and **Jack Teagarden** also appear.

EPISODE NOTES. 1. The town of Mayberry is located in Mayberry County. 2. Opie swears that Barney is the best crossing guard the school has ever had. 3. Andy has Barney chalk tires, a job Barney hates. When Barney is sheriff for a day, he makes Andy chalk tires. 4. Greendale City Hall was erected in 1902. 5. When Barney believes he is going to be the high sheriff of Greendale, he refers to the town as another Dodge City. Floyd says Greendale is a quiet and peaceful town. 6. During the episode, both Andy and Barney lock themselves in cell #2. Later, Barney locks himself in cell #1. For the record, cell #1 is Otis Campbell's usual cell. If a person is standing directly in front of the cells, cell #1 is to the right and cell #2 is to the left. 7. Barney's "Manhunt" theme is played throughout the episode. 8. Barney compares the Welch-Osgood dispute to the case of Willoughby *vs.* Perkins. 9. In this episode, Willow Street and Woods Way are said to be two of the most quiet and peaceful streets in Mayberry. The real Willow Street, located in Mount Airy, is also known to be a very peaceful and quiet street.

"The Farmer Takes a Wife"

Episode #45. Air date: 1-1-62. Writers: Charles Stewart and Jack Elinson. Director: Bob Sweeney.

Jeff Pruitt is a gregarious, gentle giant of a farmer. He has come to town in search of a wife. He tells Andy and Barney he has recently broken up with his old girlfriend, Bertha, because she is a farm gal and he wants his wife to be more feminine, like city gals are. Big Jeff tells Andy and Barney that with his good looks, strength, and successful farm, it shouldn't take more than two days to find a suitable spouse. Jeff enjoys food, farming and picking up women—literally!

Barney and Thelma Lou decide to help Jeff by playing cupid. Thelma Lou holds an all-female party at her house (Barney refers to it as a hen party) and invites Andy and Barney to bring Jeff along to check out some of Mayberry's most eligible women. Barney goes berserk when Jeff picks Thelma Lou.

Jeff pursues a relationship with Thelma Lou by escorting her around town, picking her handfuls of sweet peas, calling her sugar plum, and telling her she is "juicier than a barrelful of corn squeezins'." Barney tells Thelma Lou to "nip it in the bud," but she actually likes the attention and gets a kick out of seeing Barney jealous. When Barney sees Jeff and Thelma Lou together, Andy has to physically restrain his wiry deputy from getting clobbered by the much larger Mr. Pruitt.

Finally, Andy and Thelma Lou devise a plan that will make Jeff leave her alone without hurting his feelings. Their plan is to turn Jeff into a city slicker. They teach him proper etiquette and make him buy the largest available suit at the local men's clothier, Carroll's of Mayberry. Andy tells Jeff that Thelma Lou is a city gal and he can't dress the way he did when he dated Bertha. Next, Jeff visits Thelma Lou and she serves him finger sandwiches for supper. Jeff is incredulous. He is used to a supper where he devours an entire leg of lamb with all the trimmings, like Aunt Bee served him. Andy shows up and tells Jeff that Thelma Lou has decided she wants to live in the city after she and Jeff get married. He goes on to tell the bewildered farmer that Mayberry real estate agent Tom Biggers has some houses in mind. Jeff finally explodes when Andy tells him of three possible jobs for him in Mayberry: (1) a guard at the bank; (2) a helper in the vegetable department at Crowley's Market; and (3) a shoe salesman at Harvey Willick's shoe store. Jeff rips off his jacket and tie and calls off the wedding plans. He says he's going back to Bertha. As he is leaving, Barney storms into the house and challenges Jeff to a fight. Jeff tells him he can have Thelma Lou, and Barney believes it was his bravery that scared away the much stronger man. A very confident Deputy Fife tells Andy and Thelma Lou, "The bigger they come, the harder they fall." Then he grabs Thelma Lou and says, "To the winner belongs the spoils, baby!"

CAST NOTES. Regulars: **Andy Griffith, Don Knotts, Ronny Howard, Frances Bavier,** and **Betty Lynn.**

Alan Hale, Jr., turns in a great performance as Jeff Pruitt. Hale's father, Alan Hale, Sr., was a noted actor in his own right. He appeared in numerous movies in the 1930s and 1940s with Errol Flynn. The younger Hale is well known for his role as the Skipper, Jonas Grumby, on *Gilligan's Island* from 1964 through 1967. It's interesting to note in the episode that Jeff Pruitt referred to Barney as "little buddy." Gilligan fans know that the Skipper often referred to Gilligan as his "little buddy." Could Hale have been inspired by this episode to use this term a few years later in *Gilligan's Island?* We think so.

Adoree Evans appears as one of Thelma Lou's friends at the hen party. Her name was Mary. **Bob McQuain** portrays Joe Waters.

EPISODE NOTES. 1. The following Mayberry businesses may be seen in this episode: Lamps and Shades, the Florist Shop and the Golden Rooster Snack Bar. 2. Jeff (literally) "picks up" a girl named Avis on Main Street. 3. Jeff Pruitt drives a pickup truck. His license plate number is R-24877. 4. Joe Waters parks illegally in front of the courthouse. The license plate number on his truck is the familiar DC-269. 5. Jeff tells Andy that his old girlfriend Bertha can milk cows, call hogs, and pick tobacco as well as he can.

"Keeper of the Flame"

Episode #46. Air date: 1-8-62. Writers: Jack Elinson and Charles Stewart. Director: Bob Sweeney.

Opie joins a secret kids' club called the Wildcats. The four members of the club are all schoolmates, and they periodically meet in a barn owned by a crotchety old farmer named Jubal Foster. The club members are sworn to secrecy, and if anyone breaks the code, he will be struck by "the curse of the claw." Opie can't tell Andy he's a member of the club, or the fact that his job is the Keeper of the Flame, which means it's his job to keep the sacred candle that is lit at the beginning of every meeting.

Jubal complains to Andy about the boys using his barn without permission, and he ticks off the sheriff by saying Opie was one of the "brats" he ran off his farm. What Mr. Foster is actually afraid of is that the kids will discover the illegal still that's hidden in the barn.

Later, Jubal knocks over a lamp while checking the still, and the barn goes up in flames. Naturally, Jubal blames Opie and his friends for causing the fire. Andy doesn't believe Jubal until Aunt Bee discovers matches and the sacred candle hidden under Opie's pillow. Andy questions his son over and over. Finally, Opie admits to being at Jubal's but denies starting the fire. Andy is convinced that Opie is responsible for the fire, so he and Barney go to the Foster farm, where Andy is prepared to pay for the damages. It is a hot day, so while Jubal is telling Andy that the bill will be around $700.00, Barney goes to get a drink of water. He accidentally drinks some of Jubal's homemade brew. In a hilarious scene, a highly inebriated Barney attempts to tell Andy about his discovery. Once Andy investigates the situation, he arrests Jubal Foster for operating an illegal still and setting fire to his own barn.

Next, Andy apologizes to Opie and goes on to tell him that when he was a child, he once belonged to a secret club and his role was also Keeper of the Flame. When his father discovered Andy's job, he gave him a safer "flame"—a flashlight! So, Andy passes along the flashlight to Opie, who now becomes the Keeper of the Flashlight for the Wildcats.

MEMORABLE SCENE. A drunken Barney repeating "Jubal, Jubal, Jubal, Jubal."

CAST NOTES. Regulars: **Andy Griffith, Don Knotts, Ronny Howard,** and **Frances Bavier.**

Everett Sloane stars as Jubal Foster. Sloane was a member of Orson Welles's legendary Mercury Players in the 1930s and 1940s. He appeared in such film classics as *Citizen Kane* (1941) and *Lust for Life* (1956). Sloane also wrote the lyrics to the theme song of *The Andy Griffith Show*, "The Fishin' Hole." Even though the lyrics were never performed on the show, numerous recordings are available for those interested. Two of these are "Songs, Themes and Laughs from the Andy Griffith Show," issued by Capitol Records in 1961, and "The TV Theme Song Sing-Along Album," released by CBS Special Products in 1985. Andy Griffith sings the song on both of these albums.

Flip Mark appears as the leader of the Wildcats. **Terry Dickinson** portrays another member of the club. Dickinson had previously appeared as Sheldon, the bully, in episode 33, "Opie and the Bully."

Grace Lenard and **Robert Gallagher** provide the radio voices. **Mark Rodney** also appears.

EPISODE NOTES. 1. Andy states that Mayberry County has a volunteer fire department. 2. Andy allows Opie to do some chores around the courthouse in order to earn money to pay his weekly membership dues to the Wildcats. 3. Aunt Bee enjoys listening to an unnamed radio soap opera. Celia Gordon and a man named John are two of the characters. Andy enjoys poking fun at Aunt Bee for listening to the melodramatic program.

"Bailey's Bad Boy"

Episode #47. Air date: 1-15-62. Writers: Leo Solomon and Ben Gershman. Director: Bob Sweeney.

A spoiled rich kid named Ronald Bailey is arrested after speeding through Mayberry on his way to Miami. Bailey is also accused of sideswiping Fletch Dilbeck's produce truck. He denies the speeding, reckless driving, and hit-and-run charges until an incriminating stalk of celery in the back of his convertible does him in. Once Ron is arrested, Andy tells him he'll be locked up in the Mayberry jail for a few days until Circuit Judge Parker arrives for the trial. Bailey, acting like the smart-aleck 19 year old he is, threatens Andy by calling his influential father, John Judson Bailey, who according to Ron has the power to strip Andy and Barney of their jobs.

Andy takes Ron with him and Opie on a fishing trip, and he also goes to the Taylors' home on Sunday because the Mayberry courthouse and jail officially closes on Sundays. While at Andy's, Ron witnesses Opie's admission to his pa that he broke Mrs. Purdy's window with a ball. Andy's punishment is to take away Opie's allowance until the debt is paid in full. Opie accepts Andy's decision, but

Ron asks the sheriff why he didn't "bail the kid out of the jam." Andy explains that Opie must learn responsibility.

The next day arrives and so does John Judson Bailey's shrewd lawyer, Arthur Harrington. Mr. Harrington has bribed Fletch Dilbeck with a brand new truck, and now Fletch sheepishly swears that Ron didn't cause the accident. Andy knows he's beaten, but as he's about to release Ron, the young man disagrees with Mr. Dilbeck's account and accepts full responsibility for the accident. When Mr. Harrington asks Ron how he will explain these happenings to his father, Andy pipes in with the following line: "Tell him the boy busted a window and he wants to stand on his own two legs."

CAST NOTES. Regulars: **Andy Griffith, Don Knotts, Ronny Howard, Frances Bavier,** and **Hal Smith.**

Bill Bixby stars as Ronald Bailey. Bixby is well known as the star of such television hits as *My Favorite Martian, The Courtship of Eddie's Father,* and *The Incredible Hulk.* He also directed numerous television shows, including *Blossom,* prior to his untimely death in 1993.

Jon Lormer portrays Fletch Dilbeck. Lormer appears in several roles in this series. He appeared in a host of television series, including *Barney Miller, Batman, Ben Casey, The Big Valley, Bonanza, Columbo, Dennis the Menace, The Fugitive, Lassie, The Mary Tyler Moore Show, Medical Center* (an episode called "The V.D. Story!"), *Mission: Impossible, Rhoda, Star Trek* (as Dr. Haskins in the pilot episode called "The Cage"), *The Twilight Zone, Wendy and Me* and *The Wild Wild West.* Lormer appeared in several movies, including *I Want to Live!* (1958), *The Gazebo* (1959, with Glenn Ford), *Where the Boys Are* (1960), *The Second Time Around* (1961, with Andy Griffith), *Dead Ringer* (1964, with Bette Davis), *The Singing Nun* (1966), *The Sand Pebbles* (1966, with Steve McQueen), *Getting Straight* (1970, with Candice Bergen and Harrison Ford), *Doctor's Wives* (1991, with Gene Hackman and Dyan Cannon), *Rooster Cogburn* (1975, with John Wayne and Katharine Hepburn), *The Boogens* (1982), and *Beyond the Next Mountain* (1984).

John Graham appears as Arthur Harrington.

EPISODE NOTES. 1. Andy assigns Barney to watch the bicycles at the movie house. No reason is given as to why he is doing this. Maybe there is a bicycle thief in Mayberry. 2. The visiting hours at the Mayberry jail are 2:00 P.M.—4:00 P.M. daily, except Sunday. 3. While most of the vehicles used in the series are Fords, Fletch Dilbeck's truck is a Chevrolet. 4. Barney gets angry at Ronald Bailey for insisting on listening to loud rock 'n' roll music on his transistor radio while he's in jail. 5. In this episode, Barney is living in the back room of the courthouse. 6. Ron is originally locked up in cell #2, but when Otis stumbles in drunk, young Mr. Bailey is shifted to cell #1, because cell #2 is where Otis always sleeps. (However, this represents an inconsistency with other episodes. In episodes 44, 106, and 155, it is made clear that Otis is accustomed to sleeping in cell #1.) 7. Barney hums "Bringing in the Sheaves" in order to help Otis fall asleep. Ron Bailey views this spectacle in disbelief. 8. When the Mayberry courthouse and jail closes on Sundays, Andy puts Otis in charge of taking messages and locking up the place after he sobers up and leaves. 9. Andy Gump is one of Barney's favorite characters in the Sunday funny papers. 10. Andy, Aunt Bee, Opie, and Barney regularly make homemade ice cream on Sundays. In this episode, the flavor of the day was strawberry.

"The Manicurist"

Episode #48. Air date: 1-22-62. Writers: Charles Stewart and Jack Elinson. Director: Bob Sweeney.

Voluptuous and talkative Ellen Brown stops in Mayberry while on her way to Nashville on the Southern Bus Lines. She noticed the sign on the outskirts of town proclaiming, "Mayberry—The Friendly Town." Ellen is mulling over a marriage proposal from a man named Pierre, who lives in a large unnamed city, probably Raleigh. Ellen is a manicurist, or as she puts it, she does nails. She works at the same place of business where Pierre works. Ellen begs Floyd to give her a job, and he finally gives in when she agrees to work on a commission basis only. However, since no one in a town as small as Mayberry has ever wanted or needed a manicure, Ellen has trouble getting started. The men in town love looking at her but want absolutely nothing to do with a manicure.

In an uncharacteristic moment, Andy remarks to his cronies in Floyd's Barbershop that Ellen won't last 24 hours in Mayberry. Unfortunately, Ellen overhears his comment. She emphatically tells him that she is leaving and that the people of Mayberry should take down their sign that welcomes strangers to "the Friendly Town." Andy saves the day by volunteering to be Ellen's first customer. Floyd calls him "a prince of a man," and Ellen begins to believe that Mayberry isn't so bad after all. Next, Andy remarks to Barney, Mayor Pike, Sam (the hardware store owner) and a few others about how much he enjoyed the experience of receiving a manicure from such a gorgeous gal like Ellen. The others reluctantly heed his advice and wind up enjoying their manicure as much as Andy did.

A problem arises when the Mayberry wives begin forbidding their husbands to hold hands with a beautiful single lady. Floyd pleads with Andy to explain the situation to Ellen. When Andy speaks to her, she misunderstands and believes he's asking for her hand in marriage! Before he can explain, Ellen tells him how flattered she is by his proposal, but she has decided to go back to the big city and marry Pierre. Andy breathes a long sigh of relief, but the men in Mayberry are upset because they are losing their manicurist. No need to worry; Floyd comes to the rescue by advertising a new manicurist on duty. Mayor Pike excitedly rushes to be the first customer of the new girl, but he should have gone back to his office. The new manicurist turns out to be none other than elderly Emma Watson. Floyd tells everyone he specifically hired Emma in order to keep the peace with the married women of Mayberry.

MEMORABLE SCENE. Mayor Pike, Barney, Floyd, Sam and an unnamed butcher describing what they did on Sunday, while gawking at Ellen Brown's shapely legs. What did they do on Sunday? Mayor Pike shot three rabbits; Barney did nothing; and Sam caught a half-dozen trout. Floyd and the butcher said nothing. They were too busy staring!

CAST NOTES. Regulars: **Andy Griffith, Don Knotts,** and **Howard McNear. Dick Elliott** returns as Mayor Pike. This is Elliott's final appearance in the series. **Cheerio Meredith** returns as Emma Watson. No explanation is given as to why her last name changed from Brand in the first season to Watson in the second season.

Barbara Eden stars as Ellen Brown. Eden has appeared in numerous television shows and movies over the years. She is best known as Jeannie on the long-running hit *I Dream of Jeannie.*

Sherwood Keith appears as Sam. **Frank Warren** appears as the unnamed butcher. In subsequent episodes, his character will be referred to as Art, and later on, he will be known as Art Crowley, from Crowley's Market.

EPISODE NOTES. 1. Floyd nearly skewers Barney with his barber scissors while admiring Ellen Brown. 2. Barney warns Ellen to be extra careful with his trigger finger during his manicure. 3. If you are lucky enough to catch the complete uncut version of this episode, you will hear Barney saying some *very* uncharacteristic remarks about Ellen Brown. For instance, when Floyd asks him how he would treat a girl like her, Barney responds, "a little rough" and he would "rough her up a little," because "women like her expect this type of treatment." It's a wonder that this type of dialogue made it through the production staff of the show, or the censors at CBS in 1962. It's no wonder this scene is not in most of the syndication packages.

"The Jinx"

Episode #49. Air date: 1-29-62. Writers: Jack Elinson and Charles Stewart. Director: Bob Sweeney.

Barney claims that a kindly old man named Henry Bennett jinxed him into losing a game of checkers against Floyd by standing over his left shoulder during the match. Next, Barney reminds Floyd, Sam, and an unnamed butcher that during the horseshoe pitching contest on Labor Day, Henry patted Virgil Hosh on the back while Virgil was pitching a perfect game. Virgil proceeded to lose the match after Henry touched him. Floyd tells everyone that during the opening day of the Little League baseball season, his son Norman dropped a fly ball, right after Henry had returned a foul ball to the playing field. It just happened to be the *same* ball. Andy comes in and overhears the story. He reminds Floyd the dropped fly was the *only* ball hit to his son during the entire ball game! Nonetheless, superstitious Barney Fife is convinced Henry is a jinx. He gets a book from his grandmother titled *Signs, Omens, Portents and Charms to Ward Off Bad Luck* in order to keep Henry from hexing him.

Andy tries to disprove Barney's theories by inviting Henry to accompany him and Barney to the opening day fishing sweepstakes. Andy and Barney have won the sweepstakes the past three years for having the best catch of the day. Barney is outraged when Andy tells him Henry is joining them, and he refers to his book for lucky charms and chants to combat Henry's presence. At the fishing contest, things go well until Andy's boat springs a leak and starts sinking fast. Barney blames Henry, while Andy blames Earl Gilley's poor caulking job on the boat.

Now, Henry starts believing he is a jinx and decides the best thing he could do is to leave Mayberry. Andy scolds Barney and his cohorts for acting foolish and for being inconsiderate to a lifelong friend. Collectively, everyone agrees to try to restore Henry's confidence. Their plan is to rig the upcoming church social drawing in order for Henry to win the grand prize, a portable television. The plan is to draw the number 44 from a hat. Everyone in attendance has the winning number, but all have agreed to stay silent and let Henry claim the prize. When Andy reads off the winning number, no one, including Henry, steps forward to accept the television. Barney discovers Henry drew the number 6 7/8 — the hat size tag! Now, Henry believes he has jinxed himself, but Andy and Aunt Bee remind him he's quite a lucky man indeed to have such a large amount of friends willing to make him feel like a

winner. Henry agrees and decides to stay in Mayberry after all. Now, if only Barney could be convinced — but that's asking a bit too much.

CAST NOTES. Regulars: **Andy Griffith, Don
Knotts, Ronny Howard, Frances Bavier,** and
Howard McNear. Sherwood Keith returns as Sam.
Frank Warren returns as the unnamed butcher.

John Qualen stars as Henry Bennett. Qualen
has one of the most recognizable faces of any character actor in the history of film. From the 1930s
through the 1960s, Qualen was a favorite of legendary director John Ford. He appeared in such
Ford classics as *The Long Voyage Home* (1940), *The
Grapes of Wrath* (1940), and Qualen also appeared
in *Casablanca* (1943) and *Anatomy of a Murder*
(1959). It is ironic that he played a person with bad
luck in "The Jinx," because, as a friend of ours put
it, "He was always the guy in the movies who had
his land taken from him, or had his cows stolen
from his farm, or had his wife and daughter taken
by Indians."

Clint Howard appears as the cowboy-clad
youngster at the church social. He is unbilled in the
credits. In future episodes, Clint will return in the
same outfit as Leon, the little cowboy who loves
those peanut butter and jelly sandwiches. The son
of Rance and the younger brother of Ron, Clint
Howard was born in Burbank, California, on April
20, 1959. Like Ron, he had a busy career as a child.
His first regular role was as Stanley in *The Baileys
of Balboa* (1964-1965). This was followed by the
popular series *Gentle Ben*, in which he played Mark
Wedloe (1967-1969). In 1974, he was Steve in *The
Cowboys*. After appearing in his brother's film *Gung
Ho*, he starred in the 1986-1987 television series of
the same name. He played a man named Googie.
In 1992 he was seen regularly on a short-lived series
called *Space Rangers*. Clint has guest-starred in
many series including *Bonanza* (the episode "All Ye
His Saints," he plays a child whose father is critically wounded by Indians), *The Fugitive, Marcus
Welby, M.D., The Monroes, Nanny and the Professor,
The Odd Couple, The Patty Duke Show, Please Don't
Eat the Daisies, The Red Skelton Show, Seinfeld* (as a
serial killer!) and *Star Trek*. In the latter, he
appeared as Balok in the episode called "The Cor-
bomite Maneuver." He also lent his voice, as Roo,
to a 1970 animated special, *Winnie the Pooh and the
Honey Tree*. He has appeared in many made-for-
television movies, such as *The Red Pony* (1973),
Huckleberry Finn (1975, with his entire family, parents Rance and Jean and brother Ron), *The Death
of Richie* (1977), and *Cotton Candy* (1978). He co-
wrote this with Ron Howard, who directed the film.
Clint appears as Corky MacFearson. He has
appeared in such theatrical films as *The Courtship of*

Eddie's Father (1963, with brother Ron), *Talion,* aka
An Eye for an Eye (1966), *The Gentle Giant* (1967,
which became *Gentle Ben* on television), *The Jungle
Book* (1967, lending his voice to this Disney animated classic), *The Wild Country* (1971, with brother
Ron), *Salty* (1973), *Eat My Dust* (1976, with Ron
and Rance Howard), *Grand Theft Auto* (1977, with
Ron and Rance Howard, who co-wrote the script;
this was Ron's first directorial effort), *Rock n' Roll
High School* (1979), *Evilspeak* (1982), *Night Shift*
(1982, directed by Ron Howard), *Splash* (1984,
directed by Ron Howard), *Gung Ho* (1985, directed
and executive-produced by Ron Howard), *Cocoon*
(1985, directed by Ron Howard), *The Wraith* (1986),
End of the Line (1987), *Freeway* (1988), *Tango and
Cash* (1989, with Sylvester Stallone and Kurt Russell), *B.O.R.N.* (1989, with Rance Howard and
Hoke Howell), *Parenthood* (1989, directed by Ron
Howard; Clint appears as Lou, the irate loudmouth
dad, and Rance appears as a college dean), *Silent
Night, Deadly Night Part 4 — Initiation* (1990), *Backdraft* (1991, directed by Ron Howard), *Disturbed*
(1991, with Malcolm McDowell), *Far and Away*
(1992, directed by Ron Howard, starring Tom
Cruise; Rance Howard also appears), and *The Paper*
(1994, directed by Ron Howard; Rance Howard also
appears). Note for trivia buffs: In 1978, Clint
attended Pepperdine College, where he majored in
Journalism.

Sherman Sanders also appears.

EPISODE NOTES. 1. Barney applies the following practices which he obtained from the book,
*Signs, Omens, Portents and Charms to Ward Off Bad
Luck*: (1) To ensure good luck before a coming
event, rub the head of a redheaded man. If a man
with red hair cannot be obtained, a boy will do.
During the episode, Barney rubbed Opie's head and
the head of a man appropriately named Red. (2)
While fishing with Andy and Henry in the boat,
Barney rubs a rabbit's food and recites chants he has
learned from the book. (3) Barney has Floyd, Sam,
and the unnamed butcher do and say the following
things when Henry Bennett enters Floyd's Barbershop: Touch a rabbit's foot, turn all hand mirrors
face down, put their right hands over their heads in
order to touch their left earlobes, close their eyes
and repeat the following chant: "Wynkum, Pyn-
kum, Nodimus Rex, protect us all from the man
with the hex." 2. Barney describes to Andy how a
person with "hexum" qualities puts jinxes on people — a scientific fact, Barney says, discovered by a
man named Buzz Fluhart. Andy says this "fact" is
the biggest crock of nothing he has ever heard. Barney retorts that people like Andy are always poking fun at great minds like "Edison, the Wright
Brothers and Buzz Fluhart." 3. Henry Bennett drives

a Ford pickup truck. His license plate number is the familiar DC-269. 4. Barney says that Cole Porter records "have that certain effect" on Thelma Lou. 5. According to Floyd, last year's grand prize at the church social was a transistor radio, without an ear plug. 6. The townsfolk in Mayberry square dance at the church social. A man named Sandy does the calling at the dance. 7. Raffle tickets for the portable television cost 50 cents each. 8. With Barney present, Opie beats his pa at checkers. Andy teases his superstitious deputy by blaming him for the loss. In fact, Andy calls him, "Bad Luck Barney." 9. Henry Bennett calls Barney "a great big sap." 10. Barney wears his dapper salt and pepper suit to the church social. 11. Barney gets a real kick out of telling Andy that if he should happen to get into a game of cards or checkers after visiting with Henry Bennett, he will be somebody's pigeon. 12. In the episode, Andy states that Earl Gilley's failure to properly caulk his boat caused it to sink during the fishing contest. The real Mr. Gilley is named Earlie, and he and Andy Griffith have been friends for many years. He runs an auto repair shop in Pilot Mountain. By the way, Earlie married Lorraine Beasley, who happens to be Andy Griffith's cousin. Her name was also used in the series. We will note the use of Mr. Gilley's name in four other episodes.

"Jailbreak"

Episode #50. Air date: 2-5-62. Writer: Harvey Bullock. Director: Bob Sweeney.

State police investigator Mr. Horton comes to Mayberry in search of Clarence "Doc" Malloy and his accomplice. The two are wanted by the F.B.I. for interstate flight and for stealing the payroll from a furniture factory. Mr. Horton tells Andy to stay away from the search and chase chicken thieves while the "pros" do all the hard police work.

Mr. Horton and his group quickly capture Malloy and place him in the Mayberry jail. Against Andy's wishes, Barney poses as a fellow prisoner in order to learn the whereabouts of Malloy's partner in crime. The charade fails when Malloy sees a newspaper clipping of Barney hanging on the wall. The picture is taken from the time Barney solved the Walker Drugstore robbery. Malloy quickly overpowers the deputy in disguise and escapes.

Next, Andy discovers from Mayberry's dry cleaner, H. Goss, that Malloy's accomplice is a female. So, without the support of the state police, who are even more upset with our heroes since they learned of Malloy's escape, Andy and Barney track the fugitive couple to the Half Moon Trailer Park

on River Road in Mayberry. After Barney peers in a window and sees two newlyweds making out, he discovers Doc Malloy's trailer. He is even more surprised to see that Mr. Horton has been tied up and taken hostage. He reports this to Andy, and they try to decide their next move. In a hilarious scene, Barney takes it upon himself to commandeer Malloy's vehicle, while the couple and Mr. Horton are in the attached trailer. Barney proceeds to fly around Mayberry until Andy is finally able to stop him. An easy arrest is made of a shaken-up Doc Malloy and his girlfriend. As Andy is untying Mr. Horton, he tells him, rather sarcastically, that he and Barney captured two more chicken thieves.

CAST NOTES. Regulars: **Andy Griffith, Don Knotts, Ronny Howard,** and **Howard McNear. Frank Warren** appears as Art. Warren was finally given a name, after appearing as the unnamed butcher in the past few episodes.

Ken Lynch stars as Mr. Horton.

Veteran character actor **Allan Melvin** makes his first of many appearances in the series. He usually appears as a crook or a tough guy. In this episode he portrayed Clarence "Doc" Malloy. Melvin was born in Kansas City, Missouri, but was raised in New York City. His face and voice are familiar to anyone who has ever watched television. He held the following regular series roles: Corporal Henshaw on *The Phil Silvers Show* (1955-1959), Sergeant Charlie Hacker on *Gomer Pyle, U.S.M.C.* (1965-1969), Sam, the butcher (his character's last name was revealed to be Franklin) on *The Brady Bunch* (1969-1974), and Barney Hefner on both *All in the Family* and *Archie Bunker's Place* (1973-1983). Those of us who were children in the 1960s will also recognize his voice, which Melvin lent to dozens of Saturday morning cartoon characters, including Bristol Hound, Bumbler, Barney Google, Sergeant Snorkel, and Magilla Gorilla. He made many guest appearances in series such as *Arnie, The Dick Van Dyke Show, Green Acres, Mayberry R.F.D.,* and *Perry Mason.* He even had a voice role as a demon in an episode of *Kung Fu.* Interestingly, he also appeared in a 1972 comedy pilot called *Man in the Middle.* It was produced and written by Harvey Bullock and Ray Saffian Allen, two important writers from *The Andy Griffith Show.* Melvin also appeared in the 1968 movie *With Six You Get Eggroll.* This movie was directed by Mayberry alum Howard Morris (aka Ernest T. Bass).

Fred Sherman appears for the first time as Mayberry's tailor and dry cleaner, H. Goss. In subsequent episodes, the nosy cleaner will be referred to as Fred Goss. Sherman was born in 1905 in Woodland Hills, California. He died on May 20, 1969. In the 1950s he had two regular television roles: He was Burt Purdy on *Cimarron City*, and he was also in *Hey, Mulligan*. Among the other series he appeared on are *The Adventures of Jim Bowie, Perry Mason*, and *I Love Lucy* (as a drunk in the episode "The Diner"). Among Sherman's many movies are *Behind Green Light* (1946), *Chain Lightning* (1950, with Humphrey Bogart), the classic *Some Like It Hot* (1959), and *Twist All Night* (1961).

Bob McQuain appears as the bridegroom. **Sally Mills** appears as the bride. **Rita Kenaston** appears as Malloy's girlfriend.

EPISODE NOTES. 1. Floyd Lawson owns a shaggy dog named Sam. This pooch appears to be the same one known as "Blue" in episode 128, "Barney's Bloodhound." 2. Barney says Andy's address is 24 Elm Street. 3. The Mayberry Grand Theatre can be seen in this episode. 4. Barney is reading a book titled *Penitentiary*. 5. Barney's "Manhunt" theme is played throughout the episode. 6. When Barney was Malloy's cellmate, he said his nicknames were "Puddintame," "Fingers," "Chopper" and "Mad Dog." He makes sure that Malloy knows that he was never known as "Tattletale." 7. Al and a man named McGinnis are two of Mr. Horton's assistants. 8. H. Goss offers a special three-hour cleaning service. He may be sloppy himself, but Mr. Goss often states to his customers, "It always pays to look neat." He also has a sign in his window stating, "When You're In A Rush, Call Us." 9. Doc Malloy's license plate number is VND-323. He and his girlfriend have a pet dog. 10. Mr. Horton gives Opie a Boys' Detective Disguise Kit. Barney puts it to good use when spying on the bride and groom at the trailer park, who complain to Andy about a peeping Tom. 11. The storyline of this episode is very similar to episode 2, "The Manhunt." Ken Lynch even appears as the state police investigator in both episodes.

"A Medal for Opie"

Episode #51. Air date: 2-12-62. Writer: David Adler. Director: Bob Sweeney.

Opie dreams of winning the 50-yard dash at the annual "Sheriff's Boys Day" track meet. Barney reminds Andy and Opie that when he was a youngster, he once won the 50-yard dash and was nicknamed "Barney the Rabbit." Andy prefers calling him "Peter Cottontail," which upsets his wiry deputy. Anyway, Barney volunteers to train Opie for the event. He has the youngster jump rope, jog, and strengthen his leg muscles. Soon, Opie has all the confidence in the world and even promises the good Lord that if he wins the first place medal, he will take it off when he takes a bath once in a while.

The big day arrives and Barney is the official starter of the events, while Andy serves as the official judge. Opie runs the race but finishes dead last. His friends Billy Johnson, Aaron Harrison, and Freddie Pruitt finish first, second, and third, respectively. Opie dejectedly leaves the track meet without congratulating the winners or even saying goodbye. When Andy returns home after the meet, he attempts to explain to his son the concept of good sportsmanship. Opie rejects the idea of being a good loser, and Andy tells the boy how disappointed he is with him.

Later, when Andy tells Barney of the situation, Barney has an idea. He says that when Opie shows up at the courthouse, he will throw a fake temper tantrum over not getting his requested salary increase. Barney reasons that Opie will be amazed at how foolish a poor loser looks.

A short time later, Opie shows up, with only Andy present. He tells his pa that he doesn't want him to be disappointed in him and he does have a better understanding of what it takes to be a gracious loser. Andy reminds him he doesn't have to be happy about losing, but he has to accept both winning and losing as a part of life. As he is finishing, Barney rushes in and immediately goes into his prearranged temper tantrum.

As soon as Opie leaves, Deputy Fife goes into a *real* temper tantrum when Andy shows him the letter stating that Barney's request for a raise *was* turned down.

MEMORABLE SCENE. Barney pooping out while riding his bike during one of Opie's training sessions.

CAST NOTES. Regulars: **Andy Griffith, Don Knotts, Ronny Howard,** and **Frances Bavier.**

Bob McQuain appears as the truck driver who makes fun of Barney while he is singing and jumping rope. **Ralph Leabow, Joan Carey** and **Pat Coghlan** also appear.

EPISODE NOTES. 1. Barney accidentally shoots off his pistol in the courthouse while practicing to be the official starter. Andy takes the gun away from him. 2. Barney used to weigh around 120 to 125 pounds, before he fell off training. 3. A boy named Joey signs up for the track meet, and another boy named Fred Stevens signs up for the 50-yard dash and high hurdles. 4. Barney sings the following rhyme, while training Opie on how to properly jump rope: "My mother, your mother, lives across the way. Every night, they have a fight, and this is what they say. Icka backa, soda cracker, icka back boo, icka backa soda cracker, out goes you." A passing truck driver overhears Barney singing this ditty and asks him if he would like to come over to his house later and play jacks. Barney calls him a smart-aleck. 5. Barney is busted because he didn't get his raise, so he calls Juanita at the Mayberry Diner (phone number 242) and suggests they stay at her house and eat frozen TV dinners. She says she wants to go to a Chinese restaurant in Mount Pilot, which advertises a family dinner for one for $2.75. Next, Opie comes in with his metal cash register full of money, and Barney gets an idea. He asks Opie if he and his family like chinese food. Opie says yes, and before you know it, Opie believes that Barney has invited the entire Taylor family to join him and Juanita at the Chinese restaurant. When Andy sees that Barney had planned to "borrow" some of Opie's money, he goes along with the charade and calls Aunt Bee. He tells her the entire dinner is Barney's treat. Barney is not amused. By the way, Barney and Opie both love egg foo yung. 6. When Barney doesn't get his raise, Andy calls him "Barney 'Mature Human Being' Fife."

"Barney and the Choir"

Episode #52. Air date: 2-19-62. Writers: Charles Stewart and Jack Elinson. Director: Bob Sweeney.

The Mayberry Choir, led by conductor John Masters, has a big problem. The group is scheduled to perform a concert, and first tenor Ralph Pritchard has had to leave the choir due to his new job's travel requirements. The upcoming concert is an important one, because if the choir is well received, they will be eligible for the state finals in Roanoke. Mr. Masters, Andy, and Aunt Bee take it upon themselves to locate a replacement for Pritchard. Aunt Bee asks Fred Mason, but he works at night. Rick Jackson is also considered, but he has recently undergone throat surgery and is no longer a tenor.

Barney Fife fancies himself as quite a tenor and tells John Masters that he has a trained singing voice. Masters believes his troubles are over and eagerly invites Barney to join the choir. The trouble is that Barney can only sing off key. After a few practice sessions, John Masters is ready to pull his hair out. The exasperated conductor asks Andy to tell Barney that he is going to be replaced. Andy realizes he must spare his deputy's feelings, so he goes along with Aunt Bee and Thelma Lou's plan of trying to convince Barney that his throat is red and swollen. The three conspirators tell Barney that resting his vocal chords is the only remedy for his condition. Unfortunately, Barney visits Doc Carruthers, who gives him a clean bill of health. Next, Andy tells Barney that talking his part would be much more dramatic than singing it. This brainstorm fails as well, because Barney simply can't keep a voice as good as his under cover.

When the situation looks hopeless, Andy comes up with a great idea. He convinces Barney to sing very softly into his microphone. He explains to his friend that the sheer power of his voice will overwhelm the audience. Unbeknownst to Barney, the microphone is dead. As Barney moves his lips, the rich baritone voice of fellow choir member Glen Cripe sings Barney's lines into a live microphone backstage. Barney is proud to be featured as a soloist, and, incredibly, he believes the voice to be his own. The concert is a success, and Barney wins $10.00 for being the outstanding vocalist at the concert.

Now Bernard Fife must gracefully retire from the choir before the finals take place in Roanoke. Having won the $10.00, he is now a professional singer who is not allowed to compete in amateur contests. John Masters, Andy, and Aunt Bee breathe a huge sigh of relief.

MEMORABLE SCENE. Thelma Lou telling Andy that Barney is a great person, "but he can't sing a lick."

CAST NOTES. Regulars: **Andy Griffith, Don Knotts, Ronny Howard, Frances Bavier,** and **Betty Lynn.**

Olan Soule appears for the first time as Mayberry choir director John Masters. He will appear in subsequent episodes involving music. Soule was born in La Harpe, Illinois, on February 28, 1909. He passed away in 1994 on February 1, in Corona, California, just shy of his eighty-fifth birthday. Soule first became famous on radio during its golden days in the 1930s and 1940s. He was heard thousands of times over the airwaves. In the 1940s, he was Barbara Luddy's leading man in the popular radio series *The First-Nighter.* (He was preceded in the role by Don Ameche and Les Tremayne.) His first regular role on television was as scientist Aristotle "Tut" Jones in the children's adventure series *Captain Midnight* (1954-1956). In 1955, Soule appeared in the live television production of *Tender Is the Night,* which was shown as part of *Front Row Center.* From 1957 to 1963, he portrayed Mr. McGunnis, the hotel manager, on the adult western series *Have Gun, Will Travel.* In 1958, he appeared in *Getaway Car,* a crime drama program which aired as part of *Studio 57.* Many television viewers will recognize Soule from his recurring roles on *My Three Sons* and *Dragnet.* On the former, he appeared as Mr. Pfeiffer from 1961 to 1963. On the latter, he was trustworthy lab technician Ray Murray in the *Dragnet 1967* series. From 1970 to 1972, he had the role of Fred Springer on the CBS comedy series *Arnie.* Nick at Nite fans may know that he frequently appeared on *Mr. Ed.* Many of us who were youngsters in the 1970s may recognize his voice, which he supplied to the caped crusader,

Batman, on the Saturday morning cartoon series *Superfriends, The New Superfriends Hour,* and *The World's Greatest Super Heroes.* Soule also appeared as a newscaster in two episodes of the live-action *Batman* series in 1966. He made over 200 appearances on television, including guest appearances in the following programs: *Alfred Hitchcock Presents, The Beverly Hillbillies, The Big Valley, Dallas, The Danny Thomas Show, The Deputy* (as a Doctor named Stoner), *The Fugitive, Gomer Pyle, U.S.M.C., Hennessy, I Love Lucy, The Love Boat, Maverick, Mayberry R.F.D., The Monkees, The Munsters, My Living Doll, Petticoat Junction,* and *The Real McCoys.* He also appeared in *The Twilight Zone* (as Mr. Smiles in the episode, "Caesar and Me"). Soule appeared in about 60 films, including the 1973 television movie pilot *The Six Million Dollar Man.* Some of his theatrical releases are *Call Me Madam* (1953, with Ethel Merman), *Human Desire* (1954), *Dragnet* (1954, with Jack Webb), *Queen Bee* (1955, with Joan Crawford), *Daddy Long Legs* (1955, with Fred Astaire), *Girl Happy* (1965, with Elvis Presley), *The Cincinnati Kid* (1965, with Steve McQueen), *The Seven Minutes* (1971—look quickly for Tom Selleck), *The Towering Inferno* (1974), and Walt Disney's *The Shaggy D.A.* (1976).

In the February 16-23, 1962, issue of *TV Guide,* the actors and actresses who portrayed the choir members were listed. They are Enrico Ricardo, Delos Jewkes, Barry O'Hara, Tom Peters, William Parsons, Marjorie McKay, Jeanne Determan, Beatrice Fisch, and Rene Aubry.

EPISODE NOTES. 1. Hazel is the name of the lady who plays the piano for the Mayberry choir. 2. Andy, Aunt Bee, and Thelma Lou also sing in the Mayberry choir. 3. Barney practices singing Juanita's name over and over in the courthouse. This drives Andy crazy. 4. The Mayberry choir sings "good old 14-A" in the hymnal, "Welcome Sweet Springtime." 5. Thelma Lou plays the piano during the episode. 6. Barney wears his salt and pepper suit to the contest. 7. The choir secretly practices (without including Barney) at the home of John Masters, on Elm Street in Mayberry. Barney overhears their voices and shows up anyway. The choir's usual practice place is the Mayberry Town Hall. 8. After Barney returns from his examination by Doc Carruthers, he tells Andy, "All God's children got a uvula." Andy responds, "Hallelujah."

"Guest of Honor"

Episode #53. Air date: 2-26-62. Writers: Jack Elinson and Charles Stewart. Director: Bob Sweeney.

It's Founders Day once again in the fair town of Mayberry. The Founders Day committee, consisting of Andy, Barney, Floyd Lawson, and grocer Art Crowley, are at a loss on how to interest outsiders in the celebration. Andy proposes that the first stranger who enters the city limits of Mayberry on the morning of Founders Day will be selected "guest of honor" for the day. The committee likes Andy's idea and decides the stranger will be met by the Mayberry band and escorted into town. Local merchants decide to do their part by donating gifts to the guest of honor, and it is decided that he or she will be given the key to the city.

The guest of honor turns out to be a traveling salesman named Thomas A. Moody. In actuality, his name is Sheldon Davis, a convicted thief and pickpocket who has just been tossed out of neighboring Pierce County for stealing the police chief's badge. After Davis makes his acceptance speech to the folks of Mayberry, all those with whom he has shaken hands discover their wristwatches are missing. Andy becomes suspicious and telephones a law enforcement official named Fred, who tells him about "Mr. Moody's" real name and his criminal record.

Andy alerts Barney and decides to allow Davis to finish the day, under *very* close scrutiny, without letting the cat out of the bag to the townspeople. Barney believes he can cure Davis and has a long discussion with the con man. Next, Barney tempts Davis into stealing his 21-jewel wristwatch with a pure gold band. Davis refuses to play along and doesn't steal the watch. Instead, he swipes Barney's key chain that holds the keys to every business in the town of Mayberry. Andy saves the day by nabbing Davis as he is departing Barclay's Jewelry Store. He tells the crook, "Oh, what a tangled web we weave, when first we practice to deceive." Later, Andy and Barney discover that Davis has an entire suitcase filled with items stolen from the citizens and stores of Mayberry. Even as he is being arrested, Davis steals Barney's badge. It seems he always had a thing about police badges.

MEMORABLE SCENE. Andy allows Barney to deputize Sam, Art, and Floyd to add extra security during the Founders Day celebration. Sam is given badge #1, Art gets badge #2, and Floyd gets badge #3. In a hilarious speech to the new deputies, Barney gets himself (and them) so fired up with emotion that even mild-mannered Floyd Lawson is screaming at the top of his lungs. On *The Andy Griffith Show Silver Anniversary Special,* aired on WTBS on October 3, 1985, Don Knotts recalled that he "laughed so hard at Howard McNear's screaming, the entire scene had to be reshot 20 times."

CAST NOTES. Regulars: **Andy Griffith, Don Knotts, Ronny Howard,** and **Howard McNear. Sherwood Keith** returns as Sam. **Frank Warren** returns as Art.

Jay Novello stars as Sheldon Davis, a.k.a. Thomas A Moody. The versatile Novello appeared in such feature films as *The Robe* (1953) and *Pocketful of Miracles* (1963). He is best known on television as Mayor Mario Lugatto on *McHale's Navy*, a role he held from 1965 to 1966. Novello returned for one more visit to *The Andy Griffith Show* in episode 141, "Otis Sues the County."

Bill Hickman also appears.

EPISODE NOTES. 1. Sheldon Davis is 5 feet 9 inches tall and drives a car with the license plate number VT-772. 2. A banner reading "Welcome to Mayberry" greets the guest of honor as he enters town. 3. Barney refers to Davis as a "kleptominerac." 4. Floyd's gift to the guest of honor is a shave and haircut. 5. Barney accidentally shoots off his revolver in the courthouse while he's deputizing Sam, Art, and Floyd. 6. Sheldon Davis stays in room 81 at the Mayberry Hotel. 7. Davis has an unseen female accomplice named Madge. He speaks to her on the telephone while he's staying at the Mayberry Hotel. 8. Crowley's Market is selected as the starting point for the tour of the town for the guest of honor.

"The Merchant of Mayberry"

Episode #54. Air date: 3-5-62. Writers: Leo Solomon and Ben Gershman. Director: Bob Sweeney.

Frazzled door-to-door salesman Bert Miller informs Andy and Barney that he is feeling "middlin'." He is tired of ringing doorbells and having to soothe his aching feet and is also suffering from the bursitis in his shoulders. Andy and Barney are sympathetic, and each purchases an item from him.

When grumpy department store owner Ben Weaver complains to Andy about Bert's illegal peddling, Andy decides to play a little joke on him. He and Barney allow Bert to stand in Crowley's lot to sell his wares. This annoys Ben, who claims that this is not a proper structure. Andy and Barney go one step further by constructing a stand and ordering some merchandise brought in from Raleigh for Bert to sell on consignment. The townsfolk flock to Bert's stand. His friendly, no-pressure salesmanship is a welcome departure from the "all business" atmosphere found at Weaver's Department store. Ben feels threatened by his new competition, and to eliminate it, he begins selling his goods at ridiculously low prices. Unfortunately for Bert, Weaver's

tactics prove effective. Poor Bert is back to square one. Andy apologizes for intervening and explains that the whole thing started out as a joke, but it simply got out of hand.

Next, Andy borrows a truck from Jim Stevens's store in Mount Pilot to haul away the unsold merchandise. When Ben Weaver sees Andy and Barney loading the truck, he mistakenly concludes that Bert has struck a deal with Jim Stevens. Andy takes advantage of the situation by coercing Ben to hire Bert "away from" Stevens, whom Weaver has always considered a threat. Now Bert will be paid handsomely and living comfortably as a salesman at Weaver's Department Store.

CAST NOTES. Regulars: **Andy Griffith, Don Knotts, Ronny Howard,** and **Frances Bavier. Will Wright** makes his final appearance as Ben Weaver.

Comic actor **Sterling Holloway** portrays Bert Miller. He is a veteran of many series, including a five-season run as Waldo Binney on *The Life of Riley*. Holloway also co-starred with Clint Howard on *The Baileys of Balboa*. His familiar voice was used in numerous commercials, and he was the voice of Winnie the Pooh on the silver screen.

Mary Lansing appears for the first time, as Mrs. Mason. She would later appear as Mrs. Rodenbach and as Mrs. Emmett (Martha) Clark. She would continue as Martha Clark in *Mayberry R.F.D.* Lansing was a regular on the 1956-1957 series *The Brothers*, playing a lady named Hazel. Interestingly, she had a role in an episode of *I Love Lucy* in which she did not appear. (Her voice was heard in episode 106 "Ethel's Birthday." Her character's name was Cynthia.) Lansing appeared in a few early "talkies," including two films made in 1930, *Happy Days* and *Just Imagine*. The latter was a sci-fi musical set in the far-flung future: 1980.

Sara Seegar appears as Mrs. Doug (Katherine) Palmer. **Bob McQuain** portrays traffic violator Joe Waters.

EPISODE NOTES. 1. Weaver's Department Store has been located in Mayberry for almost 25 years. 2. Barney purchases size 11 socks for Bert, even though he actually wears size 10½. 3. Andy buys razor blades and Aunt Bee buys an 87-cent apron from Bert. 4. Andy sings "The Crawdad Song," and he and Barney sing "Spread a Little Sunshine." 5. Opie sets up a two-cents-a-glass lemonade stand.

"Aunt Bee the Warden"

Episode #55. Air date: 3-12-62. Writers: Jack Elinson and Charles Stewart. Director: Bob Sweeney.

A youthful looking Jack Prince (Rafe Hollister).

Andy arrests Billy, Ike, Junior, and Sherman Gordon for moonshining and houses them in the Mayberry jail. When Otis Campbell shows up drunk, Andy is presented with a dilemma. The Gordon boys want to break Otis's neck for snitching on them and for buying booze from their competitors. Andy is forced to take Otis home with him, where Aunt Bee, Clara, and their friend Mary are baking 18 cakes for an upcoming church social. Otis angers Aunt Bee by singing "The Dipsy-Doodle Song" and drinking water from a vase.

The next morning, Andy puts Aunt Bee in charge of Otis for the day. Aunt Bee prepares Otis his usual breakfast: two soft-boiled, four-minute eggs, one piece of toast, and coffee with one spoonful of sugar. When Otis tells her to keep the food warm while he sleeps a little longer, Aunt Bee gets mad. She proceeds to douse him with a pitcher of water and then puts him on a strenuous work schedule, which includes mowing the yard, chopping firewood, and washing every window in the house. Otis repeatedly tries to escape, but Aunt Bee foils him at every turn. He starts referring to her as "Bloody Mary."

At the courthouse, amateur psychologist Barney Fife tells the locked-up Gordon boys that if things had worked out differently in their lives, they could have possibly held one of the following occupations: Billy — a great architect; Ike — a great violinist; Junior — a dancer; and Sherman — a dentist. In order to rehabilitate the boys, Barney gives Junior

a Mr. Potato set, Sherman a metal craft set, Ike a wood carving set, and Billy a leather craft set. Barney feels really proud of himself until Sherman makes a passkey from the metal craft set, which allows him and his brothers to escape.

Meanwhile, back at the Taylors — or, as Otis now refers to it, "the rock" — Aunt Bee believes Otis has paid his debt to society, and she makes him swear that he will *never* drink moonshine again. Otis obliges and promises that he never wants to return to "the rock" again. As he is leaving, Andy and Barney show up after recapturing the Gordon boys. Andy has brought them to "Bloody Mary," who has plenty of chores for the boys to do. The Gordon boys beg Andy for mercy, but their pleas fall on deaf ears.

CAST NOTES. Regulars: **Andy Griffith, Don Knotts, Frances Bavier,** and **Hal Smith. Hope Summers** returns as Clara.

Orville Sherman appears as Billy Gordon. **Bob McQuain** portrays Ike Gordon. **Paul Bakanas** appears as Junior Gordon. **Mary Lansing** portrays Mary, Aunt Bee and Clara's friend.

EPISODE NOTES. 1. At the beginning of the episode, Andy injured his hand while capturing the Gordon boys. Doc Zack bandaged him up. 2. Andy loves eating black jelly beans. 3. The Gordon boys' still is located in Franklin Hollow. 4. In this episode, Aunt Bee uses Roy's Laundry Service. The company makes home pickups and deliveries. There is an actual Roy's Laundry Service located in Andy Griffith's hometown of Mount Airy. It is operated by Roy Hutchins and is located on Spring Street, directly across the street from the Andy Griffith Playhouse.

"The County Nurse"

Episode #56. Air date: 3-19-62. Writers: Jack Elinson and Charles Stewart. Director: Bob Sweeney.

Mary Simpson, Mayberry's pretty county nurse, is striving to give a tetanus shot to every resident who needs one. Andy has taken a shine to Mary, and he volunteers to help her convince stubborn farmer Rafe Hollister to accept his vaccination. However, Rafe absolutely refuses to cooperate and exclaims that he has never had a shot in his life. He orders a frustrated Andy and Mary to leave him alone.

Later, when Andy is called to the mayor's office, Barney offers to accompany Mary to the Hollister farm. Barney tells her that Andy is too soft with Rafe. Unfortunately, Barney's methods also prove to be ineffective, and his stern commands are met with a smattering of gunshots. Barney reports the altercation to Andy, referring to Rafe as a mad-dog killer.

Andy arrests the ornery farmer and houses him at the jail. He then hits upon an idea. Andy tells Rafe that he understands why he refuses to take his shot. He reasons, aloud, that Rafe desires to make a martyr of himself so that others will learn from his poor example. Andy suggests that, in the near future, Rafe will injure himself, develop tetanus, and die in great agony. He sings a song that he might perform at Rafe's funeral. All of this horrifies Rafe and he agrees to take his shot. In fact, he says he will help convince others to cooperate.

Barney teases Rafe about his initial reluctance to take the shot, but he is shaken when Mary announces *he* has yet to take *his* shot. Of course, Barney does not take the news, or the ensuing shot, very well.

MEMORABLE SCENE. Andy singing "Dig My Grave with a Silver Spade."

CAST NOTES. Regulars: **Andy Griffith** and **Don Knotts**. **Jack Prince** returns as Rafe Hollister.

Julie Adams makes her one and only appearance as Mary Simpson. Adams was born Betty May Adams in Waterloo, Iowa. This former secretary has been billed as Julia, Julie, and Betty Adams at different times in her career. Her regular television roles include Denise Wilton on *General Hospital* in the early 1960s. From 1971 to 1972, she portrayed Martha Howard on *The Jimmy Stewart Show*. Exactly a decade later, she was playing Ann Rorchek, the wife of Lorne Greene's character in *Code Red*. From 1982 to 1987, she starred on *Capitol* as Mrs. Mark (Paula) Denning. Adams has appeared in many other series and specials. In the 1976 PBS drama special *Six Characters in Search of an Author*, she was "Mother" opposite Andy Griffith's "Father." Among her guest appearances on television: *Alfred Hitchcock Presents*, *Bonanza*, and *Perry Mason*. She occasionally appears as Grandma Walsh on *Beverly Hills 90210*. She also appeared in the 1973 made-for-television movie *Go Ask Alice* and the 1993 telefilm *The Conviction of Kitty Dodds*. Among her many theatrical releases are *Bright Victory* (1951), *Creature from the Black Lagoon* (1954), *McQ* (1974, with John Wayne), and *Backtrack* (1989, with Dennis Hopper and Jodie Foster).

EPISODE NOTES. 1. Andy's right hand, injured in the previous episode, is still in a cast during this episode. 2. Barney reads *The Art of Karate* and demonstrates three moves for Andy: the Bull Elk, the Hawk and the Rattlesnake. 3. Barney teases Andy about his obvious interest in the county nurse by singing "For It Was Mary." 4. Rafe states that his daddy lived to be 100 years old.

"Andy and Barney in the Big City"

Episode #57. Air date: 3-26-62. Writer: Harvey Bullock. Director: Bob Sweeney.

Andy and Barney take a bus to North Carolina's capital city. Technically, they are off duty, but they have come to meet with Police Commissioner Hodges to request funding for new law enforcement equipment. They are told their request will most likely be denied by the state's budget department because Mayberry experiences so little crime. While awaiting the budget department's decision, Andy and Barney stay at a nice hotel. Barney wishes aloud that he and Andy could solve one big criminal case, one that would make the state sit up and take notice.

While registering at the hotel, Barney notices a female guest refusing to put her jewelry in the hotel's safe. He gets concerned when he sees a man staring intently at the jewelry. Barney suspects the man may be a jewel thief. Later, as Andy and Barney dine at a French restaurant, Barney sees the man again, keeping a close eye on the woman with the jewelry. Andy chastises Barney, telling him he must stop seeing criminals everywhere he looks.

What Barney does not know is that the man is actually hotel detective Bardoli, a former police officer. Bardoli is especially alert because he has seen notorious jewel thief C.J. Hasler in the hotel. Detective Bardoli has warned Hasler he will be watched.

Later, as he leaves to visit the police station, Andy literally bumps into Hasler. Barney ends up having a conversation with the con man, who introduces himself as newspaper owner C.J. Hoffman. Barney tells him about his suspicions. C.J. states that it is likely the thief has already taken the jewelry (an emerald necklace). "Hoffman" suggests he and Barney should go to the woman's room to see if, indeed, the necklace is gone.

Meanwhile, Andy is enjoying his visit with the police. He glances through a book of mug shots and sees a familiar face: C.J. Hasler.

Back in the hotel, Barney and Hasler break into the woman's room. C.J. easily pockets the jewelry, then exclaims to Barney that it is gone. Next, Detective Bardoli comes by to check things out. Barney quickly shoves him into a closet and locks him in. He and C.J. rush out of the room. Barney is confident he has captured the crook.

In the lobby, Barney and C.J. run into Andy

and Police Sergeant Nelson. Suddenly, Andy realizes why the mug shot of Hasler looked so familiar. He quickly frisks the crook and finds the necklace. Barney is confused, but Andy tells Sergeant Nelson the credit for this capture belongs to Barney, for doing such a masterful undercover job. The stunned deputy is embarrassed when he discovers that the man whom he locked in the closet is the house detective. Things look much brighter for Barney the next day when the local paper hails him as a hero. The article refers to him as "intrepid" and "fearless." Commissioner Hodges tells Andy and Barney the extra funding request will almost certainly be approved.

MEMORABLE SCENE. Barney ordering dinner in a French restaurant. Not wanting to look like a hick, he points to items on the menu. It turns out he has ordered snails and brains. Andy took no chances and asked for a steak, a baked potato, and green beans.

CAST NOTES. Regulars: **Andy Griffith, Don Knotts, Ronny Howard,** and **Frances Bavier.**

Les Tremayne, most famous as a suave leading man in radio shows of the 1930s and 1940s, portrays C.J. Hasler. Tremayne was once named one of the three most distinctive voices in America. The other two were Bing Crosby and President Franklin Roosevelt.

Allan Melvin returns. This time he portrays Detective Bardoli. **Peter Leeds** appears as Sergeant Nelson. **Arte Johnson,** best known as the *"very interesting"* guy on *Rowan and Martin's Laugh-In* in the late 1960s and early 1970s, appears as the hotel clerk. **Roger Til** appears as the waiter at the French restaurant. Also appearing are **Robert S. Carson, Ottola Nesmith** and **Thomas Myers.**

EPISODE NOTES. 1. Barney wears his salt and pepper suit throughout this episode. 2. Barney refers to the big city as "the asphalt jungle." 3. When Barney signs the hotel register, he signs, "Barney Fife, M.D." Questioned by Andy, he says the initials stand for Mayberry Deputy. 4. Sergeant Friendly Dean shows Andy the mug shot book. 5. Andy refers to Barney as "Fearless Fife." 6. Andy and Barney stay in room #920 for $7.00 per night. The woman with the jewelry stays in room #420. 7. Hasler's mug shots are dated 9-15-1959. He is listed as 54 years of age, 5'9" tall and weighing 132 pounds. He has brown eyes. The mug shot number is 75249. 8. The "big city" referred to in this episode must be Raleigh, the capital of North Carolina, even though it is never mentioned by name. 9. Aunt Bee packs Andy's suitcase for the trip. She also sends along some picalilly relish and a bag of sandwiches. 10. Opie loses a baby tooth and Barney has him say "Simple Simon sells seashells by the seashore."

"Wedding Bells for Aunt Bee"

Episode #58. Air date: 4-12-62. Writer: Harvey Bullock. Director: Bob Sweeney.

When Mayberry's Dry Cleaner, H. Fred Goss, invites Aunt Bee to a dance, she politely refuses. Her friend Clara Johnson tells her that she should have accepted. Clara believes that Bee is unwittingly hampering Andy's social life. She explains that until Bee marries and settles down, Andy will not feel free to pursue a wife. Aunt Bee finds a grain of truth in these words, and she decides to have Mr. Goss over for supper.

Fred is an incessant gossip, and he is constantly complaining about the hardships dry cleaners face each day. Aunt Bee can scarcely tolerate Fred, but she believes she is doing what is best for her family. Andy believes that Aunt Bee is in love with Fred, so he encourages their relationship. After explaining to Opie about "that marrying kind of love," Andy casually remarks to Aunt Bee that she has "that deep love" for Mr. Goss. He becomes suspicious when she makes no comment. Aunt Bee finds herself unable to keep up the charade, and she begins to weep. When she reveals the reason for her sudden interest in Mr. Goss, Andy is surprised. He tells her, "Among folks that love each other, like we do, nothing can be best for *us* unless it's best for *you.*" Aunt Bee takes comfort in those words. She is relieved when Andy helps her end her unfortunate relationship with H. Fred Goss.

CAST NOTES. Regulars: **Andy Griffith, Ronny Howard, Frances Bavier,** and **Hal Smith. Hope Summers** returns as Clara Johnson. **Fred Sherman** returns as H. Fred Goss.

EPISODE NOTES. 1. Otis has his own key to the courthouse. 2. Aunt Bee asks Andy if he is taking any of the following ladies to the dance: Alice Stapleton, Cissy Wainwright, or Stell Parsons. 3. Fred Goss charges $1.00 to clean Andy's dress suit. 4. According to Fred, gravy makes awful spots, and grass stains and ink stains are hard to remove. He especially dislikes dealing with rhinestone and plastic buttons, flocking, and paper taffeta. 5. Some Fred Goss gossip: Mrs. Doug Palmer regularly brings in her husband's suits for cleaning. Those suits are often stained with elderberry wine. Mrs. Rick Jackson brought in one of her husband's suits recently, and it had a blonde hair on it. (Mrs. Jackson is a brunette.) Gilley Parker's suit pocket contained a poker chip. Gilley's wife, Alice, thinks it odd that his pants manage to get so wrinkled when he wears them to "choir practice." Wayne Devereaux carries a picture of Myrna Loy in his suit pocket. 6. Fred has never married. 7. Opie claims that he hates brushing his teeth. 8. In a rare occurrence on the series, Opie makes reference to his mother. 9. The viewer gets a rare glimpse of the Taylors' bathroom. 10. On many occasions, Frances Bavier stated that "Wedding Bells for Aunt Bee" was her all-time favorite episode.

"Three's a Crowd"

Episode #59. Air date: 4-9-62. Writers: Jack Elinson and Charles Stewart. Director: Bob Sweeney.

When Barney overhears Andy and county nurse Mary Simpson planning an evening at her home, he suggests that he could bring Thelma Lou and make it a party for four. Mary is too polite to reject the idea. Later, at Mary's, they sing and talk and have a nice time. Barney entertains his friends by playing his bongo drum. He is unaware that Andy and Mary would have preferred to have had the evening to themselves. However, Thelma Lou is not. She asks Barney to take her home early. Just as Andy and Mary are getting comfortable, Barney returns! He unintentionally ruins a potentially romantic night.

The following afternoon, Andy asks Barney to straighten out the courthouse file cabinet. Andy hopes that this tedious task will keep Barney at work while he and Mary enjoy the evening together. Unfortunately, Barney finds a new way to intrude: by telephone. It seems that he cannot locate a particular file. He repeatedly calls Andy at Mary's. Later, when he finally finds the file, he comes by Mary's to tell Andy. This is not Andy's idea of a romantic evening.

The next day, Andy candidly tells Barney that he wants to be alone with Mary. Barney says that he understands, but he actually believes that Andy is going to propose marriage to her! The excited deputy tells Thelma Lou, Aunt Bee, and many others about the upcoming nuptials. The happy gathering decides to drop in on the couple that evening and surprise them with an impromptu picnic. When they arrive at Mary's, they discover that she and Andy have left. Barney leads the gang in search of the couple. Meanwhile, Andy and Mary have driven to a secluded area and are finally having a romantic evening. Just as they are about to kiss, Barney and company surprise them. As the celebration begins, an exasperated Andy and Mary agree to begin courting.

CAST NOTES. Regulars: **Andy Griffith, Don Knotts, Frances Bavier,** and **Betty Lynn.**

Sue Ane Langdon portrays Mary Simpson in this episode. Langdon was born in Paterson, New Jersey. She studied acting under two masters, Lee Strasberg and Herbert Berghof. In 1958 she was a regular on the syndicated variety show *Go Set Go.* From 1959 to 1961, she was Kitty Marsh on *Bachelor Father.* In 1962, she was a performer on *The Jackie Gleason Show.* She won a Golden Globe Award in 1971 for her portrayal of Lillian Nuvo on *Arnie* (1970-1972). During the 1978-1979 season, she was Rosie Kelley on *Grandpa Goes to Washington.* In *When the Whistle Blows* (1980) she portrayed Darlene Ridgeway. She also appeared on numerous dramatic anthology programs early in her career. Her many guest-starring roles include appearances on *Perry Mason, Three's Company, Bonanza, The Love Boat, The Man from U.N.C.L.E., The Dick Van Dyke Show, Police Story* and *Hart to Hart.* Among her many films are *The Great Impostor* (1961, with Tony Curtis), *Roustabout* (1964, with Elvis Presley), *Frankie and Johnny* (1966 with Elvis Presley), *The Cheyenne Social Club* (1970, with Henry Fonda and Jimmy Stewart), and *UHF* (1989, with Weird Al Yankovic).

EPISODE NOTES. 1. Barney wears his salt and pepper suit while playing the bongo drum at Mary's. 2. Barney's favorite pizza topping is mozzarella. He also loves pepperoni. 3. Thelma Lou's home phone number is 247 in this episode. 4. Andy refers to Barney as "Phantom Fife." 5. Mary mentions the Powell Family. They are said to be county residents. 6. Barney says he can play "La Cucaracha" on his bongo drum. 7. The foursome sings "Seeing Nellie Home" at Mary's. 8. Andy sings "I Wish I Was a Red Rosy Bush" to Mary. 9. Andy wants to take Mary to Franklyn Woods. It features a lake and a berry patch.

"The Bookie Barber"

Episode #60. Air date: 4-16-62. Writers: Ray Saffian Allen and Harvey Bullock. Director: Bob Sweeney.

Floyd's dream is to someday own a two-chair barbershop. His dream seems to be coming true when a stranger named Bill Medwin comes to town. Mr. Medwin tells Floyd that he has been a big city barber for many years and is now semi-retired. He asks Floyd if he could work as a second barber in his shop. He would have his own equipment and would supply his own customers. Best of all, he would work solely on commission. Floyd eagerly agrees to the deal, which seems too good to be true.

Shortly after Medwin moves in, Andy becomes intrigued when he notices the same customers returning to the new barber's chair on a daily basis. Later, Aunt Bee tells Andy that Sarah, the switchboard operator, listened in on Medwin's numerous phone calls. Sarah told Aunt Bee that she believes he is a playboy because she kept hearing phrases such as "Tiger Lil not coming home until ten to one" and "Lindy Lou didn't show at all." Andy recognizes the unusual terminology and realizes that Medwin is using the barbershop as a front for a bookie operation.

Andy discusses the situation with Barney. They need to catch Medwin with such evidence as betting slips and large amounts of cash. But before any plan of action is chosen, Barney decides to take a gamble on his own. As Andy leaves to handle another matter, Barney dresses up as an old lady and attempts to get Medwin to take a $2.00 bet. The crooked barber and his surly "customers" are not fooled. Moments later, Barney makes a grab for the telltale black bag. He is outnumbered as a struggle ensues, but Andy returns just in time to help out.

The contents of the bag confirm Andy's suspicions. Medwin and his gang are arrested and extradited back to the big city. Floyd, who was home eating lunch during the arrest, remains blissfully ignorant of the illegal actions of his partner.

CAST NOTES. Regulars: **Andy Griffith, Don Knotts, Ronny Howard, Frances Bavier,** and **Howard McNear.**

Veteran character actor **Herb Vigran** portrays Bill Medwin. **Tom Monroe** and **Harry Swoger** appear as barbershop customers. **Taggart Casey** and **Joe Stannard** also appear.

EPISODE NOTES. 1. Mr. Medwin charges customers 80 cents for a shampoo and $1.50 for a facial. 2. Opie's friend Joey appears in this episode. 3. Andy visits the town of Triplett in this episode, to see a fellow named Stuart Simmons. 4. Mayberry's second grade teacher is Mrs. Cox. Opie and Joey think Barney looked like her when he dressed as an old lady. 5. Barney says, "compelsion complex," meaning to say, "compulsion complex." 6. One of Floyd's customers is a man called Gordon. Another man named Ed tries to make an appointment at Floyd's. 7. Floyd jokes that he is so busy, he might develop "barber's claw" from gripping the shears. 8. Barney worries that Mayberry might become known as "the gateway to Monte Carlo." 9. This is the only episode that features Floyd's "Two chairs — no waiting" sign. 10. When you visit Mount Airy, North Carolina, you will want to see Floyd's City Barbershop. It is owned and operated by Mr. Russell Hiatt. You can pick up t-shirts, hats, and other souvenirs that feature the phrase "Two chairs — no waiting."

"Andy on Trial"

Episode #61. Air date: 4-23-62. Writers: Jack Elinson and Charles Stewart. Director: Bob Sweeney.

Andy travels to Raleigh to locate noted newspaper publisher J. Howard Jackson and bring him back to Mayberry. Two weeks earlier, Andy ticketed the businessman for speeding. Mr. Jackson was issued a summons to appear before the Mayberry justice of the peace (Andy) within a few days. He chose to ignore the summons.

Now, a very irritated Mr. Jackson, accompanied by his lawyer, reluctantly returns to the small town to stand before Andy. He pleads guilty and is fined $15.00. Upset by having to travel that far to pay such a small fine, the irate publisher hurls several insults at Andy and leaves the courthouse vowing revenge. When he returns to Raleigh, he orders one of his reporters, Jean Boswell, to go to Mayberry and dig up all the "dirt" she can find on Andy, then twist it into a scathing article against the sheriff. He wants Andy's reputation destroyed.

The lovely Ms. Boswell poses as a student majoring in government at Hillside University in Raleigh. She tells Andy and Barney she is writing a thesis on small town administration. Barney offers to help her in any way he can. He escorts her around town, and she encourages him to speak freely about differences between his and Andy's methods of law enforcement. While enjoying refreshments at the diner, Ms. Boswell's flattery and coaxing finally pay off. Barney criticizes Andy's reluctance to strictly enforce every law. He cites three specific examples, stating that (1) Andy mollycoddles Otis; (2) Andy lets "chronic jaywalker" Emma Watson go unpunished; and (3) Andy sometimes uses the squad car for unofficial business, such as delivering groceries from Art Crowley's market to an ailing Emma Watson.

Days after Ms. Boswell's brief visit, Roger Milton from the state attorney's office comes to Mayberry. He shows Ms. Boswell's newspaper article to a dumbfounded Andy and Barney. The article has no byline, but it is titled, "Does The Sheriff Run The Town, Or Does The Town Run The Sheriff?" In the article, Ms. Boswell has used Barney's simple statements to suggest malfeasance with public funds and a shocking disintegration of law enforcement.

Mr. Milton informs Andy that the article merits a hearing, to be held in Mayberry the next day. The sole judge will be a commissioner. Unfortunately, Andy must be suspended from his duties until he is cleared of wrongdoing. Barney is appointed as acting sheriff. Needless to say, the lawmen are stunned and confused.

The next day, they discover that Ms. Boswell wrote the article and that she works for Mr. Jackson. Both attend the hearing. Ironically, Barney is called as the key witness against Andy. He is bombarded by the prosecutor and forced into admitting to his statements to Ms. Boswell. When the commissioner asks Barney to step down from the stand, the visibly shaken deputy demands, and is granted, a chance to elaborate. In a hard-hitting and heartfelt defense of Andy, Barney admits he got carried away, bragging to a pretty woman. He calls Andy a great sheriff and points out that, to the townspeople, he is much more than a sheriff — he is a friend. He ends his remarks by revealing Andy's philosophy about enforcing the law: "When you're dealin' with people, you do a whole lot better if you go not so much by the book, but by the *heart*."

Noting the state has no evidence against Andy, the commissioner dismisses the charges.

MEMORABLE SCENE. Barney testifying in defense of Andy. This is one of the series' most important and most touching moments.

CAST NOTES. Regulars: **Andy Griffith, Don Knotts,** and **Hal Smith.**

Roy Roberts portrays vengeful publisher J. Howard Jackson. Roberts' best known roles were as Harrison Cheever on *The Lucy Show* (1965-1968) and as Mr. Bodkin on the long-running series *Gunsmoke* (1965-1975).

Former model, beauty queen, and one-time television game show hostess **Ruta Lee** portrays the lovely Ms. Jean Boswell. **Robert Brubaker** portrays Roger Milton. **Byron Morrow** appears as the commissioner. **Sally Mansfield** portrays Mr. Jackson's secretary, Miss Fenwick. **Richard Vath** also appears.

EPISODE NOTES. 1. Barney tells Ms. Boswell the Mayberry Hotel is the town's only hotel, but in subsequent episodes, the Palmerton Hotel, the Gibson Hotel, and the Gem Hotel will be shown. 2. In trying to impress Ms. Boswell, Barney tells her there are expansion plans for the courthouse. These supposedly include a new up-to-date crime lab, a new wing of cell blocks, a dispensary, a "rec" hall, and a chapel. 3. Andy says Barney likes to smoke a cigar when he's feeling "special sporty."

"Cousin Virgil"

Episode #62. Air date: 4-30-62. Writers: Phillip Shuken and Johnny Greene. Director: Bob Sweeney.

Barney tells Andy that his young cousin, Virgil, is coming from New Jersey to visit for a few days. He suggests that Virgil could help out around the courthouse. Andy recalls that Barney once described his cousin as "clumsy" and a "goofball." Barney assures him that Virgil has changed. However, things start off on a bad note when they discover that Virgil missed his bus. Andy and Barney finally find him walking into town. Later, when he is invited over for supper with the Taylors, Virgil's clumsiness ruins the meal. Upon leaving Andy's, he crashes the squad car into the Taylor's garage. Virgil means well, but he can't manage to do anything right.

Andy warns Barney to keep Virgil away from the courthouse, but Barney allows his troublesome cousin to sweep up. This seems easy enough, but Virgil manages to wreak havoc by breaking a cabinet window. Soft-hearted Barney then gives him another easy task. He asks him to polish the jail cell keys. Meanwhile, Otis wakes up in his cell. He's anxious to get to a job interview. Virgil presents the freshly polished keys to Barney. Unfortunately, the keys no longer work because Virgil's sandpapering wore the teeth down. Barney becomes angry at, and embarrassed by, his cousin. He lashes out at him verbally and then leaves the courthouse.

While Barney is thinking of a way to get Otis out of his cell, Opie arrives at the courthouse. He shows Andy a wooden cowboy and a wooden dog that Virgil had carved and given to him. When Andy compliments Virgil on his fine craftsmanship, the young artist replies that he did the work when he was alone. He explains that he always panics when someone is watching him work or when someone is expecting something from him. Andy realizes that it is confidence and not competence that Virgil lacks. He sets a toolbox in front of Virgil and asks him to get Otis out of his cell. Otis looks away, and Andy retires to the back room. Left to his own devices, Virgil succeeds.

MEMORABLE SCENE. Andy catching Barney taking an afternoon nap at work.

CAST NOTES. Regulars: **Andy Griffith, Don Knotts, Ronny Howard, Frances Bavier,** and **Hal Smith.**

Michael J. Pollard portrays Virgil. Pollard has enjoyed a lengthy career in movies and television. He specializes in rather exotic characters. His most notable film role to date remains his portrayal of C.W. Moss in the 1967 classic *Bonnie and Clyde.*

Rance Howard, father of Ron and Clint Howard, appears as the bus driver. Howard is an accomplished actor, writer, producer, and director and it is widely believed that his relationship with Ron was the model for Andy's relationship with Opie. Howard served in the Special Services

Division for the U.S. Air Force. He wrote some plays while in the service, and throughout his career he has written and directed many plays. He and wife Jean introduced their 18-month-old son Ronny to acting in the 1956 feature film *Frontier Wagon*. In 1959, the trio traveled to Vienna to film *The Journey*. Young Ronny would soon make a splash on television as Opie in *The Andy Griffith Show*. Rance Howard appeared with his son in a handful of episodes. (Rance received story credit for an episode of *The Andy Griffith Show* called "The Ball Game." The episode was based on the time that Rance umpired an informal softball game during Ron's childhood, and called Ron out during a close play. To this day, Ron still believes his father made the wrong call!) Rance Howard also worked with son Clint from 1967 to 1969, portraying Henry Broomhauer, the Wedloe family friend, on Clint's series, *Gentle Ben*. In the 1970s, Rance, Ron, and Clint formed Major H Productions. Howard once appeared with Vic Morrow, in *Combat!* He has appeared in several projects for television, including an episode of *Kung Fu* (as Sheriff Howard). He played Aaron in the 1974 made-for-television movie *The Locusts*; Pap Finn in the 1975 television movie *Huckleberry Finn* (which starred the entire Howard family); the deputy in the 1976 television movie *State Fair*; Myron Faraday in a 1975 *ABC Out of School Special*, "The Skating Rink," and Principal Bremmercamp in the 1978 television movie *Cotton Candy* (which starred Clint Howard and was directed by Ron Howard). He also appeared in the 1979 television movie *Flatbed Annie and Sweetiepie: Lady Truckers*. In 1981, he and son Ron co-wrote, co-produced and co-starred in the 1981 television movie *Through the Magic Pyramid*, which Ron directed. This work was nominated for an Emmy in 1982, under the category of best children's program. (Unfortunately, it lost to *The Wave*.) In 1983, Howard portrayed Doc Wilson in the hit miniseries *The Thornbirds*. In 1986, he portrayed the minister who wed Barney and Thelma Lou in *Return to Mayberry*. In 1993 Howard appeared in a television ad for Wausau Insurance. He also appeared in two very popular shows, *Coach* and *Seinfeld*. Rance Howard has appeared in many theatrical movies over his career, including *Frontier Wagon* (1956, with Ron), *The Journey* (1959, with Ron), *The Music Man* (1962, with Ron; Rance was Oscar Jackson), *Talion* (1966, with Clint), *Cool Hand Luke* (1967, as the sheriff, with Paul Newman), *The Bloody Trail* (1972), *Where the Lillies Bloom* (1974), *Chinatown* (1974, with Jack Nicholson), *Eat My Dust* (1976, with Ron Howard), *Grand Theft Auto* (1977, starring and directed by Ron; Rance served as associate producer and appeared as Ned Slinker), *Love Letters* (a.k.a.

Passion Play, 1983), *The Lonely Guy* (1984, with Steve Martin), *Splash* (1984, directed by Ron; Rance appears as Mr. McCullough), *Creator* (1985), *Cocoon* (1986, directed by Ron; Rance appears as a detective), *Gung Ho* (1986, directed by Ron; Rance appears as Mayor Zwart), *B.O.R.N.* (1989, with Clint Howard and Hoke Howell), *Parenthood* (1989, directed by Ron; Rance appears as a college dean in a fantasy sequence), *Far and Away* (1992, directed by Ron). In 1993 he appeared with Jeff Bridges in *Fearless*. In 1994 he appeared in *The Paper* (directed by Ron) and *Ed Wood* (directed by Tim Burton).

EPISODE NOTES. 1. Virgil's bag was carried into town aboard a Southern Buslines bus out of Macon. The vehicle's plate number is RH 572. 2. Miss Gratham is the only person to exit the bus in Mayberry. 3. The bus stop is located in front of Franklyn Pharmacy in Mayberry. 4. Barney and Virgil each wear a salt and pepper suit to dinner at Andy's. 5. Otis's job interview is with Oscar Skinner at the Mayberry Feed and Grain Store. The business was established in 1890. 6. In an attempt to free Otis from his cell, Barney tears open the back wall of cell #1 by attaching a rope to the cell window bars and to the squad car, which he then drives a few yards. 7. Virgil changed buses in Currituck, but when the Macon bus made a "freshen up" stop in Springville, he didn't get back to the bus in time. He had bought a funny postcard for Barney and then walked one and a half miles to mail it. The postcard pictured a fisherman with a crab pinching his rear end. The caption read, "Boy! They sure are biting down here!" 8. Barney claims that his mother's side of the family is very sensitive. They're also fun. 9. Virgil's father is a cabinetmaker and woodcarver. 10. Barney describes himself as "completely coordinated, keen, sharp, and alert."

"Deputy Otis"

Episode #63. Air date: 5-7-62. Writers: Fred S. Fox and Iz Elinson. Director: Bob Sweeney.

Otis is distraught when he discovers that his brother Ralph and Ralph's wife, Verlaine, are coming to visit. He has misled the couple into believing he's one of Andy's deputy Sheriffs. Otis explains to Andy that he was always the black sheep in his family. His brother Ralph was always the one who would do well in life. Otis simply could not bear to admit that his family was right.

Andy wants to help Otis save face, so, much to Barney's chagrin, he appoints him a temporary deputy. He'll even get to wear a uniform. Otis is extremely grateful.

When Ralph and Verlaine arrive, they are stunned to discover a sober and successful Otis. Ralph never really believed Otis would be anything but a drunk. He remains skeptical because Otis always had a fondness for booze. Later, Ralph leaves Otis's house to take a walk in the countryside. A nervous Otis goes to the courthouse to speak with Andy. He tells him he's certain his brother is actually trying to find a way to discredit him.

Suddenly, Ralph stumbles into the courthouse, drunk. He proceeds to lock himself up, explaining that this is how he does it back home. Otis is shocked to discover his brother is exactly like him. Otis tells Ralph he's embarrassed and ashamed of him. Ralph tells Otis he's going to change his ways, because he wants to achieve the respect that Otis has. If he only knew....

CAST NOTES. Regulars: **Andy Griffith, Don Knotts, Ronny Howard, Frances Bavier,** and **Hal Smith. Dorothy Neumann** returns as Mrs. Otis (Rita) Campbell.

Character actor **Stanley Adams** portrays Ralph Campbell. Adams guest-starred in a very popular episode of the classic television series *Star Trek* (in the episode "The Trouble with Tribbles," he portrays Cyrano Jones). He has also appeared in numerous television and movie roles.

Amzie Strickland returns. This time she portrays Mrs. Ralph (Verlaine) Campbell.

EPISODE NOTES. 1. Andy and Barney get a letter from the Hubacher brothers, who are inmates at the state prison. (Letters from the Hubachers have also arrived in episode 11, "Christmas Story," and 26, "The Inspector.") According to the letter, the fellows celebrated their second anniversary with a cell block party. Junior sang "My Little Gray Home in the West." It made the warden cry. Andy and Barney plan to visit them some Sunday. 2. Otis can read labels only when he's *not* wearing his glasses. 3. Andy, Barney, and Otis all have their own set of courthouse keys. 4. Barney gets all worked up when Andy deputizes Otis. He is against any kind of falsifying.

SEASON THREE

In this outstanding season we are introduced to such memorable characters as Ernest T. Bass, the Darlings, the fun girls, Malcolm Merriweather and Gomer Pyle. Andy begins dating Peggy Macmillan, but before the season is through, he will discover Helen Crump. This season is a treasure trove for devotees of the series. A.C. Nielson Co. rating for the 1962-1963 season: 29.7; rank: 4.

"Opie's Rival"

Episode #64. Air date: 12-3-62. Writer: Sid Morse. Director: Bob Sweeney.

Opie and Andy are the best of pals; in fact, they are "blood brothers." They enjoy fishing, swapping stories, and being together. But Opie senses a change in their relationship when Andy begins dating Peggy Macmillan. Suddenly, Opie believes his pa would rather spend his spare time with a pretty woman than with his eight-year-old son. In an attempt to keep Andy and Peggy apart, Opie feigns an illness. His ploy is initially successful as his worried father breaks a date in order to stay home with him. Andy reschedules the date for the following evening, when he will meet Peggy at her home.

The next day, Peggy finds Opie playing by himself in the courthouse. When she remarks upon his rapid recovery, the youngster says that he was not ill the night before. This intrigues Peggy, who has come by to tell Andy of a slight change in their evening plans. She leaves a note for Andy, telling him to meet her at the drugstore instead of at her house. When Peggy leaves the courthouse, Opie throws the note away. Later that evening, Andy waits outside of Peggy's house, having never gotten word of the change of plans. Peggy, who has been pacing in front of the drugstore, had called Aunt Bee earlier and told her to tell Andy of her whereabouts if he should call. Unfortunately, Andy calls when Aunt Bee is momentarily away from the phone. Instead, Opie answers and "forgets" to relay the message.

Eventually, Andy meets up with a very angry Peggy. She believes that he has stood her up twice.

Andy puts it all together and confronts his son. Opie admits his deception and explains that he feels he is no longer an important part of his father's life. Andy explains that a man enjoys the company of a woman with whom he can travel, go to dances, and talk about pretty things. However, nothing or no one will ever change the special relationship between himself and Opie. Comforted by this knowledge, Opie happily accepts Peggy. In fact, they become "blood brothers" as well.

MEMORABLE SCENE. Andy changing the lyrics to the song "Cindy."

CAST NOTES. Regulars: **Andy Griffith, Ronny Howard,** and **Frances Bavier.**

Joanna Moore appears for the first time as Peggy Macmillan. Moore appeared on many anthology series in the 1950s and 1960s. She also appeared in such series as *Alfred Hitchcock Presents, Bat Masterson, Bewitched, The Dick Powell Show, The F.B.I., The Fugitive, The Greatest Show on Earth, Hawaiian Eye, Judd for the Defense, The Man from Galveston, Maverick, McCloud, My Three Sons, Nanny and the Professor, The Virginian* and *Wagon Train.* She has made many movies, including *Slim Carter* (1957), *Touch of Evil* (1958, with Orson Welles), *The Last Angry Man* (1959), *Follow that Dream* (1962, with Elvis Presley), *Walk on the Wild Side* (1962, with Jane Fonda), *Son of Flubber* (1963), *Never a Dull Moment* (1968, with Dick Van Dyke), *Countdown* (1968, directed by Robert Altman), *The Dunwich Horror* (1970), *The Hindenburg* (1975, with George C. Scott) and *Moving Targets* (1987). Moore was formerly married to actor Ryan O'Neal and is the mother of Oscar-winning actress Tatum O'Neal and actor Griffin O'Neal.

EPISODE NOTES. 1. According to Andy, the

spirits of the fire, water, and air are Budjum Snark, Brillen Tramp, and Grovely Barch, respectively. 2. Aunt Bee's friend Katherine Palmer is said to be a little under the weather during this episode. 3. Andy, Opie, and Peggy sing "Cindy." 4. According to Andy, a man named Isaac Walton "wrote the book" on fishing.

"Andy and Opie — Bachelors"

Episode #65. Air date: 10-22-62. Writers: Jim Fritzell and Everett Greenbaum. Director: Bob Sweeney.

Aunt Bee is going out of town for three or four days to visit her Aunt Louise. Before leaving, she worries that Andy and Opie might not take proper care of themselves, so she asks Peggy Macmillan if she would mind looking in on them from time to time. Moments after Peggy answers that she would be happy to help out, Aunt Bee is on her way out of town, courtesy of Southern Buslines.

When Floyd discovers Andy's situation, he begins to tease him. He says that Peggy now has the perfect opportunity to get him thinking about marriage. Andy is not amused. He believes that he and Opie can get by without any help. That evening, however, when Andy burns supper to a crisp, he begins to doubt himself. Luckily, Peggy stops by and fixes a wonderful candlelight dinner. Later, she even tucks Opie into bed. The next day, Floyd teases Andy even more by pointedly humming "The Wedding March."

Peggy's visits occur daily and her meals are appreciated, especially by Opie. Meanwhile, Floyd's words of warning begin to have the ring of truth, and Andy exclaims that he will put some distance between himself and Peggy. Later, Andy calls her and says that he and Opie would like to spend an evening alone. Peggy says she understands. That night, Andy serves up a mess of weenies and beans...albeit a bit charred. Peggy does show up later to let Andy know that she has no ulterior motives. She simply enjoys keeping company with him and Opie. This relaxes Andy, and he thanks Peggy for her kindness. Opie is grateful that she is cooking for them again. He will not miss Andy's home cooking.

CAST NOTES. Regulars: **Andy Griffith, Ronny Howard, Frances Bavier,** and **Howard McNear. Joanna Moore** returns as Peggy Macmillan.

Ray Lanier appears as the impatient bus driver.

EPISODE NOTES. 1. Barney is vacationing in Raleigh, enjoying his usual routine, which includes getting a corner room at the Y, watching others play ping pong, getting his hair cut, and getting his shoes shined. 2. Barney and Floyd both love tapioca pudding. 3. Andy makes "great" chicken and weenies and beans. 4. Ollie is a customer of Floyd's. He makes a four o'clock appointment. 5. Opie's pal Johnny Paul Jason claims the following: Chewing tar is good for the teeth; if you lick the point of an indelible pencil, you will die in a minute and a half; and eating burnt food will give you a good singing voice. 6. Peggy sings "The Crawdad Song" and she and Andy sing "Down in the Valley."

"Mr. McBeevee"

Episode #66. Air date: 10-1-62. Writers: R. Allen Saffian and Harvey Bullock. Director: Bob Sweeney.

Opie is at the age where he particularly enjoys utilizing his vivid imagination. Andy plays along when Opie pretends to be a cowboy named Tex, with a horse named Blackie. Barney isn't so thrilled by imagination. He's a bit gullible and he takes everything literally. He actually believed Andy had bought a horse for Opie.

Andy is amused when Opie begins telling him about a man he met while playing in the woods. He says his name is Mr. McBeevee and that he walks among the treetops and wears a big, shiny silver hat. Later, Andy is concerned when his young son displays a dulled hatchet and claims that Mr. McBeevee gave it to him. Andy believes Opie must have found it somewhere, perhaps at Mr. Eddinger's Carpentry Shop. He orders the boy to take it back to wherever he found it. Opie is disappointed, but he does return the hatchet — to Mr. McBeevee. The odd-sounding character does exist. He works on phone lines for the telephone company. He wears a hard hat, as Opie described, and he does have to climb trees to get to trouble spots.

Mr. McBeevee cheers up the long-faced youngster by blowing smoke out of his ears. Because Opie has kindly picked some apples and berries and fetched some spring water for him, the burly lineman rewards him with a quarter. Opie shows it to his pa and to Barney. He further describes Mr. McBeevee as having "12 extra hands" (his tools) and jingling when he walks (the sound of the tools dangling from his tool belt).

Andy has heard enough. Imagination is one thing, but outright lying is another. Opie offers to lead his father to see Mr. McBeevee for himself. Unfortunately, the lineman has momentarily left the area to pick up another worker. Andy accuses his son of lying. He makes repeated attempts to get Opie to say that he made everything up — that Mr.

McBeevee is as imaginary as Blackie. A distraught Opie can't prove he is telling the truth. but he looks Andy in the eye and asks, "Don't you believe me?" Andy's doubts disappear. He tells Barney that he may not believe the story, but he believes in his son.

Andy returns to the woods to contemplate the matter. He utters the words "Mr. McBeevee" in a discouraged tone of voice, and suddenly his utterance is answered. The mystery man emerges and descends from the treetops. Andy could not be more surprised or more relieved. His faith in his son was justified.

CAST NOTES. Regulars: **Andy Griffith, Don Knotts, Ronny Howard**, and **Frances Bavier**.

Karl Swenson, a veteran radio actor in the 1930s and 1940s, is best known to television viewers as Lars Hanson on the long-running series *Little House on the Prairie*. He is terrific here as Mr. McBeevee.

A gentleman by the name of **Thurston Holmes** also appears in this episode. He is Karl Swenson's stunt double.

EPISODE NOTES. 1. Mr. McBeevee's unseen co-workers are Mr. Travers and a man named Charlie. 2. The truck driven by Mr. McBeevee has the license plate number J-86449. 3. Doc Harvey is referred to in this episode.

COMMERCIAL. During the original CBS broadcast of "Mr. McBeevee," an advertisement for Jell-O pudding was aired at the conclusion of the program. It began with Andy, Opie and Barney sitting in the kitchen at the Taylors' home, enjoying Jell-O pudding. There is an open window over the sink, directly behind Andy. Opie asks Andy if he can take some Jell-O chocolate pudding out to his horse. Barney is annoyed by this apparent resumption of the imaginary cowboy game. Andy scolds Barney for not believing there's a pudding-loving horse outside. He points out a few reasons a horse could love Jell-O pudding, such as its nutritious content (it's made with milk) and the free recipes on every box. Barney turns away. Just then, the head of a black horse pokes through the window. As Barney turns back and gapes in disbelief at the horse, Andy says, "I wouldn't lie to you about Jell-O chocolate pudding!" He turns to the camera to recommend Jell-O to the viewers, then thanks the audience and bids them goodnight.

"Andy's Rich Girlfriend"

Episode #67. Air date: 10-8-62. Writers: Jim Fritzell and Everett Greenbaum. Director: Bob Sweeney.

Peggy enjoys her dates with Andy. Their outings are of a simple and relaxing nature, such as an evening spent by the lake. She has only been in Mayberry for two weeks, and she and Andy are just getting to know one another.

Andy discovers that Peggy's father is a wealthy businessman. He owns the R&M Grain Elevators in Raleigh. When Andy relates this fact to Barney, he catches an earful. Barney believes the rich are pampered all their lives. When they tire of the good life, they seek out ordinary people to go out with. He tells Andy that Peggy is simply using him as a toy and that the relationship will almost certainly fail. Andy dismisses this as nonsense.

One evening, he takes Peggy out to a nice French restaurant in Raleigh. Unfortunately, Andy has a miserable time. Peggy, who has traveled extensively, has to explain the menu to him. Andy believes his lack of sophistication makes him stick out like a sore thumb. After the date, he tries to avoid Peggy, and when she calls, he makes excuses as to why he can't go out. Peggy is confused and angry.

One evening they meet, quite by coincidence, at the lake. Andy admits that he didn't believe he was sophisticated enough for her. She tells him he's acting like a snob and that his perceptions about the rich are unfounded. She says she loves being with him no matter what they do or where they go. Andy is very relieved. Now that the situation is resolved, they may resume their relationship.

CAST NOTES. Regulars: **Andy Griffith, Don Knotts, Frances Bavier**, and **Betty Lynn**. **Joanna Moore** returns as Peggy Macmillan.

Donald Lawton and **Warner Jones** appear as employees at the French restaurant in Raleigh.

EPISODE NOTES. 1. Andy does a good imitation of a hawk. 2. Both Thelma Lou and Peggy have brothers. 3. Andy and Barney once started on a trip to New Orleans, but Andy's Model A Ford burned out a bearing near DeQueen Junction. Andy ended up selling the car for $12.00. 4. In a rare tone, Andy tells Barney to shut up. 5. Both Andy and Barney became Boys Scouts second class in the same month. 6. Barney once took second place, behind Andy, in a penmanship contest. 7. Barney was best man at Andy's wedding and is Opie's godfather. 8. Andy mentions that he has taken Peggy to the Weenie-Burger in Mayberry. As a teenager, Andy Griffith worked at the real Weenie-Burger in Mount Airy, North Carolina. He washed dishes and made milk shakes. The restaurant was owned by his first cousin, Evin Moore. 9. Andy, Barney, Peggy, and Thelma Lou eat at Mom's Diner. It features home cooking. 10. Peggy works as a nurse at the hospital in Mayberry. 11. Raleigh is said to be 55 miles from Mayberry.

"Barney Mends a Broken Heart"

Episode #68. Air date: 11-5-62. Writer: Aaron Ruben. Director: Bob Sweeney.

Andy's plan to spend an evening with Peggy is spoiled when he discovers she is entertaining an unexpected visitor. A little angry, he resigns himself to staying home and reading a magazine. Andy goes to the courthouse to pick up his magazine, and Barney questions him about his canceled date. The well-meaning deputy believes Andy and Peggy have broken up and that Andy is brokenhearted. He takes it upon himself to find a new girl for Andy.

Barney and Thelma Lou drop by Andy's, bringing along one of Thelma Lou's friends, Lydia Crosswaithe. Andy is in no mood for company and is not happy about this sudden find-a-girl-for-Andy movement, but he manages to be polite. Unfortunately, Lydia has no personality. She speaks in a monotone and has virtually no interests. The only thing she and Andy have in common is that neither knows how to play bridge. Even thick-headed Barney eventually realizes there is no chemistry between the two, and he takes the women home, much to Andy's relief.

But Barney doesn't give up his search for a girl for Andy. He calls Skippy, a woman he met once in Mount Pilot. He asks her to call her friend Daphne and tell her he has a guy she might enjoy meeting. He tells Skippy to meet him and his friend at the Tip Top Cafe.

Once again Andy's quiet evening at home is disrupted. Barney manages to persuade Andy to come with him to the cafe by telling him he received a telephone tip about the owner of the cafe being suspected of serving liquor illegally. Once there, Andy quickly surmises that the accusation is false. He is ready to leave, but then Skippy and Daphne arrive. Deep-voiced Daphne is immediately attracted to Andy, but the feeling is not mutual. Andy politely tries to tell the women the evening is over, but Daphne's muscular boyfriend, Al, interrupts. The scene gets rather ugly, and Andy ends up with a black eye.

The next day, Andy seriously warns Barney to restrain himself from trying to solve his problems, real or perceived. Peggy stops by the courthouse with a report on school vaccinations and discovers Andy's shiner. She apologizes for having to break their date, and Andy apologizes for walking off in a huff. All is well once more.

CAST NOTES. Regulars: **Andy Griffith, Don Knotts, Ronny Howard, Frances Bavier,** and **Betty Lynn. Joanna Moore** returns as Peggy Macmillan.

Jean Carson is introduced as Daphne. (Daphne and Skippy will be referred to as "the fun girls" in subsequent appearances.) Carson, not to be confused with an English comedienne by the same name, was born in Charleston, West Virginia, the daughter of Alexander and Sarah Carson. At age four, she enrolled in Vera Baxter Watson's dance studio. She appeared in school plays and was in the Charleston acting group known as the Kanawha Players. During this time, she appeared in such productions as *Charley's Aunt.* She traveled with Billy Bryant's Showboat doing light musical comedies. Her first was *Carmen,* for which she received $5.00 per week. She attended Carnegie Tech College (now known as Carnegie-Mellon University), and after her freshman year, she joined a summer stock company. Among their productions were *Jason, A Goose for a Gander* (with Gloria Swanson), and *The Dangerous Woman* (with Zasu Pitts). Carson also appeared on several radio programs, such as *Grand Central Station, Modern Romance, My True Story,* and *Suspense.* She won a promotional contest conducted by romance magazines (sponsors of some radio programs) and was chosen as "Miss ABC." She performed in the radio program *Broadway Is My Beat.* In 1948, she appeared in *Bravo,* which was the final collaboration between writers Edna Ferber and George S. Kaufman. She appeared in *Two Blind Mice* and was selected as one of the 12 most promising newcomers to the stage for the 1948-1949 season by Theater World Magazine. Other plays include *Anniversary Waltz, Bird Cage,* for which Carson received a Tony nomination; *Men of Distinction*; and *Metropole.* Carson is also a veteran entertainer on television. She had a regular role as a woman named Rosemary on *The Betty Hutton Show* from 1959 to 1960. She was also a regular on *The Red Buttons Show* in 1952. In 1953, she was a regular on the summer replacement series *The Larry Storch Show.* She made many guest appearances on dramatic anthology programs and in numerous other series, including *Boots and Saddles, Bronk, The Chevy Mystery Show, Court of Last Resort, The Colgate Comedy Hour, Dante, Death Valley Days, December Bride, Ellery Queen, Eye Witness, The Farmer's Daughter, Gomer Pyle, U.S.M.C., The Joey Bishop Show, Kraft Theater, Lock Up, M Squad, Mama, Man Without a Gun, The Milton Berle Show, Perry Mason, Peter Gunn, 77 Sunset Strip, Untouchables, The Tom Ewell Show, The Trap, Wagon Train, The Walter Winchell File, Wendy and Me, Your Lucky Strike Theater,* and *Your Show of Shows.* One special episode of *The Twilight Zone* ("A Most Unusual Camera") was written specifically for Carson by Rod Serling. As mentioned earlier, Carson has done much work on the stage. She was still active in the 1990s with the Palm Desert Community Theater in Palm

Springs. Recent productions include *The Elephant Man, I Hate Hamlet, On Golden Pond, Surprise,* and *Steel Magnolias.* In 1993, she was named best performer in a comedy by the Desert Theater for her work in *Surprise.* She has appeared in several films. We've listed a few here: *A Date with a Dream* (1953), *The Phoenix City Story* (1955), *I Married a Monster from Outer Space* (1958), *Sanctuary* (1961; Carson's scenes ended up being cut from the film), *One Man's Way* (1964), *Gunn* (1967), *Warning Shot* (1967), *The Party* (1968), and *Fun with Dick and Jane* (1977, with Jane Fonda). In 1994, Carson co-authored a book with author Lee Grant, entitled *More Than Just a Fun Girl from Mt Pilot — The Jean Carson Story.* The book details Carson's career in the entertainment field and contains a good amount of material about her Mayberry experiences. Other notes of interest: Carson once auditioned for the job of providing a voice to Betty Rubble on *The Flintstones.* (Bea Benederet eventually won the role.) Carson's son, Tracy Parlan, made a few appearances on *Happy Days* and also served as Henry Winkler's double. Her other son, Carson, owns his own advertising agency.

Joyce Jameson appears as Skippy. Jameson was born on September 26, 1932, in Chicago and died on January 16, 1987. She was a fine comedienne who managed to build a nice career in a short amount of time. She was a regular performer on *Club Oasis,* a 1958 variety program, and on *The Spike Jones Show* in 1960. She also appeared as Colleen Middleton on the daytime serial *General Hospital* in the late 1970s. Her enthusiastic voice was also heard on the popular cartoon series *The Scooby Doo and Scrappy Doo Show.* Jameson appeared in several dramatic anthology programs, such as *The Bob Hope Chrysler Theater, The G.E. Theatre,* and *Playhouse 90.* She made guest appearances in the following programs: *Adam 12, Alfred Hitchcock Presents, Barney Miller, Baretta, The Big Valley, The Bob Newhart Show, Charlie's Angels, Comedy Playhouse, Columbo, C.P.O. Sharkey, The Danny Kaye Show, The Danny Thomas Show, The Donald O'Connor Show, The Don Rickles Show, The Ed Sullivan Show, Emergency, F-Troop, The Fall Guy, Gangbusters, The Girl from U.N.C.L.E., Gomer Pyle, U.S.M.C., Gunsmoke, Hogan's Heroes, The Hollywood Palace, Ironside, The Jack Benny Program, The Jerry Lewis Show, The Lucy Show, The Man from U.N.C.L.E., McHale's Navy, McMillan & Wife, The Mort Sahl Show, The Munsters, My Favorite Martian, Pat Boone in Hollywood* (a 1968 special), *Perry Mason, Police Woman, The Red Skelton Show, Rhoda, The Rockford Files, The Steve Allen Show, The Twilight Zone, The Virginian,* and *The Waltons.* For a short time, Jameson hosted her own talk show in Los Angeles. She also appeared on *The Dick Van Dyke Show* (in an episode entitled "A Day in the Life of Alan Brady," she appears as Blanche, a flirtatious party guest). She appeared in several television movies, including *The Victim* (1972), *Promise Him Anything* (1975), *The First 36 Hours of Dr. Durant* (1975), *The Love Boat* (the first of 3 pilots to the long-running series), and *The Wild Wild West Revisited.* Among her numerous movies are *Showboat* (1951, her film debut), *Phfft!* (1954, with Jack Lemmon), *The Apartment* (1960, with Jack Lemmon), *Tales of Terror* (1962), *The Balcony* (1963, with Peter Falk), *The Comedy of Terrors* (1964), *Good Neighbor Sam* (1964, with Jack Lemmon), *Boy, Did I Get a Wrong Number* (1966, with Bob Hope), *Frankie and Johnny* (1966, with Elvis Presley), *The Split* (1965, with Gene Hackman), *Company of Killers* (1970), *Death Race 2000* (1975, with David Carradine and Sly Stallone), *Hustle* (1975, with Burt Reynolds), *Scorchy* (1976, with Connie Stevens), *The Outlaw Josey Wales* (1976, with Clint Eastwood), *Every Which Way but Loose* (1978, again with Clint Eastwood), *Pray TV* (1980), *The Man Who Loved Women* (1983, again with Burt Reynolds), and *Hardbodies* (1984). Jameson appeared in such stage productions as *Billy Barnes Revues, Venus at Large, Kismet,* and *Guys and Dolls.* She also studied acting under the legendary instructor Lee Strasberg and later taught improvisational comedy. She earned her masters degree in Theatre Arts from U.C.L.A.

Michael Ross portrays Al. Ross would later appear in the television movie *Salvage* and the series *Salvage 1,* both of which starred Andy Griffith. **Fred Beir** portrays Peggy's unexpected guest, Don. Beir would later have a regular role on the long-running television serial *Another World.* **Josie Lloyd** makes her first appearance as the none-too-vibrant Lydia Crosswaithe. In earlier episodes, Lloyd appeared as Mayor Pike's daughters, Juanita and Josephine. She would return for one more appearance as Lydia Crosswaithe in episode 147, "Goober and The Art of Love."

EPISODE NOTES. 1. Peggy's guest is an old friend from college named Don. They had not seen each other for three years. They shared a table in chemistry class in school. Don is now a pharmacist and was on his way to a pharmacist convention in Miami when he decided to come and visit. 2. Thelma Lou's home phone number is given as 247. 3. Barney mispronounces therapeutic as "therapetic." 4. Opie is shown playing with marbles in this episode. 5. Opie's friend Matt Merlus explained to him what it meant to be "stood up." 6. Barney wears his salt and pepper suit when he brings Lydia over to Andy's. 7. Skippy's phone number is given as Mount Pilot 327. 8. Barney says Mount Pilot is 12 miles from Mayberry, and he jokes that Mayberry rolls up the sidewalks at 9 P.M. 9. Barney had met both Skippy and Daphne at the Tip Top Cafe in Mount Pilot a few weeks earlier. 10. Skippy calls Barney "Bernie," and Daphne's salutation to Andy is a throaty, "Hi, Doll!" 11. Skippy suggests the foursome go to a place in Harnett that has dancing and everything, or to a pizza place near the county line. That place serves beer! Daphne suggests they go to the gigolo Club in Yancey. They have a floor show there. 12. Barney would be content to go to Daphne's and watch a George Raft movie on television. 13. Al calls Andy "Curly," then refers to Andy and Barney as "Squirts." 14. Some facts about Lydia Crosswaithe: (1) She was born in Greensboro; (2) She works in Mount Pilot; (3) She hates the outdoors and gets "the herpes" when she is out in the sun; (4) She hates the guitar, but does not mind the clarinet or the saxophone; (5) She hates "chit chat" but does not mind ordinary conversation; and (6) She says "Lydia" means "native of Lydia" in ancient Greece.

"Andy and the New Mayor"

Episode #69. Air date: 10-15-62. Writers: Harvey Bullock and R. Allen Saffian. Director: Bob Sweeney.

Mayberry has elected a new mayor, a strict administrator by the name of Roy Stoner. He and Andy get off to a rather rocky start when Andy misses a meeting between the mayor and other town officials. Mayor Stoner is appalled by the way Andy runs the courthouse. He strongly believes Andy should always carry a gun. The mayor finds several "improprieties" when he pays a visit to the courthouse to look over some papers. First, he opens the top drawer of Andy's desk and is surprised to find Opie's recently caught trout. Before Barney can explain why the fish is there, the mayor notices a baby in cell #2. Andy explains that Mrs. Ambrose often asks him and Barney to watch her son, Jeremy, while she shops downtown. The worst infraction occurs when the mayor witnesses Andy preparing to release moonshiner Jess Morgan before he has served his full sentence. Andy explains that Jess has to get his crops harvested and he's giving him three days to do it. Then, Jess will voluntarily return to jail. The mayor is outraged and forbids Andy to release the prisoner. However, after the mayor leaves, Andy keeps his deal with Jess and allows him to go.

Barney is frantic that the mayor will discover that Andy disobeyed his order. He keeps the courthouse locked up and tries to avoid Mayor Stoner.

When the mayor catches Barney in an unguarded moment and visits the courthouse, Barney hides under the covers of the cot in cell #1, hoping Mayor Stoner will believe Jess is still incarcerated. Unfortunately, the ruse backfires: The mayor believes Morgan has been left unguarded. Incensed, Mayor Stoner storms out to locate Andy, who is unaware of Barney's deception. Andy admits he released Jess. He tries to calm the mayor by assuring him that Morgan will return by 5 P.M.

When Jess fails to return, Andy, Barney, and Mayor Stoner drive to the Morgan farm. Jess is found sitting way up high in a tree in the woods near his home. He refuses Andy's order to come down. The mayor then finds out the hard way why Jess refused to come down: An angry bear waits at the tree trunk. Luckily, the mayor escapes with nothing hurt but his pride, and he is inclined to agree when Andy suggests he can run the courthouse very well without future interference.

CAST NOTES. Regulars: **Andy Griffith, Don Knotts,** and **Ronny Howard.**

Parley Baer appears for the first time as the blustery Mayor Roy Stoner. Baer has had numerous roles in radio, television, and movies. From the 1940s through the early 1960s, Baer took part in well over 8,500 radio shows. He was best known on radio as Chester on *Gunsmoke* from 1952 to 1961, but fans of *Lum n' Abner* and *Amos and Andy* will recognize him, too. Baer once worked as a ringmaster and lion tamer for the Ringling Brothers Barnum and Bailey Circus! It seems likely that many of his loud and blustery vocalizations could be traced back to his experiences with the circus. (Ironically, he acted as a technical advisor on 1977's *Circus of the Stars.*) His first regular role on television was as Darby in *The Adventures of Ozzie and Harriet* from 1955 to 1961. Then came *The Andy Griffith Show* and the role of Mayor Roy Stoner. In 1966, he portrayed Mr. Hamble on the short-lived series *The Double Life of Henry Phyfe.* In the mid-1980s he appeared occasionally as Buck, president of the Beaver Lodge, on the hit series *Newhart.* All told, Baer has appeared on nearly 1600 television programs including guest appearances on such shows as *The Addams Family* (many appearances, usually as Insurance Agent/City Commissioner Arthur Henson), *Beverly Hills 90210, Bonanza, Death Valley Days, The Don Rickles Show, The Fresh Prince of Bel Air, The Fugitive, Gomer Pyle, U.S.M.C., Green Acres, Hello, Larry, I Dream of Jeannie, I Love Lucy, L.A. Law* (as a judge), *The Lucy Show, Major Dad, Mrs. G. Goes to College, The Outer Limits, Petticoat Junction, Quantum Leap, Rango, Temple Houston, The Virginian, Wagon Train,* and *WKRP in Cincinnati.* He has also appeared in many Disney projects on television, including *Bristleface* and *The Strange Monster of Strawberry Cove*. He appeared in a special episode of *Bewitched* entitled "Sisters at Heart." (This episode was written by an English class from Thomas Jefferson High School in California. It won the Governor's Award at the 1971 Emmy Awards Ceremony. The episode dealt with the ugliness of prejudice, and Baer portrayed the racial bigot, Mr. Brockway.) Baer also appeared in the very last episode of *Bewitched*. Among his notable television movies are *Punch and Jody* (1974, with Glenn Ford), *True Grit* (1978, with Warren Oates), *Rodeo Girl* (1980) and the made-for-cable movie *Roswell* (1994). He has taken part in many television commercial campaigns, most notably as the voice of one of the elves in the Keebler cookie ads. You may also have seen him as a grandfather in ads for Osco Drugs as a town loafer gossiping with a friend in ads for Prowl Herbicide. He has also appeared in ads for Monterey Mushrooms. Baer's movie career has spanned over four decades. A few of his notable films are *Union Station* (1950), *People Will Talk* (1951, with Cary Grant), *Deadline U.S.A.* (1952, with Humphrey Bogart), *The Young Lions* (1958, with Marlon Brando), *The F.B.I. Story* (1959, with Jimmy Stewart), *Wake Me When It's Over* (1960, with Don Knotts), *Gypsy* (1962, with Natalie Wood), *Bedtime Story* (1964, with Marlon Brando and David Niven), *The Brass Bottle* (1964, with Barbara Eden; this was the forerunner to television's *I Dream of Jeannie*), *The Ugly Dachshund* (1966), *Where Were You When the Lights Went Out?* (1968, with Doris Day), *The Skin Game* (1971, with James Garner), *Like a Crow on a June Bug* (a.k.a. *Sixteen*, 1972) *White Dog* (1982, with Kristy McNichol), *Doctor Detroit* (1983, with Dan Aykroyd), *Chattanooga Choo-Choo* (1984, with Barbara Eden), and *Dave* (1993).

Roy Engel, who appears in minor roles throughout the series, is featured here as Jess Morgan. **Janet Stewart** portrays Mrs. Ambrose. **Helen Kleeb** appears as Mrs. Jess Morgan.

EPISODE NOTES. 1. Barney wears his salt and pepper suit to take Juanita out. 2. Barney likes to park with Juanita on Willow Lane near the duck pond. 3. The mayor orders that No Parking signs be put up on Willow Lane. It seems the area has become something of a lover's lane. 4. Barney tells Juanita he will bring a new Ted Weems record to her house. He claims the music "soothes the savage" in him. 5. Barney's questionable aftershave is Nuit de Paris (Paris Night). On the bottle it says: "Capture the fragrance of Riviera rose petals and the passion of the Mediterranean moon in a rugged he-man scent." Teasing him, Andy adds: "Caution: User should wear gloves." He and Opie think it smells like paint. 6. Fraser's Store is located in May-

berry. They sell licorice whips, among other items. 7. Mayor Stoner's license plate number is the familiar VT-772. 8. Andy was an hour and six minutes late for his meeting because he was fishing with Opie.

"The Cow Thief"

Episode #70. Air date: 11-29-62. Writers: R. Allen Saffian and Harvey Bullock. Director: Bob Sweeney.

Two Mayberry farmers, Wetty Huff and Tate "Fletch" Fletcher, have reported a cow missing from each of their farms. The cows did not just escape; they were stolen. The only clue to the mystery was left at the Fletcher farm: three sets of footprints. Mayor Stoner has no confidence in Andy's investigative ability, so he calls for help from "a real professional" from Raleigh. Barney takes offense at the idea of an "interloper" and plans to give him "the big freeze." Meanwhile, Andy notices that ex-convict Luke Jensen is back in town. Andy refers to him as a "bad penny" and plans to keep an eye on him.

William Upchurch, a special investigator from Raleigh, arrives. Barney's "big freeze" quickly melts when Mr. Upchurch mistakes him for the sheriff and then compliments him for his special report on safety procedures on country roads. He liked Barney's catchy slogan, "Walk on the left side after dark and you'll wind up playing harp!"

Andy, Barney, Mr. Upchurch, and Mayor Stoner go to Fletch's farm to view the footprints. Mr. Upchurch makes a moulage (a plaster cast) of the footprints. Barney is fascinated by the investigator's methods. The others virtually ignore Andy's common-sense approach. Andy suspects Mr. Upchurch's theory, that three culprits stole the cow, is wrong. Yes, there are three sets of footprints, but if they were made by three thieves, where are the *cow's* prints? Andy suggests that one man put shoes on the cow and led it away from the farm. Andy suspects Luke Jensen was the culprit. Later, with help from Tate Fletcher, Andy sets a trap to capture the crook red-handed.

The mayor and Mr. Upchurch choose to ignore Andy's "harebrained" idea, but, in a beautiful display of loyalty, Barney stands by Andy. It seems he remembers a time when another Mayberry mayor called Andy harebrained. It was when Andy decided to hire Barney to be his deputy! Andy's theory proves to be right on target, and the befuddled mayor and Mr. Upchurch look on in amazement as Andy catches the thief, Luke Jensen, and hauls him away.

CAST NOTES. Regulars: **Andy Griffith, Don Knotts**, and **Ronny Howard. Parley Baer** returns as Mayor Stoner.

Malcolm Atterbury, who portrayed Grandfather Aldon on television's *Apple's Way* (1974-1975), appears as Luke Jensen. **Jon Lormer** portrays Tate Fletcher. Lormer can be seen in several roles in this series. Among them is another "Fletch." (In episode 47, "Bailey's Bad Boy," he was Fletch Dilbeck.) **Ralph Bell** portrays special investigator William Upchurch.

EPISODE NOTES. 1. When nearsighted Luke Jensen is caught, he has mistaken Fletch's bull for a cow. The bull put up a fight. 2. Investigator Upchurch nicknamed the three fictitious thieves in his theory "Able, Baker, and Charlie." 3. Barney's theme, "The Manhunt," is played as he exits Tate Fletcher's cabin along with Mayor Stoner and Mr. Upchurch. 4. Luke Jensen had been recently released from the Asheville County Jail. 5. Luke Jensen's dog is called Mac. 6. Tate Fletcher's wife is named Cornelia. 7. A man named Ed works for *The Mayberry Gazette*. 8. Earlie Walker's trash can is mentioned in this episode. 9. Aunt Bee cleans out the attic, and among the items she discards is an umbrella stand shaped like an elephant's foot. We wonder if co-writer Harvey Bullock recalled this unusual item when he worked on the 1986 television movie *Return to Mayberry*. In the movie, Ernest T. Bass, prompted by an unscrupulous businessman, makes giant footprints with monster feet made from plaster. Hmmm....

"Floyd the Gay Deceiver"

Episode #71. Air date: 11-26-62. Writer: Aaron Ruben. Director: Bob Sweeney.

Calling himself "a miserable, deceitful wretch," Mayberry's guilt-ridden barber tells Andy that he is ready to skip town and go to Nashville. His panic stems from deception. Floyd is a member of a Lonely Hearts Correspondence Club and has been regularly corresponding with a wealthy widow named Madelyn Grayson. Now Ms. Grayson has written him and said she is coming to meet him. This sounds harmless enough, until Floyd informs Andy that he has led her to believe he is a millionaire businessman.

Although Andy suspects that Ms. Grayson may be misrepresenting herself as well, he decides to help Floyd out. Andy has been entrusted by the Cliff Deavereaux family to watch over their lovely home in Mayberry while they are in New Orleans for a few days. Andy allows Floyd to use the home during Ms. Grayson's visit. He even enlists Aunt Bee to be Beatrice, his maid! Floyd is very grateful and calls Andy "a prince of a fellow."

Ms. Grayson arrives in a fancy Ford convertible, and suddenly Andy finds himself posing as Andrew Paul Lawson, Floyd's son. When Opie innocently walks in on this game of deception, he is passed off as Floyd's younger son. Ms. Grayson seems pleased with them all and tells Floyd she is glad to find he is as he described, and not another phony. She claims to have been taken advantage of by several deceitful men. Ms. Grayson enjoys Floyd so much, she announces she may spend the entire week with him.

Andy tells Floyd — by now a nervous wreck — that Ms. Grayson must be told the truth. Poor Floyd is unable to break the news, so the task falls on Andy's shoulders. Andy calmly explains to Ms. Grayson that he is actually the sheriff. Before he can continue, Ms. Grayson, believing her own deception has been uncovered, admits she is a fraud. She confesses that she routinely poses as a wealthy widow in order to sponge money off of wealthy men. Andy hides his surprised reaction and asks her to leave immediately. When he discovers that Floyd's only concern is for Ms. Grayson's feelings, he decides against revealing *her* deceit. Floyd's a very sensitive guy — that is, for a miserable, deceitful wretch!

CAST NOTES. Regulars: **Andy Griffith, Ronny Howard, Frances Bavier**, and **Howard McNear**.

Doris Dowling, who may be best known for her role as Irene Adams on the 1960s television series *My Living Doll*, portrays Madelyn Grayson.

EPISODE NOTES. 1. Ms. Grayson claimed to own homes in Baltimore and Palm Beach. 2. Floyd took a course in Latin while attending barber college. His teacher was fond of the phrase "Tempus edax rerum," which means "Time heals everything." 3. Andy says that, in her maid outfit, Aunt Bee looks like "Fifi, the upstairs maid." 4. As a girl in Sunday school, Aunt Bee played the queen in the play, *Six Who Pass While the Lentils Boil*. 5. Andy comments that Floyd "looks good enough to be put in a J.C. Penney window. 6. Posing as Floyd's son, Andy says he's studying to be a chiropractor. 7. Floyd has blue eyes. He calls them azure. 8. Floyd had sent Ms. Grayson a "touched-up" photo of himself. 9. While waiting for Floyd to open his shop, Andy says "howdy" to a fellow named Alvin.

"The Mayberry Band"

Episode #72. Air date: 11-19-62. Writers: Jim Fritzell and Everett Greenbaum. Director: Bob Sweeney.

The ragtag Mayberry band is looking forward to the upcoming annual band festival in Raleigh. At a town council meeting, Andy asks Mayor Stoner to sign a travel voucher for the band. The mayor refuses to do so, arguing that the band is the worst in the entire state. As accurate as the mayor's statement may be, Andy knows how much the festival means to the band. He tells the mayor the band has improved and asks him to come listen to them. The mayor reluctantly agrees to hear the band play at least half a chorus of "Stars and Stripes Forever."

Meanwhile, Freddy Fleet and His Band With a Beat make a stop in Mayberry to get a bite to eat. They are en route to Raleigh to play at a dance. Andy and Barney get to meet the band's new trumpet player, Phil Sunco. Barney picks up some of the musician's hip lingo, such as "chickie baby," but cannot seem to master the musician's handshake.

Mayor Stoner listens to the town band's wretched rendition of John Philip Sousa's famous march. The experience only increases his determination not to sign a voucher. The band is very upset, of course.

Andy decides to try some deception. He takes advantage of the presence of Freddy Fleet's band by coercing a few of them to masquerade as members of the Mayberry band. Next, Andy asks Mayor Stoner to come and watch the band play as they march down Main Street. Andy tells him the band plays much better when they are marching. Incredibly, the charade works, and Mayor Stoner gives in and signs the voucher. It is only when the actual town band leaves by bus (playing their way out of town) that the mayor realizes Andy has pulled the wool over his eyes (and ears).

CAST NOTES. Regulars: Andy Griffith, Don Knotts, Ronny Howard, and Howard McNear. Parley Baer returns as Mayor Roy Stoner.

Thom Carney portrays Mayberry band member Burly Peters. Joseph Sirola portrays Freddy Fleet. Norman Leavitt, who would later become filling station owner Wally in the series, appears here as a town councilman named Ralph. William Eben Stephens appears as trumpet player Phil Sunco. Also appearing are Burt Mustin, Sherwood Keith, and Frank Levya.

EPISODE NOTES. 1. In previous episodes, the visiting professional band was known as "Bobby Fleet and His Band with a Beat." Perhaps Bobby and Freddy are brothers! 2. A gentleman named Merle serves on the Mayberry town council. He is the chairman of the dance committee for this year's Apricot Blossom Festival. He announces that the traditional decorations, Japanese lanterns, are not available. The council decides to replace them with balloons. 3. A gentleman named Ralph is also a councilman. He likes to say "Hear, Hear!" 4. In the Mayberry band, Andy plays tuba, Floyd plays trombone, a man named Carl plays first clarinet, and a fellow by the name of Burley Peters plays the snare drum. Barney is the newly named standby cymbalist. 5. Barney purchased a pair of cymbals (Andre Kastelonitz Marchers) from Cymbal City, a shop in Chicago. They have leather handles and cost $18.50. Also available were a lesser pair that had leatherette handles and cost $14.50. 6. "Stars and Stripes Forever" is song number 12 in the Mayberry band's brown book. 7. Andy tells Freddy that it is "Bug Month" and he and Barney must inspect their bus for "Interstate Pest Control." Actually, this is just a ruse Andy uses to coerce the Fleet band to help the Mayberry band out. 8. The Mayberry Feed and Grain Store and Franklyn Pharmacy are seen in this episode. 9. Floyd is one of the founders of the Mayberry band. 10. Barney wears his salt and pepper suit to the band festival in Raleigh, although we see him without his jacket. 11. Mayor Stoner says hello to Miss Johnson and a boy named "Little" Wendell, two Mayberrians watching the band march down Main Street. 12. The town band leaves Mayberry on a Mayberry School District school bus. 13. Opie wins a bugle and 10 free lessons as a door prize at the movie house in Mayberry.

"Lawman Barney"

Episode #73. Air date: 11-12-62. Writer: Aaron Ruben. Director: Bob Sweeney.

Two big and mean out-of-town farmers, Matt and Neal, are illegally selling produce along the roadside in Mayberry. Barney orders them to cease their activity and move along. The men intimidate and threaten him until he makes a speedy retreat to the safety of the courthouse. Shortly after this incident, Andy notices the men and orders them to leave town. They can see that Andy will not be intimidated and begin to pack up their goods. The men tell Andy that his deputy had previously ordered them to leave and they did not take him seriously because he acted like a "clown" and a "scared rabbit." Andy replies they shouldn't have messed with Barney, because he has a violent streak. He claims Barney may act frightened when initially confronted, but he usually returns with a vengeance. He warns them Barney is known by several nicknames, including Barney the Beast, Fife the Fierce, and Crazy Gun Barney. The farmers agree to get out of town as soon as possible.

Andy returns to the courthouse and tells Barney he wants him to go chase away the two farmers who are selling produce in back of Dexter Street. He figures this will give his deputy a real boost of confidence. Barney tries to get out of going, but Andy makes the request an order. As Barney is arriving on the site, the men catch a glimpse of him, and they quickly leap into their truck and leave. A confused but triumphant Deputy Fife returns to the courthouse.

Meanwhile, Floyd is enjoying a bottle of pop at Wally's Filling Station when Matt and Neal pull in to get some water to fill their truck's leaking radiator. Barney honks as he drives by the station, not noticing the two farmers. Floyd and Wally joke about Barney's false bravado and his reputation of being overzealous. Matt and Neal realize they've been hoodwinked. They tell Floyd to be sure and let Barney know that they are returning to their selling spot, and that they are looking forward to having the deputy as a customer.

Floyd goes to the courthouse and tells Andy everything the men said, unaware that Barney is in the back room, listening. Andy tells Barney that *he* will get them to leave by teaching them to respect the law. Barney decides to tag along with Andy. Just before reaching their destination, Barney tells Andy he wants to face the men alone. The brave deputy then solemnly confronts them, and, in a rare display of true courage, handles the situation perfectly.

CAST NOTES. Regulars: **Andy Griffith, Don Knotts, Ronny Howard**, and **Howard McNear**.

Allan Melvin returns. He portrays Neal, one of the farmers illegally selling produce. **Orville Sherman** also returns to the series to portray Matt. **Bob McQuain**, who appears in several episodes (usually in small roles), portrays an unnamed man relaxing with Floyd and Wally. **Norman Leavitt** makes his first appearance as Wally, owner of Wally's Filling Station.

EPISODE NOTES. 1. Barney's "Manhunt" theme is played during and after his showdowns with Matt and Neal, and also when Andy confronts the men. 2. Andy tells the farmers that Barney always does these things just before he turns violent: (1) clears his throat; (2) tugs at his collar; and (3) beats his fist against his holster. 3. According to Barney, Otis uses cheap hair oil, which stains his pillowcases. 4. Barney says stalking is his number one job. 5. Floyd claims Wally has the best pop in town, in terms of variety. Two kinds are Nectarine Crush and Huckleberry Smash. 6. Floyd calls Wally a "scamp." 7. Wally refers to Barney, sarcastically, as "Fearless Fife." 8. Floyd says Barney uses his gun to start the potato sack race at the Masons' picnic. 9. Andy and Opie play darts inside the courthouse. 10. Barney accidentally shoots out the squad car's left rear tire. 11. Matt and Neal jokingly suggest

that maybe Barney is "Wyatt Earp," "Marshal Dillon," "The Lone Ranger," or "The Lone Ranger's *horse*, Silver."

"Convicts-at-Large"

Episode #74. Air date: 12-10-62. Writers: Everett Greenbaum and Jim Fritzell. Dorector: Bob Sweeney.

Three female convicts, Big Maude Tyler, Jalene Naomi Connors, and a "lady" named Sally, have escaped from state prison and are holed up at Charlie O'Malley's lakeside cabin, just outside of Mayberry. Floyd and Barney have been fishing at the lake and have no knowledge of the prison break. As the pair head back home, Floyd's car runs out of gas near O'Malley's cabin. The women quickly capture the unsuspecting pair and plan to use them as hostages. Big Maude forces Barney to telephone Andy and tell him that he and Floyd are spending the night with Charlie O'Malley. After he hangs up, Barney tries to think of ways of escaping, while Floyd seems content being a prisoner. Sally tells Barney that he reminds her of one of her old boyfriends named Al, whom she met at the Cascade Club in Toledo. Everyone at the cabin, including Floyd, starts referring to Barney as "Al."

When Big Maude sends Floyd and Sally into Mayberry to buy groceries, Andy sees them and believes his two buddies are having a big party with some female companions at the cabin. Andy's lighthearted suspicions turn to concern when he meets Charlie O'Malley after Floyd and Sally have sped away. Charlie explains he has just returned home from Detroit and has not been at his cabin.

Andy and Charlie go to the cabin and quickly capture Sally and Naomi as they are getting water from an outdoor well. Andy is able to signal Barney that he needs to get Big Maude out the front door. Deputy Fife does his best Rudolph Valentino and tangos Big Maude right out the door and into Andy's waiting handcuffs. Meanwhile, inside the cabin, a totally oblivious Floyd scolds Big Maude and "Al" for letting the hamburgers on the oven burn. Andy gets a kick out of this.

The next day, Barney gets ticked when none other than Floyd gets credit in *The Mayberry Gazette* for single-handedly capturing the female prisoners. The headline states: "Local Barber Captures Escaped Convicts." Under the headline is a large picture of Floyd Lawson, with a big smile on his face.

CAST NOTES. Regulars: **Andy Griffith and Don Knotts. Howard McNear** makes his final appearance prior to suffering a severe stroke. He would return in episode 119, "Andy Saves Gomer."

Reta Shaw stars as Big Maude Tyler. Shaw would later appear in episode 116, "The Song Festers," as Barney's voice teacher, Eleanora Poultice. **Jean Carson** appears as Jalene Naomi Connors. Carson is well known to fans of *The Andy Griffith Show* as Skippy, one of the "Fun Girls." **Jane Dulo** portrays Sally. Dulo is well known as Agent 99's mother on *Get Smart*. **Willis Bouchey** appears as Charlie O'Malley.

EPISODE NOTES. 1. Big Maude Tyler's prison number is 38216. She is also known as Clarice Tyler, Maude Clarice Tyler, Annabelle Tyler, and Ralph Henderson. She is 5 feet 6 inches tall and weighs 175 pounds. 2. Jalene Naomi Connors is described as slender with blonde hair. Her prison number is 5831. She stands 5 feet 4 inches tall and weighs 115 pounds. She is a convicted husband-beater. In fact, when she hears her and her ex-husband's favorite song on the radio, she breaks a vase over Floyd's head in a fit of anger. 3. Sally's prison number is 1000. She refers to Floyd as "Charlie Chase." Sally and the other two "convicts-at-large" enjoy dancing. 4. Floyd drives an old car that has the license plate number RD-757. 5. Charlie O'Malley's father-in-law owns the company Jenson's Orthopedic Loafers. They are well-to-do. 6. Floyd and Sally's grocery list includes one pound of sugar, two pounds of coffee, four dozen eggs, four loaves of bread, ketchup, fruit, and four pounds of hamburger. 7. Big Maude refers to Barney as "Slim." 8. Where did Floyd get the gas to drive into town for groceries? If you recall, the reason why Floyd and Barney went to O'Malley's cabin was to get gas for the car. They never mentioned whether they found any at O'Malley's.

"The Bed Jacket"

Episode #75. Air date: 12-17-62. Writers: Harvey Bullock and R. Allen Saffian. Director: Bob Sweeney.

Andy credits his fishing pole, "Eagle-Eye Annie," for bringing him luck as a fisherman. Mayor Stoner envies Andy's angling success and offers to buy the pole from him, but Andy turns him down.

Aunt Bee's birthday is coming up, and she warns Andy and Opie not to buy her anything that isn't sensible. Andy's practical purchase is two dozen preserve jars, while Opie wisely chooses a salt and pepper set.

Meanwhile, a frilly bed jacket in the window of Lukens Style Shop has captured Aunt Bee's atten-

tion. She does her best to hint to Andy that she would love to receive it as a gift. She even drops hints on Mayor Stoner's non-listening ears in the hope that he will tell Andy. The mayor, who has just purchased guest towels from Lukens Style Shop as a "welcome home" gift for his wife, Mabel (who was away for a month visiting her sister), decides instead to buy her the bed jacket. Because he's due to hold a meeting, he asks Andy to exchange the towels for the bed jacket, which is the only one in stock.

While leaving F. Wakefield's Beauty Salon, Aunt Bee and Clara notice Andy going into Lukens. When Aunt Bee sees Andy buying the bed jacket, she is overjoyed. She can scarcely wait until the next day to open her fabulous birthday gift.

Needless to say, Aunt Bee is devastated when the bed jacket is not among her gifts. Unable to hide her disappointment, she leaves the room in tears. Just then, Clara Johnson comes by. She asks Andy how the bed jacket looks on Aunt Bee. A previously puzzled Andy now understands the situation.

Andy hurries over to the mayor's house and offers to buy the bed jacket. The mayor decides to use it as a bargaining chip. He tells Andy he can have the jacket if he will sell his beloved fishing pole for $15.00. They is an easy decision for Andy. Although he likes "Eagle-Eye Annie," his love for Aunt Bee knows no boundaries.

Andy returns home, and before Aunt Bee can explain her odd reaction to her gifts, he tells her that she ran out so fast, she neglected to open her other present. Aunt Bee's reaction when she discovers the bed jacket makes Andy feel terrific. Later, he tells Opie about the deal he made with the mayor. Andy says "Eagle-Eye Annie" always brought him pleasure and, even though she now belongs to Mayor Stoner, she continues to make him happy.

Ironically, Andy gets "Annie" back in another deal with the mayor. It seems Mrs. Stoner heard that her husband had purchased a bed jacket. Now, she believes he must have given it to another woman! Andy agrees to explain the situation in exchange for the pole. In the end, everyone is happy...except for the mayor, who has lost $15, the bed jacket, and a great fishing pole.

CAST NOTES. Regulars: **Andy Griffith, Ronny Howard,** and **Frances Bavier. Parley Baer** returns as Mayor Stoner. **Hope Summers** returns as Clara. This time her surname is Johnson, not Edwards.

Dabbs Greer returns. This time he's a sales clerk. **Mary Lansing** also returns. She appears as Mrs. Lukens.

EPISODE NOTES. 1. The bed jacket is pale

blue with little flowers, a little bow at the neck, and puffed sleeves. 2. Mayor Stoner once offered to pay $27.50 for "Eagle-Eye Annie." 3. Andy and Opie keep their fishing poles on a rack in their living room. 4. Andy does a "garbage report" for the mayor. 5. Opie loves chocolate cake.

"Barney and the Governor"

Episode #76. Air date: 1-7-63. Writers: Bill Freedman and Henry Sharp. Director: Bob Sweeney.

A few Mayberrians, including Jud, notice the governor's car parked illegally in front of the Post Office. They bring it to Barney's attention, and the deputy automatically begins writing a ticket. He doesn't realize whose car it is. A chauffeur comes over to the car and tells Barney that the official vehicle is for the governor's use. Barney would like to back down, but pride gets in the way. He issues the ticket.

Privately, Barney worries his action may have been foolish, if not career-threatening. He tells Andy about it and receives approval from him. However, when the mayor hears about it, he's outraged. He demands that Andy call the governor and apologize. Andy refuses, and the mayor finally makes the call. The governor shocks the mayor by telling him that Barney should be commended for doing his duty. In fact, the governor will be in the vicinity of Mayberry later that day, and he plans to stop by the courthouse to shake Barney's hand.

Meanwhile, Barney remains unaware of all of this because he has been attending to his school crossing guard duty. When he returns to the courthouse, he finds only a drunken Otis. The town drunk has decided to make it a long weekend. He wants to avoid having to deal with celebrating the anniversary of his marriage. He has secretly spiked the spring water in the cooler just outside his cell.

Barney discovers that the governor is coming, but he does not know why. He is certain he will be fired. Upset, he paces the courthouse floor and drinks a few cups of the water. In a matter of minutes, Barney is smashed. Andy finds his deputy staggering around and takes him home to try to sober him up quickly. Before leaving, he tells Otis to tell the mayor, when he comes by, that he and Barney will be back soon.

Mayor Stoner is upset when he learns of their absence. The governor is due to come by very soon. It is a rather warm day, and the mayor begins drinking from the water crock.

Hot and cold showers, along with copious amounts of coffee, bring Barney back to sobriety.

Andy explains why the governor is coming, and the two lawmen head back to the courthouse. The governor is waiting there, patiently. He is apparently alone except for Otis. When Barney walks in, the governor is happy to shake his hand. Seconds later, the governor leaves, and Andy and Barney are shocked to discover a drunken Mayor Stoner in the back room.

Otis is given a couple of extra days in jail when Andy discovers the spiked water.

MEMORABLE SCENE. Mayor Stoner's telephone conversation with his "very close friend," the governor.

CAST NOTES. Regulars: **Andy Griffith, Don Knotts,** and **Hal Smith. Parley Baer** returns as Mayor Roy Stoner. **Burt Mustin** returns as Jud.

Carl Benton Reid, who played "the man" in *Burke's Law* from 1965 through 1966, portrays Governor Ed. No surname is given. **Joe Hamilton** and **Bob McQuain** make appearances as unnamed townsfolk. **Rance Howard,** father of Ron and Clint, appears as the governor's chauffeur.

EPISODE NOTES. 1. Strangely, the license plate on the governor's car reads A1A, Noth Capolnja 62. Above the letters on the plate is the slogan: DRIVE SAFELY. (Perhaps the strange spelling is to prevent any legal problems with a plate actually reading "North Carolina.") 2. Jud calls Mayberry's deputy "Ol' Eagle-Eye Barney." 3. A drunken Barney calls Andy "Mike." 4. Otis tells Andy that Barney may appear to be drunk due to the fallout that has affected the milk supply.

"Man in a Hurry"

Episode #77. Air date: 1-14-63. Writers: Everett Greenbaum and Jim Fritzell. Director: Bob Sweeney.

It's a quiet Sunday morning and Malcolm Tucker, the owner of Tucker Industries in Charlotte, experiences car trouble two miles outside of Mayberry. Mr. Tucker is in a hurry to return to Charlotte for a big business meeting on Monday. Sunday is a day of rest in Mayberry—a fact that collides with Mr. Tucker's hectic lifestyle. Wally, the filling station owner in Mayberry, prefers to sit on his porch and read *Moon Mullins* in the comics, rather than be bothered by an out-of-town businessman with car problems. He assures Mr. Tucker that he will repair his car first thing in the morning. This doesn't satisfy Mr. Tucker, so he turns to Gomer Pyle for help. When Gomer proves to be no help at all, Mr. Tucker explodes and steals Gomer's truck. Andy catches him but, under the conditions, refuses to press charges. Instead, Andy takes Mr. Tucker home with him for one of Aunt Bee's famous Sunday dinners.

Mr. Tucker simply cannot relax. He refuses to eat, and when he attempts to use the telephone, he discovers that the elderly Mendelbright sisters, Maude of Mayberry and Cora of Mount Pilot, tie up the party line every Sunday. They like to gab about why people's feet fall asleep and other interesting subjects. This is all too much for Mr. Tucker to take. He reminds everyone that scientists are sending rockets to the moon, yet two old ladies tie up the Mayberry phone lines talking about people's feet falling asleep. Why does that happen?

Mr. Tucker finally calms down for a minute when he joins Andy and Barney in a beautiful version of the hymn, "The Church in the Wildwood." The calm is suddenly broken by Gomer, who informs Mr. Tucker that he has enlisted the aid of his cousin Goober to fix the car. Unfortunately, as Andy observes, this news only serves to get Mr. Tucker "all keyed up" again. He erupts with impatience at Barney's lazy, repetitive recital of his plans for the evening ("go home, have a nap and then go to Thelma Lou's to watch a little TV") and is distinctly unimpressed with Andy's achievement of peeling an apple without breaking the peel.

Finally, Gomer returns and assures Mr. Tucker that his car is ready for the road. Gomer and Goober refuse to accept any payment for their work, explaining that it was a real honor to work on such a fine piece of machinery. They did take one liberty: Gomer took Goober's picture by the car with the hood up.

As Mr. Tucker gets ready to depart, he looks into the faces of people who are living the type of life that is a faded childhood memory to a big businessman. Suddenly, Charlotte doesn't seem so important, and an extra day of relaxation may just be what the doctor ordered. At the conclusion of this outstanding episode, Malcolm Tucker is sound asleep in a chair on the Taylors' front porch, holding the fully intact peel of an apple that *he* peeled.

CAST NOTES. Regulars: **Andy Griffith, Don Knotts, Ronny Howard,** and **Frances Bavier.**

Robert Emhardt turns in an outstanding performance as Malcolm Tucker. Emhardt appeared as a character actor in numerous movie and television roles. He would return to Mayberry in episode 187, "The Foster Lady."

Jim Nabors appears for the first time in the series as Gomer Pyle. On *The Andy Griffith Show Silver Anniversary Special,* aired on WTBS on October 3, 1985, Don Knotts stated that a real-life experience inspired writer Everett Greenbaum to create the character of Gomer Pyle.

William Keene appears for the first time as Reverend Hobart M. Tucker. (He is not related to Malcolm Tucker.) While never a regular in any series, Keene played a variety of roles, both dramatic and comedic, including appearances in *The Addams Family, The Big Valley, The Fugitive, Get Smart, Green Acres, The Joey Bishop Show, Lassie, Mayberry R.F.D.* (still as Reverend Tucker), *Perry Mason* and *The Twilight Zone.* He also appeared in a *Mission: Impossible* episode in 1966. (In this chilling episode, entitled "Memory," he portrayed the evil Janos Karq, known as "the Butcher of the Balkans.")

Norman Leavitt portrays Wally.

EPISODE NOTES. 1. Buzz Jenkins is accused of stealing chickens from Al's Poultry Headquarters in Mayberry. 2. Barney borrows 50 cents from Andy to buy a Sunday newspaper and some frozen Sunny June Bars for Thelma Lou. 3. Opie says his friend Johnny Paul Jason swears that if you put a horsehair in "stagnation" water, it will turn into a snake. 4. Malcolm Tucker smokes cigars. 5. Wally can take a motor apart and put it back together again before your eyes. He also has a public telephone at his filling station. 6. Goober takes his motor boat out on the water every Sunday. 7. Barney wears his customary salt and pepper suit to church and to Sunday dinner at the Taylors'. 8. Goober's telephone number is 371J. 9. The Mendelbright sisters talk about a girl named "Moosie." 10. It's obvious that Mr. Tucker is not related to the Buffalo Tuckers'. Charlotte Tucker married a lens-grinding man from Hutchison, Kansas, who fell down a lot. 11. Andy tells Mr. Tucker that Gomer Pyle is studying to become a doctor. 12. Aunt Bee hums "Rock of Ages" and Andy and Barney sing "Go Tell Aunt Rhody" on the Taylors' front porch. 13. Aunt Bee gives Mr. Tucker some chicken to eat while he's driving back to Charlotte. It's better than the food you get on the road. 14. Opie claims a penny is lucky if it's been run over by a train. 15. When Mr. Tucker decides to stay overnight at the Taylors', Opie is thrilled, because he'll get to sleep on an ironing board set up between two chairs. That's adventure sleeping!

"The Bank Job"

Episode #78. Air date: 12-24-62. Writers: Jim Fritzell and Everett Greenbaum. Director: Bob Sweeney.

Barney reads about a series of robberies that have occurred in nearby Marshall County. Careless merchants and apathy are the root cause of the lack of property protection, according to a statement released by the beleaguered county's Sheriff Wilson. Barney believes the conditions in Mayberry are ripe for a similar crimewave. To display his seriousness about the situation, he begins to call Andy "Chief" and to pontificate about carelessness and indifference. The Sheriff recognizes the speech pattern: A Glenn Ford movie, G-Men, has been playing at the Grand Theatre, and apparently, Mr. Ford's character made an impression on Barney.

The wary-eyed deputy takes a walk through the Mayberry Security Bank and notices an alarming lack of security. Asa, the bank's elderly guard, is caught napping; a cash drawer, full of money, is left open; and the door to the bank's vault is ajar. Barney awakens Asa and tells him he is conducting a security check. Asa remarks how Barney's demeanor reminds him of Glenn Ford. Barney is not amused. He discovers that Asa's gun is missing some screws and falls apart quite easily. Deputy Fife is disgusted when he sees Asa's bullets, which are green with mold. Barney reports his findings to the bank president, Mr. Meldrim. To Barney's chagrin, both Mr. Meldrim and Harriet, the bank's head teller, observe that he sounds like Glenn Ford.

Barney remains undaunted and becomes determined to show everyone just how vulnerable the bank is. He dresses up as the "cousin" of the bank's regular cleaning lady, Mrs. MacGruder, and goes to work. He tells Harriet he's filling in for Mrs. MacGruder because she is ailing with "fungus of the knee." As he positions himself near the bank vault, Harriet realizes who he is and alerts Mr. Meldrim, who decides to startle Barney just for fun. When Meldrim shouts "Stop, thief!" Barney panics and ends up locking himself in the vault. Unfortunately, the bank vault is on a timer and will not open again until 8 A.M. the next day. Asa is sent to the filling station to alert Gomer to bring an acetylene torch. Harriet runs out to summon Andy.

As Gomer blazes away at the vault, Barney breaks through the wall and ends up in an adjacent beauty shop. He returns to the bank and tells an unsympathetic crowd about the weak walls of the vault and the absence of an alarm system. He then storms out of the bank in utter frustration, not to mention a little humiliation.

Meanwhile, Barney's worst fears are being realized. A con man named Ollie was in the bank during Barney's summation of the bank's lack of security. He intended to cash a bad check, but when he hears what an easy mark the bank is, he convinces his partner, a fellow named Mort, to help him rob the place.

The next morning, Mr. Meldrim is held up while opening the bank. Mort, the holdup man, is wearing a mask and brandishing a revolver. At first,

Mr. Meldrim believes that Barney is up to his old tricks, so he's not alarmed. Then Harriet, en route to work, sees the masked man in the bank window. She asks Andy to come with her to the bank and put an end to Barney's shenanigans. Asa arrives before they do and is quickly disarmed. By now, both Mr. Meldrim and Asa know the man is *not* Barney Fife.

Andy and Harriet enter the building, and while Andy tries to talk with the man he thinks is Barney, Harriet's scream splits the air: She sees Barney walking down Main Street. Andy gestures for Asa to make a sudden move away from the crook. When he does, the thief attempts to fire Asa's gun at Andy. The gun falls apart, and Andy easily apprehends the man. Meanwhile, con man Ollie is nervously waiting outside the bank when Barney stops to cite him for overtime parking. Just then Andy comes out of the bank with Mort, who yells, "Beat it!" to warn his partner. Barney ends up making a quick capture. The deputy is very surprised when Andy informs him of the robbery attempt.

The whole ordeal becomes big news, and Barney finally gets some satisfaction in knowing he was right. Glenn Ford would no doubt be very proud of him.

CAST NOTES. Regulars: **Andy Griffith, Don Knotts,** and **Jim Nabors.**

Lee Krieger and **Al Checco** portray the potential bank robbers, Mort and Ollie. Checco would go on to appear with Don Knotts in *The Reluctant Astronaut* (1967) and *How to Frame a Figg* (1971). He also appeared with Andy Griffith in *Angel in My Pocket* (1969).

Charles Thompson appears as Asa Breeney, security guard at the Mayberry Security Bank. He would return in future episodes again as Mr. Breeney, but also as Asa Bascomb, the night watchman at Weaver's Department Store, and as Doc Roberts. Thompson had guest roles in such series as *Bonanza, Green Acres, Gunsmoke, Lassie,* and *Malibu Run.* He appeared in several motion pictures, including *The Naked City* (1948), *Teenage Caveman* (1958, directed by Roger Corman), *Hot Rods to Hell* (1967), *The Trouble with Girls (And How to Get Into It)* (1969, starring Elvis Presley), and *Dreams of Glass* (1970).

Warren Parker portrays bank president Mr. Meldrim. **Frances Osborne** portrays Harriet, the bank teller. **Mary Lansing** returns. This time she's seen as Mrs. Rodenbach, a patron at the beauty shop. **Clint Howard** makes another delightful appearance as Leon, the little cowboy who is always offering up a bit of his peanut butter and jelly sandwich.

EPISODE NOTES. 1. Asa has "the misery" in

his back. 2. Andy remembers when he was a boy and his dad persuaded Asa to show young Andy his gun. He allowed Andy to slip the gun under his belt. It was so heavy, it fell out and knocked a buckle off his knickers. 3. Barney cites two examples of carelessness in Mayberry: (1) Earl Johnson leaves his car keys in the ignition all the time (Andy explains that the key broke off in the ignition last spring and cannot be removed); and (2) There is no night light on in the office at the Mayberry Ice House (Andy says that's because it keeps the night watchman awake). 4. A teasing Andy calls Barney "Glenn," in reference to Glenn Ford. 5. There is a hardware store down the street from the Mayberry Security Bank. 6. The drugstore's businessman's special in this episode is a hollowed-out tomato stuffed with avocado and raisins. Andy suggests that Barney order it, top it off with a lemon phosphate, and then go watch the men change the marquee at the Grand Theatre. 7. Andy promises Mrs. Kelsey he will ensure that her laundry gets taken in, off of her clothesline, while she is in Mount Pilot. It was Mrs. Kelsey's clothes that Barney wore while posing as Mrs. MacGruder's cousin. While "cleanin," he sang "Dear Old Donnegal." 8. Barney's "Manhunt" theme is played as he leaves the beauty shop and heads back (in women's clothing) to the bank. 9. Leon offers his sandwich to Barney and to Mr. Meldrim. Both decline. 10. The headline in *The Mayberry Gazette* after the attempted bank robbery read, "Bank Hold-Up Foiled Here." 11. Barney complains that, for the third time, the newspaper has misspelled his name. This time his last name was listed as "Fike." When Barney calls *The Mayberry Gazette* reporter, Mr. Butler, the reporter apologizes and calls him "Howie." 12. After Asa scrubs his bullets clean, Andy proclaims that Asa and Barney have the most beautiful bullets in town.

"One-Punch Opie"

Episode #79. Air date: 12-31-62. Writer: Harvey Bullock. Director: Bob Sweeney.

Opie is dismayed when he discovers his pals following a wayward young boy named Steve Quincy. The 9-year-old smart-aleck would rather swipe apples than go fishing, and he likes to call Opie "Dopey." This doesn't sit well with Opie, but he won't fight Quincy, because it wouldn't look good for the sheriff's son to do so. Andy advises Opie to try to find something to like about Quincy, who is new in town. Opie agrees to give Steve another chance.

The Quincy boy dares Opie to throw a stolen apple at a street light. Opie does, but intentionally makes a bad throw so he won't hit it. Quincy makes a couple of snide remarks and then proceeds to break the light. He and the others run off when they see Andy coming down the street. Opie is left holding the (stolen) apples. Andy surveys the situation and orders Opie to round up the whole gang and bring them to see him at the courthouse. All of the boys show up except for Steve Quincy. Andy tells the others he will report any future wrongdoing to their fathers.

Sometime later, Andy decides to take Opie and his friends fishing. Before that can occur, grocery store owner Mr. Foley reports that a gang of boys ran by his store, marked up his window and stole some tomatoes. He adds that one boy — indicating Quincy — hit him with a few thrown tomatoes. Andy has heard enough. He decides to speak with the father of every boy in the gang.

After Opie overhears Andy telling Barney about how Quincy is a bad influence on the usually well-behaved gang, he decides to confront the bully. To his surprise, Steve Quincy turns out to be all talk and no action, as his cowardly reaction to Opie proves. The other boys are very relieved to be able to be themselves again. Opie has regained his friends without even throwing a punch.

MEMORABLE SCENES. 1. Barney teaching Opie how to handle rowdies. 2. Barney's incarceration speech to the boys. 3. Leon closing the cell door on Barney, then offering him a bite of his sandwich.

CAST NOTES. Regulars **Andy Griffith, Don Knotts, Ronny Howard,** and **Frances Bavier.**

Scott McCartor portrays Steve Quincy. **Kim Tyler,** who is best known for his portrayal of Kyle Nash on the television series *Please Don't Eat the Daisies* (1965-1967), portrays Billy Gray, one of Opie's friends. **Stanley Farrar** makes an appearance as Mr. Foley. **Clint Howard** returns as Leon.

Richard Keith makes his first appearance as Johnny Paul Jason. Keith was born in Lafayette, Louisiana, on December 1, 1950. His surname then was Thibodeaux. In the mid-1950s, famed bandleader Horace Heidt took note of the young boy's ability to play the drums and brought him to Los Angeles as part of his traveling "Youth Opportunity Show." Keith was billed as "the World's Tiniest Professional Drummer." From 1954 to 1955, Keith played the role of Wallace Grant on the television serial *First Love.* At the age of five, he tested for the *I Love Lucy* series, and in 1956, he was given a seven-year contract by Desilu Studios. From 1956 to 1960 he portrayed little Ricky Ricardo on *I Love Lucy.* (Episodes from 1957 to 1960 were produced under the title *The Lucy-Desi Comedy Hour.*) Oddly, he was never billed in the credits, leading to widespread, though erroneous, speculation that Desi Arnaz, Jr., was playing Little Ricky. Later came the role of tall-tale teller Johnny Paul Jason on *The Andy Griffith Show*. Keith made guest appearances in several series as a boy, including *The Phil Silvers Show, The Joey Bishop Show,* and *The Lucy Show* (in 1964). In 1965, he returned to Louisiana, where he formed a Christian rock 'n' roll band called "David and the Giants." He also worked in the oil business. More recently, he (along with other former child stars) has appeared on the television talk show *Geraldo*, hosted by Geraldo Rivera. Today, his Christian rock 'n' roll band is called "The Lively Stones." He has reverted to his original surname. (Incidentally, it was Desi Arnaz who "Americanized" his name.) He writes music and performs occasionally. He married an accomplished ballet dancer and instructor, and he manages a ballet company in Jackson, Mississippi. Mr. Thibodeaux's autobiography, "Life After Lucy," was released in the summer of 1994. In August of 1994, he appeared on the syndicated television series *Inside Edition*.

EPISODE NOTES. 1. Some gossip from Aunt Bee: The Quincy family has recently moved from Richmond to Mayberry. They are renting Charlie Eaver's home on Grove Street. Mr. Quincy is a traveling salesman who sells farm implements. Mrs. Quincy was previously married (to a serviceman) and, just prior to moving to Mayberry, had an operation on her foot. 2. Barney warns Andy that there's only one way to deal with any child's misbehavior: "Nip it in the bud!" 3. Barney accidentally locks himself in cell #1 while speaking to Opie and his friends. Later, Leon closes the wrong "door" and locks Barney in cell #2. 4. The five named members of Opie's group (of six) are Opie Taylor, Steve Quincy, Carter French, Jr., Billy Gray, and Johnny Paul Jason. 5. Barney mispronounces "inoculated" as "inarculated." 6. Barney tells Opie and his friends that incarceration means "no more carefree hours; no more doing what you want whenever you want; and no more peanut butter and jelly sandwiches." 7. This episode's theme is reminiscent of episode 34, "Opie and the Bully."

"High Noon in Mayberry"

Episode #80. Air date: 1-21-63. Writers: Jim Fritzell and Everett Greenbaum. Director: Bob Sweeney.

In 1952, Andy shot and wounded a man named Luke Comstock, who had just robbed a filling station in Mayberry. Comstock fired at Andy while attempting to flee the scene of the crime. Andy returned fire and subsequently made the capture. Comstock spent the next six months laid up in the hospital due to the bullet wound in his leg. He was then imprisoned.

Andy finds himself recalling the past when he receives a letter from Comstock. The letter states that he has wanted to set things straight for a long time, and he's coming to pay Andy a visit. Barney, alarmed by the ominous wording, tells Andy that the ex-convict surely has revenge in mind. He advises Andy to leave town for a few days or, at the very least, carry a gun. Andy flatly refuses to do either.

Believing Andy needs around-the-clock protection, Barney deputizes an unwilling Otis and Gomer. He orders them to act as bodyguards for Andy without letting the sheriff know he's being protected. Because of their clumsy attempts at secrecy, however, Andy quickly discovers what the bodyguards are doing. He tells Barney he appreciates the thoughtfulness, but protection is unnecessary.

Later, Barney reports that Otis and Gomer spotted a suspicious-looking man getting off of a bus in downtown Mayberry. The man was walking with a limp and carrying a leather shotgun case. A short time passes, and Andy gets a telephone call from Comstock. Luke says he's in town and will be coming to see him in a matter of minutes.

Andy admits to Opie that he's a little nervous. He asks Aunt Bee to take Opie and go next door to Clara's for awhile. Aunt Bee secretly telephones Barney and asks him to keep an eye on the situation. Barney arms Gomer and gives Otis a rope, and the trio heads to Andy's house, arriving shortly after Luke does.

Luke tells Andy that during his stay in the hospital, he reevaluated his life and began devoting himself to education. He developed an interest in mathematics and electronics, and today he owns a successful chain of television repair stores in Cleveland. He believes he owes his success to Andy. As a gift of appreciation, he presents him with a new shotgun. Andy is delighted, as well as a little relieved.

Meanwhile, Barney and his fellow deputies are witnessing the sight of Luke holding the shotgun and Andy standing before him with his hands in the air! (Andy is actually depicting the wing span of the northern geese—he calls them "honkers"— he plans to hunt.) Barney springs into action. He opens the fuse box on the side of Andy's house and turns off the lights. Then he, Otis, and Gomer run to the back of the house. Their plan is to run into the house and take Comstock by surprise.

Andy and Luke go outside to check the fuse box. Suddenly, they hear a great commotion coming from inside the house. When Andy rushes back inside, he finds the three hapless deputies hopelessly entangled in their own rope.

CAST NOTES. Regulars: **Andy Griffith, Don Knotts, Ronny Howard, Frances Bavier, Jim Nabors,** and **Hal Smith.**

Leo Gordon portrays Luke Comstock. Gordon has had a lengthy career in television and movies. Among his credits are his portrayal of Hank Miller on the television series *Circus Boy* (1956-1958) and his appearance in 1983's epic television mini-series *The Winds of War* as General Benton.

Dub Taylor also appears.

EPISODE NOTES. 1. Aunt Bee's bedroom is shown briefly. 2. Andy answers Miss Peterson's call for help. Her cat, Fluffy, who has kittens, is stranded on the rooftop of the Peterson home. 3. Andy and Barney play five games of dominoes in this episode. 4. Luke Comstock arrives in Mayberry on bus #78 out of Raleigh. The bus is driven by a man named Alf. 5. Barney owns 1/8th of a share of stock in the Amalgamated Oxidation and Aluminum Corporation of America, along with Floyd, Wally, and "some of the boys." He receives a dividend check in the amount of 27 cents. 6. Barney refers to Andy as "one of the all-time greats." 7. Andy keeps an unloaded revolver on top of Aunt Bee's china cabinet. The bullets are kept in a drawer.

"The Loaded Goat"

Episode #81. Air date: 1-28-63. Writer: Harvey Bullock. Director: Bob Sweeney.

The highway department is blasting with dynamite in order to provide Mayberry with an underpass. The frequent and loud explosions unnerve some of the townsfolk, as well as their pets. Farmer Cy "Hudge" Hudgins brings his pet goat, Jimmy, into town for a couple of reasons: He had promised the goat that he would, and because Jimmy is so jittery due to the blasting, Cy was afraid to leave him at home by himself.

Cy has come to town to run a few errands. He ties Jimmy to a bench just outside of the courthouse. Jimmy manages to get himself free and begins to roam around. When Cy returns, he is alarmed to discover his goat is gone. He notifies Andy and Barney, who join in the search for Jimmy. Opie tells Andy he saw a goat in back of the hardware store, hanging around an old shed. When Andy and Barney investigate, they are alarmed to find the shed full of dynamite. It's a storage shed for the blasting

Andy and Barney face an explosive situation with Jimmy (the loaded goat).

crew. Unfortunately, they also discover evidence that Jimmy has been there: his rope and some partially eaten sticks of dynamite. Needless to say, this has turned into a potentially explosive situation.

Before long, Jimmy finds his way to the courthouse, and Cy is so angry at him he wants to give the goat a swift kick. Andy and Barney return just in time to stop him from doing it. They know Jimmy must be treated with "kid" gloves. They put him in cell #2, which they pad with Otis's mattress and pillows. Hay is supplied, in great amounts, for Jimmy to eat. The hope is that the hay might "cushion his insides."

Andy sends Barney to summon Mr. Burton, the blasting engineer on the highway crew. Burton tells the men that it appears they have done all they can to ensure Jimmy won't explode. Burton orders that the blasting be halted in order to avoid a chain reaction.

Andy sends Cy home, and then he and Barney leave to retrieve more hay and padding for Jimmy's cell. During their absence, Otis drunkenly stumbles into the courthouse and drags Jimmy out of his cell. When the lawmen return, they find one very angry goat. In a desperate attempt to calm Jimmy, Andy asks Barney to play a tune on his french harp. It works! Andy puts this discovery to good use. He and Barney gently lead Jimmy outside and walk him to a nice big meadow well outside of town, where he can safely graze until the danger "passes."

Andy and Barney later return to the courthouse and begin to clean up Jimmy's old jail cell. While they are putting things away in the back room, Cy and Mayor Stoner come in to await Andy and Barney's return. They are unaware that the lawmen are in the back room. Suddenly, they hear an explosion. They are horrified, because they are certain the blast must have come from Jimmy. They figure Andy and Barney must have perished, too. An amused Andy and Barney listen to Mayor Stoner deliver an impromptu and poignant eulogy. Finally, they step out of the back room and explain that Jimmy is fine, and, obviously, so are they. Andy had recently notified Mr. Burton that he could resume blasting. Cy is just happy that Jimmy, Andy, and Barney are alive. An angry and embarrassed Mayor Stoner storms off.

CAST NOTES. Regulars: **Andy Griffith, Don Knotts, Ronny Howard, Hal Smith,** and **Parley Baer.**

Forrest Lewis portrays Cy Hudgins. **Bing Russell** portrays blasting engineer Mr. Burton.

EPISODE NOTES. 1. Cy brings Jimmy into Floyd's Barbershop. Cy wanted a haircut, but Floyd was out to lunch. According to Andy, Floyd takes an hour or more for lunch because he believes that if he returns to work immediately after eating, the food will go right to his legs. 2. Cy tells Mayor Stoner that folks are saying the main reason he pushed so hard to get an underpass for Mayberry is because the highway will run right past his brother-in-law's filling station. 3. A rear entrance to Barclay's Jewelry Store in Mayberry is shown. 4. Otis initially mistakes Jimmy to be his Uncle Nat. 5. Old Miss Vickers calls the courthouse after every blast. She worries it means that Yankee cannons are approaching. Andy tells her, "We're still hanging onto Richmond!"

"Class Reunion"

Episode #82. Air date: 2-4-63. Writers: Everett Greenbaum and Jim Fritzell. Director: Charles Irving.

Barney's landlady, Mrs. Mendelbright, has asked Barney to remove his old trunk from her cellar. She needs the space to grow mushrooms. Andy helps Barney move the trunk, which will be stored in the Taylors' garage. Unfortunately, the trunk's rotted bottom falls out and the contents are spilled. As the men stoop to pick up the fallen belongings, two items catch Andy's eye. First, he asks Barney about a big rock he saw. Barney explains that the rock once belonged to his father and sat on his desk. The elder Fife used to let young Barney strike matches on it and light his father's pipe. Barney says his father always got a big kick out of it.

The other item needs no explanation. It is *The*

Cutlass, Barney's copy of his and Andy's high school yearbook. Andy enjoys thumbing through it. He had not seen one in years, because Aunt Bee gave his copy away to a "disease drive." He and Barney reminisce about their high school years. Barney fondly remembers a girl named Ramona Wiley. He was in Social Studies 1A with her and claims she was wild about him. She nicknamed him "Tweaky" and signed his yearbook "Always, Ramona." Barney will never forget one special note she wrote: "Barney, beloved.... The tears on my pillow bespeak the pain that is in my heart." Barney says it was a one-sided relationship.

Andy, on the other hand, had a full-fledged high school romance with a popular student named Sharon Despain. They were voted "Couple of the Year" during their junior and senior years. Andy confesses that the old adage about one's first flame never quite burning out is very true. He'll never forget Sharon. The last he heard of her, she was working as a designer in Chicago.

The Cutlass unleashes a flood of warm memories, and Andy gets an idea. He decides a class reunion is in order. He will form a committee to organize it. Barney is excited by the idea, too. They enlist the help of one of their classmates, Mary Lee, who takes care of the details and mails out the invitations. Later, when she announces that at least 28 former classmates will be coming to the reunion, she tempers the good news by saying that Sharon Despain has not been heard from. Andy had really been looking forward to seeing her again.

Barney is happy to hear that Ramona will be coming, although she is now Mrs. Harry Becktoris. Barney hopes Harry is not the jealous type. Maybe Ramona can, somehow, control herself. Andy is a bit melancholy, but Barney assures him they will have the time of their lives, no matter what. Andy cheers up, and he, Barney, and Mary Lee sing The Mayberry Union High School song.

The big night finally arrives, and the class of 1945 is well represented. The entertainment is provided by Carl Benson's Wildcats. It's the original band that was organized in Andy's high school days, except, now, Carl's mother plays the saxophone. One of the numbers they play is "Chattanooga Choo-Choo." Meanwhile, Andy and Barney are spending much of the evening near the punch bowl, and they discover that it is difficult to recognize some of their classmates. Barney resorts to quickly scanning the yearbook to identify people, but the results are hilariously hit and miss.

Barney's encounter with the former Ramona Wiley appears to contradict his account of her. She remembers Andy, but has absolutely no recollection of Barney. In fact, she mistakes him for the bartender. Barney desperately tries to make her remember him, even quoting her love note, but it's to no avail. Andy tries to lessen Barney's disappointment by telling him, "She's covering up. She's fighting it." He then confesses to Barney that he's a little disappointed Sharon couldn't make it to the reunion. Moments later, several of his classmates direct his attention to the entrance. Sharon Despain has arrived!

It appears Andy and Sharon's romance is immediately rekindled. They share a slow dance and then decide to take a walk outdoors. They wind up sitting in a garden area. After sharing a kiss, they wonder why things didn't work out for them as a couple. Sharon recalls that they had a big argument on graduation night, in a similar setting. Oddly, neither of them can remember what the argument was about, or why they went their separate ways.

Andy asks Sharon if she will stay in town awhile, but she answers that she cannot. She has to get back to her job in Chicago. She and Andy begin to discuss the advantages of living in a big city versus the virtues of living in a small town. Soon, they begin bickering, with each defending his own lifestyle. Sharon believes that a person cannot fulfill his or her potential in a town like Mayberry. Andy claims to be very happy in his hometown and argues that happiness is the ultimate goal in life.

Suddenly, Andy develops a sense of déjà vu. It was this major difference of opinion that led to their breakup years ago! Each wanted to go his own way, and their choices have worked out well in both cases. The couple decides to share a last dance together, as two old friends.

As the evening concludes, Andy and Barney are alone, discussing the reunion. They agree that the evening was a rousing success, but it was rather sad to see that everyone is growing old. In a spontaneous and poignant moment, Andy and Barney sing their high school anthem, and they agree that the tears on their pillows *do* bespeak the pain that is in their hearts.

CAST NOTES. Regulars: **Andy Griffith** and **Don Knotts**.

Peggy McCay portrays Sharon Despain. McCay is best known for her portrayal of Caroline Brady, mother of Bo, Roman, Kimberly, and Kayla on the long-running daytime serial *Days of Our Lives*.

Barbara Perry portrays Mary Lee. Perry would return in episode 176, "The Return of Barney Fife," as a similar character named Floss.

Paul Smith portrays Ramona Wiley's husband, Harry Becktoris. Mr. Smith had regular roles in a couple of series worth noting. First, he was Captain Martin in the television version of *No Time for Sergeants* (1964-1965). Later he appeared as Ron Harvey on *The Doris Day Show* (1969-1972).

Also appearing are **Don Haggerty, Frank Behrens, Virginia Eiler,** and **Molly Dodd**.

EPISODE NOTES. 1. Mrs. Mendelbright got the idea about growing mushrooms from an ad in a magazine. Its headline read, "Grow Mushrooms For Fun And Profit." Barney and Andy have seen the ads, which feature such testimonials as: "V.J. of Cincinnati reports earning up to $600 a month," and "S.T. of Texarkana says 'My spare time is now a money-making proposition.'" 2. Last year, Mrs. Mendelbright sent away for a machine that tore car ties into long shreds of rubber. Barney says she wove them into floor mats, purses, seat covers, and other attractive items. Andy says he remembers the ad for those machines. He says he recalls one testimonial: "R.A. says old tires sent my daughter through beautician's college." 3. Barney says he has his mother's family frame. He was painfully thin at age 17; in fact, he could reach into a milk bottle and retrieve an egg. 4. Andy and Barney's classmates include (among others) Sharon Despain, Ramona Wiley Becktoris, Jarvis Eldred, Lillian Becker, Pearlie Mae Dubois, Mary Lee, Edna Thoate, Jack Sweet, Ralph Haynes, Nate Bracey, and Jack Egbert. 5. According to Andy, eight or nine classmates still live in Mayberry. 6. The last address Mary Lee had for Sharon Despain was in Philadelphia. 7. Barney mistakes Ralph Haynes to be another classmate, Jack Sweet. Ralph's wife was on the debate team at Paul Revere High School in Chicago. Andy says she reminds him of a classmate named Edna Thoate, who was on the debate team at Mayberry Union High. 8. Barney reads in *The Cutlass* that Ralph Haynes participated in wrestling, boxing, football, basketball, pole vaulting, weightlifting and the mile run. He recalls that Ralph was always sweating. 9. Nate Bracey greets Andy and Barney with, "You two chicken thieves!" He and his wife have taken dance lessons. 10. Ramona and Harry Becktoris have two children, one boy and one girl. 11. Barney wears his salt and pepper suit to the reunion. 12. Information from *The Cutlass*: Andrew Jackson Taylor: second vice-president; 4H; secretary of the Philomathian Society (according to Andy, it's a group that got together once a week and cut out current events to paste in a book.) Barney was nominated to be in the club, but Jack Egbert did not like him. Andy reported that fact to Barney, who cried. Now, Barney says, "Jack Egbert was no *prize!*" As for Bernard Milton Fife: board of directors — tin foil drive; hall monitor; volleyball court maintenance crew; and Spanish club. 13. Music plays an important role in this episode. When Andy is reunited with Sharon, Carl Benson's Wildcats are playing "I Love You for Sentimental Reasons," and during his last dance with her, the band plays the traditional last dance tune "Goodnight, Sweetheart." The music for the Mayberry

Union High School song was composed by Earle Hagen. 14. According to Everett Greenbaum, co-writer of this episode, *The Cutlass* was the name of Jim Fritzell's yearbook from his high school in San Francisco. Most of the lyrics from Mayberry Union High (rooting for "the orange and blue") came from the song for Greenbaum's alma mater, Bennett High School in Buffalo, New York. Orange and blue were that school's colors. Jack Egbert was a next-door neighbor of Greenbaum's. Ramona Wiley was someone the writer's wife knew in Arkansas. Sharon Despain went to school with Jim Fritzell. Finally, the line "The tears on my pillow bespeak the pain that is in my heart" comes from a true experience Mr. Greenbaum had in grade school. He had a big crush on a girl named Jane Clark. A fellow classmate thought he'd play a prank on young Everett. He put a gift-boxed miniature ivory elephant on Greenbaum's desk along with a note that included the memorable line and was signed "Jane." Years passed before Greenbaum realized he'd been tricked.

This information was included in the February 22, 1994, edition of *The Bullet* (Volume 9, Issue 3). It is the official newsletter of The Andy Griffith Show Rerun Watchers Club and is edited by Jim Clark. Professor Neal Brower has written a series of columns about *The Andy Griffith Show* which have been included in the newsletter. The information supplied by Mr. Greenbaum about this episode comes from the feature "Professor Brower's Class."

"Rafe Hollister Sings"

Episode #83. Air date: 2-11-63. Writer: Harvey Bullock. Director: Charles Irving.

The annual Ladies League Musicale will be held in Mayberry this year. Barney believes he will be chosen to represent his town, and he prepares excitedly for his audition. He is not sure what song he'll sing, but "Tico Tico," "Moon of Manicura," and "The Umbrella Man" are all strong contenders. As he is practicing, Farmer Rafe Hollister drops by the courthouse on an errand and listens to Barney's wretched rendition of "Believe Me If All These Endearing Young Charms." Rafe begins singing the song in order to show Barney how it should be sung, and he does so beautifully. Much to Barney's chagrin, Andy encourages Rafe to audition, too.

After the auditions, Barney believes he did very well. He overhears Mayberry's choir director, John Masters, say that thanks to Andy, a wonderful voice will represent Mayberry. When Masters mentions that the voice belongs to Rafe, Barney's ego takes a

beating. He dejectedly admits to Andy that his audition did not go well. In fact, he was stopped in the midst of crooning "Chiribiribin!" He claims the selection was over their heads.

When Mayor Stoner and Mrs. Jeffries, the head of the Mayberry chapter of the Ladies League, meet with John Masters and are told that Rafe Hollister won the audition, they are unhappy. The mayor orders Andy to tell Rafe he did *not* win. The mayor and Mrs. Jeffries object to Rafe's appearance and his manner of dress (overalls). Mrs. Jeffries claims that the Ladies League is "dedicated to the *finer* things." Andy is very upset with this snobbish and unfair decision, but he does go to see Rafe. However, when he sees how excited and proud the farmer and his wife, Martha, are, he decides he cannot let them down.

The mayor is very unhappy when he discovers that nothing has changed. He says Rafe is "seedy looking," and he holds Andy responsible for the reaction from the crowd at the upcoming musicale, which the mayor believes will be quite negative. Andy believes that he can at least solve the problem of Rafe's appearance by surprising him with a new suit of clothes. Knowing that Rafe would not accept charity, Andy tells him the clothes are owed to him because he spent time in the Mayberry jail last year. Andy tells Rafe he forgot to pick up his "government-issued" clothes upon his release. Unfortunately, to Rafe, the clothes are a prison all by themselves. When Martha tells Rafe he looks good enough to get buried, Rafe replies, "I feel like I'm fixin' to!"

Mayor Stoner and Mrs. Jeffries catch a glimpse of Rafe in his suit during a practice session. Mrs. Jeffries deems his new duds "acceptable enough" and then adds, "as long as he doesn't *associate* with anyone." This insensitive remark is made within earshot of Rafe and his wife. It hurts them and certainly does not sit well with Andy.

The big night arrives, and Rafe is the last to perform. Included in the crowd are Mayor Stoner, Mrs. Jeffries, and the president of the Ladies League, Mrs. Dennis, all sitting next to one another. To their disbelief, Rafe appears on stage in his customary attire. Andy happily supplies the music with his guitar, and Rafe performs splendidly. Mrs. Dennis tells the mayor that Rafe is wonderful, and she remarks that it was a great idea to have him appear in informal clothing. It made his musical selection seem much more authentic. She asks Rafe to "favor us with another selection." As Rafe launches into "New River Train," even super-snobs Mrs. Jeffries and Mayor Stoner find themselves clapping along.

MEMORABLE SCENES. 1. The entire "Believe Me If All These Endearing Young

Charms" scene. 2. Barney singing "a cappella" to the tune of "La Cucaracha."

CAST NOTES. Regulars: **Andy Griffith, Don Knotts, Ronny Howard,** and **Parley Baer** (in his final appearance on the series as Mayor Stoner). **Jack Prince** returns as Rafe Hollister. **Olan Soule** returns as John Masters.

Isabel Randolph returns to the series. This time she's Mrs. Jeffries. **Ottola Nesmith** portrays Mrs. Dennis. **Kay Stewart** portrays Mrs. Rafe (Martha) Hollister.

EPISODE NOTES. 1. Barney wears his salt and pepper suit to the musicale. 2. Barney says "larnyx" instead of "larynx." 3. Barney uses a honey-and-water spray for his throat. Andy calls it "bug spray." Barney claims that all the big singers, including Nelson Eddy, Tex Ritter, and Ferlin Husky, use it. 4. Aunt Bee asks Rafe to take a bushel of fresh-picked string beans to the courthouse. They will be prepared for a Ladies League supper following the musicale. 5. The singing tryouts and the musicale itself are held at Mayberry's town hall. 6. Rafe says that when he greases his shoes, all the cats in town follow him. 7. Rafe was arrested in April of 1962 for moonshining. He spent 10 days in jail. His case number was 68456735. He lives on Willow Creek Road. 8. Rafe's first song at the musicale is "Look Down That Lonesome Road." 9. Opie sings "The Crawdad Song" twice — once by himself, and once with Andy.

"Opie and the Spoiled Kid"

Episode #84. Air date: 2-18-63. Writers: Jim Fritzell and Everett Greenbaum. Director: Bob Sweeney.

Opie has become acquainted with a new boy in town named Arnold Winkler. Arnold is a spoiled brat who believes he can get away with anything. He rides his new bicycle on the sidewalk, nearly knocking over several pedestrians on Mayberry's Main Street, including Barney and a lady named Mrs. Rodenbach.

When Arnold discovers that Opie gets a mere quarter-a-week allowance and has to do chores to get it, he tells Opie that he's being taken advantage of. Arnold doesn't have to work for his allowance and believes that no kid should. Opie decides to quietly demand that his father raise his allowance to 75 cents (the amount Arnold gets), and he says he should not have to do any chores. Opie is obviously uncomfortable making these demands, and he takes it well when Andy flatly refuses to comply.

Barney, who has been reading the magazine sec-

tion of the Sunday newspaper, tells Andy that the article he read is about the use of discipline in child-rearing. He believes that strict discipline is beneficial.

Arnold tells Opie that "man to man" talks always fail. He advises Opie that throwing a temper tantrum will get him whatever he wishes. He says it always works. Arnold tells Opie how to throw a tantrum: (1) Hold your breath; (2) kick a table leg in anger; and (3) roll around on the floor, kicking your feet and pretending you can't stop crying.

Later, Barney stops Arnold for riding his bicycle on the sidewalk and warns him not to do it anymore. Just moments after that, Arnold is back on the sidewalk. This time he nearly bowls over Andy, who decides to impound the boy's bike for a week or two. Arnold gets angry and threatens to tell his father. Andy encourages him to do that and asks him to have his dad come to the courthouse.

Next, Opie makes another demand for "more pay, no work." Andy doesn't budge. Opie then throws a very unconvincing tantrum. It has no effect. Moments later, Arnold and his father, Simon, drop by to demand that Andy return the boy's bicycle. Andy suggests that, since Mr. Winkler appears unwilling to take responsibility for his son, he might just lock the elder Winkler up. Arnold yells that he doesn't care if his dad is jailed or not; he just wants his bicycle back. Mr. Winkler is shocked to hear these words. He realizes that his boy has no respect for him. He sees the error of his ways and tells Andy he is going to sell the bicycle. Arnold loudly protests and turns on the waterworks as his father leads him to an old-fashioned wood shed out back, where Arnold will get a good (and long overdue) spanking.

Opie, having witnessed the ugly scene, apologizes to Andy for *his* recent antics. He says he will gladly work for his 25-cents-a-week allowance. Andy, knowing how hard it must have been for his son to apologize, raises his allowance by two cents a week.

CAST NOTES. Regulars: **Andy Griffith, Don Knotts,** and **Ronny Howard.**

Ronnie Dapo portrays Arnold Winkler. **Harlan Warde** appears as Simon Winkler. **Mary Lansing** returns as Mrs. Rodenbach.

EPISODE NOTES. 1. Barney and Andy gossip about Mr. and Mrs. Arthur Tarbocks. Mrs. Tarbocks is getting gray, and Arthur is thinking of moving his family out of Mayberry because he believes people gossip too much. 2. Mrs. Rodenbach and Mrs. Edith Blessing gossip about the Tarbocks, too. 3. Barney claims to have a photographic mind. 4. The Winkler family recently moved from Raleigh to Mayberry. 5. Arnold Winkler always calls Opie "Taylor." 6. Arnold's new bike is an Intercontinental Flyer, a gift from his dad. It cost $70.00. 7. In order to earn his weekly allowance, Opie must clean the garage, take out the ashes, keep the wood box filled, and set the table every night. 8. The following men are featured in the new "Wanted" posters at the courthouse: Henry "Shopping Bag" Leonetti (wanted for grand larceny), $4,000.00 reward; Max "the Tongue" Rasmussen (wanted for grand theft auto), $1500.00 reward; and Benjamin Schuster, a.k.a. Benji Schuse or Benny Chute (wanted for forgery), $3,000.00 reward. 9. Barney is sensitive about being call "sensitive." 10. At one point, Barney calls himself "high-spirited." Later, he denies that he is. 11. Barney calculates that if Opie got 75 cents a week for his allowance, he would make $40.00 per year. 12. Barney was a sickly child, but even then, he was bigger than his dad, who was "sicklier." 13. Arnold Winkler spent 2 weeks in summer camp at age seven. 14. With his allowance raised to 27 cents a week, Opie plans to buy a bell. Then, he will save up to buy a bike to put under it.

"The Great Filling Station Robbery"

Episode #85. Air date: 2-25-63. Writer: Harvey Bullock. Director: Bob Sweeney.

The Mayberry squad car needs a new carburetor installed, so Andy stops by Wally's Filling Station. Gomer Pyle is the attendant because Wally has gone to the Jefferson County seat for a week. At the filling station, a citizen, Mr. Carter, complains to Andy that a young man named Jimmy Morgan stole his truck battery. Jimmy has had several minor skirmishes with the law before, and Andy, wanting to help the young man out, asked Mr. Carter to hire him as a delivery boy. Andy had hoped that the responsibility of a job would keep Jimmy on the straight and narrow.

When confronted, Jimmy claims to have merely borrowed the battery in order to test a starter motor he built. He accidentally broke the battery but fully intends to replace it. Mr. Carter doesn't believe the story and asks Andy to arrest Jimmy. Andy refuses, and instead of jailing Jimmy, he allows him to work with Gomer, who is backlogged with repair work. This way, Gomer gets some needed help, and Jimmy can make some money to replace Mr. Carter's battery. Mr. Carter isn't happy about this second chance for Jimmy. He warns Gomer to watch Jimmy because he has "sticky fingers."

While Wally is away, Gomer allows the Hanson brothers, Jed and Prothro, to park their car inside of Wally's building.

The following day, Andy proclaims that Jimmy did good work on the squad car. However, his happy news is overshadowed by Gomer's announcement that someone stole Wally's new tools overnight. Jimmy was the last person to use them, and he was also responsible for locking up the building.

Andy and Barney find no signs of a break-in, and Barney believes they have an open-and-shut case against Jimmy. Andy suggests that Barney stake out the station at night. Barney also rigs up a camera to take a picture when the thief opens the front door of the station. Despite these preparations, that night, while Barney and Gomer's backs are turned, someone quietly robs the station. The next day, Gomer reports that among the stolen items were four flashlights, six fan belts, and two sets of battery clips.

Barney is certain that the camera captured the crook's image. He sends Gomer to the drugstore, where Mrs. Mason will develop the film. Meanwhile, Andy has brought Jim Morgan in for questioning. When Gomer returns, he, Andy, and Barney eagerly open the newly developed photo. They are shocked to discover that the camera snapped a great photo—of Barney! It seems Barney accidentally triggered the camera as he set it up. While they are looking at the photo, Jimmy, who has maintained his innocence the entire time, flees the courthouse.

Andy and Barney search in vain for Jimmy. That night, Gomer tells them he drove past the filling station and noticed someone walking around inside. Andy and Barney go check it out and discover the intruder is Jimmy. They see him at the cash register, and they watch as he wires it to a set of truck batteries. The men assume Jimmy is going to try to blow the register open. As they move in to make the capture, they hear a scream. It comes from Prothro Hanson, who is getting, literally, the shock of his life. It turns out that Hanson has been hiding in the trunk of his car and stealing from the station. Jim was bound and determined to stop the robberies and clear his good name. He is completely vindicated, and the great filling station robberies are now a thing of the past.

CAST NOTES. Regulars: **Andy Griffith, Don Knotts, Ronny Howard,** and **Jim Nabors.**

Pat Colby, who appeared in episode 10, "Stranger in Town" as Bill Matthews, portrays Jimmy Morgan. **Willis Bouchey** returns to the series, this time as Mr. Carter. **Jack Shea** portrays Jed Hanson. **Johnny Silver** portrays Prothro Hanson.

EPISODE NOTES. 1. Barney phones Juanita, the waitress at the Bluebird Diner. He greets her with "cock-a-doodle-do." He recites to her a love poem of his own composition. 2. Barney sets up an intercom in cell #2. The other speaker is put on Andy's desk. Barney wants to use it to communicate with the prisoners and to listen in on any escape plans. He calls it "Our own little spy in the sky." 3. Andy calls Barney "Mr. Marconi." 4. Gomer sells regular and high test gasoline. The cost is 30 cents per "ding" at the pump. 5. Andy says Mr. Carter's truck battery would cost $12.95 to replace. 6. Barney says "electronally" instead of "electronically." 7. Gomer Reads "Captain Marvel" comic books.

"Andy Discovers America"

Episode #86. Air date: 3-4-63. Writer: John Whedon. Director: Bob Sweeney.

Opie dislikes his new schoolteacher, Miss Crump. One of the subjects she teaches is history, which is not one of Opie's favorites. He complains that she gives out too much homework. He and the other boys in class refer to the new teacher as "Old Lady" Crump. Andy is sympathetic to his son's plight. As a boy, Andy also found history difficult. He and Barney had a mean old teacher named Miss Thickett, who Barney says "must have been 107 years old." Andy tells Opie to do the best he can in school, but, if he doesn't know an answer, he should tell Miss Crump that he "comes by it naturally."

At school, Miss Crump—who is definitely *not* an old lady—gets upset when Opie tells her his father said history was not important. His pals all proclaim that they feel the same way. Miss Crump is stunned by this sudden revolt, and, in anger, she doubles homework for all the boys in class. Later, Opie and his friends report the "unfair" burden to Andy, who receives an unexpected visit from the irate young teacher. She orders him, in no uncertain terms, to "Stay out of my business!"

Later, Opie and his friends tell Andy that one of the boys, Howie Pruitt, overheard two teachers saying that Miss Crump may quit teaching. That prospect makes the boys happy, of course. Andy however, does not like this gleeful reaction, and realizes he must do something to get the boys back on the right track and help save a young teacher's job. He uses some reverse psychology on the boys. First, he agrees with them how great it will be to not have to study history. He adds that they won't have to hear about such things as "Redcoats, cannons, muskets, and guns." His words create some exciting imagery in the boys' heads, and they urge him to explain about the American Revolution, which he does so colorfully that even Barney finds himself entranced. The boys are shocked to hear that history books are chock-full of such stories.

Andy suggests the boys form a history troupe and call themselves the Mayberry Minutemen. Their motto could be "Always Ready with the Answers." He tells them that they must pass "a fitness test." He asks them to memorize the list of dates that Miss Crump gave them.

The boys return to school with a new enthusiasm about history. A previously disheartened Miss Crump is delighted and surprised to witness this remarkable change of attitude. Later, after discovering Andy's role in all of this, she tells him how pleased she is. Andy confesses he handled the situation incorrectly at first and is very happy to have been able to help.

Thus Andy and Helen begin what will prove to be a long relationship on a good note, despite a rather rocky beginning.

MEMORABLE SCENE. Barney explaining the Emancipation Proclamation.

CAST NOTES. Regulars: **Andy Griffith, Don Knotts, Ronny Howard, Frances Bavier,** and (introducing) **Aneta Corsaut** as Miss Helen Crump.

Joey Scott, Dennis Rush, and **Richard Keith** portray Opie's classmates. They respectively portray Whitey Porter, Howard "Howie" Pruitt, and Johnny Paul Jason. Dennis Rush had a substantial television career as a child, appearing in several series, television ads and movies. He appeared as Horrible Horace in a memorable installment of *My Favorite Martian.* He also appeared on *Wagon Train, Perry Mason,* and *The Lucy Show.* He appeared in ads for such products as Downy detergent, Jif peanut butter and Nestea instant tea. His first movie was *Man of a Thousand Faces* in 1957. He also appeared in the 1966 film *Follow Me, Boys!* Rush, now a successful restaurateur in California, graduated with honors from San Diego State University He majored in American History. Guess Andy's Mayberry Minutemen idea was a pretty good one!

Episode Notes. 1. Helen Crump replaced Miss Warner as Opie's teacher. 2. Barney claims that history was one of his best subjects. 3. Opie and his classmates recite The Pledge of Allegiance at the start of every school day. 4. The name Howard Pruitt (used for one of Opie's classmates) belongs to a Mount Airy native.

"Aunt Bee's Medicine Man"

Episode #87. Air date: 3-11-63. Writer: John Whedon. Director: Bob Sweeney.

Aunt Bee is beginning to feel her age. She is distraught when an acquaintance, Augusta Finch, who was her age, passes away. Andy points out that Miss Finch was often in poor health, while Aunt Bee has always enjoyed good health. Aunt Bee will not be consoled. Andy asks her to make an appointment with Doc Andrews for a checkup, but she refuses because he always tells her, "We're no spring chickens anymore!"

Opie tells Aunt Bee about a man who is out on the street talking to a large group of folks. The man, Colonel Harvey, is a traveling "medicine man" who claims to have been kidnapped by Indians when he was a boy and says he was adopted by an Indian chief. He is hawking Colonel Harvey's Indian Elixir, which he claims will cure one's ills and restore health and vitality. An interested Aunt Bee listens to him and purchases two bottles of the wondrous elixir for $1.00 each. She is so charmed by the smooth-talking con man that she invites him to supper.

Andy and Barney check out the show moments after Aunt Bee leaves. They are surprised to find that Colonel Harvey does have a legal permit to sell his wares on the street (which he obtained from the Mayberry County Clerk). Even though they smell a rat they are powerless to stop him.

Meanwhile, Aunt Bee *is* rejuvenated by the elixir. Andy and Barney find her merrily playing the piano and singing "Toot Toot Tootsie" with Opie! Her energy seems boundless. Barney and Andy would believe her to be drunk, if it were not for the fact that she is a teetotaler. But as Barney reaches into Andy's closet to retrieve a raincoat, he discovers a half-empty bottle of Colonel Harvey's Indian Elixir. Andy asks Barney to take it to Doc Andrews and have him analyze its ingredients.

Meanwhile, Aunt Bee's supper guest arrives, and Andy is surprised to discover the guest is Colonel Harvey. After a delicious meal, Colonel Harvey impresses Opie with smoke signals and hand gestures that the Shawnee Indians taught him. He boasts, "The Shawnee. I lived among them. *They're devils!*"

Aunt Bee is impressed, too. In fact, she invites Colonel Harvey to address the Ladies Aid Church Committee when they meet at her home tomorrow. He happily accepts.

The next day, Barney returns from Doc Andrews' office with alarming news: The elixir is 85% alcohol. Barney is anxious to arrest Colonel Harvey right away, but Andy believes that if he did, Aunt Bee would never forgive him. He decides to wait until after the con man finishes addressing the ladies' group. When the time seems about right for the end of the meeting, Andy heads home, only to find a gassed Aunt Bee leading her drunken friends in a chorus of "My Chinatown." He announces he

is raiding the "party" and proceeds to arrest the entire group.

As he sobers them up in jail, the women slowly realize that they have been duped. They are embarrassed and angry. Barney arrests Colonel Harvey, who receives some criticism from all the ladies as they are released. In the end, Andy and Aunt Bee share a good laugh about the whole embarrassing affair.

MEMORABLE SCENES. 1. Colonel Harvey showing Opie Indian smoke signals and speaking "the Shawnee language." 2. A tipsy Aunt Bee calling Andy "Sheriff Matt Dillon" and referring to Barney as "Chester."

CAST NOTES. Regulars: **Andy Griffith, Don Knotts, Ronny Howard,** and **Frances Bavier.**

John Dehner portrays Colonel Harvey. Dehner had a long career in radio, film, and television. He was a regular on *The Don Knotts Show* (1970-1972), portrayed Cy Bennett on *The Doris Day Show* (1971-1973), and played Admiral King in the 1983 miniseries *The Winds of War.* A former animator for Walt Disney Studios, Dehner served as an Army publicist during World War II, recording the exploits of General George S. Patton.

Mary Lansing, Kathryn Hart, Jewel Rose, Ruth Packard, and **Noreen Gammill** appear as unnamed members of the Ladies Aid Church Committee.

EPISODE NOTES. 1. Aunt Bee gives the Taylors' address as 332 Maple Road. (In episode 50, Barney gave Andy's address as 24 Elm Street.) 2. Barney tries to make himself look like a publicity photo of Rock Hudson. 3. Doc Andrews charges $5.00 per visit. 4. Andy says Aunt Bee is such a teetotaler that she will not allow even a fruitcake in the house, on account of "a brother she had."

"The Darlings Are Coming"

Episode #88. Air date: 3-18-63. Writers: Everett Greenbaum and Jim Fritzell. Director: Bob Sweeney.

The eccentric and superstitious Darling family appears for the first time in the series. Leaving their home in the mountains, Briscoe Darling and his five adult offspring come into Mayberry in a weathered old truck. The radiator overheats, and Briscoe stops in front of a horse trough and begins using his hat to scoop up water for the car. He claims it takes 11 hatfuls to fill 'er up.

Andy notices this activity and comes to tell Briscoe that he is breaking two town ordinances simultaneously: parking in front of a trough and misuse of a trough. He lets them off with a friendly warning. Briscoe inquires as to where he and his family could find a night's lodging, and Andy directs him to the Mayberry Hotel.

The family has come to town to welcome home Private First Class Dudley A. Wash. He has just been honorably discharged from the U.S. Army and is coming home (by bus) to marry his sweetheart, Charlene Darling, Briscoe's youngest child and only daughter. The couple have been pledged to marry since they were five years old. The family will meet Dud when he gets off the bus the next morning.

Briscoe checks into the hotel alone, taking a single room. Once there, he lowers a rope outside his window, which his family uses to sneak in. They bring their musical instruments with them because they need to practice for Charlene's wedding. Hotel clerk John Masters (moonlighting from his job of choir director?) hears the music and is certain that Briscoe is not alone in his room. He summons Andy, who eventually catches the younger Darlings as they sneak back out of the room. Andy tells the family they will have to find somewhere else to stay if they wish to play their instruments. The family obliges, but their next lodging is an empty building on private property. Andy has to move them out. While doing that, he offers to allow them to stay at the courthouse. They gratefully accept.

Aunt Bee feeds them, and Andy joins them in playing a couple of songs. Charlene takes an immediate liking to Sheriff Taylor, which makes him uncomfortable. Briscoe keeps an eye on Andy, believing him to be chasing Charlene.

The next morning, everyone is eagerly awaiting the imminent arrival of Dud Wash...well, everyone but his bride-to-be! Charlene has Andy cornered in the courthouse. Andy does his best to fight off her amorous advances. Briscoe chides Andy for playing "hard to get" and tells him he will have to fight Dud for Charlene's affections. After all, says Briscoe, "It's the natural law of tooth and claw."

Dud arrives and quickly wins Charlene's heart when she discovers that he kept all of the letters she sent him. He also has kept her hair ribbon and the remainder of the mountain gladioli she gave him on the day he left to serve his country. He keeps all such valuables in his money belt. As justice of the peace, Andy marries the happy couple in the courthouse.

The Darlings will be returning to Mayberry every so often, sometimes causing a little trouble for Andy, but always tickling our funny bone.

CAST NOTES. Regulars: **Andy Griffith** and **Frances Bavier**. **Olan Soule** returns as John Masters.

Members of the popular bluegrass band **The Dillards** appear as the Darling boys. They are **Doug Dillard** as Jebbin ("Doug" in later episodes), his real-life brother **Rodney Dillard** as Rodney, **Mitch Jayne** as Mitch, and **Dean Webb** as Other, pronounced oh-ther. In future episodes, Webb's character is known as Dean.

Denver Pyle portrays Briscoe Darling, father of the Darling clan. Pyle is a veteran of many television series and movies. Elsewhere in this book is a large listing of Pyle's acting credits. **Maggie Peterson** portrays Charlene Darling.

Hoke Howell portrays Dudley A. Wash. Howell is perhaps best known as Ben Jenkins from the television series *Here Come the Brides* (1968-1970). However, many folks may recognize him from his Hardee's commercials (and others). Howell has appeared on such series as *The Blue Knight, Bewitched, The Brady Bunch, Columbo, Green Acres, Kung Fu, The Munsters,* and *Quincy, M.E.* He also appeared in a 1970 comedy pilot written by Lawrence J. Cohen and Fred Freeman called *The Shameful Secrets of Hastings Corner,* in which he played Pa Fandango, patriarch of the Fandango clan. His son was portrayed by Barry Williams, who at the time was starring in *The Brady Bunch.* Howell has appeared in many movies, including *Shenendoah* (1965, with Jimmy Stewart), *Marlowe* (1969, with James Garner), *The Klansman* (1974, with Lee Marvin), *Framed* (1975), *From Noon to Three* (1976, with Charles Bronson), *Grand Theft Auto* (1977, directed by and starring Ron Howard), and *Far and Away* (1992, directed by Ron Howard and starring Tom Cruise). He also appeared in the 1994 made-for-cable movie *Roswell.*

EPISODE NOTES. 1. Briscoe Darling plays the jug. He tells Andy he can get banjo and guitar sounds—in fact, any sound—out of the jug. (This is his attempt at covering up for the rest of his family.) 2. Charlene sings and dances. Rodney plays the guitar, Jebbin plays banjo, Other plays the mandolin, and pipe-smoking Mitch plays bass fiddle. 3. The Darling boys aren't very talkative. Although they sing in most of the episodes in which they appear, this is the only episode in which they speak. They thank Aunt Bee for their supper and bid her good night. The Darling boys may remind viewers of the villains in the 1972 movie *Deliverance.* They may have inspired the creation of the backwoodsmen Larry, Darryl, and Darryl on the 1980s television hit *Newhart.* 4. Charlene refers to Andy as a "Perty man" and says he's "beautiful preserved." 5. Dud Wash spent three years in the Army. He brought back a "tiger eye" ring for Charlene. He bought it in Spokane, Washington. 6. Briscoe likes to say "More power to you." 7. A single room, without a bath, at the Mayberry Hotel (which Briscoe takes) costs $1.75 per night. A single room with a bath goes for $2.50 per night. Briscoe's room is #27. 8. John Masters takes a supper break about 8:00 P.M. 9. Briscoe claims that Other doesn't have much of a personality. 10. Even John Masters knows that a "907" is a law against dipping one's hat in a horse trough. 11. The trough's inscription says: "David Mendelbright, 1870–1933. Let No Horse Go Thirsty Here." 12. A "317" is a law against occupancy of private property without permission. 13. Dud Wash arrives on a Southern Buslines bus out of Macon, Georgia. 14. Andy's usual fee for performing a marriage is $2.00. He waives the fee for the Darlings in favor of a song. 15. Briscoe calls Andy "Sheriff Justice" after the wedding ceremony. 16. The Darlings play a couple of unnamed instrumentals, plus "Dooley," "Tearing Up Your Old Clothes for Rags," "Salty Dog" (featuring Charlene), and "Cindy." They don't play "Keep Your Money in Your Shoes and It Won't Get Wet," because it makes Charlene cry. However, they do play "Slimy River Bottom," despite the fact that it makes her cry.

"Andy's English Valet"

Episode #89. Air date: 3-25-63. Writer: Harvey Bullock. Director: Bob Sweeney.

Malcolm Merriweather, an English valet, is bicycling across the U.S.A. He loves the charm of small towns, so he's trying to visit as many as possible while on holiday. He stops in Mayberry and inadvertently causes a minor traffic mishap: He is reading a road map and not paying attention to the road when he pulls in front of Fletch Roberts's delivery truck. The damages to Fletch's truck amount to $40.00, but Malcolm doesn't have the money for the repairs. Andy feels sorry for the nice foreign visitor, so he allows him to work off the debt by doing repair work at his home. When Malcolm proves to be useless as a handyman (he breaks a window with a ladder), he begs Andy to allow him to be the Taylors' cook and butler. Andy obliges, because Aunt Bee is away visiting her sister Florence. Malcolm has been Colonel Chumley's gentleman's gentleman for the past eleven years in his native Heckmondwike, England.

Malcolm prepares fine meals, and Andy and Opie like him, but Andy cannot get accustomed to some of Malcolm's ways, such as helping him get dressed every morning, making him wear his police cap and tie to work, dressing formally for dinner, drawing his bath in the evening, and chauffeuring him to the courthouse every morning. Late one evening, Malcolm overhears Andy and Barney talking on the front porch about these "English traits"

in a rather negative way. With his feelings hurt by the remarks, Malcolm leaves Andy and Opie a goodbye note claiming "urgent business" and quietly departs.

The next morning, Andy discovers from Opie that Malcolm may have overheard the conversation from the previous night. Andy has a hunch where Malcolm may be, and sure enough, he locates him leaving town on his bicycle. Andy apologies for the misinterpreted remarks and tells Malcolm that his presence is needed at the Taylor household. Malcolm happily returns and remains with Andy and Opie until Aunt Bee comes home from her visit.

As the episode concludes, Malcolm bids farewell to the Taylors, hops on his bicycle, and continues his sightseeing tour of America's small towns. Cheerio, Malcolm!

CAST NOTES. Regulars: **Andy Griffith, Don Knotts, Ronny Howard**, and **Frances Bavier**.

Bernard Fox makes his first of three appearances on the series as Malcolm Merriweather. A real bobby-dazzler of an actor, Mr. Fox has appeared on many American television programs, although his only regular role was as the warlock medicine man Dr. Bombay on *Bewitched*. He had previously appeared on that series in an episode called "Disappearing Samantha," in which he played a character named Osgood Rightmire. Speaking of classic series, he appeared in three episodes of *The Dick Van Dyke Show*. (He appeared as Ogden Darwell in "Girls Will Be Boys," in which Richie is bullied by a girl. In another episode, titled "Never Bathe on Saturday," he was a detective who is called to Rob and Laura's hotel room when Laura gets her toe stuck in the bathtub spigot. Finally, in "Teacher's Petrie," he was Laura's flirtatious writing teacher, Mr. Caldwell. Mayberry alum Cheerio Meredith also appeared in this episode.) Fox also made recurring appearances as Colonel Crittendon on *Hogan's Heroes*. Among the many series in which he made guest appearances are *The Adventures of Huck Finn* (as the voice of Jason, the servant) *The Danny Thomas Show, F-Troop, The Farmer's Daughter, The Girl from U.N.C.L.E., I Dream of Jeannie, I Spy, The Jeffersons, Lou Grant, Love, American Style, The Man from U.N.C.L.E., M*A*S*H, McHale's Navy, The Monkees, Murder She Wrote, The Partridge Family, Perry Mason, The Queen and I, Simon & Simon, Tammy, Twelve O'Clock High*, and *The Wild Wild West*. He appeared in the 1972 television movie *The Hound of the Baskervilles* and in the 1980 television movie *Gauguin the Savage*. Mr. Fox is also familiar with stage work. He starred in the 1990 play *Sextet*. He has also appeared in many motion pictures, including *Home and Away* (1956), *The Safecracker* (1958), *The List of Adrian Messenger*

(1963, directed by John Huston), *Strange Bedfellows* (1965, with Rock Hudson), *Hold On!* (1966, with Herman's Hermits), *Munster, Go Home!* (1966, directed by Earl Bellamy), *Star!* (1968, with Julie Andrews), *$1,000,000 Duck* (1971), *Big Jake* (1971, with John Wayne), *Herbie Goes to Monte Carlo* (1977, with Don Knotts, *The Rescuers* (1977; animated, with the voices of Bob Newhart and Eva Gabor), *Zone of the Dead* (1978), *The Private Eyes* (1980, with Don Knotts and Tim Conway), *Yellowbeard* (1983, with Richard "Cheech" Marin and Tommy Chong), and *18 Again* (1988, starring George Burns).

Bob McQuain portrays Fletch Roberts.

EPISODE NOTES. 1. The traffic mishap between Malcolm and Fletch Roberts occurred in front of the Mayberry Feed and Grain Store. Malcolm was trying to locate Route 43 when he caused the accident. 2. A lady named Miss Snyder lives next door to the Taylors. 3. Aunt Bee knitted a scarf for her sister Florence. 4. Malcolm finds Andy's long-missing police cap in the back of the cupboard. 5. A lady named Maggie usually cleans the Taylors house when Aunt Bee is out of town. 6. Malcolm refers to Andy as "Constable." 7. Opie enjoys Malcolm's magic tricks and roly-poly pudding. Malcolm can make paper trees and ladders. He also enjoys painting faces on eggs. 8. Clara Edwards lets Andy borrow her car. Her license plate number is DF-153. Andy mistakenly refers to her as "Flora" during the episode. 9. Barney originally thought Malcolm was from Canada.

"Barney's First Car"

Episode #90. Air date: 4-1-63. Writers: Jim Fritzell and Everett Greenbaum. Director: Bob Sweeney.

Barney has his heart set on spending his $300.00 life savings on a good used car. He answers a newspaper ad for a 1954 Ford sedan. The ad was placed by a kindly elderly lady from Mt. Pilot named Mrs. Lesh. She claims the car belonged to her late husband Bernard (a coincidence?) and was only used to go to church on Sunday and to her Aunt Martha's on Thanksgiving. Andy and Mrs. Lesh urge Barney to test-drive the car and have Wally at the filling station give it the once-over. Barney will have nothing to do with this because he trusts Mrs. Lesh completely. When she overhears Barney saying that he wants to spend his entire nest egg of $300.00, Mrs. Lesh states that her late husband's funeral expenses, coupled with lawyer fees, property and inheritance taxes, equal $297.50. Barney happily pays $297.50 for the car and instructs

Mrs. Lesh to donate the remaining $2.50 to Bernard Lesh's favorite charity.

Next, Barney invites Andy, Thelma Lou, Gomer, Aunt Bee, and Opie to join him on the car's maiden voyage. Barney looks spiffy in his salt and pepper suit as the crew climbs into the car. But after passing the beautiful Johnson farm, the car literally falls apart.

Later, Gomer states that Wally verified the car was a piece of junk. Wally found problems with the plugs, points, bearings, valves, rings, starter switch, ignition wires, water pump, fuel pump, oil pump, clutch, clutch bearings, clutch plate, brake lining, brake shoes, brake drums, radiator hose, and radiator hose cover, as well as sawdust in the differential and transmission. Andy and Gomer agree that sawdust in the differential and transmission will make worn-out gears run fine for a short time. It's one of the oldest tricks in the book. To add insult to injury, Gomer also says the car could use a good wash.

Andy and a very disillusioned Barney attempt to drive the car back to Mt. Pilot and return it to "Hubcaps" Lesh. Unfortunately, the heap breaks down for good just outside of Mayberry. Andy walks to a telephone and asks Gomer to bring a tow truck. As Andy and Barney are waiting for Gomer to arrive, they both fall asleep. They are awakened when the feel the car being towed. By sheer chance, one of Mrs. Lesh's tow trucks has mistakenly picked up the "abandoned" car to take it to her chop shop. The driver is unaware of Andy and Barney's presence. Upon arriving at the shop, Andy and Barney are able to easily arrest Hubcaps Lesh and her henchmen.

Barney's next prospective car deal comes from a lady named Mrs. Rose Temple. She has a 1959 Ford that has only been driven to church on Sundays. In fact, Mrs. Temple's nephew is the minister of the church. Barney lives by the motto "Once bitten, twice shy" and believes that Mrs. Temple is another Hubcaps Lesh. He then proceeds to blow the deal of a lifetime. All Andy can do is shake his head in disbelief.

CAST NOTES. Regulars: **Andy Griffith, Don Knotts, Ronny Howard, Frances Bavier, Jim Nabors,** and **Betty Lynn.**

Veteran television and movie actress **Ellen Corby** stars as Mrs. Myrt "Hubcaps" Lesh. Corby is well known for her role of Grandma Esther Walton on *The Waltons.*

Allan Melvin returns to the series. This time he appears as Mrs. Lesh's accomplice, Jake. (Mrs. Lesh claims he's her nephew.) **Hallene Hill** portrays Mrs. Rose Temple, and **Tom Allen** appears as her nephew, the minister.

EPISODE NOTES. 1. On *The Andy Griffith Show Silver Anniversary Special*, aired on WTBS on October 3, 1985, Andy Griffith selected "Barney's First Car" as his all-time favorite episode. 2. Andy claims it takes about an hour to drive from Mayberry to Mt. Pilot. Mrs. Lesh states it took her four hours to make the same trip, because she never drives over 25 miles per hour, and she gives the car a 10-minute rest every half-hour. (In either case, the distance represents an inconsistency with information given in other episodes, in which Mt. Pilot is said to be 12 miles from Mayberry. See episodes 68 and 126 for examples.) 3. Mrs. Lesh claims to owe $140.00 for her late husband's funeral expenses. Bernard Lesh was laid to rest by the Pilot Pines Funeral Home in Mt. Pilot. 4. Barney first considered buying a 1949 Hudson Terraplane. The car was described in the ad as a "fixer-upper" because it has been crushed by a 30-ton semi-trailer. The cost for this gem is 12 good laying hens or the cash equivalent. 5. Barney refers to himself as "Mr. Independent Wheels." 6. The license plate number on Barney's piece of junk is GP-780. 7. Mrs. Lesh's telephone number in Mt. Pilot is MP-3791. The license plate number of her tow truck is DF-153. 8. Barney tells Andy that he once bought his mom and dad a septic tank as an anniversary present. Andy tells him, "You're a fine son, Barn." 9. Barney, Andy, Thelma Lou, Gomer, Aunt Bee, and Opie sing "Old MacDonald" as they are riding in Barney's car. 10. Gomer has a tendency to get car sickness. 11. The Johnsons have a pretty red barn on their beautiful farm. 12. There is a discrepancy between this episode and an earlier one. In episode 4, "Runaway Kid," Barney is said to own an automobile, but in "Barney's First Car," this fact is never mentioned. 13. This episode earned the writers, Jim Fritzell and Everett Greenbaum, the prestigious Writer's Guild of America Award, for best writing in a comedy or variety series.

"The Rivals"

Episode #91. Air date: 4-8-63. Writer: Harvey Bullock. Director: Bob Sweeney.

Opie is experiencing first love. The object of his affection is a pretty classmate named Karen Burgess. He tries hard to impress her. He gives her a tour of the courthouse, offers to carry her school books, and even does a handstand. He tells her that, in Floyd's opinion, it will not be long before he will need to shave. To Opie's dismay, Karen appears unimpressed.

Barney and Thelma Lou sympathize with Opie.

Veteran character actor, Allan Melvin appeared as a tough guy in numerous episodes of the *Andy Griffith Show.*

Barney recalls that when he was Opie's age, he was smitten with a girl named Vickie Harms. He met her at an ice cream parlor. Young Barney loved raspberry snow cones, but he would always offer Vickie a bite. However, she always played a nasty trick on him. She would bite off the end of the cone, suck out all the syrup and leave him with nothing but ice. Barney says she thought she was hot stuff because her daddy was a civil service worker.

Thelma Lou tries to lift Opie's spirits by spending more time with him. She includes him in her activities, much to the chagrin of Barney, who finds himself odd man out. He begins to resent Opie's unintentional interference.

Opie tells Andy that he has gotten over Karen. He now considers Thelma Lou to be his girl! Because it is Saturday, he expects to spend the entire day with her. He asks Andy for some ideas about what he and Thelma Lou could do together. Andy cleverly makes Opie understand that grown women and little boys have completely different interests. In fact, he makes any date with a woman sound very dull, especially to a boy Opie's age.

Meanwhile, Karen has begun to miss the attention she got from Opie. She has quietly become envious of Thelma Lou. She shows up just as Opie leaves the courthouse for a potentially deadly dull date with Thelma Lou. When Opie sees Karen, he loses all interest in pursuing a grownup. The youngsters decide they will spend the day together. They have all sorts of things they can do, such as go to the movies, ride their bikes, and enjoy a soda at the drugstore. Opie asks his pa if he will explain things to Thelma Lou so she won't be hurt. Andy promises to try to let her down easy.

CAST NOTES. Regulars: **Andy Griffith, Don Knotts, Ronny Howard,** and **Betty Lynn.**

Ronda Jeter appears as Karen Burgess.

EPISODE NOTES. 1. The viewer gets a rare glimpse of Thelma Lou's kitchen in this episode. 2. Karen takes piano lessons. 3. Mr. Foley runs a grocery store in Mayberry. 4. Opie's bedtime is 8:30 P.M. 5. Opie sometimes climbs Mr. McGinnis's apple trees. 6. Andy calls Barney "Tiger." 7. Barney creates a nonexistent girlfriend named Sally. 8. While showing Karen the courthouse, Opie points out the file cabinet, the gun rack, the jail cells, and the door he goes through when he takes the trash out. 9. Mrs. Purvis calls Andy because her cat is on her roof. 10. Opie tells Andy that when he is with Karen, he gets a lump in his throat, his ears ring, and his knees get all squiggly. Andy says it is either love or a bad case of the measles. 11. Thelma Lou invites Opie to her house for fudge brownies and her homemade peach ice cream. 12. Barney wants to park by the duck pond with Thelma Lou. 13. Barney tells Andy that although Opie is one of the nicest kids in town, he is also a pest.

"A Wife for Andy"

Episode #92. Air date: 4-15-63. Writer: Aaron Ruben. Director: Bob Sweeney.

Barney tells Andy he should find a wife for himself and a mother for Opie. He tells the sheriff that a man who keeps putting marriage off will become irritable and desperate. Andy claims he is neither irritable nor desperate and says he will marry when he finds a woman who is right for him.

Barney decides to send one dozen of Mayberry's eligible young women to Andy's house so the lonely sheriff can look them over. He gets the women there under false pretenses, telling them that Thelma Lou wants to meet with them at Andy's house. After the ladies arrive, Barney pops in to see if Andy has found "Miss Right." Andy is angry, and the women are confused over this preposterous situation.

Still, Barney keeps his eyes open for a possible mate for Andy. He sees Andy walking with Opie's schoolteacher, Miss Helen Crump, which prompts

him to ask Thelma Lou to invite each of them to supper. Neither Andy nor Miss Crump knows that the other has been invited. They are surprised to discover this fact when they arrive for the meal.

Barney comes to believe he has made a mistake getting Andy and Helen together when Helen admits she can't cook and that she would continue teaching even if she were married. Barney tries to bring the evening to an early end.

The following day, Barney is appalled when Andy thanks him for bringing him and Helen closer together. Barney tells him that Helen is the wrong woman for him. Andy disagrees and says he's going to go out with her whether Barney likes it or not.

That evening, in a desperate move, Barney arranges for Mayberry's eligible ladies to return to Andy's. Barney figures that Helen will come over, see Andy surrounded by lovely young women, and leave. Andy has the last laugh when he reveals to Barney that he is picking Helen up at her place. The couple are going to Mount Pilot for a Chinese supper. An embarrassed Barney is left to face a house full of irate women.

CAST NOTES. Regulars: **Andy Griffith, Don Knotts, Ronny Howard, Frances Bavier, Aneta Corsaut,** and **Betty Lynn.**

Barbara Perry portrays Lavinia, one of the town's eligible women. **Janet Stewart** portrays Lorraine Beasley. Thelma Lou says Lorraine is too young for Andy. Others appearing include **Janet Waldo** as Amanda and **Rachel Ames** as Rosemary. Ms. Ames would soon become better known to many viewers as Audrey on the television daytime serial *General Hospital*. Prior to this appearance she was a regular on the police drama *The Line-up* as Officer Sandy McAllister.

EPISODE NOTES. 1. Prospective women for Andy include Lavinia, Amanda, Rosemary, and Blanche. A woman named Annabelle is not in the running, since she's married. 2. Andy gets mad at Barney and tells him to shut up. 3. Doc Harvey is referred to in this episode. 4. Clara injured herself while lifting her oven. She was trying to clean up some spilled bacon grease. Aunt Bee says Clara is now walking crooked. 5. Opie says a boy named Matt Merlus is his best friend. 6. Andy tries to read "The Legend of Sleepy Hollow" to Opie. It's a favorite, and Opie refers to its as "The Headless Horseman." 7. Andy says that leg of lamb is his favorite dish. 8. Barney wears his salt and pepper suit to dinner at Thelma Lou's. 9. The character of Lorraine was named after a real person. Lorraine Beasley was the name of Earlie Gilley's wife before she married. Lorraine and Earlie are citizens of Pilot Mountain, North Carolina.

"Dogs, Dogs, Dogs"

Episode #93. Air date: 4-22-63. Writers: Everett Greenbaum and Jim Fritzell. Director: Bob Sweeney.

Andy and Barney are eagerly awaiting the arrival of a state investigator, who will inspect the jail and determine if the Mayberry courthouse is in need of any additional funds.

Opie finds a stray dog and brings him into the courthouse. Andy suspects the little pooch is hungry and, much to Barney's chagrin, feeds one of Barney's sandwiches to the mutt. Barney also protests when Andy gives the dog Barney's dessert, a Mr. Cookie Bar. When Barney brings his lunch to work, he normally packs three sandwiches (on salt-rising bread), plus a Mr. Cookie Bar. He eats two of the sandwiches for lunch and saves the third until late in his workday, when he gets a sinking spell. The dessert is eaten later for a sugar pick-me-up.

Opie is happy when Andy allows him to take the dog home. However, the dog escapes while Opie tries to make a bed for him in the backyard. Opie reports this loss to Andy. Later, Andy, Opie, and Barney are surprised to discover that the dog Opie found is back at the courthouse — with three more dogs. Barney tries to blackmail Otis, saying he will bar him from jail unless he takes the dogs home with him, but Otis refuses. Andy makes the same request, in a gentler fashion, and Otis reluctantly complies. Unfortunately, Otis later reports that the dogs ran off as soon as he got home. Moments later, the four dogs return to the courthouse, along with seven others!

The men are in a quandary over what to do with the dogs. Otis suggests they should be taken to the pound. This idea is okay with Opie, until he hears Otis say that if no one claims the dogs, they will be gassed.

Andy and Opie think the situation over while drinking a bottle of pop at the filling station. Meanwhile, Barney decides to solve the problem by luring the dogs into the squad car, using his last sandwich (Otis used one to get the dogs to follow him home). Barney takes the dogs to a large open field in the country, just a few miles outside of town. Later, he explains his actions to Opie and Andy. Barney says they'll be better off outdoors, where they can run and jump. Opie is not so sure, and his doubts multiply when a heavy thunderstorm begins.

Barney tells Opie not to worry. He says that dogs do not get struck by lightning because they are so low to the ground — unlike, say, giraffes. He also says their fur provides insulation against the rain.

Opie is especially worried about the first dog, the one he brought in. He knows the dog is a "trembler." Barney assures him that the bigger dogs will look after him. Actually, Barney is growing ever more uncertain about the dogs' safety. To convince himself, he continues talking about how dogs look after one another, still comparing them favorably to giraffes. He gets so worked up that he gets angry at giraffes, calling them the selfish type, always looking out for themselves. As the storm worsens, Barney admits he's as concerned about the dogs' welfare as Opie is, and the trio leave at once to retrieve them and bring them back to the safe, dry courthouse.

Soon, Andy gets a call from state investigator Somerset, who says he'll be arriving shortly. Barney asks Opie to take the dogs out back until Mr. Somerset finishes his investigation.

Andy and Barney are dismayed when the investigator refuses to listen to their requests. Mr. Somerset tells them he believes the jail is not lacking in any regard. The additional funding appears doubtful at best. Suddenly, the dour inspector is bowled over by the dogs! Opie explains that he could not hold them back any longer. Andy and Barney are quick to apologize to Mr. Somerset, but this proves unnecessary. It seems the investigator is a dog lover. He has two labradors and a beagle. The presence of the dogs seems to bring about a change in Mr. Somerset's personality. He informs Andy that he will do all he can to secure the funds he and Barney desire.

Later, Andy and Barney take it upon themselves to find good homes for all 11 dogs. After that is accomplished, the men return to the courthouse, exhausted but happy. Then a man named Clint Biggers appears and informs them that the dogs belong to him! So Andy and Barney set out to retrieve every pooch, bringing this doggone funny episode to an end.

MEMORABLE SCENES. 1. Barney attempting to convince Opie (and himself) that the dogs will weather the storm, and wandering into a diatribe on those "selfish giraffes." 2. Andy preparing a hangover cure for Otis.

CAST NOTES. Regulars: **Andy Griffith, Don Knotts, Ronny Howard,** and **Hal Smith.**

Robert Cornthwaite, who was known as John James Audubon on the television series *The Adventures of Jim Bowie* (1956-1958), appears as Mr. Somerset.

Roy Barcroft appears as Clint Biggers. Barcroft portrayed ranch owner Jim Logan in *Spin and Marty*, which was broadcast as part of the television series *The Mickey Mouse Club* (1955-1958). He was also in its spin-off versions.

EPISODE NOTES. 1. The Mayberry Grand

Theater is shown in this episode. 2. Otis claims soda pop is bad for his liver. 3. Among the items Andy and Barney would like to purchase for the sheriff's department: new cots, more guns, and brown belts. 4. Barney recites the following quote: "The quality of mercy is not strain'd. It droppeth as the gentle rain from heaven." The quote is from William Shakespeare's play *The Merchant of Venice*, which was first published in 1600. The quote is from act IV, scene 1. Actually, the quote is incomplete. The rest of the verse is: "…upon the place beneath. It is twice blest — it blesseth him that gives and him that takes."

"Mountain Wedding"

Episode #94. Air date: 4-29-63. Writers: Jim Fritzell and Everett Greenbaum. Director: Bob Sweeney.

Briscoe Darling comes to Mayberry and requests Andy's aid to get rid of a mountain wild man named Ernest T. Bass. It seems that Ernest T. is in love with Charlene Darling Wash, whom Andy has recently married to ex-serviceman Dud Wash. Ernest T. claims the wedding was not valid because Andy is a justice of the peace and not a regular preacher. Ernest T. has terrorized the Darling family by throwing rocks through their cabin windows in an effort to gain Charlene's attention. Ernest T. tries to impress Charlene by telling her that he's the best rock-thrower in the county. He also tells her that he can do 18 chin-ups and he's saving his money in order to buy a gold tooth.

Andy and Barney decide to go to the Darlings' cabin in the mountains. At the cabin, the two Mayberry lawmen convince Charlene and Dud to have an honest-to-goodness preacher perform a wedding ceremony in order to satisfy Ernest T. Bass. Unfortunately, Mr. Bass has other plans in mind. He vows to stop the "second" wedding. He continues to throw more rocks through the Darlings' windows and threatens to kidnap Charlene. After Andy stops Dud from going after Ernest T., he tells the entire Darling clan he has a plan to end Mr. Bass's threats. He has Barney disguise himself as Charlene, by wearing her wedding gown with the veil pulled completely down over his face. At the outdoor ceremony, Ernest T. takes the bait and kidnaps Barney. This allows the actual wedding to take place.

When Ernest T. Bass discovers he's kidnapped Barney, he doesn't seem to mind at all. In fact, Ernest T. actually takes a "fancy" to Barney. Needless to say, Barney does not return the compliment,

and at the end of the episode, everyone comes to the conclusion that Ernest T. Bass truly is a nut.

CAST NOTES. Regulars: **Andy Griffith** and **Don Knotts**. **Denver Pyle** returns as Briscoe Darling. **Margaret Ann Peterson** returns as Charlene Darling Wash. **The Dillards** return as the Darling boys. **Hoke Howell** returns as Dud Wash.

Howard Morris stars in his first of five appearances as Ernest T. Bass. Veteran character actor **Dub Taylor** appears as the preacher.

EPISODE NOTES. 1. Barney Fife meets the Darling family for the first time in this episode. He was on a bus trip to Charlotte with his mother when Andy married Charlene and Dud in episode 88, "The Darlings Are Coming." 2. Barney is able to wake up from a sound sleep when someone snaps his fingers. 3. In this episode, the Darlings performed the following songs: "Dooley," "Leaning on the Everlasting Arms," "The Anniversary Waltz" a.k.a. "Dance Til Your Stockings Are Hot and Raveling," and one unnamed instrumental. One song they didn't perform was "Never Hit Your Grandma with a Great Big Stick" because it makes Charlene cry. 4. Briscoe and his boys considered killing Ernest T. Bass, but Briscoe said they "kinda hated to go that far." 5. During the episode, Ernest T. Bass's cousin tells Dud Wash that Ernest T. went into the woods to kill a mockingbird. 6. At the cabin, Charlene offers Andy and Barney some hog backbone and fish muttle for supper. The lawmen say thanks, but no thanks. 7. Ernest T. tries to impress Charlene by singing "Old Aunt Maria" while banging on an empty gas can. Charlene turns down Ernest T. Bass's request to sing "Eatin' Goober Peas."

"The Big House"

Episode #95. Air date: 5-6-63. Writer: Harvey Bullock. Director: Bob Sweeney.

Two bandits who had holed up in an abandoned barn near Route 43 (about five miles from the Mayberry County line) have been captured. They are temporarily jailed in Mayberry until two Memphis detectives can arrive to return them to Tennessee. Meanwhile, Andy joins in the hunt for their two partners in crime, who are believed to be on the lam in the area. Barney decides that he and Andy need a third man, so he deputizes Gomer. He assigns him to serve as a lookout atop the courthouse after giving him a crash course on looking like a deputy.

As Barney soon discovers, Gomer makes a poor look-out. He sleeps on the job, and when he's suddenly awakened, he always drops his rifle over the edge of the building. Even worse, Andy finds himself having to order Gomer not to put the rifle in his own mouth. Andy believes Gomer would be put to better use if he would pick up all the lights and decorations on the roof top. They are leftover from Christmas. Actually, Andy had asked Barney to do the chore.

Soon, the two former fugitives are brought in, and Barney gives them some food for thought. Doing his best to intimidate the men, Barney refers to the jail as "the Rock." He says the rules are as follows: (1) "Obey all rules"; and (2) "Do not write on the walls, as it takes a lot of work to erase writing on the walls." Barney tells Andy the crooks should get no frills. He wants to give them what they can expect at "the Big House": A cot, a blanket, and a cracked mirror.

Barney believes he has the crooks' respect, but they are just waiting for an opportunity to escape. They get such a chance when Andy leaves to investigate a call from Carter French, who saw two suspicious men on his property. The felons intentionally provoke Barney into conducting a shakedown in their cell. While Barney performs the needless search for weapons, etc., the men easily slip out the door unnoticed. Luckily, Andy is still outside and nearby. He captures the crooks and returns them to a chagrined and embarrassed Barney.

Moments later, Barney absentmindedly leaves the cell keys in easy reach of the bandits, who escape as the deputy is preparing coffee. Again, Andy easily recaptures them.

Later, the two detectives from Memphis arrive. They believe the crooks' comrades will make an attempt to set their friends free. As the plainclothed detectives stake positions outside the courthouse, Andy sends Barney to the roof to assist Gomer. Meanwhile, the on-the-lam crooks are nearby, casing the courthouse from a car. Barney sees the detectives hiding behind bushes and, mistaking them for the crooks, captures them. Next, the real crooks come in, stick Barney into a cell, and proceed to free their buddies. Barney now has lost all four crooks, as one of the detectives points out.

Andy is outdoors and manages to get the drop on the gang. Gomer nearly foils the capture by dropping his rifle and knocking the gun out of Andy's hands. But it is Gomer's clumsiness that saves the day. When he accidentally kicks a basket of light bulbs to the ground, the resulting popping noises fools the gang into believing Andy has a machine gun. They stop dead in their tracks, and Andy brings them in. Andy credits Barney with coming up with the "clever scheme," thereby salvaging Barney's reputation in the eyes of the detectives.

CAST NOTES. Regulars: **Andy Griffith, Don Knotts, Ronny Howard,** and **Jim Nabors.**

Veteran character actor **Billy Halop** appears as Tiny, one of the first pair of crooks jailed. Halop is best remembered as one of the famed Dead End Kids from the movies.

Jack Lambert portrays Doc, the crook jailed with Tiny. Lambert had a regular role on television's *Riverboat* (1959-1961), as Joshua.

George Kennedy, a veteran of countless television appearances and movies, portrays an unnamed Memphis detective. Kennedy won an Oscar as best supporting actor for *Cool Hand Luke* (1967), in which he portrayed prisoner Clarence "Dragline" Slidell.

Also appearing: **Bob McQuain** (as a state police lieutenant), **Richard Angarola** as Detective Morley, with **Lewis Charles**, and **Arthur Kendall.**

EPISODE NOTES. 1. The viewer gets to see much more of the courthouse exterior than usual in this episode. 2. Andy, Barney, Opie, and Gomer listen to the account of the initial capture on the courthouse radio. 3. Police Chief Benson gave the orders to temporarily house the bandits in Mayberry. 4. The first pair of prisoners ate their meals in cell #1 and slept in cell #2. 5. A car parked near the courthouse bears the very familiar license plate AY-321. 6. From the courthouse roof, Gomer saw (1) Miss Fletcher get splashed with mud, when Pete Dooley's truck hit a mud hole; (2) Viola McConker sneaking out to her barn to have a pinch of snuff; and (3) Sue Ella Sawyer and her son walking down the street. 7. Doc jokingly refers to one of the detectives as Pete, in order to convince Barney that he knew him. 8. While training Gomer in the quick draw, Barney witnesses his protege smashing the bookcase glass. Barney orders him to be more careful, then proceeds to shoot his own gun off in its holster.

SEASON FOUR

In another season of great episodes, we bid adieu to Gomer Pyle and say "Hey" to his hilarious cousin, Goober. A.C. Nielsen Co. rating for the 1963-1964 season: 29.4; rank: 5.

"Briscoe Declares for Aunt Bee"

Episode #96. Air date: 11-28-63. Writers: Everett Greenbaum and Jim Fritzell. Director: Earl Bellamy.

Andy receives word of a disturbance at Nick's Cafe. When he investigates, he discovers that the Darling family are the cause of the trouble. Briscoe had wandered into the kitchen area to watch the cooks prepare food. This caused a bit of a scene, and the family was eventually refused service. Andy invites the mountain-born brood to have supper with him and even allows Briscoe to watch Aunt Bee prepare the meal.

Aunt Bee, ever the gracious hostess, makes certain Briscoe and his boys get plenty to eat. Briscoe misinterprets her hospitality as a sign of romantic interest. After supper, Aunt Bee recites a poem, and Briscoe believes the poem was aimed at him. He openly declares for Aunt Bee, stating his desire to marry her. Aunt Bee is understandably horrified, then flabbergasted when Briscoe refuses to take "no" for an answer. The only thing Andy and Aunt Bee can do is to ask him to take things slowly.

In the middle of the night, Aunt Bee is awakened by Briscoe, who stands on the lawn and serenades her with the song "Low and Lonely." This tactic does not succeed, of course, so Briscoe makes a drastic change in his strategy. He kidnaps Aunt Bee and takes her to his cabin in the mountains. He leaves a note for Andy, who makes a quick trip to retrieve his aunt. He chastises Briscoe for his illegal action, but Briscoe vows he will never give up in his quest to secure Aunt Bee's hand in marriage.

Andy comes up with an idea and manages to get a reluctant Aunt Bee to go along with his plan. Andy leaves after Aunt Bee tells Briscoe he has won her heart. The mountain man is thrilled, until she begins acting like a slave driver. She soon has Briscoe and his boys cleaning out the cabin, taking baths, and acting civilized at the dinner table. The straw that breaks the camel's back, according to Briscoe, is the fact that every now and then, Aunt Bee raps his hand with a wooden spoon.

Aunt Bee may be neat, reverent, an excellent cook, and a humble woman, but being beaten to death by a wooden spoon is just too much for Briscoe to take. He retracts his proposal, even though it means making a breach of promise. Andy's plan is a success, and a very relieved Aunt Bee returns to town, relatively unscathed.

MEMORABLE SCENE. The Darlings dining at the Taylors, especially Briscoe hollering for "taters," which inspires Opie to holler too. When Andy admonishes the boy, Briscoe reminds his boys not to holler while eating.

CAST NOTES. Regulars: **Andy Griffith, Ronny Howard,** and **Frances Bavier. Denver Pyle** returns as Briscoe Darling. Note that he is listed as "Brisco" in the credits. **The Dillards** return as the Darling boys.

EPISODE NOTES. 1. At the Taylor house, Andy and the Darling men play "Dueling Banjos" and another instrumental named "Doug's Tune." 2. Opie and Andy sing "Dan Tucker." 3. The poem Aunt Bee recites is "A Fading Flower of Forgotten Love" by Agnes Ellicott Strong. Aunt Bee and her sister, Florence, used to recite it at family gatherings. Briscoe calls the poem "rose poetry." 4. When Andy praises Aunt Bee's cooking, she exclaims "Oh, flibbertigibbet!" 5. Briscoe says his boys are bad cooks. The other night, according to Briscoe, they made hoot owl pie. "Perfectly good hoot owl…just plumb wasted!" 6. Andy suggests that the Darlings play "Dirty Me, Dirty Me, I'm Disgusted with

Myself." They decline, because the song makes Briscoe cry. 7. The Darling men wolf down Aunt Bee's supper, which includes pot roast with pearly onions and baked potatoes. 8. Opie protests that when he has to stay with Miss Marker, a neighbor, she feeds him grits and prunes. Andy reminds him that young 'uns in Norway have to eat hardtack and raw fish. (Hardtack is a cracker-like biscuit, well known to U.S. military personnel. It is sometimes called a "sea biscuit.") 9. Briscoe describes himself as a "tiller of soil and feller of trees." He likes to show off his muscles. 10. Besides his undying love, Briscoe tells Aunt Bee that, if she marries him, she will gain the constant devotion of his fun-loving, warm, and amusing sons and a sturdy hand-built cabin with all its furnishings and pure iron nails. 11. This is the only "Darling family" episode without Charlene.

"Gomer the House Guest"

Episode #97. Air date: 11-4-63. Writers: Jim Fritzell and Everett Greenbaum. Director: Earl Bellamy.

Wally is upset with Gomer because he spends too much time telling stories to some of his customers, while others get impatient waiting for service. In fact, Wally notices one impatient patron driving away in disgust. This incident causes Wally to fire Gomer, which puts Gomer out of both a job and a home because his living quarters were in a back room at the station. There, he had a one-burner stove, a wooden egg crate, forks, salt and pepper, and other luxuries.

Gomer asks Andy if he can stay in one of the cells at the courthouse for a few days. A sympathetic Andy invites him to stay at the Taylors' until he finds a new job. It is an invitation Andy will soon regret.

Gomer turns out to be a real nuisance. He talks throughout an episode of the television series "Shep and Ralph" (a story of a man and his dog), ruining it for Andy and his family. When Gomer decides to do some chores for the family to earn his keep (since Andy won't accept any rent payment), he chooses to do them overnight. He does some sawing, and while trying to repair the toggle switch on Aunt Bee's vacuum cleaner, he turns on the machine. These escapades wake up the entire family. Finally, Andy gets him to prepare for bed. Alas, Gomer gargles loudly and than sings "No Account Mule" over and over, annoying Andy.

The next morning, an exhausted Andy bluntly tells Gomer that due to the racket last night, he did not get much sleep. Gomer apologizes and vows to be more quiet. Sure enough, in the evening, Gomer retires when the family does and quietly reads his comic book in bed. Unfortunately, two of his former customers come by the house asking for Gomer's appraisal of the condition of their automobiles. This situation creates such a din that Andy's neighbors wake up and complain.

The next morning, Andy, Opie, and Aunt Bee are unusually cranky with each other. They realize they are not getting enough sleep. Andy becomes determined to tell Gomer he must find other arrangements. Meanwhile, he goes off to work as usual, where he demonstrates that his grumpiness is evenhanded: He begins handing out tickets to any driver whose automobile is in poor repair. He discovers a lot of offenders. He also discovers that Wally's business has dwindled drastically since he fired Gomer. Then, Andy finds out just how much Gomer means to Mayberry. When he returns home, he finds Gomer chatting with his old customers, who have missed his stories as much as his mechanical skills. Andy orders all of them to follow his car, and they parade straight to Wally's, where Andy points out that Gomer *is* Wally's business. Wally needs no coercion to rehire Gomer. Andy suggests to Wally that he could improve Gomer's "kitchenette" by providing an extra burner and an icebox. Wally readily agrees and even adds some fresh paint and some groceries to make his prized employee more comfortable.

CAST NOTES. Regulars: **Andy Griffith, Ronny Howard, Frances Bavier,** and **Jim Nabors. Joe Hamilton** returns as Jase.

Trevor Bardette makes his only appearance as Wally. Bardette was born in Nashville, Arkansas, on November 19, 1902, and he passed away in 1978. The former engineering major (he attended both the University of Oregon and Northwestern) appeared in well over 100 movies. He made several guest appearances on television, too, in series such as *Jeff's Collie, Perry Mason, The Twilight Zone, The Adventures of Superman,* and *Gomer Pyle, U.S.M.C.* (an episode entitled "Hello, Dolly"). Among his better-known movies are *They Won't Forget* (1937), *Abe Lincoln in Illinois* (1940), *The Westerner* (1940, with Gary Cooper), *The Big Sleep* (1946, with Humphrey Bogart and Lauren Bacall), *Destry* (1954, with Joel McCrea), and *Mackenna's Gold* (1969, with Gregory Peck).

Lee Krieger is Merle Dean. **Forrest Lewis,** a very familiar face in the series, portrays Willie Jack in this episode. **Roy Engel** portrays Luther.

EPISODE NOTES. 1. Gomer entertains his pals Jase, Merle Dean, Luther, and others with the following story: One day, he and a friend named Birdy Blush were fishing in a pond near a rock known as

"Lover's Leap Rock." It is so named because legend has it that a Confederate colonel jumped from it and drowned after being spurned by a Yankee woman. Anyway, Birdy bet Gomer 30 cents that (Gomer) would be unable to catch a trout in the pond. Gomer took the bet, baited his hook with limburger cheese and a slice of onion, and caught a trout. Birdy couldn't believe it and claimed it was a catfish, but it was a big rainbow trout. Gomer says Birdy sounds like a jay bird when he gets excited. When Jase hears the story, he comments that although he's lived in Mayberry for 40 years, he never knew the name of the rock by the pond Gomer mentioned. 2. Opie's allowance is given as 25 cents a week. Note that in episode 84, "Opie and the Spoiled Kid," Andy raised his allowance to 27 cents. Sounds like Opie's been slacking off in his chores! 3. On the fictional television show "Shep and Ralph," Ralph is a man and Shep is his dog. In this episode, young Dave is Ralph's cousin. Dave gets trapped in a mine shaft on Potter's Peak. 4. Gomer once had a dog that had two names. One of the names was "Sport." He was sweet, but dumb. One time, while Gomer's house burned, Sport went to stay at the neighbor's rather than alert the Pyle family. Luckily, a flame licked Gomer's hand and woke him up. He still has the scar on his right hand. 5. Luther's car has been running "rough." Merle Dean's truck needs new shock absorbers. Willie Jack's car has bad brakes. When ticketed by Andy, Willie Jack says, "You're getting to be just like Barney Fife!" 6. Opie wrote his chores on his wrist so he'd remember them. For the record, his chores are taking care of the lawn, trash, garage, and ashes. (In episode 84, filling the wood box and setting the table were also among his duties.) 7. Gomer applies for a job as a butcher at the market. When Andy asks "Do you *know* anything about cutting meat?" Gomer answers, worriedly, "Do you think they'll ask me that?"

"The Haunted House"

Episode #98. Air date: 10-7-63. Writer: Harvey Bullock. Director: Earl Bellamy.

Opie hits a baseball thrown by a friend and breaks a window at the abandoned old Rimshaw house. Both boys are nervous about retrieving the ball because the house is rumored to be haunted. As they approach the door, they hear a spooky noise that scares them away. They go to the courthouse and tell their story to Andy and Barney. The men tell them it was probably just the whistling wind. Andy warns them to stay out of the house because

it is likely that the floorboards are loose. Then, sensing that Barney was putting up a false front when he said there was nothing to be afraid of, Andy asks his deputy to go get the ball for the boys. While it is clear that Barney doesn't want to do it, he can't back out now. When Gomer suddenly comes by, Barney quickly enlists him to come along.

The nervous deputy enters the house first—"Age before beauty," says Gomer. Unfortunately, they don't get much farther than the boys did. Ghostly moans send them scrambling for the door.

Back at the courthouse, Andy chides Barney for failing to get the ball and for believing the house is haunted. Barney says he recalls that when old man Rimshaw died, his last wish was for his home to remain undisturbed. Otis Campbell chimes in with rumors he has heard: the walls move, the eyes on the portrait of Mr. Rimshaw seem to follow a person around the room, and axes float through the air.

Andy dismisses all this as nonsense, and he goes to the Rimshaw house with Barney and Gomer in tow. They quickly locate the baseball, and despite objections from his cohorts, Andy insists they look around the place. While he wanders off into another room, Barney and Gomer slowly move around the room, looking scared to death. Suddenly, Gomer disappears! Barney panics, and Andy returns. Gomer suddenly reappears. He had inadvertently stepped into a closet or something. The eerie thing is, Gomer says that someone or something pushed him back out. Next, Andy notices that the wallpaper above the fireplace is peeling and the wall is warm. Barney suggests that maybe an old tramp has been using the fireplace.

Andy ventures upstairs and asks Barney and Gomer to check out the cellar. Gomer correctly surmises that the cellar is downstairs. When Barney opens the cellar door, he sees an ax. Too scared to go down the stairs, he softly inquires, "Any old tramps down there?" then quickly shuts the door. Gomer tells Barney that legend has it that Rimshaw put chains on his hired hand and then killed him with an ax.

Barney notices the eyes on the Rimshaw portrait following him. When he tells Andy, Andy responds that it's probably just a trick of the light.

Barney knocks on the wall—and his knock is answered. Andy gets the same result when he knocks. Suddenly, Andy appears frightened. He loudly orders, "Let's get out of here!" Barney and Gomer quickly bolt out of the house, but Andy remains. He has a plan in mind.

Suddenly, we see Otis and notorious moonshiner Big Jack Anderson in the house. They are laughing, and Big Jack is quite proud of the fact that his scare tactics worked. He has found the perfect spot for his still, and claims he could probably stay there for twenty years.

As they come out of their hiding place, believing the house is empty, they get the shock of their lives. They witness an ax hanging in the air, a baseball rolling down the stairs, and the eyes moving on the portrait. They make tracks leaving the house. Meanwhile, Barney has bravely determined he must go rescue Andy, so he comes in the rear entrance. He see the suspended ax and hears moaning. He nearly passes out from fright before Andy can explain things.

The lawmen later use the infamous ax to smash Big Jack's still. Andy captures Anderson and surrenders him to Federal Agent Bowden of the Alcohol Control Division. Mr. Bowden has been after the tough and tricky outlaw for years. As usual, Andy generously shares the capture credit, in this case with Barney and Gomer.

CAST NOTES. Regulars: **Andy Griffith, Don Knotts, Ronny Howard, Jim Nabors,** and **Hal Smith.**

Ronnie Dapo portrays Opie's unnamed friend. In episode 84, "Opie and the Spoiled Kid," he portrayed Arnold Winkler. **Nestor Paiva** appears as Big Jack Anderson. **James Seay** appears as Agent Bowden.

EPISODE NOTES. 1. Opie's friend believes that no one can hit Whitey Ford's "dipsy doodle" pitch. Opie disagrees. He says Mickey Mantle could, by using his special grip and his old bat. 2. Barney wants to give a sobriety test to Otis, so he asks him to skip rope while reciting a verse. Barney gives him an example of a verse: "Call for the doctor, call for the nurse, call for the lady with the alligator purse." Otis finally makes up a verse: "Slow it down and let me in, or I'll go out and get some gin!" 3. Barney refers to *The Twilight Zone* in this episode. 4. Another verse recited by Barney is the same as the one he said in episode 51, "A Medal for Opie." It goes as follows: "My mother, your mother, lives across the way, every night they have a fight, and this is what they say: icka backa soda cracker, icka backa boo, icka backa soda cracker, out goes you!" 5. Three years after this episode was made, Don Knotts starred in the movie *The Ghost and Mr. Chicken.* The projects share several similarities.

"Ernest T. Bass Joins the Army"

Episode #99. Air date: 10-14-63. Writers: Jim Fritzell and Everett Greenbaum. Director: Dick Crenna.

While driving by the post office in the squad car, Andy and Barney notice a pile of men battling someone trapped beneath them. When order is restored, the lawmen discover that wild mountain man Ernest T. Bass is at the bottom of the pile. The army has a recruiting office located inside the post office building, and Ernest T. was bumping the other men out of line in an effort to be first. Incredibly, he wants to enlist in the army.

The recruiting sergeant comes outdoors to see what the commotion was about. Andy warns the sergeant that he would be wise to overlook Ernest T. when he tries to enlist, but the sergeant says the army wants and needs every able-bodied man. Ernest T. retorts that he *is* able-bodied. When he brags about his physical capabilities (he can, among other things, tote a full-grown mule on his shoulders for five miles), the sergeant likes his spirit. He believes he can handle Ernest T. Andy and Barney walk away, shaking their heads.

Ernest T. acts up during his physical, and the sergeant realizes he should have listened to Andy and Barney. He tells Ernest T. that the army, regretfully, cannot accept him. This deeply disappoints and angers Ernest T. He vows revenge against the recruiting center and Andy.

The sergeant stops by the courthouse on his way to Mount Pilot and warns Andy that Ernest T. has begun his rampage. He broke a window at the recruiting center. Moments later, the courthouse window is broken by a rock with a note attached. The note blames Andy and says every window in the state will be broken. It is signed, "Ernest T. Bass, ex-serviceman."

Barney wants to throw a dragnet over the town and go all-out with bloodhounds and tear gas. Andy believes his deputy is overreacting. However, phone calls to the courthouse indicate that Ernest T. has made a good start on his threat. Soon, Andy and Barney manage to capture the elusive rascal in front of the barbershop. Barney locks him up in cell #2.

The next morning, Barney is shocked to discover that the man sitting next to him as he eats breakfast at the diner is none other than Ernest T. He was just sitting there reading the newspaper. Ernest T. refuses to say how he escaped. Barney, taking no chances, leads Mr. Bass back to jail at gun point. He locks up the spare key to the cells in the file cabinet, rather than stowing it in the desk as usual. Barney calls Andy and then leaves to pick him up for work. When he and Andy enter the courthouse moments later, they find that Ernest T. has escaped again. They soon discover he is continuing to break windows.

The men search long and hard for the escapee, but to no avail. Then Andy notices delivery men carrying a new window to the courthouse. He figures that where there is glass, there's bound to be Bass, so he keeps a wary eye out. Sure enough, Ernest T. pops up, ready to break the window. However, a bumbling Barney accidentally beats him to it.

Apparently tiring of the chase, Ernest T. locks himself up. When Andy and Barney confront him, they discover that Ernest T. didn't really want to join the army. All he wants is a uniform. He says he has been blessed with good looks, brains, and personality, and he claims to be a good kisser. In short, he has everything ... except for romance. He says that three or four girls back in the mountains would have him if he only had a uniform. He cites an example: Jelsick Sturman came home from the service wearing a uniform, and the girls flocked around him. Ernest T. believes a uniform is his key to finding romance.

Andy can think of only one small-sized uniform that is handy, and Barney is wearing it. He manages to persuade Barney to give up his uniform. Ernest T. leaves with a smile and a salute, and proudly marches off toward his mountain home.

MEMORABLE SCENE. Ernest T. getting his army physical.

CAST NOTES. Regulars: **Andy Griffith** and **Don Knotts. Howard Morris** returns as Ernest T. Bass.

Allan Melvin, a very familiar performer in this series, portrays the unnamed army recruiting sergeant. **Paul Smith**, who appeared as Harry Becktoris in episode 82, "Class Reunion," portrays the army doctor.

Alice Backes portrays Olive, a waitress at the diner. She had a regular role in television's *Bachelor Father*, as Vickie, from 1957 through 1958. **Tom Myers** and **David Lipp** also appear.

EPISODE NOTES. 1. Some Andy and Barney gossip: (1) Mrs. Macknight has lost a lot of weight. The doctor said she had to...her ankles were too skinny to hold up all that heft. (2) Mrs. Devereaux is ugly as homemade soap and her husband Charlie is no prize. (3) Cecil Gurney won't admit to having two sets of false teeth. The two cut the gossip when Viola Slatt is spotted. Barney claims *she* is the town's biggest gossip. 2. Ernest T. calls the army doctor "Mr. Medico." 3. Ernest T. does not yet have a gold tooth, but is saving up for one. When he gets it, he will knock out three front upper teeth and put the gold tooth in the middle. This way the tooth will stick out when he dances. 4. At the diner, Andy and Barney get a great deal. For 80 cents, they get three vienna sausages (heavy on the tomato puree) and a slice of bread with a pat of butter on a paper dish. Andy says they were also served more than an ample portion of succotash. Barney tips Olive, their

waitress, a quarter because he doesn't know Andy has already done the same thing. When he discovers this fact, he has thoughts of taking the quarter back. Andy stops him by reminding him that Olive is a widow with four children. 5. Barney says that a #2 Amber Alert means that he or Andy will be alert at all times. 6. Andy receives courthouse calls from the following people: Merlin Bracey saw Ernest T. break a street light in front of Miss Megginson's house. Hannah Lou Smith reports that someone broke two panels out of her greenhouse. Finally, hardware store owner Richard Farrar reports that his store's window was busted. 7. At the diner for breakfast, Barney, who "isn't very hungry," orders orange juice, a bowl of cereal, a stack of wheats, three eggs, bacon, buttered white toast, hash brown potatoes, and coffee. Ernest T. passes him the sugar. 8. Jack's Bar is shown in Mayberry. 9. Barney's deputy uniform came from Raleigh and is made of genuine whiplash cord. 10. Barney finds a fork under Ernest T.'s cot. He believes that is what he used to make his escapes. Barney locks himself and Andy in cell #2 to test the theory. It doesn't work. 11. In explaining to the sergeant about Ernest T.'s character, Andy recalls the incidents which took place at the Darling cabin when Charlene married Dud (for the second time). Refer to episode 94, "Mountain Wedding."

"The Sermon for Today"

Episode #100. Air date: 10-21-63. Writer: John Whedon. Director: Dick Crenna.

It is Sunday morning in Mayberry, and like most of their neighbors, the Taylors are going to church. Andy and Opie relax on the front porch. Opie is listening to his pa read "Little Orphan Annie" aloud from the Sunday comics section of the newspaper. Aunt Bee is hurriedly dressing for church. Their regular preacher at the All Souls Church, Reverend Hobart M. Tucker, has invited a guest minister from New York City to deliver today's sermon. He is Dr. Harrison Everett Breen, a noted author. The title of his sermon is "What's Your Hurry?" Andy is reluctant to attend church today, because he has been "taking from Reverend Tucker" for years. Aunt Bee points out that both men are on "the same side." Clara Johnson rides to church with the Taylors. Barney and Gomer are going, too.

Dr. Breen's message is about the unfortunate acceleration of the pace of life. It seems that few people are taking time to relax and enjoy life. He reminds the congregation of days gone by, when people took time to enjoy old-fashioned band concerts on Sundays. He challenges them with the question, "What's your hurry?" Dr. Breen's fine sermon would be better suited to a more urban congregation, but he is warmly congratulated after the service. Of course, not *everyone* was paying attention. Barney nodded off briefly, only to be nudged by Andy, who was also fighting the urge to sleep. Gomer snored loudly enough to bring the sermon to a temporary halt, until the fellow sitting next to him elbowed him. Opie amused himself by catching a fly and holding it up to his ear.

Aunt Bee invites Dr. Breen to come over for dinner, but he must decline because he has to hurry to Mount Pilot to deliver another sermon. He adds that he may be able to drop by and join the family for coffee when he returns.

After a delicious dinner, Andy, Aunt Bee, and Barney reminisce about the band concerts of the past. Aunt Bee sees no reason why it could not be done today. Before long, the three become inspired to organize a band concert for that very evening. Aunt Bee and Clara begin working on mending the town band uniforms. Barney and Gomer plan to repair the old bandstand, while Andy hurries to organize the town band. A sense of excitement and optimism is in the air. Andy sends Gomer to ask his cousin, Goober, to help. Unfortunately, Goober is busy washing his car. He is going to take his mother visiting, but he will not allow her to ride in a dirty car. Goober says, "Hey," though, and he allows Gomer to borrow his tools. The only drawback is, only a relative of Goober's can use his tools.

After a while, the concert appears to be a pipe dream. The band uniforms need much mending and are mildewed. Clara blames cheap thread and poor storage. She and Aunt Bee find themselves bickering with each other. The bandstand, which is presently located across the street from the Mayberry Feed and Grain Store, is in poor shape, too. Gomer is reluctant to crawl under it because he believes there might be spiders there. Barney argues with him. Meanwhile, Andy is having trouble with the rusty town band. There are eight members (counting Andy) in the band, including Luther, a hard-of-hearing saxophonist. The band is horribly out of tune. Their version of "The Skater's Waltz" must be heard to be believed. The band members begin blaming one another for their awful sound.

Before long, it becomes clear that there will be no concert. Everything essential for a concert is in a sorry state of disrepair. A sweet idea has ended on a sour note. The exhausted gang gathers to relax on the Taylors' porch. Just then, Dr. Breen stops by to explain that he is sorry that he cannot join them for that cup of coffee he spoke of earlier. He must rush back to New York. He observes how serene and relaxed everyone looks, and he remarks that they look like folks who have just listened to an old-fashioned band concert! As he bids them adieu, Gomer exclaims "Oh, Reverend! We ain't relaxed. As a matter of fact, we're pooped!" Before Gomer can completely spill the beans, quick-witted Andy turns the tables on the departing preacher by stating that Gomer was just saying, "What's your hurry?"

MEMORABLE SCENES. 1. Gomer, Barney, Andy, and Opie sitting through church. 2. Andy and Barney on the porch, discussing whether to go to the drugstore for ice cream.

CASE NOTES. Regulars: **Andy Griffith, Don Knotts, Ronny Howard, Jim Nabors,** and **Frances Bavier. Hope Summers** returns as Clara. **William Keene** returns as Reverend Hobart M. Tucker, D.D. (Doctor of Divinity).

David Lewis portrays Dr. Harrison Everett Breen. **Forrest Lewis** appears as Luther. **Roy Engel** appears as an unnamed trumpet player, and **Joe Hamilton** portrays an unnamed clarinetist in the Mayberry band.

EPISODE NOTES. 1. Andy plays the tuba in the town band. He stores the horn in his garage. 2. Andy borrows Louise Palmer's sewing machine for Aunt Bee, to aid her and Clara in mending the band uniforms. 3. Barney wears his salt and pepper suit to church. 4. Andy guesses that the "Little Orphan Annie" comic strip is 42 or 43 years old, although Annie is probably Opie's age. 5. According to Andy, preaching begins at 11 o'clock. 6. Barney claims that everything he eats goes to muscle. He claims his mother was the same way. 7. Gomer enjoys watching Goober washing his car. 8. Barney creates a poster that reads "Concert tonight — Relax to music under the stars." Andy uses a nifty bit of logic to convince him that the sign is unnecessary.

"Opie the Birdman"

Episode #101. Air date: 9-30-63. Writer: Harvey Bullock. Director: Dick Crenna.

Barney helps Opie make an old-fashioned slingshot as Andy looks on. He wants his son to enjoy himself, but he cautions him to be careful with it. Opie assures his pa that he will only shoot at "tin cans and stuff." Barney tells Opie that he was an expert with a slingshot when he was a lad. He decides to demonstrate his best trick shot, the tailgunner, for Opie and Andy. He asks Opie to hold up a mirror, which will reflect the target, the courthouse trash can. Barney stands with his back to the target and then peers over his shoulder into the mirror. When he fires, the ammo misses its mark and breaks a window in the bookcase. Andy uses this accident to remind Opie to only fire his weapon outdoors.

Opie has fun just pretending to shoot at people and other outdoor targets. Suddenly, he notices something in a tree in his front yard. He takes aim and shoots. Much to Opie's surprise, a bird falls to the ground. At first, Opie refuses to believe the bird is dead. He tries to help it fly away. He *pleads* for it to fly. When he realizes that he has killed the bird, he is devastated. He runs, sobbing, to his room.

At the dinner table that evening, Opie scarcely touches his meal. Andy tells Aunt Bee that he found a dead songbird in the yard. He believes that the neighbor's cat is responsible. Aunt Bee refutes the theory because she knows that the neighbor, Mrs. Snyder, and her cat have been away for over a week. Guilt-stricken Opie leaves the table and dashes upstairs to his room.

Andy easily deduces what has happened, and he confronts his son. Opie admits that he killed the bird and that he is sorry. Andy knows that in this case, being sorry won't suffice. He opens Opie's window and tells him that the plaintive chirps he hears are of young birds calling for their mama, who will never return. Instead of whipping the boy, he tells him to sit and listen to the birds awhile.

By the following morning, Opie has decided that he will act as a surrogate mother to the orphaned birds. He gathers them a breakfast of bugs and worms and feeds them as they sit in their nest. Later, when Mrs. Snyder's cat returns to town and is heard prowling around, Andy transfers the three young birds to a large white cage, which he hangs on the front porch. Opie names the birds Wynken, Blynken, and Nod. Andy, worried that Opie might become too attached to the birds, is quick to remind him that he will have to release them someday. Despite this warning, Opie does become attached. He diligently and lovingly cares for them.

One morning, as Andy and Barney gaze at the birds, Andy remarks that they are mature enough to be released. Barney makes a brief attempt to convince him otherwise, but he knows better. Andy brings up the subject with Opie, who is understandably reluctant to set them free. Andy tells him that the one final thing the birds' mother would have done is to set her children free. Opie realizes that he must release them. He has had nagging doubts about his effectiveness as mother to the birds, but those doubts disappear as Wynken, Blynken, and Nod fly away and inhabit the trees in the front yard. A relieved Opie wistfully remarks that the cage looks empty. Andy agrees, but before turning around to go inside, then adds, "But don't the trees seem nice and full?"

MEMORABLE SCENES. 1. Barney showing Opie how the birds communicate with each other. 2. Barney's account of David and Goliath.

CAST NOTES. Regulars: **Andy Griffith, Don Knotts, Ronny Howard,** and **Frances Bavier.**

EPISODE NOTES. 1. Mr. Snyder is going to do some work for Andy. 2. Mrs. Snyder was away visiting her sister. 3. Johnny Paul Jason told Opie, "If you touch a bird, it's gonna die." Barney rejects that notion as superstition. He claims it will only stunt the bird's growth. 4. When Opie sticks his tongue out as he works on the slingshot, Barney tells him to put his tongue in, because he might bite it off. The advice goes unheeded, and we note that Barney sticks his tongue out too. 5. Barney says keen, sharp eyes and a good set of pinchin' fingers made him a slingshot master. Some of his most successful shots were over-the-mountain, behind-the-barn, and under-the-bridge. 6. Aunt Bee planned to use a recipe she saw in the newspaper—"ham loaf with green beans, Chinese style." She began preparing the food, then she notices that the rest of the recipe was continued on page 7. Unfortunately, she had used that page to line the trash pail. 7. Barney lends Opie his tweezers to help free the birds so the birds won't be frightened by the smell of a human. 8. Barney mispronounces "safari" as "safairy." 9. Barney tells Opie that he should never take a wild bird into a house because it is scientifically and biologically wrong. Besides, a bird in the house means there is going to be a death in the family. 10. Otis left his pocket transistor radio in the courthouse, and Andy uses it to play a joke on Barney. When Barney brings in a bowl with two goldfish in it, Andy secretly activates the radio. Barney believes the fish are actually talking to each other. 11. Barney claims that the greatest cause of goldfish death in the U.S. is overfeeding.

"A Black Day for Mayberry"

Episode #102. Air date: 11-11-63. Writer: John Whedon. Director: Jeffrey Hayden.

Two U.S. treasury agents come to Mayberry to inform Andy that an armored truck, bearing over $7 million in gold bricks, will be passing through town on its way to Fort Knox. The shipment, which originates in Denver, should arrive in Mayberry at 4:30 the next afternoon. When it comes, it will stop at the filling station for gas, and the driver and guards will have a bite to eat at the diner. It will be Andy and Barney's responsibility to guard the gold at that time.

Andy explains to Barney that this matter is

strictly top secret. Barney assures him that nary a word will be said. Moments later, "Tight Lips" Barney spills the beans to Juanita, the waitress at the Bluebird Diner.

While Andy is away, checking the roads within the county, Barney dons a trench coat, hat, and pipe and wanders over to the Mayberry Hotel. He asks the desk clerk, Asa, if he has seen any suspicious characters lately. Asa has only seen one: Barney! The deputy is not amused. Barney explains that he is working undercover. To his astonishment, he discovers that Asa knows about the gold shipment. In fact, Asa explains, just about everybody in town knows about it.

Later, Andy and Barney go to Wally's filling station just to check it out. To their surprise, they discover that Gomer knows about everything, too. He heard about it from Lauralee Hobbs at the dime store. Andy quickly realizes that Barney's lips were not as tight as he claimed they'd be.

The next day, Andy is mortified to see half the town lined up along Main Street. They're all there to welcome the gold shipment. Someone is selling hot dogs, balloons, and other items, and a carnival atmosphere prevails. A couple of citizens hold up a banner that reads, "Mayberry Welcomes Gold Truck." Andy and Barney are distraught when they realize they have little time to change the situation. In fact, the truck arrives moments later. Andy apologizes to the federal agents, and they point out that the mission must go on as planned. Andy finally succeeds in getting the crowds to disperse by informing them that they are interfering with government business and government property.

As things quiet down, Andy, Barney, and a recently deputized Gomer follow the truck to Wally's. Andy will stand outside of the truck to guard against any intruder, Gomer will fill the truck's tank with gas, and Barney will trade places with the guard who is minding the gold. Meanwhile, the agents will eat.

For a few minutes, things go smoothly — that is, until Gomer almost floods the inside of the truck with gas when he mistakes a gun port for the gas tank. Barney is a nervous wreck, and Andy has to walk away from the scene momentarily to disperse the few sightseers that remain. Barney gets curious and takes a look at the gold bricks. To his horror, the bricks are actually gold-painted boxes filled with sand! He yells to attract some attention, but when the guards rush over to investigate and Barney tries to get out of the truck, they push him back in and the truck speeds away. Andy and Gomer jump in the squad car and give chase. Andy manages to get ahead of the truck, using a shortcut, and he blocks

the road. Once questioned by Andy, the agents explain that the truck is merely a decoy. When Barney discovered the fake gold, he figured the agents were actually crooks. The agents had to quiet him down so he would not broadcast their secret. They were merely going to drop him off at the county line. The real gold shipment is going by way of Raleigh.

CAST NOTES. Regulars: **Andy Griffith, Don Knotts, Ronny Howard, Frances Bavier**, and **Jim Nabors**. **Clint Howard** returns as Leon, the little cowboy who is always offering Barney a bite of his partially eaten peanut butter and jelly sandwich.

Rance Howard appears as one of the treasury agents. Howard is the father of Ron and Clint Howard.

Ken Lynch returns to the series. This time, he is an FBI agent. Lynch made a career out of portraying law enforcement officials.

Doodles Weaver, a comic actor who was once part of the Spike Jones and the City Slickers musical comedy troupe, appears as Regis, a tax protester. Weaver, brother of former NBC president Pat Weaver and uncle of movie actress Sigourney Weaver, was born Winstead Sheffield Weaver. He once joked that he changed his name to Doodles because "it sounded more dignified." His mother refuted that explanation. She says she nicknamed him Doodles because he had big ears and looked like a doodle bug.

Familiar faces **Joe Hamilton** and **Roy Engel** appear as Mayberry townsfolk. **Charles P. Thompson** portrays Asa. In this episode, he is the clerk at the Mayberry Hotel. Also appearing are **Phil Arnold** as the hotdog vendor, and **Alex** and **Leslie Barringer**.

EPISODE NOTES. 1. One of the many people awaiting the gold shipment in Mayberry is a protester named Regis. He came from his home in the woods to carry a sign that reads, "Down with the gold standard. Vote for the single tax!" After exchanging insults with some members of the crowd, he asks Gomer to hold his sign, then walks away. 2. Barney wears his salt and pepper suit under his undercover gear while paying a visit to the Mayberry Hotel. 3. Asa tells Barney that he would just like to *wave* at the gold. 4. Opie wonders aloud if free samples will be handed out when the truck comes. 5. Opie, who is standing with Aunt Bee when we first see him on Main Street, is later seen standing atop the squad car with Leon, who is holding a balloon. Look for this unusual brotherly scene when the gold truck comes to town and Andy orders the crowd to go home.

"Opie's Ill-Gotten Gain"

Episode #103. Air date: 11-18-63. Writer: John Whedon. Director: Jeffrey Hayden.

Andy is concerned when he sees Opie doing his arithmetic homework at the breakfast table. Doing one's homework in a last minute rush is not the way to insure good grades. Opie tells his father that he is not worried about his grades because he believes that his teacher, Miss Crump, likes him.

When report cards come out, Opie surprises Andy with great news: He received straight A's. Andy can hardly believe it. He is very proud of his son. Aunt Bee bakes Opie's favorite pie, Butterscotch Pecan. Andy proudly shows Barney the report card. Barney exclaims that Opie may be a genius, and he tells Andy that he should have Opie's I.Q. tested.

The following day, an apologetic Miss Crump informs Opie that she made a mistake in transcribing his grades. Opie did not get all A's. In fact, he got one F—in arithmetic. Opie goes from elation to dejection. He does not immediately mention this turnabout to Andy or Aunt Bee.

Later, Andy purchases a new bike, with a bell on it, to surprise his bright son. When Opie discovers it, he is thrilled—until he learns that Andy bought it because of his outstanding marks. Feeling guilty, Opie declines to ride it and explains that he has studying to do. Andy, Aunt Bee, and Barney cannot understand Opie's curious behavior. Andy reckons "that's the way you get all A's!" Barney recalls that his father used to tell him, "Get your nose out of them books and get some fresh air!" Then young Barney would be sent to the cellar to sift the ashes!

Opie makes several attempts to tell his father what really happened, but Andy is too busy bragging about the grades his boy got. When Opie overhears Andy tell Aunt Bee that he has been boasting about his son to the fellows at the barbershop, it is just too much for him to take. He decides to run away.

Miss Crump pays Andy a visit at the courthouse and quickly discovers that he is unaware of the report card mix-up. She explains the situation, and Andy goes home to talk it over with Opie. To his dismay, he finds only a note telling him that his son has run away from home. Andy goes looking for him and soon finds him walking down a country road. Opie tells him what happened and explains that he had tried to tell him before, but he did not want to disappoint his father. So, he decided to run away until he could accomplish something that would make his pa proud of him.

Andy confesses that he gave much more importance to the grades than he should have. He realizes that he made it difficult for Opie to come to him with the truth. He tells Opie that he is proud of him because he is who he is. He adds that all he will ever ask of him is that he do the best he can. Opie's frown quickly becomes a smile. He responds to his father's support by earning a B+ on his next arithmetic test.

MEMORABLE SCENE. Barney reciting the Preamble to the Constitution of the United States.

CAST NOTES. Regulars: **Andy Griffith, Don Knotts, Ronny Howard, Frances Bavier,** and **Aneta Corsaut.**

EPISODE NOTES. 1. Opie claims that Barbie Tyler gets good grades because she is Miss Crump's pet. 2. Opie keeps his nutrition money in his shoe. He uses that money to purchase a mid-morning snack. 3. Barney claims that kids are too pampered today. When *he* was young, there were no food breaks. Anyone caught chewing anything in school had to stay after school and clap erasers. 4. Barney claims to have gotten all A's once. The teacher made a fuss over him, and his classmates hated him. To remedy this, he buckled down and got bad marks. 5. Barney digs up his eighth grade history book. While in eighth grade, on one page he wrote these words: "This book belongs to Bernard P. Fife. If lost or stolen, please return to Bernard P. Fife. (signed) Bernard P. Fife." On the next page it says: *The History of the United States of America* by Bernard P. Fife. Barney had pasted his name over the author's name. 6. Andy suggests that Aunt Bee should have a title bestowed on her, such as "Miss Fried Chicken of Mayberry." 7. Andy brags that he should photograph Opie's report card and show it off to Edgar Beasley, who is always bragging about his young'un. 8. Opie thought that he might run away and join the navy. 9. Barney pronounces Einstein as "Einsteen."

"Up in Barney's Room"

Episode #104. Air date: 12-2-63. Writers: Jim Fritzell and Everett Greenbaum. Director: Jeffrey Hayden.

For the past five years, Barney has enjoyed living at the Mendelbright Park Apartments. His landlady, Mrs. Mendelbright, is a kindly elderly woman, but she strictly enforces two rules that Barney routinely breaks: She does not allow cooking in tenant's rooms, and she forbids the use of light bulbs that are stronger than forty watts. Barney has a hot plate in his room and cooks his own meals occasionally. He also uses a seventy-five watt bulb.

Andy stops by Barney's apartment to give him his paycheck. Barney is cooking up some home-made chili. Suddenly, Mrs. Mendelbright comes to his door, and Barney hides the evidence in the dresser. The smell of chili and crackers leads Mrs. Mendelbright to discover that Barney has been cooking. She becomes upset when she sees that the hot plate has scorched her mother's dresser. She complains about the seventy-five watt bulb and points out that she knows that Barney sleeps with the light on. Barney calls her "snoop" and "bulb-snatcher," after which she orders him to move out. Mrs. Mendelbright knows that the room will not be vacant for long. She has recently met a smooth-talking charmer by the name of Oscar Fields. He has just inquired about a room.

Andy invites Barney to stay at his house, but Barney, calling himself "Mr. Independent," decides to move into the back room at the courthouse. He invites Thelma Lou over to see his new digs. That evening, as Andy and Opie are walking home after a movie, they notice the courthouse lights switching off and on. They investigate and discover that Barney had gotten a bit too fresh with Thelma Lou. An embarrassed Barney tries in vain to hide his lipstick-covered face from Opie. Andy tells Barney that he must seriously look for new, more permanent lodging.

Five days pass, and Barney has not found anything that comes close to what he had at Mrs. Mendelbright's. Andy urges him to talk to her and ask if he may have his old room back. Andy even offers to accompany him. Barney reluctantly okays the idea, but exclaims, "I will not crawl!" Of course he does. Mrs. Mendelbright accepts his apology, but informs him that she is selling the house and moving to Raleigh. She and Mr. Fields are getting married! Barney is immediately suspicious about this whirlwind romance, but he and Andy wish her well. Privately, Barney tells Andy that he hopes the marriage will end in a quickie Mexican divorce.

Later Barney runs into Mrs. Mendelbright as she is leaving the Mayberry Bank. She tells him that she has just withdrawn her entire savings of $3,600.43. It will serve as her share of the down payment on her future home in Raleigh. Barney is alarmed. He believes that she is about to be victimized by Mr. Fields. He tells Andy, who reluctantly agrees to ask the state police to check out Mr. Fields' background.

While they await a reply, Barney breaks out some sweet cider and reminisces about the past five years. He and Mrs. Mendelbright used to sit on the porch every evening, sipping cider and counting cars. He said that Mrs. Mendelbright reminds him of his mother. Andy agrees that she is a good

woman. They both recall the time their church presented her with a white bible. She is the most faithful member the church has. Barney even comes close to tears as he recalls the time Mrs. Mendelbright washed his hair because he had such a bad sunburn he could not raise his arms. A couple of cups of cider later, Barney is slurring words and making little sense. Andy discovers that the cider has turned hard. Barney is drunk.

Meanwhile, Mr. Fields, having discovered another bottle of hard cider that Barney left behind, begins plying Mrs. Mendelbright with it. She too gets a bit gassed. As she goes upstairs to retrieve her "valoose" (meaning "valise"), Mr. Fields grabs her purse.

Back at the courthouse, Andy receives the information from the police. Oscar Fields, a.k.a. "Otto Feldman" and "Norman Feldspar," is a notorious con man, bigamist, and extortionist. Andy manages to sober Barney up enough to hurry over to Mrs. Mendelbright's house. They arrive just in time to nab Fields as he is leaving. As Andy hauls him away, Barney and Mrs. Mendelbright make everything right again with heartfelt words and a tender embrace. Not only does Barney get his room back, Mrs. Mendelbright lowers his rent from $6.00 to $5.00 per week, allows him to cook whenever he wishes, and tells him he may use a 100 watt light bulb.

CAST NOTES. Regulars: **Andy Griffith, Don Knotts, Ronny Howard,** and **Betty Lynn.**

Veteran character actor **J. Pat O'Malley** portrays Oscar Fields. O'Malley's most notable television role was as Bert Beasley on *Maude* from 1975 through 1977.

Enid Markey, who enjoyed a long career as a television and film character actress, portrays Mrs. Mendelbright. She portrayed Jane in the very first Tarzan movie, *Tarzan of the Apes* (1918). She was born on February 22, 1896, in Dillon, Colorado, and died on November 16, 1981. Her only regular role on television was as Aunt Violet Flower in the 1960-1961 series *Bringing Up Buddy.* She appeared in an early 90-minute drama in 1948's *Stage Door* as Judith Canfield. She made guest appearances in such series as *Please Don't Eat the Daisies* and *Gomer Pyle, U.S.M.C.* (In the latter, she played Gomer's grandma in "Grandma Pyle, Fortune Teller.") Most of her movies were silent ones, such as *Battle of Gettysburg* (1914). One well-known talkie she appeared in was *The Boston Strangler* (1968, with Tony Curtis).

EPISODE NOTES. 1. A sign in front of Mrs. Mendelbright's house declares: "No children, No pets, No cooking, No vacancies." 2. Mrs. Mendelbright believes that Barney's work is dangerous and that Barney is underweight. 3. Andy says that Barney's chili is so spicy it makes his head all wet. 4. Barney mispronounces "herbs" by pronouncing the 'h'. 5. Barney has bound volumes of *True Blue Detective* magazine, dating from 1959. They feature good stories such as "I Married a Fink," "How It Feels to Pull the Switch," and "I Picked a Pocket and Paid." 6. Barney's wall sports a Mayberry High School pennant. His room also features an old orange crate, which he uses for shelving. 7. The dresser that Barney scorched with his hot plate had been bussed to Mayberry all the way from Fort Lauderdale. 8 According to Mrs. Mendelbright, Barney is afraid of the dark. 9. Barney wears his salt and pepper suit while showing Thelma Lou his room at the courthouse. 10. Opie and Andy take in a Gregory Peck movie. Opie notes that Mr. Peck spoke with a funny accent, but, in the last picture they saw him in, he talked like Andy does. Andy explains that as an actor, Mr. Peck has mastered both southern and northern accents.

"A Date for Gomer"

Episode #105. Air date: 11-25-63. Writers: Everett Greenbaum and Jim Fritzell. Director: Dick Crenna.

Thelma Lou's shy and homely cousin, Mary Grace Gossage, is coming to Mayberry for a visit. The annual Chamber of Commerce dance is scheduled to be held during Mary Grace's stay, and Thelma Lou informs Barney that she will not attend the dance unless he can help locate a date for her cousin. Barney consults with Andy, and together they enlist Gomer Pyle to take Mary Grace to the dance. However, shortly after being introduced to her on the night of the dance, Gomer suddenly excuses himself and leaves Thelma Lou's without explanation. Mary Grace is hurt, but she insists that Thelma Lou, Barney, Andy, and Helen should go to the dance without her. They do, although Thelma Lou is reluctant to go.

A short while later, Gomer returns to Thelma Lou's with a corsage for Mary Grace. He explains that he had noticed that Helen and Thelma Lou had one and she did not. Mary Grace is touched by his thoughtfulness. The couple realizes they now have no vehicle to take them to the dance, but it hardly matters. They decide that they would rather stay at Thelma Lou's and get better acquainted.

Meanwhile, Thelma Lou is too upset to dance. She insists that they leave and return to comfort her forsaken cousin. They are surprised to discover Gomer and Mary Grace dancing and having a great time.

CAST NOTES. Regulars: **Andy Griffith, Don Knotts, Ronny Howard, Frances Bavier, Jim Nabors, Aneta Corsaut,** and **Betty Lynn.**

Mary Grace Canfield, best known for her hilarious portrayal of carpenter Ralph Monroe on the hit series *Green Acres*, portrays Mary Grace Gossage.

EPISODE NOTES. 1. Thelma Lou's house number is 830 on an unspecified street. 2. Barney buys Thelma Lou some West Indian Licorice Mocha Delight ice cream from Murphy's House of the Nine Flavors. The treat cost Barney 40 cents, but Thelma Lou reimburses him. 3. Freddy Fleet and His Band with a Beat perform at the dance. 4. The dance features Japanese lanterns as decorations, a door prize, and a buffet supper. 5. For his date with Mary Grace, Gomer purchases a pair of yellow socks, a purple tie with an acorn pattern, an $8.00 pair of shoes with brass buckles on the side, and a brown belt with an imitation mother-of-pearl horseshoe buckle. 6. Gomer states that Barney is worldly and "swayve" (suave). As evidence, Gomer points out that Barney has been out with waitresses and even a registered nurse. 7. Barney wears his salt and pepper suit to the dance. 8. Andy ran into Al Becker and a big collie dog at Norman's Groceteria where Mrs. Speers works. None of Andy's friends seem to know Al. 9. Thelma Lou gets angry and gives Barney a bloody nose. 10. Old Mr. Perkins is a stag line regular at dances in Mayberry, while Nate Bushy always brings his mother. 11. Mayberrian Luke Taft likes to "hit the sauce." 12. "Skinny" Griffin is a bird-hunting friend of Gomer's. 13. Barney says "knave" for "naive." 14. For historical purposes, it is worth noting that this episode aired just three days after President John F. Kennedy was assassinated.

"Citizen's Arrest"

Episode #106. Air date: 12-16-63. Writers: Everett Greenbaum and Jim Fritzell. Director: Dick Crenna.

Shortly after reminiscing with Andy about serving as his deputy for ten years, Barney arrests Gomer for making an illegal U-turn. Gomer protests, and a large crowd soon gathers. Barney tells Gomer that even if he were not a deputy, he would still be obligated to make a citizen's arrest. He writes Gomer up, handing him a ticket fining him $5.00. Then he pulls away in the squad car, making a U-turn. Gomer begins shouting, "Citizen's arrest!" and insists that Barney write himself a ticket. Andy arrives on the scene, and to Barney's dismay, he insists on it, too. An irate Barney stubbornly refuses to pay the fine and jails himself. Andy tries to talk some sense into him, but Barney has made up his mind. Before long, the hardheaded deputy resigns. (He appears to be a little upset when Andy readily accepts the resignation.)

Gomer is distraught when Opie tells him that Barney has quit. He decides to stage a phony robbery at the filling station, hoping that a big case will inspire Barney to get back to work. The plan succeeds. However, Barney cites Gomer for a false alarm. Then, as Barney pulls away from the scene, he makes a U-turn. Of course, Gomer begins hollering, "Citizen's arrest!" again.

Back at the courthouse, Barney apologizes to Andy for behaving the way he did. Andy merely places his deputy's letter of resignation in his file, which, incidentally, happens to hold several similar letters of resignation written by Barney over the past ten years.

On *The Andy Griffith Silver Anniversary Special* aired on October 3, 1985, on WTBS, Jim Nabors picked "Citizen's Arrest" as his favorite episode.

MEMORABLE SCENES. 1. Barney attempting to smoke a cigarette. 2. Otis teasing Barney about being in jail.

CAST NOTES. Regulars: **Andy Griffith, Don Knotts, Ronny Howard, Frances Bavier, Jim Nabors,** and **Hal Smith.**

Joe Hamilton and **Roy Engel** appear as Mayberry townsfolk.

EPISODE NOTES. 1. Gomer subscribes to *Mechanics Monthly* magazine. 2. A man named Pinkley was Mayberry's Sheriff in 1931. He was followed, chronologically, by Fred Paley, Dale Buckley, and Andy Taylor. 3. In 1931, Purcell Branch, father of Tyler Branch, was arrested for disturbing the peace, which is a misdemeanor. He drove his Reo Flying Cloud down Mayberry's Main Street with the cut-out open. According to Barney, "In those days, everybody thought they were Lucky Lindy." 4. A man named Freeburger once arrested Barney's father for speeding. Oddly, Freeburger was not in law enforcement. He was a sewer inspector. 5. Otis believes he is in *The Twilight Zone* when he sees Barney in jail. 6. Andy and Barney harmonize on the song "Tell My Darling Mother I'll Be There." 7. Otis took his first drink 27 years ago (1936). 8. Barney's middle initial is given as "P." 9. Barney received his first revolver as deputy in August of 1953. 10. Barney jails himself in cell #2. Cell #1 is Otis's cell. 11. Barney claims that people seem to like his smile. 12. The code for a U-turn is "911." A "912" is code for insulting the intelligence of an officer. 13. Barney calls Gomer a "boob." 14. Otis sings, "I'm Sorry I Broke Your Heart, Mother."

"Gomer Pyle, U.S.M.C."

Episode #107. Air date: 5-19-64. Writer: Aaron Ruben. Director: Aaron Ruben.

Gomer startles Andy with the announcement that he has enlisted in the United States Marine Corps. He was influenced to do so when he read about the Marines and the exploits of a much-decorated Marine named General Lucius Pyle (no relation to Gomer). Andy believes that Gomer is not cut out to be a Marine, but he offers to drive Gomer to the base in Wilmington, hoping that he can talk him out of joining the armed services. Unfortunately, Gomer is late in reporting, and he is reprimanded by his drill instructor, Gunnery Sergeant Vincent Carter. He is forced to sing the "Marine Corps Hymn" while wearing a bucket on his head.

Gomer manages to stay on Carter's bad side merely by being his friendly, easygoing self. Sergeant Carter is certain that Gomer will fail the first inspection for new recruits and will be discharged from the service. He finds a certain comfort in that thought. However, Andy knows that Gomer would be heartbroken if that occurred, so he has a chat with Carter. Andy cleverly leads the sergeant to believe that Gomer is the son of General Lucius Pyle. Sergeant Carter believes he is being tested by the Corps. He knows he cannot let the son of a legend fail inspection, so he gives Gomer a crash course on being a good Marine. When Batallion Commander Colonel Watson makes his inspection, he comments that Gomer presents the image of the ideal Marine. This praise comes as a relief to Sergeant Carter. He is not amused, however, when he discovers that General Pyle never had children. Thanks to Andy and to an unwitting Sergeant Carter, Gomer will remain in the Marine Corps.

CAST NOTES. Regulars: **Andy Griffith** and **Jim Nabors.**

Frank Sutton plays Sergeant Vince Carter. He would continue the character in the spin-off series. Sutton also co-starred with Jim Nabors on *The Jim Nabors Hour,* a variety series that ran from 1969 to 1971. His best-known movie appearance was as the brother of Ernest Borgnine in *Marty.* Sutton died in 1974.

Frank Albertson portrays Colonel Watson, the commanding office. **Eddie Ryder, Karl Lucas, Alan Reed, Jr.,** and **Charles Myers** also appear in the episode.

EPISODE NOTES. 1. The Marine base is named Camp Wilson. 2. Gomer was late in reporting due to a tire problem. The tire had a leaky valve. 3. Gomer wished he had time to go to Raleigh to get an eagle tattoo on his arm and then have the word "Mother" tattooed beneath it. 4. Sergeant Carter tells Gomer that wearing a bucket on one's head will improve the voice and help one to think better. 5. Gomer wants Andy to let him know when Ida Carrington gets the cast off of her broken leg, and whether Miss Hook finds her lost Boston Bulldog. 6. Gomer sings the "Marine Corps Hymn" to Andy. He knows the lyrics because one year, Nelson's Funeral Parlor had the lyrics printed on the back of their calendars. (Nelson's Funeral Parlor could have a connection with an actual funeral home in Mount Airy, Moody's Funeral Parlor, once known as the Nelson-Moody Funeral Home.) 7. Sergeant Carter likes to repeat the phrase "I can't hear you" to his recruits. 8. Gomer's fellow recruits trick him into putting on Sergeant Carter's dress blue uniform. 9. This episode served as the pilot for the popular series *Gomer Pyle, U.S.M.C.* (1964-1970).

"Opie and His Merry Men"

Episode #108. Air date: 12-30-63. Writer: John Whedon. Director: Dick Crenna.

Opie and his friends are playing Robin Hood in Crouch's Woods near the lake when they run into a hobo. Before long, the hobo is reminding them how Robin Hood stole from the rich to give to the poor. The hobo points out that life has not been kind to him. He tells the boys that, many years ago, he saved an infant boy from a horrible death. It seems that the hobo was once a "fire" man for the C.B. & Q railroad. He risked his life to save the baby and suffered a leg fracture as a result. The hobo was left with a game leg. He claims that the child he rescued is now president of a supermarket. The boys, seeing how little the hobo has to eat, go about stealing food from their own homes to feed him.

Andy discovers what Opie and his merry men are doing, and he asks the gang to take him to meet this extraordinary fellow. Andy sizes up the hobo accurately and quickly. He tells the man that there are several jobs available to him and that he will even rent him a room in town until he can decide which job to take. The hobo obviously does not want to work, and when Andy gives him an opportunity to run off, he does. The boys notice that his "game" leg wasn't slowing him down at all. They realize that their generosity was wasted on a scoundrel.

CAST NOTES. Regulars: **Andy Griffith, Don Knotts, Ronny Howard,** and **Frances Bavier.** The hobo is portrayed by **Douglas Fowley.**

Fowley is best known as Doc Fabrique and Doc Holliday on the popular television series *The Life and Legend of Wyatt Earp.* **Richard Keith** appears as Johnny Paul Jason, **Dennis Rush** as Howie Pruitt, and **Joey Scott** as Whitey Porter.

EPISODE NOTES. 1. The hobo is known to Barney as "Weary Willie." The deputy had twice before run him out of Crouch's Woods. 2. Barney says he used to love reading "childish" (meaning "childhood") classics. He claims that he was an "avaricious" reader. He meant to say "avid," or perhaps "voracious." 3. When Barney gets mad, a vein on his neck sticks out. 4. Opie beats Barney in a game of checkers.

"Barney and the Cave Rescue"

Episode #109. Air date: 1-6-64. Writer: Harvey Bullock. Director: Dick Crenna.

Today, many of Mayberry's citizens will enjoy a town picnic. Andy, Helen, Barney, and Thelma Lou are going. Unfortunately, before the picnic, Barney mistakes Mayberry Security Bank president Mr. Meldrim and a bank examiner for bank robbers. The ensuing public ridicule bothers Barney, and he initially refuses to go on to the picnic. However, Andy assures him that they will find a nice, quiet spot away from the crowd.

At the picnic, Andy and Helen decide to explore a mine cave. Its nickname, according to Andy, is the Lost Lover's Cave. The name begins to ring true when Andy and Helen witness part of the cavern collapsing behind them. Fortunately, Andy notices an exit at the opposite end of the cave, and he and Helen escape without injury. What they cannot know is that Barney and Thelma Lou entered the cave awhile after them. Barney saw the cave-in occur. He and Thelma Lou logically believe that Andy and Helen are trapped inside.

Barney alerts the picnicking townsfolk and organizes a rescue operation. Meanwhile, Andy and Helen have hitched a ride home to clean up. They overhear a radio report about Barney's rescue effort, and Andy realizes that unless he and Helen are found in the cave, Barney will be ridiculed even more.

He and Helen will not let that happen. They return to the cave unnoticed and find a spot near the cave-in to slump over and look appropriately exhausted. When Barney succeeds in "rescuing" them, the town hails him as a hero.

CAST NOTES. Regulars: **Andy Griffith, Don Knotts, Ronny Howard, Jim Nabors, Aneta Corsault,** and **Betty Lynn.** **Warren Parker** returns as Mayberry Security Bank president Mr. Meldrim.

Joe Hamilton portrays Choney Lathan, and **Roy Engel** appears as Jud.

EPISODE NOTES. 1. Barney claims that if a bat or a moth lays eggs in your hair, you will go crazy. 2. The license plate number of the truck that Andy and Helen get a ride from is H-14105. 3. Gomer said that his cousin, Goober, once got lost in a cave while chasing a skunk. The skunk's scent led him back out, and Goober made it into a pet. 4. Gomer says his cousin Goober is ugly, but not stupid. 5. Sarah (the never-seen switchboard operator) says that her mother hurt her hip when she fell at the bowling alley. 6. Helen makes an apple crumb pie, while Thelma Lou prepared fried chicken for the picnic. 7. After the rescue, the headline of *The Mayberry Gazette* reads, "DEPUTY FIFE HERO IN CAVE RESCUE." A picture of Barney is featured. This front page will be seen framed on a courthouse wall for years to come.

"Andy and Opie's Pal"

Episode #110. Air date: 1-13-64. Writer: Harvey Bullock. Director: Dick Crenna.

A boy named Frederick Bowden III and his mother are new to Mayberry. They hail from Erie, Pennsylvania, but they're going to be living in "the Friendly City." They are currently staying with Miss Edwards. The boy is Opie's age, and the two youngsters quickly get to know each other. The lad from Erie is known as "Trey" because he is a third. Trey's father is deceased. Trey's wide-eyed response when Opie mentions that *his* father is sheriff of Mayberry makes it obvious that the boy longs for a father figure.

Andy gives special attention to Trey, allowing him to hold Barney's unloaded gun and taking him on lake patrol (a treat usually reserved for Opie). Of course, Opie's nose gets bent out of joint. In fact, he grows quite jealous. When Trey drops in on one of Opie's top-secret football practices, the two get into a shoving match, instigated by Opie. Barney drops by and stops the action. He tells Opie that if Andy knew he and Trey were fighting, he would probably not allow him to play with Trey. That statement sparks an idea in Opie's head, and soon he is walking into the courthouse with his face covered in bandages. He tells Andy that he and Trey had a fight. Andy takes a peek under a bandage and discovers that Opie is absolutely unharmed. He realizes that Opie has pushed away a friend simply because he mistakenly believed Trey was interfering in their relationship.

To illustrate to Opie how a friend feels when he is intentionally excluded, Andy tells Barney that he would prefer he not come along on their usual fishing outing. Barney, unaware of Andy's little game, is very hurt. When Opie sees Barney's reaction, he realizes that Trey is probably feeling the same way. Opie apologizes to Trey, and on the following day, the boys join Andy and Barney for a day of fishing. Opie gives Trey his prized genuine, full-size, regulation football, which was once used in a State College football game. Andy says his son gave Trey more than that: He gave him a genuine, full-size, regulation *friend*.

CAST NOTES. Regulars: **Andy Griffith, Don Knotts, Ronny Howard,** and **Frances Bavier. Richard Keith** and **Dennis Rush** return as Johnny Paul Jason and Howie Pruitt, respectively.

David A. Bailey appears for the first time as Trey Bowden, a role he would play in several episodes. Bailey appeared throughout the 1960s in a variety of television shows, such as *Dennis the Menace* and *Bewitched*. He also appeared in some movies, including *One Man's Way* (1964) and the Disney flick *Follow Me Boys!* (1966).

EPISODE NOTES. 1. Trey has a nine-bladed knife. He also has a model plane with a gasoline motor. 2. Barney accidentally fires his gun while explaining gun safety to Trey on the Taylors' front porch. 3. Barney's nicknames for his gun are Old Roscoe, Heater, the Old Persuader, Rod, or, as Andy says, Revolver. 4. Opie's football jersey sports the number 14. He is the quarterback. Johnny Paul and Howie are two of his teammates. When Opie calls, "55, 66, 77, 88 and 99," it means everybody out for a pass. 5. June 23, 1952, was an eventful day in Mayberry. It was a hot Saturday afternoon and Barney was upset because Andy "beat him to the punch" in escorting the state's queen of the Apricot Festival. Andy gave her a tour of the furniture factory, the beaver dam, and the diner. Barney had purchased a new shirt at Patterson's (for $3.95) just for the occasion. Though he denies it, Barney has clearly not recovered from all the resentment he felt back then. 6. Miss Moran was Andy and Barney's fourth grade teacher. That was when they first started hanging out together. 7. Juanita was a waitress at the diner in 1952. 8. Gomer (and Barney) believe that Jesse Pearson, owner of Pearson's Sweet Shop, may be running an illegal contest. Anyone who finds a pink center in one of the peppermints purchased at the shop wins a free peppermint. If a green center is found, the lucky winner gets a flashlight. Gomer is peeved because he has purchased 22 peppermints and each had just a plain white center. 9. Opie and Trey become blood brothers, using red barn paint to mark their arms.

"Aunt Bee the Crusader"

Episode #111. Air date 1-20-64. Writer: John Whedon. Director: Coby Ruskin.

Aunt Bee's egg salesman and friend, Mr. Frisby, informs her that the county has notified him that his house is being condemned. The county is constructing a stretch of highway that will run through Mr. Frisby's current property. If he does not move out voluntarily, he will be forcibly evicted. Obviously, Mr. Frisby is unhappy about the situation. He tells Aunt Bee that he was born on that land, as was his father. Yet he seems resigned to leaving. He appears to be a dejected and rather pathetic individual.

Aunt Bee is appalled by his story. She tells him that she will have a word with Andy. Meanwhile, Mr. Frisby promises Opie that he can have his beloved rooster, Beauregard ("Beau"), after he is evicted. The only requirement is that Opie build the bird a suitable coop. Opie is thrilled, and he soon begins making plans to do that. In a giving mood, apparently, Mr. Frisby gives Aunt Bee his mustache cup. It is decorated with her favorite flower, the rose.

Later, Aunt Bee turns to Andy to try to help her friend. Unfortunately, Andy can do nothing to change the situation. If forcible eviction becomes necessary, Andy must be the one to do it. Aunt Bee tells Andy that he should be more interested in running off moonshiners, not good folks like Mr. Frisby. Andy insists that, as a county employee, he must do his duty. He reasons that the highway is sorely needed to make it more safe and easy for emergency vehicles to get about. As it is now, they have to go around by Fisher's Pond and cross a wobbly old bridge. When Aunt Bee accuses Andy of disliking Mr. Frisby, he admits that she is right. However, he tells her that his distaste for the man has no bearing on his duty to enforce the law. He reminds Aunt Bee that Mr. Frisby will be well compensated for giving up his land. An angry Aunt Bee believes that Andy has no regard for Mr. Frisby's emotional welfare. When Andy discovers the gifts that Mr. Frisby has given or promised to Aunt Bee and Opie, he suspects that the man is playing on their sympathy. Ultimately, Aunt Bee stops speaking to her nephew. Andy insists that the interests of a community must come before individual interests.

Aunt Bee and many of her female friends picket the courthouse, hoping to pressure Andy into getting the county to halt its plans. They only succeed in frightening Barney.

Later, Andy gets word that the Highway Department is about to bulldoze the Frisby farm. He and Barney go to the farm to ensure that Mr. Frisby has vacated the premises. When they arrive, they discover that he has not. In fact, Aunt Bee and her friends are blocking the bulldozer's path. The group sings "We Shall Not Be Moved," and they chant in unison, refusing to obey Andy's orders to disperse.

Andy begins moving Mr. Frisby's belongings out of the shack, while Opie and Barney go to the henhouse to free the chickens. Opie becomes concerned when he is unable to find Beau. When he does find him, he brings him to Andy and exclaims that the rooster is ill. Beau *is* acting strangely, crowing wildly and staggering around. Andy quickly recognizes that the bird is drunk! Opie says he found the rooster in a cellar, under the henhouse. He adds that he found a trap-door. This sounds very suspicious to Andy. He asks Barney to keep the women busy while he investigates the situation.

Moments later, Andy emerges from the henhouse, carrying a still. He said he found five more illegal stills in the cellar beneath the henhouse. It seems that eggs are not the *only* product that Mr. Frisby sells.

The women are rightfully upset, and they let Mr. Frisby know what they think of him. Later, Aunt Bee apologizes to Andy for her foolish behavior. Andy accepts her apology and then candidly admits that he never trusted "that sneaky old buzzard."

MEMORABLE SCENE. Barney's "third degree" questioning of Otis.

CAST NOTES. Regulars: **Andy Griffith, Don Knotts, Ronny Howard, Frances Bavier,** and **Hal Smith.**

Charles Lane, a veteran character actor, portrays Mr. Frisby. Lane is best known for his portrayal of Homer Bedlow on the hit series *Petticoat Junction* (1963-1968). He also may be recognized as Mr. Barnsdahl from *The Lucy Show.*

Mary Lansing, often seen in this series in various roles, appears as one of Aunt Bee's crusading friends. **Noreen Gammill** also appears.

EPISODE NOTES. 1. Aunt Bee tells Otis that she prays for him. She suggests that he speak with Reverend Tucker about his drinking problem. (*Otis's* problem, not the Reverend's.) 2. Barney gets caught up in Aunt Bee's anger at the county. He calls all county employees "a bunch of goldbrickers and deadheads." Andy reminds him that they themselves are county employees. 3. Among the protest signs the women carry are "The County Has No Heart"; "Is There No Mercy?"; "Don't Patronize This Jail"; "Stop The Land Grab" and Aunt Bee's sign, "Sheriff Taylor Is Unfair." 4. To try to keep the ladies busy, Barney asks them to sing, "Row, Row, Row, Your Boat." 5. Some of the women's chants are "Stand your ground," "Move us, too," and "We will not sing."

"Barney's Sidecar"

Episode #112. Air date: 1-27-64. Writers: Jim Fritzell and Everett Greenbaum. Director: Coby Ruskin.

To the dismay of Andy, Barney purchases a World War I motorcycle (model RJ300), complete with a sidecar, at a war surplus auction held in Mount Pilot. Barney claims he can use it to catch speeders on Highway 6, by setting up a "checkpoint chickie." Barney also shows Andy the accessories he bought. These include a helmet, goggles, a leather jacket, gloves, and gauntlets. He is a sight to behold, yet the ensuing public ridicule does not discourage him. He hands out several warning tickets to truck drivers, even though Andy has always allowed truck drivers to go a little over the posted speed limit to enable them to climb the uphill area of Highway 6, known as Turner's Grade.

Thanks to Barney's zealousness, the truckers begin to avoid the speed trap by driving through town at all hours. This annoys everyone. Barney angers the townsfolk further when he starts handing out tickets with a vengeance. The good people of Mayberry have had enough of this motorcycle menace. Even Aunt Bee finds herself suggesting that a wire be strung, neck high, across the road, in order to bring Barney and his motorcycle to an abrupt end.

At his wit's end, Andy uses Opie's wood burning set to create a plaque, which he conceals under the sidecar seat. He then "discovers" the plaque and shows it to Barney. The newly inscribed piece of wood reads: "First motorcycle to cross the Marne River — Battle of Chateau Thierry, 6-12-18. Passenger: Black Jack Pershing. Driver: Corporal Nate Jackson, A.E.F." Obviously, Andy says, the motorcycle has historical significance. He convinces a reluctant Barney to do his patriotic duty and donate his beloved motorcycle and sidecar to the Mayberry National Guard Armory.

CAST NOTES. Regulars: **Andy Griffith, Don Knotts, Ronny Howard,** and **Frances Bavier.**

Joe Hamilton returns. This time he is a prankster named Jase. **Virginia Sale,** best know as Selma Plout on the hit series *Petticoat Junction,* portrays Mrs. Beggs. **Rodney Bell, Ray Kellogg, Hal Landon,** and **Jerry Brutsche** also appear.

EPISODE NOTES. 1. Mrs. Beggs nearly got run off of Highway 6 by a woman speeder. Mrs. Beggs's sister, Tillie, was the victim of a bad dentist in Nashville as a child and, as a result, has very long teeth. In school she was nicknamed "the Beaver." 2. Andy has to make a trip to the Millstone farm in this episode. 3. Opie received the wood burning set as a birthday present. 4. Neither Barney nor his mother can stand for anyone else to wear their hats. 5. Andy calls Barney "Baron Von Richtofen." 6. Charlie Phelps transferred the Mayberry insignia onto Barney's sidecar. 7. Barney stops Edgar J. Masters' truck at "checkpoint chickie." He also stops a truck bearing the license plate L-73218. 8. The Feed and Grain store in Mayberry is shown in this episode. 9. Mayberry has no psychiatrist. 10. Barney refers to the Smithsonian Institution as "The Smith Brothers' Institution." 11. Some of the World War I veterans who reside in Mayberry are a man named Al, Burt Stevens, and the Milo boys. 12. Andy pulls over a *tank* on Highway 6, believing it to be another of Barney's outlandish purchases. However, the driver is Major Hobart of the Army's Twenty-second division, on his way to a military display. 13. The famous World War I song "Over There" is put to good use in this episode.

"My Fair Ernest T. Bass"

Episode #113. Air date: 2-3-64. Writers: Everett Greenbaum and Jim Fritzell. Director: Earl Bellamy.

Guess who is back in Mayberry, wreaking havoc? Yes, it's mountain wild man Ernest T. Bass. This time, he has crashed a social at Mrs. Wiley's home. The hostess describes the following events to Andy and Barney: First, a man burst into the house uninvited, demanding to meet a woman. Next, he stuck his hand in the punch bowl, ate every bit of the watermelon rind, and topped that off by soaking paper napkins in the punch and throwing them at the ceiling. A guest named Mr. Schwump managed to pinch the crazed man, but it did not end the rampage. He just giggled and jumped away. Finally, when Mrs. Wiley ordered him to leave, the man lost all control, tossed a rock through one of her windows, and ran off.

Although Mrs. Wiley and her guests did not know the man, Andy is positive it can only be Ernest T. Bass. He and Barney conduct a lengthy search, even checking under two houses. Exhausted by their efforts, they return to the courthouse, only to discover that the elusive Ernest T. Bass has jailed himself.

Atop Andy's desk is the uniform that Barney

had previously given him (see episode 99, "Ernest T. Bass Joins the Army") so that Ernest T. might be able to attract a girl back home. Ernest T. Bass once believed that wearing a uniform would make him irresistible. He brought it back because it simply did not work out that way. His explanation for his recent misbehavior is that he is lovesick and lonely. He explains that he tried courting Hog Winslow's daughter, Hogette (it's a French name). He found a pretty rock, tied a pretty note to it, and even made a pretty toss — right through her window. Unfortunately, the rock hit Hogette on the head. The resulting wound needed seven stitches. Now she is engaged to the taxidermist who sewed up her head, and Ernest T. has just about given up on romance. He threatens that he might just find a cave and "hermitize" himself. Andy takes pity on him and decides to attempt to help him. He will clean him up and teach him to act more like a gentleman.

Andy discovers that Ernest T. is a very slow learner. First, he tries to teach him manners at the dinner table. Next, he works on the social manner of how to properly enter a room. Barney is present at Andy's to witness the spectacle of Ernest T. Bass bouncing down the staircase and leaping into a chair. Barney tells Andy that he is fighting a hopeless cause. Still in hilarious fashion, Barney tries to help by pantomiming entering a room.

Andy works very hard trying to improve Ernest T.'s diction. He asks him to repeat the phrase "How do you do, Mrs. Wiley?" many times. Ernest T. has the annoying habit of talking through his nose. He tells Andy that he does it on purpose so he can talk whilst he eats. Nevertheless, Andy keeps working with him. His plan is to pass Ernest T. off as a Raleigh man named Oliver Gossage. Andy actually does have a cousin by that name, though family and friends call him "Ollie."

Andy outfits Ernest T. in brand new clothing. The transformation is so complete that even Barney fails to recognize him. Andy chooses Mrs. Wiley's weekly social to showcase his creation. If Ernest T. goes unrecognized by Mrs. Wiley, then Andy has truly accomplished something amazing. As Barney, exclaims, "If you wrote this into a play, no one would believe it!"

Incredibly, the charade appears to be working. Ernest T. is the picture of restraint. He limits himself to uttering only the short phrases Andy rehearsed with him. Mrs. Wiley speaks to Ernest T. privately, and she believes that he is from back bay Boston. She tells Andy to encourage "Mr. Gossage" to dance with her niece, Ramona Ancrum. Ernest T. dances Ramona out to the front porch and tells her about his good manners. She is impressed. He brags about his strength, and he wins her over when he lifts her off the ground!

Mrs. Wiley summons all of her guests to participate in a tag dance. This proves to be Ernest T.'s undoing. He wants to dance only with Ramona, who he calls "Romeena." When he is tagged by another man, he does give her up — briefly. He, in turn, politely tags the fellow back, so that he can resume his dance with Ramona. When the man does not respond, Ernest T. becomes irate and breaks a vase over the man's head. Suddenly, Mrs. Wiley recognizes who Oliver Gossage really is. She calls him a "creature," which further enrages Ernest T. He begins to go after *her*, even reaching for a chair to use as a weapon. Fortunately, Andy and Barney somehow manage to wrestle him out of the house.

When he calms down, Ernest T. sincerely thanks Andy for trying to help him, and resigns himself to bachelorhood. However, all ends well when Ramona comes running to him and tells him that she would love to spend more time with him. They celebrate their newfound joy by running around like children and madly hopping over tree stumps. As Andy puts it, "There really is a woman for every man!" If they wrote this into a play, no one would believe it.

CAST NOTES. Regulars: **Andy Griffith, Don Knotts, Ronny Howard,** and **Frances Bavier. Howard Morris** returns as the incomparable Ernest T. Bass.

Jackie Joseph, a wonderful light comedic actress who had featured roles in both *The Bob Newhart Show* and *The Doris Day Show,* portrays Ramona Ancrum. **Doris Packer,** a familiar character actress who had two different roles on the long-running series *The Many Loves of Dobie Gillis,* appears as Mrs. Wiley.

EPISODE NOTES. 1. Barney has borrowed a book entitled *Psychological Aspects of the Law.* 2. Barney refers to *The Count of Monte Cristo.* 3. Barney wears his salt and pepper suit to the social at Mrs. Wiley's. 4. A woman named Mildred serves refreshments at Mrs. Wiley's. 5. Barney claims that the ladies at the social are all "dogs." He tells Andy that "if you flew a quail through the house, every woman in the place would point!" 6. This episode mentions the events that took place in episode 99, "Ernest T. Bass Joins the Army." 7. Barney pronounces "demure" as "demore." 8. Ramona Ancrum is the granddaughter of "Rotten Ray" 'Ancrum. Mr. Ancrum came down from the hills in 1870 and burned the town of Mayberry down. Soon afterward, he opened the Ancrum Charcoal Company, which still exists. 9. Ernest T. tells Ramona that he once hoisted a goat into the air while a veterinarian gave it a shot. 10. The mysterious Mr. Schwump makes his debut in this episode. Avid fans of this series know to look for him in a crowd. He appears in several episodes and is easy to spot. He is the grinning man with a bad toupee. 11. Obviously, this episode was inspired by George Bernard Shaw's play *Pgymalion*. It was made into a film of the same title in 1938, and set to music in the Broadway smash *My Fair Lady*.

"Prisoner of Love"

Episode #114. Air date: 2-10-64. Writer: Harvey Bullock. Director: Earl Bellamy.

Barney has his evening planned. As he and Andy relax in front of the courthouse, Barney states that he will go home, change, and then go over to Thelma Lou's and watch "that George Raft movie" on television. Thelma Lou will probably prepare a pan of cashew fudge.

Moments later, Sergeant Jacobs, of the state police, calls Andy and informs him that his men will be bringing in a recently captured prisoner for the evening. Either Andy or Barney will have to spend the night at the courthouse. Barney is anxious to get away and is relieved when Andy agrees to stay. He asks Barney to delay leaving for a few minutes while he runs over to the drugstore to pick up a magazine. During this time, the prisoner is brought in. Barney is shocked when he discovers that the prisoner is a gorgeous woman. The police inform him that she has been charged with grand larceny for stealing jewels. They believe that she may have a partner who is still on the loose. She will be jailed in Mayberry until the manhunt ends.

Barney is quickly mesmerized by her beauty. He falls all over himself scrambling to find a match to light her cigarette. Andy returns, but he is initially unaware of the female prisoner. Barney, enchanted by the woman, informs Andy that *he* will be happy to stay. Andy believes that Barney is merely being polite, and he sends his unselfish deputy home.

Suddenly, Andy catches his first glimpse of his voluptuous prisoner and does a double take. He shares a few awkward exchanges with her, but then Barney unexpectedly returns. He states that he has already seen the George Raft movie, and anyway, it's a deputy's duty to watch any prisoner. Both men are there when the lady requests an extra pillow, and both hurry to accommodate her. To give her some privacy, they drape a bed sheet over her cell. After bidding her good night, they turn off the courthouse lights. The lamp in her cell is still lighted, and the

lawmen enjoy a glimpse of her shapely silhouette as she undresses and readies herself for bed.

A drunken Otis spoils this voyeuristic moment by barging into the courthouse. He complains about his cell, which has been scavenged by Andy and Barney in order to make their prisoner more comfortable. The men realize that Otis cannot stay. Barney loses the coin toss that decides who will escort Otis to his home.

With the lights back on, the lovely prisoner asks Andy if he will sit and talk. He is delighted to oblige. After awhile, she thanks him for not asking why or how she ended up in this situation. Moments later, she seems to be having trouble opening a case in her cell, and Andy volunteers to help open it. Inside the cell, Andy is overwhelmed by his strong attraction to her. Just as they are about to kiss, Barney returns. Andy manages to exit the cell before his deputy actually walks in the door. Andy realizes that he must put some distance between himself and temptation, so he tells Barney that he has decided to go home after all. Yet the prisoner remains on Andy's mind. The scent of her perfume has rubbed off on his shirt collar, reminding him of the intimate moment they shared. Meanwhile, Barney has been lured into the woman's cell and is attempting to unlock her case.

As Andy is contemplating the evening's events, he suddenly bolts from his porch and makes a beeline for the courthouse. He arrives just in time to nab the pretty prisoner as she is escaping. Her departure had gone unnoticed by Barney, who was still working diligently on her case.

Later, when the state troopers come to retrieve the prisoner and take her to Raleigh, Andy and Barney watch her continuing to work her feminine charms as she had so effectively on them. As Andy says, "Well, you can't blame a girl for tryin'."

CAST NOTES. Regulars: **Andy Griffith, Don Knotts, Frances Bavier,** and **Hal Smith.**

Susan Oliver, a familiar character actress who may be best known for portraying Laura Horton on the popular soap opera *Days of Our Lives* in the mid-1970s, stars as the alluring (and unnamed) prisoner. **James Seay,** who appeared as Agent Bowden in episode 8, "The Haunted House," here portrays a state policeman.

EPISODE NOTES. 1. Shy Mayberrian Henry Gilley dated Tyla Lee Vernon for 16 years before he finally got the nerve to propose. She accepted, and they live in a little yellow house, two up from the corner (from the courthouse). 2. Barney finds himself locked inside cell #1, the lady prisoner's cell, after she leaves. 3. Once again, Barney gives his middle initial as "P." 4. Otis's doctor told him that moonshine would blind him sooner or later. 5. Otis escaped from Barney three times as he was being taken back home. 6. The state policeman who puts the "prisoner of love" in the squad car is named Fred. 7. The unnamed prisoner was given the name Angela Carroll in an unproduced script. Perhaps it was decided that the lack of a name added to the sense of mystery. This episode is very sensual and unique.

"Hot Rod Otis"

Episode #115. Air date: 2-17-64. Writer: Harvey Bullock. Director: Earl Bellamy.

Otis surprises Andy and Barney when he purchases a car. They believe that Otis will not be responsible enough to operate the automobile safely. Otis points out that he has had a driver's license for years but did not own a car. In order to earn enough to buy a convertible, Otis worked at an (unspecified) night job for a month. Barney decides to spy on Otis to ensure that he drives only when he is sober.

One night, when Otis gets drunk during a party at Charlie Varney's house, Andy and Barney see him passing out next to his new automobile. They haul him off to jail, where they play a trick on him. Hoping to discourage him from wanting to drive, they awaken him from his stupor, and then they ignore him. Otis notices that they are talking about how tragic it is that he was killed while driving drunk! They sing a mournful song and put on a convincing display of sorrow. Otis believes he is dead. He passes out again, and is quickly revived by Andy and Barney. Otis realizes he is alive. He tells them that he had a nightmare. He adds that he is glad that he sold his car to his friend Charlie Varney earlier that evening. He had been uncertain that he could refrain from drinking and driving, so he sold the car to eliminate any risk. Andy and Barney are very relieved.

MEMORABLE SCENE. Barney using little toy cars to test Otis's reactions to hypothetical traffic situations.

CAST NOTES. Regulars: **Andy Griffith, Don Knotts,** and **Hal Smith.**

EPISODE NOTES. 1. Andy recites the tale of "Jack and the Beanstalk" to Otis to help him fall asleep. 2. Otis loves fairy tales such as "Rumplestilskin." 3. Barney says "facitious," meaning to say "facetious." 4. Otis's license plate number is (the much used) AY-321. 5. Otis buys booze at the County Line Cafe near Mount Pilot. 6. Andy refers to the Two Mile Hill and the Old Plank Road in this episode. 7. Barney shakes down a gumball machine outside of the grocery store. 8. Barney jok-

ingly says that Otis may have gone to an alligator farm in Florida. 9. Andy and Barney sing "The Vacant Chair," a song about family members mourning their loved one killed in the Civil War. The subject of the song, Lieutenant John William Grout of Massachusetts, was killed in the battle of Balls Bluff, Virginia, in October 1861. The following month, Henry S. Washburn wrote a poem about the Grout family's anguish. The words were set to music by noted songwriter George F. Root.

"The Song Festers"

Episode #116. Air date: 2-24-64. Writers: Jim Fritzell and Everett Greenbaum. Director: Earl Bellamy.

Choir Director John Masters is at his wit's end. The Mayberry choir is lacking a good tenor soloist, and the Chorale Concert is just days away. Barney has been filling the vacancy in practices, but his vocal ability is limited. Barney, however, is not aware of his limitations. He has been taking voice lessons from Miss Eleanora Poultice. Miss Poultice compares Barney to a former client named Leonard Blush. Mr. Blush walked in off of the street one day, and two years later, he was singing "The Star-Spangled Banner" at the opening of the County Insecticide Convention! Nowadays, he has his own radio show on the third Tuesday of every month. It originates from Mount Pilot on station YLRB. His rise to fame was "meteoric," as Miss Poultice says.

Andy tries to prepare Barney for a letdown by warning him that John Masters may find a good tenor, and if he does, the deputy will be replaced as soloist. Barney believes he has little to fear.

One day at practice, John Masters and his choir overhear someone singing outside of the building where they are rehearsing. The beautiful music is coming from Gomer Pyle. He was changing a tire on Mr. Masters' car when he began to sing. John is anxious to audition Gomer. When he does, he realizes that he has found his tenor soloist. He asks Andy to explain things to Barney. Andy tries to cushion the blow, but the news breaks Barney's heart.

One day, while Gomer practices, Barney sits alone in the next room. When he believes the building is empty, Barney begins to envision himself at the big concert, ready to deliver a solo. But reality seeps in, and he is devastated. He sings softly and sadly. Unbeknownst to Barney, a friend has been watching.

The big night comes, and Gomer hoarsely informs Mr. Masters that he has lost his voice. He explains that he had been flushing a radiator and somehow the antifreeze squirted him in the face. He will be unable to sing. This is very upsetting to the choir director, because the program is due to begin very shortly. Andy and Gomer indicate that Barney knows the solo part and, in a pinch, could handle the job. Andy scrambles to locate Barney. He finds him at Miss Poultice's home. A stubborn Barney refuses initially, but Miss Poultice shames him into agreeing to perform.

Moments before the concert begins, Gomer unintentionally reveals his charade by yelling, "Sing it good, Barney!" A quick-thinking John Masters incorporates Gomer back into the choir as the curtain rises.

The chosen selection is "Santa Lucia." When it is time for the solo, both Barney and Gomer are reluctant to step forward. The rest of the choir anxiously holds a very long note. Barney and Gomer nod at each other to go ahead. They step forward, then retreat, in unison. Andy finds the solution. He brings himself, Barney, and Gomer forward, and they perform the solo as a trio.

Their performance is a big hit, especially with Miss Poultice. She believes that the threesome should embark on a singing career. If not for their deciding to keep their day jobs, they just might have eclipsed The Beatles.

CAST NOTES. Regulars: **Andy Griffith, Don Knotts, Frances Bavier,** and **Jim Nabors. Olan Soule** returns as choir conductor John Masters.

Reta Shaw, who previously appeared in episode 74, "Convicts-at-Large," returns to the series as Barney's voice teacher, Miss Eleanora Poultice. **Barbara Griffith,** the wife of Andy Griffith when this episode was filmed, appears as Sharon, a member of the choir. She can be seen standing next to Barney during the practices and at the Chorale performance.

EPISODE NOTES. 1. Barney wears his salt and pepper suit to Miss Poultice's and to the Chorale Concert. 2. Barney mispronounces "larynx" as "laranyx." 3. Barney's "Laranyx and Voice Box Calisthenic": "Me They Me They, IOU, IOU, IOU." 4. Miss Poultice teaches piano and the dance lessons, too. 5. Barney tells Andy that Leonard Blush does all the vocals on the Ethel Page Organ Recital shows. Andy only recalls a canary singing in the background. About 10 years ago, Miss Page and her canary performed on Sunday afternoons at the Pot O'Honey restaurant. 6. John Masters states that Mayberry has a population of 2,000. 7. Andy says that tenor Bruce Flower could only sing high after a fight with his mother. 8. When Andy tells Barney that he is being replaced as a soloist, Barney asks if either Morton Downey or Kenny Baker is being considered as his replacement. 9. Gomer is scheduled to recharge the car battery of a woman named Miss Drum. 10. A lady named Hazel plays the piano for the choir. 11. Mr. Masters states that the choir arrangement for their featured song, "Santa Lucia," came from New York. 12. Gomer claims that he not only pumps gas and changes tires, but does engine work as well. This is an amazing advancement for him. In previous episodes, he left such work to Wally. 13. Barney's warm-up song is "Now Is the Month of Maying." 14. Ric Ricardi supervised the choral music used in this episode.

"The Shoplifters"

Episode #117. Air date: 3-2-64. Writers: Bill Idelson and Sam Bobrick. Director: Coby Ruskin.

An upset Ben Weaver complains to Andy that his department store is being robbed. He has discovered that, according to his inventory, several items are missing, including a silver tea set. Ironically, business has been good lately, with folks coming from out of town to shop at the store. Ben asks Andy to provide police protection. Andy urges him to keep a watchful eye on the situation, and he lets Mr. Weaver know that he and Barney will do the best they can.

That evening, Barney calls off his date with "the only girl (he) ever really gave a hoot about," Thelma Lou. He plans to hang around Weaver's Department Store in hopes of catching the thief. He does this without the knowledge of Andy, Mr. Weaver, or Asa Breeney, the store's elderly night watchman. Before Barney arrives at the site, however, Mr. Weaver quietly enters his store in order to determine if Asa is, as Andy inferred, napping on the job. To his dismay, Andy is right. Ben starts to awaken the dozing guard, but he hears a noise outside. The noise is actually Barney, checking to ensure that the doors are locked. Because Ben entered from the rear door, Barney finds the rear entrance unlocked. Alarmed, he enters the building cautiously and puts his bullet in his gun. Then Ben mistakes Barney for an intruder, and vice versa. It is difficult to see who is who in the darkened building. The confusion leads to minor mayhem, especially when Andy drops by and turns on the lights. Barney causes such a commotion that even Asa jumps to his feet.

Once calm is restored, Ben lays the blame for the thefts at the feet of the sleepy watchman. However, Andy points out that the robberies must be occurring while the store is open; otherwise, the thieves would use the cover of night to rob Weaver of his entire inventory. Ben is aghast at the thought of shoplifting, but concedes Andy is probably right.

The next morning, Barney tells Andy he believes Ben might be staging the thefts so he can collect the insurance. Andy dismisses the idea as "hogwash," even though his deputy is dying to take a look in the trunk of Weaver's car. Andy states that Ben is one of Mayberry's most respected businessmen and one of the town's most loyal churchgoers.

Andy asks Barney to just walk among the customers at Weaver's and try to be inconspicuous. Instead, Barney places himself in the sporting goods section and poses as a mannequin. Of course, his cover is blown before long, and Mr. Weaver believes the effort was useless and ridiculous. However, Barney believes that he has discovered a shoplifter, and he rushes over to a little old lady and demands to see the contents of her bag. The woman is indignant, but she does allow the lawmen and Mr. Weaver to watch as she reveals that all she has is her knitting and her bible. Barney is flabbergasted, and Mr. Weaver is profusely apologetic. He angrily orders Andy to make Barney leave the premises.

As the lawmen stand outside the store, Andy explains to Barney he did a couple of things wrong. First, he should have been absolutely certain the woman was guilty. Secondly, he should never have made a shoplifting arrest inside the store. Rather, he should have waited until she was outside. Otherwise, she could claim she intended to pay.

When the accused woman exits the store, Andy detains her. He asks Barney to retrieve a bathroom scale from the store. Meanwhile, the outraged woman threatens to sue the store, which upsets Ben greatly. When Andy finally weighs her, Barney and Mr. Weaver are surprised when the petite woman weighs in at 163 pounds! Andy opens her overcoat to reveal a large cache of jewelry and silver. As Barney exclaims, "She's a traveling pawnshop." Andy had become suspicious when he accidentally bumped into her in the store and she "clanked." He adds that "Little old ladies ought not *clank*," and Barney chimes in with, "Unless they're headed for the *clink*!" Case closed.

CAST NOTES. Regulars: **Andy Griffith, Don Knotts, Ronny Howard**, and **Frances Bavier. Charles P. Thompson** returns as Asa Breeney. **Clint Howard** returns as Leon.

Tol Avery, who will appear in various roles in this series, makes his first and last appearance as Ben Weaver. Avery enjoyed a long career in television and film. He had regular roles in two television series: *The Thin Man* (1957–1958), as Lt. Steve King, and *Slattery's People*, (1964–1965), as Bert

Metcalf, Speaker of the House. Avery appeared in many anthology drama productions. His guest-starring roles are numerous. Among them are roles in: *Batman, Dragnet, Mission:Impossible, Mr. Ed, Room 222, The Wild Wild West, Maverick, F-Troop, Gomer Pyle, U.S.M.C.*, and *Get Smart*. Among his better known movies are *Where Danger Lives* (1950, one of several films he made with Robert Mitchum), *North by Northwest* (1959, an Alfred Hitchcock classic), *Hotel* (1967), and *Maurie*, the Maurice Stokes story (1973).

Lurene Tuttle, who portrayed Annabelle Silby in episode 8, "Opie's Charity," appears as the unnamed shoplifter. **Mary Lansing, Jewel Rose**, and **Elizabeth Harrower** all appear as customers in Weaver's store.

EPISODE NOTES. 1. Some of Andy and Barney's gossip: (1) Mrs. Burton is a sweet little woman, but her husband, Sam, likes to hit "the sauce"; (2) Dick Rennicker wears a toupee; and (3) Barney says there is a story going around about lingerie shop employee Myra Koonce. We never get to hear the full story, but, it has something to do with "that fellah who came through from Chattanooga." 2. Barney mispronounces "lingerie" as "lanjerie." 3. The lady shoplifter manages to steal Barney's gun. 4. Mrs. Larch catches Barney hiding behind a rack of clothes at Weaver's Department Store. 5. Asa Breeney evidently has three jobs. Besides acting as Weaver's night watchman, we have seen him as a part-time desk clerk at the Mayberry Hotel and as a security guard at the bank. 6. Weaver's Department Store is located at 501 Main Street. 7. Barney is amused by a beer can opener that has a tiny umbrella attached to it. He is told by Ben Weaver to either pay $1.25 for it or put it back on the counter. 8. Thelma Lou's telephone number is given as 596. (In episode 68, it was 247.) 9. A sign above the employee's coffeepot at Weaver's says: "Don't Forget to Feed the Kitty." 10. Barney hates it when Andy gets "obtuse." 11. Barney claims that Andy is wrong when he says Ben Weaver "knows every hymn in the book." He tells Andy to watch Ben the next time "Leaning On the Everlasting Arms" is played. He claims Ben doesn't know the words....he just moves his lips. 12. Leon offers Andy and Barney a bite of his partially eaten peanut butter and jelly sandwich. He offers it to Barney when the deputy is acting as a mannequin. 13. Barney states that he weighs 132 pounds. 14. This episode earned the writers, Bill Idelson and Sam Bobrick, the prestigious Writer's Guild of America Award for Episodic Comedy Writing.

"Andy's Vacation"

Episode #118. Air date: 3-9-64. Writers: Everett Greenbaum and Jim Fritzell. Director: Jeffrey Hayden.

The daily grind is getting to Andy, and he is receptive to Barney's suggestion to take some time off. During his one-week vacation, Andy plans to read his favorite magazine, *National Geographic*, and do a little gardening at home. Meanwhile, Barney deputizes Gomer, and the (less than dynamic) duo manage to cause some minor mayhem in town. They annoy Andy, who finds that he can't have a moment's peace. In order to get away from it all, Andy heads for the mountains.

Back at the courthouse, Barney is given a prisoner to guard. The state police caught the man after he escaped from Lentwood Prison, some 400 miles from Mayberry. Barney promises maximum security, which means he will keep the jail cell keys in the desk drawer. Of course, the prisoner soon escapes, much to Barney's dismay. The felon flees to the mountains — where he happens to run into Andy.

Andy's experienced eyes tell him that this man is not your average camper. He quickly captures the man and handcuffs him to a tree before heading to a ranger station for additional help. Unfortunately, Barney and Gomer, who have come to the mountains to find Andy, mistakenly set the escapee free. Next, Barney mistakes a returning Andy for the crook and jumps him from behind.

After explaining the mistake, Barney and Gomer continue bumbling around, while Andy recaptures the prisoner once and for all.

CAST NOTES. Regulars: **Andy Griffith, Don Knotts, Frances Bavier,** and **Jim Nabors.**

Allan Melvin returns. He portrays the escaped prisoner. **Dabbs Greer** and **Molly Dodd** portray a husband and wife who beat up on each other. **James Seay** portrays the unnamed state policeman.

EPISODE NOTES. 1. Barney tells Gomer that a deputy must always polish the back of his shoes. 2. Andy tells Barney and Gomer that a badge is the lawman's most important item. 3. Hugo Hotflash is a German World War I veteran, and a good friend of Barney's. 4. Barney and Gomer lock themselves in cell #1. They also handcuff themselves. 5. A man named Arthur wants to make sure that his place of business is checked daily while Andy is on vacation. 6. Gomer ticketed Bunny Caldwell for parking in front of Mr. Martinelli's meat market during "no parking" hours, which are between 9:30 and 11:30 A.M. on Tuesday and Thursday. 7. Mrs. Cruteck's cat, Queenie, is stuck in a tree and afraid to climb down. 8. Barney claims he has logged 10 years in law enforcement. 9. Gomer tells Barney that, if they get separated in the woods, he will imitate an owl. He also suggests that Barney imitate a squirrel, so they can locate each other. 10. The sign at Wally's Filling Station blew down during a wind storm. 11. As in episode 78, the newspaper again misspells Barney's surname as "Fike." 12. An irate Andy gives a combative husband and wife the following options: Pay a $10 fine or begin serving a 10-day jail sentence. 13. Andy's final solution to his need for a vacation is to give *Barney* a week off.

"Andy Saves Gomer"

Episode #119. Air date: 3-16-64. Writer: Harvey Bullock. Director: Jeffrey Hayden.

Andy discovers Gomer napping on the job at Wally's filling station as a small fire smolders in a barrel of oily rags. He easily puts the flames out after waking Gomer. The sleepy-eyed pump jockey believes that Andy saved his life. In order to repay the debt, Gomer begins doing everything he can for the entire Taylor family. In one extreme example, he chops up 7 years' worth of firewood for the family's fireplace. He believes that nothing is too much for the man, and the family of the man, who saved his life.

Gomer quickly becomes a nuisance, and Andy grows desperate in his desire to undo Gomer's feeling of obligation. He stages a gas leak at the courthouse and arranges for Gomer to find him "passed out" on the floor. Gomer almost bungles the rescue by succumbing to the gaseous fumes, but Andy makes certain that Gomer believes he has just saved the sheriff's life. Thus the debt no longer exists. Ironically, the story does not quite end here. Gomer, believing that Andy is accident-prone, decides to continue to help him out during his spare time.

MEMORABLE SCENE. Opie catching Andy pretending to be passed out.

CAST NOTES. Regulars: **Andy Griffith, Ronny Howard, Frances Bavier,** and **Jim Nabors. Howard McNear** makes a welcome return to the series after suffering a debilitating stroke. His last appearance had been in episode 74, "Convicts-at-Large."

EPISODE NOTES. 1. The fire was caused by Wally. He carelessly tossed his cigar stub into a barrel of oily rags. 2. Opie normally cuts the grass at home on Saturdays. 3. Gomer brings Andy some freshly caught fish for breakfast. He also washes and waxes the patrol car, washes the courthouse windows, trims the Taylors' hedges, and picks flowers for Andy. These are just some of the things Gomer does to reward the man who saved his life. 4. A Mayberry man named Carter French, Sr., calls to tell Andy that they are having a boiled dinner, followed by cribbage, at the firehouse. 5. The Taylors use cell #1 as a temporary hideout from Gomer in order to have dinner without interference. 6. Opie's friend Tommy Griff has a new cement driveway at his house. All the neighborhood kids want to roller skate on it. 7. Barney is vacationing in Raleigh. He is with his cousin Virgil, who was seen in episode 62, "Cousin Virgil." Barney writes a letter to Andy, who reads it aloud to Floyd and Opie.

COMMERCIAL. During the original airing of this episode, a commercial for Post Toasties, featuring Andy, Opie, and Aunt Bee, appeared. In the opening shot, it's breakfast time at the Taylors'. Andy and Aunt Bee are sitting at the kitchen table, drinking coffee. Suddenly, Opie pops into the room, carrying a book. In response to a query from Andy, Opie explains that it's a book on magic. He asks if Andy knows any tricks. Andy agrees to show him one. Picking up an ear of corn from the table, he asks, "How would you like to have Post Toasties for breakfast?" Opie's response is enthusiastic, so Andy shucks the corn. Inside are Post Toasties flakes! Opie is very surprised. Andy, pouring them from the husk into a bowl, explains that these light, crispy flakes are "cracklin' with fresh corn flavor." Opie tries to reproduce the trick himself, but the ear of corn he shucks proves to be just another ear of corn. Andy, filling Opie's bowl with cereal, declares that Opie will have to get his Post Toasties from the box — but "they're every bit as cracklin' fresh."

"Bargain Day"

Episode #120. Air date: 3-23-64. Writer: John Whedon. Director: Jeffrey Hayden.

Aunt Bee prides herself on being a thrifty shopper. However, this admirable quality sometimes leads her to make unwise purchases. Andy tries to make her see that a bargain is not always a bargain. Some time ago, at an auction, Aunt Bee purchased a freezer. She believed that she saved over $100 at that time, but Andy points out that the freezer has merely been sitting idle on the back porch.

Clara informs Aunt Bee of a new butcher shop that has just opened. It's called Diamond Jim's, and the store sells meat at bargain prices. Aunt Bee purchases 150 pounds of beef. She stocks her freezer, but is disheartened when it fails to work properly. (To make matters worse, the meat is tough.) Andy tells Aunt Bee to call the Mount Pilot repairman. However, in an effort to save money, Aunt Bee asks

Gomer to take a look at it. He is unable to fix it, and the freezer quits working altogether. The meat will soon be thawing, so Aunt Bee must act quickly. Though she is initially too embarrassed to ask her regular butcher, Mr. Foley, to store the meat for her, Mr. Foley very kindly consents when she does ask. However, Andy refuses to allow him to be responsible for Aunt Bee's mistake. Instead, Andy surprises his well-meaning aunt by buying her a brand new freezer.

CAST NOTES. Regulars: **Andy Griffith, Ronny Howard, Frances Bavier,** and **Jim Nabors. Hope Summers** appears as Mrs. Clara Johnson in this episode.

Frank Ferguson appears as butcher Mr. Foley for the first time. He previously appeared as Wilbur Pine in episode 1, "The New Housekeeper," and in other roles on the series.

EPISODE NOTES. 1. When Opie appears on the front porch bare-chested, Aunt Bee refers to him as a naked savage. 2. Andy had planned on buying some shoes for Opie at Finley's. However, Aunt Bee already got a pair. They were discounted from $6.50 to $4.89 at a Mount Pilot outlet store. Unfortunately, the shoes are too big for Opie, and they squeak. 3. Aunt Bee buys sugar in bulk. 4. Mr. Foley converses with a woman named Mrs. Ritter on the telephone. 5. In the freezer, Gomer finds a golf ball, a mousetrap, and an inspection tag. The tag says, "Serviced by Ed's Refrigeration, March 3, 1951." 6. Andy talks to a man named Merle on the telephone. 7. The Mount Pilot repairman once charged Aunt Bee $7.00 to put a fuse in Andy's refrigerator. 8. Mr. Poultice does work for Louise Palmer. 9. Andy purchases a new freezer from a Mount Pilot business. The brand name is Super Freeze.

"Divorce, Mountain Style"

Episode #121. Air date: 3-30-64. Writers: Jim Fritzell and Everett Greenbaum. Director: Jeffrey Hayden.

Charlene Darling Wash hitchhikes her way from her mountain home to the courthouse. She says she has come to do an errand and asks Andy and Barney to take her for a drive. Although she is acting very mysterious and secretive, Andy agrees to do as she wishes. She asks him to stop near an oak tree. Then, using a shovel borrowed from the trunk of the squad car, she digs a hole and drops in a small bag she had been carrying. She then fills in the hole. Barney wonders if someone in the mountains is sick and Charlene is doing this to help them recover. Maybe *Charlene* is sick with the bursitis or warts, he suggests. Charlene motions for Andy to stand on her right. When he does, she chants a mysterious incantation, draws a circle in the dirt, and announces that she has just divorced Dudley D. Wash. She further explains that because Andy was standing on her right during the incantation, they will be married during the next full moon. Andy is flabbergasted.

Charlene tells Andy she divorced Dud because she caught him looking and grinning at Idele Bushy during last Sunday's preaching. She is also angry at Dud for staying out for long periods of time, fox hunting with Hasty Burford. Charlene believes he and Hasty just sit around drinking hard cider, and punching each other in the arm and hollering, "flinch." She feels that her husband no longer loves her.

Charlene has always been attracted to Andy, and often calls him "lover sheriff." The attention makes Andy uncomfortable, however. He takes her back in the squad car, while Barney goes to the library to find a book on mountain superstitions.

To Charlene's dismay, her family is waiting at the courthouse. Briscoe is angry that she left her husband. He says that Charlene is lucky to have Dud. They live in a house with a wooden floor, and Dud hardly ever beats her. Charlene tells her pa that the deed has been done — the divorce proceedings have been buried. She announces that Andy will be her new husband when the next full moon appears. The family accepts it, and as usual, Andy finds it impossible to win an argument with the Darlings.

Later, Barney returns with a book titled *Mountain Folklore*. He believes he has found an antidote to the divorce. According to the book, "If the intended should dig up the proceedings before the moon becomes full, the divorce proceedings are null and void." Andy says all of this is nonsense. Just then, an angry Dud Wash bursts into the courthouse and begins yelling at Andy. He challenges Andy to fight him, but the annoyed sheriff simply disposes of him by throwing him outside.

Andy reluctantly agrees to go with Barney and dig up the divorce proceedings. They are stopped, however, by the Darling clan, who had figured they might try to fight the inevitable.

Andy discovers there will be a full moon on the next night. He can't help feeling a little anxiety. Barney doesn't help when he tells Andy to look at the bright side of the situation. After all, the deputy continues, Charlene is a very pretty woman with a good singing voice and a love of music. He adds that Briscoe and his boys would not be too hard to live with, if they cleaned themselves up. Anyway,

Gilligan himself (Bob Denver) stars as Dudley D. Wash in "Divorce, Mountain Style."

Opie needs a mother. Andy can scarcely believe his ears. The entire situation is outlandish.

Barney scans the library book, looking for an answer. He finds the following: "If a rider dressed in black rides east to west on a white horse in the light of a full moon, passing a bridegroom, he is cursed and the union is cursed." This just may be the solution that will get Andy out of this mess.

On the night of the full moon, Andy has Barney dress in black clothing. Despite Barney's fear and reluctance, he agrees to ride a horse. Somehow, Andy finds a white horse in Mayberry, and he instructs Barney to wait a half-hour while he sets the Darlings up to witness the event. Andy knows the family will come for him and that they will all proceed to Preacher Winslow's house, where Andy is expected to marry Charlene.

Andy returns to the courthouse only to find the entire Darling clan already there. Pesky Dud Wash drops in to try again to fight Andy. This time, two of the Darling boys take him away.

Soon, Charlene and Andy, followed by her family, are walking toward the preacher's house. Andy tries a couple of stall tactics, which are mildly successful. Suddenly, a *sneezing* rider dressed in black (Barney is allergic to horse hair!) comes riding. However, he is riding north to south. The Darlings continue on. Then Dud comes running out of Preacher Winslow's house and begs Charlene to take him back. He professes his love for her and promises to never look at Idele Bushy again. Meanwhile Barney has corrected his course, and Andy points him out to the family. They recognize this as the curse of the white horse. The divorce is declared null and void, and Andy breathes a huge sign of relief. Charlene will remain married to Dud.

Everyone celebrates this happy turn of events with music and dancing at the courthouse.

CAST NOTES. Regulars: **Andy Griffith, Don Knotts**, and **Howard McNear. The Dillards** return as the Darling boys. **Denver Pyle** returns as Briscoe Darling. **Maggie Peterson** returns as Charlene Darling Wash.

Bob Denver, who is known by millions as Gilligan on the much-loved, but savagely critiqued, series *Gilligan's Island*, and as beatnik Maynard G. Krebs on *The Many Loves of Dobie Gillis*, portrays the annoying Dudley D. Wash. Denver was born in New Rochelle, New York on January 9, 1935. He is most famous for the above-mentioned roles, each of which he continued in several television reunion movies. Among his other regular roles: In *The Good Guys* (1968-1970) he starred as part-time cabby and diner owner Rufus Butterworth. (No reunion movies for this one...yet!). He lent his voice to two cartoon versions of *Gilligan's Island* in the 70s and 80s. He also starred as Junior in the 1975-1976 live action children's program *Far Out Space Nuts*. He has guest-starred on many series, including *Dr. Kildare, I Dream of Jeannie, Fantasy Island, Herman's Head*, and *ALF*. Denver has also appeared in several theatrical releases, including *Who's Minding the Mint?* (1967, directed by Howard Morris), *The Sweet Ride* (1968), and *Back to the Beach* (1987). In 1994, Bob Denver wrote a book titled *Gilligan, Maynard & Me*.

EPISODE NOTES. 1. Nelson's Hardware Store is located in Mayberry. Barney tells Andy that he and Thelma Lou gazed at its new window display, which featured a transparent plastic tool kit for bicycles. Andy says he prefers the solid black ones, because what he keeps in his bicycle kit is *his* business. 2. Barney says that the shovel Charlene uses is official police equipment. 3. The contents of the bag Charlene buried: one beak of an owl, four tail feathers from a chicken hawk, a piece of bacon, and a broken comb. 4. Dud Wash calls Andy a "home wrecker." 5. Andy states that Charlene is fifteen years younger than himself. 6. Two more items found in the book *Mountain Folklore*: "If you put a willow chip under a dog's head while he's dreaming, and then put it under your own pillow, you'll have the same dream." Plus, "If you wear a ruby ring while riding an old horse, the horse will go mad." 7. Barney hates to wear black. He believes it makes him look thin. 8. As a child, Barney sat on the hood of his Uncle's Hudson Terraplane and had his picture taken. 9. The Darlings sing "Shady Grove" and "Boil Them Cabbage Down." The latter song makes Charlene cry, but Briscoe urges her to try to control herself. 10. To stall the wedding procession, Andy pretends to have a sore foot, so Charlene offers another incantation. The ailing party is supposed to have a buckeye in his pocket during the incantation. 11. Perkin's Realty Office is located on Main Street in Mayberry.

"A Deal Is a Deal"

Episode #122. Air date: 4-6-64. Writers: Bill Idelson and Sam Bobrick. Director: Jeffrey Hayden.

Opie, along with several other boys in Mayberry, is attempting to sell an ointment called Miracle Salve, door-to-door. Whoever sells the most will win a pony, courtesy of the Miracle Salve Company, located in Mount Pilot. None of the youngsters are having much success. Opie has sold only a few jars (three to Andy and at least one to Barney). Apparently, the salve is useless. Barney complains that it did not clear up his crow's feet. The ointment claims to cure poison ivy, athlete's foot, prickly rash, complexion, and spring itch. It sells for 35 cents per jar.

One of Opie's friends, Trey Bowden, sends his jars back to the company and later receives an unsettling response. The salve company says how disappointed they are with him and states they are putting Trey on a "blacklist." Trey notifies his friends, and they decide to ask Barney about the letter. The alarmed deputy explains that being blacklisted means that you cannot get a job. Barney decides to play "hardball" and dictates a letter to the salve company, in which he threatens to sue them. He tells Opie to sign the letter, "Bernard P. Fife, Attorney at Law."

When Andy learns of the blacklist letter, he tells the boys not to worry about it. The company is merely trying to intimidate them into trying harder to sell their salve. Barney decides to discard his letter, but he comes up with another idea. He tries to convince Andy to join him in a visit to the salve company. Andy refuses to go, and he expects his deputy to forget about the entire matter. However, without Andy's knowledge, Barney gets Gomer to agree to go with him.

Once they arrive at the company's Mount Pilot office, Barney introduces himself as a veterinarian named Dr. U.T. Pendyke, and Gomer calls himself

Opie Taylor, Sr., father of Opie Taylor of Mayberry. Gomer tells the two company owners that little Opie experimented with the salve on the family's mangy dog. The mange quickly cleared up, and he contacted his veterinarian, Dr. Pendyke. Barney exclaims that he tried the salve on six of his mangy animals. To his amazement, the mange disappeared in 24 hours. The owners are stupefied. They believed their product was useless. Dr. Pendyke says that he and Mr. Taylor would like to buy up their entire stock, including any unsold jars still in Mayberry. They tell the excited owners they plan to sell the salve to veterinarians and drugstores. The owners agree to do it. Barney and Gomer leave, confident that the owners are burning up the phone lines to sell their product directly to drugstores and veterinarians.

A day or two later, it appears that the charade worked. Opie and his friends receive letters from the company asking them to return any unsold jars. Each boy that returns the salve will receive $1.00. A smug Barney and Gomer begin to tell Andy of their recent exploit, but they are interrupted by a phone call from a very upset Aunt Bee. It seems that the Miracle Salve Company has delivered 946 jars of salve to the Taylors' house and made the bill out to "Opie Taylor, Sr." A sheepish Barney and Gomer have a lot of explaining to do.

Barney tries to enlist Opie and eight other boys to sell the salve for Gomer and himself, but the boys want nothing more to do with the stuff. It looks like the men are about to discover for themselves the difficulties of selling an unwanted and useless product.

MEMORABLE SCENES. 1. Opie trying to awaken a napping Barney. 2. Barney and Gomer's visit to the Miracle Salve Company.

CAST NOTES. Regulars: **Andy Griffith, Don Knotts, Ronny Howard, Frances Bavier,** and **Jim Nabors. Richard Keith, David A. Bailey,** and **Dennis Rush** return as Johnny Paul Jason, Trey Bowden, and Howie Pruitt, respectively.

George Petrie appears as Lenny, one of the owners of the Miracle Salve Company. **Lewis Charles** portrays Lenny's unnamed partner.

EPISODE NOTES. 1. Mrs. Farley called Barney and asked him to retrieve her cat, who was stuck up a tree. Ultimately, it came down by itself. 2. Andy and Barney used to sell flower seeds when they were kids. The flowers were guaranteed to bloom, night and day, for six months. Barney still has five packs of the seeds. 3. The Miracle Salve Company is located in an office building, room #106, in Mount Pilot. The building also houses the offices of Ideal Construction Company and the law firm of Lonas, Hill, and Davison (room #108). 4.

Barney wears his civilian trademark, the salt and pepper suit, when he visits the salve company. He also wears a pair of wire-rimmed glasses as part of his Dr. U.T. Pendyke persona. 5. As "Dr. Pendyke, D.V.M.," Barney speaks in a deep, nasal voice. He says his "practice" is limited to small animals, such as dogs, cats, birds of all kinds and small sheep. He claims Miracle Salve is much better than the salve he formerly used, "Molly Harkin's Mange Cure." He also mentions his "colleagues," Dr. Webster and Dr. Neely. 6. Gomer uses a very deep voice as "Opie Taylor, Sr." 7. The Mayberry Security Bank can be seen in this episode. 8. According to Barney, you fight fire with fire, and you deal with a fox by "outfoxing" him.

"Fun Girls"

Episode #123. Air date: 4-13-64. Writer: Aaron Ruben. Director: Coby Ruskin.

Andy and Barney are working late so they can be free the next night to take Helen and Thelma Lou to a dance. Around 7:00 P.M., Barney leaves to pick up some supper at the diner. Helen and Thelma Lou stop by the courthouse to see if Andy and Barney will accompany them to the movie house. Andy explains why they cannot, and says that he and Barney are looking forward to taking them to the dance.

After they leave, Gomer and his cousin Goober drop in. They're going to the movies, too. Tonight's film is a romantic comedy starring Cary Grant. Gomer introduces Goober to Andy. Goober, prompted by Gomer, proceeds to do some imitations for Andy. His hilarious repertoire includes Cary Grant, Edward G. Robinson, and "Chester" (the deputy who walked with a pronounced limp) from the popular television series *Gunsmoke.*

After Gomer and Goober leave, Barney finally returns. Unfortunately, while at the diner, Barney ran into Daphne and Skippy, the "fun girls" from Mount Pilot. Of course, they insisted on coming back to the courthouse with the sheepish deputy. They want to dance, visit, and make out in the jail cells. Andy is upset by their shenanigans and mutters to Barney that he wants the women out. He orders his deputy to take them back to the diner. Andy is upset when he discovers that Barney has promised to take them home. Skippy will cuddle up to Barney on the way home, but what about Daphne? She complains, loudly, when Andy initially refuses to ride along with them. Reluctantly, he is talked into it. Unbeknownst to this unlikely foursome, an astonished Helen and Thelma Lou, fresh from the movie house, witness them leaving.

The next morning, Andy is sore at Barney, mainly because of the work that went undone the previous night. Barney can tell that Andy is sore because the sheriff always works his jaw muscles when he's angry. Andy just wants to get the work done and forget about everything else.

Barney spots Thelma Lou and Helen shopping across the street. When he and Andy approach them, they are given the cold shoulder. Puzzled by this reaction, they mention the dance, only to hear a scorned Thelma Lou suggest they should take the women they were with the previous night. "They look like *fun girls*," she adds. The women leave, and the startled and chagrined lawmen realize they are dateless. Andy sarcastically says, "Well, I guess we could take Daphne and Skippy to the dance."

Later, Andy tries to explain things to Helen, but she refuses to listen. Andy resigns himself to staying home. He reasons that he'd rather stay home than stand in the stag line with Old Man Schwump. Barney, however, has other ideas. On the evening of the dance, he brings Daphne and Skippy to Andy's house. An angry and embarrassed Andy is obliged to introduce the girls to Aunt Bee and Opie. Barney, decked out in his salt and pepper suit, does succeed in getting Andy to come to the dance, but before they leave the house, Andy growls, "When this is over, I'm going to *kill* you!"

At the dance, Andy and Barney are surprised to discover that Helen and Thelma Lou are sitting with Gomer and Goober. When the women see that Andy and Barney have dared to bring the fun girls, they immediately ask their dates to dance.

Andy tries to get Helen's attention on the dance floor, but to no avail. Finally, he requests the band to play a switch-your-partner number. Eventually, Andy ends up with Helen, and Barney hooks up with Thelma Lou. The men do their best to explain the entire situation, and they are soon forgiven. Everyone in the room applauds when they hear Barney, who was yelling to be heard above the music, telling Thelma Lou, "You're the only girl I love!" Then the reunited quartet notices that the "fun girls" have hit it off with Gomer and Goober. They could not be more pleased (or relieved).

Later in the evening, after taking Helen and Thelma Lou home, Barney asks Andy to drive by the courthouse. He wants to look and see if Otis has checked in for the weekend. They are shocked to find Gomer, Goober, and the fun girls inside. It seems that when Gomer offered to take the girls home, they told him that Barney had promised to take them. So, Barney, accompanied by ride-alongs Gomer, Goober, and a disbelieving Andy, takes Daphne and Skippy back to Mount Pilot once and for all.

CAST NOTES. Regulars: **Andy Griffith, Don Knotts, Ronny Howard, Frances Bavier, Jim Nabors, Aneta Corsaut,** and **Betty Lynn. Joyce Jameson** and **Jean Carson** reprise their role from episode 68 as Skippy and Daphne, the fun girls.

This episode introduces **George Lindsey** as Gomer's cousin Goober. Lindsey remained on this series until it ended. He continued as Goober in the very popular spin-off series, *Mayberry R.F.D.*, in which he was featured even more prominently.

Dick Winslow appears as Earle, the band leader at the dance.

EPISODE NOTES. 1. Goober imitates Cary Grant by uttering quickly, "Judy Judy Judy Judy Judy." For Edward G. Robinson, he screws up his face and says, "Okay, you guys, Alright, you guys. Come on, you guys. Beat it, you guys." When he imitates "Chester" of *Gunsmoke*, he walks around with a highly exaggerated limp. Goober also "sews up" his fingers (at the dance). 2. Goober never misses a Cary Grant film. He studies him. 3. Goober always says "Yo" for "Yes." He picked that up which serving in the National Guard. 4. This is the only episode of *The Andy Griffith Show* in which Gomer and Goober appear together. 5. Andy calls Barney "Mr. Fix It" three times in this episode. 6. Barney claims to have a low sugar blood content. He means a low blood sugar count. 7. For his supper, Barney planned to order the following items from the diner: two chili-size burgers with chopped onions, ketchup, piccalilli, and mustard, a side of french fries, a slab of rhubarb pie, and a chocolate malt. 8. Sarah, the switchboard operator, apparently has a cold in this episode. Andy advises her to drink a lot of hot juices. 9. Daphne says she has never been in a jail before, except to visit friends. 10. Daphne and Skippy argue over which one of them has a friend named Al. 11. Daphne suggests that she and Skippy would like Andy and Barney to go to Mount Pilot's Kit Kat Club with them and they can all have a beer. 12. Skippy jokes that the son of a cop usually grows up to be a gangster. 13. Barney mentions that he learned how to crochet from his mother. In fact, he'd thought of crocheting an afghan for Andy. It would feature the official state colors and have the words "Bless This House" on it. 14. During the first dance, the band plays "Carolina in the Morning." This is also when Goober is "sewing up" his fingers for Helen and Thelma Lou. During the switch-partners number, the song "When the Saints Come Marching In" is played. 15. Andy calls the bandleader Earle. This was his way of recognizing Earle Hagen, who did such a tremendous job with the music throughout the series. 16. Mr. Schwump returns. He can be seen at the dance.

"The Return of Malcolm Merriweather"

Episode #124. Air date: 4-20-64. Writer: Harvey Bullock. Director: Coby Ruskin.

Merry Englishman Malcolm Merriweather, still on his bicycle tour of America, returns to Mayberry to say hello to Andy. Malcolm has plans to go to Gettysburg, but he's finding it difficult to finance his tour. He has taken on odd jobs and served as a butler during his long journey, just as he did for the Taylor family about a year ago. Andy is happy to see him again and hires Malcolm to help an overburdened Aunt Bee with her household chores. Aunt Bee prepares the guest room for Malcolm.

The native of Heckmondwike, England, wants to do all he can to help out Andy and his family, but Aunt Bee is upset when she discovers that Malcolm is doing virtually all of her chores. He does everything — from cooking to escorting Opie to his friend Jimmy Farrington's birthday party. Andy and Opie both notice a change in Aunt Bee. Opie tells Malcolm that Aunt Bee used to sing while she worked around the house, but she isn't singing now. Malcolm begins to wonder if his presence is making Aunt Bee feel useless.

Aunt Bee begins spending most of her time in bed, insisting she feels ill. She skips going to church. She won't even join Andy and Barney for Sunday dinner. Thus, she's still in bed when Barney rings the dinner bell (a signal for Malcolm to service dinner) and the efficient and proper valet comes stumbling out of the kitchen, apparently quite drunk. He makes a real mess of dinner, and the ensuing ruckus causes Aunt Bee to come downstairs to see what is happening.

Barney advises Andy to "get rid of the wino," after he discovers a telltale empty bottle of cooking sherry in the kitchen. When confronted, Malcolm begins to cry. He announces he will leave as soon as possible. An understanding Aunt Bee rationalizes that Malcolm had simply taken too much of the workload upon himself.

Andy, very surprised by Malcolm's bizarre outburst, makes a startling discovery: Malcolm merely emptied a bottle of sherry down the drain! He was only pretending to be drunk. After he overhears a very sober Malcolm saying goodbye to Opie, Andy realizes that Malcolm did what he did all for the sake of making Aunt Bee feel needed again.

Before Malcolm departs, Andy tells him, with a knowing look, that he appreciates everything he has done for the Taylor family. Clearly, Malcolm is just as thankful for Andy and his family. So, with love in his heart, and a little cash in his pocket, the kindly Englishman leaves to continue his tour.

CAST NOTES. Regulars: **Andy Griffith, Don Knotts, Ronny Howard**, and **Frances Bavier. Bernard Fox** returns as Malcolm Merriweather. Malcolm's previous appearance was in episode 89, "Andy's English Valet."

EPISODE NOTES. 1. Barney claims to have a low "sugar blood" content and says he is ruled by a clock in his stomach. If he doesn't eat by noon, he gets a headache. 2. Andy dubs Aunt Bee "Miss Luncheon Tray." 3. In his previous trip to Mayberry, Malcolm caused a traffic accident because he was bicycling on the left side of the road. In this episode, he causes an accident because he is riding in the middle of the road. 4. Barney tells Malcolm that the U.S. won the battle of Bunker Hill in 1776. Malcolm corrects him by telling him the British won, not only at Bunker Hill, but also at Lexington and Concord. Barney blurts out that at least the U.S. won the war. 5. Malcolm compliments Aunt Bee by calling her a real bobbydazzler. 6. Malcolm creates a paper ladder out of a torn newspaper. 7. Barney believes Andy has a warped sense of humor. 8. For a lunch at the courthouse, Malcolm serves Andy and Barney cornish pasty (meat and potatoes at one end and plum pudding at the other). 9. Malcolm puts some hair tonic from England on Opie's hair. 10. Malcolm performs magic tricks at young Jimmy Farrington's birthday party. 11. Barney compliments Malcolm on his tasty beef stew. Malcolm says his secret is using a double dollop of cooking sherry. This information alarms Barney because he is due to go on duty. 12. Aunt Bee's soup ladle is kept in a drawer in the bottom of the stove, and the soda crackers are stored on the top shelf of the pantry. 13. Barney calls the supposedly drunken Malcolm an English Otis. 14. Opie eats Sunday dinner at the Lewis's house in this episode. 15. Opie acknowledges that Malcolm cooks and cleans as well as Aunt Bee, but says she has him beat when it comes to giving hugs.

COMMERCIAL. At the end of the original broadcast of this episode, a commercial for Sanka ran before the final credits. In the opening shot, Andy, coming from the kitchen, carries a coffee tray into his living room. Addressing the camera, he delivers a speech extolling the virtues of Sanka. When he finishes, Opie suddenly pops up from behind the couch, asking for "a wrestle." Gently pulling Opie's head onto his shoulder, Andy looks toward the camera and bids the audience goodnight.

"The Rumor"

Episode #125. Air date: 4-27-64. Writers: Everett Greenbaum and Jim Fritzell. Director: Coby Ruskin.

Andy notices Helen shopping inside Sterling's Jewelry Store and drops in to say hello. She is buying a charm bracelet as a graduation present for her niece. She asks store owner Fred Sterling to make the bracelet smaller. She'll be back to pick it up in a couple of days. Barney sees Andy and Helen in the store, gazing at jewelry and then sharing a quick kiss. He gets the idea that the couple are buying a ring and that an engagement announcement is forthcoming! He tells Thelma Lou about this, and she gets just as excited as he is. He tells her to keep this knowledge to herself for now. Barney, of course, then immediately informs Aunt Bee, who is overcome with tears of joy. Andy and Opie are perplexed by Aunt Bee. She breaks into tears for no apparent reason, especially when she is near Andy. When Opie asks his pa about it, Andy says that women just naturally do that sometimes. He suggests that maybe she heard a song which reminded her of an old romance. Opie wonders aloud if the liver they are having for dinner has triggered the outburst. Barney cannot help but smile around Andy, whom he calls "Old Mr. Transparent." Andy remains puzzled.

Helen is just as confused by Thelma Lou's behavior. When Thelma Lou discovers that Helen is going to stop by the jewelry store to pick up an item, she is ecstatic.

Barney decides a surprise party should be thrown for the newly engaged couple. The party will be on Friday (just a couple of days away). Aunt Bee and Thelma Lou call their friends and arrange for them to each bring a covered dish to the party. Each will also chip in to buy the happy couple a nice gift. Aunt Bee, knowing that Andy and Helen will live at the Taylor house, decides that her present will be a newly decorated bedroom. Barney manages to keep Andy busy at the courthouse so the work at home can be accomplished. Andy's room, which had reminded Aunt Bee of an elephant's nest, is transformed into a bedroom designed with a woman in mind. It has a canopied bed, new wallpaper, new curtains, and is freshly painted. Barney determines that Andy will hate it because it is "kissy" looking.

On Friday night, Barney and Thelma Lou tell Andy and Helen they are being treated to supper at one of the town's fine eateries. Actually, they are merely stalling to give the party-givers time to set up for the surprise. Gomer is chosen to act as look-out to warn everyone when he sees the guests of honor approaching. His warning signal is to hoot like an owl, but when the quartet arrives, Gomer cannot hoot because he has a mouthful of food. So, Andy and Helen are not surprised, at least not in the conventional sense. They are, however, dumbstruck when they discover that everyone believes they are engaged. As Aunt Bee proudly displays the new bedroom, Andy explains that he and Helen are not getting married. Everyone is disappointed, and Barney is embarrassed. Andy insists that the party continue. He tells everyone they will get their money back and announces he is giving his bedroom to Aunt Bee. Now, she will have the lovely room she always wanted.

In a private moment, Andy apologizes to Helen for the embarrassment of this awkward situation. He tells her that he may not be marriage-minded now, but he might be someday. Helen feels the same way. She says she is not ready to give up teaching yet, anyway. They realize that the party and the gifts are symbols of the love and generosity of their family and friends.

CAST NOTES. Regulars: **Andy Griffith, Don Knotts, Ronny Howard, Frances Bavier, Howard McNear, Jim Nabors, Aneta Corsaut,** and **Betty Lynn.**

Rance Howard, Molly Dodd appears as Lillian, and **Mary Lansing** appear as friends of Andy and Helen at the party. Each of these actors have made appearances on the series. **Ronda Jeter** also returns. This time she portrays Ethel, one of Helen's students. **William Newell** appears as Fred Sterling, owner of Sterling's Jewelry Store.

EPISODE NOTES. 1. Andy greets a woman named Miss Cleta on Main Street. He compliments her for wearing a pretty black oilcloth coat. 2. Sterling's Jewelry Store is located on Main Street in Mayberry. 3. Thelma Lou asks Barney not to throw his education in her face. Barney replies that he can't help being a student of humanity. 4. Opie has a lizard, which he keeps in a lizard house. 5. Barney says "boodoor" instead of "boudoir." 6. Opie spends a night at the Belfasts' home. 7. The Friday night special at the diner is catfish casserole. This is, apparently, unappealing to both Barney and Thelma Lou. 8. Barney lost the little black book containing the names of each contributor to the surprise party and the amount of money each spent. However, he claims he remembers who gave what. 9. Gomer tells Barney to never call *him* dumb again, after Barney's misunderstanding is revealed. 10. Once again, Mr. Schwump appears, this time at the surprise party.

"Barney and Thelma Lou, Phfftt"

Episode #126. Air date 5-4-64. Writers: Bill Idel-son and Sam Bobrick. Director: Coby Ruskin.

While Andy and Barney are busy at the court-house filling out monthly reports, Deputy Fife begins talking about the movie date he had with Thelma Lou the night before. The movie was about a lovely and talented girl who ends up falling for a big sloppy goof. Barney found the scenario to be unrealistic and far-fetched, but Thelma Lou loved it. Andy admits he has seen the picture, and that he liked it, too.

Thelma Lou's telephone call disrupts the con-versation. She needs Barney to take her to Mount Pilot for a dental appointment. Unfortunately, the squad car is at Wally's, being repaired. Andy sug-gests she take a taxi, but Barney nixes the idea as too costly. Moments later, Gomer stops by the court-house to announce that Wally will not have the car fixed until later in the day. He then volunteers to drive Thelma Lou to Mount Pilot. Barney is grate-ful, but Andy kids him that he's liable to lose his girl to Gomer. Barney replies that he has no reason to worry about losing Thelma Lou because "I've got that little girl right in my hip pocket!" Gomer leaves to go get Thelma Lou, and during the drive he innocently repeats what Barney said. Thelma Lou is furious.

Later in the day, Gomer returns the squad car and tells Barney that Thelma Lou treated him to a fine lunch in Mount Pilot. Barney is a little sur-prised. He says Thelma Lou has never bought *his* lunch. In fact, they always go dutch treat. Andy jokes that "sometimes, pretty girls go for a shaggy type of guy, and Gomer is pretty shaggy!" Barney is not amused.

Thelma Lou disappoints Barney by telling him she is too busy to have their standing Tuesday night date. This upsets Barney's usual routine of "watch-ing that doctor show" on television at Thelma Lou's. He and she would sit on her couch, with a pan of cashew fudge between them. But this week, Andy finds Barney sitting alone at the courthouse Tues-day evening. The lawmen proceed to walk down Main Street, doing a night check. Barney is very upset when he spies Thelma Lou and Gomer mer-rily entering the movie theater together.

The next day, Andy tries to console Barney by saying that he doubts Gomer and Thelma Lou have a serious relationship. However, he angers Barney by reminding him that he has occasionally stepped out on Thelma Lou. He cites Juanita, the waitress at the diner, as one of Barney's other women. Gomer stops by the courthouse, and Barney refuses

to speak with him. In fact, he storms out of the building.

Andy talks with Gomer and discovers the con-tent of his conversation with Thelma Lou. He tells Gomer he believes Thelma Lou is using him to try to make Barney jealous. Andy claims that if a fel-low ever got too serious with Thelma Lou, she would probably go running back to Barney. This give Gomer an idea. He gives Thelma Lou candy, hoping to make her believe he is serious about her. While Thelma Lou prepared a pot of coffee, Gomer calls Andy and informs him of his plans to make her scheme backfire. Unbeknownst to Gomer, Thelma Lou overhears this conversation and decides to add a twist to her scheme. When Gomer asks her if she will be his steady girl, she horrifies him by saying yes.

Meanwhile, a brokenhearted Barney makes his way to the home of his lost love, hoping to some-how make things right. But he glances through a window and sees her giving Gomer a big kiss.

Now very upset, Barney goes to see Andy. A confused Gomer arrives at Andy's moments later. Gomer attempts to explain his predicament to Andy, while Barney is challenging him to fight. Gomer believes he has no choice but to marry Thelma Lou, because she kissed him —flush on the jaw! Andy manages to calm the confused Gomer and the combative Barney, and he drives them over to Thelma Lou's. While Barney waits in the car, Andy and Gomer confront her. Andy decides to try a ridiculous tactic. He tells Thelma Lou she must marry Gomer, because of the kiss. She confesses she was only getting revenge for the trick Gomer was pulling. Andy suggests she could "take the kiss back," thereby undoing the engagement obligation. Thelma Lou kisses Gomer again, making her a free woman. Gomer is very relieved, too. At this point, Andy brings Barney in, and he and Thelma Lou quickly reconcile. Barney agrees there will be no more talk about her being in his hip pocket. The couple vows to make their Tuesday night date unbreakable, unless three days' notice is given. As far as marriage is concerned, Barney later reveals that he and Thelma Lou share the motto "Marry in haste, repent in leisure."

CAST NOTES. Regulars: **Andy Griffith, Don Knotts, Jim Nabors**, and **Betty Lynn**.

EPISODE NOTES. 1. Barney wears his salt and pepper suit on his movie date with Thelma Lou, and on Tuesday night after his date is canceled. 2. While walking home from the movies, Barney and Thelma Lou gaze at a blue sofa and a green rug dis-played in a store window. Thelma Lou comments, "It's smart," but Barney prefers to have a leather chair. He says he wants a den that smells like real leather and also smells of pipe tobacco. The den would contain good books and a dog. No ladies, including Thelma Lou, would be allowed in his den. 3. Barney describes his job as "nerve-wracking." 4. Barney says Mount Pilot is 12 miles from Mayberry. 5. Gomer says his Mount Pilot lunch, which included 3 eggs and 6 flapjacks, must have "set Thelma Lou back" over 70 cents. 6. Barney, again, refers to Andy's "warped" sense of humor.

"Back to Nature"

Episode #127. Air date: 5-11-64. Writer: Harvey Bullock. Director: Coby Ruskin.

Andy and Barney are about to take Opie and ten of his friends on a camping trip to the woods. Barney is especially gung-ho about the weekend outing and claims to be an expert woodsman and a pioneer at heart. Gomer reluctantly agrees to go along, although it will mean missing a Preston Foster movie on television.

The boys sing "There Ain't No Flies on Us," as they make the long hike to the campsite. Barney would sing along, if only he could catch his breath. The first night, the gang huddles around the campfire and sings "John Jacob Jingleheimer Schmidt." Andy entertains them with a ghost story. This succeeds in frightening Barney and Gomer, who then find themselves unable to fall asleep for awhile.

The next morning, one of the boys, Trey Bowden, tells Andy that Opie is missing. Andy orders everyone to stay put while he searches for his son. When he returns, with Opie in tow, he discovers that Barney and Gomer have taken off to look for the boy, too. They were going to look for him near the northern slope.

Moments later, Andy's friend Fletch drives up in his pickup truck. He has brought some archery equipment for the boys. He also brings a couple of roasted chickens, compliments of Aunt Bee. Andy asks Fletch to keep the boys busy while he goes searching for Barney and Gomer.

Meanwhile, Barney, the expert woodsman, is completely lost, although he will not admit this fact to Gomer. They are both quite hungry, because they left the campsite before breakfast. Several hours have now passed. Barney brags that he could build a trap to catch a pheasant if he had some string. Obligingly, Gomer produces a spare shoelace. It seems he always carries an extra one with him. Barney is put to the test. Miraculously, he does manage to make a trap, but he seriously doubts it will work. Then he begins bragging that he knows how to start a fire by rubbing two sticks together. He says

this believing that Gomer has some matches. However, this is not the case, and Barney's attempts to start a fire "the pioneer way" fail. He asks Gomer to go check the snare while he works on starting a fire.

Andy has spotted Gomer and quietly approaches him. Gomer confirms that he and Barney are lost. He tells Andy that the laugh will be on Barney, once the boys find out that the deputy is not at all the expert woodsman he claims to be. Andy tells him that it would really hurt Barney if he were ridiculed. Gomer understands and agrees to go along with Andy's plan to help Barney save face. Andy gives Gomer some matches and instructs him to put the match heads into the fire-maker Barney fashioned. Gomer does this while Barney is off gathering twigs. When Barney returns, he is very surprised when his stick-rubbing seems to have started a campfire. This prompts Gomer to call him "a regular Daniel Boone." While a stunned Barney wanders off to gather more twigs, Andy hands Gomer a roasted chicken, which he has skewered with a stick. He tells Gomer to go and hold it over the fire. He also tells him that, later, he will hear a strange bird call, and when he does, he should identify it as the call of a lake loon.

Barney returns and is absolutely amazed to see Gomer holding a fully cooked bird over the fire. Gomer explains that the trap worked and he quickly plucked the wild pheasant and began cooking it. Barney can only conclude that it cooked so quickly because a fire started by sticks is bound to be hotter than a fire started by matches.

From a safe distance, Andy enjoys the other chicken. Later, he makes a bird call. Gomer hears the call and brings it to Barney's attention. Barney claims it is the call, not *merely* of a lake loon, but of a web-footed, red-crested lake loon. He says they can follow the sound and it will lead them to the lake and on to the campsite. Barney turns out to be right, of course, and Andy gathers the boys to welcome home their pioneering friends. They cheer Barney and eagerly listen to the story of his recent exploit—that is, until he starts in with his tired old speech about self-reliance and communing with nature.

MEMORABLE SCENE. Andy telling his ghost story around the campfire.

CAST NOTES. Regulars: **Andy Griffith, Don Knotts, Ronny Howard, Jim Nabors,** and **Howard McNear. Richard Keith, Dennis Rush,** and **David A. Bailey** all return as Opie's friends, Johnny Paul Jason, Howie Pruitt and Trey Bowden, respectively.

Willis Bouchey appears as Fletch.

EPISODE NOTES. 1. Opie wandered away from the camp to pick some berries for breakfast.

2. Barney says a person starts a fire by "constriction," meaning to say "combustion." 3. Barney refers to his eyes as his "baby blues." 4. Barney is upset because the new gas pump at the filling station scratched the squad car. 5. Floyd doesn't like automatic lather machines. He prefers to make his own lather in a mug. He loves the sound the lather makes as it is being mixed in the mug. It goes "klep, klep, klep." 6. Andy's ghost story tells about an old hermit who lived in the woods near the campsite, who believed a valuable treasure was buried in the vicinity. While searching for it, he was attacked by a bear, who bit off one of the hermit's arms. The hermit killed the bear with a knife and eventually found the treasure. Using the money he found, he purchased a new arm. This was not a regular artificial arm; it was made of gold. One day, the old hermit died, and a thief, who had heard about the golden arm, came and stole it. Legend has it that, to this day, the hermit's ghost wanders around, looking for his long-lost golden arm and crying out, "Whoooo? Who stole my golden arm?" *Was it you?* 7. This episode marks Jim Nabors' final filmed appearance on *The Andy Griffith Show*. The following television season featured his own series, *Gomer Pyle, U.S.M.C.*

Its pilot episode aired as part of *The Andy Griffith Show* (episode 107, "Gomer Pyle, U.S.M.C.") on May 19, 1964. It was seen by television viewers as his final appearance on the parent series.

COMMERCIAL. A commercial for Grape Nuts, featuring Andy and Barney, was shown during the original airing of this episode. It begins with Andy inside the courthouse, reading. Barney enters from the back room, carrying a breakfast tray. He announces that it's "Grape Nuts breakfast time." Andy reacts with pleasure and starts to pour the Grape Nuts into a bowl, but Barney reminds him that they have to exercise first. Andy is annoyed and tries to talk Barney out of it, but Barney says that they have to "keep slim and trim" by exercising as well as eating foods like Grape Nuts. He takes the bowl away from Andy, and he and Andy start doing deep knee bends. Together they recite as they exercise, "A Grape Nuts breakfast fills you up, not out, fills you up, not out...." As Andy chants and exercises, Barney secretly retreats to the desk and begins eating Andy's cereal. Andy continues his exercises, and Barney looks into the camera and announces, "Delicious!"

SEASON FIVE

America's beloved deputy Barney Fife departs Mayberry near the end of this season. Fortunately, there's lots of entertaining episodes to keep our spirits up! A.C. Nielsen Co. ratings for the 1964-1965 season: 28.3; rank 4.

"Barney's Bloodhound"

Episode #128. Air date: 10-26-64. Writers: Bill Idelson and Sam Bobrick. Director: Howard Morris.

Ralph Neal, an escapee from the state penitentiary, is being pursued in the Mayberry area. Neal is five feet ten inches tall, weighs 165 pounds, and is said to be armed and dangerous. Inspired by this news, Barney Fife goes out and gets an old shaggy dog from Henry Choate in order to track the escaped convict. Barney tells Andy that old "Blue" is part bloodhound, but Andy is not impressed with Blue's looks or his poor tracking instincts. In fact, Andy doesn't believe that Blue can even locate his own food dish. When Barney attempts to practice some tracking exercises with his prize pooch, old Blue responds only to Floyd's lollipops and Barney's silent dog whistle, which absolutely drives the hound crazy. Andy gets annoyed with Barney when his determined deputy insists on taking Blue along on the manhunt for Neal.

When Andy and Barney reach the wooded area by the lake, where Neal has been spotted, they go their separate ways in search of the escapee. Surprisingly, Blue leads Barney directly to Neal, who is fishing in the lake. Neal gets the drop on the unsuspecting deputy and captures him. He takes Barney to an abandoned cabin and holds him hostage. To make matters worse, Blue seems to be doing everything in his power to help the criminal. For example, Barney attempts to escape while Neal is sleeping, only to be foiled by Blue's loud barking. Blue also licks and bites Barney's hands instead of loosening the ropes that have him bound up. Neal appreciates Blue's assistance, and the convict actu-ally starts to like Barney's bloodhound. Meanwhile, Andy has discovered the wanted poster of Neal that Barney was carrying, and he also finds Barney's police hat lying on the ground near the lake. Naturally, he comes to the conclusion that his deputy has been captured by Neal.

A short time later, Andy locates the cabin and is able to signal a plan of escape to Barney. Unfortunately, the plan backfires when a mix-up occurs, and now both officers are taken hostage. But when Neal attempts to leave the cabin with Andy and Barney, he has trouble getting Blue into the squad car. Andy remembers how Blue reacted to the silent dog whistle, and he suggests to Neal that if he blows the whistle, Blue will come right to him. Sure enough, Neal takes the bait and blows the whistle. Blue bolts right at him and proceeds to knock Neal to the ground. Andy is able to make an easy arrest, and Barney is one proud deputy with his crime-fighting dog.

At the jail, Barney accidentally locks himself and Andy in cell #1, while Neal is housed in cell #2. Blue is sitting in front of both cells, with the key that will open either cell in his mouth. In a close call, Andy once again remembers the dog whistle, and the good guys get the key.

CAST NOTES. Regulars: **Andy Griffith, Don Knotts,** and **Howard McNear.**

Noted character actor **Arthur Batanides** stars as Ralph Neal. Batanides has appeared in countless television and movie roles, usually as a tough guy or criminal. **James Seay** portrays the first state trooper, and **Brad Trumbull** appears as the second state trooper.

Howard Morris, best known to fans of *The Andy Griffith Show* as Ernest T. Bass, provides the voice of WMPD's radio announcer and the operatic

134

singing voice of Leonard Blush. Mr. Morris also directed this episode. This is the first of eight episodes directed by Howard Morris.

EPISODE NOTES. 1. Andy and Barney enjoy listening to Leonard Blush's radio show on the "voice of Mt. Pilot," WMPD. Mr. Blush is known as the "Masked Singer." His rendition of the song "Sylvia" is interrupted by the news of Ralph Neal's escape from the state pen. Leonard Blush was introduced as Eleanora Poultice's prize pupil in episode 16, "The Song Festers." 2. Barney swears that the phrase "vis á vis" means hand-to-hand combat. 3. Ralph Neal changes clothing with Barney at the cabin, in order to look like he's the deputy and Barney's the crook. 4. The cabin in which Andy and Barney are held captive is owned by the Forbes family of Mayberry. 5. Blue resembles the shaggy dog that Floyd Lawson owned in episode 50, "Jailbreak." In that episode, the dog's name was Sam.

"Family Visit"

Episode #129. Air date: 10-5-64. Writers: Jim Fritzell and Everett Greenbaum. Director: Howard Morris.

Aunt Bee, longing to see her out-of-state relatives, invites her baby sister, Nora, and her family to come visit for a weekend. Nora and her husband Ollie live in Lake Charles, with their young sons Roger and Bruce. All four are decent folks, but each can be a royal pain in the neck. Andy finds himself having to share his bed with Ollie, which proves to be quite unpleasant. Ollie snores loudly and moves around a lot, a bleary-eyed Andy tells Aunt Bee later. Ollie annoys Andy during the day, too—especially when he turns on the squad car siren. Nora becomes a bit of a pest to Andy as well. She is constantly trying to match him up with a Lake Charles widow named Racine Tyler. Although Aunt Bee loves her sister, she admits she isn't crazy about how Nora has taken over her kitchen. Opie is miserable, too. He has to share his bed with his cousins, and Roger keeps sticking his foot into Opie's back. If company (like dead fish) begins to smell after three days, as someone once said, imagine how the Taylors feel when Nora and Ollie announce that they have decided to extend their stay to one full week. Next, Ollie begins to bully traffic violators, and he uses his kinship to Andy to justify acting like a lawman.

Two prison escapees are reported to be in the vicinity of Mayberry. After Andy learns of their capture, he comes up with an idea. He calls for his Uncle Ollie to "help track down the outlaws."

Tough-talking Ollie proves to be all talk, no action. Andy is not surprised when he returns home to find Ollie hurriedly getting his family together and heading back to Lake Charles.

CAST NOTES. Regulars: **Andy Griffith, Ronny Howard, Frances Bavier,** and **Howard McNear. Richard Keith** returns as Johnny Paul Jason.

James Westerfield, who portrays John Murrel in *The Travels of Jaimie McPheeters,* guest-stars as Ollie.

Maudie Prickett, who will be seen later in this series in the recurring role of Mrs. Edna Sue Larch, portrays Nora. Prickett enjoyed a lengthy career in television. She was born in 1915 and passed away on April 14, 1976. She had recurring roles on the following series: *The Jack Benny Show* as Jack's secretary, Miss Gordon (1950-1965); *Fury* as Aunt Harriet (1955-1968); *Hazel* as Rosie, a maid friend of Hazel's (1961-1966). You may also recall her as Cassie Murphy on the 1957-1958 series *Date with the Angels* or as Mrs. Ratchett on *The Tammy Grimes Show.* In 1965, she appeared as a maid on *Gallagher,* a mini-series from *Walt Disney's Wonderful World Of Color.* She appeared on several pilots, too, such as the 1955 pilot *Johnny Belinda* as Maggie MacDonald and the 1958 pilot *Belle Starr* as Miss Piper. She has made guest appearances in many series, including *The Adventures of Superman* (billed as "Maude"), *Bewitched* (several episodes as Tabitha's nursery school teacher, Mrs. Burch), *The Donna Reed Show, Dragnet, Get Smart, Gomer Pyle, U.S.M.C., Gunsmoke, Lassie, Love, American Style, Mayberry R.F.D.* (as Myrtle), *My Three Sons,* and *Room for One More.* She appeared in many fine movies, including *The Model and the Marriage Broker* (1951, directed by George Cukor), *Stars and Stripes Forever* (1952), *The Legend of Tom Dooley* (1959, with a young Michael Landon), Alfred Hitchcock's classic *North by Northwest* (1959), *I'll take Sweden* (1965, with Bob Hope), *The Maltese Bippy* (1969, with Dan Rowan and Dick Martin), and *Sweet Charity* (1969, directed by Bob Fosse).

Kenneth Butts portrays Roger, and **Billy Booth,** who is best known as Dennis Mitchell's pal, Tommy Anderson, on the hit series *Dennis the Menace,* portrays Bruce. The credits have the children's roles reversed.

Forrest Lewis portrays Mr. Mundt.

EPISODE NOTES. 1. Andy acknowledges a man named Eli and his wife as they walk to church. 2. The sermon mentioned in this episode is on the subject of Cain and Abel. 3. Four generations of the Beamon family attend church in Mayberry together. Their names are Claude, Sr., Claude, Jr., "plain" Claude, and Claudette. Each has the characteristic Beamon overbite. 4. Andy and Ollie used to play baseball together when they were younger. 5. Ollie's license plate number is the familiar AY-321. He drives a maroon two-door car. 6. The Mayberry Gas Works is mentioned. It has a blacktop parking lot. 7. Mr. Mundt owes $2.00 for parking in front of a fire hydrant. Ollie calls him a firebug. 8. Harry's Trout Pond has recently opened in Mayberry. It is located about two miles east on Miles Road. 9. Racine Tyler's husband left her $4,000 (his life insurance), a bakery, and a three-year-old bakery truck. Her home phone number is 439-7123. 10. The Bears are a baseball team in Mayberry. 11. Three prisoners escaped from the state prison in Meehawken, South Carolina. Two were members of the notorious Felts brothers gang. 12. Andy's second cousin, Todd, is a wiper on an oil tanker. He will not return to America "because of a girl in Cleveland, Ohio." 13. Although it is never stated, it is implied that the city of Lake Charles is in Louisiana.

"Aunt Bee's Romance"

Episode #130. Air date: 10-19-64. Writer: Harvey Bullock. Director: Howard Morris.

Aunt Bee receives a letter from an old beau that she hasn't seen in more than twenty years. His name is Roger Hanover and he's been living in Raleigh. By the way, Mr. Hanover happens to be an eligible bachelor. Aunt Bee invites him to come to Mayberry for a visit. She fixes her hair and buys new clothes for the big event. Andy remarks that she "looks good enough to take to Chinatown." When Roger arrives, he and Aunt Bee hit it off, but Andy and Opie instantly dislike the old codger. Roger is constantly cracking bad jokes and playing childish pranks. For example, he likes to wear Halloween masks at the breakfast table. Another one of his favorite (and most annoying) jokes is that when he shakes hands with a stranger, he pulls his hand up at the last second and says, "Hang it on the wall."

Even though Roger's obnoxious behavior bothers Andy and Opie, they tough it out, because Aunt Bee seems to be having the time of her life, and as Andy says, "There's some good in everybody." But one day, Roger approaches Andy and tells him that he's planning to propose to Aunt Bee, *unless* Andy gives him $400.00 to go to Florida. Andy is now aware that Mr. Hanover is not only a jerk, he's also a con man. Without hesitation, Andy decides to call Roger's bluff. This plan works, and Roger Hanover mercifully leaves on the next train for Florida. Andy doesn't have the heart to tell Aunt Bee about the extortion attempt, but is pleased to

hear her say at the conclusion of the episode that "a little of Roger goes a long way." We couldn't have said it any better ourselves.

CAST NOTES. Regulars: **Andy Griffith, Ronny Howard, Frances Bavier,** and **Howard McNear.**

Wallace Ford stars at the irritating Roger Hanover. Ford has appeared in such classic feature films as *Spellbound, Harvey, The Rainmaker,* and *A Patch of Blue.*

EPISODE NOTES. 1. Three of Aunt Bee's pen pals are Mrs. Deacon, who is the head of the Ladies Auxiliary in Raleigh; Donna Forbes, an arthritis sufferer, who recently moved to Raleigh from Mayberry; and Rita Akin, who is an old friend of Aunt Bee's. 2. Opie gets to go on a school field trip to a bakery in Raleigh. He and his classmates get to watch them make doughnuts. 3. When Roger Hanover arrives in Mayberry, he gives Aunt Bee a box of candy. 4. Roger is a cigar smoker. 5. Floyd tells Andy that Calvin Coolidge, not Mark Twain, said, "Everybody complains about the weather, but nobody does anything about it." 6. Roger tells Floyd that the barbershop should be called a "clip joint." Andy has to explain this joke to the dumbfounded barber. This is odd, because in episode 20, "The Beauty Contest," Floyd submitted an ad in the Founder's Day program stating, "Compliments of Floyd's Tonsorial Parlor—The Best Clip Joint in Town." 7. Roger ruins one of Andy's electrical cords when he tries to repair it. This further endears Roger to Andy. 8. Andy sarcastically tells Roger that he (Andy) is a giant when it comes to potting petunias. 9. Aunt Bee prepares Roger some sandwiches to take with him on his trip to Florida.

"Barney's Physical"

Episode #131. Air date: 9-28-64. Writer: Bob Ross. Director: Howard Morris.

The sixteenth of May proves to be a bittersweet day for Barney. It is the day he marks his fifth anniversary as Mayberry's deputy, but it is also the day that the learns he may soon lose his job. Andy is informed that all sheriffs' deputies must meet new civil service requirements for height and weight. The minimum standards are set at 5'8", 145 pounds. The physical will be given in one week, and Barney finds himself about seven pounds shy of the weight requirement, and almost one inch shy of the height standard. Maybe it's possible for Barney to meet the weight goal, but a grown man suddenly gaining an inch in height sounds impossible. Andy says, however, that it can be done. He remembers when Asa Bascomb had a pinched nerve in his neck. Doc

Harvey prescribed a harness for Asa. The contraption worked, and Asa claimed it made him "a good half inch" taller! Barney decides to try it. Asa sets him up with the harness, and we do mean *up*....Barney hangs in a closet! Obviously, it is a bit uncomfortable, but completely safe. Asa advises him to use the harness three or four hours per day. Meanwhile, Aunt Bee's cooking is putting on the needed weight. Incredibly, Barney reaches the height requirements, too.

Everything looks positive with just a day or two prior to the physical. Then, disaster strikes. Barney develops a severe case of hiccups and is unable to eat. On the day of the physical, his hiccups are gone, but he is now two and one-half pounds shy of the requirement. It appears certain that he will soon lose his job. However, Andy comes up with a brilliant solution: He attaches a very heavy chain to Barney's ID tag. This brings Barney's weight to the required 145 pounds, and Barney passes.

MEMORABLE SCENE. Opie charging his friends a nickel to watch Barney "hanging himself."

CAST NOTES. Regulars: **Andy Griffith, Don Knotts, Ronny Howard, Frances Bavier, Howard McNear,** and **Betty Lynn. Charles Thompson** returns, this time as Asa Bascomb. In other episodes, he is seen as Asa Breeney. (Mr. Thompson has had other roles in this series, too.) **Richard Keith** and **Dennis Rush** return as Johnny Paul and Howie.

Larry Thor appears as Mr. Bronson at the civil service office in Mount Pilot.

EPISODE NOTES. 1. Barney and Thelma Lou first met at Wilton Blair's funeral in 1960. 2. Barney wears his salt and pepper suit to the courthouse before going to Mount Pilot for his physical. 3. Andy wears his uniform, with a tie, in his two trips to Mount Pilot. 4. A deputy named Hanson is weighed just prior to Barney. 5. Barney gets several suggestions as to how to get rid of hiccups. One, from Floyd, is to inhale the air produced by an electric fan. 6. Barney receives a stainless steel waterproof wrist watch from Andy, Aunt Bee, Thelma Lou, Floyd, and Opie in recognition of his five-year anniversary. The inscription on the back bears the numeral 5. 7. Barney says that his usual weight varies between 138 and 138½ pounds. 8. Floyd says that Barney usually gets his hair cut every third Monday. He says that Barney's ears wing out, giving him lots of room to work. He says that Barney will never be bald, because he has a "loose scalp." By the way, Floyd says Barney is a good tipper. 9. Thelma Lou brings Barney a double-rich vanilla malted with two raw eggs in it, to help him gain weight. 10. There is a bent lamp post on the corner of Maple Street.

"Opie Loves Helen"

Episode #132. Air date: 9-21-64. Writer: Bob Ross. Director: Aaron Ruben.

Opie develops a crush on his teacher, Helen Crump. He spends his entire savings, 80 cents, to buy her a gift. After looking at numerous silk handkerchiefs, he finally decides to buy a pair of ladies' stockings. Andy believes the gift is for a young girl, and he asks his son if the wrapped present is a jigsaw puzzle, a box of fishing hooks, or a model airplane. Needless to say, when Andy sees the stockings, he's absolutely stunned. He tells Opie the gift is not appropriate, and suggests a box of candy or flowers would have been a much better idea. Confused, Opie goes to noted playboy Barney Fife seeking advice. Barney is also unaware that Helen is the subject of Opie's desire. Deputy Fife has the youngster recite a love poem, taken from T. Jonathon Osgood's book *Poems of Romance*, over the phone to his "girlfriend."

Helen interrupts Opie's recitation and tells him that she needs to see him in person. Opie tells Barney, and both are ecstatic. Before the youngster arrives at Helen's house, however, she phones Barney and tells him the true story. Barney is very embarrassed, and a short time later, he fills Andy in on the situation.

At Helen's, Opie gives her the stockings, which she politely refuses. Andy soon arrives and explains to his son that Helen is his girl. Opie is satisfied to end his "relationship" with Helen when he realizes that someday she may become his mother. At the conclusion of the episode, Opie is back with his old girlfriend, Sharon McCall. He is carrying her books home from school and plans to play stoop ball with her. Andy breathes a big sigh of relief.

MEMORABLE SCENE. When Barney calls the diner, he accidentally calls Frank "sweetie pie," mistaking Frank for Juanita, or "Neet," as he likes to call her. Barney asks Juanita to go to the drive-in movies with him. Frank is one of Juanita's coworkers at the diner.

CAST NOTES. Regulars: **Andy Griffith, Don Knotts, Ronny Howard,** and **Aneta Corsaut. Richard Keith** returns as Johnny Paul.

Mary Lansing portrays the beleaguered sales clerk, Miss Primrose. **Ronda Jeter** appears as Sharon McCall. **Betsy Hale** appears as Betty Ann.

EPISODE NOTES. 1. Andy and Barney's nickname for one of their old schoolteachers, Mrs. Von Roeder, was "the beast of the fourth floor." The mischievous duo once put ink in her thermos bottle, a tack on her chair, and a garter snake in her desk drawer. 2. Helen Crump teaches her students how to waltz, in order for them to keep alive the tradition of community dancing, which was a large part of the social life of their ancestors. Opie's usual waltz partner, Sharon McCall, was absent because her brace got loose and she bit down on it. Helen substitutes as Opie's partner, and the class dances to a recording of "My Darlin' Clementine." (This and other dances in this episode were staged by Jennie Gold.) 3. Barney took Thelma Lou to Morrelli's restaurant on her last birthday. They feasted on the deluxe special, consisting of pounded steak `a la Morrelli, for a mere $1.85, minus the shrimp cocktail, of course. Morrelli's has red checkered tablecloths, and the cooks there pound their own steaks. They also have great minestrone. They have a moody gypsy violinist, whom Barney tipped a quarter. Barney says patrons are allowed to bring a bottle into the restaurant. He goes on to say that Andy should take Helen to this fine establishment. 4. Opie's original savings was 62 cents. The remaining 18 cents came from returning soda pop bottles for the deposit money. 5. Andy and Barney have dated Helen and Thelma Lou, respectively, for two years. 6. A picture of George Washington hangs on the wall in Helen's classroom. 7. Opie and his classmates hold a collection drive for the Red Cross. 8. In elementary school, Andy had a big crush on an older girl named Barbara Edwards. 9. Barney refers to Andy as "Daddy Long Legs." 10. Opie tells Barney that he only knows two poems. They are "I had a dog named Spot…" and "The boy stood on the burning deck…" 11. After Barney discovers that Opie was reciting T. Jonathon Osgood's poem to Helen, he tells Andy things were less complicated when kids hated their teachers. 12. Opie attached the following note on the card bearing Helen's gift:

> Dear Miss Crump
> XXXXXXXXXXXX
> XXXXXXXXXXXXXXXXX
> Your Friend
> Opie

"The Education of Ernest T. Bass"

Episode #133. Air date: 10-12-64. Writers: Everett Greenbaum and Jim Fritzell. Director: Alan Rafkin.

Ernest T. Bass returns to Mayberry demanding an education. It seems that his girlfriend Ramona, or as Ernest T. calls her, "Romeena," doesn't believe that getting a gold leaf tooth and shaving the back of his neck is good enough. She will not marry him unless he gets an education. Ernest T. threatens to break every window in town unless he gets educated. Andy promises to help. He enlists the aid of Helen, who allows Ernest T. to attend classes along with her fifth grade students.

Having Ernest T. for a pupil proves a big challenge for Helen. When she tries to teach her class the proper grammar for the sentence "The possum hid under the rock," Ernest T. makes a big issue about how to actually remove a possum from under a rock. (He has personal experience in this matter.) Needless to say, he continually acts up in class until Helen can stand no more. In frustration, she smacks him on the hand with a ruler. At that moment, Ernest T. declares that he's in love with Helen and will not leave her alone until she feels the same way toward him. Everywhere Helen goes, Ernest T. is not far behind. He even throws a rock through her window in the middle of the night, with a note attached to it that says, "I love you!" Later, Andy and Barney discover that as a child, Ernest T. was hit on a daily basis by his mother. The pair come to the conclusion that Ernest T. is using Helen as his "mother figure."

Andy believes he can solve the problem if he can just teach Ernest T. some facts about geography, English, and math, and get him back to the hills (and Ramona). Andy reminds Ernest T. that he once stated he loved Ramona more than his cow or his .22 rifle. That evening, Andy has Ernest T. recite and write all of the words he knows in one complete sentence. It goes: "No hunt for wear, open and close, no credit." In geography, Ernest T. states the United States is bordered on the west by either Old Man Kelsey's woods, Old Man Kelsey's creek, or Old Man Kelsey's ocean. (Old Man Kelsey is one of Ernest T. Bass's neighbors, back in the hills.)

The next day, Andy has Ernest T. display all of his knowledge for Helen and Barney at the courthouse. Helen gives him a diploma for learning. The ceremony is actually quite touching. Barney is so moved that he has to fight back tears. The plan works, and Ernest T. stops bothering Helen and heads back to the hills to show off his diploma to Ramona.

Unfortunately, we haven't heard the last of Ernest T. Bass, because he later returns to Mayberry and starts breaking windows all over town. Evidently the diploma wasn't what Ramona wanted after all.

MEMORABLE SCENE. Ernest T. Bass showing us his unique way of adding 25 + 25.

CAST NOTES. Regulars: **Andy Griffith, Don Knotts, Ronny Howard,** and **Aneta Corsaut. Howard Morris** returns as the crazed Ernest T. Bass. **Ronda Jeter** returns as Sharon (McCall).

EPISODE NOTES. 1. Andy uses Opie's first-grade reader to teach Ernest T. Bass proper grammar. 2. Ernest T. learned to wash his food before consuming it from a possum and raccoon with whom he once lived for six months. Ernest T. also learned that a muskrat grabs the first female that comes along, and they live happily ever after. 3. Ernest T. asks Andy to be his "brother figure." 4. At school, Opie does the multiplication table for the number nine on the blackboard. 5. Barney says Sigmund Frude, rather than Sigmund Freud. 6. Ernest T. got his gold tooth for one dollar at a local sign company. 7. Barney prefers not to eat lunch at the drugstore, because everything there tastes like medicine. 8. The lunch special at the Mayberry Diner is chicken wings, rice, and mixed vegetables. Barney claims the chickens must have done a lot of flying, because their wings are so small. 9. Mr. Schwump, the mysterious man in the bad toupee, appears sitting with Andy on the bench outside the courthouse.

"Man in the Middle"

Episode #134. Air date: 11-2-64. Writers: Gus Adrian and David Evans. Director: Alan Rafkin.

Barney and Thelma Lou break up after an argument about their dating habits. Thelma Lou claims that Barney never takes her anywhere, and she implies that he is rarely willing to spend money when they do go out. An upset Barney bends Andy's ear, ranting and raving about the argument. Andy does his best to be supportive. He suggests that things will look much brighter after Barney gets a good night's sleep and "cools off" a bit. Barney does not think so. He says he's going to swear off women. However, the next thing you know, a repentant Barney is apologizing to Thelma Lou. She apologizes too, and the argument is a thing of the past. Barney laughingly remarks that Andy suggested maybe Thelma Lou and Barney were not meant for each other. Actually, it was Barney who said it — but now Thelma Lou is angry with Andy.

The next day, Andy gets snubbed by Thelma Lou. When he asks Barney why she is upset with him, Barney tells him. Andy reminds his deputy who actually made the offensive remark. They argue briefly.

An angry Thelma Lou goes to Helen to tell her what Andy said, hoping to get some sympathy. Instead, Helen tells her she cannot believe that Andy would say such a thing. Soon, Thelma Lou gets very offended when Helen says she is acting childish. She and Helen stop speaking to each other. Thelma Lou tells Barney what Helen called

her, and the peeved deputy pays a visit to Andy, who remarks that sometimes Thelma Lou *is* childish. The men argue. Andy calls Barney "childish," and Barney calls Helen a "dame." Fortunately, this argument doesn't last long. They reconcile the following morning.

Next, Barney decides to try to get Thelma Lou and Helen to reconcile. He calls them both to come to the courthouse. There, he tells then that he and Andy are friends again, and he quotes Andy's remark about how silly it was to let a remark made by a "third party" (meaning Helen) come between them. Helen is offended that Andy referred to her in such a manner. Thelma Lou agrees with Helen and is upset too! When Andy gets the cold shoulder from Helen, he is puzzled. Barney tells him what happened. Andy can hardly believe Helen took offense at his innocent remark.

Barney and Thelma Lou make up with each other. Then, Thelma Lou hatches a plan to get their friends back together. She persuades Helen to go on a blind date. Barney talks Andy into the same thing. Andy and Helen are surprised when they realize they are one another's mystery date. Fortunately, each uses this opportunity to apologize, and their dispute is resolved. Ironically, Barney and Thelma Lou end up rekindling their original argument! Fortunately, they soon resolve it, bringing this strange period of misunderstandings to a merciful end.

MEMORABLE SCENES. 1. Andy catching Thelma Lou with mussed hair and Barney with a lipstick-covered face. 2. Barney telling Andy that his blind date is a woman named "Grace" at the same time that Thelma Lou says the date's name is "Millie." They compromise, and Barney refers to her as "Millie Grace."

CAST NOTES. Regulars: **Andy Griffith, Don Knotts, Aneta Corsaut,** and **Betty Lynn.**

EPISODE NOTES. 1. Barney and Thelma Lou's usual dating routine is as follows: On Sundays, they meet at church. On Tuesdays, Barney joins her at her place for television. On Thursdays, they order the special at the diner. On Friday nights, when Barney is on duty, Thelma Lou joins him for a cup of coffee at the courthouse. 2. After their last argument, Barney tells Thelma Lou that he's decided they'll have no more specials at the diner. Instead they will splurge and order a steak sandwich for $1.25 and have both salad *and* soup. 3. Barney wears his salt and pepper suit throughout most of this episode. 4. Andy likes Helen to wear her green dress when they go out. 5. Helen enjoys hearing Andy sing "The Fox," usually with Barney. 6. Andy sings "I Wish I Was a Red Rosy Bush" to Helen. 7. The movie playing in Mayberry during this episode is

The Monster from Out of Town. 8. Barney and Thelma Lou have been an item for five years. 9. Mayberrian Jed McIntyre has lived alone for 25 years. He smiles a lot and talks to himself. 10. Barney says the man who wrote the following must have been some kind of a nut: "So deep a friendship hath one man for another, that no female caress shall ever tear it asunder."

"Barney's Uniform"

Episode #135. Air date: 11-9-64. Writers: Bill Idelson and Sam Bobrick. Director: Coby Ruskin.

A man named Fred Plummer has been getting on Barney's nerves lately. Plummer, a recently hired employee at Foley's Market, has been warned by the deputy to stop sweeping sidewalk debris onto Main Street. Barney approaches him for the fourth time and issues a ticket, charging him with littering a public thoroughfare, and he fines him $4.00. Fred is irate, but agrees to pay the fine. However, he tells the wiry lawman that if he ever catches him out of uniform, he will break every bone in his body. Naturally, Barney is intimidated by the threat. He begins wearing his uniform everywhere.

Barney is evasive when Andy questions him about wearing his uniform to church and even on his day off. Eventually, he tells Andy about Fred's threat. He then produces a piece of paper, showing that he is a member of the Mount Pilot Judo Society. Barney used to take lessons, then slacked off, but he has recently returned to the ancient Oriental art under the instruction of Mr. Izamoto. He tells Andy that he wears his uniform to *protect* Fred. He says that it is only his uniform that keeps him from going after Mr. Plummer. Of course, Andy doesn't believe that, but he lets the subject go. He knew about the situation because Plummer came by earlier to pay his fine, and he told Andy about his "beef" with Barney.

Andy decides to pay a visit to Barney's judo instructor in Mount Pilot. He discovers that although Barney is a good student who tries hard, he is not well-versed in the art. He is called "the chicken" by his classmates, because he has weak bones (that would snap easily) like a chicken's. Andy gets an idea. He informs Mr. Izamoto of Barney's situation, and the instructor agrees to help out. He will masquerade as Barney, under the cover of darkness.

Back in Mayberry, Andy tells Plummer that Barney will be in his civvies tonight because he is going to the charity dance. He warns Fred that Barney knows judo and may not hesitate to use it if the need arises. Brash Mr. Plummer snickers, "I'll judo him!" Andy lets him know about what time to expect Barney, too.

Later, Fred waits for Barney to leave the courthouse and come walking past the market. Sure enough, here he comes, wearing his civvies, just as Andy told him. Fred pounces and is promptly manhandled. Using a couple of basic judo maneuvers, and garbed all the while in Barney's salt and pepper suit, Mr. Izamoto leaves Fred a bit bruised and battered.

A short time later, Andy convinces Barney that an officer of the law is always an officer, whether he is wearing a uniform or not. A lawman must command respect. Barney agrees to wear his civilian clothes to the dance. He'll wear his salt and pepper suit, of course, because he bought it for dances. He says it's perfect for doing the dip.

As Andy and Barney start to drive off, Andy suggests that maybe Barney ought to go talk to Fred and straighten him out. He tells Barney he has a feeling that Fred is still at work. Barney approaches with some trepidation, only to discover Fred huddled up in the alley. Barney is shocked when his wary nemesis treats him with respect and awe. Ignorance is bliss, and in this case, it's a confidence booster. Barney can be himself again.

MEMORABLE SCENE. Barney practicing judo on Andy.

CAST NOTES. Regulars: **Andy Griffith, Don Knotts, Ronny Howard,** and **Frances Bavier. William Keene** returns as Reverend Hobart M. Tucker.

Allan Melvin returns to the series in another "heavy" role, this time as Fred Plummer. Japanese character actor **Yuki Shimoda** portrays judo instructor Mr. Izamoto.

EPISODE NOTES. 1. Fred Goss, Mayberry's dry cleaner, misplaces Barney's salt and pepper suit for a few days. It was accidentally sent to a Mr. Fitz in Siler City. 2. Barney takes Thelma Lou to Glifford's Department Store in Mount Pilot to shop for toiletries. 3. The Mount Pilot Judo Society is located between Peggy's Beauty Salon and William's Interiors. Ted's Pet Shop is two doors down. 4. Barney's theme, "The Manhunt," is played after his final confrontation with Fred Plummer. 5. Andy calls Barney "Tiger." 6. Barney reads *The Art of Judo* by Professor Matzamoto. 7. The Mayberry Charity Dance is at 8 P.M. on Wednesday. The cost is $3.00 per couple. 8. Sunday's sermon was titled "The Dice Are Loaded Against the Evil-doer."

"Opie's Fortune"

Episode #136. Air date: 11-16-64. Writers: Ben Joelson and Art Baer. Director: Coby Ruskin.

While walking home from school, Opie finds a man's black leather change purse alongside the road. It contains $50.00 in currency, but no clue as to who the owner might be. He turns it over to Andy, who tells him that he will hold it for one week. If no one shows up to claim the money, Opie may keep it. The excited youngster does a lot of window shopping. Indeed no one does report losing the money, and at the end of the seventh day, Opie is $50.00 richer. Andy strongly advises him to spend only $10.00 and put the remainder in his new piggy bank.

Moments after an ecstatic Opie leaves the courthouse, Barney notices a lost and found ad in the recently delivered *Mayberry Gazette*. It states that Parnell Rigsby, of Bannertown, R.F.D. 1, lost the money in the vicinity of Mayberry. Andy knows the money must be returned to its rightful owner, but when he sees how happy Opie is, he decides to pay Mr. Rigsby right out of his own pocket. This touches Barney. He and Andy drive to the Rigsby farm.

Meanwhile, Opie comes to the courthouse to show Andy his newly purchased fiberglass rod and reel. Finding the place empty, he practices casting inside the building. Just then, in walks Parnell Rigsby, looking to report his lost change purse. He leaves his message with Opie and returns home, where he finds Andy and Barney about to leave Bannertown after leaving the money with Mrs. Rigsby. Parnell is grateful to get his money back. He mentions that he talked to Opie at the courthouse, and says the boy appeared to know nothing about the lost money.

An upset Andy returns home to talk with his son. He discovers that Opie has broken his piggy bank and taken off with the money. Finding him at the sporting goods store, he takes the boy to the courthouse and is just about to scold him when Opie explains his actions. He was *returning* the rod and reel. He knew that it was wrong to keep something that belongs to someone else. He had to break his bank in order to get the remaining money out. He gives the $50.00 to his chagrined father. Andy is very proud to have such an upstanding young son. To reward Opie, Andy buys him the rod and reel.

CAST NOTES. Regulars: **Andy Griffith, Don Knotts, Ronny Howard,** and **Frances Bavier.**

Jon Lormer portrays Parnell Rigsby. **Mary Jackson,** who appears in various roles in the series, appears as Mrs. Rigsby. She is best known as Emma Baldwin from the classic television drama *The Waltons*. (Emma and her sister are renowned for their "tonic.") **Bill McLean** portrays Mac, the clerk at the sporting good store. In the episode, Andy refers to him as "Max."

EPISODE NOTES. 1. One of Barney's old girlfriends was Phoebe Gilbert, now operator of Phoebe's Beauty Salon. Barney once took her to the Blu-Vue. (The Blu-Vue is the real name of the first motel in Mount Airy, N.C.) Phoebe has a brother named Limley Gilbert. Interestingly, long after this episode aired, *Gomer Pyle, U.S.M.C.* had an episode in which Gomer was teamed with a military trained German Shepherd. Gomer named the dog Limley Gilbert. 2. Ted's Pet Shop is shown in this episode. Mount Pilot has a Ted's Pet Shop, too. Perhaps it is a chain. 3. Earl Pike purchased a new car for his son's birthday. His son is 57 years old. 4. Virginia Beasley and Earlie Gilley announce their engagement in *The Mayberry Gazette*. A real Earlie Gilly does indeed exist and lives in Mount Airy's sister city, Pilot Mountain. He married Andy Griffith's cousin *Lorraine* Beasley (not Virginia). 5. Two desserts that Barney loves are tapioca pudding and chocolate layer cake. 6. Barney once found a $1.00 bill. He spent it all on a girl. 7. Rhoda Apfel is getting married. It was announced in *Mayberry After Midnight*, a regular feature of *The Mayberry Gazette*. This column is written by 16-year-old Red Akins. 8. A Mayberry couple, Howard and Lorraine Felcher, are getting a divorce. Lorraine is a drinker. 9. Bannertown is the real name of a North Carolina town, just two miles from Mount Airy.

"Goodbye, Sheriff Taylor"

Episode #137. Air date: 11-23-64. Writers: Fred Freeman and Lawrence J. Cohen. Director: Gene Nelson.

Andy is seriously considering a job offer from his friend Herb Mason of Raleigh. He has been asked to join the Hogarth Detective Agency, which is located there. If Andy accepts, it would mean leaving Mayberry. Andy has been sheriff for 12 years, and he feels that maybe it is time to make a change. Andy tells Barney that if the job in Raleigh pans out, he would like him to fill the vacated sheriff's position.

Andy goes to Raleigh to check things out, leaving Barney as acting sheriff. Barney hires Goober, Otis, and Jud as his deputies. Then the mayhem begins: Opie's friend George gets his head stuck in a sewer drain; Little Jimmy Jackson falls and skins his knee while Otis is acting as the school crossing guard; and Jud helps himself to some free fruit, which angers Harry, who runs the fruit stand. The grand finale is a major traffic jam orchestrated by Goober. Barney confides to Floyd that he does not want to be sheriff.

Andy returns, and Barney believes that the sheriff has made up his mind to leave. In desperation, Barney asks Goober and Floyd to stage robberies at their businesses, thus creating a crime wave. Barney hopes that Andy will stay on as sheriff to fight this sudden outbreak of crime. Andy easily sees through the scheme. Finally, Barney admits to Andy that he does not want to be sheriff. Andy tells him he realizes that, and he then informs him that he has decided to stay on as the sheriff of Mayberry. That is great news for Barney, and for Mayberry.

CAST NOTES. Regulars: **Andy Griffith, Ronny Howard, Don Knotts, Frances Bavier, Howard McNear,** and **Hal Smith. George Lindsey** returns as Goober. **Burt Mustin** returns as Jud.

Andrew Duncan appears as a truck driver. **Janet Stewart,** who can be seen in various roles in this series, portrays Mrs. Jackson.

EPISODE NOTES. 1. This is the first episode in which Goober is seen wearing his trademark beanie. 2. When George gets his head stuck in the sewer drain on Maple Street, Barney contacts the Mayberry Department of Public Works. 3. Andy delivers a gun permit to a man named Ben Lucas. 4. Andy and Opie both had trouble with spelling at school. 5. It costs Floyd 20 cents to clean each of his barber towels. 6. Barney pays each deputy $5.00 for his work. 7. The license plate number on Goober's pickup truck is M-37905. 8. Barney calls Goober, Jud, and Otis deputies #1, #2, and #3, respectively. 9. There once was a big accident at the intersection of Fourth and Main streets. It involved a garbage truck and a hook and ladder truck. 10. Floyd says that he would hate to lose Andy as a customer because he has soft but strong, easy-to-cut hair. Also, Andy never fidgets in the chair. 11. Floyd claims that the traffic jam created by Goober is the worst he has seen since the 1939 World's Fair.

"The Pageant"

Episode #138. Air date: 11-30-64. Writer: Harvey Bullock. Director: Gene Nelson.

The Mayberry Centennial Pageant is featuring a play about the founding of the town of Mayberry. The lead female role of "Lady Mayberry" is offered to Clara Edwards (who has played the role in the past), while Aunt Bee is in charge of sewing all the costumes. Secretly, Aunt Bee believes she could be

a great Lady Mayberry. In fact, as a child in West Virginia in the 1920s, Aunt Bee had the lead role of Alice in a church play called *The Little Princess.* It was directed by the Reverend Dargood, and Bee's performance received rave reviews.

Suddenly, Clara is forced to drop out of the play because her sister in the town of Saberton has taken ill. Next, Aunt Bee convinces the play's director, John Masters, to give her the coveted role. In the play Andy portrays English settler James Merriweather; Doris Williams is his wife, Mary; and Barney Fife appears as Indian Chief Noogatuck.

When the time comes for Aunt Bee's first rehearsal, she turns out to be a terrible actress. Even after numerous rehearsals, her acting doesn't improve at all. John Masters is forced to ask Andy to inform Aunt Bee that she will have to be replaced. Knowing this would break her heart, Andy tries to come up with a different plan of action. Meanwhile, Clara Edwards is able to return to Mayberry because her sister's health has improved. John Masters asks Clara to take over the role of Lady Mayberry, but she refuses, due to her lifelong friendship with Aunt Bee.

Andy now sees a way to settle this situation. He asks Clara to take over Aunt Bee's household duties at the Taylor home, because with all the rehearsals, Aunt Bee simply doesn't have the time to clean house, go shopping, and prepare meals. Clara happily obliges and wishes Aunt Bee luck with the play. Then with Aunt Bee present, Clara does a beautiful rendition of Lady Mayberry's soliloquy, which begins Act II of the play. Andy's sly plan succeeds, and Aunt Bee willingly hands over the reins of Lady Mayberry to the much better actress. Also, Aunt Bee didn't want Clara in her kitchen anyway.

MEMORABLE SCENES. 1. Barney's poor performance as Chief Noogatuck. The topper occurs when he chokes while smoking a peace pipe with James Merriweather. Barney also refuses to remove his Indian headdress, even when he's not rehearsing. 2. Opie and Barney trading tongue twisters. Barney just can't seem to say the line "Rubber baby buggy bumpers" four times in a row without flubbing up.

CAST NOTES. Regulars: **Andy Griffith, Don Knotts, Ronny Howard,** and **Frances Bavier. Hope Summers** returns as Clara Edwards. **Olan Soule** returns as John Masters.

Barbara Perry appears as Doris Williams. **James Brewer** portrays Duane, the author of the play.

EPISODE NOTES. 1. The town of Mayberry was founded in 1864 and (like the real town of Mount Airy) is located in the northern part of North Carolina. 2. Barney explains the Latin meaning of the word centennial to Andy and Opie. He doesn't believe Andy is telling Opie the truth when he tells the youngster that a centipede has 100 legs. 3. Mrs. Armbruster is an "itty bitty" lady who works at the Mayberry library. She was considered as a replacement for Clara, but John Masters preferred a taller woman for the role. 4. Opie refers to confectioner's sugar as "conventionery" sugar. This amuses Aunt Bee. Opie loves to eat Aunt Bee's fresh-baked brownies. 5. Barney states that Eleanora Poultice is his speech instructor. You may recall that Ms. Poultice was his voice teacher in episode 116, "The Song Festers." 6. In the play, the town of Mayberry was originally known as Happy Valley. Also in the play, Chief Noogatuck refers to James Merriweather as "Laughing Face" and "Pale Face." 7. Barney refers to the theatre as "Heartbreak Alley." 8. As Lady Mayberry, Aunt Bee refers to Chief Noogatuck as "Chief Noggatook." 9. When Clara takes over the role of housekeeper at the Taylors', she promises to bake her famous apple pie for Andy and Opie every day of the week. 10. At the conclusion of the episode, John Masters is trying to replace Barney in the role of Chief Noogatuck. Barney gets irate and chases the prospective "Noogatuck" off the stage.

"The Darling Baby"

Episode #139. Air date: 12-7-64. Writers: Jim Fritzell and Everett Greenbaum. Director: Howard Morris.

The Darling family returns to town along with the newest member of the family, three-month-old Andelina. She's Charlene's pride and joy. The family has come to find a young boy to become betrothed to the infant. According to mountain tradition, Andelina and the chosen male will be legally obligated to marry each other when they reach the age of consent. This sounds crazy to Andy, of course, and he gets upset when Briscoe announces that Opie Taylor is the chosen male. The Darlings are a notoriously stubborn bunch, and Andy cannot convince them to forget the idea. The Darlings consider the betrothal a done deal.

All that remains is the signing of the contract, designed by the family's preacher, Reverend Opel. In a shocking turn of events, Andy and Opie agree to sign the document. Barney cannot believe his ears. How could Andy do this?

Just before signing, Andy chants, "Ebum Shoobem, Shoobem, Shoobem." Then he and Opie sign the paper. A jubilant Briscoe gazes at the signatures, and then is mystified as the names suddenly vanish. The elder Darling accuses Andy of practic-

ing "witchery." He immediately nixes any possibility of a marriage between the Taylors and the Darlings. Briscoe explains that, while he knows some witches and even goes to church with some, he will have no witches in his family. A little bit of ingenuity (not to mention some excellent disappearing ink!) sends the superstitious Darling family back to their mountain home.

MEMORABLE SCENE. Barney getting gassed on mulberry squeezings.

CAST NOTES. Regulars: **Andy Griffith, Don Knotts, Ronny Howard**, and **Frances Bavier. The Dillards** (Rodney and Doug Dillard, Dean Webb, and Mitch Jayne) return as the Darling boys. **Denver Pyle** returns as Briscoe Darling. **Maggie Peterson** returns as Charlene Darling Wash.

EPISODE NOTES. 1. Opie reads a book titled *Twenty Scientific Tricks a Boy Can Do at Home.* It was written by Seymour Shreck, author of *Fun in a Garage on a Rainy Day.* Opie discovers how to slip an egg into a milk bottle, turn a wishbone into rubber (soak it in vinegar), and make disappearing ink. 2. Andelina's dowry includes an 8' x 10' cottage on the back twenty. It needs a roof and fresh mud on the floor. The lucky husband will also get a cow and two acres of side hill (complete with good strong boulders). 3. Andelina was named after Andy because he has done so much for the family. 4. Barney once won a church raffle. The prize was four free haircuts. 5. Briscoe Darling's wife is deceased. She was 17 years old when she married 30-year-old Briscoe, who was her second husband. Her first husband was killed by a team of hogs. 6. In this episode, Opie is 10 and Barney is 35. 7. Aunt Bee shows Andelina to her neighbor, Mrs. Jones, who loves babies. 8. The Darlings perform the following songs in this episode: "There Is a Time" (it makes Briscoe cry), "Ebo Walker," and "Stay All Night, Stay a Little Longer." They also perform a couple of brief instrumentals. 9. The following songs are mentioned, but not played: "Wet Shoes in the Sunset," "Two Sack Full of Love," and "Will You Love Me When I'm Old and Ugly." That last one makes baby Andelina cry. 10. Barney was almost engaged to Halcyon Loretta Winslow when he was 30 years old. She was downright ugly. Barney refers to her as "Beasto Maristo." Her father owns a prune-pitting factory. He once offered Barney a ⅓ interest in his business, full use of the company car, an interest in the family home and a beautiful hillside plot in the Mount Pilot Cemetery. This was all part of the deal, if he would marry Halcyon. After lunching at Klein's Coffee House in Mount Pilot, Barney turned the deal down. The specialty at the coffee house is American cheese and garni. Incidentally, Halcyon went on to finishing school in

A rare shot of Andy Griffith and Don Knotts discussing the script during a break in filming.

the east. However, she's still "ugly, single, and pitting prunes," according to Barney. 11. Dud Wash used to hunt beaver. Now, he hunts 'possum.

"Andy and Helen Have Their Day"

Episode #140. Air date: 12-14-64. Writers: Bill Idelson and Sam Bobrick. Director: Howard Morris.

Andy and Helen realize that, due to their busy schedules, they have had precious little time together lately. Barney decides to help them out by "giving them" a Saturday. He offers to take over all of Andy and Helen's duties, errands, and chores for one day, thus making it possible for the couple to get together for a full day. The couple gratefully take Barney up on his generous offer. They look forward to a relaxing day, picnicking at Myers' Lake, located in neighboring Stokes County.

Goober Pyle will drive them there, as Barney will need the squad car.

Goober finds them a nice area, but then stays around to have a sandwich. Later, Barney shows up. These are just the first of a number of exasperating interruptions. Barney turns up two more times to inquire about trivial matters. To further disrupt the couple's day, Mr. Peterson, the county game warden, stops by and asks Andy to produce his fishing license. Unfortunately, Andy has forgotten to bring it. Mr. Peterson takes Andy and Helen to the office of the justice of the peace, where Andy uses the phone to call the courthouse. Andy does not have the $25.00 for the license infraction, so he asks Goober to tell Barney to bring the money to the office of the Stokes County justice of the peace. Goober relays the message, sort of. He recalls parts of it: Andy and Helen; justice of the peace; and $25.00 for a license.

Barney puts it all together, and concludes that Andy and Helen are tying the knot. He gathers Goober, Aunt Bee, and Opie, and the excited foursome goes to witness the wedding. When the truth is revealed, Barney is the one left blushing, not the bride.

CAST NOTES. Regulars: **Andy Griffith, Don Knotts, Ronny Howard, Frances Bavier, George Lindsey,** and **Aneta Corsaut.**

Multi-talented **Howard Morris,** who usually plays nutty wild man Ernest T. Bass, portrays a much more subdued character, George, the television repairman. Morris also directed the episode.

Colin Male portrays Game Warden Peterson. The cast credits list his character as "Wormser." Male may be familiar to fans of the 1950s television program *The Dotty Mack Show,* where he was seen as a singer.

EPISODE NOTES. 1. Barney wears his salt and pepper suit when he goes to the office of the Stokes County justice of the peace, which is located in Siler City. 2. Barney took Juanita to Morrelli's to eat, and then to her place to watch television in the dark. 3. Barney claims history was his best subject in school. 4. Andy and Barney plan to attend the Peace Officers' Bowling Tournament in Mount Pilot. 5. Andy is a deacon at church, while Helen sings in the church choir. 6. Mayberry has a hospital. 7. Wally, owner of the filling station, has a married daughter named Verdi. 8. Goober reprises his Cary Grant imitation, "Judy, Judy, Judy." 9. The double feature at the Mayberry Theater is *House of Blood* and *The Beast That Ate Minnesota.* 10. Evidently neither Andy nor Helen owns an automobile. Otherwise, they would not have had to rely on Goober to drive them to Myers' Lake.

"Otis Sues the County"

Episode #141. Air date: 12-28-64. Writer: Bob Ross. Director: Howard Morris.

Otis trips as he leaves his cell. He makes nothing out of the mishap, putting the blame on his knee, which he injured years before. Barney insists he fill out an "Accidental Injury Occurring on County Property" form. Otis believes Barney is making much ado about nothing, but he reluctantly agrees to have the document signed by a notary public. He finds one, a Mount Pilot lawyer by the name of Neil Bentley. When Bentley sees the document, he senses he has a golden opportunity to make some money. He tells Otis a lawsuit filed against Mayberry County would benefit everyone. Otis remembers hearing Andy and Barney talking about how they could use more funding. He does not want to sue his friends, but Bentley insists Otis would actually be doing them a *favor* by doing so.

He points out that Otis would be compensated for his "injury," the county would have to improve the condition of the courthouse, and, of course, the lawyer would get his percentage of the judgment against the county. Otis falls for the shyster's misrepresentations and consents to the lawsuit.

When Andy and Barney are informed of Otis's $5,000 claim against the county, they are very upset. Mr. Bentley meets with Andy and urges him to encourage the county to settle out of court. Andy, sensing the falsity of the lawsuit, will not comply.

Barney makes a hilarious but futile attempt to wheedle the truth out of Otis and get him to admit that the fall was not the fault of the county. Barney only manages to get drunk, along with Otis, and the two end up singing "Sweet Adeline." The whole sorry situation was recorded by Barney on a reel-to-reel tape recorder.

The county's chief attorney, Mr. Roberts, arrives in Mayberry to try to determine if the county is liable. While reenacting the event at the courthouse, Otis suddenly remembers that he tripped over his own suit jacket as he left his cell. A sheepish Mr. Bentley leaves the premises, and the lawsuit is forgotten.

CAST NOTES. Regulars: **Andy Griffith, Don Knotts, Hal Smith,** and **Howard McNear.**

Jay Novello, who appeared in episode 53, "Guest of Honor," as Mayberry's honored guest and con man, Sheldon Davis, here portrays lawyer Neil Bentley. **Bartlett Robinson,** who was radio's original "Perry Mason," portrays Mr. Roberts.

EPISODE NOTES. 1. Otis claims that he initially injured his knee while playing football with his wife. 2. Floyd was in the courthouse, along with Barney, when Otis fell. If a trial had ensued, Floyd would have been the county's star witness. 3. Neil Bentley's office number is 205. 4. Mayberry does have a notary public, a bank employee named Mary Pleasance. However, she and a woman named Dixie Bell Edwards are out of town during this episode. Together, they are hunting black bear at Great Dismal Swamp. 5. Floyd has a sister. 6. Floyd says he always enjoys a midmorning cup of coffee. 7. Mr. Schwump returns. He grabs some bench time with Andy and Barney outside of the courthouse.

"Three Wishes for Opie"

Episode #142. Air date: 12-21-64. Writer: Richard M. Powell. Director: Howard Morris.

Barney purchases a "magic" lamp at a police auction in Mount Pilot. It had been confiscated from a group of traveling gypsies. The gullible deputy believes the lamp is inhabited by the spirit of an eighteenth-century gypsy genie named Count Ist Van Telecky.

Opie arrives at the courthouse, and Barney has him select some of the cards that accompanied the lamp. Opie draws two flaming torches, which means the Count has granted the youngster three wishes. Opie's first wish is for a jackknife. Lo and behold, Andy walks through the door and gives his son a jackknife! Opie's second wish is to get a B in arithmetic, because Andy has promised him a trip to the Raleigh Zoo if he can achieve this grade. In a close call, according to Helen Crump, Opie gets the desired B. Now Barney is *really* excited. He brings in Floyd and Goober as witnesses and, in the backroom of the courthouse, all three watch as the magic cards (two unicorns) grant Barney one wish. He wishes for the fingerprint set that he had ordered over six months earlier. He no sooner gets the wish out of his mouth when the fingerprint set is delivered to the courthouse. Floyd and Goober are speechless as a visibly shaken Deputy Fife states, "Count Ist Van Telecky lives!"

The time has come for Opie to make his third and final wish. He manages to utter only the first few words of it when Barney interrupts him. The deputy interprets that Opie's wish is for Andy and Helen to get married. Barney spreads the word all over Mayberry about the pending marriage, and Andy has to take an irate Helen Crump aside to explain the strange story that led to the announcement of their upcoming nuptials.

This was not Opie's wish. He actually wished for Helen to be his teacher in the sixth grade, during the next school year. Meanwhile, Andy and Helen tell Barney there are definitely no wedding plans. A dejected Deputy Fife reluctantly throws the magic cards and the lamp in the garbage. At that moment, Opie comes in and explains his actual wish to everyone present. A stunned Helen tells Andy, Barney, and Opie, that she was just informed she is being transferred from the fifth to the sixth grade. The switch will take effect at the start of the next school year. After hearing this, a confident Barney retrieves the magic cards and lamp from the garbage, and the Count is back in business.

In the next day's edition of *The Mayberry Gazette*, the "Mayberry After Midnight" section reports that Andy and Helen have announced their wedding plans. The wedding will most likely take place in June. Barney swears that he didn't have anything to do with the article. Only Count Ist Van Telecky knows for sure.

CAST NOTES. Regulars: **Andy Griffith, Don Knotts, Ronny Howard, Howard McNear**, and **Aneta Corsaut. Burt Mustin** returns as Jud. (The cast credits list him as "Judd." In all other episodes, he is listed as Jud.) **George Lindsey** returns as Goober. Lindsey's role of the likeable character Goober Pyle will steadily increase in upcoming episodes. He will become a full-time regular as the season progresses.

EPISODE NOTES. 1. An angry Helen tells Andy that he believes he's Mayberry's answer to Cary Grant. 2. Andy says hello to a couple named Willie and Pearl who are walking in front of the courthouse. 3. Andy was the person who delivered the fingerprint set to the courthouse. He was at the Mayberry Post Office when it arrived. A postal worker named Clint gave it to him. 4. Barney swears that E.S.P. means "Extra *Sensitive* Perception." 5. At the police auction in Mount Pilot, Goober buys a roll of copper tubing for 30 cents. Andy claims he could have got the same copper tubing in Mayberry for 16 cents. 6. Barney reads a book called *Psychic Phenomena*. It is written by Dr. Merle Osmond. Dr. Osmond lives in Boise, Idaho, and was a guitar instructor before he became involved with the psychic world. 7. The exceptional musical scores used in the episodes of *The Andy Griffith Show* are often taken for granted. Special credit must be given to music director Earle Hagen and music editor Ken Johnson for their tasteful use of the eerie music in this enjoyable episode.

"Barney Fife, Realtor"

Episode #143. Air date: 1-4-65. Writers: Bill Idelson and Sam Bobrick. Director: Peter Baldwin.

Barney has decided to try his hand at selling real estate after an enthusiastic meeting at the diner with Mayberry realtor Ernie Slummer. He will receive a 5 percent commission on every transaction. When Andy hears Barney mention that the Williams family may soon put their home on the market, it piques his interest. Andy has always liked that house. Barney claims that Andy could sell his home for $24,000 and purchase the Williams' place for just $3,500 more. Andy admits it is an enticing idea.

Later, Andy finds Opie attempting to sell his damaged bicycle to a boy named Howie Williams. Opie's asking price is $5.00. Andy points out the problems, and the Williams boy declines to buy it. Andy explains to Opie about "fair dealin'," being open and honest.

Meanwhile, Barney has been busy getting his clients, Harry and Lila Sims, interested in seeing the Taylors' home. He surprises Andy one night when he brings the couple over, unannounced, to walk through the house. While leading the tour, Andy misleads the prospective buyers by failing to mention the house's problems. However, much to his father's chagrin, Opie is quick to set the record straight. He points out the crack in the kitchen ceiling, the faulty plumbing, and the fact that the roof leaks. Mr. and Mrs. Sims quickly lose interest in the house. Andy believes Opie is trying to get him back for spoiling his bicycle sale, but Opie insists he was just employing the "fair dealin'" principle.

Barney pleads with the Simses to have a second look at Andy's. When they do, Andy frankly admits that the 34-year-old house does have its share of problems. The Simses react peculiarly to this honesty. Suddenly they decide they *must* buy the house. Andy explains he will sell his home only if he can purchase the Williams place. Barney goes into action right away.

When Andy and Aunt Bee come to see their potential new home, the Williams's son, Howie, innocently points out the household problems there: a basement that floods easily and a crack in the furnace. Ultimately, Andy and Mr. Williams decide to stay put for the time being. This is all upsetting to Barney, who decides to leave the real estate game and become a part-time used car salesman.

CAST NOTES. Regulars: **Andy Griffith, Don Knotts, Ronny Howard,** and **Frances Bavier.**

Dabbs Greer, a fine character actor who has appeared in hundreds of series, portrays Harry Sims. **Amzie Strickland** returns to the series, this time as Lila Sims. **Dennis Rush,** who previously was seen as Howie Pruitt in several episodes, returns. This time he is Howie Williams. **Harlan Warde** portrays Mr. Williams.

EPISODE NOTES. 1. Barney wears his salt and pepper suit when he shows houses. 2. Mr. Ferris is a plumber who lives in Mayberry. 3. The Clarks and the Mortons are real estate clients of Barney's. 4. The Simses reside on Elmwood Street in Mayberry. 5. Barney exclaims that Aunt Bee keeps her home in "apple pie order."

"Goober Takes a Car Apart"

Episode #144. Air date: 1-11-65. Writers: Bill Idelson and Sam Bobrick. Director: Peter Baldwin.

Andy has a sheriff's safety conference to attend in Mount Pilot. He expects to be away for a day and a half. Because Barney is vacationing in Raleigh, Andy needs to find someone to stay at the courthouse. A man named Shorty had agreed to

help Andy out, but later canceled. He will, however, take over as a temporary crossing guard.

Goober informs Andy that he will be happy to stay at the courthouse. Andy reluctantly consents to let Goober do it. However, the happy-go-lucky mechanic almost blows the opportunity when he doesn't show up at the courthouse when Andy is ready to go. Andy finds him working on Gilly Walker's carburetor at Wally's Filling Station. Goober promises Andy that he will go straight to the courthouse as soon as he finishes repairing the car.

Later, Andy is upset when he telephones the courthouse and gets no answer. He finds Goober still working on Gilly's car, but now the car is parked just outside of the jailhouse. A disgusted Andy tells Goober to forget about helping out. Instead, he asks Aunt Bee to watch the courthouse. Just before Andy leaves, Goober begs for a final chance to help. Andy gives in and leaves town.

On his way to the courthouse, Goober is hounded by Gilly, who insists his car still isn't running right. Goober dismantles the engine and brings it inside the courthouse so he can work on it. Before you know it, Goober has dismantled the entire car and rebuilt it inside the courthouse. Floyd Lawson has witnessed much of this feat. He finds it fascinating and beautiful, while Gilly is impatient and annoyed.

When Andy returns from his trip, he finds a small crowd outside the courthouse, and Goober, Gilly, Floyd, and the car inside. Flabbergasted, he orders Goober to begin dismantling the car immediately. The frustrated sheriff leaves, only to return a bit later and find the car still intact. Floyd is sitting behind the wheel, thinking about buying the car. Andy has had enough. He orders Goober to remove the car by morning or he just might shoot him!

Andy goes home and discovers that two of his friends from the safety conference, Sheriff Jackson and Deputy Joe Watson, are coming by the courthouse to visit him. A panicked Andy rushes back to the courthouse, hoping against hope that Goober has removed the car. Alas, he has not. Everything turns out okay, however. The visiting law officers do come, but they automatically assume that Andy has taken the safety conference to heart. They believe the car to be part of the safety program that was discussed at the meeting in Mount Pilot. In fact, they ask Goober if he could set up a similar "display" in their town, Siler City.

When the men leave, Andy heaves a sigh of relief, grabs a shotgun, and then watches as Goober finally begins working earnestly to dismantle the car.

CAST NOTES. Regulars: **Andy Griffith, Ronny Howard, Frances Bavier, Howard McNear,** and **George Lindsey.**

Larry Hovis, best known as Sergeant Andrew Carter on *Hogan's Heroes,* portrays Gilly Walker. **Wally Engelhardt** and **Buck Young** appear as Sheriff Jackson and Deputy Joe Watson, respectively. **Stanley Farrar, Johnny Coons,** and **Tom Jacobs** appear as Mayberry citizens gawking at the car in the courthouse.

EPISODE NOTES. 1. Andy promises a man named Warren that he will help him with an unspecified chore when he returns from Mount Pilot. 2. Alice Nathan likes to work on her own car. Goober believes she is a Quaker. 3. Aunt Bee anticipates a phone call from her friend Doris Lacey. 4. Aunt Bee's friend Eleanor Schroder called to tell her about the car in the courthouse. 5. A man named Don Yeltin calls Andy about some business papers. 6. Sarah, the switchboard operator, has a cold in this episode. 7. Gilly wants his car fixed quickly because he is in a hurry to get to East Lake. 8. Mayberry has a phone book. 9. Andy and a Miss Corey talk via phone. She has a matter to discuss. She asks him about his trip. 10. Barney writes a letter to Andy, who reads it aloud to Goober.

"The Rehabilitation of Otis"

Episode #145. Air date: 1-18-65. Writers: Lawrence J. Cohen and Fred Freeman. Director: Peter Baldwin.

Barney decides that Otis needs to be rehabilitated, after he comes into Mayberry drunk and riding on a cow that he bought for twenty dollars from Old Man Davis. Otis actually thought he was riding on a horse. Barney reads a 25-cent magazine called *Learn a Month.* This month's topic is psychological therapy, and Barney attempts to analyze why Otis drinks like a fish. He gets no farther than giving Otis the old ink blot test before the two end up arguing over whether the ink blot was a bat or a butterfly. Ultimately, Barney gives Otis his home telephone number and instructs him to call, night or day, if he has the urge to drink booze. Otis calls Barney late one evening, from a party at the Johnson place. Barney contacts Andy, and they locate Otis. He's drunk as a skunk and once again, he's riding on the back of the cow. This time, Barney gets mad and arrests Otis for violating Municipal Code 404-B, public drunkenness and disorderly conduct. The ultimate humiliation for Otis is when Barney handcuffs him.

The next morning, an irate Otis Campbell informs Andy and Barney that he will do his drinking (and jail time) elsewhere. A concerned Andy and Barney discover from Floyd that Otis has moved on to Mount Pilot. Andy telephones Sheriff Williams in Mount Pilot, and he verifies that Otis is currently a "visitor" in his jail. Otis has struck up a friendship with a fellow drunk named Luke. Luke likes to let everyone know that his mother was a nurse.

Andy and Barney travel to Mount Pilot, and Barney begs Otis to come home. Otis is stubborn and, after conferring with Luke, decides to stay right where he is. Barney is visibly upset as he and Andy head back to Mayberry empty-handed. A short time later, however, Andy and Barney are thrilled when Otis returns home. He's drunk again and riding on the back of the same cow. In fact, he rides right through the doors of the courthouse. Later, Luke shows up with some of his drinking buddies, seeking the comforts of the Mayberry jail.

CAST NOTES. Regulars: **Andy Griffith, Don Knotts, Hal Smith,** and **Howard McNear.**

Frank Cady appears as Luke. Cady is best known for the role of Sam Drucker on *Petticoat Junction.* It is ironic that Cady would play a drunk in the same scene with Hal Smith's character of Otis Campbell. In the pilot episode of *The Andy Griffith Show,* titled "Danny Meets Andy Griffith" (which aired as an episode of *The Danny Thomas Show* in 1960), Mr. Cady appeared as Will Hoople, the original town drunk of Mayberry. Cady would go on to make one more appearance in the series. In episode 177, "The Legend of Barney Fife," he portrays Farley Upchurch, the editor of *The Mayberry Gazette.*

EPISODE NOTES. 1. Barney subscribes to *Learn-A-Month* magazine. The subject covered in the previous issue of the magazine was "Odd Facts Known By a Few." Two of these facts are (1) a horse's eyes are the same size at birth as they are when he's full grown; and (2) there are more stars in the heavens than there are grains of sand on all the beaches in the whole world. 2. Otis Campbell is a cigarette smoker. 3. Otis sings a drunken version of "Home on the Range." 4. Barney tells Otis that he looks good in the color blue. 5. Barney's telephone is on a three-way party line. 6. Floyd Lawson once helped Otis get out of a well that he had fallen into. Floyd explains that Otis was drunk at the time, and thought he had fallen in quicksand. 7. Before they discovered that Otis went to Mount Pilot, Andy and Barney thought he might have gone to Siler City, Bridgeton, or Raleigh. Otis has relatives in Siler City. 8. Floyd states, "They charge an arm and a leg for items in Raleigh."

"The Lucky Letter"

Episode #146. Air date: 1-25-65. Writer: Richard M. Powell. Director: Theodore J. Flicker.

Andy ridicules Barney when he starts to answer a chain letter. Andy says he has a very superstitious deputy. Barney says he's cautious, not superstitious. He goes on to say that he gets this trait from his mother. Andy keeps hounding Barney about being superstitious until the deputy gets mad and throws the letter in the trash.

Floyd admits to Barney that it was he who had forwarded the letter to the deputy. He also warns Barney about the bad luck waiting for those who break the chain. Sure enough, in a matter of minutes, Barney bumps his head, cuts himself shaving, gets his foot run over by a truck driven by a man named Norbert, and wrecks the squad car. Worst of all, in just a few days, he's scheduled to attend the annual pistol shooting qualifications for law enforcement officers in Mount Pilot. If he fails, he could lose his job. Poor Barney is now a nervous wreck. Andy believes Barney is bringing all the bad luck on himself, while Barney's convinced that he's simply jinxed.

Next, Barney asks Thelma Lou to go out on a date, but she's busy gluing covers back on hymn books with Edgar Coleman. Barney insinuates that she's doing other things with Edgar, and Thelma Lou tells him to get lost. Now, Barney is really at the end of his rope. As he exits the courthouse, Barney says, "Swept into the dust bin of history, exit Barney Fife."

Luckily, Andy comes up with a plan. He has Goober bring his copy of the chain letter to Barney so he may continue the chain. Barney realizes that Andy is comparing him to the non-intellectual types like Goober and Floyd. Barney refuses to forward the letter. Next, Andy has Thelma Lou attend the pistol shooting qualifications, in order to ease Barney's frayed nerves. Barney goes out and shoots a perfect round. As he's leaving, Andy and Thelma Lou discover that he was carrying a four-leaf clover and a rabbit's foot in his pocket.

Later, Barney decides to mail two copies of the chain letter in order to increase his luck. While Andy is shaking his head in disbelief, Deputy Fife proceeds to walk across the street to mail the letter. He promptly gets his foot run over for the second time. Andy comes to the conclusion that Barney is just plain unlucky.

MEMORABLE SCENE. When Andy switches hats with a sleeping Deputy Fife.

CAST NOTES. Regulars: **Andy Griffith, Don Knotts, Ronny Howard, George Lindsey, Howard McNear,** and **Betty Lynn.**

EPISODE NOTES. 1. Andy refers to Barney's superstitions in episode 142, "Three Wishes for Opie." 2. Norbert's license plate number on his truck is GP-780. 3. Barney refers to himself as "Big Barn'." 4. Barney admits he's not crazy about the number 13. 5. Barney talks to Frank at the diner when he tries to reach Juanita. As usual, Barney starts talking in a sexy voice until he realizes he's talking to Frank. 6. Goober mails two copies of his chain letter. One went to his cousin Gomer in the Marines, and the other one to his Aunt Floy. 7. After Floyd mailed two copies of the chain letter, he received a one dollar tip from a traveling salesman from Raleigh. 8. Barney accidentally shoots his pistol while it's in the holster at the shooting range. 9. Thelma Lou says that shooting a pistol is a very masculine thing. 10. While looking for Barney's discarded chain letter at the trash dump, Andy finds a fender off Buzzy Leonard's car. He also finds the January edition of a dirty magazine called *Love*. The subscriber is none other than Barney Fife! Andy and Barney also find a grocery list from a lady named Mrs. Hudgins, and a love letter written by Herbert Swindell.

"Goober and the Art of Love"

Episode #147. Air date: 2-1-65. Writers: Fred Freeman and Lawrence J. Cohen. Director: Alan Rafkin.

Andy and Barney are tired of Goober hanging around with them while they are on their dates with Helen and Thelma Lou. To remedy this problem, Andy and Barney attempt to locate a girlfriend for their painfully shy buddy. Goober admits he likes a local girl named Lydia Crosswaithe, so Andy persuades him to ask her out. Even though Andy gives Goober some helpful dating tips, his first date with Lydia is very awkward, and lasts about two whole minutes.

Barney tries to help by taking Goober to Helen's house so they can spy on her and Andy from an outside window. Barney's point is for Goober to watch the master at work, and the plan is successful, until Goober gets excited and yells some words of encouragement to an embarrassed and angry Andy and Helen.

Later, Goober gets up the nerve to ask Lydia out again, and the pair show up at Helen's while she and Andy are playing bridge with Barney and Thelma Lou. Lydia ruins the evening by complaining about anything and everything. Among her dislikes are pretzels (they lie heavy on her stomach), bowling (it hurts her back), and riding in cars (she gets car sick). Lydia is also a poor conversationalist, so Andy suggests that the group take a car drive. Lydia reluctantly goes along and hangs her head out of the window, like a sick dog. Needless to say, everyone has a rotten time.

On the next evening, Goober and Lydia invite themselves to tag along with Andy, Helen, Barney, and Thelma Lou to a dance featuring Freddy Fleet and His Band with a Beat. While everyone wants to have a good time at the dance, Goober and Lydia decide to sit and talk and just listen to the music, because, as you may have guessed, Lydia doesn't like to dance.

CAST NOTES. Regulars: **Andy Griffith, Don Knotts, George Lindsey, Aneta Corsaut,** and **Betty Lynn.**

Josie Lloyd stars as Lydia Crosswaithe. In episode 68, "Barney Mends a Broke Heart," she portrays the same character and is a friend of Thelma Lou's from Mount Pilot. In this episode, Lydia Crosswaithe and Thelma Lou have never met. Lloyd also appeared in many earlier episodes, portraying Mayor Pike's various daughters.

EPISODE NOTES. 1. Viewers get a rare glimpse of Helen Crump's house and living room. 2. Goober admires Maureen O'Sullivan, the actress who portrays Jane in the *Tarzan* movies. Goober says she is quite a swimmer. 3. Barney once got scared watching one of those mummy movies. 4. Lydia's house number is 598, but no street in Mayberry is listed. 5. Barney likes to cheat at bridge. 6. The movie currently playing in Mount Pilot is called *Raiders of Tripoli.* Andy's suggestion to see this show falls flat on its face when Lydia says that she's already seen it. 7. Goober buys Lydia a box of candy at Downey's Store in Mayberry. 8. Barney wears his salt and pepper suit to play bridge at Helen's. He also wears it to the dance. 9. While grooming for his first date with Lydia, Goober puts so much grease on his hair that it actually starts to drip down his forehead. 10. Lydia's father used to work at the lumber plant. Lydia says he hated it. 11. Once again, it's not mentioned whether band leaders Freddy Fleet and Bobby Fleet are related to each other.

"Barney Runs for Sheriff"

Episode #148. Air date: 2-8-65. Writer: Richard M. Powell. Director: Alan Rafkin.

Andy has gotten the urge to move again. An old hunting buddy of his named Ed Crumpacker has offered Andy an executive position at his St. Paul, Minnesota–based company. Andy tells Barney that he's not going to file for reelection in the upcoming sheriff's election. In fact, Andy convinces Barney to throw his hat into the ring. Later, however, Andy gets a telephone call from Ed Crumpacker, who tells him the position has been filled. It seems that the job went to a relative of someone in the company. Since Andy is not on the voting ballot, Barney takes it upon himself to organize a civic committee that launches a write-in campaign to reelect Sheriff Taylor. Barney even becomes Andy's campaign manager and coins the slogan, "Win with Taylor." Barney appoints Floyd the barber to be Andy's precinct manager from Main Street to Maple Street, Maple to Elm Street, and Elm to the Mayberry Fire Department.

Everything goes well until Barney realizes that no one in town, including Thelma Lou, took *his* candidacy seriously. Andy sees the problem and urges his deputy to start his own campaign. Barney not only starts a campaign of his own, he launches an all-out assault with loudspeakers screaming, "Fife, the people's choice, Barney Fife for sheriff, the man for the job, win with Fife." He also tries to distribute posters that proclaim, "Fife for Sheriff, Honest, Fearless, Incorruptible." Floyd tells Barney that his picture on the poster makes him look like he's smelling something.

Next, Barney challenges Andy to a public debate. Floyd is chosen as the moderator, and Barney is chosen to be the first speaker at the debate. Barney opens by citing 76 cases of malfeasance by Sheriff Taylor that have accumulated during Andy's 12 years of service. Barney explains that because of time constraints, he will discuss only three: (1) The traffic in Mayberry is completely out of control and jaywalking is rampant. (2) The sheriff's office is ill-equipped. There is no tear gas, nor are there any submachine guns. In fact, the only emergency equipment that Andy carries in the trunk of the squad car is a shovel and a rake. (3) Andy doesn't carry a gun, or a weapon of any kind on his person.

As Barney tells the large gathering about these charges, Aunt Bee stands up and yells, "Fiddle-faddle," and proceeds to call Barney a rabble rouser. Needless to say, everyone, especially Andy, is stunned by Barney's outburst. Andy's feelings are obviously hurt, but he answers each charge in a calm and rational manner. Andy's speech seems to snap Barney back to reality, and as soon as he's finished, Barney publicly endorses his best friend for reelection. Finally, everything returns to normal in Mayberry.

CAST NOTES. Regulars: **Andy Griffith, Don Knotts, Ronny Howard, Frances Bavier, Howard McNear, George Lindsey, Aneta Corsault,** and **Betty Lynn.**

EPISODE NOTES. 1. Norma's Beauty Shop and Ted's Pet Shop in Mayberry are shown. The businesses in Mayberry that wouldn't allow Barney to put his poster in their window are Floyd's Barbershop, Groceries and Meats, Dave's Coffee Shop, and the jewelry store. 2. Andy's job offer might have landed him in Europe or South America. 3. Andy explains to Opie the difference between a tortilla and a tarantula. 4. Goober sells Acme gasoline. 5. Andy makes reference to the time he considered leaving Mayberry three months earlier. This reference was to episode 137, "Goodbye, Sheriff Taylor." 6. Floyd eats a Tootsie Pop during the episode. 7. Barney's "Manhunt" theme is played when he decides to run for sheriff and as he attempts to distribute his posters. 8. At the end of the episode, Barney admits to Andy that he took about one hundred of his "Fife for Sheriff" posters and used them as wallpaper for his apartment.

"If I Had a Quarter-Million"

Episode #149. Air date: 2-15-65. Writer: Bob Ross. Director: Alan Rafkin.

While Barney is chasing a hobo away from the Mayberry railroad tracks, he stumbles over a briefcase. He gives it to Andy, who in turn takes it to Goober, a master at picking locks. Andy wants to locate the owner in order to return the case and its contents. He and Goober are stunned to find that the case contains $250,000 in cash. Andy decides to keep the briefcase in the safe at the Mayberry jail until he discovers what this is all about. He talks to the F.B.I. and discovers that the federal boys have been chasing a bank robber who pulled a big heist in Raleigh. The robber escaped after boarding the 10:18 A.M. train out of Raleigh. When the crook felt the F.B.I. breathing down his neck, he tossed the briefcase out of a window and disappeared.

Barney believes the crook will return to the area where the briefcase was discarded. He wants to start an all-out investigation, but Andy tells him to wait until the F.B.I. arrives. Barney can't wait, and without Andy's knowledge, he dons his salt and pepper suit and parades around town like a man who has just acquired a lot of money. Barney's plan is to attract the crook's attention. The dapper deputy tells Floyd the barber and Fred, the clerk at the Mayberry Hotel, that he's looking for a high-stakes, no-limit, deuces-wild poker game. Later on, Floyd cuts the hair of a stranger who expresses an interest in playing some poker himself.

Meanwhile, Mr. Brewster of the F.B.I. arrives in Mayberry and tells Andy to lay low and let the crook come to them. At the same time, Barney meets the potential poker player and starts to arrest him after the stranger states that the stolen loot was stored in bundles. Only the police and the crook would have known this fact. Barney backs down when the stranger claims to be Mr. Hennessey of the F.B.I. He shows Barney the secret F.B.I. handshake, and tells him that as a team, they will capture the real criminal, the same way the F.B.I. solved the McAlister case. Obviously, the stranger is the crook, and there is no such thing as a secret handshake or the McAlister case, but Barney falls for it, hook, line and sinker.

Next, Barney calls Andy and tells him about the current situation and what he and Mr. Hennessey are doing. Andy realizes something is wrong when Mr. Brewster shows up at the courthouse and claims he's never met Barney. Meanwhile, Barney and Mr. Hennessey pick up the briefcase at the jail and take it to Barney's apartment. Hennessey tells Barney that the real crook has been watching their every move, and it will just be a matter of time before he tries to retrieve the money from Barney's apartment. Then Hennessey and Barney will be able to make an easy arrest. Next, the bad guy puts knockout drops in Barney's glass of milk. Just as Hennessey is about to make an easy escape with the loot, he's captured by Andy and Mr. Brewster, who have figured out the criminal's plan. As Andy tries to awaken his sleeping deputy, he calls Barney "Tiger."

CAST NOTES. Regulars: **Andy Griffith, Don Knotts, George Lindsey,** and **Howard McNear.**

Hank Patterson portrays the hobo. Mr. Patterson is best known as Arnold the pig's "father," Fred Ziffel, on *Green Acres.* **Al Checco** appears as the bank robber, a.k.a. Mr. Hennessey. Mr. Checco also portrayed a bank robber in episode 78, "The Bank Job." **Robert Brubaker** appears as F.B.I. agent Frank Brewster. Mr. Brubaker appeared as state prosecutor Roger Mason in episode 61, "Andy on Trial." **Byron Foulger** appears as Fred, the clerk at the Mayberry Hotel. **Alfred Hopson** portrays the farmer.

EPISODE NOTES. 1. Barney's "expensive cigars" costs 35 cents each. He tells Floyd he plans to smoke eight of them a day. 2. A man named Ben is the manager of the Mayberry train station. 3. Floyd wonders out loud about how Barney acquired his money. He asks Barney if a relative passed away, or if he won the big prize on a television show. 4. Barney hides his gun in the back of his pants while he is on undercover duty. This causes problems: He rips his pants, accidentally shoots off the gun, and tends to lose the gun when it falls through his pants.

"TV or Not TV"

Episode #150. Air date: 3-1-65. Writers: Art Baer and Ben Joelson. Director: Coby Ruskin.

A complimentary article is written about Andy in the national sheriffs' magazine *Law and Order*. The article is entitled "Sheriff Without a Gun." (Barney likes the story until he discovers that his last name is spelled "Fice.") Andy informs Aunt Bee, Barney, and Opie that he has received a telegram from Hollywood stating that a film crew is coming to Mayberry to make a television series based on the article. Writer Allen Harvey and his female assistant, Pat Blake, arrive and tell Andy and Barney to just be themselves while they observe their everyday routine. Andy acts normal, while Barney acts like a rough and tough lawman.

It turns out that Mr. Harvey, Miss Blake, and a recent arrival, production assistant Mr. Jammel, are actually crooks. Their plan is to pretend to shoot an episode at the Bank of Mayberry so they can gain access to the vault. Barney had innocently told the trio that $50,000 in cash is usually on hand on Friday nights in the bank's vault. The crooks know from the article that Andy doesn't carry a gun, and they believe that Barney is totally incompetent. While the pretty Miss Blake flirts with Andy, Mr. Harvey and Mr. Jammel are given a tour of the bank by Barney and the bank's president, Mr. Meldrim.

That evening, Aunt Bee invites Barney and the "Hollywood gang" to dinner. Later on, as Barney is walking home, he catches the crooks robbing the bank. They quickly convince him that they are rehearsing a scene, but Andy soon arrives and actually does arrest the gang. He shows his unsuspecting deputy how the crew broke into the bank's door. Andy goes on to explain to Barney that during their after-dinner conversation, Mr. Harvey and Mr. Jammel seemed very interested in knowing what time Andy and Barney went to bed. Harvey and Jammel also made it a point to say that they would be working well into the night. Andy enlists the assistance of Floyd and Goober, whom he has just deputized. They hold a gun on the Hollywood crew while Andy takes them into custody.

CAST NOTES. Regulars: **Andy Griffith, Don Knotts, Ronny Howard, Frances Bavier, George Lindsey,** and **Howard McNear. Charles Thompson** returns as the elderly bank guard, Asa Breeney. **Warren Parker** returns as bank president Mr. Meldrim.

George Ives stars as Allen Harvey. Ives appeared as "Doc" on the television series *Mr. Roberts* from 1965 through 1966. **Barbara Stuart** appears as Pat Blake. Stuart is best known as Sergeant Vincent Carter's girlfriend, Miss Bunny Olsen, on *Gomer Pyle, U.S.M.C.* **Gavin McLeod** appears as Gilbert Jammel. McLeod is well known for his television roles of Murray Slaughter on *The Mary Tyler Moore Show* and Captain Merrill Stubing on *The Love Boat*.

EPISODE NOTES. 1. Barney played the Nelson Eddy role in *Rose Marie* in last year's Mayberry play. The drama critic in *The Mayberry Gazette* said Barney gave a stellar performance. 2. This is the only episode in which Goober's last name is given as Beasley, rather than Pyle. 3. Barney's "Manhunt" theme is played as he attempts to capture the crooks at the bank. 4. Andy's usual bedtime is between 10:00 P.M. and 10:30 P.M., while Barney's is usually 11:00 P.M. 5. Andy tells Miss Blake that the majority of law enforcement in Mayberry consists of giving parking tickets, helping young'uns across the street, and putting lids back on trash cans. 6. Mr. Jammel left his hat at the Taylors' after dinner. 7. Andy tells Miss Blake that he doesn't carry a gun because he wants folks to respect him, not to fear him because of the presence of a gun. Aunt Bee states that Andy feels "heavy on one side" when he carries a gun. 8. Barney refers to his gun as "the Old Roscoe," "Little Persuader," and "Blue Steel Baby." 9. Floyd was once deputized on Veteran's Day so he could carry the flag in the parade. Goober is always deputized on Halloween, in order to keep kids from putting orange peels, potatoes, and rotten tomatoes in the cannon located at the park in Mayberry. 10. Barney works on a television script in which he single-handedly captures a gang of bank robbers. 11. Barney refers to *Peyton Place* as "Peeton Place."

"Guest in the House"

Episode #151. Air date: 3-8-65. Writers: Lawrence J. Cohen and Fred Freeman. Director: Coby Ruskin.

Aunt Bee has a very dear friend named Minnie, who has a beautiful daughter named Gloria. The two families are so close that Aunt Bee refers to Gloria as her "cousin." Aunt Bee invites her to come from Siler City and spend a few days at the Taylor home. Gloria has recently had a lover's quarrel with her fiance, a man named Frank. Aunt Bee believes that a few days away from the broken engagement would be good for Gloria. A problem arises when Gloria, while on the rebound, falls head over heels for Andy. Aunt Bee had told him to be nice to her, so he obliges. Later, when Helen catches Gloria helping Andy with some typing at the courthouse, she gets suspicious.

At the Taylor home, Gloria refuses to accept Frank's long-distance phone calls. Instead, she accepts Andy's invitation to join him and Helen on a movie date. This makes Helen mad, and she demands that Andy set up a double date with Goober and Gloria. The following evening rolls around and the foursome goes to Morelli's Restaurant, which is famous for their $1.75 pounded steak special. Morelli's also has a large dance floor, where the patrons enjoy dancing to a jukebox. Gloria declines Goober's request to dance, preferring Andy as a partner. By the end of the evening, Sheriff Taylor is in a dilemma. Helen has told him to get lost, and Gloria has just given him a great big kiss.

Later that night, Andy goes to Aunt Bee with his problem, and together they devise a plan. Without Gloria's knowledge, Andy and Aunt Bee tell Frank to come to Mayberry. Their plan is a rousing success, and in no time at all, Gloria and Frank are headed back to Siler City, hand in hand. Andy's next mission is to patch things up with Helen. This mission also succeeds, and everything returns to normal in Mayberry.

MEMORABLE SCENE. Goober and Andy dropping their silverware so they can converse under the table at Morelli's.

CAST NOTES. Regulars: **Andy Griffith, Ronny Howard, Frances Bavier, George Lindsey, Howard McNear,** and **Aneta Corsaut.**

Jan Shutan stars as Gloria. She wasn't given a surname in the episode. Shutan is known for her role of Ruth Cramer on the television series *Sons and Daughters* in 1974. **George Spence** appears as Frank.

EPISODE NOTES. 1. Barney is in Raleigh during this episode. 2. Andy sings "There Is a Time" during the episode. This is the same tune that Charlene Darling sang in episode 139, "The Darling Baby." (It made Briscoe cry.) 3. There is a miniature golf course in Mount Pilot. It costs $1.50 for a twosome to play a round. 4. Tommy Wilson is a friend of Opie's. Tommy moved from Mayberry to Siler City. 5. Katherine Harney was a girlfriend of Andy's when he was in high school. She broke Andy's heart when she went to the prom with Vern Harris. According to Vern's mother, Andy spied on Vern and Katherine from a nearby tree as they were going to the prom. 6. Floyd relates the sad story of a Mayberrian named Agnes Drumhiller. In 1949, Agnes was stood up at the altar by a man named Horace Frizzy. After that, Agnes started drinking heavily. In fact, her brother once found her under the sink, singing and nipping at the elderberry wine. Agnes and Horace finally got married. Later she got real fat, and when she tried to dye her hair blonde, it came out bright orange. Floyd claims that

she did it on purpose to get back at Horace for standing her up at the altar.

"The Case of the Punch in the Nose"

Episode #152. Air date: 3-15-65. Writers: Bill Idelson and Sam Bobrick. Director: Coby Ruskin.

Andy and Barney are going through some old police records when Barney discovers an assault case that never went to trial. It occurred at 11:25 A.M. on August 9, 1946. The two people involved were Floyd Lawson (Mayberry's then-new barber) and grocer Charlie Foley. Andy tells Barney to forget about it, but the ever-efficient deputy insists on talking to the principals involved. Floyd doesn't remember the details, but Charlie tells Barney that he had asked Floyd for a haircut, then fallen asleep in the chair (like he always does). When he awoke, he discovered that Floyd had also given him a shave. When Floyd called Charlie a cheapskate for refusing to pay for the shave, Charlie turned around and called Floyd a crook. One thing led to another until at last mild-mannered Floyd Lawson punched Charlie Foley right in the nose.

When Floyd hears Charlie's recollection, he wholeheartedly disagrees, and an argument ensues. In order to clear everything up, Barney reenacts the crime, with the actual people involved, including Goober, who was a mere lad to five when the original fracas occurred. As Barney tries to piece together the puzzle, Floyd gets mad and punches Charlie (again) on the nose.

Before you know it, everyone in Mayberry is arguing over the case and fighting with one another. In chronological order, the following events occur: (1) Charlie Foley punches Goober in the nose; (2) Otis Campbell punches Floyd in the nose, because Otis is a distant relative of Foley's; (3) Goober punches Gilly Walker in the nose; (4) Opie's best friend Johnny Paul (who is Charlie Foley's nephew) punches Opie in the nose; (5) Lamar Tuttle (Floyd's cousin) punches Otis in the nose; and finally (6) a lady named Betty Ann telephones Andy and claims that an unnamed assailant punched her in the nose.

By this time, Andy has had enough. He severely scolds Barney for being the instigator of all the mayhem and decides to bring Floyd and Charlie together to solve this dilemma. First of all, Andy reminds Floyd and Charlie that they have been close friends for nearly twenty years. Next, he has the two men shake hands. Floyd and Charlie are suddenly reminded that in 1946, Mayberry's Sheriff Poindexter solved the original dispute in the same manner. Both men realize how foolish they've been acting, and they make up. When Barney starts to stir up the controversy once again, Floyd punches *him* in the nose!

CAST NOTES. Regulars: **Andy Griffith, Don Knotts, Ronny Howard, Frances Bavier, George Lindsey,** and **Howard McNear. Frank Ferguson** returns as Charlie Foley. **Larry Hovis** returns as Gilly Walker.

EPISODE NOTES. 1. Otis Campbell was first arrested for drinking at 2:00 P.M. on September 23, 1941. He was nabbed at the Mayberry Garden Club's flower show. Since it was his first arrest, his sentence was suspended. Barney states that Otis probably "passed out in the poppies." 2. Andy and Barney hum and then sing the hymn, "Sinners Lose All Their Guilty Stains." 3. All old police documents in Mayberry are boxed and kept in the basement of the Mayberry Firehouse. 4. Andy gets mad at Barney for bringing up the old case and in a rare fit of anger yells, "Shut up!" to his startled deputy. Also during the episode, Andy calls Barney a "nut" on two separate occasions. 5. Aunt Bee prepares a poultice for Charlie Foley's injured nose. 6. Mayberrians Robert (Bobby) Gribble and Emma Larch announce their coming nuptials in *The Mayberry Gazette.* Floyd fondly recalls that eleven years earlier, when the sidewalk was being laid in front of his barbershop, Bobby Gribble wrote the following line in the wet cement: "Bobby Gribble Hates Emma Larch." Floyd goes on to say, "Now they're announcing their coming nuptials. Ain't life funny." (Even funnier: in future episodes, Aunt Bee will have an elderly friend named Emma Larch — who is not married to Bobby Gribble.) 7. Bobby Gribble used to date Andrew Beasley's daughter. 8. In the episode, Floyd's Barbershop charges the following prices: haircuts, $1.75; flat tops, $2.00; Butch, $2.00; shampoo, 75 cents; shave, 50 cents. Floyd charges a quarter for using hair tonic.

"Opie's Newspaper"

Episode #153. Air date: 3-22-65. Writer: Harvey Bullock. Director: Coby Ruskin.

Opie's friend Howie Pruitt receives a small printing press as a birthday present. This gift inspires Opie and Howie to make their own newspaper in Howie's garage. They call their two-page newspaper *The Mayberry Sun*, and topics include the activities of their fifth-grade classmates. Besides the scores of the school's baseball team, the paper reports facts about kids, such as Karen Folker scraping her knee while chasing Bruce Newdale on the Elm Street playground; Troy Bowden forgetting his

lunch and Tommy Griff giving him a pear; and Myra Lambert preparing to portray a raindrop in the upcoming school play. Unfortunately, the paper's sales are low. Andy and Barney advise the boys to widen their scope, like the big newspapers do.

The youngsters decide to pattern their paper after the most popular section of *The Mayberry Gazette,* a gossip column called "Mayberry After Midnight." They begin eavesdropping to pick up some juicy tidbits. Opie overhears Aunt Bee saying that Mrs. Foster's chicken à la king tastes like wallpaper paste. Howie overhears Andy saying that the preacher's sermons are as "dry as dust." Later, Opie hears Barney saying that Harold Grigsby is jealous of his much younger, bleached-blonde wife, Sue, and the only reason she married him is because he owns a half-interest in the Mayberry sawmill.

Opie and Howie decide to hand out free samples of their "new and improved" newspaper. When Andy, Barney, and Aunt Bee discover what the boys have written, they desperately try to recover all the copies that were distributed. They verify that the papers were delivered on Willow Avenue and Maple and Elm streets. Luckily, only the preacher had read his paper, but he did see Andy's less-than-enthusiastic remarks about his sermons. In order to right his wrong, Andy agrees to teach Sunday school for one full month.

After Andy lectures Opie and Howie about printing this type of gossip, Opie tells him that a full second page was printed, but never distributed. In fact, Opie explains to Andy, Barney, and Aunt Bee that he and Howie bundled up the second page and watched the garbage truck pick it up. Curiosity overcomes the trio. Later that night, Andy, Barney, and Aunt Bee bump into each other at the garbage dump, desperately trying to locate the unseen second page of gossip. They finally find the bundle and, with flashlights in hand, eagerly read page two of *The Mayberry Sun.*

CAST NOTES. Regulars: **Andy Griffith, Don Knotts, Ronny Howard,** and **Frances Bavier. Dennis Rush** returns as Howie Pruitt. **William Keene** returns as the preacher, unnamed in the episode even though the cast credits list him as Reverend Martin. In other episodes, Mr. Keene's character's name was Reverend Tucker.

Burt Mustin is listed in the cast credits as Sam Benson, even though his character's name is never mentioned in the episode. **Irene Tedrow** appears as Mrs. Foster. Tedrow is known for her role of Mrs. Lucy Elkins on *Dennis the Menace.* **Kelly Thordsen** appears as Harold Grigsby, and **Vici Raaf** portrays his wife, Sue.

EPISODE NOTES. 1. Barney tells Opie that

when he attended Mayberry Central High School, he wrote a sports column for the school's newspaper called "Pickups and Splashes from Floor and Pool." Barney said his nickname was "Scoop." He confides to Andy that the column ran only one time in the paper, because it was too controversial and ahead of its time. (A note of interest is that Harvey Bullock, the man who wrote this episode, used to write a column for his school's newspaper back in his junior high days. The name of his column was "Pickups and Splashes from Floor and Pool.") As a point of reference, in episode 82, "Class Reunion" and episode 176, "The Return of Barney Fife," both Andy and Barney were classmates at Mayberry Union High School. 2. *The Mayberry Sun* costs three cents for adults and two cents for students. 3. Andy previously taught Sunday school for three years. 4. Andy mentions the name of one of Opie's friends as Troy Bowden. In previous episodes, young Mr. Bowden's name was Trey. 5. In Opie and Howie's print shop, an empty box of Frosted Flakes can be seen in the background. 6. Here is some more of Opie and Howie's fifth-grade gossip from *The Mayberry Sun*: (1) Cindy Ames had a birthday party and didn't invite her best friend, Diana. (2) Sally Tums's hair is not naturally curly, her mother rolls it up in cardboard. (3) Betty Parker lets Bobby Wilson carry her books, but does Bobby know that she writes sugar notes to Hector Styles? 7. Barney tells Andy that at Floyd's Barbershop, Fred Henry claimed that Widow Saunders is stepping out with a dish towel salesman from Raleigh. He is six feet tall and drives a fastback, wire-wheeled coupe. He took Ms. Saunders to the Half-Moon Roadhouse, where they sat on the same side of the booth and ate New York cut steaks. He didn't get her home until 1:00 A.M. Her late husband, Wilbur, left her an insurance policy of $6500.00, and she spent $97.00 of it on new slip covers that she sits on with her boyfriend. There was a rumor that she had an affair with Wilbur's hired hand, four years earlier. Barney claims that he didn't pay any attention to the above-mentioned gossip because he was too engrossed in a story about Africa he was reading in *The Geographic*. 8. Opie and Howie ran out of the letters "D" and "E" when they were printing *The Mayberry Sun*. 9. Barney blames the current rash of hot weather in Mayberry on "the bomb."

"Aunt Bee's Invisible Beau"

Episode #154. Air date: 3-29-65. Writers: Art Baer and Ben Joelson. Director: Theodore J. Flicker.

Clara tells Aunt Bee that Andy and Helen will never marry as long as she lives with Andy and remains unattached. In order to make Andy a free man, Aunt Bee makes up a story that she's dating their butter-and-egg man, Orville Hendricks of Mount Pilot. Andy and Barney do not know the man, so Barney decides to do some investigative work. He wants to make sure that Orville Hendricks is not a "chicken coop casanova," or as Barney puts it, a "Schizophreeniac." He is shocked to discover that Mr. Hendricks has a wife named Martha, and a son named Evan who helps him with deliveries. Barney tells Andy about the investigation, and Andy confronts Aunt Bee. When she swears that Mr. Hendricks is a single man, Andy decides to make a trip to Mount Pilot and have a talk with the butter-and-egg man. Mr. Hendricks is extremely shocked and upset when Andy tells him of the situation. It is mutually decided that the Taylors should find a new butter-and-egg man.

Next, Andy bumps into Clara and discovers that she was the source of the problem. Later that night, Andy sits Aunt Bee down and explains to her that both he and Helen love her and that she in no way poses a problem for their relationship. He also tells her that if one day, he and Helen do decide to get married, nothing will change. The only difference will be that Andy, Helen, Opie, and Aunt Bee will live as one happy family. This makes Aunt Bee feel much better, and soon she's flirting with their new butter-and-egg man, Farley Thurston. Fortunately, Mr. Thurston is a widower.

CAST NOTES. Regulars: **Andy Griffith, Don Knotts, Ronny Howard, Frances Bavier**, and **Aneta Corsaut. Hope Summers** returns as Clara.

Woodrow Chambliss stars as Orville Hendricks. Chambliss is known for his portrayal of Mr. Lathrop on *Gunsmoke*. He also appeared in the television epic *How The West Was Won*. **Bobby Diamond** appears as Evan Hendricks. Diamond is best known for his role of Joey Newton on *Fury*. **Lyle Latell** portrays Farley Thurston.

EPISODE NOTES. 1. Clara has a son named Gale. She has dated a man by the name of Clark Cooper for the past five years. Aunt Bee says that Mr. Cooper cuts the slits in his shoes. 2. Opie sleeps over at Johnny Paul's house during the episode. 3. Both Orville Hendricks and Farley Thurston make their deliveries to the Taylor house on Saturday mornings. Aunt Bee's usual order is three dozen eggs, one pound of whipped butter, and one pound of salted butter. The cost is $2.42. 4. Mr. Hendricks gives Aunt Bee a three-minute egg timer as a gift. 5. Helen and Andy are both Sunday school teachers. 6. Barney says that a "42-J" is a police character report. 7. Andy, Helen, and Aunt Bee play **Scrabble** at the beginning of the episode. 8. Helen says that Howie Pruitt has turned into a real monster at school. 9. The advertising on Orville Hendrick's delivery truck states: "Hendrick's/Butter & Eggs/Mount Pilot/Telephone Mount Pilot 1838." 10. The storyline of the episode is very reminiscent of episode 58, "Wedding Bells for Aunt Bee." 11. During the middle of the episode, Andy can be seen reading a copy of the *Mount Airy News* while sitting in his living room.

"The Arrest of the Fun Girls"

Episode #155. Air date: 4-5-65. Writer: Richard M. Powell. Director: Theodore J. Flicker.

Andy and Barney have to work late, so they are forced to postpone their dinner and movie date with Helen and Thelma Lou. The fun girls, Daphne and Skippy, show up in Mayberry, driving their old jalopy 45 mph in a 20 mph zone. Andy and Barney rush them out of town before Helen and Thelma Lou discover that the women have come back to try and steal their men. But Daphne and Skippy are persistent and immediately return to the courthouse, just as Andy and Barney are leaving to meet Helen and Thelma Lou for a late night snack at the diner. Andy has Barney stay with Daphne and Skippy (who want to play jail) while he goes to meet Helen and Thelma Lou. Meanwhile, the fun girls sing "Moonlight Bay," with Skippy on the ukulele, to a very upset Deputy Fife.

At the diner, Andy explains that the state police delivered two prisoners during the evening and Barney has to stay with them. Despite Andy's objections, Helen and Thelma Lou insist on visiting poor Barney at the courthouse. Andy manages to arrive first, but the charade fails when Helen and Thelma Lou catch Andy and Barney "dancing" with the fun girls. Helen and Thelma Lou leave in a huff, and an irate Sheriff Taylor emphatically sends Daphne and Skippy back to their home town of Mount Pilot.

Everything seems to return to normal after Helen and Thelma Lou accept Andy and Barney's explanation and apology. A dinner for the two couples is planned for the following evening. But just as Helen and Thelma Lou arrive for their date, they run into Daphne and Skippy. The episode concludes with Helen and Thelma Lou leaving, and Andy and Barney in another fine mess.

CAST NOTES. Regulars: **Andy Griffith, Don Knotts, Frances Bavier, Hal Smith, Aneta Corsaut,** and **Betty Lynn. Joyce Jameson** returns as Skippy, and **Jean Carson** returns as Daphne. This episode marks the final appearance of the fun girls.

The two other episodes in which they appear are episode 68, "Barney Mends a Broken Heart," and episode 122, "Fun Girls."

EPISODE NOTES. 1. The special at Morelli's Restaurant on Monday's is creamed chicken. Barney hates it. Another eatery, the Roadside Rest in Mayberry, charges extra for coffee and only gives you one dinner roll per person. The Hoffbrau Restaurant in Mount Pilot specializes in German food only. 2. The license plate number on Daphne and Skippy's car is L-5N-2. 3. The furniture store, the Palmerton Cafe, and Duncan's Hot Dog stand are seen in Mayberry in this episode. Hot dogs at Duncan's cost 15 cents each. 4. Andy and Barney had to work late because they were waiting for a telephone call from the highway department. When the call comes in, Andy speaks to two men named Wes and Monroe. They discuss extending the 50 mph speed limit on Highway 1 up to Fancy Gap. (The small town of Fancy Gap, Virginia, is located about twenty miles from Mount Airy, North Carolina, on Highway 52.) Andy promises to send Monroe some sourwood honey in exchange for a ham. 5. The fun girls play jail in Otis's home away from home, cell #1. When Otis shows up drunk in the middle of the night, Daphne and Skippy refuse to give him his cell back, and a big fight ensues. 6. Barney wears his salt and pepper suit to dinner at Andy's.

"The Luck of Newton Monroe"

Episode #156. Air date: 4-12-65. Writers: Bill Idelson and Sam Bobrick. Director: Coby Ruskin.

Newton Monroe, a 34-year-old traveling salesman, stops in Mayberry and immediately sells Goober a transistor radio and Floyd a wrist watch that gives the time, date, and temperature. Barney comes along, and Newton tries to sell him a ladies' ring called "The star of Peoria." Barney passes on the ring in favor of a genuine fur, for the unheard-of price of $13.25. Later, Andy tells Barney that Newton's goods must be stolen, because there is no way a genuine fur could be that cheap.

On the very next day, Goober's radio and Floyd's wrist watch both break, and Thelma Lou calls to tell Barney that her genuine fur has completely fallen apart. Andy and Barney confront Newton, who produces a bill of sale, proving that the goods were not stolen. What Newton doesn't have is a peddler's permit that allows him to sell his wares in Mayberry. Andy orders him not to sell another item until he obtains a permit.

A short time later, Barney catches Newton

trying to make another illegal sale before getting his permit. Deputy Fife happily hauls his prisoner in, and Andy promptly sentences Newton to five days in jail. Instead of allowing Newton to serve his time in a cell, a vengeful Barney puts him on a work detail. This is unfortunate, because Newton proceeds to accidentally destroy a water pipe, a radio, and the furnace in the courthouse, and he breaks the glass in the courthouse bookcase with the wooden end of a mop.

Poor Newton means well, but he can't seem to do anything right. He has lost any self-confidence he had, so Andy steps in to remedy the situation. He allows Newton to paint the Taylors' front porch, all by himself. Newton makes a mess of the job, but Andy and Barney secretly repaint the porch and bring Newton by later to view "his" fine work. Newton Monroe is now full of self-confidence as he heads to Mount Pilot, where Andy has set him up with a salesman's job at a hardware store.

CAST NOTES. Regulars: **Andy Griffith, Don Knotts, George Lindsey,** and **Howard McNear.**

Don Rickles stars as Newton Monroe. Rickles has been a top-draw nightclub comedian since the 1960s and has appeared in numerous television and movie roles over the years. "Mr. Insult," as he is sometimes known, starred as Otto Sharkey on the television show *C.P.O. Sharkey* from 1976 through 1978. Rickles also gave a great performance in the 1970 movie *Kelley's Heroes* starring Clint Eastwood.

EPISODE NOTES. 1. The following businesses in Mayberry are shown during the episode: Dave's Coffee Shop, Wayne's Television Repair Shop, the tax assessor's office, and the jewelry store. 2. At the beginning of the episode, Barney tells Andy that he is "going to go get a bottle of pop at the filling station, go home and take a nap, and then go to Thelma Lou's and watch a little television. Barney quoted a very similar itinerary to Andy (and Malcolm Tucker) in episode 77, "Man in a Hurry." 3. Barney is wearing his salt and pepper suit when he originally meets Newton. 4. Newton Monroe gives a 10 percent discount on his wares to men in uniform. 5. In addition to the fur, Barney bought a $2.00 pineapple skinner for Thelma Lou. 6. The license plate number of Newton's car is INH-851. 7. A man named George is a radio repairman in Mayberry. 8. Newton has a cousin named Gilbert who is a dental technician. 9. Goober states that Raleigh is located six miles from Mayberry. 10. Andy pays $17.00 to repair the water pipe that Newton destroyed. 11. According to Newton, Andy's self-confidence techniques make him feel "ept," rather than "inept." 12. Newton leaves some goodbye gifts for Andy and Barney. Barney gets a pencil sharpener and Andy gets a battery operated

Yakamoto razor. When Barney tries out Andy's razor, it grabs on to his face and won't let go. 13. The storyline of this episode is reminiscent to that of episode 62, "Cousin Virgil."

"Opie Flunks Arithmetic"

Episode #157. Air date: 4-19-65. Writer: Richard Morgan. Director: Coby Ruskin.

Andy gets upset when Helen tells him that Opie got a D in arithmetic. Long division is a particular problem for the youngster. Barney pushes Andy to improve Opie's poor math grades, because if they don't improve, a good college will never accept him. Andy reminds Barney that college is still years away, but the deputy is persistent.

Andy works with Opie, but he's simply not a good math teacher. Later, Barney frightens Aunt Bee by telling her that Opie is at a danger point and may become a dropout! Next, Barney secretly gives Opie a vocational aptitude test, and Andy finds out about it. He tells Barney to butt out and angrily tells Opie that until his grades improve, there will be no more playing football with his pals after school.

Opie decides to buckle down, but the extra studying proves to be ineffective. In fact, Opie's grades are now worse than ever, and he even loses his appetite.

When Helen discovers Andy's plan, she takes it upon herself to allow Opie to play football once again. She believes he needs to be with his friends and be a normal boy. Andy gets mad at Helen, but he backs down when she reminds him that he's acting like a hysterical parent. Andy now realizes that he has been putting too much pressure on the boy. Later that evening, Andy tells Opie that *he* is reinstating his football privileges. He also tells him to just do his best at school. This relaxed attitude starts paying dividends in no time at all, because on the next arithmetic test, Opie gets a B+.

CAST NOTES. Regulars: **Andy Griffith, Don Knotts, Ronny Howard, Frances Bavier,** and **Aneta Corsaut.** Sadly, this is Don Knott's final appearance as a regular cast member on *The Andy Griffith Show.* He will return for five memorable appearances during the last three seasons.

EPISODE NOTES. 1. Barney says his nickname in high school was "Rifle Fife." He was given this moniker because of the way he threw a football. Barney shows Opie that the proper way to throw a football is by holding it in the middle and across the seams. Opie tells him that Johnny Unitas of the Baltimore Colts holds it at the end. "Rifle Fife" has no response to this information. 2. Aunt Bee received straight As in Chemistry when she was in high school. She compared herself to Madame Curie. 3. Aunt Bee and Andy both received poor marks in math when they were in school. Guess it runs in the family. 4. Opie's pal Johnny Paul Jason is the proud owner of a #1 size chemistry set. 5. Opie keeps a picture of Aunt Bee on his bedroom dresser. 6. Barney wears his salt and pepper suit to dinner at the Taylors. 7. Barney says that Mount Pilot has a good vocational school that is dedicated to meat cutting. 8. At the beginning of the episode, a fly is driving Andy crazy at the courthouse. He finally swats it — after it lands on Helen's back. 9. Mr. Foley tells Aunt Bee that Einstein was a dropout. 10. Barney shows Andy and Aunt Bee an article he found in an old magazine at Floyd's Barbershop. The article was called "The Bleak Future Facing Our Next Generation." The name of the magazine is not given. 11. The vocational aptitude test that Barney gives Opie consists of the following questions: (1) If you had a choice, what would you do, read a book, or build a boat? Opie responds that he would build a boat in the afternoon and read a book when he went to bed. (2) If somebody were to present you with a gift, would you prefer an electric motor, or a chemistry set? After some banter, Opie decides on the electric motor.

"Opie and the Carnival"

Episode #158. Air date: 4-26-65. Writers: Fred Freeman and Lawrence J. Cohen. Director: Coby Ruskin.

The carnival is in town, and Opie and Johnny Paul visit the shooting gallery. Opie is an excellent young marksman, and he easily wins a ceramic pelican. Andy's birthday is just days away, and Opie discovers that if he can hit five consecutive bull's-eyes, he'll win an electric razor that Andy would dearly love. But the youngster is soon disappointed when he can't hit the bull's-eye even once. The cost is 25 cents for five shots, and after spending $2.75, he finally calls it quits.

Now, Opie has no razor, nor any money at all to buy a present. He asks Andy for an advance on his allowance but is turned down. In desperation, Opie asks noted marksman Goober Pyle for help. Since Goober has won the turkey shoot in Mount Pilot for the past two years, this should be easy. Four dollars and seventy five cents later, a disgruntled Goober leaves with only a celluloid kewpie doll.

Next, Goober spills the beans to Andy about Opie's shooting gallery experience. Andy makes arrangements with Goober to bring Opie back to the shooting gallery after he visits the carnival with Helen. At the carnival, Andy, dressed in his civvies, discovers that the sights on all but one gun have been bent. Before Opie arrives, Andy shows his sheriff's badge to the two operators of the shooting gallery, Pete and George. He tells them that he's going to put their names on a bunco list and distribute it to all the area carnival sites. If they don't straighten up their act, their license will be revoked. Andy also instructs Pete and George to give Opie a fair chance when he returns.

About that time, Goober and Opie show up, and Andy and Helen hide behind a nearby carnival tent. They proudly watch as Opie easily wins the coveted razor with his last quarter.

MEMORABLE SCENE. Andy in one of his more mischievous moods, standing on his front porch and barking like a dog. This causes a chain reaction, with all the neighborhood dogs chiming in.

CAST NOTES. Regulars: **Andy Griffith, Ronny Howard, Frances Bavier, George Lindsey,** and **Aneta Corsaut. Richard Keith** returns as Johnny Paul.

Billy Halop stars as George. Halop was a "Dead End Kid" in numerous movies in the 1930s, and he also portrayed Bert Munson on *All in the Family* from 1972 through 1977. **Lewis Charles** costars as Pete. Charles previously appeared as another shady businessman in episode 122, "A Deal Is a Deal." He was one of the Miracle Salve owners in that one.

EPISODE NOTES. 1. The shooting gallery uses .22 rifles. 2. Aunt Bee is giving Andy a monogrammed shirt for his birthday. 3. Johnny Paul won a baseball bat at the ring toss at the carnival. 4. At the carnival, Helen asks Andy to buy her some cotton candy. 5. Last Christmas, Opie received a tool chest that he'd asked for. He had hinted to Andy and Aunt Bee that he wanted the tool chest by writing an English composition entitled, "What I would Do If I Had a Tool Chest." He left it on the dining room table so everyone could see it. 6. Andy tells Opie that he would like a new guitar for a birthday present, but it would cost between $150.00 and $200.00. He also said he would like a couple of pairs of solid color socks, a few undershirts, or a basketball. Opie reasons that he asked for the basketball, not for himself, but for Opie, who just happens to have a basketball hoop in the backyard. 7. Johnny Paul once gave his father a necktie that he had made at school for a birthday present. His dad liked it so much that he *never* wears it. 8. Andy owns a key holder with a small flashlight inside it. It was given to him as a gift at a sheriff's convention. It even has his name on it. 9. A man named

Henry repairs bicycles in Mayberry. Another man named Harvey fills in for Goober from time to time at Wally's Filling Station. 10. Andy and Goober enjoy going hunting together. 11. Other prizes at the shooting gallery include a Swiss watch, a pearl-handled carving set from the Orient, a napkin holder with a picture of a cabin on it, a statue of a Siamese cat from the Orient, hair dryers, fishing poles, toasters, jackknifes, percolators, hunting knives, bookends, pencil sharpeners, ashtrays, thermometers, and an electric can opener. 12. Opie must not have realized that Newton Monroe had given Andy a new Yakamoto razor just two shows earlier in episode 156, "The Luck of Newton Monroe." On second thought, remember what that razor did to Barney Fife's face? No doubt Opie made a good choice after all.

"Banjo-Playing Deputy"

Episode #159. Air date: 5-3-65. Writer: Bob Ross. Director: Coby Ruskin.

After Miss Edwards and Miss Lukens complain to Andy about the suggestive dancing show at the carnival called "the Sultan's Favorite," Andy decides to see the show himself and takes Floyd the barber with him. Floyd tells Andy that he has seen the show at least five times, but he doesn't mind going one more time (the little devil). After the performance, Andy asks the manager of the show to have Flossie the dancer tone down her suggestive Arabian dance routine. The manager refuses and decides to move his act to Charlotte, where he and Flossie will join up with the Baker Brothers show. Due to a lack of money, the manager is forced to leave behind a banjo player named Jerry Miller, who portrayed "the Sultan" in the routine.

Jerry is very shy and lacks the nerve to sternly demand his $30.00 paycheck. Andy feels responsible for his dilemma, so he invites Jerry to use the cot in the courthouse for the evening and invites him to eat dinner at the Taylors'. At Andy's, Aunt Bee discovers that Jerry is from Morgantown, West Virginia. Aunt Bee lived there for five years, and it turns out that she is good friends with Jerry's parents, Robie and Irlene Miller. She persuades Andy to hire the accident-prone banjo player to help around the courthouse in Barney Fife's absence.

Against Andy's wishes, Jerry puts on a deputy's uniform, and while "patrolling" at the carnival, he attempts to break up a fight. Luckily, Andy comes along and breaks up the fight before Jerry gets hurt. Next, Aunt Bee convinces Andy to make Jerry a school crossing guard at the corner of two of May-

berry's busiest streets, Haymore and Rockford. Unfortunately, Jerry botches this assignment as well.

Later, Aunt Bee reports that her purse was stolen at the carnival. Jerry has an idea of who the purse snatchers are and takes it upon himself to arrest the culprits. Andy shows up after Jerry has confronted the crooks. As a team, they make the arrest. The episode concludes with Jerry gaining some much-needed self-confidence.

CAST NOTES. Regulars: **Andy Griffith, Ronny Howard, Frances Bavier**, and **Howard McNear**.

Noted actor, comedian, and musician **Jerry Van Dyke** stars as Jerry Miller. Jerry is the younger brother of Dick Van Dyke. Jerry is well known for his starring role of Dave Crabtree in the 1960s camp classic television show, *My Mother the Car.* He costarred with Andy Griffith in the 1969 movie *Angel in My Pocket* and in the 1970 television show *Headmaster.* Currently, he costars with Craig T. Nelson as Assistant Coach Luther Van Dam in the long-running comedy hit *Coach.*

Lee Van Cleef, a veteran tough guy in countless television and movie roles, appears as Skip, one of the purse snatchers. **Robert Carricart** portrays Frankie, the other purse snatcher. **Herbie Faye**, another veteran character actor, appears as the unnamed manager of "the Sultan's Favorite." **Sylvia Lewis** appears as Flossie. **Jean Inness, Tom Steele**, and **Bill Catching** also appear.

EPISODE NOTES. 1. This is the final black-and-white episode of *The Andy Griffith Show.* This show is also a rare example of a continuation of a previous episode. "Banjo-Playing Deputy" takes place at the same carnival used in episode 158, Opie and the Carnival. 2. The rate at the Mayberry Hotel is $3.00 per night. 3. Mayberry businesses shown include the Palmerton Cafe, Norma's Beauty Shop, and Tess's. 4. Andy makes Mrs. Clairburn move her illegally parked car after Jerry fails in being forceful with her in his role as "deputy." 5. Floyd wins a periscope and flip cards with "girlie" pictures on them at the shooting gallery. He wins a kewpie doll and a goofy-looking hat at the baseball toss. He spends $2.50 to earn these prized possessions. 6. Floyd tells Andy that he thought Calvin Coolidge said, "Speak softly and carry a big stick." It was actually Teddy Roosevelt. Floyd agrees with Andy that Coolidge *did* say, "I do not choose to run." 7. Aunt Bee's stolen purse contained the following items: a leather wallet containing $16.00 in cash; a gold ring that Bertha gave her; a membership card to the Women's Club; a rhinestone buckle; a package of bobby pins; and a brand new orange wood stick. The purse itself is worth $8.50. 8. The storyline of "Banjo-Playing Deputy," is similar to the stories used when Jerry Van Dyke portrayed Stacy

Petrie, in four episodes of *The Dick Van Dyke Show*. 9. Andy told Jerry that he had business to attend in Mount Pilot. How and why did he wind up at the carnival so quickly to break up the fight that Jerry got into? Only the producers know for sure. 10. Two cast note errors are (1) **Hope Summers** is listed in the credits as Miss Bedloe, even though Andy refers to her as Miss Edwards; and (2) **Mary Lansing** is listed as Miss Roundtree in the credits, even though Andy refers to her as Miss Lukens. 11. There once was a school crossing at the intersection of Haymore and Rockford streets in Mount Airy, North Carolina. In fact, Andy Griffith's birthplace is located at 711 Haymore Street. Today, the Andy Griffith Playhouse is located in the renovated Rockford Elementary School on Rockford Street. It features local plays and community events.

SEASON SIX

Audiences are treated to the sight of Opie's red hair and Aunt Bee's Blue Willow china as *The Andy Griffith Show* begins broadcasting in color. Mayberry welcomes a new deputy, Warren Ferguson, and county clerk Howard Sprague (and we wouldn't want to overlook Mother Sprague, would we?). Viewers fly to Hollywood with Andy, Opie, and Aunt Bee. A.C. Nielsen Co. rating for the 1965-1966 season: 26.9; rank: 6.

"Aunt Bee, the Swinger"

Episode #160. Air date: 10-4-65. Writer: Jack Elinson. Director: Larry Dobkin.

Congressman John Canfield has decided to retire and leave Washington, D.C., for the relaxed atmosphere of his old hometown, Mayberry, North Carolina. Aunt Bee lets Andy know that she would like to meet the distinguished ex-congressman, who also happens to be an eligible bachelor. Andy invites Mr. Canfield to dinner, and he and Aunt Bee are instantly attracted to each other. They soon begin dating and acting like they have the energy of teenagers. They go sightseeing, square-dancing, to the theatre, riding a bicycle-built-for-two and shooting bows and arrows (Aunt Bee even hits the bull's-eye on her first attempt). Andy and Helen can't begin to keep up with the two elder lovebirds.

Soon, Aunt Bee and John Canfield are staying out until all hours of the night. Andy is amazed at Aunt Bee's energy, until he comes home one day and finds his exhausted aunt soaking her sore and tired feet. Aunt Bee admits that she has been trying to fool Mr. Canfield into believing that she can keep up with him. When Andy goes to see Mr. Canfield, he discovers that the ex-congressman is also exhausted, and he's also soaking his tired and aching tootsies. Finally, with the help of Andy, Aunt Bee and Mr. Canfield admit the truth to each other, and this revelation allows them to relax and simply enjoy being together.

CAST NOTES. Regulars: **Andy Griffith, Ronny Howard, Frances Bavier, Howard McNear,** and **Aneta Corsaut.**

Charlie Ruggles stars as John Canfield. Rug-

gles starred in such feature films as *Ruggles of Red Gap* (1935) and *Bringing Up Baby* (1938, with Cary Grant and Katharine Hepburn). Ruggles also appeared in countless television guest roles. He may be best known as the voice of Aesop from 1961 through 1962 on the "Aesop's Fables" segment of *The Bullwinkle Show.* Ruggles also portrayed Mrs. Drysdale's father, Lowell Reddings (Daddy) Farquar, in a few episodes of *The Beverly Hillbillies.*

EPISODE NOTES. 1. This is the first episode filmed in color (though the following episode, 161, was broadcast first). Viewers can finally verify that Aunt Bee's china is the popular Blue Willow pattern. 2. Viewers get a rare opportunity to see a color shot of Aunt Bee's bedroom. She keeps a Raggedy Ann doll on a chair. 3. At the beginning of the episode, the front page of *The Mayberry Gazette* exclaims, "Congressman John Canfield returning to Mayberry." The caption is accompanied by a photo of Mr. Canfield. 4. From a newspaper article called, "Little Known Facts Known by a Few," Andy states that because, of its rare vitamin content, a person could die if he or she eats too much polar bear liver. Could this article have been taken from the *Learn-A-Month* magazine that Barney Fife subscribed to in episode 145, "The Rehabilitation of Otis"? That magazine had a feature called "Odd Facts Known by a Few." 5. Andy refers to Aunt Bee as "the prettiest girl in Mayberry." 6. Aunt Bee is a member of the weekly sewing club in Mayberry. 7. John Canfield likes to smoke cigars. 8. Andy says that Aunt Bee normally goes to bed after watching the 10:00 P.M. news. 9. A gentleman named Mr. Branch lives directly across the street from the Taylors. He never speaks to Andy, but he always acknowledges him by nodding his head. 10. Andy refers to Aunt

161

Bee and John Canfield as the "Mayberry jet set." He later calls them "Fred Astaire and Ginger Rogers." 11. Aunt Bee once again sings "My Chinatown" during the episode. She likes that one. 12. Andy claims that the pulp mill in Mount Pilot was responsible for Mayberry's sister city's rapid growth in population. 13. The Mayberry Community Center is the site for the square dance that Aunt Bee and John Canfield attend with Andy and Helen. 14. During one date, Aunt Bee and Mr. Canfield eat a fancy dinner at the Reef at Nagtin Restaurant. Aunt Bee had the fish platter with lemon and butter sauce, while John Canfield had the pounded steak. They both had lace corn bread. After dinner, the couple went dancing at the Shrine Club. Mr. Canfield is a Shriner, of course. 14. Andy whistles "There Is a Time" while playing the guitar on the porch. 15. Andy and Helen enjoy drinking cherry smash soda at the drugstore. 16. Even though Aunt Bee and John Canfield were a good match, the ex-congressman never returned to the series.

"Opie's Job"

Episode #161. Air date: 9-13-65. Writers: Art Baer and Ben Joelson. Director: Larry Dobkin.

Andy has had a chaotic day at work, which has left him very grouchy. When Opie confesses to ripping his pants and wrecking his bike (while riding "no hands" to impress pretty classmate Sharon Porter), he receives a stern lecture from his father. Andy calls him careless and irresponsible and says he needs to learn about the value of money.

Opie takes these words to heart and sets out to find a part-time job so he can earn the money to repair his bike. Aunt Bee discovers that grocery store owner Mr. Doakes is advertising to hire a boy who can work after school and on Saturdays. Opie plans to apply for the job.

On Saturday, Opie and a boy named Billy Crenshaw arrive at the store simultaneously. Mr. Doakes decides to hire both boys for one week. At the end of the week, the more productive worker will be kept on.

Although both boys are doing a fine job, Andy begins to believe that Opie has the better chance of winning a permanent position. Floyd and Goober tell him that Opie is making more deliveries than Billy. Andy insists that landing the job isn't as important as assuming responsibility and learning the value of money.

In a close call, Opie gets the job. Andy starts bragging about his son, and Goober and Floyd are proud of Opie, too. Meanwhile, Mr. Doakes allows

Billy to finish out the week because he made the decision earlier than he had planned. While talking with Billy, Opie discovers that his friendly rival needed the job to help his family pay bills. Billy's father has been ill, and the entire family needs to find work in order to make ends meet. A thoughtful and sympathetic Opie tells Mr. Doakes he's decided to play baseball rather than work.

Moments later, a very happy Billy rushes by Andy on his way home, and Andy hears the news about Opie. He is devastated. How could his boy be so irresponsible? When he finds Opie sitting quietly at home, he proceeds to give him "the business." A tearful Opie explains everything, and Andy realizes that his boy has become a man. Later, Andy hires Opie to work part-time at the courthouse.

MEMORABLE SCENE. Goober teaching Opie the proper way to apply for a job.

CAST NOTES. Regulars: **Andy Griffith, Ronny Howard, Frances Bavier, Howard McNear**, and **George Lindsey. Ronda Jeter** returns as Sharon Porter.

John Bangert portrays Billy Crenshaw. Bangert played the role of young Cornell Clayton on the television series *Margie* from 1961 to 1962. He also appeared in some guest roles on television during the 1960s including *Dennis the Menace.* **Norris Goff**, who was best known as Abner Peabody on the classic radio comedy series *Lum and Abner*, portrays store owner Mr. Doakes.

EPISODE NOTES. 1. This episode was the first of this series to be broadcast in color. 2. Events contributing to Andy's bad mood: (1) "That Leonard boy" got mad at his brother and stole his car. Then he drove it to the marsh, where he set it on fire. This set the marsh ablaze and it took all day to put it out. "That Leonard boy" is still ar large. (2) Somebody kept calling the courthouse and asking for Ethel. (3) Otis got gassed and drove his car right through the Harper's rose garden, leveling it. When Andy arrested him, Otis wanted to fight. 3. Floyd tells Andy that Mayberryian Craig Folger claims to have a cowlick, but it is actually a scar. It seems Craig's wife, Millie, hit him on the head with a broomstick handle after she caught him coming home late one night. 4. Mr. Doakes pays Opie and Billy 75 cents an hour. Goober remarks that it is good pay for a boy. He adds that one day Opie might earn as much as he does: $1.25 an hour. 5. On his way to apply for his job, Opie says hello to a Mr. Dobson, who is sweeping the sidewalk. 6. Mrs. Peters is one of Mr. Doakes's customers. 7. Floyd states that Opie could grow up to become a doctor or a lawyer. Goober says the boy could even become a civil service worker or an astronaut. Andy imagines Opie as an international financier. 8. The

Taylors routinely eat supper right at 6:00 P.M. 9. Opie inquires about a job at eight different establishments, including Floyd's and Goober's, before landing the job at Doakes Groceries and Meats. 10. Opie believes he could save enough money, working for a couple of months, to buy a new bicycle. It would be red and white with two headlights and foxtails on the handlebars. He saw the bike at the sporting goods store. 11. Andy places the following ad in *The Mayberry Gazette*: "Wanted: 11-year-old boy for part-time work after school and Saturdays. Must be bright, ambitious, and have a broken bicycle. Call Sheriff Taylor."

"The Bazaar"

Episode #162. Air date: 10-11-65. Writers: Ben Joelson and Art Baer. Director: Sheldon Leonard.

Goober complains to Andy about Mayberry's new deputy, Warren Ferguson. The eager deputy had just fined Goober for storing greasy rags in a big barrel (a possible fire hazard) and for matching pennies with Floyd. The latter offense meant a $1.00 fine for Goober and Floyd. Goober tells Andy that the townspeople are doing all they can to avoid the overzealous deputy.

Andy tries to reason with Warren and explains that enforcing the law "to the letter" is unnecessary. Unfortunately, the lecture falls on deaf ears. When Warren discovers that the Ladies Auxiliary is holding bingo games and awarding prizes to winners, he arrests the entire group! He charges them with gambling and takes the irate ladies to the courthouse. Andy cannot believe his eyes. He strongly urges Warren to drop the charges, but the stubborn deputy refuses. Instead Warren suspends the sentence, after which a relieved Andy tells the ladies they are free to go.

Moments later, Aunt Bee (who is a member of the auxiliary) realizes that she and her friends may be free, but this offense will give them all a criminal record. They march back to Andy and Warren and demand to have all charges dropped, thus erasing any record. Warren adamantly refuses to comply, and in protest, the women jail themselves. Andy storms out in anger and goes home.

Hours pass, and it is apparent that the situation will not be easily resolved. Andy finds himself confronted with several angry husbands and their hungry children. They blame him for the absence of their wives and mothers. Andy does his best to appease the group by feeding them at his home.

After supper, Andy returns to the courthouse, determined to convince Warren to drop the charges.

Warren remains unyielding. The women demand a jury trial. Absolutely flabbergasted, a sullen Andy sits on a bench outside the courthouse. Goober strolls by and unwittingly gives Andy an idea. Andy goes back inside and informs Warren he believes that the county has no case against the ladies and if a trial were held, the ladies would surely be found innocent. Warren disagrees and takes Andy's bet ($1.00) on the outcome of any such trial. At this point, Andy arrests his deputy for gambling. Using Warren's philosophy, Andy makes the deputy realize that nit-picking, when applied to the law, is ridiculous. All charges against the ladies are immediately dropped.

MEMORABLE SCENE. An angry Andy storming out of the courthouse, grabbing a rock and hurling it away. A second later, he is dismayed to hear the sound of breaking glass!

CAST NOTES. Regulars: **Andy Griffith, Ronny Howard, Frances Bavier, Hope Summers,** and **George Lindsey.**

Jack Burns joins the series as Deputy Warren Ferguson. **Amzie Strickland, Mary Lansing, Janet Stewart,** and **Claudia Bryar** appear as ladies of the auxiliary. They portray, respectively, Myra, Dorothy, Martha, and Ruth. **Joe di Reda** appears as a man named Harlan. **Sam Edwards,** familiar to fans of this series in several other roles, appears as Fred. **Pam Ferdin** portrays a young girl named Corliss. Ferdin was very active on television from the mid–1960s to the mid–1970s, supplying voices to several cartoon characters and appearing in such series as *The John Forsythe Show, Blondie* (as Cookie Bumstead), *The Paul Lynde Show,* and *Lassie* (as a blind girl).

EPISODE NOTES. 1. Goober's favorite seasons of the year (in order) are spring, summer, fall, and winter. 2. Goober says "speraneous combustion" meaning to say spontaneous. 3. Andy admits that he sometimes matches pennies with Floyd and Goober. 4. The Palmerton Movie House is located in Mayberry. 5. The familiar license plate number AY-321 appears on the plate of a car that Warren finds just barely legally parked on a Mayberry street. 6. Warren used to be a member of a men's club "back home," and he participated in charity bazaars. 7. Warren's motto is "Always be prepared." 8. Warren claims to have been born with compassion and an unusual way with words. 9. The ladies of the auxiliary have operated a bazaar for the past 18 years without a permit. 10. Andy says that Mayberry has a population of under 2,000 and that its biggest industry is making patchwork quilts. 11. Warren has been a deputy in several towns and claims to have read all the Perry Mason stories. An angry Andy tells Warren that there may be at least one story he missed: "The Case of the Pigheaded Deputy Who

Was Killed by a Berserk Sheriff." 12. Goober is specially deputized by Warren in order to aid in the roundup of the ladies of the auxiliary. 13. One of the irate ladies who is arrested calls the situation a "kangaroo court." 14. Andy refers to Warren, in a moment of frustration, as "my idiot deputy." 15. Andy tells Warren the Mayberry rules for a long, happy life, of which there are three: (1) Don't play leap frog with elephants. (2) Don't pet a tiger unless his tail's wagging. (3) *Never, ever* mess with the Ladies Auxiliary. 16. Some of the folks who eat at Andy's in this episode are Harlan and his daughter Corliss (Harlan's wife is named Ruth); Fred, his son (who is a scout) and daughter (Fred's wife is probably Dorothy, who stated earlier that her son is an eagle scout); and Dick, his two sons and daughter Pansy. 17. Opie tells Andy that he thought the pancakes Andy fixed in the past were great. They stuck a little, but it was fun eating them right from the pan. 18. The bazaar features bingo, cake sales, and a kissing booth. Warren considers charging the ladies with a morals violation because of the kissing booth.

"Andy's Rival"

Episode #163. Air date: 9-20-65. Writer: Laurence Marks. Director: Peter Baldwin.

Helen introduces Andy to Frank Smith, a member of the school board in Raleigh, with whom she will be working closely during the next couple of weeks. Their work involves evaluating and employing a new grading system. Everyone is impressed with Frank's intelligence and his many talents. He has a Ph.D. in history and is knowledgeable about wine, baseball, mechanics, and virtually any topic imaginable. He's no slouch at playing the guitar, either.

Aunt Bee encourages Andy to speak up and display his many attributes. She worries that Andy could lose Helen to a man like Frank, if he continues to "hide his light under a bush." Andy does not worry too much about the situation until Opie, Goober, and even Sarah the switchboard operator make remarks about their very favorable impressions of Frank.

Andy is elated when Helen agrees to a rare Wednesday night date. (Their usual middle-of-the-week date is on Thursday.) He plans to take her to a movie entitled *The Monster from Mars* and then to a dance at the Elks' Club.

While Andy is home getting dressed for the date, Frank tells Helen that the head of the grading project in Raleigh, Mr. Twyford, expects to see the results of their work on Thursday morning. Unfortunately, Helen has no choice but to cancel her date so she and Frank can get everything in order. This upsets Andy, but he accepts the situation. He and Goober decide to go to the movies. Afterward, they drop in at the diner for a bite to eat. Andy is surprised to find Helen and Frank sitting together inside. He and Goober join them for what turns out to be a very awkward few minutes. Helen explains they finished their project a little earlier than expected.

Andy sees Helen home, but as they approach her door, he verbally lashes out at her. He accuses her of "running with" Frank and tells her to make up her mind about who she'd rather spend her time with. Helen becomes quite angry and defensive. She tells Andy that Frank is a pleasant man and a hard worker, but he means no more than that to her. She adds that she resents the vulgar implication Andy made and that it is her business who she chooses to go out with. Suddenly, Andy realizes that he overreacted and that Helen still loves only him. The argument ends with the couple sharing a long, passionate kiss.

CAST NOTES. Regulars: **Andy Griffith, Ronny Howard, Frances Bavier, Aneta Corsaut,** and **George Lindsey.**

Charles Aidman portrays Frank Smith. Mr. Aidman has enjoyed a diverse career. He has acted, directed, and composed music. He narrated the 1985 series *The Twilight Zone* and has appeared in several films and television projects. He costarred with James Caan and Robert Duvall in Robert Altman's 1968 film *Countdown*.

EPISODE NOTES. 1. Frank and Helen are working on the Watkins Grading Manual. 2. Andy makes his Punch Supreme. Its ingredients include orange sherbet, tomato juice, root beer, and molasses. 3. According to Frank, many of the houses along North Avenue in Mayberry date back to the early nineteenth century and are antebellum in style. 4. Frank used to be an automobile racer and was a relief pitcher on his college baseball team. 5. Goober's girlfriend, Lydia Crosswaithe, has been keeping company with a butcher named James Arthur Beaslo. Mr. Beaslo wears a t-shirt with the sleeves rolled up while he chops meat so that he can show off his muscles. 6. Goober and Andy saw the film *The Monsters from the Moon* some time ago. Goober says that it was very similar to *The Monster from Mars* except the Mars monster has four sets of teeth, while moon monsters have only three. 7. Goober would like to go to Jasper to see the new tractor display. (An interesting note: although presumably Goober is referring to a town in North Carolina, the actor George Lindsey was born in

Jasper, Alabama.) 8. The school building usually closes at 7:00 P.M. 9. *The Anteaters from Outer Space* is the new movie coming to Mayberry. 10. Andy was the valedictorian of his high school class. 11. Aunt Bee says Andy used to bat the baseball clear out of sight, no matter how hard she threw it. 12. Goober says Frank is smart enough to work at a gas station. 13. At the diner, Goober orders a hamburger with ketchup, mustard, hot sauce, pickle, and onions. He gets french fries on the side and an orange drink. 14. Helen's house number is 895. It is unclear what street she lives on.

"Malcolm at the Crossroads"

Episode #164. Air date: 9-27-65. Writer: Harvey Bullock. Director: Gary Nelson.

Andy's English friend, Malcolm Merriweather, pedals his bicycle into Mayberry for a third visit. This time, however, Malcolm announces that he intends to make the friendly town his home. Andy is delighted to hear it and promises to help his friend find a job.

Earlier in the day, Andy hired mountain man Ernest T. Bass as the school crossing guard. Ernest T. was desperate for a job because he needed $12.00 to finance a honeymoon with his intended bride, Romeena (that is, Ramona). As evidence that he is willing to go all out for her, he plans to buy a tent and a lantern.

Of course, Ernest T. is hardly an ideal crossing guard. He loses his temper very easily and throws rocks at the cars who disobey his signals. Even after receiving a stern warning from Andy about the rock-throwing, Ernest T. continues his wild ways. Andy has no choice but to fire him. This firing means a temporary job for Malcolm, who is very happy to help out. Malcolm performs his duties with typical British aplomb.

When Malcolm is introduced to Ernest T., his friendly greeting is met with a growl. Ernest T. claims he can tell that Malcolm is an "Englishter," the sworn enemy of the Irish, according to mother Bass. Being part Irish, Ernest T. naturally hates him. Besides, Malcolm took Ernest T.'s job, thereby ending his chance to provide a nice honeymoon for Ramona, who will not want to marry him now. With Goober looking on, Ernest T. challenges Malcolm to fight, but the bewildered Brit is frightened off. Ernest T. yells to Malcolm that if he's still in town the following day, he will whip the fire out of him.

As Malcolm packs up his belongings, Goober tells Andy about the troublesome occurrence. Andy decides to speak with his former manservant, but before he gets the chance, Malcolm decides he will stay in town and fight. He sends word to Ernest T. that he will fight him at high noon, behind the Mayberry Garage. Malcolm asks Goober to train him, but it is obvious that any effort will be futile. Malcolm is no fighter, and both Andy and Goober realize that Ernest T. will kill him if a fight occurs. Andy tries desperately to talk Malcolm out of fighting, but to no avail. He tries to do the same with Ernest T., who absolutely refuses to back down, even under threat of being tossed into jail.

The only advice Goober can give Malcolm is to retreat and cover himself. Floyd brings a towel from his barbershop to the scene. He plans to throw it into the ring *before* the fight starts. The onslaught appears inevitable.

Shortly after Ernest T. shows up, Andy hits upon an idea. He tells Ernest T. that it will be amusing to witness two Irishmen fighting each other. Ernest T. is confused until Andy explains that Malcolm's mother was born in County Cork, Ireland. It's a white lie, but an effective one. Ernest T. refuses to fight a fellow Irishman, and proclaims Malcolm his friend.

Incidentally, Ernest T. later learns the truth, and Malcolm once again becomes his sworn enemy.

MEMORABLE SCENE. Goober imitating Cary Grant.

CAST NOTES. Regulars: **Andy Griffith, George Lindsey,** and **Howard McNear. Howard Morris** returns for the last time as the one and only Ernest T. Bass. **Bernard Fox** takes his final bow as Malcolm Merriweather. He previously appeared in episode 89, "Andy's English Valet," followed by episode 124, "The Return of Malcolm Merriweather."

Dennis Bradshaw and **Kenneth Butts** portray schoolboys Johnny and Arnie, respectively.

EPISODE NOTES. 1. Some background on Malcolm: He was a valet (or a gentleman's gentleman) to the colonel for the last six years. He can stock a wine cellar and has worked as a falcon keeper. He used to tinker with the colonel's family car, taking care of the "mechanism under the bonnet." Malcolm was a member of the Cold Stream Guard, serving as a valet to his commanding officer. (Goober tells Floyd that Malcolm was a "Cold Cream Guard.") For the record, Malcolm's mother was born in the heart of London, England, just two blocks off of Picadilly Circus. 2. There is a bulletin board located in Floyd's Barbershop, on which help wanted ads are listed. Two positions available in this episode are seamstress and hairdresser. Fletch Roberts, who works at the Mayberry Depot, has let it be known he is in need of a bookkeeper. 3. Ernest

T. says that his fiancee, Ramona, is being given a shower by her girlfriends....a plain, hot water shower! 4. Andy tells Ernest T. he will be paid $5.00 for his efforts while working as a school crossing guard. 5. Goober says he was a bully when he was a youngster. 6. At one point in this episode, Ernest T. mistakes Andy for the widow Bradshaw and hurls rocks at him. 7. Floyd brings painkillers to give to Malcolm in case a fight does take place. 8. Ernest T. tidbits: (1) He refers to Andy as "sweet" in the episode. (2) He claims to weigh 112 beautiful pounds. (3) He invites Malcolm to come eat at his cave. He has 'possum steaks which should be nice and tender, as he's been beating them with a stick. 9. This episode is the only color episode in which Ernest T. Bass appears. It is also the only color episode featuring Malcolm Merriweather.

"Aunt Bee on TV"

Episode #165. Air date: 11-15-65. Writers: Fred Freeman and Lawrence J. Cohen. Director: Alan Rafkin.

The Taylors are given a warm welcome upon their return from their trip to Hollywood. Helen, Clara, Floyd, Goober, and other friends are thrilled to see them and enjoy hearing of their exploits. Aunt Bee surprises them by revealing she was a sweepstakes winner on the "Win or Lose" game show. All but one of her prizes arrived at the Taylor house before the family returned. Aunt Bee shows them to everyone. They are a refrigerator, a dishwasher, an ice crusher, a washer and dryer, a television set, and a garbage disposal. Aunt Bee invites all of her enthusiastic friends to come over to her house when the show actually airs and watch it with her.

Her major prize is the last to arrive. It is a full-length, burnt autumn, ranch mink fur coat from Darcy Furs of Hollywood, known as "the furrier to the stars." Aunt Bee loves showing it off to her friends, who are initially happy for her, then envious, and finally upset when it becomes her sole topic of conversation. Everyone believes Aunt Bee is too wrapped up in her winnings. When she tries to organize a ladies' get-together in order to further show off her prizes, all her friends make excuses and decline the invitation.

Andy is visited by a representative from the Internal Revenue Service named Mr. Heathcote. The agent informs Andy that Aunt Bee's prizes are taxable, and that she owes $1,138.72. Andy decides to wait a couple of days before approaching Aunt Bee. When he does, he discovers that she heard

about the tax man's visit by way of the Mayberry grapevine, which in this case consisted of Goober telling Floyd, Floyd telling Warren, Warren telling Jud, and Jud telling Aunt Bee. Andy refers to this as "the Mayberry telegraph."

Anyway, Aunt Bee quietly sold all but two of her prizes, keeping only the television set and the garbage disposal. She figures it is a small price to pay. She may have lost some prizes, but she has regained her friends.

CAST NOTES. Regulars: **Andy Griffith, Ronny Howard, Frances Bavier, George Lindsey, Howard McNear, Aneta Corsaut,** and **Hope Summers.**

William Christopher portrays I.R.S. agent Mr. Heathcote. Most viewers will recognize Mr. Christopher as Father Francis Mulcahy on the hit series *M*A*S*H* (1972-1983) and its less popular sequel, *AfterMASH* (1983-1984). He was also a regular on *Gomer Pyle, U.S.M.C.* as Private Lester Hummel (1964-1969).

Real-life game show host **Jack Smith** portrays himself as host of the (fictional) "Win or Lose" game show. Mr. Smith had a brief singing career in the 1940s, before becoming host of the popular show *You Asked for It.*

Amzie Strickland and **Janet Stewart** return, as Myra Tucker and a hairdresser named Beth, respectively.

EPISODE NOTES. 1. The Taylors return to Mayberry aboard the Raleigh bus. 2. Belmont Studios arranged a limousine for the Taylors in Hollywood. Their chauffeur initially told them his name was John. Later, he confessed that he was an aspiring actor named Bob. 3. Opie had written Goober telling him he collected 22 autographs. Upon arriving home, he shows him his autograph book. Among the signatures he collected: Audie Murphy, Tony Curtis, Doris Day, Rock Hudson, Kirk Douglas, Dean Martin, and Dave Snyder. Mr. Snyder was a necktie salesman. He was wearing sunglasses, which fooled the Taylors into thinking he was a celebrity. 4. Andy tells his friends that on a tour of movie stars' homes, they saw houses belonging to Debbie Reynolds, Cesar Romero, and Jack Benny. Opie exclaims that he got to hold Mr. Romero's newspaper in his hands. Floyd uses the opportunity to remind everyone that Jack Benny is not *really* a cheapskate. 5. While in Hollywood, Andy bought a pillow with the words "Hollywood, California" on it, as well as a nice pearl necklace. Both gifts are for Helen. 6. Although we never learn what the grand prize question was on the "Win or Lose" game show, Aunt Bee's winning answer was "Cinnamon with custard filling." Goober remarks that his mother always makes that dessert with lemon filling. 7. According to Aunt Bee, Jack Smith is 44 years old. 8. Goober says minks are vicious little animals. 9. Beth, the hairdresser, lives in back of the beauty salon. She complies when Clara asks to have her hair done "Italian style." 10. Four of Aunt Bee's friends are Clara Edwards, Myra Tucker, Dorothy, and Jenny. 11. At the end of her appearance on the game show, Aunt Bee waves hello to Clara, Myra, little Johnny Paul, Helen, Jud, Otis, Floyd, and Goober. 12. Claude from the post office delivers Aunt Bee's mink. She eventually sells it to Weaver's Department Store. 13. Mr. Heathcote's license plate reads, "U.S. Government IR-51957." Andy sarcastically remarks that the agent seems to enjoy his work. 14. Goober exclaims that Aunt Bee's new ice crusher makes more noise than Mr. Wilson's fan belt.

"Off to Hollywood"

Episode #166. Air date: 10-25-65. Writers: Bill Idelson and Sam Bobrick. Director: Alan Rafkin.

Andy receives a letter from Belmont Picture Studios of Hollywood. Some time ago, an article about Andy appeared in a sheriffs' magazine. The article was entitled "Sheriff Without a Gun." Now, Belmont Studios is producing a movie based on the article. They send Andy a $1,000 check for the right to use his name.

Andy is very pleased about this unexpected windfall and plans to put the money into his savings account. Aunt Bee is so delighted about Andy's good fortune, she decides a special celebration supper is in order. She invites Helen to join the family for the evening and serves up crabmeat cocktails.

Aunt Bee believes the money should be spent on something impractical, unnecessary, and fun. Helen suggests that the family should take a trip. Andy admits that a short trip might be nice, but Aunt Bee has a more ambitious trip in mind. She wants to go to Hollywood. Opie and Helen are all for the idea, but Andy protests. However, he is outnumbered (three to one) and gives in. The Taylors are going to fly to Hollywood.

Mayberry is abuzz with the news of the trip. Virtually the entire town, including the Mayberry Band, gives Andy, Aunt Bee, and Opie a rousing sendoff.

MEMORABLE SCENE. Andy and Opie sporting their "father and son" outfits, which Aunt Bee purchased at Weaver's Department Store. She claims that the outfit is what all the little boys in Hollywood wear. Andy is not crazy about the matching clothes, and Opie thinks it is a sissy outfit.

CAST NOTES. Regulars: **Andy Griffith, Ronny Howard, Frances Bavier, Aneta Corsaut, Howard McNear, George Lindsey,** and **Jack Burns.**

Owen Bush appears as shoe store repair shop owner Mr. Jason. Mr. Bush has appeared in other episodes as various townspeople. **Maudie Prickett** returns as Edna (Sue) Larch.

EPISODE NOTES. 1. Warren reveals the following information about himself and his background: He spent 16 weeks at a sheriff's academy, finishing fourth in his class. He says that's how he got the job as Mayberry's deputy. Goober says the fact that Warren is Floyd's nephew didn't hurt his chances. Warren's brother-in-law was stationed in California during the war (probably WW II). Warren says his brother-in-law was 6'2" tall, with no waist, good-looking, with black wavy hair. The girls were all over him. Today, Warren says, he is balding, has gained 20 or 30 pounds, and has settled down with his wife and 4 children in a 3-bedroom house in Moline. He is also a member of the Lions' Club. 2. Goober cannot keep a secret. He told Floyd, a Mr. Schlummer, and George at the television store about Andy's $1,000 check, which is signed by Art Spiegel, president of Belmont Pictures. 3. Floyd advises Andy, "Don't take any wooden nickels!" 4. Goober tries to entice Andy into buying a 1958 convertible automobile from him for $600. 5. Floyd owns two acres of swampland on the north side of Mayberry. He tells Andy he would sell it to him for $150 an acre. He encourages him to put on his wading boots and go check it out. 6. Andy, Aunt Bee, and Opie once visited Andy's cousin Evin Moore in Asheville N.C. That was back when Evin was becoming a Mason. Now, Evin is a grand master with the Masons. (As it happens, Andy Griffith really does have a first cousin named Evin Moore. The real Evin Moore lives in Mount Airy and is, indeed, a Mason.) 7. The Taylors once took a short trip to Parkinson's Falls when Opie was a baby. 8. Opie says he would like to see movie stars, such as John Wayne, Elvis Presley, and Fabian, during his Hollywood trip. 9. Andy says Hollywood is 3,000 miles from Mayberry, but Aunt Bee adds that it's only 5½ hours traveling by plane. 10. Goober recommends the Taylors stay at the Starbright Hotel in Hollywood. It features a television in every room and a free morning newspaper every day. Floyd adds that the hotel also throws in a shower cap and a shoeshine rag. 11. Floyd reads an alluring description from a travel brochure for a hotel called Senior Citizen's Lodge, located on Route 66. Floyd suggests that Andy stay there. 12. Andy has a list of about 30 favors to accomplish in Hollywood. They include (1) telephoning Edna Sue Larch's second cousin in Colorado and assuring them the

Larches are doing fine; (2) notifying Hollywood talent scouts about Mr. Jason's tap-dancing, xylophone-playing niece; (3) obtaining Tony Curtis's autograph for little Eileen Hopkins; (4) standing on the corner of Hollywood and Vine and saying "hello" from Floyd; (5) taking a picture of the Pacific Ocean for Goober; and (6) getting an autographed photo of Dale Robertson for Helen's landlady. 13. The Mayberry Band plays "California Here I Come" at the big sendoff. 14. The Taylors employ Southern Buslines to get to the airport in Raleigh and fly T.W.A. to Hollywood. 15. Mr. Jason repairs the handle on a piece of Andy's luggage. He double-stitched it, but it broke off as Andy tried to carry it to the bus.

"Taylors in Hollywood"

Episode #167. Air date: 11-1-65. Writers: Bill Idelson and Sam Bobrick. Director: Alan Rafkin.

The Taylors arrive at Los Angeles International Airport and board a bus that will take them to their home for the next two weeks, the Piedmont Hotel. While rolling down Sunset Boulevard, they discover that the relief bus driver sitting behind them is from Ruby Creek, North Carolina. He points out a few famous establishments and even arranges for a quick tour of celebrities' homes along Beverly Drive.

The family discovers that their hotel room is very nice, and Opie and Andy are anxious to go swimming in the pool. Before they do that, Aunt Bee succeeds in persuading Andy to call Belmont Picture Studios and let them know he and his family are vacationing in Hollywood. A.J. Considine, director of *Sheriff Without a Gun*, returns Andy's call and invites the family to come to the set and watch them shoot some of the movie's scenes. On the set, they meet assistant director Al Saunders, Mr. Considine, and Bryan Bender, the actor who portrays Andy in the movie.

The first scene that the family sees involves "Andy" being confronted by two gun-toting outlaws, the Calhoun brothers. The calm, collected, cigar-smoking Sheriff Taylor manages to dispatch them in a barroom brawl. Andy and Opie enjoy the action, but Aunt Bee is appalled and devastated. She condemns the scene as outlandish and exaggerated. She fears that Andy will be ridiculed if the rest of the movie continues in a similar fashion. She insists that Andy order Mr. Considine to make some changes. Although reluctant, Andy tells her he will do so when they come to the studios the following day.

When the Taylors arrive back on the set, a new scene is about to be filmed. Aunt Bee will have to wait until after the scene is shot before Andy can speak with the director.

Aunt Bee is delighted when she discovers that the actress portraying her is young and glamorous. She is even more happy when she sees Hollywood's "Aunt Bee" defend her home using a rifle to repel the nasty Calhoun brothers. Suddenly, Mayberry's Aunt Bee has decided that some liberties must be taken in order to make the movie more interesting.

MEMORABLE SCENE. Andy calling Belmont Picture Studios from his hotel. He gets aggravated when he continually gets connected with the studio's tailor shop.

CAST NOTES. Regulars: **Andy Griffith, Ronny Howard,** and **Frances Bavier.**

Gavin McLeod portrays actor Bryan Bender. In episode 150, "TV or Not TV," he portrayed Gilbert Jammel. (Ironically, both episodes deal with "Sheriff Without a Gun." The earlier episode involved a proposed television series.) **Hayden Rorke,** best known for his role as Dr. Alfred Bellows on television's *I Dream of Jeannie* (1965-1970), appears as director A.J. Considine. **Eddie Quillan,** better known for portraying Eddie Edson on television's *Julia* (1968-1971), appears as the bellhop at the Taylors' hotel. **Ross Elliott,** who portrayed Sheriff Abbott on television's *The Virginian* (1967-1970), appears as assistant director Al Saunders. **Yvonne Lime,** a veteran of the classic comedy *Father Knows Best* (1954-1957) as Dotty Snow, makes a brief appearance as a T.W.A. stewardess. Veteran character actor **Herb Vigran** appears as the gate man at Belmont Picture Studios. **June Vincent** is the unnamed actress portraying Aunt Bee in the movie. **Robert Nichols** appears as the relief bus driver.

EPISODE NOTES. 1. On the bus en route to the Piedmont Hotel, the Taylors see Dino's Lounge (owned by Dean Martin), Schwab's Pharmacy (where Lana Turner was discovered), the Whiskey a Go Go (a dance club), and Blair House Motor Hotel. 2. One of the celebrity homes the Taylors see belongs to Cesar Romero. His house was at 505 Beverly Drive. Opie had his photo taken while proudly holding Mr. Romero's newspaper in his hands. Mr. Romero's maid politely asked the family to stay off of the lawn as it had just been seeded. 3. Opie wants to see the La Brea Tar Pits and Marineland, while Aunt Bee inquires about the Brown Derby Restaurant. 4. The driver of bus #60 (the Taylors' bus) is named Joe. 5. Aunt Bee intends to write a letter to one of the Smedly sisters back home. 6. The Taylors stay in room #403 at the Piedmont Hotel. 7. *Sheriff Without a Gun* is being filmed on stage 40 at Belmont Picture Studios.

8. Andy takes a picture of the bellhop standing between Opie and Aunt Bee. 9. During the Taylors visits to the studio, they sit in chairs marked "V.I.P." 10. Actor Bryan Bender signs Opie's autograph book. 11. In the movie, the Calhoun brothers try to spring their partner Harry from the Mayberry jail. 12. Aunt Bee wishes the film would depict the nice things that Andy does, such as distributing baskets at Christmas and giving safety lectures at the high school. 13. The Taylors watch "The Jerome Sanger Show" on television in their hotel room. It's a favorite of Opie's.

"The Hollywood Party"

Episode #168. Air date: 11-8-65. Writers: Lawrence J. Cohen and Fred Freeman. Director: Alan Rafkin.

The Taylors are nearing the end of their wonderful vacation in Hollywood, where the movie *Sheriff Without a Gun* is being filmed. Belmont Studios asks Andy to pose for some publicity photos with the film's beautiful leading lady, Darlene Mason. Andy reluctantly complies. He is very nervous as he is led by publicity agent Pat Michaels into Miss Mason's dressing room. She is very much at ease as the photographer (a man named Lou) starts taking pictures. Andy, of course, is quite uncomfortable. Mr. Michaels finally manages to cajole Andy to pose for one intimate, cheek-to-cheek photo with Miss Mason. This photograph is rushed to the press.

When the cozy picture appears on the front page of *The Mayberry Gazette*, Helen is deluged with phone calls from her friends and neighbors. When Andy calls her, he is surprised that she is so upset over the photo. Before he can explain the situation, Helen abruptly ends the conversation.

Upset by Helen's attitude (she called him a "Hollywood playboy"), Andy decides to turn to Miss Mason for a little comfort. He visits her at her Hollywood Marquee apartment. He finds her to be a very warm and charming woman. Miss Mason would clearly like to get to know Andy better, and she suggests they dine together. Andy makes the reservation at a posh restaurant called the Marcier. Only one obstacle stands between Andy and Miss Mason: his conscience. He tells Darlene about Helen and explains the chain of events that led him into this situation. Miss Mason understands. They enjoy a pleasant supper together.

Meanwhile, Helen decides that she should apologize to Andy for her jealous reaction. But when she calls the Taylors' room, Opie tells her that his pa is

at Miss Mason's apartment. This is the last thing Helen wanted to hear.

When Andy returns to his room just minutes later, Opie tells him about Helen's call. Andy realizes he has a lot of explaining to do. Indeed, when he returns the call, Helen quickly and angrily hangs up on him.

In order to set things straight, Andy asks Miss Mason to explain everything to Helen. She kindly obliges. Once she understands the entire story, Helen apologizes, and a very relieved Andy can finally relax.

CAST NOTES. Regulars: **Andy Griffith, Ronny Howard, Frances Bavier,** and **Aneta Corsaut.**

Lovely **Ruta Lee** appears as Miss Darlene Mason. This is Lee's second appearance in the series. In episode 61, "Andy on Trial," she portrayed deceitful reporter Jean Boswell. Lee has appeared in many television and film projects over the past four decades. She had a lead role in the pilot episode of H.B.O.'s innovative series *First and Ten* in 1985.

Veteran comic actor **Sid Melton** portrays publicist Pat Michaels. Melton may be best known for his role as carpenter Alf Monroe on the 1960s hit series *Green Acres*. He also portrayed Danny Williams' manager and uncle, Charley Halper, on *Make Room for Granddaddy* (1970-1971).

EPISODE NOTES. 1. The Taylors receive mail from Goober, and Andy gets a letter from Helen. Goober includes a clipping from *The Mayberry Gazette*, Lonnie Ladner's column "Longitudes and Latitudes." Aunt Bee reads a portion of it to Andy and Opie. It includes the information that the Taylors are still in Hollywood. 2. Goober tells of some excitement of his own at the filling station. There was a dogfight between a chow and a collie, and one of them bit through the air hose. Goober also received a shipment of new radiator caps. 3. Opie has eight autographs obtained on this trip (so far). It includes autographs of Miss Mason and Andy. 4. Mr. Michaels, taking some biographical background on Andy, stretches a few facts. He credits Andy with an extra two inches of height, and he calls Mayberry "Blueberry" and places the town in South Carolina. 5. When the photo of Andy and Darlene appears in *The Mayberry Gazette*, the headline reads "Is This Darlene Mason's Next Conquest???" The article is subtitled, "Sheriff Taylor Takes Hollywood By Storm." 6. When Andy makes a person-to-person call to Helen, he gives Helen's home phone number as 2389. 7. Aunt Bee and Opie go on a tour of Beverly Hills. Aunt Bee has heard that nowhere on earth do zinnias do better, and they say that the snapdragons also go crazy. Opie wears his Hollywood outfit on the tour. He later tells Andy that he saw a girl wearing an outfit like his.

He said it looked awful on her, too. 8. Miss Mason's phone number is Hollywood 27399. 9. Miss Mason grew up in Kansas. As a youngster, she used to play in the Whitewater Creek and catch polliwogs. 10. Some of the souvenirs that Opie will bring back to Mayberry are a pennant that says "Hollywood," a Los Angeles Dodgers pennant, a toy airplane, and a skateboard. He tells Aunt Bee that he'd like to leave his Hollywood outfit in Hollywood.

"A Warning from Warren"

Episode #169. Air date: 10-15-65. Writers: Fred Freeman and Lawrence J. Cohen. Director: Alan Rafkin.

Warren believes he has the gift of extrasensory perception (ESP). He easily convinces his uncle, Floyd Lawson, as well as Goober of his extraordinary power. Andy remains rightly skeptical. To prove his ability, Warren asks Andy, Goober, and Floyd to pick out an object in Floyd's Barbershop while he waits outdoors. Warren claims he can tell them which object they've chosen. The men choose the table nearest Floyd. Warren is put to the test. He ignores Floyd's rather obvious clues, and announces that the mirror was the object in question. When Andy informs him of his failure, Warren points out that the table is reflected in the mirror. He claims this proves he has "reflective thought waves." Floyd and Goober are astonished, and Andy is exasperated.

Helen convinces Andy to take a day off and picnic with her at Myers' Lake. Andy looks forward to a nice, relaxing day.

Warren suddenly develops a sense of impending doom. His ESP allows him to see blue, masses of green, and a man and a woman. While dining late one night with Goober, everything comes together. He believes Andy and Helen are in danger of getting hurt if they go to Myers' Lake. He and Goober rush over to Andy's house and wake him up. Warren explains his premonition and begs Andy to postpone the picnic. Andy angrily orders him to leave him alone.

The day of the picnic, Warren is desperate to keep Andy from leaving. He enlists Floyd to disguise his voice and telephone the sheriff. Floyd tells Andy that a mob of men are coming to Mayberry to rob the bank or a jewelry store. He tells him the gang is "packing *gnats*," meaning to say "Gats." Andy easily recognizes Floyd's voice, and the plan goes awry.

Next, Warren orders Goober to disable the squad car by removing the distributor cap. But this plan backfires, too. Andy merely loads up Goober's truck, and he and Helen take off. Undaunted, Warren and Goober follow them to the lake, where Andy catches them, not once, but twice.

Finally, Andy and Helen take refuge in a small boat, figuring that they can row away from their hardheaded friends. However, Warren tries to pull Andy out of the boat. When he does, the boat capsizes and dumps the unlucky couple into the lake. Helen is drenched, but otherwise okay. Unfortunately, Andy sustained a sprained wrist. The angry sheriff gets out of the water and immediately tosses Goober in. Then, glaring, he starts after Warren. The well-meaning but annoying deputy saves Andy some trouble by throwing *himself* into the lake.

Later, Warren rationalizes that, because Andy did injure himself, the premonition of danger came true after all.

CAST NOTES. Regulars: **Andy Griffith, Jack Burns, Aneta Corsaut, George Lindsey,** and **Howard McNear.**

Charles Smith appears as the unnamed counter man at the diner.

EPISODE NOTES. 1. Floyd says that Andy has "tired" hair. Actually, he is trying to get Andy to agree to a scalp treatment. The full treatment costs $3.00. The charge is $2.00 if no vibrator is used, and Floyd will charge only $1.00 if he just uses his fingers to massage the scalp. Andy declines any treatment. Floyd remarks, "It's *your* hair ... won't be for long, though!" 2. Warren's been reading a book titled *The Fundamentals of Extrasensory Perception.* He also reads magazines on the subject. One of the magazines had the story of 12-year-old Sonya Wallachauka of Warsaw, Poland. In 1928, little Sonya foresaw an avalanche. She warned her family and friends of her premonition. During the next evening, an avalanche did occur. Her warnings saved the lives of four people. Floyd, seemingly oblivious to the passage of years, remarks, "I'd like to shake that little girl's hand!" 3. Warren's mother is Floyd's sister. Floyd says Warren has her features: a high forehead and a pointy nose. 4. Sheriff Mitchell is the sheriff of Pilot County. 5. Goober say "extra senasore Perceptive" instead of "extrasensory perception." 6. Andy tells Floyd that the penalty for giving false information to a law office is 10 years. 7. Goober drives a blue pickup truck. 8. Bigg's Store is located on Main Street in Mayberry. 9. Goober orders a milkshake along with his peanut butter and tuna sandwich at the diner. He adds ketchup to the sandwich. Warren orders a hamburger. 10. By the end of this episode, Andy's left arm is in a sling. 11. Viewers get a rare glimpse of Andy's bedroom in this episode.

"A Man's Best Friend"

Episode #170. Air date: 11-29-65. Writers: Art Baer and Ben Joelson. Director: Alan Rafkin.

Opie and his new pal Tommy enjoy playing "secret agent" using a pair of miniature walkie-talkies. Unfortunately, Tommy is a spoiled brat who enjoys playing pranks. Andy and Aunt Bee believe he is a bad influence on Opie.

Goober finds a stray dog and decides to keep him as a pet. He names the dog Spot (the dog has no spots at all). He tries in vain to teach the dog some tricks.

Tommy and Opie decide to have a little fun at Goober's expense. They plant a walkie-talkie under Spot's collar and hide out in nearby bushes. Tommy supplies a voice for the dog. Initially, Goober cannot believe his ears when Spot talks to him. He is so amazed, he decides to try to find Andy. Failing to locate the sheriff, Goober broaches the idea of a talking dog with his pal Floyd. The barber mulls it over and determines that theoretically, it is possible for a dog to learn to talk. Floyd adds that if he had such a dog, he'd make a fortune.

Goober returns to the filling station and runs into Andy. Without alerting him, Goober tries to prompt Spot to say something, but to no avail. After Andy leaves, Spot tells Goober not to tell anyone that he has a talking dog. However, Goober cannot restrain himself and tells Andy and Floyd that he and Spot are leaving Mayberry as soon as Wally can find a replacement to run the station. Goober says he and his talking dog will travel around the country doing shows. Andy and Floyd chuckle at the notion, but Goober believes he will have the last laugh.

Tommy decides to take his prank one step further. As Spot, he tells Goober that a more unique act would be funnier. He suggests that Spot give the commands and Goober do the tricks. As "Spot" is putting Goober through this routine, Andy discovers what the boys are up to. Tommy and Opie flee the scene, believing they barely escaped detection.

Andy is left to break the news to Goober, and he does so as gently as possible. It was a mean practical joke. Goober is embarrassed, but he asks Andy not to be too hard on the boys, saying, "They're just kids ... they'll learn."

Andy comes up with a plan to teach the boys a lesson. He has heard Tommy say that his father plans to buy him a horse sometime when he can find one at the right price. Andy tells Tommy that while he was at the filling station, he overheard a man telling Goober about a fine young horse he was selling real cheap. He left his phone number with Goober, just in case he runs across anyone who might be interested in a bargain. Tommy and Opie get very excited and ask Andy to take them to see Goober. Before the trio heads to Wally's Andy calls Goober and tells him about the joke.

Goober plays his part perfectly. He tells Tommy that he failed to write the number down. Then he says that he told Spot the number. He then asks Spot to tell him the man's number. Tommy realizes he's out of luck. He is very disappointed as he confesses to the prank. Andy, in turn, reveals that he and Goober turned the tables on the boys as a means of revenge. The boys learn the hard way that some practical jokes aren't so funny.

Later, the boys apologize to Goober, who graciously accepts and is kind enough to forgive and forget. Tommy and Opie then invite him to play "secret agent" with them. Spot joins in the fun, too.

CAST NOTES. Regular: **Andy Griffith, Ronny Howard, Frances Bavier, George Lindsey**, and **Howard McNear**.

Michel Petit appears as Opie's friend Tommy.

EPISODE NOTES. 1. When playing "secret agent," Opie's code number is TX4, Tommy's is X21, Goober's is XY27, and Spot is known as FBI Dog. 2. Tommy's family moved from an unnamed larger town to Mayberry. Tommy's father is the chief accountant at the new shoe factory. 3. Aunt Bee says that Opie is 11 years old. 4. Andy and Floyd play checkers at the courthouse.

"Aunt Bee Takes a Job"

Episode #171. Air date: 12-6-65. Writers: Bill Idelson and Sam Bobrick. Director: Alan Rafkin.

Aunt Bee has too much time on her hands, so she applies for a receptionist's job at the newly established printing shop in Mayberry. The business is owned and operated by two newcomers to Mayberry, Ralph Kingsley and Arnold Finch. Even though Aunt Bee doesn't take dictation or type, and she's not very good with figures, she is hired — mainly because she's blissfully unaware that her employers are counterfeiters and the print shop is merely a front for an illegal operation. Not long after she starts, Andy and Warren are notified that counterfeit bills are turning up in Raleigh and some other nearby towns.

After Aunt Bee cashes her first paycheck with one of the print shop's best "customers," a Mr. Clark, she goes on a shopping spree to celebrate her very first real paycheck. She buys a $9.95 dress at Weaver's Department Store; a football for Opie at

Johnson's Sporting Goods Store; business cards for Andy that say, "Andrew Taylor — Sheriff of Mayberry" from her place of employment; and $10.00 worth of groceries from Foley's Market for a fancy meal. Everyone loves their gifts, but Andy is rather surprised to see that his business cards are printed in green ink.

Later, all of the establishments where Aunt Bee made purchases report to Andy that they have recently received counterfeit $10.00 bills. Aunt Bee overhears the news and warns her bosses to be on the lookout for the bogus bills. Kingsley and Finch begin to feel the heat of the law and close up shop. Meanwhile, Andy puts the puzzle together when he recalls that Aunt Bee had told him where she had shopped and then he remembers the color of his business cards. As Kingsley and Finch are leaving, Andy grabs Warren's pistol and shoots out the tires on the counterfeiters' station wagon. Then he and Warren make an easy capture.

CAST NOTES. Regulars: **Andy Griffith, Frances Bavier,** and **Jack Burns.**

Milton Frome stars as Ralph Kingsley. Frome was a regular on *The Milton Berle Show*, and he is also remembered for his role of Lawrence Chapman on *The Beverly Hillbillies*. **James Millhollin** costars as Arnold Finch. Millhollin has appeared in numerous movie and television roles throughout the years.

In this episode, **Jason Johnson** portrays Ben Weaver. He would reappear in later episodes. Johnson appeared in several dramatic anthology programs in the 1950s, such as *Studio 57*. He appeared in such series as *The Big Valley, The Fugitive, Lassie, The Millionaire, Mission:Impossible, One Step Beyond, Perry Mason,* and *The Twilight Zone*. In the latter series, he appeared as Jensen in the 1960 episode "The Lateness of the Hour." This was the first episode of this series to be videotaped. Johnson also appeared in the 1978 television movie *Crisis at Sun Valley*. Among his theatrical releases are *The Abductors* (1957), *Invasion of the Saucer Men* (1957), *I Want to Live* (1958, starring Susan Hayward), *Arson for Hire* (1959), *The Legend of Tom Dooley* (1959, with Michael Landon), *Cape Canaveral Monsters* (1960), and *If He Hollers, Let Him Go* (1968).

Herbie Faye returns to Mayberry. In this one, he appears as Mr. Clark. **Maggie Magennis** portrays Violet Rose Schumaker. **Don Gazzaniga** appears as Mr. Jones.

EPISODE NOTES. 1. Andy enjoys reading "Moon Mullins" in the funny papers. 2. Kingsley and Finch's print shop is located at 177 Main Street in downtown Mayberry. They took over the building that previously housed Hanson's Print Shop. In fact, Hanson's sign still appears on the front door.

The following signs appear in the new print shop: "1000 Business Cards for $2.45"; "Distinctive Job Printing — Envelopes, Letterhead, Statements, Invoices, Business Cards, Wedding Invitations — Birth Announcements — Prompt Service." 3. The following businesses in Mayberry are shown: the Mayberry Real Estate and Insurance Company; Ye Old Book Shoppe; and Norman's Groceteria. 4. Aunt Bee's job pays $30.00 a week, and she works from 1:00 to 4:00 on weekdays. 5. Aunt Bee beat out a stuck-up lady named Violet Rose Schumaker for the job. Miss Schumaker previously worked at the Mayberry Coal Company. 6. Aunt Bee has a friend named Clara Cartwright who works three days a week at the bakery in Mayberry. Clara's birthday is on August 21. Aunt Bee's birthday is on March 17, but no year of birth is given for either lady. 7. Warren claims that he can spot a counterfeit bill from a mile away, yet he looks one right in the eye at the print shop and doesn't recognize it. All of the counterfeit money consists of $10.00 bills. 8. The Mayberry Bank closes at 3:00 P.M. on weekdays. 9. Kingsley and Finch's license plate number is NRH-830. After they are apprehended, Andy locks them up in cell #2. 10. Andy speaks to a state police friend of his named Dick on the telephone. Dick informs him that the counterfeit money has turned up in Siler City.

"The Cannon"

Episode #172. Air date: 11-22-65. Writer: Jack Elinson. Director: Alan Rafkin.

It's Founder's Day once again in Mayberry! This year, something special is in the works. The plan is for the governor of North Carolina, George C. Handley, to appear at the celebration in conjunction with the arrival of the State Mobile Museum. The traveling museum houses several interesting items, such as old coins, paintings, swords, jewelry, and a prized lavaliere (a pendant) that belonged to Martha Washington.

Andy calls a special meeting of the Mayberry Founder's Day Committee. The members of the committee are Andy, who oversees all of the activities; Warren, who's in charge of security; Goober, who's in charge of transportation and assists Warren with security; Floyd, who's in charge of decorations; Aunt Bee, who's responsible for preparing the food for the governor's luncheon reception; a man named Frank Chase, who organizes the parade; and a man named John, who has the dubious honor of whipping the pitiful Mayberry Marching Band into shape. With Mayberry's mayor vacationing in Hawaii, the committee appoints Harry Bosworth, the head of the Mayberry Water and Power Company, to be the official greeter. Also, the current Potato Queen of Mayberry, Sharon Dobbins, will present a potato to Governor Handley while wearing a bikini. Aunt Bee protests this type of attire, but she's overruled. Warren and Goober are assigned to guard the State Mobile Museum, which arrives in Mayberry one day prior to the governor's appearance. Warren tells Andy that he would love to fire the old town cannon during the festivities, but Andy orders his persistent deputy to stay away from the unsafe Civil War relic.

Later on, a man named Jack convinces Warren that he's a state policeman named George Archer. He goes on to tell Warren (who's more concerned with the effort he and Goober are making to dislodge a cannonball stuck inside of the cannon) that he has been assigned to take over as the museum's official guard. Warren believes the obviously contrived story and happily turns over the museum's keys to the crook. Jack and Stella promptly start stealing items from the museum, while the Mayberry Security Team is still fiddling with the cannon just a few yards away.

Meanwhile, Governor Handley has started his speech. Suddenly, Warren accidentally fires the cannon. By a stroke of luck, the ancient cannonball strikes Jack and Stella's getaway car, and the shaken thieves are easily apprehended. Peace is soon restored, and the Founder's Day festivities are resumed.

CAST NOTES. Regulars: **Andy Griffith, Frances Bavier, Jack Burns, Howard McNear,** and **George Lindsey.**

Byron Foulger returns to the series, this time as Harry Bosworth. **Justin Smith** portrays John. **Vaughn Taylor** appears as Frank Chase. **Robert Karnes** appears as Jack, a.k.a. George Archer. **Sally Mansfield** portrays Stella. Mansfield appeared as Connie from 1961 through 1962 on *Bachelor Father.* **J. Edward McKinley** appears as Governor George C. Handley. **Douglas McCairn** appears as the driver.

EPISODE NOTES. 1. John states that "Jesse Earle Hagen," a bass player from Mount Pilot, is coming to town to play with the Mayberry Marching Band at the Founder's Day celebration. This is an inside joke. As most lovers of *The Andy Griffith Show* know, Earle Hagen wrote most of the music that was heard in every episode, and he was the composer (and whistler) of the great theme song. 2. Goober is considering buying an imitation alligator wallet for $1.95 from an ad in *Thrilling Stories* magazine. 3. Sam Edley rides his motorcycle at the rear of the parade, while Goober borrows Ear-

lie Gilley's convertible. This is not the first time Andy Griffith's old buddy from Pilot Mountain, N.C. has been mentioned on the show. However, we are not certain whether the real Earlie Gilley owns a convertible, or whether he's in the habit of loaning it to people like Goober. 4. The Mayberry Marching Band plays the Mayberry Theme Song (also used as the theme song a few years later on *Mayberry R.F.D.*) upon Governor Handley's arrival. 5. In a rare scene, Andy wears a necktie with his uniform at the Founder's Day festivities. 6. Aunt Bee serves shrimp cocktail, chicken `a la king, ladyfingers, and coffee at the governor's luncheon reception. 7. A banner in downtown Mayberry proclaims: "Mayberry Welcomes Our Governor." 8. Warren proposes the following slogan: "Mayberry's Founder's Day, May Mayberry Never Founder." It is not well received.

"Girl-Shy"

Episode #173. Air date: 12-20-65. Writers: Bill Idelson and Sam Bobrick. Director: Lee Philips.

Andy and Helen invite Warren to accompany them to Dave's Hong Kong, a new Chinese restaurant in Mount Pilot. Warren declines when he learns that Andy and Helen want him to escort Sue Anne McGrath, a new girl in town, who works at the dime store. It seems that Warren is painfully shy around women.

Later, Andy and Helen have to postpone the dinner date after Sheriff Mitchell of Mount Pilot calls Andy and asks him for assistance at a highway traffic accident. Helen initially waits at the courthouse with Warren, but a little while later, she decides to go to a movie. When she returns, Warren uncharacteristically makes a pass at her. The only recourse she has is to lock herself up in cell #2. When Andy returns from the accident, Warren denies any wrongdoing, and Andy can't believe that his shy deputy would do such a thing. What Andy and Helen don't realize is that Warren is a sleepwalker, and while sleepwalking he's influenced by the romantic leading men that he watches in the movies and on television.

After Helen is forced to lock herself in the same cell for the second time, Andy has no choice but to fire his deputy. It is only then that Warren (who has decided to leave Mayberry) confides to Goober about his affliction. Goober implores him to explain his condition to Andy, but Warren somehow comes to the conclusion that Andy would not want a sleepwalking deputy.

Finally, after watching a Fred Astaire movie and

staying up all night in order not to sleepwalk, Warren is summoned by Andy to get to the bottom of the situation. Andy also invites Helen to his house to hear the explanation, but she wants to leave as soon as she sees Warren. While Andy and Helen are bickering, they hear Aunt Bee calling for them in the living room. They are shocked to see Warren doing his best Fred Astaire imitation with Aunt Bee as a reluctant Ginger Rogers. Andy soon figures out the problem and happily reinstates his sleepwalking deputy.

CAST NOTES. Regulars: **Andy Griffith, Frances Bavier, George Lindsey, Aneta Corsaut,** and **Jack Burns.**

EPISODE NOTES. 1. Warren is originally from Boston. 2. Aunt Bee's first blind date was with a man named Orville Buck. They went ice skating, and Aunt Bee had to hold Orville up all through the evening because he had weak knees. Aunt Bee said that they didn't get along very well and that some years later, Orville was killed in an explosion. 3. Warren's favorite television show is "International Secret Agent F-45." Michael Glendon is the fictitious actor who portrays the suave and sophisticated secret agent. Warren and Goober watch an episode of the show called "Mission to Istanbul." 4. Andy says that every time Mr. and Mrs. Purvis of Mayberry get into a fight, Mr. Purvis climbs up a tree outside of their house, and Andy has to help him down. 5. When Warren is planning to leave Mayberry, he offers Goober the following items: an orange juice squeezer, a science fiction book called *Moon Men Invade Venus on Giant Bats*, a brick, and a portable television. He tells Goober that he has to ask $50.00 for the television. 6. At the conclusion of the episode, Warren handcuffs himself to his bed post when he hits the sack, just in case.

"The Church Organ"

Episode #174. Air date: 12-13-65. Writer: Paul Wayne. Director: Lee Philips.

Clara Edwards is upset. The organ that she so proudly plays during weekly church services has worn out. Goober tries to fix it, but during the hymn, "Love Lifted Me" (number 256 in the hymn book), the keys stick, and Clara runs out of the church in tears. Since Clara is a perfectionist and takes great pride in her playing, Andy, Helen, and Warren decide to form a committee in an attempt to acquire a good used church organ. The church has only $1200.00 to spend, so some shrewd wheeling and dealing is in order.

Warren discovers a classified ad in *The Mount*

Pilot Times. The ad states that a gentleman by the name of Harlan Robinson is selling a good used organ for $2,000.00. Andy and Warren visit Mr. Robinson and are impressed with the beautiful instrument, but Mr. Robinson simply can't lower the price. He needs the full amount to pay for a new barn that he desperately needs for his farm. Mr. Robinson agrees not to sell the organ while Andy and Warren try to come up with a way to raise the needed cash.

In order to make up the $800.00 difference, Andy asks the following businessmen in Mayberry to pledge $150.00 each: Floyd Lawson, Jim Slater, and two men named Rudy and Sam. Andy and Warren also pledge $150.00 each. Next, Mr. Robinson allows the Mayberry contingent to take the organ and use it at the church until all of the pledges are honored. Unfortunately, with the sole exception of Andy, all of the contributors fail to honor their pledges. Each has his own excuse: Warren's rent is due, along with two television payments and a large laundry bill; Floyd claims his business has been slow due to the low foreign exchange rate; Jim Slater's water heater blew up; Rudy's wife bought a new outfit; and Sam's son needs braces. All Andy can do is return the organ to Mr. Robinson.

A distraught Clara asks to accompany Andy and Warren to Mount Pilot. Andy doesn't care for the idea, but he allows Clara to tag along. At Mr. Robinson's home, Clara discovers that he's a single man. By using her feminine charms and serenading Harlan with a spontaneous version of "Some Enchanted Evening," Clara makes certain that the permanent location of the organ will be at the church in Mayberry.

MEMORABLE SCENE. Andy has to quiet a mischievous Opie for laughing at Clara's broken organ at church.

CAST NOTES. Regulars: **Andy Griffith, Ronny Howard, Frances Bavier, Howard McNear, Aneta Corsaut, Jack Burns,** and **Hope Summers. William Keene** returns as Reverend Tucker.

Woodrow (Woody) Chambliss stars as Harlan Robinson. Chambliss previously appeared as Orville Hendricks in episode 154, "Aunt Bee's Invisible Beau." **Bert Remsen** appears as Jim Slater. In 1980 and 1981, Remsen appeared as Mario on *It's a Living*. **Robert B. Williams** portrays Sam. In 1977 and 1978, William appeared as Martin Mull's father, Garth Gimble, Sr., on *Fernwood 2-Night*. **Pitt Herbert** appears as Rudy.

EPISODE NOTES. 1. Before she got the new organ, Clara played "Love Lifted Me" during church services because the song doesn't contain too many flats. 2. The church choir practices on Wednesday nights. 3. Andy claims that Reverend

Tucker's sermons on happiness are his best. After the new organ has been secured, Reverend Tucker's new sermon is "Seek and Ye Shall Find." 4. Harlan Robinson lives on Oakmont Road in Mount Pilot. 5. During pledge time, Floyd urges Jim Slater to "give 'til it hurts." 6. The first hymn sung after Clara receives the new organ is "Bringing in the Sheaves." 7. Glenn Cripe sits behind the Taylors at church. 8. In celebration of receiving the new organ, the entire church congregation sings "Leaning on the Everlasting Arms." 9. Opie pledges the 60 cents that Johnny Paul owes him toward the new organ. A problem occurs when Opie has to fight Johnny Paul on Sunday in order to acquire the money. 10. Warren tells Andy that he used to be in the wholesale fish business. He lasted for over three months. 11. A gentleman named Jim Slate is a resident of Mount Airy, North Carolina. Could he have been the inspiration for the character Jim Slater? Only Andy knows for sure. 12. Mystery man Mr. Schwump appears in this episode. He can be seen sitting directly to the left behind Clara at church. He wears glasses as he sings from the hymn book.

"Otis the Artist"

Episode #175. Air date: 1-3-66. Teleplay by: Fred Freeman and Lawrence J. Cohen. Story by: Bob Ross. Director: Alan Rafkin.

Warren is a member of Mayberry's adult art class and is currently interested in mosaics. He believes that creating art is a great way to relieve everyday pressure.

Warren meets Otis Campbell for the first time when the infamous town drunk comes stumbling to his jail cell on a Friday night. Warren refuses to mollycoddle him and, in fact, orders Otis to go home. Otis refuses to leave, and when he attempts to fight the deputy, Warren arrests him for assaulting an officer. Otis therefore gets to stay in his cell after all.

The next morning, Warren prepares a hangover cure for Otis and tries to interest him in mosaics. Otis is not enthusiastic about moving ceramic tiles around, but the persistent deputy finally gets him to try. Surprisingly, Otis takes to it like a duck takes to water. He is proud of his first creation, which can best be described as a crude depiction of a cow. Warren encourages him, and Otis decides to give this art piece to Andy. Warren decides to hang it over Andy's fireplace. It is an eyesore as far as the Taylors are concerned. Andy takes it down and hides it in a closet.

Warren is quite pleased with Otis's progress. His goal was to give Otis a new hobby to replace his old one (drinking). He arranges for his protege to speak to those in attendance at the next art class.

On the night of his speech, Otis stops by the Taylors' home and notices that his art is no longer hanging above the fireplace. Opie is embarrassed as he explains that his father put it in a closet. This hurts Otis, and he reverts to his original hobby. He shows up late, and drunk, at the art class. He manages to utter a few words to the confused gathering before he disappears.

Warren worries when a day and a half passes and he has not seen hide nor hair of Otis. Finally, a drunken Otis shows up at the courthouse and displays his new mosaic to Andy and Warren. To their amazement, it is a beautiful landscape. Otis explains that, after he realized his initial work was rotten, he discovered that he does his best work when he is "just a little gassed!" Now, he has two hobbies!

CAST NOTES. Regulars: **Andy Griffith, Ronny Howard, Frances Bavier, Jack Burns, Hal Smith,** and **George Lindsey.**

EPISODE NOTES. 1. The local hardware store sells mosaic kits. Opie buys one. 2. Otis has an imaginary dog, whom he calls Spot. He tries to sic it on Warren. Later, a real dog accompanies a drunken Otis as he stumbles into the courthouse, but he is apparently invisible to his master. 3. When Otis threatens to do his drinking in Mount Pilot or Siler City, Warren threatens to blacklist him from every jail within a 500-mile radius of Mayberry. This is how Warren coerced Otis to try mosaics. 4. A drunken Otis warbles a line or two from "If I Had the Wings of an Angel." 5. Goober studied art in Bible School one summer. 6. Aunt Bee belongs to the art class. She says her class has 10 members and meetings are on Wednesday evenings. She enjoys painting with water colors. 7. Warren's hangover remedy combines sassafras, root beer, sorghum molasses, a raw egg, and hot sauce. This concoction is similar to the hangover cure that Andy prepared for Otis in episode 93, "Dogs, Dogs, Dogs." 8. *The Monster that Ate Minnesota* is the movie currently playing in Mayberry. Goober has seen it 10 times. 9. Goober and Andy are among the many townspeople who come to hear Otis address the art class. 10. Otis's weekday job is at the furniture factory, where he is a glue-dipper. This is the only mention of his job in the series. 11. Mr. Schwump returns. He can be seen at the art class.

"The Return of Barney Fife"

Episode #176. Air date: 1-10-66. Writers: Sam Bobrick and Bill Idelson. Director: Alan Rafkin.

Andy is delighted to hear that Barney is coming to Mayberry to visit and to attend their high school reunion. Barney has been working in the traffic division of the Raleigh Police Department and has recently been promoted to the fingerprint section. He is in charge of the files N through R (Nab to Rossisky). He's been living in the corner room at the Y, of course.

Barney has not forgotten about Thelma Lou, the only girl he ever loved. She moved away from Mayberry about a month after he left for Raleigh. Barney is hoping she will come back for the reunion. He is ecstatic when his wish comes true. For a while, it appears that time has not changed things between them. Unfortunately, Barney's hope of rekindling the relationship are dashed when he is introduced to Thelma Lou's husband of six weeks. His sorrow and regret is somewhat lessened when a former classmate, Nettie Albright, reveals that she has always had a crush on him.

MEMORABLE SCENE. Barney trying to drown his sorrow with nonalcoholic punch.

CAST NOTES. Regulars: **Andy Griffith, Ronny Howard, Frances Bavier,** and **Aneta Corsaut. Don Knotts** returns as Barney Fife in his first of five guest appearances.

Burt Mustin returns. This time he is "old man" Crowley. He has previously appeared as Jud, Burt, Jubal, and "the old geezer." **Barbara Perry** appears as Floss, who is in charge of organizing the reunion. Perry appeared, in a very similar role, as Mary in episode 82, "Class Reunion." **Ted Jordan,** better known as Nathan Burke from 1964 to 1975 on the long-running television western *Gunsmoke,* portrays Thelma Lou's husband, Gerald Whitfield. **Virginia Sale** and **Edna M. Holland** appear as two of Barney's old teachers.

Alberta Nelson portrays Nettie Albright. Nelson would soon essay the role of Goober's well-endowed girlfriend, waitress Flora Mallerby. Nelson made relatively few guest appearances on television, but there are a couple that may stick in many viewers' minds. First, she appeared as Ritchie's schoolteacher, Miss Reshovsky, in an episode of *The Dick Van Dyke Show.* (The episode, "Go Tell the Birds and Bees," dealt with Ritchie's erroneous retelling of the facts of life.) She also made an appearance as Flora in an episode of *Mayberry R.F.D.* titled "Emmett's Retirement." Nelson appeared in many "beach" movies throughout the 1960s, almost all of them costarring Frankie Avalon and/or Annette Funicello. The most popular of these were *Beach Party* (1963), *Beach Blanket Bingo, Dr. Goldfoot and the Bikini Machine,* and *How to Stuff a Wild Bikini* (all 1965), and *The Ghost in the Invisible Bikini* (1966).

EPISODE NOTES. 1. In episode 82, "Class Reunion," the graduating year is given as 1945. In this episode, the class graduated in 1948. 2. Barney drives a blue 1960 Ford Edsel in this episode. The car has a 1961 grille. 3. While in Mayberry, Barney stays in Andy's spare room, which comes complete with a night light. Aunt Bee has also prepared for his visit by buying air freshener and antacid tablets for him. 4. Barney has a credit card and owns an Italian suit that has pockets "on the slant." He wears his salt and pepper suit, along with a monogrammed shirt, to the reunion. This is the first time viewers can see the suit in color. 5. Barney comes bearings gifts: for Opie, a fingerprint set with an official ink pad; for Aunt Bee, some handkerchiefs imported from Tijuana; and for Andy, a tie clip that can be worn on the front of his shirt. Barney says, "It's smart!" 6. Andy and Barney sing the Mayberry Union High School song twice: first while relaxing on Andy's porch, and then while riding in Barney's car. 7. Barney's "Manhunt Theme" is played upon his arrival in Mayberry. 8. One of Barney's old teachers, Miss Fenton, asks him if he still gets nosebleeds. 9. Alfred Kitcherly, who used to drive an old Essex that had "Hey, Toots!" written on the side and who once blew up the chemistry class, was one of the reunion attendees. Some of the others not previously mentioned are Peterson, Rayburn, and Andy's old flame, Sharon Despain, who appeared in episode 82, "Class Reunion." Also returning from that episode were Carl Benson's Wildcats, who performed at both reunions. In this episode, librarian Mrs. Hartzell plays the saxophone. Carl's mother must've skipped this gig. 10. Classmate Bonnie Johnson has gained a lot of weight since she got married. 11. Nettie Albright has dyed her hair blonde and now lives in Asheville. 12. Barney's salary is $95.00 a week, and he receives a $125.00 Christmas bonus. 13. Gerald Whitfield and Thelma Lou reside in Jacksonville. He is a foreman of a wrecking crew. 14. This episode brings a sad and abrupt ending to Barney and Thelma Lou's relationship and marks the final appearance of **Betty Lynn** in the series. This was the only color episode in which she appeared. Viewers can finally see that she had lovely auburn hair.

"The Legend of Barney Fife"

Episode #177. Air date: 1-17-66. Writer: Harvey Bullock. Director Alan Rafkin.

Barney's car is in need of a new fuel pump, which Goober intends to order from Mount Pilot. Since this means that Barney will be spending another day visiting in Mayberry, Andy is eager to introduce Barney to the man who replaced him as deputy, Warren Ferguson. Although Barney is reluctant, he is surprised and flattered when he discovers that Warren idolizes him. The young deputy considers Barney to be a legend. The two men get along famously.

It's a great day for Barney, until he answers a telephone call from Warden Hix, the director of the county work farm. The warden explains that a convict named Avery Noonan has escaped and may be heading toward Mayberry. Noonan has vowed to take revenge on Barney since he arrested him a year ago. A shaken Barney orders Goober to reinstall his car's old fuel pump. Unfortunately, the fittings are too worn to be of any use. Unable to leave, Barney tries to make himself scarce.

When Andy answers a second call from Warden Hix, he discovers why Barney is so nervous. Warren then gets a tip that Noonan is hiding out at the Mayberry depot. He urges Barney to join in on the manhunt. Andy assures Barney that everything will be fine. Warren senses Barney's nervousness, and he begins to have doubts about the legendary and heroic Deputy Fife. But, once again, Andy saves Barney's reputation by setting up a situation where his hapless former deputy can make the arrest with no trouble. Barney will always be a legend in Warren's eyes.

After the arrest, Barney tells Andy to give the capture credit to Warren when he reports the story to the newspaper.

CAST NOTES. Regulars: **Andy Griffith, Frances Bavier, Jack Burns, George Lindsey,** and **Howard McNear. Don Knotts** returns in his second of five guest appearances as Barney Fife.

Frank Cady appears as Farley Upchurch, reporter, photographer, and publisher of *The Mayberry Gazette.* Cady appeared in a couple of episodes in this series and was the original town drunk, a man named Will Hoople, in the series pilot. **Harry Holcolmb** portrays Warden Hix. **Ted White** portrays the escaped convict, Avery Noonan.

EPISODE NOTES. 1. Barney wears his salt and pepper suit until he changes into his old uniform. 2. When Barney was a youngster, his idol was Skeets Gallagher. Skeets was the sidekick to Tailspin Tommy. In the early to middle 1930s, Tailspin Tommy and his friend Skeeter were popular comic book heroes. The characters also appeared in live-action movie serials. 3. Barney's license plate number is the familiar AY-321. 4. Barney takes three lumps of sugar and a little cream in his coffee.

"Lost and Found"

Episode #178. Air date: 1-24-66. Writers: John L. Greene and Paul David. Director: Alan Rafkin.

While painting a dresser, Aunt Bee discovers a pretty pearl-and-gold pin that was given to her many years earlier by her Aunt Martha. No sooner does she show off the pin to Andy and Opie than it mysteriously disappears. Aunt Bee and Opie turn the house upside down, but the pin cannot be found. Warren believes it was stolen, so he deputizes Goober to help him find the thief. They question George Barstow, the Taylors' butter-and-egg man, and a boy named Thompson, who delivers the newspaper. When Goober asks Clara Edwards if she took the pin, she promptly slaps him in the face.

As usual, Warren and Goober's theories are completely wrong. Later, the "dynamic duo" haul in a hungry vagrant who swears that he committed the theft. The truth is that he only wanted a free meal and a roof over his head. Andy orders Warren and Goober to let him go.

Finally, Andy notifies his insurance agent, Ed Jenkins. Since the pin was covered by Andy's homeowner's policy, a mysterious disappearance claim is filed. Ed Jenkins reluctantly sends Aunt Bee a claim check for the estimated value of the pin, $275.00. She uses the money to buy a garbage disposal. Opie loves to put his toast into the disposal and hear it crunch. Andy reminds him not to waste food.

When things calm down, Aunt Bee decides to go back and finish painting the dresser. She is stunned to discover Aunt Martha's pin in her painting smock. She sheepishly tells Andy, who proceeds to call Ed Jenkins in order to explain the situation. An explanation becomes unnecessary when Warren and Goober fight over the pin and drop it into the garbage disposal, where it is destroyed once and for all. Andy thinks quickly and tells Ed that he was calling to thank him for the speedy and courteous service in processing the claim.

CAST NOTES. Regulars: **Andy Griffith, Ronny Howard, Frances Bavier, George Lindsey, Jack Burns,** and **Hope Summers.**

Jack Dodson stars as Ed Jenkins. This was Dodson's first appearance on *The Andy Griffith Show.* This role paved the way for the character of Howard Sprague, which began later in this sixth season of shows.

Arthur Malet appears as the unnamed vagrant. In 1986 and 1987, Malet portrayed a butler named Bobby on the television sitcom *Easy Street.*

EPISODE NOTES. 1. Aunt Bee mentions her cousin Oliver in this episode. 2. Opie recently got an A in art class at school. 3. Aunt Bee promises to pay Opie a quarter for helping her paint the dresser. 4. Sarah Smedley comes down with the flu, and Aunt Bee has to take over her job of running the cookie booth at the upcoming bazaar. Aunt Bee has operated the booth for the past three years. For this year's bazaar, she bakes 26 dozen cookies. 5. Andy refers to Warren as "Sherlock Holmes." 6. A contradiction occurs in the episode. In episode 165, "Aunt Bee on TV," Aunt Bee won a garbage disposal, among other game show prizes. She sold most of her prizes to pay the IRS, but retained the garbage disposal and a television. In this episode, however, she claims to have given up the disposal that she won in Hollywood.

"Wyatt Earp Rides Again"

Episode #179. Air date: 1-31-66. Writer: Jack Elinson. Director: Alan Rafkin.

A promoter named Fred Gibson brings his Wild West show to the fair town of Mayberry. Fred's business card proclaims, "Gibson's Wild West Show — East Or West, Gibson's The Best." The feature attraction is a frail little man with glasses named Clarence Earp. Fred states that Clarence is the great-nephew of famed lawman Wyatt Earp. The folks in Mayberry are not impressed with Clarence's physical attributes, until he beats an apparently much stronger Warren Ferguson at arm wrestling and then soundly defeats Goober Pyle in a regular wrestling match. Andy gets concerned when Opie and his pals begin heeding Clarence's personal code of the west, which is "The man who can fight, is the man who is right."

Meanwhile, Fred has set up his show at the Mayberry fairgrounds, where Clarence demonstrates his prowess at lassoing, knife throwing, and performing the quick draw. When Andy tells Fred and Clarence that the Earp name has somewhat diminished over the years, an irate Clarence Earp challenges Sheriff Taylor to a duel at high noon on the following day. Andy researches the Earp family history at the Mayberry library and discovers there never was a descendant named Clarence.

Finally, Fred confesses to both Andy and Clarence that his star performer is not related to the Earp family. Fred goes on to say that when he first met the young man, Clarence had no self-esteem. In order to boost his ego, he completely made up the entire Wyatt Earp tale.

At the conclusion of the episode, Fred promotes Clarence as a direct descendant of the famous boxer Jack Dempsey. He refers to him as Clarence (Kid) Dempsey, and offers the sum of $50.00 to anyone who will step into the ring with "the Kid."

CAST NOTES. Regulars: **Andy Griffith, Ronny Howard, Howard McNear, George Lindsey,** and **Jack Burns**. This is the final episode in which Jack Burns appeared. **Richard Keith** returns as Johnny Paul Jason.

Veteran character actor **Pat Hingle** stars as Fred Gibson. On the silver screen, Hingle has appeared in such films as *On the Waterfront* (1954), *Splendor in the Grass* (1961), *The Gauntlet* (1977), and *Norma Rae* (1979). On television, Mr. Hingle appeared with Dennis Weaver on *Stone* in 1980. He portrayed Chief Paulton.

Richard Jury costars as Clarence Earp, a.k.a. Clarence (Kid) Dempsey.

EPISODE NOTES. 1. Fred and Clarence have made 15 tours across the United States. 2. The last traveling show that passed through Mayberry featured a fire-eater known as the Great Mandrake. Floyd recalls that the show didn't last long because the fire department had to keep putting the Great Mandrake out. 3. Warren won a month's supply of mint jelly for being the arm wrestling champion at last year's Founder's Day picnic. 4. Warren ends up losing a 50-cent bet to Fred Gibson when Clarence beats the Mayberry deputy two consecutive times at arm wrestling. 5. Floyd claims always to have been a patron of the theatre. 6. The Mayberry Grand Theatre and Bigg's New and Used Furniture Store are shown. 7. A man from Mayberry named Harvey Kester used to repair Gloria Swanson's radio set. 8. Floyd tells Andy that, in his opinion, he would have been a high stakes gambler in the Old West, while Andy would most likely have been a barber. 9. Fred Gibson's license plate number on his car is the familiar DF-153.

"Aunt Bee Learns to Drive"

Episode #180. Air date: 2-7-66. Writer: Jack Elinson. Director: Lee Philips.

Aunt Bee, who has never learned to drive, is growing weary of depending on Andy to provide her with transportation. One day, she becomes intrigued with a car that Goober is trying to sell. She tells him she needs a car, but she is not sure how Andy will react to the notion of her learning to drive. She tells Goober she will bring up the subject at supper. Goober says he'll come by with the car afterward.

Unfortunately, Goober shows up before Aunt Bee has said anything to Andy, letting the cat out of the bag. Opie and Helen are very excited for Aunt Bee, but Andy is dead-set against the idea of her driving. Ultimately, however, he concedes that the decision is Aunt Bee's to make. Goober will act as her driving instructor.

Aunt Bee obtains a learner's permit, which allows her to drive only when a licensed driver is with her. She gets off to a very rocky start, but slowly makes progress.

One day, a worker for the township of Mayberry asks Aunt Bee to move her parked car forward a few feet so that some branches may be cut from a tree in the yard. Since no one else is home, she decides to do it. Unfortunately, she accidentally throws the car into reverse, causing the car to scrape up against a tree. The side of the car has sustained a fair amount of damage. Aunt Bee is very upset, embarrassed, and worried about what Andy will say. She tells Helen, who helps her hide the damage by covering the affected area with Opie's Scout tent.

Later, Aunt Bee decides to confess to Andy, but he keeps her from doing so by complimenting her on her progress. He tells her he is very pleased to know that she is a careful driver.

When Andy comes home from work, he becomes momentarily distracted and runs into the rear end of Aunt Bee's car. There is no damage, but when he uncovers the car, he is shocked to see the big dent. He apologizes profusely to Aunt Bee and chastises himself for the accident. A guilt-ridden Aunt Bee cannot let Andy take the blame, so she confesses. Andy is relieved and disappointed at the same time, but tells her that even the most experienced drivers make mistakes, too.

Aunt Bee proudly passes her driver's exams and purchases the car from Goober.

MEMORABLE SCENE. Floyd telling Andy that he read in the paper that the dingo dog is indigenous to Australia.

CAST NOTES. Regulars: **Andy Griffith**, **Ronny Howard**, **Frances Bavier**, **Aneta Corsaut**, **Howard McNear**, and **George Lindsey**.

Raymond Kark portrays the Mayberry township worker named Lowell.

EPISODE NOTES. 1. The car Aunt Bee buys was previously owned by Jed Coontz. Its seats are broken in well, because Jed weighs over 290 pounds. Aunt Bee pays $295.00 for the black Ford Sunliner convertible. Its license plate number is the very familiar AY-321. Several vehicles in the series had this plate number, including cars belonging to Barney and Otis. 2. Andy orders a young man named Sonny to ride his bicycle closer to the curb. This was the distraction that led to Andy bumping into Aunt Bee's car. 3. Among Andy's favorite foods are pork chops, beans, fresh fruit, and chocolate pudding. 4. Mr. Schwump appears, very briefly. Don't blink or you'll miss him walking by in the background when Goober is showing his car to Aunt Bee.

"Look Paw, I'm Dancing"

Episode #181. Air date: 2-14-66. Write: Ben Starr. Director: Lee Philips.

This episode, which was appropriately aired on Valentine's Day, begins with Opie playing practical jokes on Andy and Aunt Bee. He shakes Andy's hand with a joy buzzer (he had already gotten Aunt Bee twice with it) and hides a spring snake in Andy's newspaper. This can only mean one thing: It's time for Opie's annual school party. Every year practical jokes abound with the boys, while the girls keep to themselves. Opie's joy is short-lived however, when he discovers that this year's party is going to be a dance. He is a notoriously poor dancer. In fact, at last year's church social, he stepped all over Sharon Porter's toes while attempting to dance with her. Miss Crump believes the time is right for her twelve-year-old students to learn how to trip the light fantastic in order to be better prepared for future social events.

Opie tells Andy that he doesn't want to go, and his pa tells him that is fine. It seems that Andy wasn't much of a dancer either when he was a youth. Later, however, Aunt Bee and Helen coerce Andy into suggesting to Opie that he attend the dance. Aunt Bee even tries to help Opie by teaching him a few steps, but he is still reluctant to go. Meanwhile, Helen has asked Andy to be a chaperon with her at the dance, so Opie now feels that he is obligated to attend.

At the dance, all the kids are out on the dance floor having a ball, except for Opie, who quietly sits by himself in a chair. Andy tries in vain to get him out on the floor, but what turns the trick is Helen forcing a reluctant Andy to cut a rug with her. Opie and his classmates get a kick out of Andy's fancy footwork and watching Helen getting caught up in the music. Opie's inhibitions are gone, and before the night is over, he dances five times with his favorite girl, Sharon Porter.

MEMORABLE SCENE. Floyd declaring that as a youngster, Andy hid in a barn during his school dance. He also tells Goober that Andy was a real stick-in-the-mud when he was a kid. Goober and Floyd start laughing so hard at this remark that Andy runs out of the barbershop in embarrassment.

CAST NOTES. Regulars: **Andy Griffith**, **Ronny Howard**, **Frances Bavier**, **Howard McNear**, **George Lindsey**, and **Aneta Corsaut**. **Richard Keith** returns as Johnny Paul. **Ronda Jeter** returns as Sharon Porter.

Opie's classmate named Bruce, who is shown getting a haircut from Floyd on credit, is not listed in the cast credits.

EPISODE NOTES. 1. Johnny Paul has an unnamed sister. 2. Opie is a washroom monitor at school. 3. Andy watches a baseball game on television at Helen's house. 4. The Roadhouse in Mayberry is a rock 'n' roll bar. 5. A man named Arnold Pruitt works at the record store in Mayberry. 6. Floyd suggests to Aunt Bee that the following list of "current" songs could be used in order to teach Opie how to dance: "Roses of Piccardy," "Yes, We Have No Bananas," and "Poor Butterfly." An exasperated Aunt Bee tells Floyd that she remembers those songs from when *she* was a little girl.

"Eat Your Heart Out"

Episode #182. Air date: 2-28-66. Writers: Art Baer and Ben Joelson. Director: Alan Rafkin.

Goober falls hard for Flora Mallerby, the new waitress at the Mayberry Diner. He is shy, so he asks Andy to go to the diner with him and tell Flora nice things about him. Andy obliges and proceeds to tell Flora the following: (1) Goober hit and rang the bell not 17, but 18 times at the county fair; (2) Goober has been the wrist wrestling champion of Mayberry for the past four years; and (3) Goober once took a carburetor apart and put it back together in 38 minutes and 12 seconds, a personal record. Unfortunately, Flora hears none of Goober's triumphs. She's too busy falling in love with Andy. Andy senses what's happening and discourages it, but a lovesick Goober is completely oblivious to the situation.

Later, Andy warns his buddy not to rush into a relationship, but Goober confides that he has finally found his true love. In order to get away from this mess, Andy decides to go crow hunting out in the woods. Who should turn up but Flora, who feigns a sprained ankle so that Andy is forced to carry her back to the car and drive back to Mayberry. Floyd and many other witnesses see Andy carrying her out of the car. Flora picks this most inopportune moment to plant a big kiss on Andy's lips.

Floyd relates this event to Goober, who promptly goes to Andy and challenges him to a fight. Andy is forced to tell him the truth about Flora and how she came on to him without any encouragement. Goober backs down and leaves the courthouse very depressed. Andy takes it upon himself to remedy this sorry situation. He goes to Flora and tells her exactly how Goober feels about her. This finally prompts her to aim her attention in the right direction.

CAST NOTES. Regulars: Andy Griffith, George Lindsey, Howard McNear, and Aneta Corsaut.

Alberta Nelson appears as Flora Mallerby for the first time. She had previously appeared as Nettie Albright in episode 176, "The Return of Barney Fife."

EPISODE NOTES. 1. Floyd recalls that Ephraim and Martha Terwilliger's youngest daughter, Honey, dated Hollis Pudney for years, but ended up marrying Hollis's brother instead. 2. Goober claims that the Mayberry Diner has the best mashed potatoes in town. 3. When Andy meets Flora for the first time, he and Goober both order the meatloaf plate. Flora gives Andy the larger portion. The next day, Andy and Goober have the diner deliver their pot roast special to the courthouse. Flora personally makes the delivery and ignores Goober completely. Instead, she sets up Andy with a red checkered tablecloth and gives him the larger portion of roast beef. At the conclusion of the episode, after Flora's change of heart, she gives Goober the larger portion of the meatloaf plate. 4. Goober throws a kiss to Flora over the phone, but she has already hung up. 5. Andy and Helen go to a movie in which an irate wife shoots her unfaithful husband. 6. A spiteful and jealous Flora serves Andy a large and perfectly cut piece of apple pie. On the other hand, she literally throws a small and botched-up piece of pie to Helen. 7. The candy store in Mayberry is shown. 8. The music that plays throughout this episode during the diner sequences is similar to music composed by Max Steiner for the 1959 motion picture *A Summer Place.*

"The Gypsies"

Episode #183. Air date: 2-21-66. Writer: Roland Maclane. Director: Alan Rafkin.

Four wandering Gypsies come to Mayberry in order to sell worthless merchandise, which they claim is priceless. The gypsies are Murrillos, the leader of the group; Queen La Farona, Murrillos's booze-guzzling mother; Sabella, Murrillos's pretty sister; and Sylvio, Murrillos's best friend. Andy warns the group not to sell any of their "priceless" merchandise to the townspeople, but they ignore his warning. First, Murrillos sells Aunt Bee a ceremonial shawl that once belonged to a Gypsy princess name Terranoya. He also sells her some earrings that were supposedly worn by an ancient Gypsy queen named Vincenta. All told, Aunt Bee pays $8.00 for the shawl and $4.50 for the earrings. Next, Goober has his fortune told to him by Sabella's 600-year-old crystal ball. The cost is $3.00 a shot. Even Clara Edwards buy some earrings.

After Andy hears about these "bargains," he

Jamie Farr of M*A*S*H fame appears as Sylvio in "The Gypsies."

marches down to the Gypsies' camp and orders them to leave by nightfall. In retaliation, Queen La Farona puts a curse on the town of Mayberry. She is joined by the rest of the group in a ritual that will supposedly cause a drought. Andy believes the curse is pure hokum, but sure enough, a long dry spell ensues. The Gypsies are camped just outside of the county line on Cranston's farm, and they have promised to bring rain if they are allowed to return to Mayberry.

After ten consecutive days of dry weather, the townspeople are driving Andy crazy with pleas to bring the Gypsies back. The farmers are worried, and vegetable prices have skyrocketed. (Tomatoes have gone up to 54 cents a pound at Foley's Market.) The pleas fall on deaf ears as Andy refuses to believe in the curse.

The truth is that the Gypsies are able to forecast the weather by tuning in their short-wave radio to station CQL in Greenland. When the Gypsies discover that rain is predicted within 72 hours on the Eastern Seaboard, they go into town and announce that they are merciful Gypsies and will bring rain in three days. Andy demands that they leave town at once. Of course, when the rain does come three days later, the townspeople want the Gypsies back more than ever. Just when Andy looks like a fool, Goober stumbles across the short-wave radio, and the Gypsies' charade is discovered.

Later, the Gypsies sell the radio to Andy in lieu of bail money. He is not amused to discover that they have removed all of the electric components contained inside the radio.

CAST NOTES. Regulars: **Andy Griffith, Ronny Howard, Frances Bavier, George Lindsey, Aneta Corsaut,** and **Hope Summers.**

Veteran character actor **Vito Scotti** stars as Murrillos. Scotti was a regular on *The Flying Nun* from 1968 through 1969. He portrayed police captain Gaspar Formento. Scotti also made two memorable guest appearances on the cult classic *Gilligan's Island.* (In the first one, an episode entitled "The Friendly Physician," he takes the castaways to his laboratory for experiments. The second episode is "Ring Around Gilligan." In this one, Scotti uses a magic ring to hypnotize the castaways into robbing Fort Knox. Of course, the plan fails.) On *The Dick Van Dyke Show*, Scotti appeared in an episode called "Give Me Your Walls." (He portrayed an eccentric house painter who painted Rob and Laura Petrie's home.)

Jamie Farr appears as Sylvio, even though the cast credits incorrectly list his character's name as Grecos. Mr. Farr is well known for his role as the cross-dressing Corporal Max Klinger on the sitcom *M*A*S*H.*

Francesca Bellina appears as Sabella. **Argentina Brunetti** portrays Queen La Farona. **Jason Johnson** steps out of his role as Ben Weaver to portray a Mayberry citizen named Mr. Bluett.

EPISODE NOTES. Soda pop costs 10 cents a bottle at the filling station.

"A Baby in the House"

Episode #184. Air date: 3-7-66. Writers: Bill Idelson and Sam Bobrick. Director: Alan Rafkin.

Aunt Bee is thrilled! Her niece Martha from Jacksonville has asked her to take care of her six-month-old daughter, Evie Joy, while she and husband Darryl attend her sister Grace's wedding in Jersey City, New Jersey. Aunt Bee reads the baby book *From the Cradle to Junior College* by Dr. Walker, in order to prepare herself for the task. Goober has even pitched in by loaning Aunt Bee some of his old baby toys, including "Buster," his all-time favorite Teddy Bear; a checkerboard, and a cigar box that he loved to open and close when he was a baby.

Unfortunately, Aunt Bee's happiness is short-lived. It seems that every time Aunt Bee picks up Evie Joy, the baby starts crying. Aunt Bee confides to Helen that for some unknown reason, Evie Joy hates her. Out of desperation, Aunt Bee enlists the aid of Andy, Opie, Goober, and even an out-of-town kitchenware salesman to hold the baby during feeding time.

Later, while Aunt Bee is grocery shopping, Opie and his friend Pete feed Evie Joy some blueberries. When Aunt Bee returns, she panics when she sees that the child has a blue face. She instinctively grabs Evie Joy and summons Andy and Opie to immediately call a doctor. Aunt Bee is relieved when Opie explains the situation. Andy remarks to Aunt Bee that she is holding the baby but the baby is not crying. Andy states that Evie Joy had previously sensed Aunt Bee's nervousness, but now feels safe in her arms.

CAST NOTES. Regulars: **Andy Griffith, Ronny Howard, Frances Bavier, George Lindsey,** and **Aneta Corsaut.**

Jim Connell appears as Darryl. Connell portrayed Junior on the television sitcom *Run Buddy Run* from 1966 through 1967. He was also a regular on *Donny and Marie* from 1976 through 1979. **Candace Howard** appears as Martha. **Alvy Moore** portrays the unnamed door-to-door kitchenware salesman from the Martin Phillips Company. Moore is well known for his role of double-talking county agent Hank Kimball on *Green Acres.* **Ronnie Dapo** returns to the series, this time as Opie's friend Pete. The infant who portrayed Evie Joy is not listed in the cast credits.

EPISODE NOTES. 1. Goober claims that he didn't talk until he was five years old. 2. Darryl states that Evie Joy likes to be held when she's fed. Her feeding times are 8:00 A.M., noon, 4:00 P.M., and 8:00 P.M. 3. Aunt Bee used to correspond by mail with an unnamed lady from Buffalo, New York. 4. Dr. Walker's baby book, *From the Cradle to Junior College* has sold more than 65,000 copies, according to Aunt Bee. 5. Andy keeps a picture of Aunt Bee on his bedroom dresser. 6. Opie claims that Evie Joy will often make a face that makes her look like Benjamin Franklin. 7. On one of the days that Evie Joy cries constantly, Andy had to stay up the previous night breaking up a fight between two brothers, Jed and Carl Darling. The fight started when Jed told Carl there is no Santa Claus. It is not mentioned whether Jed and Carl are related to Briscoe Darling and his clan. 8. Opie's first class of the day at school is gym. 9. At the end of the episode, Helen sings the lullaby "Golden Slumbers," accompanied by Andy on guitar.

"The County Clerk"

Episode #185. Air date: 3-14-66. Writers: Bill Idelson and Sam Bobrick. Director: Alan Rafkin.

Jack Dodson appears for the first time as the intelligent but shy county clerk of Mayberry, Howard Sprague. Howard has one major drawback: his mother. He's something of a mama's boy.

Helen coerces Andy to ask Howard and the pretty county nurse Irene Fairchild to join them on a double date at Morelli's Restaurant. Howard's widowed mother doesn't like the idea of letting her boy out of her grasp for one minute. Despite this, Howard goes and has a great time dining and dancing with Miss Fairchild. Unfortunately, he makes the mistake of phoning home, and his mother promptly claims to be ill. He is forced to cut the evening short in order to go home and check on his mother. Helen gets upset over the situation and forces Andy into coming up with some kind of solution.

Andy visits Mrs. Sprague and compliments her on how she has devoted her life to her only son. He also tells her that she needs a social life of her own, in order to achieve a balance. Unfortunately, Mrs. Sprague misinterprets Andy's suggestion and accompanies Howard, Irene, Andy, and Helen on their next double date at Morelli's. To make matters worse, Mrs. Sprague dances with a disenchanted Andy until 2:00 A.M.

MEMORABLE SCENE. Helen's way of persuading Andy to do her bidding.

CAST NOTES. Regulars: **Andy Griffith, Ronny Howard,** and **Aneta Corsaut.**

As noted earlier, **Jack Dodson** appears as Howard Sprague for the first time. Mr. Dodson had previously appeared as an insurance agent named Ed Jenkins, in episode 178, "Lost and Found."

Mabel Albertson, a character actress of note, makes her first of many appearances as the doting Mrs. Sprague. Albertson was born in 1901 and died on September 28, 1982. She had a long career on television, including regular roles in the following series: *That's My Boy* (1954–1955) as Henrietta Patterson; *Those Whiting Girls* (1955 and 1957) as Mrs. Whiting; *The Tom Ewell Show* (1960–1961) as Grandma Irene Brady; and *Accidental Family* (1967–1968) as Mrs. Sheppard. Viewers may remember her as Darrin Stevens's mother, Phyllis, on *Bewitched,* or as Donald Hollinger's mother, Mildred, on *That Girl.* She made a variety of guest appearances on such series as: *The Adventures of Superman, Dragnet, Gunsmoke, The Mary Tyler Moore Show, The Munsters, No Time for Sergeants, The Paul Lynde Show, Pete 'n' Tillie, The Time Tunnel,* and *The*

Wild Wild West. She appeared in a few television movies, including *The House That Would Not Die* (1970) and *Ladies of the Corridor* (1975). Her movie career spanned over twenty years, and included such gems as *Forever, Darling* (1956, with Lucille Ball and Desi Arnaz), *The Long Hot Summer* (1958, with Paul Newman and Joanne Woodward), *Don't Give Up the Ship* (1959, with Jerry Lewis), *All the Fine Young Cannibals* (1960, with Natalie Wood; the British music group Fine Young Cannibals took their name from this film), *A Period of Adjustment* (1962, with Jane Fonda and Jack Albertson, Mabel's brother), *Barefoot in the Park* (1967, with Robert Redford and Jane Fonda), *On a Clear Day You Can See Forever* (1970, with Barbra Streisand and Bob Newhart), and *What's Up Doc?* (1972, with Ryan O'Neal and Barbra Streisand).

Jim Begg appears in a brief cameo as a prospective bridegroom seeking a marriage license. **Colleen O'Sullivan** portrays his young prospective bride. This is the first of a few appearances by Jim Begg. He has worked as a writer, producer, and actor on television and in the movies. He had a regular role as the mailman on the 1973 series *Ozzie's Girls* and appeared in a couple of little-remembered pilots in the 1960s. From 1973 to 1975, he lent his voice to the CBS animated series *Bailey's Comets*. He worked as a writer on the animated series *The Partridge Family: 2200 A.D.* from 1974 to 1975 (along with Rance Howard). He lent his voice to the character called Scootz on the cartoon series *The Cattanooga Cats*. He guest-starred on such series as *Bewitched*, *The Mother-in-Law*, and *That Girl*. He produced the 1982 television movie *The Kid with the Broken Halo* starring Gary Coleman and Robert Guillaume. Begg has appeared in several movies, including *Village of the Giants* (1965, with Ronny Howard), *The Ghost and Mr. Chicken* (1966, starring Don Knotts), *Catalina Caper* (1967, with Little Richard), *The Cool Ones* (1967, directed by Gene Nelson), *It's a Bikini World* (1967, with the Animals), *The Love God?* (1969, starring Don Knotts), *Grand Theft Auto* (1977, directed by, and starring Ron Howard), *The Cat from Outer Space* (1978, with Ken Berry), *Leo and Loree* (1978, executive-produced by Ron Howard), and *Death Wish II* (1982, starring Charles Bronson).

Nina Shipman portrays Irene Fairchild.

EPISODE NOTES. 1. As county clerk, Howard Sprague requests Andy to provide him with Mayberry's 1953 accident report for a statistical study he's doing on how accidents are related to population growth. 2. Andy and Howard were high school classmates but were not close friends. 3. Opie gets a quarter for sweeping out the courthouse. 4. Opie claims that Howard Sprague throws a baseball like Aunt Bee. 5. A marriage license costs $3.00 at the Mayberry county clerk's office. 6. Irene Fairchild took over Howard's old office in Room 201 at the Mayberry County Building. He moved to a larger office in Room 203. Irene discovered a t-shirt that Howard had put in a file cabinet in his old office. Embarrassed, he explained that he had taken off the shirt on a particularly hot day. 7. Mrs. Sprague always refers to Andy as "Andrew." Miss Fairchild refers to Howard as "Howie." 8. Dr. Burnside is Mrs. Sprague's physician. 9. Howard and his mother often play bridge with the Albrights. 10. At the end of the episode, Helen attempts to coerce Andy into setting up a date between Mrs. Sprague and a fellow Mayberrian named Mr. Judson. Andy can only roll his eyes in wonder at his cupid-playing girlfriend.

"Goober's Replacement"

Episode #186. Air date: 3-28-66. Writers: Stan Dreben and Howard Merrill. Director: Alan Rafkin.

Goober persuades Wally to let his girlfriend, Flora, take his place at the service station while he goes on a much-needed, week-long fishing trip with his pal Lou. Goober stays at a place called Martin's Cottages near a lake. He writes Andy and says he hopes that Wally isn't losing too much business due to his absence. On the contrary, Flora has become the most popular gas jockey in North Carolina. As Floyd says, "Goober is not quite the same in slacks." Many of the male customers drive around town just to use up gas so they can return and fill up their gas tanks. Consequently, Wally is setting sales records daily.

When Goober returns, he sees that his services are obviously no longer required. Goober tells Flora to keep the job because he has his sights set on bigger things. Flora is so busy concentrating on charts and graphs in order to further improve business that she doesn't take the time to consider Goober's feelings.

When Goober has no luck in landing a job, Andy steps in and coerces Ben Weaver to hire him as a sales clerk and cashier at his department store. Goober fails miserably at Weaver's and is let go. He considers moving to Mount Pilot to work for Earlie Gilley at his garage.

As Goober is pondering the situation, Andy spots Flora going into the Mayberry Diner. He goes in and has a chance to have a one-on-one visit. He proceeds to do a masterful job of convincing her that while she could be a success in business, she would be sacrificing a happy and prosperous social life. Flora decides to quit, Goober takes his old job back, and everything returns to normal.

CAST NOTES. Regulars: **Andy Griffith, Ronny Howard, Howard McNear,** and **George Lindsey. Alberta Nelson** returns as Flora Mallerby. **Jason Johnson** returns as Ben Weaver. This was Johnson's second and last appearance in this role. He has previously appeared as Ben Weaver in episode 171, "Aunt Bee Takes a Job." **Maudie Prickett** returns as Edna Larch. **Charles Smith** returns as the counter man at the Mayberry Diner, appropriately named Charlie.

Cliff Norton appears as Wally. This was his only appearance as the owner of Wally's Filling Station. Born in Chicago, this comic actor was especially prominent during television's early years. He has had regular roles on many series, including *Garroway at Large* (1949-1951), *Your Show of Shows* (1950-1954), *The Public Life of Cliff Norton* (1952), *The Dave Garroway Show* (1952-1954), *Pete and Gladys* as Newton Norwood (1960-1962), *It's About Time* as Boss (1966-1967), and *Where's Huddles?* (the 1970 prime-time cartoon series) as Ed Huddles. When the space-age cartoon series *The Jetsons* was revived in the 1980s, Norton lent his voice on a regular basis. He has made scores of television appearances on such popular series as *Green Acres* (in the series' final episode, "The Ex-Secretary"), *The Munsters, The Bob Newhart Show, Bewitched, The Odd Couple, The Lucy Show, Ben Casey, Love, American Style, Get Smart, Dream On, The Wild Wild West* and *The Dick Van Dyke Show.* (In the latter, he portrayed a game warden in the episode in which Ritchie is "attacked" by a woodpecker.) Norton has appeared in many movies, including *The Ghost and Mr. Chicken* (1966, with Don Knotts) and *Funny Lady* (1975, with Barbra Streisand and James Caan).

According to the cast credits, **Burt Mustin** appears as "the old geezer." **David Azar** appears as one of Flora's admiring customers at Wally's.

EPISODE NOTES. 1. Horace Flood couldn't fill in for Goober at Wally's because he was studying electronics. Louis Jordan was considered, but he was going on the fishing trip with Goober. 2. Wally sells Acme regular and super gasoline. A quart of premium motor oil costs 45 cents. Wally also owns and operates a laundry business in Mayberry. 3. Goober borrows Andy's rod and reel to take on the fishing trip. 4. While on the fishing trip, Goober catches three fish. He uses the same grasshopper as bait to catch all three fish. 5. A Mayberrian named Mrs. Lewis calls Andy to complain about the kids in her neighborhood making too much noise while she is trying to take a nap. 6. When Goober is having trouble locating a job, he considers trying to find a

job at a service station in Raleigh. He also asks Floyd if he would hire him as a barber at Floyd's Barbershop. Floyd turns him down flat and explains that it takes years to learn how to cut hair properly. 7. In this episode, Goober drives a light blue pickup truck. 8. One of Goober's (many) favorite dishes is pounded steak. 9. Flora orders a tuna salad sandwich, hold the mayo, and a cup of coffee at the Mayberry Diner. 10. No reason is given as to why Flora is no longer working as a waitress at the Mayberry Diner. 11. Earlie Gilley is once again mentioned. You may recall that the real-life Mr. Gilley resides in Mount Airy's sister city, Pilot Mountain, North Carolina, and is married to Andy Griffith's cousin, the former Lorraine Beasley.

"The Foster Lady"

Episode #187. Air date: 3-21-66. Writers: Jack Elinson and Iz Elinson. Director: Alan Rafkin.

Andy finds Willard Foster standing near his damaged car on Juniper Road at the outskirts of Mayberry. Mr. Foster explains that he swerved to avoid hitting a cow and lost control of his car, which slid into a ditch. Andy calls Goober at Wally's Filling Station from Mr. Foster's car phone. Mr. Foster resides in Raleigh, where he is the founder and president of Foster's Furniture Polish. Goober is especially impressed because he likes the pretty spokeswoman used in the company's commercials. Mr. Foster believes that too many people pay attention to the models and not the product.

Andy tells him that Aunt Bee pays attention to the product; in fact, she has used it for years. Mr. Foster is delighted to meet her when Andy invites him over for lunch while Goober tends to his car. Aunt Bee waxes enthusiastic about the merits of the polish. Mr. Foster begins to toy with the idea of using a real housewife in his ads. Sensing an opportunity, Aunt Bee hints that she would make a good spokesperson. Finally, Mr. Foster asks her to become "the Foster lady." The commercial will be shot inside the Taylors' home. Aunt Bee is overjoyed.

Goober and Floyd give Aunt Bee the star treatment, applauding her as she passes by. Floyd jokes that "no matter what happens, we can always say, 'We knew you when!'" He also dubs her "Mayberry's lady of the hour." Aunt Bee still cannot believe this turn of events. She recalls when she once sat in the second balcony and watched actress Clara Kimball Young perform. Now, *she* is in the spotlight! Andy admits, "This is a big year for the Taylors ... Elizabeth and Aunt Bee!"

The camera crew arrives, and a nervous Aunt Bee begins her sales pitch. The nervousness wears off after a couple of takes, but it soon becomes evident to everyone (except Aunt Bee, Floyd, and Goober) that acting is not one of her strong points, although she tries very hard and even writes a jingle for the company.

During a break in the filming, Andy confers with Mr. Foster and director Jim Martin. They agree that Aunt Bee is not working out. When Jim mentions that viewers would laugh at her, Mr. Foster decides that maybe Aunt Bee is the perfect choice after all, since humor is often effective in advertising. Andy balks at the notion of Aunt Bee being exploited in such a manner.

Because Aunt Bee believes she is doing a good job, Andy has to come up with a way to get her to resign without telling her about Mr. Foster's plans. He tells her that because she will be busy with contracts, interviews, and fan mail, he will be hiring someone to cook and clean for him and Opie. The thought of someone else in her kitchen, plus the realization that she would miss her friends and her social activities, prompts Aunt Bee to happily decline to become the Foster lady.

Martha Carruthers of Pleasantville, using much of the dialogue from Aunt Bee's takes, soon becomes the Foster lady. She even sings Aunt Bee's jingle.

CAST NOTES. Regulars: **Andy Griffith, Ronny Howard, Frances Bavier, George Lindsey,** and **Howard McNear.**

Robert Emhardt, who was previously featured in episode 77, "Man in a Hurry" as Malcolm Tucker, portrays Willard Foster. Stand-up comedian and comic actor **Ronnie Schell** appears as director Jim Martin. Schell was also a regular on *Gomer Pyle, U.S.M.C.* He portrayed Gomer's pal, Duke Slater. Real-life staffers from *The Andy Griffith Show*—hair stylist Eva Kryger, director of photography Sid Hickox, and crewman Burt Taylor—appear as part of the commercial crew. Kryger plays a makeup artist. **Marc London** portrays assistant director Bob Saunders. The real-life A.D. for this episode was Robert Saunders.

EPISODE NOTES. 1. According to Andy, Mr. Foster's car went into the ditch about one and a half miles from the lake. 2. Mr. Foster's car phone number is KG62114. His car's license plate number is SD-561. His address is 403 Elm Street in Raleigh. 3. Goober's phone number at Wally's Filling Station is 363. 4. Floyd tells Mr. Foster that he has used Foster's Furniture Polish for years. He says that he would like to be "the Foster man," should the need ever arise. 5. The Foster Furniture Polish Company sponsors the television series "The Rex Benson Show." The series features Rex Benson and the Sing-Songers.

"The Battle of Mayberry"

Episode #188. Air date: 4-4-66. Writers: Paul David and John L. Greene. Director: Alan Rafkin.

The Mayberry Gazette is celebrating its fiftieth anniversary. In honor of the event, the publisher of the newspaper, Farley Upchurch, goes to the Mayberry Grade School and tells Opie and his classmates that the newspaper is sponsoring a contest for the paper that best describes the legendary (and bloody) Battle of Mayberry. The battle took place over 200 years ago, and the combatants were the settlers and the Indians. Mr. Upchurch goes on to say that the student with the best paper will receive a gold medal and will have his or her paper printed on the front page of the golden anniversary edition of *The Mayberry Gazette*.

All of the townspeople are excited about the contest, because many of them had ancestors in the battle. For example, Andy, Aunt Bee, and Opie had an ancestor named Carlton Taylor. They believe he was a colonel and was one of Mayberry's first settlers. Andy claims that the town of Mayberry was almost named "Taylortown" in honor of Carlton. Floyd's ancestor was Colonel Caleb (Stonewall) Lawson. Floyd claimed that Stonewall killed 14 Indians in the battle. Goober's ancestor was Colonel Goober Pyle, of the North Carolina Seventh Cavalry. Clara Edwards's ancestor was her great-great grandfather, Colonel Edwards. Clara said that he led his troops into the battle with the cry, "Come on boys, do you want to live forever?" Clara even has this inspirational ode embroidered on a pillow. Sarah, the telephone operator, also claims to have had an ancestor who was a colonel in the battle. On the other side, Tom Strongbow, Mayberry's local Cherokee Indian, had an ancestor named Chief Strongbow who was a hero on the Indians' side. Tom refers to the battle as "the victory of Tuckahoosie Creek." He and Andy argue about the outcome of the battle. Needless to say, expectations in Mayberry are high for an outstanding paper.

Opie is confused by the conflicting stories, and Andy agrees to take him to the library in Raleigh, where the youngster discovers the sad truth. According to the May 18, 1762, edition of the Raleigh newspaper, the so-called Battle of Mayberry was actually a farce. The settlers and the Indians only yelled some taunts and insults at one another. The only victims were three deer and one scrawny cow by the name of Bessie Lawson! Bessie was owned by one of Floyd's ancestors. Poor Bessie was mistaken for a deer. Later, the settlers and the Indians went hunting together and then got drunk on corn liquor. They soon became friends.

Andy, Aunt Bee, and Opie are understandably devastated by the shocking news. What makes matters worse is that Andy has always taught his son to be honest, so Opie is compelled to write the awful truth. Andy and Aunt Bee pray that his paper will not be selected as the winner because they expect that all of their friends with "colonels" in the great battle may never speak to them again. Unfortunately, Helen Crump states that Opie's paper is far and away the most honest and truthful one she received, and regardless of the consequences, she declares him the winner of the contest. The townspeople proceed to give the Taylors the silent treatment for one full week.

Finally, in his weekly radio broadcast, the governor of North Carolina, who had caught wind of the story, commends Opie and the entire town of Mayberry for their honesty and for the way their ancestors were able to peacefully solve a dispute. Goober leads all of the Taylors' friends in a rousing chant of three cheers for Opie.

CAST NOTES. Regulars: **Andy Griffith, Ronny Howard, Frances Bavier, Aneta Corsaut, Howard McNear, George Lindsey,** and **Hope Summers.**

Clinton Sundberg appears as Farley Upchurch. Sundberg appeared in such feature films as *Easter Parade* (1948), *The Barkleys of Broadway* (1949), and *Hotel* (1967). It is interesting to note that Frank Cady portrayed Farley Upchurch in episode 177, "The Legend of Barney Fife."

Arthur Malet appears as the man who loafs around Floyd's Barbershop. His name is Purvis. Malet portrayed a vagrant in episode 178, "Lost and Found."

Norm Alden portrays Tom Strongbow. A veteran of many television shows and movies, Alden may be best known as Coach Leroy Fedders on *Mary Hartman, Mary Hartman.* In that show, Coach Fedders met his demise by falling asleep and drowning in a bowl of soup that Mary (Louise Lasser) had prepared for him.

EPISODE NOTES. 1. Opie speaks to a Mayberrian named Mr. MacGruder about the Battle of Mayberry. 2. The title of Opie's paper is "The True Story of the Battle of Mayberry." 3. Tom Strongbow is a farmer who resides at Rural Route 3, Box 222, in Mayberry. 4. The cost of admission to the Grand Theater in Mayberry is 25 cents for balcony seats and 35 cents for the orchestra area. The theater's name has a real-life connection. The Grand Theater existed in downtown Mount Airy during Andy Griffith's childhood. It was located a few doors down from the Snappy Lunch and the City Barbershop. Today, the building that once housed the Grand Theater is the Greene Finance Corporation.

"A Singer in Town"

Episode #189. Air date: 4-11-66. Writers: Stan Dreben and Howard Merrill. Director: Alan Rafkin.

Keevy Hazelton, a noted singer and entertainer, comes to Mayberry for a much-needed fishing vacation. Keevy is a well-known star who even has his own television show in Raleigh. Aunt Bee and Clara ask a reluctant Andy to invite Keevy to supper so that they can perform an original song, "My Hometown," for him. They wrote and performed it three years earlier as part of the ceremonies on Flag Day, and it was very well received. They hope Keevy will like it so much that he'll record it and sing it on his program. Mr. Hazelton has often specialized in songs about towns. He had a million-seller with a song called "Texarkana in the Morning." Some of his other hits include "Abilene" and "Mobile."

Keevy accepts the pot roast dinner invitation, but falls fast asleep during Aunt Bee and Clara's performance of "My Hometown." The next day, against Andy's wishes, Aunt Bee, Clara, and Clara's wacky accordionist nephew, Ferdie, go to Keevy's hotel room with the hope of performing the song. Keevy's business manager, Bill Stone, convinces him to perform "My Hometown" on his television show. It seems that the show's ratings have been sagging and many sponsors have abandoned the show. A song by two local ladies may just be what the doctor ordered.

A major problem occurs during rehearsal when Keevy turns the lovely ballad into a rock 'n' roll song, complete with go-go dancers. Aunt Bee and Clara get extremely mad and threaten to sue the singer unless he performs the song properly during the actual show. Keevy believes that if he sings the song the way the ladies want him to, his image will be destroyed. However, when Keevy and Mr. Stone see that Aunt Bee and Clara mean business, the singer reluctantly obliges. Fortunately, the song and his performance are both a smashing success.

CAST NOTES. Regulars: **Andy Griffith, Ronny Howard, Frances Bavier, Howard McNear, George Lindsey,** and **Hope Summers.**

Jesse Pearson stars as Keevy Hazelton. Pearson is best known for his performance as Conrad Birdie in the 1963 hit movie *Bye, Bye Birdie.* Pearson also portrayed a successful singer in an episode of *The Beverly Hillbillies* entitled "Teenage Idol." His name in that episode was Johnny Poke.

Tom D'Andrea appears as Bill Stone. D'Andrea portrayed Jim Gillis from 1953 through 1958 on the successful sitcom *The Life of Riley.* **Joel Redlin** appears as bug-eyed Ferdie. **Byron Foulger**

returns as Leroy. **Edgar Hess** portrays the stage manager.

EPISODE NOTES. 1. Floyd says that he wears long underwear even when the temperature reaches 70 degrees. 2. Opie gets Keevy Hazelton to accept Aunt Bee's pot roast dinner invitation by telling him that the special at the Mayberry Diner is chicken croquettes, which are awful. The Taylors eat dinner at 6:00 P.M. daily. 3. Three of Mayberry's female teenagers who get Keevy Hazelton's autograph are Doris, Gertrude (Gertie), and Karen. Keevy says that he once dated a girl named Karen. 4. Goober takes a color picture of Keevy for himself and one for Floyd. He also has Leroy, the clerk at the Mayberry Hotel, take a picture of him with his arm around Keevy. 5. Clara says that she gets thrown off key when Ferdie taps his foot while she's trying to sing "My Hometown." 6. Keevy introduces Aunt Bee and Clara to his television audience as "two ladies who are going to make Tin Pan Alley sit up and take notice." 7. After the success of "My Hometown," Aunt Bee and Clara receive fan mail and begin writing a song about Venice, Italy.

SEASON SEVEN

Floyd Lawson moves on at the end of this wonderful color season. Audiences also bid farewell to the Darling family but say hello to Mayberry's fix-it man, Emmett Clark. A.C. Nielson Co. rating for the 1966-1967 season: 27.4; rank: 3.

"Opie's Girlfriend"

Episode #190. Air date: 9-12-66. Writer: Budd Grossman. Director: Lee Philips.

Helen's niece, Cynthia, from Wheeling, West Virginia, is in Mayberry for a visit. She and Opie are the same age, and Andy and Helen want them to be friends. After some prompting by his pa, Opie reluctantly shows the little girl around town. He gets upset when Cynthia proves to be his superior when it comes to athletics. Goober advises Opie to find something that he can do better than her. He tries football, but Cynthia proves to be a much better player. In frustration, Opie picks a fight with her. After he pushes her, Cynthia promptly gives Opie a (well-deserved) black eye.

Opie leads Andy to believe that he received the shiner while protecting Cynthia's honor. Andy comes to the conclusion that the Blake boy (a known bully, who's a full two inches taller than Opie) must have picked on the poor little girl and Opie rushed to her aid. Goober thinks that another well-known bully, that Cosgrove boy, could have been the culprit. Both theories are shot down when Andy discovers the truth from Opie's friend Billy. Opie finally admits that he did fight Cynthia, but swears that she picked the fight by cheating at football. Opie is obviously lying, but Andy stands by his son's story.

That evening, Andy and Helen get into a huge argument over the situation. After Andy leaves, Helen tells Cynthia that it might be a good idea to give in and allow Opie to excel in some area, such as roller skating. By doing this, Opie's fragile male ego can be satisfied. The plan is a success.

MEMORABLE SCENE. Opie, in a feeble attempt to hide his black eye, wearing sunglasses at the dinner table.

CAST NOTES. Regulars: **Andy Griffith, Ronny Howard, Frances Bavier, Howard McNear, Aneta Corsaut,** and **George Lindsey.**

Mary Ann Durkin stars as Cynthia. **John Reilly** appears as Billy.

EPISODE NOTES. 1. Opie reminds Andy of the time he was forced to go to a school dance. This is a reference to episode 181, "Look Paw, I'm Dancing." 2. Opie is the president of his seventh-grade class. 3. Cynthia's favorite subject in school is history. Opie's is lunch. 4. Aunt Bee says that Dr. Anderson warns his patients to be aware of foreign objects in the eye. 5. Andy claims that Helen beat him at bowling because he wasn't wearing his regular bowling shoes. He was forced to wear rented ones. At the conclusion of the episode, Andy defeats Helen at bowling. He gives the credit for his victory to his own shoes, which he was wearing this time.

"The Barbershop Quartet"

Episode #191. Air date: 9-26-66. Writer: Fred S. Fox. Director: Lee Philips.

The Mayberry Barbershop Quartet is looking forward to the Sheriff's Annual Barbershop Quartet Contest, which will take place in Mount Pilot. The Mayberry Quartet, consisting of Andy, Howard, Burt, and a man named Wally, has been victorious in the contest for the past two years. If they win this year, the grand prize trophy will be theirs to keep forever. It would look mighty fine on permanent display in Mayberry. Furthermore, Andy is especially anxious to win because his main competition is a quartet led by Sheriff Blake Wilson of Mount Pilot. Andy admittedly does not like the man.

Disaster strikes when Howard comes down with a cold just two days before the contest. The ailment directly affects Howard's throat. After trying every cold remedy known to man, Howard realizes that the group will have to replace him with another high tenor.

Andy holds an open audition at the courthouse, but a satisfactory replacement eludes the quartet. Suddenly, prisoner Jeff Nelson begins to sing. Andy cannot believe his ears. Nelson has a beautiful tenor voice. The problem is that Nelson is an unsavory character who has been jailed before for fighting and stealing chickens. He is currently serving time for pick-pocketing. Despite pleas from Burt, Wally, and interested onlooker Floyd, Andy refuses to allow Jeff Nelson to participate.

Andy remains steadfast in his refusal until obnoxious Sheriff Wilson stops by to offer his "condolences" and then arrogantly states that the trophy will look better displayed in a big town like Mount Pilot. This attitude angers Andy, and he changes his mind. He will allow Jeff to sing with the quartet, but he makes him swear that he will not try to escape.

Upon arriving in Mount Pilot, Jeff breaks that promise and escapes into the woods, where he happens upon a hobo named Kelly. Ironically, the two men have met before, as prisoners in the town of Bixby. Kelly states that he, too, was once a prisoner in Mayberry. He claims that Andy Taylor always treated him with respect. Jeff agrees that Andy is a good man. This realization leads to a change of heart. Jeff decides to return just in time for the contest.

With Jeff securely handcuffed to Andy, the quartet gives a wonderful (and winning) performance. The prized trophy will remain in Mayberry forever.

MEMORABLE SCENE. Floyd anxiously asking, "What are you gonna *do*, Andy?"

CAST NOTES. Regulars: **Andy Griffith, Ronny Howard, Frances Bavier, Jack Dodson,** and **Howard McNear. Burt Mustin** returns as Burt. The closing credits list him as "Jud" once again. **Sam Edwards** returns as Tom Bedlow.

Hamilton Camp portrays Jeff Nelson. Camp is a former child actor and folk singer who has appeared in many television projects. He portrayed Andrew Hummel in the sitcom *He and She* (1967-1968) and Arthur Wainwright on the comedy series *Too Close for Comfort* (1981). He is an alumni of the renowned comedy troupe Second City.

Blackie Hunt appears as Wally. **Ken Mayer** appears as Sheriff Blake Wilson, although the credits list him as "Sheriff Blake." **Vernon Rich** appears as Mr. Johnston. **Harry Arnie** appears as Mr. Kelly, the hobo.

EPISODE NOTES. 1. The Mayberry Barbershop Quartet performs "Beautiful Isle of Make Believe" at the contest. In practice, they sing "In the Gloaming," in case they are called upon to do an encore. Aunt Bee fills in for Howard during one practice. Burt complains that her voice is squeaky. 2. Opie is a member of a kids' quartet. The boys' voices are changing, so it makes no difference which part they sing in the quartet. 3. Howard's mother is in Raleigh during this episode. 4. Burt advises Howard to keep his throat warm by wrapping a beaver pelt around it. 5. Howard is allergic to penicillin. 6. Suggested tenors to replace Howard are (1) Fred Callahan (Burt's suggestion). Floyd points out that Fred has passed away; and (2) Cliff Parmaley (Wally's idea). Andy says that Cliff is hard of hearing and sings so loudly that he drowns out everyone else. 7. Among those actually auditioning to replace Howard are Tom Bedlow (Andy tells him he's too short for the quartet), Perry Plummer, and Bill Watkins. 8. A Mr. Johnston registers all quartet contestants in Mount Pilot. 9. The Mayberry Quartet is scheduled to perform at 8:30 P.M., as the final contestants in the Mount Pilot contest. The Mayberrians use dressing room F. 10. Floyd tells Sheriff Wilson that Jeff Nelson is a famous singer who has sung at the Metropolitan Opera in New York City. 11. Aunt Bee, Opie, Floyd, and Howard are among the Mount Pilot audience who witness the Mayberry quartet's award-winning performance. 12. A Mayberry Bowling League exists. Andy is teamed with Howard, Goober, and a man named Frank.

"The Lodge"

Episode #192. Air date: 9-19-66. Writers: Jim Parker and Arnold Margolin. Director: Lee Philips.

Mrs. Sprague gets upset when Andy invites Howard to become a member of his lodge, the Regal Order of the Golden Door to Good Fellowship. Andy tells Mrs. Sprague that the members generally have a meeting, drink refreshments, horse around, tell jokes, and play cards and checkers. Mrs. Sprague is scared of losing her only companion to a bunch of non-intellectual types. She tells Goober that Howard's deceased father was a compulsive gambler and she is certain that Howard shares his father's weakness for cards.

When the day comes for the lodge members to

cast their secret vote on Howard's membership, they are all reminded that one black ball amongst all the white balls in the ballot box will nullify a new member's enrollment. After all the votes are cast, Sheriff Taylor, who serves as the lodge's voting proctor, confidently pulls out one while ball after another. Floyd is so sure of Howard's approval that he exclaims "He's in like Flynn." But Andy's chin just about hits the floor as he pulls out the one and only black ball in the box. With a look of disbelief on his face, Andy states, "Somebody's blackballed Howard Sprague." Goober had decided to protect Howard by blackballing him from the lodge, but it takes Andy a while to discover who did the deed. He calls Cyrus Tankersley, the president of the lodge, and asks him to call a special meeting in order to change the mind of the "blackballer" and call for a second vote. Howard stops by the lodge as Andy is addressing the card-playing members. He bumps into Goober, who is serving as the Keeper of the Door for this particular month. When he spots Howard, Goober rushes into the lodge like a madman and disrupts all of the card playing. Andy questions Goober about his strange behavior in the presence of Howard. Goober finally explains his conversation with Mrs. Sprague. Howard and Andy tell him that Mrs. Sprague has a tendency to exaggerate sometimes. A much-relieved Goober happily approves Howard for membership.

Later, Howard shows that he does have quite a penchant for playing cards. Maybe Mrs. Sprague was right after all.

CAST NOTES. Regulars: **Andy Griffith, Ronny Howard, Frances Bavier, Howard McNear, George Lindsey,** and **Jack Dodson. Mabel Albertson** returns as the high-strung Mrs. Sprague. **George Cisar** returns as Cyrus Tankersley. **Sam Edwards** returns to Mayberry, again as Tom Bedlow. **Burt Mustin**'s character is listed as "Jud" in the case credits once again, but he is referred to as "Burt" in the episode.

Ralph Rose portrays a lodge member named Clete.

EPISODE NOTES. 1. The secret password at the lodge is "Geronimo." 2. As the Keeper of the Door, Goober wears a red turban with green tassels and a large gold key and chain around his neck. 3. Mrs. Sprague had made dinner reservations for her and Howard at a Chinese restaurant called Ching Lee's on the night that Howard went to his first lodge meeting. 4. Howard tells Andy that in the past 23 years, girl births have outnumbered boy births by 94 percent, practically 2 to 1. Andy says that he likes the odds. At first Howard doesn't understand the joke, but he later uses it at the lodge with Andy's approval. Later, Howard buys a joke book in order to learn some new jokes to use at the lodge. 5. *Something About Blondes* is currently playing at the movie theater in Mayberry. 6. Lou and Charlie are two other lodge members. 7. Floyd tells Andy that a person in Mount Pilot had his mobile home stolen. A concerned Floyd asks Andy to check and see if his house is still there. 8. The lodge serves beer, root beer, and soft drinks. Howard enjoys drinking the lodge's root beer. Floyd tells Howard that root beer was invented by the Indians and is a very healthy drink. He mentions that "you don't see many sick Indians." 9. Burt serves as the lodge's secretary. Part of his job is to take and report the minutes of the lodge meetings. 10. According to Howard, his father was never a gambler. He only played gin rummy at home with Mrs. Sprague. 11. Mr. Schwump (and his bad toupee) appears as an unnamed lodge member.

"The Darling Fortune"

Episode #193. Air date: 10-17-66. Writers: Arnold Margolin and Jim Parker. Director: Lee Philips.

In the Darlings' final visit to Mayberry (and the only color episode in which they appear), they have sold some of their land to the county of Mayberry for the sum of $300.00. With this newly acquired fortune, Briscoe declares that his boys can now "afford to feed some extra mouths." This can only mean that the mountain family has come to town to find wives. The Darling boys proceed to bird-dog the single girls in Mayberry from the steps of the Gem Hotel, in the park, and in front of the Mayberry Diner. Andy deputizes Goober to keep an eye on the clan. The Darling men find the pickin's slim in Mayberry and are about to leave town when they notice an owl in broad daylight. The superstitious family believe in the mountain folklore known as the omen of the owl. The omen states that if you see an owl in the daytime, the first female you see after the owl sighting is your bride-to-be. Unfortunately, the first female the Darling boys see is Helen Crump. The only question is which one of the Darling boys Helen will fall for.

Andy tries his best to keep the Darling clan away from her, but they prove to be quite persistent. They even serenade Helen in the middle of the night with a version of "There Is a Time," even though this one makes Briscoe cry. At his wit's end, Andy discovers that a counter-omen is the only thing that will break the original omen. In this case, it is seeing another owl in the daytime. Andy enlists the aid of Goober for the following plan of action: He has the Darlings come to his house at 9:00 A.M.

to sign a marriage license. Meanwhile, Andy has Goober hang a stuffed owl, which usually resides on the mantel at the lodge, from a tree outside of his house. Even though Goober hangs and "flies" the owl in odd positions (including upside down), the Darlings fall for the trick. Andy is thrilled, and Helen breathes a huge sigh of relief.

CAST NOTES. Regulars: **Andy Griffith, Frances Bavier, Aneta Corsaut,** and **George Lindsey. Denver Pyle** makes his final appearance as Briscoe Darling. **Margaret Ann Peterson** and **the Dillards** also appear for the last time as Charlene and the Darling boys.

EPISODE NOTES. 1. Briscoe refers to Goober as "Big Ears" because he is nosy. 2. Songs performed are a few instrumentals by the Darling boys, "There Is a Time," and a rousing version (sung by Charlene) of "Salty Dog." 3. The Gem Hotel is shown. The Gibson Hotel of Mayberry is also featured. 4. Before the Darlings got headlights on their truck, Doug would have to get on the hood with a lantern in order for the family to drive at night. 5. Briscoe describes his boys in the following way: Dean is his only short son, but he's fun-loving; Mitch is strong as an ox, and almost as bright, and also has fine chiseled features where a chisel hit him right across the jaw; Rodney is jittery; and Doug is tall. 6. Goober states that the Mayberry Drugstore is serving corned beef sandwiches for lunch. 7. Andy calls Doug Darling a "caution," and Briscoe refers to Helen as a "society gal." 8. Aunt Bee serves steak, potatoes, black-eyed peas, and muffins for the Darling clan. Briscoe says that he uses sour mash in his muffins. Later in the episode, Aunt Bee serves the Darlings lunch. 9. Andy states that Helen is "just crazy" about Rodney. 10. Deputy Goober Pyle refers to Andy as "chief." Andy gives him the deputy's badge that he's always begging for. 11. Goober is superstitious. He will not step on any cracks in the sidewalk because he doesn't want to break his mother's back. 12. No mention is made as to whether Charlene is still married to Dud Wash, or the whereabouts of her daughter, Andelina.

"Aunt Bee's Crowning Glory"

Episode #194. Air date: 10-10-66. Writer: Ronald Axe. Director: Lee Philips.

Aunt Bee is tired of having to fix her hair every time she attends the many church and social events that are part of her busy schedule. With the support of Bernice, her hairdresser, and Helen Crump, she buys a blonde wig. She plans to wear it for the first time to Clara Edwards's house, where a reception is being held in honor of Reverend Leighton, a visiting minister from Raleigh, who also happens to be an eligible bachelor.

Andy throws a fit when he sees the wig for the first time as the Taylors and Helen are leaving for the reception. He tells Aunt Bee that everyone will stare at them and it will be a very embarrassing situation. He also says that the Taylor family has lived in the county of Mayberry for three generations and they've always used their own hair. Nonetheless, Aunt Bee will not be swayed, and with the encouragement of Helen and Opie, she goes to Clara's proudly sporting her new hairpiece.

At the reception, all of the elder ladies are vying for Reverend Leighton's attention, but when he spots Aunt Bee, she has his undivided interest. While Clara, Mrs. Larch, and Maggie Peters say awful things about the wig (behind Aunt Bee's back, of course), Aunt Bee and Reverend Leighton are having the time of their lives. He comments that the people of Mayberry impress him because they are down-to-earth and do not have a pretentious bone in their bodies. Aunt Bee sheepishly nods in agreement.

On Sunday, Reverend Leighton is invited by Reverend Tucker to deliver the sermon. Inspired by what he has seen in Mayberry, his sermon is entitled "Be Yourself." Later, he is invited to the Taylor home for dinner. After Andy and Aunt Bee do some fancy footwork and trickery to assure that she has on her wig for the early-arriving minister, Aunt Bee decides to confess. She confides to the Reverend that she has been wearing the wig. Reverend Leighton is understanding and assures Aunt Bee that she was simply being fashionable, not pretentious.

At the conclusion of the episode, Clara Edwards also buys a blonde wig.

CAST NOTES. Regulars: **Andy Griffith, Ronny Howard, Frances Bavier, Howard McNear, Aneta Corsaut,** and **Hope Summers.**

Ian Wolfe stars as Reverend Leighton. Wolfe was a distinguished character actor in numerous television shows and many classic motion pictures. His movie credits include the 1935 version of *Mutiny on the Bounty* (with Clark Gable), Alfred Hitchcock's *Saboteur* (1942), and *Rebel Without a Cause* (1955, with James Dean).

In this episode, **Carol Veazie** portrays Mrs. Larch. **Ruth Thom** appears as Maggie Peters. **Janet Stewart** portrays Bernice.

EPISODE NOTES. 1. Floyd claims that he knows all of Reverend Tucker's sermons by heart. 2. Helen says that Aunt Bee is the best cook in Mayberry. 3. Floyd relates the sad story of Fluffy Johnson. It seems that Fluffy worked at the gas company in Mayberry, and she had a crush on a gentleman by the name of Orville Portnoy, who worked at the Mayberry Bakery. She once had a bad time trying to impress Orville when she wore false eyelashes and fingernails. When she met him, both the eyelashes and the nails fell off. Poor Fluffy went home in tears (and without Orville). 4. Reverend Leighton initially accepts an invitation to be the new minister at a church in Mount Pilot, but his congregation in Raleigh pleads for him to stay. He decides to remain in Raleigh. 5. Floyd claims that the hair for wigs comes from China. He pulls and picks at Aunt Bee's wig during church services. Andy tells him to stop. 6. Opie shows Reverend Leighton some card tricks. 7. Clara serves chopped-egg canapes among her hors d'oeuvres at the reception. 8. The congregation signs "Bringing In the Sheaves" during Reverend Leighton's visit to the Mayberry church. 9. Andy sings and plays guitar on one of Reverend Leighton's favorite hymns, "On Jordan's Stormy Banks."

"The Ball Game"

Episode #195. Air date: 10-3-66. Story: Rance Howard. Teleplay: Sid Morse. Director: Lee Philips.

Opie is excited. His baseball team, the Mayberry Giants, is going to pay its arch rival, the Mount Pilot Comets, in the biggest baseball game of the season. The winner of the game will advance to the state championships in Raleigh.

Out of the blue, home plate umpire Earlie Gilley takes ill, and Goober, who is the coach of the Mayberry Giants, asks Andy to replace him. Andy refuses, stating that since his son is on the team, it would not be appropriate. Goober clears it with Mr. Carlin, the coach of the Mount Pilot team, and virtually everyone in town, including Mrs. Sprague, believes that Andy is fair and honest and will do a fine job. Andy asks if he can umpire the bases, rather than call the balls and strikes. Goober tells him that Mr. Hendricks, the other umpire, has a bad leg and can't squat. Andy reluctantly takes the job.

The day of the game arrives, and everyone from both towns shows up at Mayberry Field. The game is nip-and-tuck, and as the Mayberry Giants are coming to bat in the last inning, they are trailing the Comets 6 to 5. (One interested observer is Howard Sprague. Howard is covering the game for *The Mayberry Gazette* because the usual sports reporter, Blanton Fuller, is in Siler City covering a fishing derby. Howard's usual beat is the garden column.) Opie, the Mayberry Giants' second baseman, comes to bat with two outs, no one on base, and his

team is down by one run. On a two-strike, no-ball pitch, he smacks a long drive over the center fielder's head. Floyd thinks it is a homer for sure, but the outfielder retrieves the ball and fires it to the cutoff man just as Opie is reaching third base. Andy realizes that his son is going to try to score, and he prepares to make the call. In a bang-bang play, Andy calls Opie out at the plate. With this call, the Mayberry Giants' dreams of going to the state championships come to an abrupt end. The entire Mayberry team, led by Goober and Opie, converges on Andy. Even Aunt Bee yells that Opie was safe and that Andy was supposed to help his son.

Later, everyone in town except Helen and Howard gives Andy the cold shoulder, including Aunt Bee and Opie. Even a little dog angrily barks at him. Goober reluctantly and silently fills up Andy's gas tank, and Floyd tells him that he needs to make an appointment in order to get a haircut. Both Goober and Floyd remind Andy that he would be treated like a king in Mount Pilot, because they love him there. Things finally come to a head when Andy and Helen stop at the Mayberry Diner after taking in a movie. Floyd, Goober, and Howard are sitting at the next booth, and while Howard watches, both Floyd and Goober start chiding Andy once again. This time Andy explodes and tells them off in no uncertain terms. He and Helen leave the diner in disgust.

Goober reminds Howard to be sure and "tell it like it is" in his newspaper column that will appear in the following day's edition of *The Mayberry Gazette.* Howard takes a different approach and writes an article in defense of Andy, reminding readers that Andy took on the job of umpire as a favor. He points out that because the town thrust that responsibility onto Andy, it was now the town's responsibility to accept his decisions "in the spirit of good sportsmanship." He also challenges Andy's critics to volunteer for umpire duty themselves, adding, "Frankly, I don't think we'll get too many offers."

Everyone reads the article, and each in his own way apologizes to Andy.

Incidentally, Opie was definitely safe. As the call was being made, Helen snapped a picture that proves this point. She shares this secret with Aunt Bee and then, after swearing Aunt Bee to secrecy, tears up the picture.

MEMORABLE SCENE. Goober's "hit one for the old Goober" speech to Opie.

CAST NOTES. Regulars: **Andy Griffith, Ronny Howard, Frances Bavier, Howard McNear, Aneta Corsaut, George Lindsey,** and **Jack Dodson.**

John Reilly appears as one of Opie's teammates named Billy.

EPISODE NOTES. 1. The Mayberry Giants' team colors are orange and white. The Mount Pilot Comets' colors are navy blue and white. 2. Floyd says that being the manager of the Mayberry Giants has made Goober "power mad." 3. The "Mayberry Theme Song," which later became the theme song for the series, *Mayberry R.F.D.*, is played before the baseball game. 4. The bank in Mayberry is now referred to as the City Bank. 5. Aunt Bee states that Andy is the head of the Good Government League and has been a member of the church choir for five years. 6. Floyd says that Mount Pilot has a four-chair barbershop. 7. Goober's baseball signals to his players are as follows: (1) Wiping his hands across his chest means to hit, (2) Tugging at the bill of his cap means to bunt, (3) Grabbing his belt buckle means to take a pitch. Jackie Sims of the Mayberry Giants can't seem to remember the hit sign. 8. Johnny Adams is the lead-off hitter for the Mount Pilot Comets. 9. The license plate number of the car that Goober is working on is SD-561. 10. This story was written by Ron and Clint Howard's father, Rance. Rance Howard appeared in numerous episodes of *The Andy Griffith Show*, but this was the only episode that he wrote. In Stephen J. Spignesi's excellent book *Mayberry My Hometown* Spignesi interviews Rance, Ron and Clint Howard. Ron picks "The Ball Game" as one of his favorite episodes. Rance swears that the story is based on an actual incident in which he umpired a softball game at Ron's birthday party. 11. Earlie Gilley is once again mentioned. We do not know if the real-life Mr. Gilley of Mount Airy umpires baseball games. 12. This episode was appropriately aired just two days prior to the 1966 World Series, between the Baltimore Orioles and the Los Angeles Dodgers. For the record, the Orioles won the series, four games to none.

"Goober Makes History"

Episode #196. Air date: 12-19-66. Writers: John L. Greene and Paul David. Director: Lee Philips.

Andy, Helen, Floyd, Howard, Goober, and a few others decide to attend an adult American history class. The night class is being taught by Bill Lindsey at the Mayberry Grade School. Goober suffers from a lack of historical knowledge and self-confidence. After a few embarrassing moments in class, he decides to drop out. He goes on a three-week fishing trip, but forgets to take along his razor. When he returns home, Goober is sporting a full beard.

Goober looks so different that even Floyd doesn't

recognize him. Andy spots him and remarks that he looks like "the Thinker." Aunt Bee tells him that he resembles a philosopher, while Floyd says he looks "brainy." When Goober asks Floyd to shave off the beard, Floyd reminds his pal that there hasn't been a beard in Mayberry for ten years. Floyd goes on to say that he will be happy to shape it up, but he will never shave off such a magnificent work of nature.

In no time at all, the flattering comments go to Goober's head, and he decides to return to the American history class. He now has way too much self-confidence, and his persistence in offering his views drives everyone around him crazy. Even his best friends start avoiding him at every turn, but he keeps turning up like a bad penny. Finally, an exasperated Andy screams at him that he is acting like a jerk and it doesn't hurt to listen to others every once in a while. Goober is initially hurt by this outburst, but soon he understands the error of his ways and returns to his old likable self, minus the beard.

MEMORABLE SCENES. 1. Andy pretending to be asleep so he can avoid listening to Goober. 2. Opie quizzing Andy about the American Revolution, the Articles of Confederation, and the Stamp Act.

CAST NOTES. Regulars: **Andy Griffith, Ronny Howard, Frances Bavier, Howard McNear, Aneta Corsaut, George Lindsey,** and **Jack Dodson.**

Sandy Kenyon appears as Bill Lindsey. The cast credits incorrectly list Richard Bull in this role. Kenyon has appeared in countless television shows, including regular roles as Jim Lucas on *Love on a Rooftop* from 1966 through 1967 and as Reverend Kathrun on *Knots Landing* in 1984 and 1985.

Vivian Rhodes portrays an adult student named Maggie Kohler. **Christina Burke** portrays a student named Edna.

EPISODE NOTES. 1. Howie Forman has a bad habit of chewing on Opie's pencils at school. 2. Aunt Bee once had a beau with brown hair, blue eyes, and a red beard. She says that "he was just a riot of colors." 3. The Gem Hotel and Rooms in Mayberry is shown in this episode. 4. Howard studies up on the quotations of Charles Cotesworth Pinckney, who is (incorrectly) credited with the slogan, "Millions for defense, but not one cent for tribute." Andy quoted this motto to Opie when he was troubled by a young extortionist in episode 34, "Opie and the Bully." For a complete history of this quotation, check the Episode Notes of episode 34. 5. Floyd trims Goober's beard for no charge. Goober promises to give him a free radiator flush in return. 6. Andy says that Floyd is Goober's best friend, while Floyd claims that Andy is Goober's best friend. 7. Portraits of George Washington and

Abraham Lincoln appear on the walls of the class-room. These two portraits may also be seen on the walls of the meeting room of the Mayberry Town Council in episode 248, "Opie and Mike." 8. Shorty Watson once owned and operated a grocery store in Mayberry. One time, Goober, Shorty, and a few other friends went on a fishing trip to Troublesome Creek. 9. A man named Bill tries to avoid chatting with Goober in front of the courthouse. 10. Howard Sprague makes paper dolls in order to fight boredom while Goober rambles on during class.

"The Senior Play"

Episode #197. Air date: 11-14-66. Writer: Sid Morse. Director: Lee Philips.

Helen is put in charge of the Mayberry High School senior play. She encourages the students to break away from previous themes, such as histori-cal and Victorian fare. She instructs the kids to express themselves and allows them to do a play that contains rock 'n' roll music and dancing. Mr. Hamp-ton, the high school principal, witnesses a dress rehearsal and blows a fuse. He is appalled by the music and dancing. He makes it perfectly clear to Helen that a play which contains such obvious exhi-bitions of disgraceful behavior will not be tolerated. He threatens to cancel the play unless Helen and the students change it to something respectable, like a play depicting the lifestyle of his own youth.

After Helen calms down, she comes up with a shrewd plan of action. She alters the play to include dances like the Charleston and Black Bottom Stomp of the 1920s. She also adds songs and clothing from Mr. Hampton's era. Helen and the students, with lead actors Homer and Estelle, treat Mr. Hampton to a special preview of the revised play. He imme-diately sees that his era was not quite as calm and respectable as he would like to remember. With no recourse, Mr. Hampton comes off his high horse and allows the students the freedom to do their own play, using their own music and dances. He even dances with Helen at the party after the play.

MEMORABLE SCENES. 1. Goober doing his patented imitations of *Gunsmoke*'s Chester, Edward G. Robinson, and Cary Grant for Andy. Goober asks Andy if he can name the person he is imitat-ing when he is taking off on Edward G. Robinson. Andy innocently replies, "Floyd?" 2. Howard explaining what everybody means at the volatile meeting between Helen and Mr. Hampton.

CAST NOTES. Regulars: **Andy Griffith, Howard McNear, Aneta Corsaut, George Lindsey**, and **Jack Dodson**.

Leon Ames stars as Mr. Hampton. Ames is best remembered for his many movie roles, which include *Meet Me in St. Louis* (1944, with Judy Gar-land) and *The Postman Always Rings Twice* (1946). On television, he was Clarence Day, Sr., on *Life with Father* from 1953 through 1955. On the tele-vision version of *Father of the Bride*, he took over Spencer Tracy's movie portrayal of Stanley Banks. Viewers of *Nick at Nite* may recognize Ames as Gor-don Kirkwood on *Mr. Ed*. He also appeared in memorable episodes of *The Beverly Hillbillies, My Three Sons*, and *The Jeffersons*.

Mary Jackson returns to the series. This time she portrays the home economics teacher, Miss Vogel. She had previously appeared as Parnell Rigsby's wife in episodes 136, "Opie's Fortune." **Chuck Brummit** appears as Homer. **Cynthia Hull** portrays Estelle.

EPISODE NOTES. 1. Helen appeared in a few plays during her college days. 2. Howard is the trea-surer of the high school. The budget for the play is only $38.00. 3. Miss Vogel is in charge of all the costumes in the play. She suggested that the play should be a series of skits depicting great moments in history. Mr. Hampton and Howard liked her idea. Helen and the students hated it. 4. While in high school, Floyd appeared in *The Mikado*. He claims to have been the backbone of the drama club. He sings "A Wandering Minstrel" from the afore-mentioned operetta. Goober joins in on a pitiful duet. 5. Floyd says that Helen is a wonderful girl and the salt of the earth. 6. Helen plays the piano at rehearsals. 7. A man named Charlie is in charge of the lighting for the play. 8. Andy and Goober assist in painting the sets for the play.

"Big Fish in a Small Town"

Episode #198. Air date: 11-28-66. Writers: Bill Idelson and Sam Bobrick. Director: Lee Philips.

Andy, Goober, Floyd, and Opie are preparing for the opening day of the fishing season. It starts promptly at 6:30 on the following morning. For the past seven years, all of the aforementioned anglers have had dreams of catching an elusive silver carp whom they've nicknamed "Old Sam." Old Sam has achieved legendary status in Mayberry and at Tucker's Lake, which is his home.

A problem arises when Howard Sprague, a novice fisherman, asks Andy if he can accompany the group. Andy reluctantly invites him, even though Floyd and Goober believe that Howard will make a lot of noise and scare away all of the fish, including Old Sam. The next morning, Howard arrives at Andy's at 6:00, fully equipped for a day of fishing. He has taken the scientific approach, which includes bringing a depth finder, a water temperature gauge, a net, an umbrella, a tray, a flashlight, and a portable radio, among other items. Howard even brings a picnic basket filled with two roasted chickens, a quart of potato salad, and a lemon pie.

At Tucker's Lake, Howard continually snags his line in trees, rocks, and the seat of his pants. Finally, he casts his line using some of his potato salad as bait and promptly catches Old Sam. Howard is thrilled. He puts the silver carp in a tank in front of the courthouse for people to look at.

Later, Howard is asked by the Raleigh Aquarium to donate his prize catch, and he obliges. Andy, Floyd, Goober, and Opie lament that Old Sam is gone, and they are especially upset that Howard donated the legendary fish to an aquarium. A few days later, Opie accompanies Howard to Raleigh, where they stop in to visit Old Sam. Howard proudly reads the plaque that sits beneath Old Sam's tank. It states, "Silver Carp, Caught in Mayberry, North Carolina. Donated By Howard Sprague." Opie tells Howard that the aquarium is nice, but Tucker's Lake just isn't the same anymore. Howard reconsiders and happily returns Old Sam to his rightful home. Everyone is thrilled, and the race is back on to see who can catch the "Big Fish In A Small Town."

CAST NOTES. Regulars: **Andy Griffith, Ronny Howard, Howard McNear, George Lindsey**, and **Jack Dodson**.

Sam Reese appears as the photographer who takes Howard's picture with Old Sam.

EPISODE NOTES. 1. Andy uses size #6 fish hooks. 2. Goober's cousin tells him to use a piece of banana peel with red yarn as bait. 3. Opie started fishing at the age of four. 4. Goober claims that Tucker's Lake is also loaded with rainbow and bluegill. 5. One time, Floyd's cousin on his wife's side ruined an entire day of fishing for Floyd and Goober by constantly sloshing the water around and scaring away the fish. 6. According to Opie, the deepest spot in Tucker's Lake is ten feet. 7. Two of Andy's friends, Cyrus and Burt, are also trying to catch Old Sam. 8. Howard states that 90 percent of lake fish are caught when the water temperature is 68 degrees. 9. Goober also likes to fish at a place called Warrior River. 10. Mr. Schwump appears as an interested party peering at Old Sam in front of the courthouse.

"Mind Over Matter"

Episode #199. Air date: 10-31-66. Writers: Ron Friedman and Pat McCormick. Director: Lee Philips.

Andy brings the squad car to Wally's Filling Station and asks Goober to check out the steering. Shortly after Goober gets behind the wheel, a car driven by a young woman smashes into the rear of the squad car. Goober is fine, except for the fact that he swallowed his chewing gum. He does admit to a minor "crick" in his back, but says it's nothing a soak in a hot bathtub can't cure. The lady driver is very apologetic. She had been reaching to turn off her car radio as she pulled up to the pump, and that moment of distraction resulted in the accident. Because there was no damage done to either car and because the lady appears to have learned her lesson, Andy does not issue a ticket.

Later, Goober goes to Floyd's Barbershop to borrow some ointment for a minor scratch. He relates the mishap to Floyd, who reacts with alarm. Floyd recalls that a similar accident once happened to Johnny Harris, a former Mayberrian. Johnny complained of a "crick" too, then twinges of pain, until he was diagnosed with whiplash. Floyd tells Goober about the whiplash test, which consists of putting yours fists tight against your chest, raising your elbows and trying to make them touch over your head! Poor Johnny couldn't get his elbows back down. When he died he had to be buried in an extra-wide coffin. Of course, this unlikely story has an effect on Goober, who begins to feel much worse. As Goober leaves, Floyd warns him to watch out for hardening of the back and bids him goodbye with, "We wouldn't want to lose *you*, boy!"

Aunt Bee and Opie run into Floyd at the market, and he tells them about Goober. They stop at Wally's to get gas and to check on their friend. Goober is now walking very stiffly and slowly, but he says he will probably be okay. Then Aunt Bee relates the sorry tale of Willis Cundiff, who had a similar accident. Poor Willis started out with just a "crick" and soon went back to work. Then it got worse and he ended up in traction at the hospital in Mount Pilot. He's been there for months and has not improved.

Suddenly, Goober is on the verge of collapse. Aunt Bee takes him home, where she can see to his needs. She puts him in Andy's room.

When Andy comes home, he is astounded to discover this turn of events. Doctor Bennett examines Goober and states that he has a classic case of whiplash and will need complete bed rest for at least six weeks. He tells Andy to give Goober a deep back massage for 20 minutes, five or six times a day.

The Taylors wait on Goober hand and foot. Andy helps out with the massages and grooming and even lugs the family television set up to his room. Aunt Bee makes sure he is well fed (even sacrificing Andy's steak), and Opie helps out by keeping Goober supplied with comic books.

After talking with Aunt Bee and Floyd, Andy realizes that Goober's problem is purely psychosomatic. His suspicion is verified when he catches Goober sleeping with his arms comfortably raised over his head. He attempts to explain that the trouble is all in his mind, but Goober angrily denies it.

Doctor Bennett listens to Andy's theory and concurs. He advises Andy to try to catch Goober while he is awake, but in a relaxed, unguarded moment.

Andy catches some heat when Goober realizes he is being tested. However, while protesting, Goober finds himself raising his arms high above his head. Goober is cured!

Incidentally, Andy's test was to toss a football at Goober when he isn't looking. After the miraculous cure, Goober tosses the ball to an unguarded Andy, who ends up falling and injuring his shoulder.

CAST NOTES. Regulars: **Andy Griffith, Ronny Howard, Frances Bavier, George Lindsey,** and **Howard McNear.**

Sue Taylor appears as the lady driver. **George Selk** appears as Doctor Bennett.

EPISODE NOTES. 1. Goober borrows mercurochrome from Floyd. It can be found next to the bay rum. 2. Floyd neglected to tell Goober that Johnny Harris was kicked in the head by a mule. 3. Aunt Bee left out the fact that Willis Cundiff is 91 years old. 4. Goober claims that he was once a star football player. 5. Andy has to sleep on a cot in the spare room while Goober is a house guest. 6. Opie reads comic books to Goober. Opie borrowed some new comic books from his friend Pete. Goober's new favorite comic book hero is Crabmonster. Crabmonster masks his monster identity in the guise of Mark Steele, a mild-mannered hygiene instructor at Boys High School. He drinks a secret formula that transforms him into Crabmonster, enemy of crime. In the issue Opie is reading from, Crabmonster is trying to capture the evil Professor Scolar.

"Politics Begin at Home"

Episode #200. Air date: 11-7-66. Writer: Fred S. Fox. Director: Lee Philips.

A Mayberry councilman named Ralph has resigned and moved away, leaving a vacant seat on the town council. Andy suggests that Howard Sprague would be a fine replacement. Floyd and Goober agree. As a group, they approach Howard and ask him to consider becoming a candidate. Floyd promises, "The machine will back you 100 percent!" Andy says he is certain that Aunt Bee can convince the ladies of Mayberry to vote for Howard. Modest Mr. Sprague decides to throw his hat into the ring.

Meanwhile, at a Garden Club Meeting, Clara Edwards surprises Aunt Bee by nominating her for town council. Aunt Bee admits she knows nothing about politics, but her friends convince her to enter the race.

Later, Aunt Bee tells Andy she is going to run for the town council. It is an awkward moment for Andy, because he has already promised his (and Bee's) support to Howard. He tells Aunt Bee that other folks may be better qualified for the position. Before he can say anything further, Howard, having already heard about Aunt Bee's candidacy, stops by to congratulate her. He tells Andy that, under the circumstances, he will understand if he wants to withdraw his support. However, Andy truly believes Howard is the best person for the job and sticks with him. An upset Aunt Bee begins giving Andy the cold shoulder.

The Taylors' home becomes Aunt Bee's campaign headquarters, and Clara acts as her campaign manager. Opie creates a poster that says, "Miss Bee Taylor For Progressive Government." Meanwhile, Howard uses Floyd's Barbershop as his headquarters. Floyd racks his brain to come up with a catchy slogan and also to come up with a way to win the "Indian vote." It doesn't seem to matter that there is only *one* Indian living in Mayberry. Floyd thinks the Indian vote can be won with the slogan "Preserve the buffalo."

Andy believes an open debate between Howard and Aunt Bee would be helpful to the voting public. Both candidates agree to stand before their constituency at the town hall and answer questions.

Aunt Bee's stock answer to every question is "If it is the will of the people, it shall be done." Howard gives intelligent, thoughtful replies, quoting facts and figures to support his proposals. Before long, it becomes very apparent that Howard is the better candidate, and Aunt Bee graciously bows out of the race and pledges her support to him. Andy is relieved when Aunt Bee implies that the cold shoulder days have come to an end.

After the debate, Howard asks Aunt Bee to head the committee for the beautification of Elm Street. Aunt Bee says she would like to remove all the elm trees and replace them with magnolia trees.

She believes this will provide more shade and make the street (which would likely be renamed Magnolia Street) the loveliest thoroughfare in town.

CAST NOTES. Regulars: **Andy Griffith, Ronny Howard, Frances Bavier, Jack Dodson, Howard McNear, George Lindsey,** and **Hope Summers.**

Maxine Semon appears as Tillie Kincaid. **Ruth Thom** appears as Ella. In later episodes, Thom will appear as Myrtle.

EPISODE NOTES. 1. Floyd spent 4 years on the town council, years ago. He says they were four of the stormiest years in Mayberry's political history. The township was rife with corruption, including the famous drinking fountain scandal. It seems that someone hooked up a hot water line to the fountain and then tried to cover it up. 2. Aunt Bee states that at the last meeting of the Garden Club, Tillie Kincaid gave a review of the book *Roses Are the Backbone of Your Garden*, by Mabel J. Mosley. Tillie summed up the theme as "Save the insecticide, but do not spare the fertilizer." 3. Tillie suggests that Elm Street would look nicer if only the Wallravens would paint their home. 4. Aunt Bee would like to see a dam and a water wheel installed, once the bridge on Baker Street is completed. 5. Howard has been county clerk for two years. 6. Opie gets a high D on his latest history test. 7. Some of Floyd's slogan ideas for Howard are "Win with Wilkie, "a landslide for Landon," and "Tippecanoe and Tyler, too." 8. Among Aunt Bee's posters are "Vote for Bee Taylor" and "Beautify Mayberry." The banner at her headquarters says, "Bee Taylor For Town Council." 9. Among Howard's posters is "Sprague — The Man For The Job." His headquarters is framed by a banner reading, "Howard Sprague For City Councilman." 10. Clara arranges for Aunt Bee to speak at the Booster Club Luncheon as well as before the Literary Guild. Lillian Hartzell has offered to accompany Aunt Bee and play her saxophone. Aunt Bee believes that Lillian's version of "Flight of the Bumblebee" livens up an audience. 11. Ella asks the first question at the debate. She wants to know the candidates' positions on erecting a new bridge over Parker's Creek on Old Branch Road. Howard suggests that taxpayers could save a great deal of money by building a bridge one block away, on Baker Street, and repairing the existing bridge for pedestrian usage. 12. Goober asks about getting a new sewer system for Main Street. Howard believes that the old sewers should be repaired and that the 200-foot run between first and second streets should be the focus of the town's attention. 13. Howard says that building a new road to connect with the state highway would be a waste of the taxpayers' money.

"A New Doctor in Town"

Episode #201. Air date: 12-26-66. Writers: Ray Brenner and Barry E. Blitzer. Director: Lee Philips.

Dr. Bennett, Mayberry's beloved physician for the past 40 years, has decided to retire. He is being replaced by a young man named Dr. Thomas Peterson. Many of the residents of Mayberry, most notably Floyd and Clara, believe that the new doctor is too young and inexperienced to be an adequate physician. Floyd and Clara also do not like the fact that Dr. Peterson has a sense of humor, likes to play golf, and enjoys going out on Saturday nights.

Andy decides to invite Dr. Peterson, along with Helen, Floyd, and Clara, to the Taylor house for a turkey dinner. Andy believes that if Floyd and Clara get to know the good doctor, they will like him. Unfortunately, the exact opposite occurs. When Dr. Peterson attempts to carve the turkey, he practically destroys everything in sight. Floyd remarks that "a man on an operating table wouldn't have had a chance."

Later that evening, after Dr. Peterson has left, Andy and Helen try to change Floyd's mind. Then Opie comes into the room, complaining that his throat is extremely sore. Andy inspects his tonsils and discovers they are severely inflamed. Helen is shocked when Andy tells his son to gargle and fails to contact Dr. Peterson.

On the next day, Helen coaxes Andy to take Opie to the new doctor's office. Dr. Peterson confirms that Opie's tonsils need to be removed. Now, it is apparent that Andy has been just as skeptical about Dr. Peterson as Floyd and Clara. When he suggests to Aunt Bee and Helen that he may take Opie to Mount Pilot for the surgery, Helen can't keep quiet any longer. She admonishes Andy for his distrust of the young doctor and says that if he chooses to take Opie to an out-of-town physician, Dr. Peterson may as well pick up and leave Mayberry for good. So it is up to Andy whether Mayberry will have a doctor or not.

An apprehensive Andy decides to take Opie to Dr. Peterson, who performs the surgery, assisted by Nurse Oakley. The operation is a success, and now Floyd says he will let Dr. Peterson examine his sinus problems. Clara says that she will let the new doctor take a look at her 25-year-old neuralgia condition.

CAST NOTES. Regulars: **Andy Griffith, Ronny Howard, Frances Bavier, Howard McNear, Aneta Corsaut,** and **Hope Summers.**

William Christopher stars as Dr. Thomas Peterson. Christopher previously appeared as IRS

William Christopher

agent Mr. Heathcoate in episode 165, "Aunt Bee on TV." **Sari Price** appears as Nurse Oakley.

EPISODE NOTES. 1. Dr. Bennett was the doctor who delivered Opie. 2. Dr. Peterson is 25 years old and drives a convertible. His license plate is #SR-490. He also has another license plate affixed to his car. This license plate number is MBB-624. 3. The Mayberry business Biggs New and Used Furniture Store can be seen in this episode. 4. The Taylors' address is given as 14 Maple. (In episode 87, it was 382 Maple; in episode 50, it was 24 Elm.) They usually eat dinner at 7:00. (In episode 189, their dinnertime was 6:00.) 5. Opie's bedtime is now 9:00 P.M. Andy states that youngsters need a good 10 hours of sleep. 6. Dr. Peterson likes to joke about his tender age. When folks ask him if he is old enough to have a doctor's license, he responds, "No, I only have a learner's permit." Floyd and Clara do not find this amusing. 7. At the conclusion of the episode, Opie decides that when he grows up, he wants to be a doctor.

"Opies Finds a Baby"

Episode #202. Air date: 11-21-66. Writers: Stan Dreben and Sid Mandel. Director: Lee Philips.

Opie and his friend Arnold find an abandoned baby boy on the steps of the Mayberry courthouse. Opie wants to tell his pa about it, but Arnold con-

vinces him not to because he's sure that the baby would be put in an "orphan asylum." Since the baby came complete with extra diapers and a full bottle, the boys load him into a shopping cart (courtesy of Foley's Market) and take him to their clubhouse in Opie's backyard.

In order to find a good home for the baby, Opie and Arnold proceed to ask some personal questions of a few of Mayberry's more prominent citizens, including Helen and Goober. Andy gets concerned when he hears about Opie and Arnold's embarrassing queries. Andy, who is totally unaware of the baby, decides that Opie needs a father-and-son "facts of life" session. Andy begins stumbling into his chat with Opie when he is interrupted by the parents of the infant, Mr. and Mrs. Garland of Mount Pilot. Andy is puzzled by the Garlands' questions until Opie explains the situation and leaves to get the baby.

Meanwhile, Mrs. Garland explains to Andy that she and her husband had gotten into a bad argument, and in a moment of desperation, she left the baby at the courthouse. Both parents acknowledge their mistake and promise that it will never happen again. Andy decides to let them have the baby back, after first threatening to call the welfare department and then giving them a stern lecture about responsibility and a promise that he will notify the sheriff of Mount Pilot about the situation.

Opie and Arnold are thrilled, and Andy is proud of the way he handled the much-dreaded father-and-son talk with Opie. Andy doesn't realize that Opie had already learned the facts of life at school, and Opie doesn't have the heart to tell his well-meaning pa.

CAST NOTES. Regulars: **Andy Griffith, Ronny Howard, Frances Bavier, Aneta Corsaut,** and **George Lindsey.**

This episode marks the first of two appearances by Mayberry's most distinguished star of the future, **Jack Nicholson.** He portrays Mr. Garland. Nicholson would later appear as Marvin Jenkins in episode 223, "Aunt Bee the Juror." Jack Nicholson has been nominated for and won several Academy Awards for movie gems such as *One Flew Over the Cuckoo's Nest* (1975) and *Terms of Endearment* (1983).

Sheldon Golomb makes his first of many appearances as Arnold Bailey. Golomb would later be billed as Sheldon Collins. He appeared as Arnold in *Mayberry R.F.D.* (in an episode entitled "Mike's Losing Streak"). He had a regular role in the daytime drama *Guiding Light,* for a short time in the 1960s. Collins made several guest appearances during his childhood, including roles on *My Three Sons, Storefront Lawyers,* and *The Dick Van Dyke Show.*

(In the latter, he appeared in an episode written by Ben Joelson and Art Baer. It was titled "Buddy Sorrell-Man and Boy." The nicely crafted story dealt with Buddy [Morey Amsterdam] studying for his long-put-off bar mitzvah.) Collins also appeared in a zany 1966 movie called *The Russians Are Coming! The Russians Are Coming!* That film provided Alan Arkin with his first starring role.

James McCallion portrays Lou Bailey, Arnold's father. This is the only episode in which Arnold's father appeared, even though he is referred to in subsequent episodes. McCallion, a native of Glasgow, Scotland, portrayed Mi Taylor in the television version of the movie *National Velvet*.

Janie Kelly appears as the frantic Mrs. Garland.

EPISODE NOTES. 1. Arnold tells Andy that when he grows up, he also wants to be a sheriff who doesn't carry a gun. Arnold plans to use an Australian bullwhip instead. Arnold also tells Opie that he caught a shark while fishing at Hopkins Creek. Opie tells him that he's nuts. 2. Arnold deduces that the baby is a boy because of the blue blanket in the basket. Arnold's younger brother also had a blue blanket when he was an infant. 3. Lou Bailey tells Andy that he had hoped Andy would tell Opie about the facts of life, and in turn, Opie would tell Arnold. This way, Mr. Bailey would not have to deal with the delicate subject. Goober claims that his daddy told him about the facts of life using the out-of-date birds-and-bees scenario. He suggests that Andy use the story about the mackerel's swimming downstream. Andy corrects him by pointing out that it is salmon, and they swim upstream. 4. Other than Helen and Goober, Opie and Arnold ask Sarah the telephone operator, a lady named Miss Cripps, an unnamed young woman with five children, and an unnamed elderly gentleman (who appreciated the thought) if they would like to have a baby. 5. Arnold has read a lot of books, including *Oliver Twist*, which makes him an expert on "orphan asylums." Arnold also tells Opie that he read in a book that it costs $26,000 to raise a child from birth through college. It costs even more if the child wants to become a doctor. 6. Mr. and Mrs. Garland drive a Ford Mustang. Their license plate number is RSR-640.

"Only a Rose"

Episode #203. Air date: 12-5-66. Writers: Jim Parker and Arnold Margolin. Director: Lee Philips.

At a Mayberry Garden Club meeting, Mr. Simmons announces that his seed company will judge the club's upcoming flower contest. Blue ribbons will be awarded in the following divisions: snapdragon, gladioli, pansy, and hybrid rose. The hybrid rose winner will receive special recognition. Not only will this award include a cash prize, but the rose will be propagated at the Simmons nursery and will be featured in the next seed catalog, along with a photo of the grower.

Clara Edwards has a knack for growing prizewinning roses. She has won in that category for the past seven years. When Aunt Bee mentions that she may enter the contest, Clara does not worry. Still, she asks her friend Tillie Kincaid to do a little spying. Tillie is a next-door neighbor to the Taylors.

Aunt Bee has labored for over a year to grow a quality hybrid rose. She has cross-pollinated a Mrs. Pinkney Variegated Red with an Alma Swarthout Sunset Pink. It is due to bloom just days before the contest. Aunt Bee hopes she can compete with Clara's Snow Valley White Rose. Tillie overhears Aunt Bee telling Andy that it bothers her that Clara acts so uppity. She reports this to Clara, who is offended by the remark.

Aunt Bee and Clara have had a competitive friendship since they attended Sweetbriar Normal School together. Aunt Bee tells Andy that even then, Clara always had to be the best.

Finally, Aunt Bee's "Deep Pink Ecstasy" comes to full bloom. It is absolutely gorgeous. Andy leaves to retrieve his camera from the courthouse, while Aunt Bee races to register for the contest. Opie's friend Billy arrives at the Taylors', and soon the boys are tossing a football around in the backyard. Unfortunately, one of Opie's passes sails into Aunt Bee's rose and breaks it at the stem. Opie is extremely upset because he knows how much the rose means to Aunt Bee. He tries to tape it up so it won't show. When Andy returns to snap a few pictures of it, he doesn't notice anything wrong.

The next morning, Opie discovers that the tape did little good. Aunt Bee's rose is dead. He confesses to Andy, who breaks the news as gently as possible to Aunt Bee. She is heartbroken, of course. Still, she insists on attending the flower show. Andy attends with her. Opie tells them he will join them later.

Clara can't resist making a cute remark to Aunt Bee about her sudden withdrawal from the competition. Andy informs her that the rose was accidentally destroyed.

Just as Clara is announced as the winner of the hybrid rose division, Opie shows up and presents Aunt Bee with an 8 x 10 color photograph of the rose. Opie had it made from a negative. Aunt Bee is delighted to see her beautiful rose once again. Clara is awestruck when she sees the photo. She takes it to the winner's platform with her and addresses the gathering. She tells them what happened to Aunt Bee's rose and then shows the crowd the picture. She states that although she wanted to win for an eighth consecutive year, a rose such as Aunt Bee's Deep Pink Ecstasy has no rivals. With the permission of Mr. Simmons, Clara awards the blue ribbon to Aunt Bee, who is moved by the unselfish and sincere gesture from her lifelong friend.

MEMORABLE SCENE. Floyd telling Andy to stop blocking the sun from his pansies.

CAST NOTES. Regulars: **Andy Griffith, Ronny Howard, Frances Bavier, Howard McNear,** and **Hope Summers. Maxine Semon** returns as Tillie Kincaid. **Ruth Thom** returns as Ella Carson. **John Reilly** returns as Opie's friend Billy.

Richard Collier appears as Mr. Simmons.

EPISODE NOTES. 1. Some of the members of the Mayberry Garden Club are Aunt Bee, Floyd, Clara, Ella Carson, Tillie Kincaid, Ella Baskins, and Mr. Schwump (who is sitting in the first row when the flower contest is announced). Floyd wins the blue ribbon for his pansies. His only competition was from Ella Baskins. 2. A lady named Alma serves as entry clerk at the flower show. 3. Snails and bugs, particularly aphids, are the bane of any flower grower. Clara advises, "Spray, spray, spray!" She also says that the Simmons Seed catalog has been the Mayberry Garden Club's planting bible for many years. 4. Aunt Bee and Clara played basketball together at Sweetbriar Normal School. Aunt Bee was the backbone of the team, while Clara was the best dribbler. 5. While preparing Aunt Bee for the bad news about her rose, Andy reminds her that the really important things in life are one's health, having enough money to live on, good friends, a sound mind, good weather, and pep. 6. Andy suggests that he, Opie, and Aunt Bee could dine at the Copper Kettle in Mount Pilot. 7. Aunt Bee and Clara sing the Sweetbriar Normal School song on the Taylors' front porch.

"Otis the Deputy"

Episode #204. Air date: 12-12-66. Writers: Jim Parker and Arnold Margolin. Director: Lee Philips.

Two men named Fred and Larry have just robbed the bank of Mount Pilot to the tune of $6,000. They are thought to be hiding out in the vicinity of Mayberry. In fact, Andy speaks on the phone to a law enforcement officer named Ed about the possibility of the bank robbers taking Route 88 near Franklin Junction, which is just outside of town. Otis stumbles into the courthouse and tells

Andy that he noticed two strangers in that area, and they were staying at the abandoned Carson shack. Otis was up there visiting his stash of booze. Andy tells both Otis and Howard that he is going to investigate. At the Carson shack, Andy trips over Otis's stash and is easily captured by the crooks.

Meanwhile, back at the courthouse, Howard and Otis are worried. They decide to form a two-man posse. While Howard walks home to get his car, Otis proceeds to get gassed on a bottle of booze that Andy put in a desk drawer. Howard comes back and reluctantly takes Otis with him for directions, but advises his drunken partner to remain in the car.

Howard is soon captured, and Otis stumbles his way to right outside the window, where Andy and Howard are tied to chairs. He promptly passes out cold. Andy and Howard try to revive their drunken savior by throwing cups of water begrudgingly given to them by Larry. After two failed attempts, including one thrown right in Andy's face, Howard awakens Otis, who makes enough noise to distract the crooks. He knocks Fred in the head with a bottle of booze, and Andy and Howard free themselves and capture Larry.

MEMORABLE SCENE. A drunken Otis singing the tune "Go Tell Aunt Rhody." He starts crying when he sings the line, "The old gray goose is dead."

CAST NOTES. Regulars: **Andy Griffith** and **Jack Dodson.** This episode marks the final appearance of **Hal Smith** as the lovable town drunk, Otis Campbell.

Joe Turkel appears as Fred. **Charles Dierkop** portrays Larry. Dierkop appeared as Detective Pete Royster from 1974 through 1978 on *Police Woman.*

EPISODE NOTES. 1. Otis states that Andy is his best friend. 2. Howard quotes the theories of Dr. Emile Sharlock to Fred and Larry. Dr. Sharlock wrote that any criminal can be rehabilitated into becoming a good citizen. Initially, Fred tells Howard to "shut up" about Dr. Sharlock's theories. At the conclusion of the episode, Howard tries one more time to convince Fred about the theories. This time, Fred punches him in the stomach. 3. Observant viewers should note that after Otis gets doused by the two cups of water and wakes up, his shirt is still wet, but his pants are bone dry.

"Don't Miss a Good Bet"

Episode #205. Air date: 1-2-67. Writer: Fred S. Fox. Director: Lee Philips.

Goober is curious about a man who has come to Mayberry. He tries to discover just who the stranger is, but gets nowhere. While Goober and Floyd are talking about this situation, the mystery man comes into the barbershop. He tells Floyd that others in town have told him that the Mayberry barber is one of the most successful businessmen in town. He introduces himself as George Jones, and says he has a business proposition that could be financially lucrative for himself and his future investors. Needless to say, Goober and Floyd are all ears.

Mr. Jones begins to speak of the legend of Ross's Raiders and the alleged $100,000 in gold that is buried three miles outside of Mayberry, near Hopkins Creek. Floyd and Goober chuckle and tell Mr. Jones that folks have tried for years to locate the treasure. Mr. Jones impresses them by declaring that he has an authentic map detailing the spot where the treasure is buried. He claims that his great aunt, who died three months ago, was an ancestor of one of the raiders. This map was found hidden inside her family bible.

Before agreeing to invest $100 each, Floyd and Goober examine the map. It looks authentic enough to them. Mr. Jones says he would like to have three more investors, because renting the necessary digging equipment is costly. He says he wants to do the job right. Jones would keep 50 percent of the treasure, with Floyd, Goober, and the other investors splitting the remainder. The prospect of making $10,000 apiece is incentive enough for Floyd and Goober to invest. Together, they try to convince Andy to invest, but the wary sheriff wants no part of the venture. In fact, he warns his friends that they may get taken. Goober believes that Mr. Jones is on the up and up. He says, "If they've got a family bible, he's from good stock!"

Andy may be adamant about his refusal to invest, but Aunt Bee and Helen decide to take a gamble. Each becomes a $100 investor. Andy can only shake his head in disbelief. The ladies believe *they* will have the last laugh.

Unable to secure a fifth investor, Mr. Jones informs the others that they'll have to make do with only $400 worth of equipment, which he will bring to the digging site the following morning. Later in the evening, however, greed gets the best of Andy, and he, too, invests $100. He asks Mr. Jones to keep his participation a secret.

The next morning, Floyd and Goober patiently wait for Mr. Jones at the treasure site. He never appears. It is soon discovered that Jones purchased a one-way ticket to Miami, Florida, and left town with the money.

Aunt Bee, Helen, Floyd, and Goober are openly upset and also embarrassed that they were hood-

winked so easily. They hail Andy as the only one with any sense. If they only knew.....

Incidentally, Andy later receives word that Jones was captured in Miami as he got off the train. The money, $500, was all there and would be returned to Mayberry. Andy relates this to the investors, who are quite puzzled. $500! Just *who* was the fifth investor? Andy manages to mumble that, uh, he'll ask around.

CAST NOTES. Regulars: **Andy Griffith, Ronny Howard, Frances Bavier, Howard McNear, George Lindsey**, and **Aneta Corsaut**.

Roger Perry portrays con man George Jones. Perry portrayed Mr. Charles Parker on the long-running comedy series *The Facts of Life*. He also appeared as John Costello from 1982 to 1985 on the nighttime television serial *Falcon Crest*.

Dick Ryan portrays Mr. Wilson, who works at the Mayberry Depot.

EPISODE NOTES. 1. According to Andy, Ross's raiders were a group of men during the Civil War who showed allegiance to neither Union nor Confederate troops. They stole valuables from both sides. Once, they robbed a Union payroll train and took away over $100,000 in gold, which they promptly buried. They were later caught and sentenced to life in prison. Some believe that the ill-gotten booty is still buried. 2. Floyd, who was named after his mother's brother, is secretary of the Downtown Businessman's Club. 3. A candy shop in Mayberry is shown in this episode. 4. Goober and Floyd talk about what they'd do if they got a share ($10,000) of the treasure. Goober would likely buy his own gas station and hire someone to run it. He'd come by a couple of times a week to collect the profits. He would also purchase some fancy clothes, such as "one of those black suits that glistens when the sun hits it." Floyd would renovate his barbershop. He'd push out the shop in back and turn it into a five-chair affair. That would be "big time," he says. He does not care whether he could fill all the chairs, because he will still be the only barber in town.

"Dinner at Eight"

Episode #206. Air date: 1-9-67. Writer: Budd Grossman. Director: Lee Philips.

Aunt Bee is going to Raleigh for a couple of days to visit her sister, Ellen. Opie and his Boy Scout troop are going on an overnight camping trip. Andy is just looking forward to spending some time at home alone.

After dropping Opie off at Scoutmaster Stevens's

home, Aunt Bee asks Goober to look in on Andy from time to time. Unfortunately for Andy, Goober believes he has a better idea. He tells Andy he is going to stay with him so he won't feel lonely. Andy protests, but Goober insists on staying.

Opie returns home because he forgot his scout ax. As he and Goober hurriedly search for it, impatient Scoutmaster Stevens toots his car horn a few times. The situation becomes more frantic when Goober answers two phone calls (from Howard and Helen) in quick succession. He takes their messages, but fails to write them down. Meanwhile, Opie finally finds his ax (in his underwear drawer) and leaves.

Later, Andy comes home and discovers that Goober has made a splendid spaghetti supper. Goober claims to use a special secret ingredient in his spaghetti sauce, which he reveals to be oregano. Andy enjoys three helpings and is just about to retire to the living room when Goober remembers that Howard called. He tells Andy that Howard is expecting him to come over for supper. He also recalls that Helen called a Young People's Club meeting. Unfortunately, Goober has attributed the messages to the wrong people.

An annoyed Andy dutifully shows up at Howard's for supper. The Spragues, having just eaten, are unprepared for their surprise guest. However, Howard's mother warms up the leftovers and is able to serve Andy a hot plate of ... spaghetti. Mrs. Sprague tells Andy that her spaghetti sauce has a secret ingredient, and the recipe has been handed down through five generations of the Sprague family. Of course, the secret is that Greek spice known as oregano.

The well-fed sheriff returns home up to his eyeballs in spaghetti. He wants nothing more than to go to bed. However, Helen calls and is quite upset because Andy is over an hour late for supper. A sheepish Goober apologizes to Andy for the message mix-up. Andy's reaction is "Now, I'm going to Helen's and eat my *third* supper, and then I'm coming back ... and I'm going to *kill* you!" No jury would convict him.

Helen's Uncle Edward has been visiting her, and he tells Andy that his niece has prepared a fine spaghetti supper! Edward prepared the sauce, which just happens to contain a secret ingredient. It took Edward several hours to wheedle it out of a famous Italian chef in New York City. Needless to say, it's oregano. Andy picks at his food, claiming to be on a diet.

Meanwhile, Opie has suddenly returned home because his camping trip was rained out. Since Opie is hungry and there are no leftovers from supper, Goober phones Helen, who tells him to send the boy right over.

When Opie notices that Andy is not eating heartily, he reminds him that it is wrong to waste food. Andy had lectured him on that subject at breakfast. Trapped by his own philosophy and scrutinized by Helen and her Uncle Edward, Andy has no choice but to dig in.

When Aunt Bee gets back, she remarks that Andy looks as if he has not been eating well. She decides to prepare a quick and easy meal for him. Something tells us that's the last plate of spaghetti Andy will subject himself to for a long time to come.

CAST NOTES. Regulars: **Andy Griffith, Ronny Howard, Frances Bavier, George Lindsey, Jack Dodson,** and **Aneta Corsaut. Mabel Albertson** returns as Mrs. Sprague.

Emory Parnell, best known as Chester Riley's boss on *The Life of Riley,* portrays Helen's Uncle Edward.

EPISODE NOTES. 1. Aunt Bee's sister, Ellen, planned ahead for Aunt Bee's visit. First, she'll host a luncheon, then they'll attend a handicraft exhibit at the old people's home. After resting for an hour or two, they'll dine at the Armenian restaurant She-Bobs in Raleigh. Everything there is wrapped up in grape leaves. Ellen wants Aunt Bee to make a return visit when it's time for the Strawberry Festival. 2. Scoutmaster Stevens leads troop #44 (Opie's troop). He shows the boys how to keep warm by putting hot rocks in their sleeping bags. He was going to demonstrate how to make pancakes out of powdered eggs, oatmeal mix, and water over an outdoor fire, but it rained. Aunt Bee's comment: "As a cook, I think it was fortunate the rains came when they did!" 3. Andy purchases the following foods at the market: wild mushrooms, canned oysters, chili sauce, pickled avocados, chocolate syrup, and shrimp enchiladas. 4. Howard goes shopping for his mother. On his list: oatmeal, 2 quarts of whole milk, a dozen brown eggs, a container of yogurt, and three dozen oranges (his mother likes him to get plenty of vitamin C during the flu season). 5. Howard neglects to rinse the backs of just-washed plates. His late father had the same bad habit. 6. When Goober finds Andy play-acting in an old jacket, he asks him if he is rehearsing for another play at the lodge. 7. Aunt Bee packs five pairs of socks in Opie's scout pack, just in case the ground is damp. Mr. Stevens assured her that the troop would have occasional bivouacs (rest stops). 8. On the 1985 WTBS presentation *The Andy Griffith Show Silver Anniversary Show,* host Don Knotts announced that this episode was selected by George Lindsey as his all-time favorite.

"Andy's Old Girlfriend"

Episode #207. Air date: 1-30-67. Writer: Sid Morse. Director: Lee Philips.

Andy's old girlfriend, Alice Harper, who has been living in New York, returns to her hometown after a ten-year absence. She had planned to stay at a hotel while her old home was being cleaned and painted, but Aunt Bee insists that she stay in the guest room at the Taylors'. Andy is very happy to see her, and they reminisce about old times.

Helen gets upset when Andy introduces her to Alice as "Opie's schoolteacher." Later, Andy explains to Helen that there is nothing but friendship between him and Alice. To prove his point, he fixes up Alice with Howard, and the foursome spend an evening dining and dancing at Morelli's restaurant. Howard had a crush on Alice when they were in high school, but did nothing about it because she was Andy's girl.

The evening is such a smashing success that both couples agree they should get together more often. Alice suggests that they all spend a weekend at her family's cabin near the lake. Everyone likes the idea.

At the cabin, Andy finds it impossible to sleep, due to Howard's loud and continuous snoring. He decides to take a walk in the woods. There he runs into Alice, who, like Andy, couldn't sleep. Her reason was different, though. She says it was too quiet to sleep. Soon, Andy decides that they should return to the cabin. Alas, they lose all sense of direction and get lost.

Meanwhile, Howard and Helen have awakened to realize that their roommates are gone. Although nothing is said, both come to the conclusion that there is some hanky panky going on. They return to their rooms.

Andy and Alice do not find their way back to the cabin until 6:30 A.M. Alice treats the situation humorously, which annoys a deadly serious Andy. He asks her to follow his plan. They'll pretend that they woke up and decided to surprise Helen and Howard by preparing breakfast.

Of course, when Andy tells Helen that he slept "very soundly" during the night, she knows that he is lying. Howard quickly informs Andy that Helen knows he was out with Alice. Andy tries to tell Helen the entire truth, but she is in no mood to listen. Instead, she runs off into the woods. Suddenly finding herself lost, she begins to panic. By the time Andy comes to her rescue, she has realized that Andy's story just might be plausible after all.

CAST NOTES. Regulars: **Andy Griffith, Ronny Howard, Frances Bavier, Aneta Corsaut, George Lindsey,** and **Jack Dodson.**

Joanna McNeil guest-stars as Alice Harper.

EPISODE NOTES. 1. Andy and Alice remember the first time they went to the fair together and rode the ferris wheel. They got stuck on the very top, and a frightened Andy began screaming. 2. Once, Alice stood up in a canoe she and Andy were riding in. 3. Helen returns a muffin tin that she had borrowed from Aunt Bee. 4. Howard brushes his teeth with an electric toothbrush for 15 minutes in the morning and 15 minutes in the evening. When he sleeps, it's usually on his stomach. 5. Andy fixes corn flakes for breakfast. 6. Andy says he has known Helen for about five years and that she came from Kansas. 7. Goober had been reading spicy romantic stories, but he gave them up for science fiction.

"The Statue"

Episode #208. Air date: 2-20-67. Writer: Fred S. Fox. Director: Lee Philips.

The Mayberry Civic Improvement Committee, which consists of Howard, Andy, Aunt Bee, Floyd, Goober, and Clara Edwards, has $1200.00 to invest in a project. Howard, who serves as chairman, has an idea. He would like to have a statue erected and dedicated to the town's greatest benefactor. Clara suggests that Andy's great-great grandfather, Seth Taylor, deserves to be so honored. Howard had the same thought in mind. Andy and Aunt Bee are very flattered. Seth Taylor's accomplishments are legendary. He built the first sawmill, organized the Mayberry Chamber of Commerce, gave some of his land to Mayberry, and loaned the town money during the crisis of 1874.

All agree that Seth Taylor is the right choice ... that is, all but Floyd. He believes that his ancestor Daniel Lawson, Mayberry's first Indian agent, is more deserving. However, the majority rules, and the decision is final.

Howard appoints Aunt Bee as head of the Artistic Committee, and she pays a visit to a stone mason named Brian Jackson. Mr. Jackson will do the job for $1200.00, using old photographs of Seth as a guide. He works with a 5'7" block of granite, despite the fact that Seth was a taller man. Floyd, still arguing that his choice was best, announces that Daniel Lawson *was* that short.

The statue turns out beautifully. It is decided that a dedication ceremony will take place in front of town hall on the Mayberry Square. A proud Aunt Bee works on the speech she will give.

Not long before the grand unveiling, Mr. Simmons, head of the Simmons Seed Company of Mount Pilot, brings bad news to the Taylors. It seems that he has proof that Seth Taylor and *his* ancestor, Winston Simmons, were two of the biggest swindlers of the nineteenth century. He shares the proof with Andy and Aunt Bee, who are devastated by this revelation.

Aunt Bee agonizes over what to do. She decides that ruining Seth's fine reputation at this late date would serve no good purpose, and she attempts to deliver her speech. However, she bursts into tears halfway through, and Andy explains everything to the confused committee.

Ironically, it is Floyd who saves the day. He suggests that, if Seth Taylor had not made his unscrupulous business deals, Mayberry would have turned out to be an industrial boom town instead of the nice, peaceful community it is. Everyone agrees, and Aunt Bee is able to proudly continue her speech and oversee the unveiling of Mayberry's only statue.

CAST NOTES. Regulars: **Andy Griffith, Frances Bavier, Jack Dodson, Howard McNear, George Lindsey,** and **Hope Summers. Richard Collier** returns as Mr. Stuart Simmons. He first appeared, in the same role, in episode 203, "Only a Rose." **George Cisar** returns as Cyrus Tankersley.

Dal McKennon portrays Brian Jackson. McKennon co-starred as Cincinnattus on television's *Daniel Boone* from 1964 to 1970. He also provided the voice of Archie Andrews in several cartoon series.

EPISODE NOTES. 1. The Mayberry Women's Bridge Club meets in the Mayberry Town Hall. 2. Before the group decides on a statue, Clara suggests using the money to plant flowers in flower boxes and put them along the railings of the bridge over Parker Creek. This is on the main road from Raleigh. Andy says he'd like to rezone the property at the end of Main Street for commercial stores and development. Floyd opposes Andy's idea. He thinks there would be too much confusion and traffic. 3. Andy has Seth Taylor's chin and Opie has Seth's eyes, according to Aunt Bee and Clara. 4. Brian Jackson's business sign reads: "Brian Jackson — Stone Mason — Head Stones and Art Objects." According to Howard, Mr. Jackson creates over 90 percent of the tombstones used in the community. Mr. Jackson's wife ran off with a traveling man. 5. Seth Taylor's swindles involved convincing Mayberrians that a big railroad terminal was going to run through their town. Then, using political influence and bribery, he saw to it that the railroad would be put in Mount Pilot. He bought up land in Mayberry and then sold it at incredibly inflated prices. Next, he bought up land in Mount Pilot for next to nothing. This resulted in Mayberry's sister city becoming an industrial city of 30,000 people. Seth and his cohort, Winston Simmons, became millionaires. 6. Clara and Howard decide to declare an annual Seth Taylor Day. 7. Floyd claims that all the children in Mayberry (population 1,800) have good teeth. 8. Mayberrians believe their town is the garden city of the state.

"Aunt Bee's Restaurant"

Episode #209. Air date: 2-6-67. Writers: Ronald Axe and Les Roberts. Director: Lee Philips.

Aunt Bee is a very superstitious lady. She finds a "lucky" penny and decides to invest $400.00 to become a partner in a new Chinese restaurant venture with Charlie Lee. Together, they remodel the recently closed Spare Ribs Tavern restaurant, where Charlie cooked for the owner, Mr. Hendricks. They hire Charlie's nephew, Jack Lee, as the waiter. Jack is a Phi Beta Kappa student currently working on his master's degree in psychology at the University of North Carolina. Aunt Bee serves as hostess, while Charlie handles all the cooking duties.

"Aunt Bee's Canton Palace" opens and is a smashing success. Aunt Bee and Charlie take in over $80.00 on the first night of business. Andy, Helen, Goober, and Howard all feast on the Chinese cuisine, and Aunt Bee joins them after they finish their meal. Together, they are all given fortune cookies, including Aunt Bee. Their fortunes read as follows: Goober — "You are going to meet a tall handsome stranger"; Helen — "Spend the day with good friends"; Howard — "Be considerate of others, it will return many fold"; and Andy — "Try to avoid temptation in the coming week." Aunt Bee does not reveal her fortune and leaves the table in a hurry. Later that evening, Andy discovers that her fortune was "Beware of new business ventures, they can prove costly."

Being the superstitious type, Aunt Bee panics and starts to drive Charlie and Jack crazy with menu and decorative suggestions that are totally unnecessary. Finally, Andy persuades Aunt Bee to sell her share of the partnership. The new partner turns out to be none other than Jack Lee. Andy is surprised to discover that a college-educated person such as Jack decided to become a partner after opening a fortune cookie that said, "This is your lucky day."

CAST NOTES. Regulars: **Andy Griffith, Frances Bavier, Aneta Corsaut, George Lindsey,** and **Jack Dodson.**

Keye Luke, a veteran character actor and Charlie Chan's number one son in the movies, stars as Charlie Lee. **Lloyd Kino** portrays Jack Lee. **Jason Johnson** appears as "The Man" and **Ruth Thom** as "The Wife." Aunt Bee refers to her as Ella, so evidently her character was intended to be Ella Carson, as in episode 203, "Only a Rose." They were patrons at Aunt Bee's Canton Palace.

EPISODE NOTES. 1. When the Spare Ribs Tavern closed, Charlie Lee had planned to go back to his old hometown Pittsburgh and work at Wong Soo's Canton Palace. 2. Aunt Bee sings "My Chinatown" to Andy. She says it is one of her favorite tunes. 3. "Aunt Bee's Canton Palace" is located on Main Street in downtown Mayberry. 4. Howard is particularly fond of water chestnuts in his Chinese food. 5. On opening night at Aunt Bee's Canton Palace, Andy and his friends order the following dishes: Andy, Helen, and Goober go for the $1.95 Chow Mein dinner. Goober was going to opt for the smaller $1.65 Chow Mein dinner, until Andy said that he was picking up the tab. Howard orders the Ling Chi Chi (with only one Chi—a printer's error on the menu) chicken plate and a bowl of what Jack Lee refers to as a Chinese matzoth ball soup.

"Floyd's Barbershop"

Episode #210. Air date: 2-13-67. Writers: Jim Parker and Arnold Margolin. Director: Lee Philips.

Mayberry realtor Harry Walker received word that the Robinson family, former Mayberrians who now reside in California, are putting their Mayberry property up for sale. They own the building which has been the site of Floyd's Barbershop for the past 28 years. Naturally, Floyd begins to worry about his future. Whoever buys the building may not wish to keep him on as tenant. His worries disappear when Howard Sprague decides to purchase the property and continue the status quo. All Howard expects is a 5 percent profit on his investment.

Mr. Walker informs Howard that due to a new tax bill and increasing insurance premiums, he would be wise to raise Floyd's rent. Otherwise, he will not get a good return on his investment. But when Howard tells Floyd that his rent must be increased from $50.00 to $65.00 per month, Mayberry's only barber erupts with anger. He calls Howard a robber and a scavenger. He accuses him of trying to "crush the little man and drive him into the ground." Floyd vows to vacate the premises in 24 hours, and he tears up the lease.

Howard is discouraged and disappointed by his friend's reaction, but he realizes he must find a new tenant (preferably a barber). Meanwhile, because all the other buildings along Main Street are occupied, Floyd drives to Mount Pilot to research the possibility of opening a shop there.

Later, Floyd tells Andy he believes he's found a great place. The existing shop is located next to a Deli-Time Snack Bar and a pickle-bottling plant. The shop has two chairs, mirrors on both walls, and an automatic lather machine. Floyd says, "It's the big time!"

With no barbershop to loaf around in, Goober, Cyrus Tankersley, Mr. Schwump, and others use the courthouse as their gathering place, much to the dismay of Andy. Opie regrets the loss of the barbershop too, because Aunt Bee is bound and determined to cut his hair. Andy can find no place to do his paperwork because "the office is a checkers parlor and home is a barbershop."

Howard finds a potential buyer in a Mr. Coefield, who owns a chain of barbershops. Coefield is only interested in making a profit. He says he will fix the place up with stainless steel walls and mirrors and discard the much-used bulletin board and checkers table. He will not tolerate horseplay or idle visitors. He offers to pay $75.00 a month in rent, but Howard wants time to think things over.

Andy manages to bring Howard and Floyd together at the courthouse, under the pretense that he wants the men to shake hands and part on friendlier terms. Using a brilliant bit of reverse psychology, he tells both men they will each be better off financially. Then he denigrates the property by calling it "a stupid piece of real estate." Floyd and Howard start to defend the institution that was Floyd's Barbershop. Floyd recalls that it had a "homey touch" and Howard adds that the place had "atmosphere." They defend the town loafers as friends who filled the shop with good conversation and stimulating discussion. They lament that it is a shame to see things change. Suddenly, both men realize that things don't *have* to change. Howard offers to come down $7.50 on the rent, and Floyd agrees to go up $7.50. It's a deal! Floyd's Barbershop will remain a Mayberry landmark.

MEMORABLE SCENE. Andy getting defensive when Opie tells Aunt Bee how the men loaf around at Floyd's Barbershop.

CAST NOTES. Regulars: **Andy Griffith, Ronny Howard, Frances Bavier, Howard McNear, Jack Dodson,** and **George Lindsey. George Cisar** returns as Cyrus Tankersly.

Dave Ketchum, best known as undercover Agent 13 on *Get Smart,* portrays hard-line realtor Harry Walker. **James O'Rear** portrays prospective barbershop buyer Mr. Coefield. **William Challee** appears as a checkers-playing citizen.

EPISODE NOTES. 1. "The Mayberry Theme" is played at the beginning of this episode. 2. Goober drives to Mount Pilot to see a sexy foreign film, titled *La Vie des Femmes.* 3. Harry Walker's company is the Harry Walker Real Estate Company. Harry is a typical high-pressure salesman. He makes such dubious statements as "The aircraft industry has its eye on Mayberry." 4. Floyd has cut Andy's hair since Andy was a youngster. Floyd fondly recalls that young Andy used to mistake shaving cream for ice cream. 5. Goober and Cyrus Tankersly play checkers. Later, Andy plays Cyrus, and Cyrus plays a town loafer. 6. Floyd's Barbershop uses red and purple ceramic tile in the back room. 7. On the lease Howard has drawn up for Floyd, the rent increase is stated in clause #6. 8. Howard's "For Rent" sign says his phone number is Mayberry 397. 9. Goober states that there has not been any bad blood in Mayberry since "that Ferguson girl" beat up Harold Lovett. 10. Aunt Bee states that she used to cut her brother's hair years ago. 11. Desperate to avoid getting a haircut from Aunt Bee, Opie threatens to ride his bike to a barbershop in Mount Pilot. After all, it's only a six-hour ride from Mayberry. (Unless Opie's mighty slow on his bike, this suggests an inconsistency with the distance established in previous episodes. Both 68 and 126 place the distance at 12 miles.) 12. Mr. Schwump returns. this time he appears reading a newspaper inside the courthouse.

"A Visit to Barney Fife"

Episode #211. Air date: 1-16-67. Writers: Bill Idelson and Sam Bobrick. Director: Lee Philips.

Andy takes a bus to Raleigh to visit Barney, who is now a detective at the police bureau. He gives Andy a tour of the office, and the sheriff quickly realizes that Barney is not well respected by his peers. In fact, he seems to be little more than a glorified gofer.

Barney informs Andy that there will soon be a job opening at the bureau and encourages him to apply. Of course, Andy is quite satisfied with his current job.

Barney has moved from his corner room at the Y into a boarding house run by "Ma" Parker. He introduces Andy to Ma and her adult children, sons Leroy and Henny and beautiful daughter Agnes Jean, who likes to flirt with the former deputy.

While still at the bureau (or "the brain center," as Barney likes to say), Andy had learned that Raleigh is suffering a rash of supermarket robberies. Barney tells him that there must be a leak at the bureau, because every time a specific area is staked out, a robbery occurs elsewhere in the city. Andy becomes concerned when he hears Barney tell the Parker family details about planned police activities involving the robberies. Barney assures him that the family is just showing an interest in his work.

Barney tells Andy that he has made an appointment for him to meet with Captain Dewhurst and apply for a job. Andy candidly tells the captain that he is not interested in the position. He is shocked to discover that the job up for grabs is Barney's. Andy realizes that he must make Barney look good in the captain's eyes in order to save his job.

Andy becomes suspicious when he notices that the Parker clan goes shopping together late at night and return with very few items. When another robbery occurs at a southside supermarket, Andy tags along with Barney to the crime scene. (Barney mistakenly handcuffs the store manager.) Soon afterwards, Andy realizes that the stakeouts always fail because Barney unwittingly tips off the thieves: the Parker family!

Andy tricks the family into believing that the southside will no longer be the focus of the police's attention. He then convinces Barney to join him at (the southside) Super Bargain Market after closing hours. Barney thinks it's a waste of time, but sure enough, Andy's suspicions prove to be right, and a surprised Barney gets credit for the capture.

Thanks to Andy, Barney's job is saved, and he finally gets some much-needed respect from his peers.

CAST NOTES. Regular: **Andy Griffith. Don Knotts** returns in his third of five special appearances on the series, as Raleigh detective Barney Fife.

Veteran character actor **Richard X. Slattery**, who may be best known as "Murph" on the 76 Gasoline Station commercials, portrays Captain M.L. Dewhurst. Slattery was a New York City policeman for 12 years before pursuing a full-time acting career in 1958. Among his regular roles in a series are First Sergeant John McKenna in *The Gallant Men* (1963–1964), Captain John Morton on *Mr. Roberts* (1965–1966), and Commanding Officer Captain Buck Buckner on the Don Rickles series *C.P.O. Sharkey* (1977–1978). Slattery has appeared in several pilots and mini-series, including *Rich Man, Poor Man, Book II* and *Of Men, of Women*. He co-starred in the first pilot for *Wonder Woman* in 1974. He has guest-starred in dozens of series, including *Bewitched, Bonanza, Mayberry R.F.D., Mr. Terrific, No Time For Sergeants, The Odd Couple, The Partridge Family, Rawhide, Room 222,* and *The Waltons*. Slattery has made several motion pictures, including *Butterfield 8* (1960, with Elizabeth Taylor, who won an Oscar for her role), *The Boston Strangler* (1968), *The Secret War of Harry Frigg* (1968, with Paul Newman), *Walking Tall* (1973, with Joe Don Baker), *Herbie Rides Again* (1974, with Helen Hayes), and *The Apple Dumpling Gang Rides Again* (1979, starring Don Knotts and Tim Conway).

Betty Kean portrays Ma Parker. **Margaret Teele** appears as Agnes Jean Parker. **Richard Chambers** and **Gene Rutherford** portray, respectively, Henny and Leroy Parker. **Robert Ball** portrays Mr. Oldfield, manager of the Super Bargain Market. **Luana Anders** portrays Miss Clark, **Peter Madsen** appears as Mr. Peterson, and **Charles Horvath** portrays Al Jenkins. All three characters work with Barney.

EPISODE NOTES. 1. From his boarding house room window, Barney can get a glimpse of City Hall. His room features a private sink, a double bed, a real leather chair, and two pieces of art: "The Laughing Cavalier" and "Blue Boy." Barney's walls also feature his Mayberry High pennant and his framed *Mayberry Gazette* headline and story about his heroic cave rescue. (Refer to episode 109, "Barney and the Cave Rescue.") 2. Barney wears his salt and pepper suit throughout this episode. 3. Barney's "Manhunt Theme" is played after he captures the Parkers. 4. Barney once arrested a minister for loitering. The minister is currently threatening to sue him. 5. When Andy Griffith was in high school, his girlfriend was named Angie Jean. Is it a coincidence that the beautiful woman in this episode is called Agnes Jean?

"Barney Comes to Mayberry"

Episode #212. Air date: 1-23-67. Writer: Sid Morse. Director: Lee Philips.

Mayberry is buzzing with excitement because movie star Teena Andrews is returning to her hometown, where her new motion picture will be premiered. Teena was known as Irene Flogg before she went to Hollywood. She went to school with Andy and Barney back in her ugly duckling days.

Most of the townsfolk gather at the depot to await her train, and Andy is no exception. However, he's there to welcome home another passenger: Barney Fife. Barney is taking a few days' vacation from his detective job in Raleigh. He is totally unaware that Teena is on his train. (He mistakes the warm welcome from the crowd to be for him!) Andy fills him in on everything. Barney never realized that Teena Andrews used to be Irene Flogg, a girl he dated years ago. Andy suggests that they should drop by her room at the Mayberry Hotel and say hello.

Teena has little recollection of Barney and Andy, but her publicity agent, Harold Carson, suggests that she ask Barney to be her escort to the premiere. Needless to say, Barney is delighted. The premiere is a sold-out smash, and Barney is interviewed by a television reporter from station KNC at the event.

Afterward, back in Teena's hotel room, Barney tries to get romantic with the actress. His advances go unnoticed, mainly because Teena is quite tired. Besides, she has an early morning radio interview and needs her beauty sleep. She agrees to have lunch with Barney the next day. She ends the evening by giving him a big "thank you" kiss.

The next day, lovestruck Barney gets his heart broken when he discovers that Teena has left town. It seems she has flown back to California to be with her fiance. Andy tries to console his friend, but the dejected detective decides to cut his vacation short and return to Raleigh.

Upon his return to work, Barney discovers that two female receptionists have suddenly developed an interest in him. They saw the newspaper photo of him and Miss Andrews taken at the premiere. Things are finally looking up for Barney.

CAST NOTES. Regulars: **Andy Griffith, Ronny Howard, Frances Bavier, Aneta Corsaut,** and **George Lindsey. Don Knotts** makes his fourth special return appearance in the series. His fifth and final appearance will be in episode 240, "Barney Hosts a Summit Meeting." **Luana Anders** returns as Miss Clark, and **Patty Regan** returns as Renee. Both characters work with Barney.

Diahn Williams portrays Teena Andrews. She may be best known for her role as Terry in the television series *Harry's Girls.* She also made guest appearances in such series as *Get Smart* and *I Spy.* She was also featured in the 1976 movie *Deadly Hero.*

Chet Stratton appears as publicist Harold Carson. **Christine Burke** appears as Teena's secretary, Harriet. **Steve Dunne** portrays a television reporter who interviews Barney and others at the premiere. Dunne hosted the game show *Truth or Consequences* before Bob Barker took over. **Ollie O'Toole** appears as the man seated next to Barney on the train. **Mary Lou Taylor** also appears.

EPISODE NOTES. 1. The Mayberry Band plays "The Mayberry Theme" as Barney's train pulls into the depot. 2. Barney wears his salt and pepper suit throughout much of the episode. He wears a double-breasted tuxedo to the movie premiere. He rented it from Giggleheimer's. 3. Andy refers to Barney as "Ol' Tiger Fife." 4. According to Andy, the train only comes through Mayberry once a day. 5. Andy used to help Irene Flogg with her homework. 6. Miss Andrews stays in room #7 at the Mayberry Hotel. Her publicist, Harold Carson, and her secretary, a lady named Harriet, stay at the hotel, too. 7. While making dinner reservations, Barney asks the maitre d' to put a bottle of the restaurant's best red wine on ice. He is informed that red wine is traditionally served at room temperature. 8. The episode ends with a brief exchange between Aunt Bee and Andy. Both admit they miss Barney, and Andy says, "I guess there's just one Barney Fife."

"Helen the Authoress"

Episode #213. Air date: 2-27-67. Writer: Doug Tibbles. Director: Lee Philips.

Helen Crump has written a book titled "Amusing Tales of Tiny Tots." Roger Bryant, the head of the Bryant Publishing Company in Richmond, has contacted her about publishing the book. He even sends her an advance of $1,000.00 in order to obtain the exclusive rights to her book. Needless to say, Helen is ecstatic. She asks Andy to accompany her on the trip to see Mr. Bryant in Richmond.

At the publishing company, Mr. Bryant introduces Helen to cover designer Robling Flask and to Harold Mosby, "the best promotion man in the business." All are impressed by her work, and Roger Bryant even mentions the possibility of a complete series of books. But two problems suddenly arise. First, all of the men at the publishing company either ignore Andy or refer to him as "Sandy" and "Taylor Sanders." Second, they tell Helen that the name "Crump" will have to be changed. Harold Mosby comes up with a pen name for her: "Helene Alexion Dubois."

Later, Andy gets mad when Floyd, Goober, and Howard kid him about how Helen will support him after they are married. He is also distressed because Helen becomes so involved in rewriting parts of the book that Andy becomes little more than her servant. When she tells him that she and Roger Bryant will be working on the book for one straight week, the normally composed sheriff explodes in anger. This is the proverbial straw that broke the camel's back.

In retaliation, Andy asks Mavis Neff, who works at the drugstore, for a date. Mavis has quite a reputation for being forward. In fact, Floyd tells Howard that when Harvey Bunker was dating her, he was asked to give up his job as scoutmaster. Andy and Mavis end up at the diner, where they run into Helen and Roger Bryant. Mavis falls all over Andy, and Helen leaves in anger.

Later that evening, Andy stops at Helen's house and apologizes. He also explains why he had gotten so upset. They make up, and everything returns to normal. Helen's book inspires Aunt Bee to begin writing a cookbook, and even Opie starts working on a book entitled "What It's Like to Be the Son of a Sheriff."

CAST NOTES. Regulars: **Andy Griffith, Ronny Howard, Frances Bavier, Howard McNear, Aneta Corsaut, George Lindsey,** and **Jack Dodson.**

Keith Andes stars as Roger Bryant. Andes appeared in such movies as *The Farmer's Daughter* (1947) and *Tora! Tora! Tora!* (1970). He also appeared with Glynis Johns in the 1963 television comedy *Glynis*.

Laurie Main portrays Robling Flask. Main succeeded the late Sebastian Cabot as the narrator of the *Winnie the Pooh* cartoons, specials, and recordings.

Tom Palmer appears as Harold Mosby. **Kathrin Victor** appears as Roger Bryant's secretary, Miss Fain. **Diane Deininger** also appears.

Elaine Joyce turns in a very funny performance as the "Marilyn Monroe" of Mayberry, Mavis Neff. Joyce was married to entertainer Bobby Van and was a regular on *The Don Knotts Show* in 1970 and 1971. She also appeared with Knotts in the 1971 feature film *How to Frame a Figg* and with Rory Calhoun in the 1980 cult movie classic *Motel Hell*.

EPISODE NOTES. 1. Andy states that the name of Crump carries a lot of class in the state of Kansas. 2. Goober says that Potter's Cave is a tourist site in Mayberry. 3. During this episode, the high school in Mayberry is being sandblasted. 4. Howard enjoys putting raw eggs in his malted milkshakes. 5. A full page ad about Helen and the book appears in the *Mount Pilot Bugle and Sun*. 6. Mavis Neff claims that root beer floats make her "bubbly wubbly" all over. 7. In *Best Bets*, a television magazine, Andy spots a documentary about forest rangers that he and Helen plan to watch. After that, they plan on watching an Eddie Bracken movie.

"Goodbye, Dolly"

Episode #214. Air date: 3-6-67. Writers: Michael L. Morris and Seaman Jacobs. Director: Lee Philips.

Mayberry's milkman, Walt Simpson, has delivered milk for many years using a wagon pulled by a horse named Dolly. When Walt's company, Dogwood Dairy Farms, informs him that, for the sake of efficiency, Dolly will be replaced by a truck, the milkman decides to buy the horse from the company.

Walt informs the Taylors that Ben Curtis will take over deliveries for 4 or 5 days while he vacations near Raleigh with his brother. He asks Opie to feed Dolly for him and offers to pay the boy $5.00

for his efforts. Opie is eager to accept, but Andy reminds him about the time when he was a newspaper boy. It seems that Opie turned his interest to football and Andy ended up delivering the papers. Opie vows to be responsible, and Andy maintains a "wait and see" attitude.

Opie runs into trouble on his first trip to Walt's farm. Dolly absolutely refuses to eat. Goober, who is in the area fixing Earl Foster's fuel pump, stops by to see what's going on. After Opie fills him in, Goober tells the boy that he once had a canary named Louise who also refused to eat. Figuring that Louise was lonesome, Goober put a mirror in her cage, and it worked like a charm. Goober finds a mirror in the barn, and he allows Dolly to see her reflection (which Goober refers to as "Old Paint"). Unfortunately, this tactic doesn't work on Dolly. Opie has to give up for a while or be late for school.

The next day, Opie tempts the horse with an apple and then some sugar, but Dolly still refuses to eat.

Howard Sprague tells Opie that he once had a pony named Fido who would only eat in the afternoon. Opie is anxious to see if Dolly might do the same, but Andy reminds him that first he must mow the lawn. Opie offers to pay his friend Arnold a quarter if he will try to feed Dolly. Arnold agrees to do it, but for 65 cents.

Opie is upset when Arnold brings Dolly to the Taylors' house. Dolly didn't eat, and Arnold says she felt warm to him. Actually, he's scared the horse will die. When Arnold was younger, he had a cat that wouldn't eat, and it died after only three days.

Opie decides to try to hide Dolly in the garage, hoping that no one will discover her. However, during supper, Dolly makes a ruckus, and Opie has to spill the beans. Andy wants to take Dolly home immediately, but Aunt Bee believes that the horse may be ill. Dolly stays overnight, and Doctor Roberts pays a visit the next morning. He says that Dolly is quite healthy. Aunt Bee wonders if Dolly just simply misses Walt.

When Walt returns, Dolly still refuses to eat. Everyone is puzzled, until Opie sees the old girl backing up to her old wagon. Suddenly, Walt realizes that Dolly misses her job. Unfortunately, the old horse-drawn wagon days are gone, but Opie comes up with a great solution. He attaches one end of a long rope to the back of Walt's dairy truck and the other end to Dolly's harness. The next time we see Walt, he's driving his truck slowly, and a happy Dolly trails behind, believing she still plays a major role in the dairy business.

Dolly is back to her old self. In fact, she is eating like a horse.

CAST NOTES. Regulars: **Andy Griffith, Ronny**

Howard, Frances Bavier, George Lindsey, and **Jack Dodson. Sheldon Golomb** returns as Arnold Bailey.

Charles P. Thompson returns to the series, this time as Dr. Roberts. **Tom Tully,** who played Matt Grebb in television's *The Line-Up,* appears here as Walt Simpson.

EPISODE NOTES. 1. Goober claims that a horse can live off its fat for seven days. Also, he tells Opie that when he was a boy, a day's work consisted of rising before daylight, chopping the neighbors' kindling, feeding chickens, slopping hogs, delivering groceries for the general store, sweeping up, and pumping gas at his daddy's gas station. He was paid a quarter per day. He quit after the first day. 2. Aunt Bee took Clara's advice and put just a touch of nutmeg in her apples as they cooked. This made for a tasty apple pie. 3. Sally Higgins is a friend of Aunt Bee's. 4. One of the Taylors' next door neighbors is Fred Hartley. 5. Opie refuses to accept any payment from Mr. Simpson. 6. Howard is looking forward to retirement. He has an annuity that pays off when he is 60 years old. He tells Andy and Goober what a typical day for him will be when that time comes. He'll wake up, have breakfast, read the paper, putt around the garden a bit, have lunch at the diner, spend a couple of hours visiting friends, go home, read the evening paper, have dinner, and go to bed. When Howard realizes how dull this sounds, it appears that he is going to reconsider his retirement plans.

"Opie's Piano Lesson"

Episode #215. Air date: 3-13-67. Writers: Leo and Pauline Townsend. Director: Lee Philips.

Clara Edwards has given piano lessons to youngsters for many years. Aunt Bee informs Andy that one of Clara's students, young Douglas Lewis, has just moved to Raleigh with his family, thus freeing Miss Edwards to take on another student. Aunt Bee tells Andy that he should encourage Opie to take Clara's twenty-lesson course. Andy believes that his son would not be interested in taking piano lessons. He reasons that boys like to spend their time fishing, playing football, and fooling around. But, to satisfy Aunt Bee, Andy does ask his son if he'd be interested in taking the course. He is surprised when Opie answers yes. Andy makes him promise to devote himself to the lessons and to practicing.

Clara gives Opie two lessons per week and tells him he must practice two hours every day. Opie's practice hours are from 3:30 P.M. to 5:30 P.M.

Opie's football team is introduced to Flip Conroy, a famous ex-pro football player. Flip has returned to Mayberry to work in his father's business. He has agreed to coach the team in his spare time. Opie and his teammates are excited, but Flip insists that they come to practice for two hours a day after school. Opie has a problem. How can he be two places at once? He tries to get out of piano practice by telling his father that he needs a month or so to limber up his fingers. Andy tells him that piano practice is the best way to do that.

Opie tries to devote time to both activities, but Coach Conroy gets annoyed when the boy shows up late for practice. At one point, when Opie doesn't show up for practice, the coach sends a group of his players to give the budding Liberace an ultimatum: Come to practice or quit the team. Opie explains his problem to his pals. His friend Arnold, the team's manager, is very sympathetic and comes up with a temporary solution. He will play the piano while Opie goes to football practice. Arnold took lessons from Miss Edwards some time ago. Because he is merely the manager, his presence at practice is not very important. But it *is* important to have someone play piano because Aunt Bee, who is next door making a quilt with Mrs. Edna Sue Larch, is always listening for Opie's practicing.

Upon hearing the well-played music, Aunt Bee is surprised. Opie's sour notes had driven her to distraction before, and she can hardly believe the improvement. She decides she will go home and praise her nephew.

Andy arrives home before she does and, upon seeing Arnold, demands an immediate explanation. Arnold opts to go get Opie instead. As Opie rushes home, Arnold fills Coach Conroy in on everything.

Andy expresses his disappointment to Opie. He tells him that there are more important things than football, and orders him to stick with piano practice. Just then, Coach Conroy stops by and suggests that it is possible for Opie to pursue both activities. To prove his point, Flip sits down at the piano and plays it expertly!

The solution proves to be a simple rescheduling. From now on, Opie will practice the piano *before* school. This works out great for Opie and the team. When Opie tells his father, during his 6:00 A.M. practice, "There's time for everything!" a groggy Andy replies, "Except sleep!"

CAST NOTES. Regulars: **Andy Griffith, Ronny Howard, Frances Bavier,** and **Hope Summers. Sheldon Golomb** returns as Arnold Bailey. **Maudie Prickett** returns as Mrs. Edna Sue Larch.

Rockne Tarkington portrays Coach Flip Conroy. Mr. Tarkington portrayed Rao, the village veterinarian, on television's *Tarzan* from 1966 to 1968.

He also appeared in a recurring role on *Matt Houston*.

Richard Bull portrays Mayberry Junior High School teacher Mr. Jackson. Mr. Bull portrayed the doctor on the television cult favorite *Voyage to the Bottom of the Sea* from 1964 through 1968. He may be best known for his role of Nels Oleson on *Little House on the Prairie* from 1974 through 1983.

Johnny Jenson appears as Tim, the back-up quarterback on Opie's team. **Kirk Travis** appears as Opie's teammate, Joey. **Chuck Campbell** appears as an unnamed teammate.

EPISODE NOTES. 1. When Aunt Bee insists that knowing how to play the piano can make a person popular, Andy remarks that, when he was a boy, the most popular kid was Harvey Belfast. Harvey couldn't tell the difference between the songs "Let's Have Another Cup of Coffee" and "Tea for Two." 2. Aunt Bee says that the first requirement of a piano player is that he must have clean hands. 3. The Taylors' piano needs to be tuned. Aunt Bee hopes to catch piano tuner Mr. Higby the next time he passes through town. 4. Flip Conroy played college football before playing for ten years with the New York Giants. 5. Opie is both the quarterback and captain of his football team. 6. Black performers had been cast as extras in other episodes of *The Andy Griffith Show*, but this episode is the first and only one to feature a black actor.

"Howard the Comedian"

Episode #216. Air date: 3-20-67. Writers: Michael Morris and Seaman Jacobs. Director: Lee Philips.

Andy, Floyd, and Goober believe that Howard Sprague is the funniest man in town. Howard recently served as master of ceremonies at the Lodge Banquet. His jokes had the entire lodge membership rolling in the aisles. Floyd tells Howard that he should pursue comedy as a career. Howard modestly remarks that he is quite content serving as Mayberry's county clerk.

Andy, Aunt Bee, and Opie watch an amateur talent show called "Colonel Tim's Talent Time." It airs weekly, originating live from studio WASG in Raleigh. After hearing Andy rave about Howard's jokes, Opie remarks that Mr. Sprague should be on the program. Andy tries to encourage his friend to do that, but Howard is reluctant.

A curious Howard finds some jokes in a book titled *Jokes for All Occasions*, and he tries a few on Opie. Somehow, they sound stale and lifeless. Opie suggests he try personalizing the jokes, and suddenly, Howard has an angle. He uses the citizens of Mayberry as the butt of his jokes.

Andy accompanies Howard to the television studio in Raleigh. The show will be seen throughout North Carolina. Aunt Bee, Opie, Floyd, Goober, and Clara gather around the Taylors' television set, anxious to see Howard knock 'em dead. By the time he finishes his unintentional attack on his friends, however, the only person left laughing is Opie. Andy congratulates Howard and tells him he's liable to be the toast of the town back home. Instead, Howard gets the cold shoulder from most of his friends, even though he tries to explain that he did not intend to offend anyone. No one appreciates being used as material for his jokes.

This is all very upsetting to Howard, but as he worries alone, something happens that changes the attitudes of his friends. Suddenly, strangers passing through town seek out Andy, Goober, and Floyd. They mention that they saw Howard on television and decided they just had to meet the people he spoke about. Floyd and Goober are very flattered and excited about being famous. Meanwhile, Aunt Bee receives calls from several friends from whom she hadn't heard in years. Clara gets a telegram inviting her to address the Ladies' Historical Society of Summitville. Both ladies are delighted.

Howard, unaware of this change among his friends, calls them to come together. He makes a formal apology and informs them that he has decided to cancel a scheduled return appearance on "Colonel Tim's Talent Time." He is very surprised when everyone encourages him to go back to the show and perform with a clear conscience. In fact, they begin to provide him with material about themselves! The "Merry Madcap of Mayberry" just may have a new career ahead of him.

CAST NOTES. Regulars: **Andy Griffith, Ronny Howard, Frances Bavier, Jack Dodson, Howard McNear, Hope Summers,** and **George Lindsey.**

Dick Haynes, who starred in the 1945 Rodgers and Hammerstein musical *State Fair*, appears as Colonel Tim. **Dick Curtis,** a veteran of many western movies and a regular on *The Jonathan Winters Show*, portrays Bill Hollenbeck. **Tol Avery,** who once played Mayberry's Ben Weaver, appears here as a man passing through town.

EPISODE NOTES. 1. Goober refers to Howard as "Mayberry's #1 comedian." 2. Howard says that his Uncle Carl had a good sense of humor. 3. According to Floyd, Harry Blake is going to ask Howard to perform at the Elks Club in Mayberry for the annual Hijinks Show. 4. A man named Nevin Thorpe appears on "Colonel Tim's Talent time." He is a one-man band and plays a poor rendition of "The Blue Danube." Also appearing on the program are Agnes Jean Babcott, who twirls her baton to "When the Saints Go Marching In"; a boy soprano; and a gentleman from Fayetteville who tells jokes. 5. Colonel Tim takes credit for launching the careers of the following folks: Ossie Snake, Rosa Mae Johnson, and Jughead Peters and His Aristocrats. 6. Colonel Tim's sign-off is "Well, it's 'bye for now and bless you all." 7. The book *Jokes for All Occasions* was compiled by a person with the surname of Pepe. 8. Opie renews his bicycle license for fifty cents a year. 9. Before Howard leaves for Raleigh, Floyd gives the comedian a trim, while Goober waxes his blue station wagon. After the program, Floyd tells Howard he should get his next haircut from "that poodle trimmer in Mount Pilot." 10. Howard nervously calls Colonel Tim "Captain Tom" and "Colonel Tom." 11. Aunt Bee receives telephone calls from Mabel Pollack, Billy Sensibaugh, and Charles Humboldt. 12. Floyd tells a stranger that he supplies Howard with much of his material. Floyd asks the man if he has heard the one about the zebra that fell in love with a pair of pajamas. 13. Colonel Tim introduces Howard as "the Merry Madcap of Mayberry." 14. "The Mayberry Theme" is played as Howard takes the stage.

"Big Brother"

Episode #217. Air date: 3-27-67. Writer: Fred S. Fox. Director: Lee Philips.

The local Sheriff's Association is becoming involved in promoting a Big Brother program. This involves asking responsible adult males to help out underprivileged or misguided boys by befriending them and providing them with good role models. Howard Sprague volunteers, and school principal John Tracy pairs him with a bright but undisciplined young man named Tommy Parker. Tommy and his older sister, Betty, live in Mayberry, and their parents travel with a carnival seven months out of the year.

Howard's initial meeting with Tommy does not go well. He tries to talk baseball with him, but the young man realizes that his Big Brother has no expertise on the subject. Because Howard is studying to take a civil service exam, he informs Tommy that they will be studying together three nights per week.

Howard meets Tommy's pretty sister and is immediately attracted to her. Betty works as a professional dancer at the Embassy Dance Hall in Mount Pilot. Tommy notices Howard's attraction to Betty and decides to use it to his advantage. He makes a point of telling Howard that Betty has to commute by bus every night she works. He claims it is a torturous commute to Siler City, where Betty must catch a second bus to Mount Pilot. Howard is sympathetic.

After a few meetings, Tommy tells Howard that he will be glad to study alone, if Howard would give his sister a ride to work. Assured that Tommy will hit the books, Howard hits the road with Betty. He then spends the entire evening dancing with Betty in Mount Pilot. Tommy spends the evening loafing around at home. This becomes an established routine.

After a few weeks, Mr. Tracy informs Andy that Tommy's grades have not improved. This puzzles Andy, because he believes Howard has been doing all he can to help the youngster. He soon discovers, by way of Sarah, the switchboard operator, that Howard has been spending all of his free time at the Embassy Dance Hall. An angry and disappointed Andy confronts Howard there. Howard makes a feeble attempt to rationalize his behavior, but the enraged sheriff abruptly ends the conversation by refusing to accept his excuses.

The next day, after being informed by his sister about the dance hall confrontation, Tommy pays Andy a visit. He confesses that he took advantage of Howard's infatuation with Betty in order to get out of studying. He admits he is saddened and confused to see how a man like Howard Sprague could so easily lose sight of his goals.

Andy confronts Howard again and lets him have it with both barrels. Howard really does regret his negligent behavior.

Ironically, the situation ultimately has a positive effect on Tommy, who becomes determined to study and not lose sight of his goals. Before long, his grades are vastly improved. Meanwhile, Howard continues to see Betty, but not at the dance hall. They study together at the Mayberry library.

CAST NOTES. Regulars: **Andy Griffith, Jack Dodson, Howard McNear,** and **George Lindsey.**

Peter Hobbs, who essayed the role of patriarch Peter Ames on the long-running serial *The Secret Storm*, portrays principal John Tracy.

Elizabeth MacRae, who is most remembered for her role as Gomer Pyle's girlfriend, Lou Anne Poovey, on *Gomer Pyle, U.S.M.C.*, portrays Betty Parker. Her melodic voice can also be heard in the 1964 Don Knotts film *The Incredible Mr. Limpet* as Lady Fish. She appeared with Gene Hackman in the 1974 film *The Conversation.*

Scott Lane portrays Tommy Parker. He had the costarring role of cadet Gary McKeever in the television series *McKeever and the Colonel.*

EPISODE NOTES. 1. Goober says he was an only child. 2. Floyd and Goober think the Big Brother program is a good idea. In fact, they offer to volunteer. 3. Howard mistakenly refers to the St. Louis Dodgers, meaning to say the Los Angeles Dodgers. Then, he refers to the St. Louis Orioles, meaning to say the St. Louis Cardinals. Later, he reads a sports magazine and discovers that former St. Louis Cardinal Stan Musial had a lifetime batting average of .344.

"Opie's Most Unforgettable Character"

Episode #218. Air date: 4-3-67. Writers: Michael Morris and Seaman Jacobs. Director: Lee Philips.

Opie and his classmates are assigned to write an essay about the most unforgettable character they have known. Opie has trouble deciding who to write about until Aunt Bee suggests that Andy would be an ideal subject. The boy agrees and decides to spend a full day observing his father at work. Unfortunately, he discovers that Andy's average day is rather uneventful. Opie notes that his father beat Goober two games out of three in checkers, bawled Floyd out for sweeping his customer's hair clippings onto the street, and changed the ribbon in his typewriter.

Aunt Bee advises Opie to write about his father's philosophy. Opie questions Andy about his outlook on life and receives a glib reply. After Aunt Bee informs Andy that he is his son's most unforgettable character, the proud father gives Opie a more thoughtful answer. His philosophy is, "Do unto others as you would have them do unto you."

Andy is anxious to hear how Opie does on his paper. His son usually receives good grades in English, and Andy believes a story about himself will do very well. However, he is crushed when he discovers that Opie got an F. He questions Helen Crump about the paper, and he gets upset when she informs him that the poor grade was due to the lackluster content rather than any grammatical errors. Opie will have to do a rewrite.

Determined to give Opie something to write about, Andy tells him that he once earned a dollar for catching a wildcat with his bare hands. To Andy's chagrin, Aunt Bee adds that the poor animal was so ill, it could barely walk.

Later, Andy impresses Opie by recounting his days as a pitcher on his high school baseball team. One year, he sustained a broken middle finger on his throwing hand that never set right. It left him with a crooked finger and caused him to change his grip. He developed a hard-to-hit pitch which he dubbed "the wobble ball." He threw a no-hitter against Mount Pilot. Goober remarks that Mayberry *lost* that game 10 to 0 because Andy walked 17 men.

While glancing at a horsefly through his microscope, Opie gets an idea. He decides to write his paper on Dr. Lou Bailey, the father of his friend Arnold. Ironically, and unbeknownst to Andy, Arnold writes his paper on Sheriff Taylor.

Andy is thrilled when he discovers that Opie got an A on his rewrite, until he learns that he was not the subject. But his ego is soothed a bit when Arnold reveals that Andy is *his* most unforgettable character. By the way, Arnold got an A too.

Opie tells his father that he discovered that when you write about people you are close to, somehow it comes sounding sort of sissy. Andy understands.

CAST NOTES. Regulars: **Andy Griffith, Ronny Howard, Frances Bavier, Aneta Corsaut, Jack Dodson,** and **George Lindsey. Sheldon Golomb** returns as Arnold Bailey.

Joy Ellison returns, this time as a young girl named Betsy.

EPISODE NOTES. 1. Prior to suggesting Andy as an interesting subject for Opie, Aunt Bee suggests he write about egg man Mr. Bristol or Howard Sprague. (Mr. Bristol talks to his chickens as if they were people. Howard single-handedly reorganized Mayberry's entire sewer system.) Andy suggested that Goober might make a good subject. (Opie started a paper on Goober, but its 42 words fell far short of the required 500-word essay.) 2. Aunt Bee says that Andy has the most exciting job in town and that he is certainly a colorful man. Andy says he was a "devil-may-care young scalawag" when he was Opie's age. 3. Otis Campbell has been doing his drinking in Mount Pilot of late. 4. Andy says that the last time he fired one of his police rifles was when he started a potato sack race at a church picnic. 5. Andy refers to Lucy Burnett's Dry Goods Store in Mayberry. 6. Goober recently enjoyed his finest weekend of fishing. He caught 7 perch and 6 large-mouth bass. 7. Opie uses Andy's old piggy bank. Andy recalls the first dollar he ever put into it. It was the bounty that the county paid him for catching the wildcat. 8. In this episode, Floyd's Barbershop is *not* located adjacent to the courthouse.

"Goober's Contest"

Episode #219. Air date: 4-10-67. Writers: Ron Friedman and Pat McCormick. Director: Lee Philips.

After a silly dispute over tire inflation with Goober, Floyd vows never to patronize Wally's Fill-

ing Station again. Besides, Floyd has found another gas station, one that has a contest called "Line-Up for Loot." (He won $4.00 there.) Wally notices a decline in business because several of his competitors are having such contests.

Wally decides to put Goober in charge of a similar giveaway. The contest will be called "Grab-Bag for Cash." A total of $200.00 will be given away. There will be twenty $2.00 winners, twenty $3.00 winners, fourteen $5.00 winners, and just three $10.00 winners. Unfortunately, when Goober writes down the amount of the prizes, he writes the total down, too. Hammond's Print Shop surmises that $200.00 is the grand prize. Mr. Hammond and his apprentice, Joe, print up the winning cards, along with losing ones that say, "Better luck next time." All the cards are then put in envelopes and delivered to Wally's.

The contest works like a charm. Wally's is as busy as ever, and there have been several winners. After Aunt Bee wins $5.00, Andy decides to try to talk Floyd into coming back to Wally's. Floyd is stubborn, and when he does return, he tells Goober that he only came back because of a civic obligation.

One envelope is awarded per five-gallon purchase of gasoline. Floyd gets three envelopes. When he opens them back at his barbershop, he is ecstatic. One of his cards is the $200.00 winner. He gives the winning ticket to Andy and asks him to tell Goober he'll be over later to pick up his money.

When Goober discovers his horrendous error, he is panic-stricken. He explains his dilemma to Andy, who advises him to tell Floyd the truth. Goober realizes he must face the music. When he does, Floyd angrily accuses him of running a fraudulent contest. He demands that the prize be awarded or he will take his case to the highest court in the land. Unfortunately, Wally cannot afford to honor the ticket.

The situation looks hopeless until Andy comes up with an idea: He arrests Goober and jails him. Floyd is shocked when he sees his old friend behind bars, wailing away on his harmonica. He is immediately sympathetic. In fact, he even offers to put up bail money to free him. Aunt Bee becomes irate when she sees the drastic measure Andy has taken. She and Floyd demand that Goober be freed at once. Andy complies with their wishes. As Floyd says, "The boy just made an honest mistake."

CAST NOTES. Regulars: **Andy Griffith, Ronny Howard, Frances Bavier,** and **George Lindsey. Howard McNear** appears for the last time as Floyd Lawson.

Rob Reiner appears as Joe, the typesetter at Hammond's Print Shop. Reiner is the son of movie director Carl Reiner, the creator of *The Dick Van Dyke Show*. Rob first gained widespread recognition when he landed the role of Michael "Meat Head" Stivic on *All in the Family*. The Emmy award–winning actor turned his attention to directing motion pictures in the 1980s. Among his outstanding directorial achievements are *Stand By Me, This is Spinal Tap, Misery*, and *A Few Good Men*.

Owen Bush returns. This time he is Mr. Hammond, the print shop owner. **Edgar Hess** portrays one of the participants in Goober's contest.

EPISODE NOTES. 1. Goober suggests calling the contest "Goober's Gusher of Gold," but Wally nixes the idea. 2. Andy strikes out with his three envelopes. 3. When Aunt Bee wins $5.00, she states that she has never won anything in her life. Apparently she has forgotten the truckload of prizes she won on the "Win or Lose" game show in episode 165, "Aunt Bee on TV." 4. Opie has seen Floyd's stubborn side. For a year now, he has tried to get the barber to part his hair on the left side, as Andy parts *his*. Floyd has refused because he says it would not fit Opie's facial contour. 5. Floyd looks through a barber catalog and orders an automatic wash-and-dry shampooer with a patented foam-free rinse control. He says it will "bring shampooing into the 20th century." 6. According to Andy, a tornado hit Mayberry about 12 years ago. Goober refers to the 1955 tornado, too. 7. Before Goober breaks the bad news to Floyd, he is offered a free haircut and a shampoo. Floyd promises to use a sweet-smelling shampoo that will make him smell like "Morris" (Maurice) Chevalier. 8. Aunt Bee's license plate number is GP-780. 9. Goober plays "If I Had the Wings of an Angel" on his harmonica. 10. Opie congratulates his father for his wisdom in scheming to resolve the contest problem. He compares Andy to the biblical King Solomon.

SEASON EIGHT

The Andy Griffith Show ends its eight-season run on a high note, ranked number one by the A.C. Nielsen company. Barney Fife makes a triumphant final guest appearance, and farmer-turned-councilman Sam Jones and his son, Mike, are introduced. They (and much of the cast) would be featured in the spinoff series, *Mayberry R.F.D.*, which enjoyed good ratings during its three season run. A.C. Nielsen Co. rating for the 1967-1968 season: 27.6; rank: 1.

"Opie's First Love"

Episode #220. Air date: 9-11-67. Writers: Ron Friedman and Pat McCormick. Director: Lee Philips.

Opie is excited about Arnold's thirteenth birthday party. Young Mr. Bailey's parents are allowing him to have a big "stag or drag" party. "Stag" means coming to the party alone, while "drag" means you bring a girl, according to Opie. Arnold plans to ask his classmate Iris to be his date. When Aunt Bee asks Opie who he will take, Andy interrupts by saying, "Mary Alice Carter." Opie has been stuck on her since the first grade. Andy teases his son about her, but Opie asks him to stop. He says she is one of his "touchy areas."

Since he has never asked a girl out, Opie is very nervous about approaching Mary Alice. When he does, she cuts him off before he can ask her out. She makes up an excuse to leave. Opie is confused.

Over the next three days, Mary Alice avoids talking with Opie. She tells her friend Iris that she is hoping that another classmate, Fred Simpson, will ask her first. When he does not, she approaches Opie and accepts his invitation. Needless to say, he is thrilled.

Opie asks Andy if he will buy him a new suit and a pair of oxblood loafers to wear at the party. Andy is more than happy to comply. Mayberry clothier Doyle Perkins outfits Opie with a lightweight blue suit.

The party approaches, and Opie calls Mary Alice to tell her that Andy and Helen will be taking them to the party in the squad car. Moments after the call, however, Fred Simpson drops by Mary Alice's house and asks her to be his date. She accepts, despite Iris's concern about how Opie will take the news.

Mary Alice calls Opie and tells him that Fred Simpson had previously asked her to the party and she simply had forgotten until now. Opie is heartbroken. At first, he tells Andy he will not be going to the party because he has a headache, but then he finally admits the true reason.

Andy relates an experience he had when he was Opie's age. It seems that a church social was coming up and Andy decided to invite a very special girl to be his date. She accepted, only to break the date at the last minute. She went with a boy named Lamar Trundle instead. Rather than sit around at home, young Andy decided to go anyway and play it cool. He ended up having a great time.

Encouraged by his father's story, Opie goes to the party. There, he finds Mary Alice Carter sitting all alone in a corner. She's angry at Fred because he dumped her shortly after the shindig began. He's been dancing with other girls and combing his hair a lot. According to Mary Alice, Fred is so conceited he makes her sick. She apologizes to Opie, and he forgives her. They spend the rest of the party talking and dancing with each other.

When Andy and Helen pick Opie up after the party, they are surprised that he is with Mary Alice. Opie explains, as he holds hands with his date, that they discovered they should have been together all along. Opie suggests that the foursome should double date, and he treats everyone to a snack at the diner.

Unwinding at home after he and Andy drop off

their dates, Opie remarks that girls are still a mystery to him. Andy's reply: "Join the club!"

CAST NOTES. Regulars: **Andy Griffith, Ronny Howard, Frances Bavier, Aneta Corsaut**, and **George Lindsey. Sheldon Collins** returns as Arnold Bailey.

Suzanne Cupito stars as Mary Alice Carter. Today, most viewers know her as Morgan Brittany. She may be best known for her portrayal of Katherine Wentworth on the popular series *Dallas* from 1981 through 1984.

Joy Ellison returns. This time she is Iris, Mary Alice Carter's friend. **Owen Bush** returns, too. He appears as Mayberry clothier Doyle Perkins, owner of Perkins' Clothing Store. **David Alan Bailey** returns, but not as Trey Bowden. He portrays Fred Simpson. **Kevin Tate** appears as George.

EPISODE NOTES. 1. The Monroe Nursery recently burned down. It was located in Mount Pilot. Aunt Bee says they used to feature some of the best azaleas she's ever seen. 2. Miss Crump's classroom is #10. 3. While Andy tries to get some paperwork done, Goober pesters him with riddles from a book he is reading. 4. Opie asks Andy to try to repair Arnold's record player. 5. Andy and Goober tease Opie about taking a girl to the party. This lack of sensitivity bothers Opie and Arnold, but they put up with it. 6. Andy asks Aunt Bee not to have Mr. Perkins make Opie's sleeves and pants 4 inches too long so the suit will fit him "seven years from now." 7. Arnold tells Opie that the party was almost ruined when his parents suggested that the kids dunk for apples. Arnold asked his folks to retreat to the kitchen for the rest of the evening. 8. At the party, a boy named George tells Opie that he believes it was wrong for Mary Alice to pull such a dirty trick on him. 9. Opie yells "hello" to a boy named Ralph and tells a girl named Bernice that she is wearing a nice-looking dress at the party. 10. Opie and Andy agree to a second double date. Next week, they'll go to the movies. 11. Opie asks Andy if he can borrow his tie that has horses on it to wear at the party. It would go well with his new suit. Andy agrees and offers to loan him his key chain. It's the one that hooks onto the belt and hangs down, leading into the hip pocket. Opie declines. 12. Episodes in this season contain more than one reference to Mayberry clothier Doyle Perkins. Andy Griffith's hometown of Mount Airy was served by a clothier named Doyle Perdue, a close friend of Andy's.

"Goober the Executive"

Episode #221. Air date: 12-25-67. Writers: Michael Morris and Seaman Jacobs. Directors: Lee Philips.

Goober is angry and confused when he discovers, from a total stranger, that Wally is selling his filling station. Wally confirms this during a telephone conversation with Goober. Because Goober has been a loyal and hard worker for 11¾ years, Wally allows him to have first refusal. Goober rather likes the idea of being a boss. He decides to ask longtime Mayberry businessman Emmett Clark how it feels to take on such a responsibility.

Emmett is the owner and operator of Emmett's Fix-It Shop, which is located in the building that once housed Floyd's Barbershop. Emmett has been in the repair business for 38 years. He tells Goober that going from mere employee to the boss can be a difficult transition.

Undaunted, Goober tries to secure a loan from loan officer Cyrus Tankersley at the Mayberry Bank. However, the loan is refused due to a lack of collateral. Cyrus tells Goober that he could ask someone to cosign a bank note. Goober turns to his friends Andy and Emmett for help.

Initially, both men refuse to cosign. The amount needed for the down payment is $2,000.00, which is too much for either man to risk. Eventually, Andy realizes that if both he and Emmett become cosigners, their risk would be cut in half. Emmett remains reluctant, but Andy finally persuades him to join in helping out a friend. Andy reminds him that Wally's has always been a moneymaker.

Soon, Goober's Service is open for business. Goober dons a suit for opening day. He has hired a young man named George to pump gas and service automobiles. Andy requests that he have the honor of becoming Goober's first customer, and he tells George to fill 'er up! Unfortunately, Goober neglected to order gasoline from the oil company. It's an embarrassing beginning for Goober, but is it an omen?

Goober purchases a copy of *Nation's Industry* magazine and begins reading about Bernard Hoddeling, a man who inherited his father's company, Consolidated Motors. Mr. Hoddeling was 36 years old at the time. The article (written by Mr. Hoddeling) tells how the pressure of the job caused him to develop migraine headaches. Consolidated Motors lost $17,000,000 in his first year as company president. Goober is sympathetic as the details of his business become so bothersome that he, too, begins having migraine headaches.

After George completes a valve job on Mr.

Perkins's car, he asks Goober where the new head gasket is. Unfortunately, Goober forgot to order it. Next, Harry, the accountant, asks Goober if he wants to keep financial records using the straight line method or the declining balance method. Goober is unsure of himself and realizes that he is unable to make any decisions. This is followed up by a run-in with a very worried Emmett. To top it off, a high-pressure representative from the Emblem Oil Company, based in El Paso, Texas, informs Goober that by selling premium gasoline along with regular and super, he can double or triple business. Goober is unable to deal with him, so he sends the man, Fred Michaels, over to Andy's house.

Andy is perplexed by the visit, and he goes to check on his friend. He is shocked to discover the station's gross business is off by 40 percent and that George has quit. A very concerned Andy reminds Emmett that, unless they can convince Goober to sell the station, they will be legally obligated to pay back the loan.

Meanwhile, Opie stops by Goober's Service and tells him about the rest of the article written by Mr. Hoddeling. It seems that the business tycoon's story has a happy ending. One year after suffering the huge setback, the company made up for it with an income of $22,000,000. The reason for this reversal of fortune was that Mr. Hoddeling realized that he must trust in his judgment and act decisively. Opie suggests that Goober should do likewise and just maybe, things might turn around for him, too.

Suddenly, Goober is a changed man. His migraines disappear, and he is not afraid to make decisions. Looks like he'll make it after all! Andy and Emmett are quite relieved when they discover this change in Goober.

CAST NOTES. Regulars: **Andy Griffith, Ronny Howard**, and **George Lindsey**. George Cisar returns as Cyrus Tankersley.

This episode was the first one filmed in which **Paul Hartman** appeared as Emmett Clark. However, viewers first saw him in episode 224, "Howard the Bowler," which aired on September 18, 1967.

Dave Ketchum, who appeared in previous episodes as realtor Harry Walker, returns. This time he is oil company agent Fred Michaels.

Bo Hopkins portrays Goober's employee, George. Hopkins has appeared in many television series and in movies. He portrayed John Cooper in the late 1970s on *The Rockford Files*, and in 1981 he was the dangerous Matthew Blaisdel on *Dynasty*. His best-known film is surely *American Graffiti* (1973), which featured Ron Howard.

James McCallion returns to the series. This time he portrays Goober's accountant, a man named Harry. He previously appeared in episode 202,

"Opie Finds a Baby," as Dr. Lou Bailey, Arnold's father.

Sam Green appears as the nameless potential buyer of Wally's. He informs Goober that the station is up for sale.

EPISODE NOTES. 1. During a recent trip to Mount Pilot, Goober purchased 14 comic books, including the new edition of "The Purple Avenger." Goober says it's all about the Grunge People. Opie, offering a trade, shows Goober his comic books, "The Space Phantom" and "The Spider Man." 2. Opie is reading *Ivanhoe* for school. Later, Goober reads it. 3. A sign (attached to a thermostat) at Wally's reads, "Treat yourself to the best." 4. According to Andy, Floyd Lawson has retired. 5. Two signs in Emmett's Fix-It Shop read, "We don't loan tools" and "No guarantee on parts sold." 6. Emmett works on Andy's cuckoo clock in this episode. He finally gets the cuckoo to come out, but it cuckoos three times at 2:00, five times at 3:00, twice at 4:00, etc. 7. Goober asks George to salute every customer like they do "on those television commercials." 8. After purchasing the station from Wally, Goober comes up with three mottos: "free air with a smile," "free water with a smile," and "the only thing we don't wipe clean is the smile on our faces." 9. Fred Michaels is the vice-president in charge of regional sales of northeastern North Carolina for the Emblem Oil Company. 10. Goober decides on using the declining balance method of bookkeeping. His reason? He and Opie liked the sound of it. 11. An IRS collector informs Goober that he owes $150.00 in taxes. Goober is pleased to have gone from "lowly mechanic" to someone who draws threats of lawsuits from "the most powerful government in the world."

"Howard's Main Event"

Episode #222. Air date: 10-16-67. Writers: Robert C. Dennis and Earl Barret. Director: Lee Philips.

Mr. Boysinger, owner of Boysinger's Bakery in Mayberry, has recently hired a Mount Pilot woman named Millie Hutchins. Howard Sprague is immediately smitten with her, and the two began dating.

All goes well, until the couple runs into sewer worker Clyde Plaunt. Clyde was Millie's last boyfriend. He tells Millie that he still wants to see her, but she gives him the cold shoulder. The next day, Clyde confronts Howard at work and orders him to stay away from Millie. If he doesn't, he will get beaten up. An intimidated Howard reluctantly breaks his date with Millie. Later, and quite by chance, Howard, Millie, and Clyde find themselves in the diner at the same time. In front of Millie, Clyde openly threatens Howard. Fortunately, Andy and Helen come by, and Clyde has to back off. However, he warns Howard that sometime he'll catch him alone, and then he will give him a good thrashing.

Howard decides that his only recourse is to never leave Andy's side. He literally becomes Andy's shadow, accompanying him to work, at lunch, at home with Helen, and even while shaving. Andy has had enough of this, and he demands to know why Howard is acting so strangely. Howard admits his fear of the tough Clyde Plaunt. Andy relates a similar situation that happened to Opie. Opie finally faced up to his bully and took a punch. Andy tells Howard that a punch in the nose hurts for a lot less time than running away from a bully.

Although reluctant, Howard decides to confront his bully. Mr. Sprague comes on strong, and Clyde gets frightened off.

Howard's newfound confidence is short-lived, however. When he confronts an obnoxious man who makes a pass at Millie, he ends up on the receiving end of a punch to the stomach.

CAST NOTES. Regulars: **Andy Griffith, Jack Dodson, Aneta Corsaut,** and **George Lindsey.**

Arlene Golonka appears for the first time as Millie Hutchins. Golonka would play a larger role in the spinoff series *Mayberry R.F.D.* as Millie Swanson, the girlfriend of Sam Jones. She was also seen from time to time on *That Girl* as Margie Myer and was a regular on the 1978-1979 series *Joe and Valerie*, in which she played Stella Sweetzer. She has made many guest appearances in pilots, specials, comedies, and dramas, including: *ABC Stage '67, Alan King's Final Warning* (a 1977 special in which Don Knotts also appeared), *Alice, The Bean Show* (a 1964 pilot), *Benson, The Big Valley, The Flying Nun, Get Smart, The Girl with Something Extra* (with Don Knotts in an episode entitled, "The Not So Good Samaritan), *Growing Pains, In the Heat of the Night, Matlock, Murder She Wrote,* and *Taxi.* She also provides her voice in the animated series *Speed Buggy.* She has appeared in several television movies, such as *The Bait* (1973), *Nightmare* (1974), and *Cops and Roberts.* She has performed on Broadway in such shows as *Come Blow Your Horn* and *One Flew Over the Cuckoo's Nest.* Golonka once taught commercial acting. She has appeared in many motion pictures, including *Love with a Proper Stranger* (1963, with Natalie Wood and Steve McQueen), *Penelope* (1966, with Natalie Wood and Peter Falk), *Welcome to Hard Times* (1968, with Henry Fonda), *Hang 'Em High* (1968, with Clint Eastwood), *Airport '77* (1977), *The In-Laws* (1979,

with Alan Arkin and Peter Falk), *Separate Ways* (1981), *Survival Game* (1987), and *Dr. Alien* (1988, with Judy Landers, Linnea Quigley and Edy Williams).

Allan Melvin returns. This time he is portraying Clyde Plaunt. **Wayne Heffley** appears as Harry, the man who flirts with Millie.

EPISODE NOTES. 1. Goober would like to learn Swedish, because he once had a customer who spoke only Swedish. 2. Goober does not own a record player. 3. Howard and Millie see a movie called *Two in Love* which stars Ed Olson and Viola Kern, at the Mayberry Grand Theater. Howard describes the film as "a three-handkerchief picture." The movie's ending involves the heroine killing herself when she realizes that her sweetheart is dead. 4. The following businesses on Main Street in Mayberry are shown: Spencer's Pipes and Tobacco, Meyer's Real Estate, Lamps and Shade, and a hardware and appliance store. 5. Andy tells Howard about events that occurred in episode 34, "Opie and the Bully." 6. Clyde Plaunt calls Howard "Ace." 7. Goober is currently dating a girl named Gloria. He claims he is only shy around women when the woman is a member of the Mayberry Softball Team. According to Goober, "They think they're so much." By the way, Gloria refuses to ride in Goober's truck. 8. According to Andy, a Mayberry man named Mr. Finney threw a rock through his wife's window because he doesn't like her. 9. Howard, Millie, and Goober go to Myers' Lake for an evening of fun. It was supposed to be a foursome, but Gloria couldn't make it.

"Aunt Bee, the Juror"

Episode #223. Air date: 10-23-67. Writer: Kent Wilson. Director: Lee Philips.

Aunt Bee is summoned to appear at the Municipal Court in Mount Pilot. She has been selected as a potential juror. Aunt Bee has never been called to jury duty before, and in fact, it has been awhile since any Mayberrian has. She is very nervous as Andy and Opie accompany her to Mount Pilot. Goober comes along, too, to lend moral support.

Aunt Bee is approved as a juror, and the trial begins. A young man, Marvin Jenkins, has been accused of burglarizing Bryce's Department Store in Mount Pilot. Among the items stolen were two typewriters, several toasters, a waffle iron, a large stereo combination, and a television set. Also stolen were many smaller items that were listed on the police report, but not mentioned in court. The total value of the stolen merchandise was estimated at over $2,000.

The prosecution has an eyewitness named Charles Keyes. Mr. Keyes, who is acquainted with the accused, testifies that he saw Marvin Jenkins coming out of Bryce's carrying a television set, after closing hours, on the night of the burglary. Because he needed a ride home, Mr. Keyes tried to get Jenkins's attention by calling out his name. This only seemed to startle Mr. Jenkins, who hurriedly loaded the television set in his truck and sped off.

Defending himself, Mr. Jenkins explains that his television set went on the blink around 9:00 P.M. on the night in question. He took it to Bryce's to see if it could be repaired. He found the front door to be locked yet the back door was ajar. However, upon entering the building, he found no one inside. As he was leaving the premises, he heard Mr. Keyes yelling, "Hey, Marvin!" Suddenly, he realized that the situation probably looked suspicious, so he quickly took off.

Before long, the jury gathers to deliberate. Every juror believes Jenkins is guilty beyond a reasonable doubt — that is, every juror except Aunt Bee. She believes that he does not *look* like a criminal. Her fellow jurors try desperately to persuade her to change her mind, but after several ballots are taken, the jury remains hopelessly deadlocked.

When Judge Cranston dismisses the charges due to the hung jury, one spectator in the courtroom becomes very upset. This gentleman, Mr. Granger, wonders aloud how Aunt Bee could find Jenkins to be not guilty. He states that Jenkins got away with a television, several toasters, and a radio, among other items. This statement makes Andy suspicious. Without fanfare, he asks the prosecutor if a radio was amongst the unmentioned stolen items. Indeed it was. When this is brought to Judge Cranston's attention, Mr. Granger is ordered to be detained for questioning. Aunt Bee's verdict is apparently justified. She received sheepish apologies from her fellow jurors, as well as a sincere word of thanks from Marvin Jenkins.

CAST NOTES. Regulars: **Andy Griffith, Ronny Howard, Frances Bavier,** and **George Lindsey.**

Academy Award winner **Jack Nicholson** graces *The Andy Griffith Show* once again. This time, he portrays Marvin Jenkins. Nicholson previously appeared in episode 202, "Opie Finds a Baby."

Rhys Williams, who appeared in many fine films including *The Corn is Green* (1945) and *Raintree County* (1957), appears as Judge Cranston.

Veteran television actor **Henry Beckman** portrays prosecuting attorney Mr. Gilbert. Beckman had the regular role of Captain Charley Clancy in the television series *Here Come the Brides.* **Tol Avery** returns to the series, not as Ben Weaver, but as jury foreman Mr. Dickinson. **Jim Begg,** seen in minor

roles occasionally in this series, portrays Charles Keyes, the state's key witness. **Emory Parnell** portrays one of the jurors. Mr. Parnell previously appeared in episode 206, "Dinner at Eight," as Helen Crump's Uncle Edward. **Richard Chambers** portrays Mr. Granger. **Tom Palmer** appears as the defense attorney. **Arthur Hanson** portrays Mr. Smith. **Pete Madsen** appears as the court clerk. **Allen Dexter** and **Frederic Downs** appear as two unnamed jurors.

EPISODE NOTES. 1. Opie once made a drawing of a horse and sent it off to an art school to have it evaluated. The reply said that he had talent, and they asked him to build on that talent by enrolling in their 12-lesson course by mail. The cost was just $98.50. Later, the art school writes him again, offering a newly developed short course for only $37.00. Opie smartly declines both offers. 2. Aunt Bee's Garden Club meets on Thursdays. She is also head of the Civic Improvement League, although she has not been actively involved in it for some time. 3. Marvin Jenkins has hazel eyes. 4. Aunt Bee and Andy watch a courtroom drama on television at home. Aunt Bee claims she can always pick out the crooks on television very easily, because they're always mean and squinty-eyed. 5. According to Goober, he "always" says, "Any worldly experience is a universal thing." 6. The truly damning piece of evidence against Mr. Granger is that his cigarette lighter was found at the scene of the crime. While watching the court proceedings, Granger complains to Andy and others that he lost his lighter. The police initially assumed that the lighter they found belonged to Mr. Jenkins, but when they discovered that he didn't smoke, they dismissed it as unimportant. It is Andy who links the lighter to Mr. Granger. 7. Aunt Bee's homemade brownies are apparently a hit with her fellow jurors. Even Judge Cranston writes and asks for her brownie recipe after the trial. 8. About 20 years later, Andy would help solve crimes as a defense attorney on television's *Matlock.*

"Howard the Bowler"

Episode #224. Air date: 9-18-67. Writers: Dick Bensfield and Perry Grant. Director: Lee Philips.

For some time now, Andy, Goober, and a man named Lou Jenkins have bowled as a team in Mayberry's bowling league. The team is sponsored by Emmett's Fix-It Shop, and shop owner Emmett Clark has spent his entire advertising budget to outfit the team with bowling shirts. Andy is looking forward to an upcoming match against a Mount Pilot team sponsored by the Trucker's Cafe.

Goober brings unwelcome news when he announces that Lou Jenkins will be in Atlanta (for business reasons) and will be unavailable for the contest in Mount Pilot. A replacement must be found or the match will be forfeited. Andy, Goober, Emmett, and even Aunt Bee and Opie mull over possible candidates to replace Lou, all of whom are rejected for one reason or another. Then Opie suggests that they ask Howard Sprague. None of the guys are enthusiastic about Howard. After all, he has only been bowling for about two months. Later, however, Howard tells his friends that his bowling has picked up of late. He now bowls on Tuesdays and Thursdays and recently converted a 4-10 split.

With time running out, the team reluctantly chooses Howard. Andy remarks, "If we're gonna lose, we might as well lose with our friends!"

Howard has a very unorthodox bowling style. He carefully measures his steps from the foul line and tries to psyche himself up by talking to himself. His methods draw laughs, but not for long.

The teams (Emmett's Fix-It Shop and the Trucker's Cafe) meet at a 10-lane bowling alley in Mount Pilot. The match begins, and Andy and company take command right away. In fact, the Mayberrians have an insurmountable lead 3/4 of the way through the match. But all eyes are focused on the unlikeliest hero, Howard Sprague. He has bowled eight strikes in a row. He couldn't bowl a perfect game, could he? A 300 game has never been recorded in the history of Pilot County.

Hank, the leader of the Mount Pilot team, offers to bet against Howard. He says his team will pay Emmett's team $40.00 if Howard finishes with a perfect game. However, should Howard fail, the Mayberry team has to shell out a meager $10.00. Against Andy's advice, Goober and Emmett take the bet.

Howard confidently rolls on...9, 10, 11 strikes in a row. Just as he is about to finish up, a power outage occurs! The power cannot be quickly restored, so the teams agree to finish the match the next evening.

Howard spends a sleepless night. The pressure is getting to him. He tries everything he can think of to relax, including reading poetry.

The next evening, Aunt Bee and Opie are among the large crowd gathered to watch Howard's final roll. Both teams agree that Howard should be allowed to take a couple of practice rolls, but both times, the ball ends up in the gutter. It is apparent that Howard has lost his timing. To the relief of Goober and Emmett, Andy manages to get the Mount Pilot team to call off the bet. Then, to the amazement of everyone, Howard throws a strike to complete his perfect game. Forgetting their joy for a moment, Goober and Emmett blast Andy for calling off the bet.

The next day, Howard's perfect game makes a great news story, complete with pictures. Knowing that Lou Jenkins will be returning to the team, Howard turns his shirt in to Andy. This bowling match meant much to Howard, and Andy realizes it. He gives the shirt back, telling him that Emmett would want him to have it. Howard will cherish it forever.

CAST NOTES. Regulars: **Andy Griffith, Ronny Howard, Frances Bavier, Jack Dodson, George Lindsey,** and **Paul Hartman.**

Norman Alden removes the Indian garb he wore in episode 188, "The Battle of Mayberry," as Tom Strongbow, and appears here as Hank, the captain of the Trucker's Cafe bowling team. **Bob Becker** appears as George, one of Hank's teammates.

EPISODE NOTES. 1. Emmett paid $8.00 apiece for the bowling shirts. 2. Andy estimates that as many as 50 to 60 people come to see a bowling match. 3. Goober's right eye usually twitches when he gets nervous. 4. Some of the possible replacements for Lou Jenkins are the pastor (Andy rejects the idea because, in the heat of a match, sometimes the language gets a little rough); Ab Winters (Emmett says Ab plays basketball on Tuesdays and Thursdays, and anyway, Ab played in a big poker game recently, so it's likely that his wife, Emmie, wouldn't let him go); Doc Springs (Andy rules him out because Doc has to tend to Cathy Hawkins, who is due to give birth); and Jeff Kingsley (Andy says Jeff has the flu). 5. According to Emmett, too much starch ruins steam irons. Goober says that his ma always used a lot of starch. 6. During the first half of the bowling match, the team from Mayberry bowls on lane number 9. They switch to lane number 10 to complete the match. 7. Goober asks a man named Joe to turn up the air conditioning at the Mount Pilot bowling alley. Joe is apparently the manager. 8. During his sleepless night, Howard reads the following verse from a Rudyard Kipling poem, entitled "**If**":

"If you can fill the unforgiving minute
with sixty seconds worth of distance run,
yours is the Earth and everything that's in it,
and which is more, you'll be a man, my son."

9. Howard also reads the last line from a poem entitled "**Casey at the Bat**" by Ernest L. Thayer: "...the mighty Casey has struck out!" 10. Andy calls Howard "Mr. 300" after the perfect game. 11. Howard states that, if Mayberry ever has a museum or a hall of fame, he would be happy to donate his bowling shirt. 12. There is a contradiction between

this episode and an earlier one. Andy states that Howard has been bowling for only a couple of months, but in episode 191, "The Barbershop Quartet," which aired on September 26, 1966, Howard was part of a team in the bowling league that included Andy, Goober, and a man named Frank.

"Opie Steps Up in Class"

Episode #225. Air date: 10-9-67. Writer: Joseph Bonaduce. Director: Lee Philips.

Andy wants to send Opie to a $10.00-a-day Saturday camp called Camp Winokee. It is said to be the best camp in the state for 12- to 14-year-old boys. Opie is 13 and has never really been away from home. Andy believes the experience will broaden Opie's horizons. Aunt Bee is against Opie going, because the rich families in Walnut Hills send their kids there. She is afraid that Opie will feel like he doesn't belong. Andy insists that kids are kids. However, when he brings up the idea about the camp to Opie, his son shows no interest. In fact, Opie says that "all the snooty kids go to that camp." Andy finally persuades Opie to go.

Andy is relieved when Opie returns from his day at camp a happy young man. He had a great time and made a few friends, one of whom is Billy Hollander of Walnut Hills. Opie tells Andy that Billy wants him to come over for lunch the next day. This is fine with Andy, but he has to go to Siler City with Helen, so he asks Aunt Bee to drop Opie off at the Hollander mansion on her way to a flower show. Opie has a nice time, and he invites Billy to come to his house the following day.

Now, Aunt Bee feels obligated to prepare a fancy lunch for Opie and his privileged pal. Her menu includes shrimp cocktail and roasted duck. When Andy comes home for lunch, he is surprised to discover the gourmet fare. After Billy leaves, Andy lectures Aunt Bee and Opie about the silliness of "putting on airs." He advises them just to be themselves.

Back in Walnut Hills, Billy's dad, George Hollander, has decided to host a father-and-son get-together. He will invite the boys who attend Camp Winokee and their fathers. Andy gets his invitation while he is chatting with Emmett. Mayberry's "Mr. Fix-It" tells Andy all about the wealthy citizens of Walnut Hills. Before long, Andy sort of forgets his own advice. He purchases a new suit from Mayberry Clothier Doyle Perkins, and he drives Aunt Bee's convertible to the Hollanders' home.

At the gathering, he is surprised to find the men dressed in casual clothes. The men are all talking

about golf and about deep sea fishing from their yachts. Just as Andy is about to fall into the "keeping up with the Joneses" trap, Opie gets his Pa's attention. He tells him that the advice he gave about being himself was right on target. Andy decides to drop all pretense and heed his own advice. Just as kids are kids, men are men. Andy rejoins the conversation and has a great time. A few of the men say they may come bass fishing with Andy at Myers' Lake.

CAST NOTES. Regulars: **Andy Griffith, Ronny Howard, Frances Bavier, Jack Dodson,** and **Paul Hartman.**

Joyce Van Patten appears as Laura Hollander. The sister of actor Dick Van Patten, Joyce began as a child star. At the age of two, she won a Shirley Temple look-alike contest. Many years later, she was a regular on *The Danny Kaye Show* (1964-1967).

Character actor **Sandy Kenyon** returns to the series. This time he portrays George Hollander. He previously appeared in episode 203, "Goober Makes History," as Bill Lindsey, the history teacher.

Ivan Bonar appears as Martin Breckenridge. Bonar portrayed Dean Hopkins on *The Adventures of Ozzie and Harriet* from 1964 to 1966. In the 1980s, he was cast as Henderson Palmer on *Dynasty II: The Colbys.*

Don Wyndham portrays Billy Hollander. **Ward Ramsey** appears as Frank Glendon. **Monty Margetts** appears as the Hollanders' maid, and **Thom Carney** appears as the Hollanders' chauffeur.

EPISODE NOTES. 1. In a conversation with Emmett, Andy states that Emerson said, "Be yourself." Emmett thinks he is referring to Fletcher Emerson, a man who used to run a hardware store in Mayberry. This Fletcher used to say things like, "Do you think the rain will hurt the rhubarb?" Andy is referring to Ralph Waldo Emerson. 2. According to a brochure, Camp Winokee offers "200 acres of untrammeled loveliness, bordering crystal clear Lake Winokee. Rugged riding trails, tennis, water skiing, a fun place!" 3. Opie tells Aunt Bee that the meal she calls "supper" is called "dinner" by the kids he met at camp. Their supper is around 11:00 P.M. or midnight. 4. Aunt Bee tells Laura Hollander that Andy works for the municipal government as an elected official. 5. At the Hollanders', Opie is served avocado salad and a hot roast beef sandwich (with no fat or gristle) for lunch. 6. According to Andy, the chicken fricassee at the diner is too fancy for him. 7. Andy is used to normal fare, such as hamburgers, cheese sandwiches, and meatloaf. 8. According to Emmett, the Hollander home has copper pipes throughout. Emmett used to service the Walnut Hills area when he had a shop in Mount Pilot. He tells Andy that George Hollander is the director of five banks. Mr. Hollander's peers are all big shots, too. Frank Glendon owns a chain of Glendon's Grocery Stores, and Martin Breckenridge is the biggest real estate broker in the state. Andy meets all of them in this episode. 9. Aunt Bee's car has 145,000 miles on it. 10. Hole number 4 at the Walnut Hills golf course is 162 yards long. According to the locals, "It's not a long course, but it's tricky."

"Andy's Trip to Raleigh"

Episode #226. Air date: 10-2-67. Writer: Joseph Bonaduce. Director: Lee Philips.

Every adult in Mayberry is looking forward to the upcoming annual Harvest Ball. This year the musical entertainment will be provided by Casper Tice and His Latin Rhythms. Sadly, because of a sudden development in an old court case, Andy must miss out on this year's festivities. He arranges for Howard Sprague to escort Helen to the ball so she won't miss out on the fun.

The court case involves an incident in which a bulldozer went out of control and struck a car in Mayberry. In the ensuing trial, Andy was called to testify. It was an uncomplicated issue, and the matter was soon disposed of. Now, however, the owner of the car has filed suit against the county, claiming to be suffering from the mishap. So Andy must travel to Raleigh to meet with Lee Drake, an attorney who needs to go over the testimony with him.

Once he arrives he is surprised to discover that Lee Drake is a woman. In fact, she is a very attractive blonde, who insists that they work at her lovely home. They work outdoors, next to her swimming pool. After an awkward beginning, Andy starts to enjoy himself, and even dons a pair of trunks to take a dip in the pool. After working for several hours, Andy and Ms. Drake enjoy a lobster dinner at her home. Later, Andy checks into a hotel to get a good night's sleep.

When he returns to Mayberry on Sunday afternoon, Andy is sporting a telltale sunburn. Goober and Emmett give him a good-natured ribbing about his exaggerated tan. Suddenly, Andy begins to believe that he'd better not tell Helen that Lee Drake is a woman, lest she get the wrong idea. After all, he wasn't unfaithful to her, but he did enjoy a sunny day with a lovely woman. When Helen asks him about Lee Drake, he describes the lawyer as "fortyish, heavyset, grim and businesslike." He explains that he got sunburned when he drove home in Aunt Bee's convertible with the top down. When Helen notices that his back is sunburned, as well,

Andy claims that he took off his shirt while tending to a flat tire on the way home.

Andy dances all around the fact that Lee Drake is a woman. In fact, he quickly changes the subject. He asks Helen to join him for a picnic at Myers' Lake on Monday.

Unfortunately, back in Raleigh, Ms. Drake receives a phone call from a Mr. Forsythe, who informs her that her request for a trial postponement has been denied. Because she needs additional information from Andy, she decides to drive to Mayberry the following day.

Goober is the first to sight Ms. Drake as she enters Mayberry. Trying to keep her away from Andy, he tells her that the sheriff went to Alaska.

When Andy meets up with her at the courthouse, he does all he can to keep her out of Helen's sight. It's not easy, because Helen is in the car just outside the courthouse, waiting to leave for the picnic. Inevitably, they do meet, and Andy is forced to introduce Helen to Ms. Drake. As the Raleigh lawyer politely excuses herself from the building, Andy tries to explain his suspicious behavior. Helen is disgusted by his lies and leaves in anger. Obviously, the picnic is off.

Later, a sheepish Andy drops in on Helen at her home. He offers her candy, as well as an apology. He is shocked to discover that she has a sunburn, too. She proudly states that she decided to go to Myers' Lake by herself. She says she had a wonderful time. In fact, she met a nice man there. When Andy asks her more about this man, Helen describes him as "fortyish and heavy set." Andy, realizing he's been had, asks her what she and this mystery man talked about. "Trust. Complete, unquestioning trust," is her reply.

Helen has gotten her revenge, but more importantly, she has made her point.

CAST NOTES. Regulars: **Andy Griffith, Aneta Corsaut, Jack Dodson, George Lindsey**, and **Paul Hartman.**

Whitney Blake portrays the lovely Raleigh lawyer Lee Drake. Blake portrayed Dorothy Baxter on the hit television series *Hazel*, from 1961 to 1965. She is the mother of actress Meredith Baxter, who delighted fans as Elyse Keaton on the long-running hit series *Family Ties*. Blake also co-created the television sitcom *One Day at a Time.*

EPISODE NOTES. 1. Goober purchases a new suit in Mount Pilot for this year's Harvest Ball. He will also wear his new cuff links, which are shaped like miniature truck tires. He received them from a new tire company as a promotional gimmick. At last year's ball, Goober wore a size 46 suit because it was all the Mount Pilot clothier had left. It was way too big, and Goober danced on his pant cuffs the entire evening. 2. According to Andy, Raleigh is more than 100 miles from Mayberry. (This is considerably at odds with the distance given in other episodes; for example, episode 67 has Raleigh 55 miles away, and 156 places the distance at 60 miles.) 3. It is Judge Conley who assigns Andy to work with Lee Drake on the court case. 4. Ms. Drake has a maid named Marie. 5. Alvin Barrows and George Brookfield are two prominent Raleigh attorneys with whom Howard Sprague is acquainted. 6. According to Goober and Emmett, the preacher is taking seven Sundays and giving a sermon each week on one of the seven deadly sins. This week the topic was sloth. Next week's sermon is on gluttony.

"A Trip to Mexico"

Episode #227. Air date: 9-27-67. Writers: Dick Bensfield and Perry Grant. Director: Lee Philips.

Aunt Bee wins the grand prize in the "Tampico Tamale Lucky Number Contest." (Her individual number was chosen). It's an all-expenses-paid, ten-day trip for two to Mexico. It appears that Aunt Bee will be forced to pick one of her two best friends, either Clara or Myrtle, to accompany her on the trip, since Andy can't take off work and Opie is stuck at school. In order to influence Aunt Bee's decision, Clara buys her a money converter, and Myrtle gives her a travel-size laundry kit. Finally, Helen comes up with a great idea. She suggests that if Clara and Myrtle pay for half of their trip, then all three friends would be able to go! Aunt Bee, Clara and Myrtle love the idea and are excited as they plan for the big day.

When the day of departure arrives, the three ladies start bickering about who gets the window seat on their TWA-bound flight to Mexico City. When they arrive in Mexico, they argue over where they should go and what they should do. The continue to argue as they enjoy a dinner and floor show featuring a flamenco dancer, who flirts with Clara; a folklore tour; the floating gardens; the Aztec pyramids; donkey rides; bullfights; Maximillian and Carlotta's palace; a mariachi band; the shrine at Guadalupe; "The Reformer"; a farmacía; and the beautiful silverware at Tasca.

Unfortunately, when they arrive back home, these good times are forgotten due to all the bickering that went on. Andy is able to remedy the situation by arranging with Elmo, the druggist and photo developer, to have all the ladies pick up their vacation pictures at the same time. Upon seeing the photos, the three friends realize that they had a great time, and all is forgiven.

CAST NOTES. Regulars: **Andy Griffith, Ronny Howard, Frances Bavier, Aneta Corsaut, Jack Dodson, Paul Hartman,** and **Hope Summers.**

Ruth Thom returns, this time as Myrtle. **Anthony Jochim** appears as Harvey, the man who delivers Aunt Bee's winning telegram. **José Gonzalez-Gonzalez** portrays the shopkeeper. **Manuel Martin** appears as the violinist and flamenco dancer who flirts with Clara. **Eddie Carroll** appears as the airport clerk. Carroll would go on to become a regular on *The Don Knotts Show* from 1970 through 1971. **Natividad Vacio** appears as the hotel clerk.

Vince Barnett appears for the first time as Elmo. Barnett was born on July 4, 1902, in Pittsburgh, Pennsylvania, and died in 1977. Educated at Duquesne and at Carnegie Tech, he became one of the pioneers of air mail piloting. In his heyday, he was known as a prankster. Among the notable figures he pulled pranks on were Franklin Delano Roosevelt, Winston Churchill, George Bernard Shaw, Henry Ford, and Charles A. Lindbergh. As an actor, his career was mostly on the big screen, although he made guest appearances on several television series including *Mayberry R.F.D.* (as Elmo), *Green Acres, The Wild Wild West,* and *My Three Sons.* He also appeared in *Girl on the Run,* a 1958 pilot. Here is a partial listing of his many movie appearances *Tiger Shark* (1932, with Edward G. Robinson), *Scarface* (1932, with Paul Muni), *Thirty Day Princess* (1934, with Cary Grant, scripted by Preston Sturges), *A Star is Born* (1937), *Seven Sinners* (1940, with John Wayne and Marlene Deitrich), *The Corpse Vanishes* (1942), *Knock on Any Door* (1949, with Humphrey Bogart), *Springfield Rifle* (1952, with Gary Cooper), and *The Rookie* (1959).

EPISODE NOTES. 1. Emmett enjoys reading "Moon Mullins" in the funny papers. 2. Howard lets Aunt Bee borrow his suitcase, which has a secret compartment for money, for her trip. 3. Emmett once went on a business trip to Akron, Ohio. He claims that Akron is a wide-open town. 4. Aunt Bee sings one of her favorites, "My Chinatown," while she is packing for the trip. 5. Emmett has a cousin who was a personal friend of the chairman of the Liquor Control Board. 6. Aunt Bee, Clara, and Myrtle's departure flight number is 17. They board at gate number 12. 7. Emmett jokingly advises the ladies not to take any wooden pesos. 8. Aunt Bee mails Opie a sombrero and a serape. He tries them on while playing his guitar. Aunt Bee also brings back sombreros for Andy, Howard, and Emmett. 9. Myrtle gives maracas to Andy, Howard, and Emmett as souvenirs. 10. When the ladies return from Mexico, Emmett greets them with a sign that states, "Welcome Home, Mayberry Jet Set." 11. Myrtle tells the leader of the mariachi band that

Clara is Ginger Rogers. 12. Clara has a barbecue fiesta upon her return from Mexico.

"Tape Recorder"

Episode #228. Air date: 10-20-67. Writers: Michael Morris and Seaman Jacobs. Director: Lee Philips.

Opie and Arnold are having a great time. They are secretly recording conversations on a tape recorder that Arnold recently received as a birthday present. Against Andy's wishes, the two boys record a conversation between Eddie Blake, a suspected bank robber, and his lawyer, Myles Bentley, while Blake is being held for questioning at the Mayberry jail. On the secretly recorded tape, Blake confesses to stealing $25,000 from a bank in Raleigh. He also offers Mr. Bentley half of the stolen loot if he will represent him. Blake goes on to say that the money is located in a dry well at Ferguson's abandoned farm on Orchard Road in Mayberry. Mr. Bentley refuses the offer and instructs Blake to find a new attorney.

When Opie and Arnold take the tape to Andy, he explains that he cannot listen to it because it was illegally obtained. He also reminds the boys to never eavesdrop again.

Later, Arnold retrieves the money from Ferguson's farm and takes it directly to Opie's room. Sure enough, in the old battered black attache case (with red lining) is $25,000 in cash.

The boys secretly go to see Blake at the jail. They inform him that, unless he decides to confess to the crime, they will turn in the loot to Andy. The plan works like a charm, and the boys let Andy believe that it was his psychological tactics that persuaded Blake to own up to the robbery.

CAST NOTES. Regulars: **Andy Griffith, Ronny Howard, Frances Bavier,** and **George Lindsey. Sheldon Collins** returns as Arnold Bailey. This is the first episode in which he used the surname Collins, rather than Golomb.

Herbie Faye returns to the series. In this one, he stars as Eddie Blake. Faye can also be seen in episode 159, "Banjo-Playing Deputy," as the manager of the carnival. In episode 171, "Aunt Bee Takes a Job," he portrayed one of the counterfeiters.

Jerome Guardino appears as Myles Bentley. Guardino is known to television fans as Officer Antonnucci on *Car 54, Where Are You?* from 1961 through 1962. **Troy Melton** appears as the State Trooper.

EPISODE NOTES. 1. Opie and Arnold secretly record a telephone conversation between Aunt Bee and Clara Edwards in which Aunt Bee gives Clara her recipe for chipped beef puffs. 2. Myles Bentley practices law and lives in Jonesboro. 3. Andy swears in Goober as an acting deputy while he goes to pick up Eddie Blake from the state police. He gives Goober the usual bent deputy's badge. 4. Opie refers to Arnold's physician father as "Doc" Bailey. Arnold's mother is simply referred to as Mrs. Bailey. 5. Eddie Blake brags about wearing a $200.00 suit. 6. At the conclusion of the episode, Aunt Bee is planning to prepare a chicken paprikash dish.

"Opie's Group"

Episode #229. Air date: 11-6-67. Writer: Doug Tibbles. Director: Lee Philips.

Opie has joined a rock 'n' roll band called "the Sound Committee." Their leader is a hip high school guitar player named Clifford Johnson. Clifford is flanked by Jesse Clayton on drums, Wilson Brown on first rhythm guitar, and Opie on second rhythm guitar.

Aunt Bee is concerned that Opie will neglect his homework and develop poor eating habits. Clara Edwards makes matters worse when she tells Aunt Bee about her brother Claude, who plays in Hippie Harrison's traveling rock 'n' roll band. Claude's undisciplined lifestyle has always worried Clara and her family.

Andy is not concerned about Opie falling into Claude's lifestyle and tells Aunt Bee not to fret. But in no time at all, Andy begins worrying as much as Aunt Bee. It begins with Opie's first gig, a birthday party given by Mrs. Roach for her daughter Brenda. The job pays five dollars a man.

Andy and Aunt Bee get upset when Opie arrives home more than two hours late after the party. Even worse, he starts getting failing grades at school.

Aunt Bee is somewhat relieved when Clara volunteers to speak to the boys at Andy's house. But when Andy and Aunt Bee arrive home, they are shocked to find Clara gleefully accompanying the Sound Committee on the piano.

Andy and Aunt Bee soon discover that Clara is going to be the group's treasurer and business manager. Opie assures his pa that band practice will not interfere with his homework, and Clara will insure that the boys will save their earnings.

By the way, there is no truth to the rumor that there is a missing scene showing Opie smoking a joint in front of Emmett's Fix-It Shop.

MEMORABLE SCENE. Opie heeding Clifford's advice to "make the scene" while talking hip with his friend Phoebe.

CAST NOTES. Regulars: **Andy Griffith, Ronny**

Howard, **Frances Bavier**, **George Lindsey**, **Paul Hartman**, and **Hope Summers**. **Sheldon Collins** returns as Arnold Bailey.

Jim Kidwell appears as Clifford Johnson. **Joe Leitch** portrays Wilson Brown. **Gary Chase** appears as Jesse Clayton.

Kay Ann Kemper portrays Phoebe, even though the cast credits incorrectly list her as Joy. Movie fans should note that in the not-too-distant future, Kemper would change her name to Kay Lenz. Lenz has appeared in such movies as *American Graffiti* (1973, with Ron Howard), *Breezy* (1973, with William Holden), and *Falling from Grace* (1992). Lenz was once married to teen idol David Cassidy.

EPISODE NOTES. 1. Aunt Bee prepares boiled beef for dinner. This is one of Andy's least favorite dishes. Mr. Bronson, the butcher at the Mayberry Meat Market, had it on special. 2. The Sound Committee practices in the Taylors' garage. 3. Goober asks Opie if he will still speak to him when his group gets as big as "the Beagles." Naturally, Goober was referring to the Beatles. By the way, Opie wasn't amused. 4. Aunt Bee warns Opie not to get electrocuted by his amplifier. The members of the Sound Committee get a good laugh at Aunt Bee's expense. 5. Andy and Aunt Bee have their hearts set on Opie becoming a Supreme Court judge when he grows up. 6. Mrs. Perkins, a neighbor of the Taylors', doesn't speak to Aunt Bee anymore because the Sound Committee practices are too loud. 7. Emmett enjoys listening to the beautiful music of the Raleigh Philharmonic Orchestra. 8. Andy suggests that Opie's group should call themselves "the Young Swingers." 9. While Emmett is repairing Opie's amplifier, Goober asks him if he wants to go out and shoot some crows. Emmett declines the offer. 10. Opie orders a bright red shirt to wear when the Sound Committee plays. He ordered it C.O.D. This doesn't please Andy, who complains that Opie has only been a musician for a few days and is already in debt. 11. When Opie was taking piano lessons from Clara, she only played one song, "The Day of the Little Bunnies." 12. Viewers may note that despite the lack of a bass guitar player, the Sound Committee has an awfully good bass sound.

"Aunt Bee and the Lecturer"

Episode #230. Air date: 11-13-67. Writers: Michael Morris and Seaman Jacobs. Director: Lee Philips.

The Mayberry Women's Club has invited noted South America expert Professor Hubert St. John to address the community at the Mayberry Town Hall. Professor St. John is the author of the book *I Know South America*. He enthralls the gathering with tales of his adventures. Aunt Bee then asks Andy to invite the professor to dinner at the Taylor home. The invitation is gratefully accepted. When Aunt Bee discovers that Clara Edwards has taken a shine to the professor, she invites her to dinner, too.

The day before the dinner, Clara, determined to get the professor's attention, spends three hours at the beauty parlor and purchases a new dress from Madame Olga's, a local dress shop. Unfortunately for Clara, the professor spends the evening staring at Aunt Bee. He is totally captivated by her. Aunt Bee finds his rapt attention to be a bit disconcerting. Clara gets jealous, develops a sudden headache, and leaves.

Later, from his hotel room, the professor telephones his son, Jonathan, and tells him that Aunt Bee is a carbon copy of his late wife (and Jonathan's mother), Ethel Montgomery St. John.

Aunt Bee and the professor picnic at Myers' Lake, and later they dine at Morrelli's Restaurant, where they enjoy spaghetti and meatballs, along with a glass or two of chianti. The professor has told her of her uncanny resemblance to his late wife. In fact, he compares everything Aunt Bee does or says to Ethel.

This is all very upsetting to Aunt Bee. She talks to Andy, who advises her that the situation will pass. When she confides in Clara, she is told that she should simply put an end to the relationship.

Unfortunately, Aunt Bee believes that a marriage proposal may be forthcoming. She tells Andy she is going to tell the professor that she doesn't wish to see him anymore. Andy tells her this will probably only make him pursue the relationship more desperately. Instead, Andy advises her to pretend to be the exact opposite of the late Mrs. St. John. Aunt Bee agrees to go along with her nephew's plan. She presents herself as a worldly swinger, which quickly douses the professor's passionate interest in her. Surprised, disappointed, and confused, Mr. St. John departs Mayberry on the five o'clock train. Before he leaves, Clara makes a last effort to win his favor, but does not succeed.

Undaunted, Clara informs Aunt Bee that she has scheduled another lecture. This one will feature an expert on Outer Mongolia. It seems that *this* lecturer has never been married!

CAST NOTES. Regulars: **Andy Griffith**, **Ronny Howard**, **Frances Bavier**, **Aneta Corsaut**, **George Lindsey**, **Jack Dodson**, and **Hope Summers**.

Veteran character actor **Edward Andrews** guest stars as Professor Hubert St. John. He has appeared in countless television and movie roles, including the 1971 movie *How to Frame a Figg*, with Don Knotts.

EPISODE NOTES. 1. After his lecture, Professor St. John autographs copies of his book. 2. Clara chairs the hospitality committee. 3. Aunt Bee serves chicken cooked in wine, a souffle, and nesselrode pie at the dinner Mr. St. John attends. 4. Andy makes his own elderberry wine. 5. According to Professor St. John, Beatrice, in Latin, means "she who makes happy." 6. Aunt Bee tells the professor that she moved in with Andy and Opie in 1959. 7. Clara calls Aunt Bee "Miss Gadabout." 8. Beulah Albright's son, Harold, was fishing at Myers' Lake when he saw Aunt Bee and the professor picnicking. 9. Ethel Montgomery St. John died 10 years ago. 10. While impersonating a swinger, Aunt Bee suggests that she and the professor should patronize a recently opened nightclub in Mount Pilot called the Bombo Pod. She tells him her motto is "live a little!" She plans an evening at the races and a visit to a little roadhouse called Patty's Place. 11. Clara tries to tempt the professor with *her* nesselrode pie. 12. Opie is in the eighth grade. 13. Mr. Schwump appears, briefly. Look for the back of his head as he sits in the audience listening to the lecture.

"Andy's Investment"

Episode #231. Air date: 11-20-67. Writers: Michael Morris and Seaman Jacobs. Director: Alan Rafkin.

Opie and his eighth-grade classmates have begun to think about what their future might be. Opie plans to go to college, but has not yet decided on a career. Andy wonders what a college education will cost, so he consults Helen. She informs him that most private college tuitions run about $15,000 for four years of study. Andy knows he cannot afford that, so he is greatly relieved when Helen tells him that a state university, such as the University of North Carolina at Chapel Hill, would cost about half as much. However, most universities have a minimum grade requirement of B. Opie's schoolwork is currently averaging out at a C+. No matter what, Andy is determined to make it possible for Opie to go to college.

After Howard Sprague urges him to look for a part-time job or start his own business on the side, Andy spots the following ad in *The Mayberry Gazette*: "Business that operates by itself. A few hours a week of your time. Minimum investment/maximum profits." The business is a coin-operated, self-service laundry franchise called Laundercoin, Inc.

Aunt Bee encourages Andy to pursue the opportunity. She knows of two similar laundries in Mount Pilot that are jammed day and night.

After meeting with Laundercoin representative Mr. Giddings. Andy purchases the franchise. Mr. Giddings assures Andy that the business will not be time-consuming. All Andy will need to do is set up the bleach and detergents every morning, make sure the coin changer is full, and return each night to empty the coin boxes. He claims this will involve only 20 minutes of attention each day.

Andy soon discovers that this is not the case. First, Aunt Bee puts too much detergent in washer #1, and soapy water leaks all over the floor. Next, Emmett absent-mindedly ruins his own shirt, but puts the blame on Andy. Then, Mrs. Edna Sue Larch gets upset when Andy issues her a parking ticket while she is patronizing his business.

Andy is trying hard not to neglect his duties as sheriff, but he finds himself spending most of his time at the Laundercoin business. This realization is driven home when state trooper Leroy Miller and Mr. Rogers, head of the State Bureau of Investigation, come to Mayberry and find Andy working at the laundry.

Andy tries to explain things, but Inspector Rogers points out that being Mayberry's sheriff must be his number one priority. Of course, Andy agrees. The men end up discussing the problems of financing their children's college education. Opie overhears them talking, and he realizes that if he can improve his grades during his upcoming high school years, he can be accepted at a fine state college. This way, he would greatly lessen the financial burden on his father.

When Opie explains his goal, Andy is very proud (and relieved). He sells his franchise to a man named Charlie Johnson and returns to being a full-time sheriff.

Later, Helen brings welcome news to Andy. Opie's grades are improving, and it is very likely that he will average at least a B during high school.

CAST NOTES. Regulars: **Andy Griffith, Ronny Howard, Frances Bavier, Aneta Corsaut, Jack Dodson,** and **Paul Hartman. Maudie Prickett** returns as Mrs. Edna Sue Larch.

Richard Collier appears as Laundercoin representative Mr. Giddings. Collier has appeared in three previous episodes: 203, "Only a Rose," 208, "The Statue," and 218, "Opie's Most Unforgettable Character." **Ken Lynch** returns, this time as Inspector Rogers. **Roy Jenson**, often used in the series, appears as state trooper Leroy Miller. **Jesslyn Fax**, who portrayed Angela on the classic series *Our Miss Brooks*, appears here as Mrs. LeGrande, one of Andy's laundry customers. **Ceil Cabot** appears as Laundercoin customer Alpha Porter.

EPISODE NOTES. 1. Aunt Bee purchased a collegiate dictionary to send to Willis Spooner, the son of her friend Louise Spooner. Willis lives in Hartford, Connecticut, and is attending a small college there. According to gossip from another friend of Aunt Bee's (Harriet Cleaver of South Bend, Indiana), the college has very low requirements. Andy remembers Willis as "the one with the adenoids," but Aunt Bee tells him that Willis's mom says that her son has had his adenoids removed and now talks like anybody else. 2. Opie has an Aunt Martha who lives near the University of North Carolina at Chapel Hill. 3. Howard Sprague went to Bradbury Business College, located on the third floor of the Essex Bank building in Mount Pilot. Howard is a proud graduate, having taken the entire year-and-a-half course. Emmett takes a few jabs at Howard's alma mater. He says the campus is "wall to wall linoleum." He cites Cyrus Whitley as an example of the average Bradbury graduate. Cyrus is now doing five years in prison for embezzlement. Emmett also calls Howard "College Boy." 4. Andy reads classifieds for three other business opportunities. They are door-to-door cosmetics sales, selling the Encyclopedia Europa, and taking orders for suits tailored in Hong Kong. 5. Andy's Self-Service Laundercoin was located on Main Street between Myers' Real Estate and Hill's Store. 6. Opie decides he would like to become a dentist, after talking to Mayberry dentist Dr. Burnside. 7. Andy was told by Mr. Giddings that he could earn up to $200 a month running Laundercoin. 8. Emmett's ruined shirt, which he washed with colored clothes, was originally white. He bought it for $3.95 at Sneedley's. 9. One of Andy's customers, Mrs. LeGrande, has lost a few pounds. She's on a diet and eats nothing but meat, chicken, fish, and steamed vegetables. 10. Alpha Porter drops off her laundry at the courthouse. 11. The University of North Carolina at Chapel Hill is the alma mater of Andy Griffith. Andy appears in some television ads promoting this historic university. These spots have been run during UNC athletic events, and they include a clip from this episode.

"Suppose Andy Gets Sick"

Episode #232. Air date: 12-11-67. Writer: Jack Raymond. Director: Peter Baldwin.

Andy comes down with a severe case of the flu, and Doc Roberts orders him to bed for a few days. But there is no rest for Sheriff Taylor. If Aunt Bee isn't trying to serve him food or change his bedding, then Goober is pestering him to be appointed temporary deputy in his absence.

An extremely reluctant Andy swears in Goober, but warns him to use some common sense, especially since Automobile Safety Progress Week is currently going on in Mayberry. He also allows Acting Deputy Pyle to use the squad car. As can be expected, Goober proves to be quite the over-zealous law enforcer. He starts arresting everyone in sight. In fact, he issues 14 citations in just one day.

To make matters worse, Emmett disturbs Andy by trying to install a reading lamp above his bed. Next, Howard arrives to complain about Goober overstepping the boundaries of an acting deputy. While all of this is going on in Andy's bedroom, Aunt Bee comes in and pleads with him to eat, and Goober wrecks the squad car while pursuing a suspect named Alvin in front of the Taylors' house. Andy threatens to kill him. The turmoil reaches its peak when Aunt Bee, Emmett, Howard, Goober, and Alvin begin screaming at Andy at the same time.

Finally, the next day mercifully arrives, and Andy feels better. He goes back to work and discovers that Goober has repaired the squad car. Andy's happiness is short-lived, however, when he finds out that Goober has made Emmett the new acting deputy. Emmett promptly wrecks the squad car in front of the courthouse.

Andy does get the last laugh when Aunt Bee tells him that Howard, Goober, and Emmett have all come down with the flu.

CAST NOTES. Regulars: **Andy Griffith, Ronny Howard, Frances Bavier, George Lindsey, Jack Dodson,** and **Paul Hartman. Vince Barnett** returns as Elmo. **Charles Thompson** returns as Doc Roberts. **Anthony Jochim** returns as Harvey. **Hollis Morrison** appears as Alvin.

EPISODE NOTES. 1. A boy named Rodney takes over for Goober at the gas station while he's acting deputy. 2. Goober issues Elmo a ticket for turning without using a signal. 3. Emmett's shoelaces are 27 inches long. 4. In Andy's absence, Howard, Goober, and Emmett form the Police Emergency Committee. 5. Doc Roberts still makes house calls. 6. Elmo's wife's name is Margaret. 7. Andy tickets Harvey for making an illegal U-turn on Main Street. 8. Aunt Bee tells Andy that Clara's nephew has the flu too. Could this be Clara's nephew Ferdie? No name is given. Ferdie was the wacky accordionist in episode 189, "A Singer in Town."

"Howard and Millie"

Episode #233. Air date: 11-27-67. Writer: Joseph Bonaduce. Director: Peter Baldwin.

After three months of dating, Howard Sprague and Millie Hutchins decide to tie the knot. They are going to be married the following week in Millie's hometown of Wheeling, West Virginia. They ask Andy and Helen to accompany them on the train ride to Wheeling and to serve as their best man and maid of honor at the wedding. Andy and Helen are happy to oblige.

During the train ride, Howard and Millie's different lifestyles and interests become quite apparent. For example, Howard wants to go to the King Arthur Pageant in Morgantown and to the Blue Rock Caverns in Virginia on their honeymoon. Millie doesn't care for Howard's rigid and precise scheduling. She prefers to do things on the spur of the moment. Her ideal honeymoon would be a trip to Las Vegas. Howard can't understand her sense of adventure. Next, Millie complains to Howard that his mustache tickles her when they kiss, and she wants him to shave it off. Howard refuses, stating that he has worn a mustache for 13 years and it is a tradition among the Sprague men to sport facial hair. They start arguing over their many differences as the train pulls into the Wheeling depot, where Millie's parents and her aunt and uncle are anxiously awaiting the arrival of the two lovebirds.

Finally, Howard and Millie mutually decide to call off the wedding. They want to keep dating, because they do love each other, but they need to learn more about one another. Howard sums it up best at the end of the episode, stating that "all couples should at least take one train ride together before tying the knot."

CAST NOTES. Regulars: **Andy Griffith, Ronny Howard, Aneta Corsaut, George Lindsey**, and **Jack Dodson. Arlene Golonka** returns as Millie Hutchins.

Roy Engel returns to the series, this time as the train conductor. **Carol Veazie** appears as the customer. **Elizabeth Harrower** appears as Millie's mother. **Steve Pendleton** appears as Millie's father. **Ida Mae MacKenzie** portrays Millie's Aunt Hannah. **Robert B. Williams** appears as Millie's Uncle Phil. Williams is known for his portrayal of Garth Gimble, Sr., on *Fernwood 2-Night* from 1977 through 1978.

EPISODE NOTES. 1. Cinnamon buns cost 7 cents a piece at Boysinger's Bakery. 2. Opie buys a dented cake for Aunt Bee at Boysinger's Bakery for $1.00. Millie tells him that the normal price is $1.25. 3. Howard treats Andy, Helen, and Millie to dinner in the dining car of the train. In order to save Howard money, Andy and Helen order the fish cake special. On the other hand, Millie orders shrimp cocktail, a porterhouse steak, au gratin potatoes, celery hearts, and fudge layer cake. 4. Howard believes that his mustache makes him look like a young Tom Dewey or Teddy Roosevelt. Millie

thinks it makes him look like one of the Keystone Cops. 5. Howard loves the Smoky Mountains. 6. Howard refers to Andy as "Soldier" two times during the episode.

"Aunt Bee's Cousin"

Episode #234. Air date: 12-4-67. Writers: Dick Bensfield and Perry Grant. Director: Lee Philips.

Aunt Bee is thrilled when she receives a special delivery letter from her cousin Bradford J. Taylor. Bradford, an international financier, is coming to Mayberry for a visit. He claims to own copper mines in Mexico, a plantation in Brazil, a 41,000-acre sheep ranch in Australia, and a paper mill in Canada. He is also the personal financial advisor to the crown prince of Denmark. Aunt Bee hasn't heard from Bradford in over two years, and Andy and Opie have never met him. Aunt Bee plans to honor him with a gala reception that is sure to be the social event of the year in Mayberry.

On the day that he is scheduled to arrive in town, Andy is shocked to discover that Bradford is riding like a hobo in one of the box cars of a freight train. Bradford explains that he has recently suffered through a series of financial setbacks and is down on his luck. Andy doesn't know what to do. How does he explain to Aunt Bee that Bradford is a failure? Bradford begs Andy not to let the cat out of the bag. Andy agrees to go along with the charade for only a couple of days, after which Bradford must leave.

At the reception, Bradford states that Aunt Bee's homemade ice cream is great and would make a fortune if it were sold internationally. Andy discourages the idea, but Bradford pursues it while Andy is in Mount Pilot on police business. Bradford suggests that the people of Mayberry can contribute financially to the ice cream venture and ultimately share in the profits.

When Andy discovers Bradford's plan, he is forced to tell Aunt Bee and Opie the truth. Andy also orders Bradford to leave town at once. Meanwhile, Aunt Bee has called a special meeting for all potential investors at her house. As they are arriving, she is still at a loss on how to explain Bradford's sudden departure.

As Bradford is attempting to leave town, he runs into the always skeptical Clara Edwards. Clara doesn't realize it, but she is about to unknowingly save the day.

At the investors' meeting, Clara bursts in and interrupts Aunt Bee (before she has had a chance to explain about Bradford) with a startling announcement. Aunt Bee and Andy are pleasantly surprised to hear Clara say that Bradford has been summoned by the state department to deal with a shipping crisis in the Far East. Aunt Bee and Andy decide not to say a word. They are content to let the townspeople believe that Bradford J. Taylor is truly a financial wizard.

CAST NOTES. Regulars: **Andy Griffith, Ronny Howard, Frances Bavier, Aneta Corsaut, George Lindsey, Jack Dodson, Paul Hartman,** and **Hope Summers.**

Jack Albertson stars as Bradford J. Taylor. Albertson is a well-known character actor who has appeared in many movies and television shows. He costarred with Freddie Prinze on *Chico and the Man* in the 1970s. He is also the brother of Mabel Albertson, Mayberry's Mrs. Sprague.

Ann Morgan Guilbert appears as Ella, the social columnist for *The Mayberry Times.* Guilbert's familiar face may be seen quite often on reruns of *The Dick Van Dyke Show.* She appeared as the Petrie's next door neighbor, Millie Helper, from 1961 through 1966. In 1971, Guilbert costarred with Andy Griffith in *The New Andy Griffith Show.* She portrayed Nora, Andy's sister-in-law.

EPISODE NOTES. 1. Aunt Bee and Bradford both grew up in West Virginia. 2. A man named Farley works at the Mayberry Post Office. He delivers Bradford's special delivery letter to Aunt Bee. 3. Bradford sneaks into Mayberry in a freight car numbered WP 754. 4. After he arrives in Mayberry, Bradford claims to have recently sold his copper mines in Mexico. He also states that he is ready to ship 10,000 head of longhorn cattle. 5. Clara states that her family was once involved in the cotton industry. 6. Aunt Bee's homemade strawberry ice cream won first prize at the county fair. 7. Bradford proposes the following names for Aunt Bee's homemade ice cream parlors: "Bee's Homemade Ice Creams," "Mayberry Pride Ice Creams," and "Bradford International Ice Creams." 8. A lady named Emily thought that Aunt Bee's reception for Bradford was the most exciting party ever in Mayberry. 9. Emmett repaired Clara's heating pad for fifty cents. Clara uses it for her chronic neuralgia problems. 10. Bradford says that Mayberry reminds him of the northern part of Mozambique.

"Howard's New Life"

Episode #235. Air date: 12-18-67. Writers: Perry Grant and Dick Bensfield. Director: Lee Philips.

After eating a pork chop dinner at the Taylors', Howard becomes attracted to the Caribbean Islands while watching Aunt Bee's favorite television show, "Travelogue." It seems that he is bored with his monotonous job and the humdrum way of life in Mayberry. To the shock of all his friends, Howard buys a one-way plane ticket to the island of St. Benedict, "the pearl of the Caribbean." He tells Andy, Goober, and Emmett that he will take a bus to the Raleigh airport, where he will fly to Trinidad and then take a boat to his personal Shangri-La.

The big day arrives, and Howard is given a proper sendoff, as well as a bongo set from his friends as a going-away gift.

When he arrives on the island of St. Benedict, Howard rents an oceanside cottage for $10.00 a month. Initially, the idea seems like a good one. Howard enjoys lying in his hammock, running along the shore, and just being away from the land of rubber stamps. He also makes friends with a native boy named Sebastian.

After a day or two, Howard goes to the island's only general store and meets four Americans, who have also left home to pursue the same carefree existence. One of the men is named Grover, and he used to be a big lawyer in Detroit. Howard sees how the years of being idle have left these men almost lifeless. All the men do is tear strips of newspaper and try to sell ships in a bottle. This scene scares Howard half to death, especially after he has a nightmare in which Andy and Aunt Bee come to the island and discover him sitting with the other zombie-like expatriates. He decides to return home, where his job is waiting for him and his friends are thrilled to see him. Howard realizes that his pot of gold lies in good old Mayberry.

CAST NOTES. Regulars: **Andy Griffith, Ronny Howard, Frances Bavier, George Lindsey, Jack Dodson,** and **Paul Hartman.**

Harry Dean Stanton stars as the unnamed proprietor of the general store. Stanton has appeared in such movies as *The Missouri Breaks* (1976), *Alien* (1979), and *The Rose* (1979). **Don Keefer** appears as Grover. **Sam Greene** portrays one of the other "zombies." His name is Wes. **Mark Brown** appears as Sebastian. A gentleman by the strange name of **Sir Lancelot** also appears (credits list him as "the man").

EPISODE NOTES. 1. Goober is a big fan of the actress Dorothy Lamour. 2. Aunt Bee had Opie pick up the pork chops that she served for dinner. They cost ninety-four cents. 3. As part of his job as Mayberry's county clerk, Howard issues business licenses, building permits, dog licenses, sales tax permits, and bicycle licenses. By the way, bicycle licenses still cost fifty cents a year. 4. St. Benedict's island is four miles long and about four miles wide. 5. A sign in the general store on the island says,

"Positively No Credit — *This Means You.*" 6. A man named Norman is another American who hangs around the general store on the island. 7. The Magazine Shop in Mayberry is shown. 8. A man named Wendell raises hunting dogs in Mayberry.

"Emmett's Brother-in-Law"

Episode #236. Air date: 1-8-68. Writer: James L. Brooks. Director: Lee Philips.

Emmett's brother-in-law, Ben Beacham, is visiting in Mayberry. He owns the Ben Beacham Insurance Agency, which is based in Raleigh but has offices throughout North Carolina. Ben is always talking about how successful he is, and he seems to delight in belittling Emmett.

Ben believes that Mayberry, Mount Pilot, and Siler City are virgin territories in need of a good insurance salesman. He offers the job to Emmett, who rejects the idea. However, his wife, Martha, encourages him to seize the opportunity to more than double his salary.

Reluctantly, Emmett closes his shop and takes a one-week training course in Raleigh. Ben even takes him to his tailor so that he can be outfitted with a new suit. However, upon his return home, Emmett discovers that he doesn't have the knack to be a good door-to-door salesman. Besides, his heart is not in the insurance business.

Martha senses Emmett's unhappiness and realizes that he only took the job to please her. His happiness is what she truly wants, and she communicates this to him in a simple but moving way. Emmett's Fix-It Shop is back in business.

CAST NOTES. Regulars: **Andy Griffith, Paul Hartman, George Lindsey, Aneta Corsaut,** and **Jack Dodson.**

Mary Lansing, who has appeared as various characters in this series, most notably as Mrs. Rodenbach, begins her featured role as Martha Clark in this episode.

Dub Taylor returns to the series. He portrays Ben Beacham, Emmett's obnoxious brother-in-law.

EPISODE NOTES. 1. Ben Beacham drives a Continental with a 340 horsepower engine. A bumper sticker on the rear of his car says, "Support Your Local Police." His license plate number is HIJ-517. The car has a vinyl top. 2. Emmett sarcastically refers to Ben as "Mr. Big." 3. Ben addresses Goober as "Mr. Goober." 4. Ben claims that Emmett could make $15,000 per year selling insurance. Emmett's Fix-It Shop income is just shy of $7,500 per year. 5. Mayberry's wealthier citizens live on the north side of town. 6. As Emmett's first customer, Andy purchases a policy for Opie that will pay the boy $1,000 when he turns 21. 7. Goober purchases a life insurance policy that will cost him $9.00 per month. 8. Andy's life insurance is paid by the state, and he gets hospitalization insurance through the Sheriffs' Association. 9. At the episode's end, Goober is selling insurance on a part-time basis for Ben. 10. This is the first of two episodes written by accomplished writer, director, and producer James L. Brooks. His second episode is 237, "The Mayberry Chef." For information about Brooks, please refer to the writers section elsewhere in this book.

"The Mayberry Chef"

Episode #237. Air date 1-1-68. Writer: James L. Brooks. Director: Lee Philips.

Aunt Bee's reputation as a cook pays off when she is asked by Carl Phillips, the owner of television station WZAZ Channel 12 in Siler City, to be the star of her own nightly cooking show. She accepts the offer to host "The Mayberry Chef" after Andy assures her that he has located a suitable cook for him and Opie. The truth is that Andy had asked a noted cook named Miss Felton, but she was already booked. Instead, he tells Aunt Bee that the hired cook is a fictitious newcomer in town named Miss Parkins. He doesn't want to tell her that he is handling the cooking chores himself, because she will give up the lucrative and popular show.

Unlike Aunt Bee, Andy is no chef, and after sampling some of his specialties, such as corned beef hash, soup, and tuna salad casserole, Opie resorts to taking vitamins and eating a huge breakfast every morning. Aunt Bee begins to smell a rat when Opie and Andy give different descriptions of Miss Parkins, and when she discovers that her immaculate kitchen is continually dirty.

Later, Aunt Bee tells Andy and Opie that she has her doubts about Miss Parkins's abilities, and she has located a new cook for the boys. The two Taylor men are pleased and surprised to discover that the new cook is none other than Aunt Bee herself. She was more than willing to sacrifice television stardom in order to care for Andy and Opie. So, like Sarah Bernhardt, Aunt Bee retires at the pinnacle of her career.

MEMORABLE SCENES. 1. Opie eating Andy's home-cooked meals. 2. Opie telling Andy that he will pay for both of their dinners at the Mayberry Diner. Andy refuses, because if they are seen eating in public, the Miss Parkins charade will be discovered.

CAST NOTES. Regulars: **Andy Griffith, Ronny Howard, Frances Bavier,** and **George Lindsey.**

Don Keefer appears as Carl Phillips. Two episodes earlier, Mr. Keefer portrayed Grover in episode 235, "Howard's New Life."

Jack Bannon appears as WZAZ's announcer, Mr. Sabol. Mr. Bannon is the son of actress Bea Benaderet (*Petticoat Junction*) and actor Jim Bannon. He would later appear as the unassuming assistant city editor, Art Donovan, on *Lou Grant* from 1977 through 1982.

Richard Poston appears as WZAZ's unnamed stage manager.

EPISODE NOTES. 1. Siler City is a 25-minute drive from Mayberry. 2. In order to film "The Mayberry Chef," Aunt Bee will be gone every week night from 5:00 P.M. till 8:00 P.M. 3. A man named Mr. Harkinson used to be Aunt Bee's butcher in Mayberry. She says that he was always a gentleman. 4. "The Mayberry Chef" airs at 6:30 P.M., which is the same time that one of Goober's favorite shows, "Rudolph Rabbit," comes on. Goober said that he will watch Aunt Bee, even though Rudolph Rabbit is going to be on Venus during Aunt Bee's premiere show. 5. A man named Charlie is the director of "The Mayberry Chef." 6. A man named Dick is one of WZAZ's stagehands. He helps Aunt Bee carry in the groceries that she uses on the show. 7. The "Mayberry Theme Song" is used to introduce "The Mayberry Chef." 8. Opie says that Aunt Bee answers all of her fan mail. 9. Aunt Bee prepared the following dishes on "The Mayberry Chef": beef casserole, chicken in a pot (not shown), and rib roast. She always cooks her rib roast at 350 degrees.

"The Church Benefactors"

Episode #238. Air date: 1-22-68. Writers: Robert C. Dennis and Earl Barret. Director: Lee Philips.

At the close of Sunday worship at Mayberry's Community Church, Reverend Tucker announces that 93-year-old Jared Hooper, who recently passed away, has remembered the church in his will. He left the sum of $500.00 and requested that it be spent on something practical and beneficial. Reverend Tucker states that the church's Finance Committee, chaired by himself, Andy Taylor, and Martha Clark, will meet and take suggestions as to how the money should be spent.

Aunt Bee and Clara Edwards try to convince the committee that the ladies' choir needs the robes they have wanted for years. Clara even models a robe before the committee, and Aunt Bee says that, at $37.50 per robe, the cost of outfitting the 12-member choir plus the organist is $487.50 (not counting state tax).

Elmo's idea is that the church should purchase a pool table for the men's club meetings. This is not given serious consideration.

Howard Sprague, who heads the Building and Safety Committee, enlists his fellow committee member Emmett Clark to illustrate his idea. Howard points out that, due to a drainage problem over the past five years, the church's foundation has settled, and the building is tilted five inches on one side. This positioning will lead to cracks and damage to the foundation. It will take about $500.00 to repair this problem.

Reverend tucker agrees with Howard's proposal, while Martha Clark sides with the ladies' choir. Elmo suggests that buying a pool table would be a nice compromise, but the idea is once again rejected.

Andy has the deciding vote, and he opts to take a couple of days to mull the situation over. In an effort to influence Andy's decision, Aunt Bee prepares and serves some of her nephew's favorite foods. She puts on added pressure by warning him that if he decides against purchasing the robes, the ladies' choir will disband.

Howard Sprague realizes that this debate is causing the church to divide, rather than stand together, so he tells Andy he will withdraw his proposal. Andy refuses to let him do so because he has made up his mind and has concluded that saving the church is much more important.

Another Finance Committee meeting is called to order, but before Andy officially announces his decision, Howard interrupts. He states that something Reverend Tucker said about Noah's Ark and the great flood has inspired him to come up with an idea that would save the church and also allow the ladies' choir to have their robes. He suggests that the other side of the church can be flooded and allowed to settle five inches, thus leveling the church. An engineer believes this plan may work. It would not cost the church a cent, so the ladies' choir could use the $500.00 to buy their robes. Everyone agrees that it sounds like a great idea.

The following Sunday, the ladies' choir is resplendent in the beautiful robes, and the leveling process is underway, thanks to Howard's divine inspiration.

However, just two weeks later, Howard admits that his plan has failed. The previously unaffected side has sunk eight inches, making the church tilt three inches the other way.

CAST NOTES. Regulars: **Andy Griffith, Ronny Howard, Frances Bavier, Jack Dodson, Paul Hartman, Hope Summers,** and **Aneta Corsaut. William Keene** makes his final appearance as Reverend Tucker. **Mary Lansing** returns as Martha Clark. **Vince Barnett** returns as Elmo.

EPISODE NOTES. 1. Opie usually tithes a quarter at weekly church services. In this episode, he attempts to sell a Canadian quarter to another boy in the congregation for 15 cents. 2. Mabel Trotter is the new soprano in the ladies' choir. 3. Emmett Clark nods off during church services. His wife, Martha, nudges him to wake up. 4. Charlie Bradshaw is a member of the Building and Safety Committee, but he is out of town during this episode. 5. Reverend Tucker doesn't always wear his high collar. He confesses to Andy that he has a short neck and sometimes, the collar kind of gets to him. The reverend visits his flock on Thursdays. 6. The new choir robes are blue with a detachable white collar made of poplin. The robes themselves consist of heavy polished cotton and are guaranteed to be wrinkle-proof. 7. Reverend Tucker recalls a time when the church was divided over whether the building should be painted or have air conditioning installed. Andy remarks that the argument still flares up when they have a hot Sunday. 8. Howard's idea was inspired by the book of Genesis, chapters 6 through 10. 9. The ladies' choir sings the following hymns: "O Grant Us Thy Evening Prayer" and "The Lord Be Gracious Unto You."

"Opie's Drugstore Job"

Episode #239. Air date: 1-15-68. Writer: Kent Wilson. Director: Lee Philips.

"Wanted! Steady job after school and on Saturdays. I'm nearly 14 years old, untrained, but willing to learn. Opie Taylor, 426." This is the ad that Opie puts in *The Mayberry Gazette* in order to find a job so he can buy a new electric guitar. Later that day, Mr. Crawford, the owner of Crawford's Drugstore in Mayberry, asks Andy if Opie is responsible enough to operate a soda fountain. It seems that Mr. Crawford's previous soda jerk, nineteen-year-old Elroy Dockins, has moved on to bigger and better things in Mount Pilot. Andy acknowledges that his son is not perfect, but if the shoe was on the other foot, he would hire Opie in a minute. Mr. Crawford heeds Andy's advice and immediately hires Opie.

After three weeks, Opie has done an outstanding job. Mr. Crawford is so impressed with Opie that he asks him to mind the store by himself for a few hours. Unfortunately, Opie breaks an expensive four-ounce bottle of Blue Moonlight perfume. He gives Arnold $64.00 to pick up a bottle of Blue Moonlight while he and his father are in Mount Pilot. Opie replaces the broken one with the bottle that Arnold brings him.

Later, Andy goes to the drugstore to buy Helen a birthday present. She has told him that Blue Moonlight is one of her favorite fragrances, so he tells Mr. Crawford he is ready to shell out the $64.00 for the perfume. Opie is shocked when he overhears Mr. Crawford tell Andy that all of the perfume bottles on display hold only colored water. The real perfume is stored elsewhere. Andy inadvertently smells the contents of the Blue Moonlight bottle and tells Mr. Crawford that it is the real thing.

After Andy leaves, Opie confesses to his boss. When Mr. Crawford notices how bad Opie feels, he intentionally breaks a bottle to show him that anyone can make a mistake.

CAST NOTES. Regulars: **Andy Griffith, Ronny Howard, George Lindsey,** and **Jack Dodson. Sheldon Collins** returns as Arnold Bailey.

Robert F. Simon stars as Mr. Crawford. Simon is best known as the first of Darrin Stephens's two fathers on *Bewitched*. The role of Frank Stephens would later go to another Mayberry guest star, Roy Roberts (see episode 61, "Andy on Trial").

Diane Deininger returns to the series as Mrs. Briggs. **Jim Begg** returns to the series. In this episode, he is Opie's first customer. He asks for a glass of water, takes one sip and a drag off his cigarette, and leaves.

EPISODE NOTES. 1. Andy's first real job was as a popcorn popper at the movie house. Old Man MacKnight was his boss. 2. Howard's first job was as a truck driver for the Mayberry transfer company. He only lasted a few days because it just wasn't for him. 3. A banana split costs 35 cents at Crawford's Drugstore. 4. Opie gets a 10-cent tip from one of his customers, Mrs. Briggs. 5. Opie's first sale of merchandise is adhesive tape to Goober. 6. While Opie is anxiously waiting for Arnold to bring him the replacement bottle of "Blue Moonlight," he accidentally puts a pickle on Goober's sundae. Later on, Goober specifically asks for a pickle to top off his strawberry sundae. This new taste sensation promptly gives him a bellyache. 7. Question we hate to ask: When Opie broke the water-filled "Blue Moonlight" bottle, how come he didn't notice that the contents had no fragrance?

"Barney Hosts a Summit Meeting"

Episode #240. Air date: 1-29-68. Writer: Aaron Ruben. Director: Lee Philips.

The Raleigh Police Department, led by Captain Dewhurst, is responsible for selecting a site in North Carolina where an East-West summit meeting could be held. The American representative is in

Washington, D.C., while his Russian counterpart is in Florida after enjoying a cruise. It is believed that North Carolina would be a fair compromise to both men, as far as traveling distance is concerned.

Still, a specific town must be decided upon. Barney suggests that Mayberry would be the perfect place, but his input falls on deaf ears. Even when the chief does decide to select Mayberry, Barney doesn't get the credit. He is, however, much to his delight, sent to his hometown to find a nice, comfortable house where privacy can be assured.

Once in Mayberry, Barney enlists Andy to help him find a suitable site. They decide to ask Mr. McCabe, when he comes home, if he will allow his mansion to be used. Barney believes it to be the perfect spot for the summit. In fact, he calls Captain Dewhurst and tells him that a site has been secured. Andy warns Barney that he may be jumping the gun. Unfortunately, Andy is proven right when Mr. McCabe returns. The elderly man is confused and uncooperative. He orders Andy and Barney off of his property.

Andy tells a discouraged Barney to place another call to Captain Dewhurst and tell him the bad news. However, Barney discovers that all concerned parties involved with the summit are en route to Mayberry. Barney is very upset, and in a moment of desperation, he begs Andy to allow his house to be used. Seeing that his friend has no other options, Andy reluctantly consents.

When the men arrive in Mayberry, their unhappiness with the chosen site is made clear. However, Barney assures privacy, and the talks begin. The key figures in the summit are Russian ambassador Mr. Vasilievich, American ambassador Mr. Clifford, and their translator, Mr. Ruskin.

The meeting soon comes to a halt when Goober, Mr. Schwump, and a few others come by to take pictures. The disgruntled parties decide to end talks for the day and retire for the evening. Aunt Bee encourages the men to stay at the house, rather than a hotel. They accept her kind invitation. To make room for their guests, Andy and Barney sleep at the courthouse.

Around midnight, a hungry Mr. Vasilievich finds his way to the kitchen and helps himself to some pickles. Moments later, he is joined by Mr. Clifford, who had the same idea. He discovers some leftover fried chicken. Next, Mr. Ruskin joins in on the refrigerator raid. Aunt Bee awakens, and upon discovering the hungry trio, she invites them to chow down on the leftover meat loaf, potato salad, and bread pudding, too. The men find the atmosphere very welcoming, and their talks continue informally as they enjoy their midnight snack.

The next morning, as Barney and Andy return to the house, they are shocked to find that the summit has ended and the parties are about to leave. They are certain that the summit failed. However, the summit meeting was quite a success, and Barney is praised for choosing the intimate site. Thanks to the relaxed atmosphere and Aunt Bee's delicious food, the men were able to reach a mutually satisfactory agreement.

CAST NOTES. Regulars: **Andy Griffith, Frances Bavier,** and **George Lindsey.** Special guest star **Don Knotts** returns for the fifth and final time since leaving the series. **Richard X. Slattery** returns as Raleigh's chief of detectives, Captain Dewhurst. **Hollis Morrison** and **Charles Horvath** return as Barney's fellow detectives, Jenkins and Peterson.

Michael Higgins appears as U.S. ambassador Mr. Clifford. **Ben Astar** portrays Soviet ambassador Mr. Vasilievich. **Alan Oppenheimer,** who essayed the role of Dr. Rudy Wells on *The Six Million Dollar Man* in the mid-1970s, and who lent his voice to several Saturday morning cartoon characters (notably Mighty Mouse), appears as the interpreter, Mr. Ruskin. **Paul Fix,** best known for his portrayal of Sheriff Micah Torrance on *The Rifleman,* appears here as Mr. McCabe.

EPISODE NOTES. 1. Barney makes a reference to the big day when a gold shipment came through Mayberry. See episode 102, "A Black Day for Mayberry." 2. Barney suggests the following Mayberry buildings as possible locations for the summit: the Kiwanis Club Meeting Hall, the basement of the Moravian church, and the banquet room at the Blu-Vue Motel. 3. Barney used to steal apples from Mr. McCabe's orchard when he was a boy. He would also play "Run, Sheep, Run," "Early, Early Oxen Free" and "1,2,3 Red Light" in his yard. Mr. McCabe used to call him a "scamp." Now, the elderly McCabe has a live-in housekeeper, who acts as his nurse. 4. Mr. Schwump appears at the summit meeting. He and Goober want to have their picture taken with the summit delegation. 5. To help make room for the guests, Opie sleeps on the couch. 6. Aunt Bee claims that her mother always said, "If you eat standing up, it goes right to your legs!" 7. Barney pronounces Vasilievich as "Vaseeliovich." 8. At one point, the chief threatens to kill Barney, but by the end of the episode, he gives Barney a couple of days off as a reward for locating the meeting site. 9. Sarah must be on vacation, as both Andy and Barney address the operator simply as "operator." 10. Barney wears his salt and pepper suit throughout this episode. 11. Barney's final words: "Those of us who chart the course of world events shall forever remain nameless." As he finishes this statement, Barney's "Manhunt Theme" is played for the final time in the series. 12. This was the

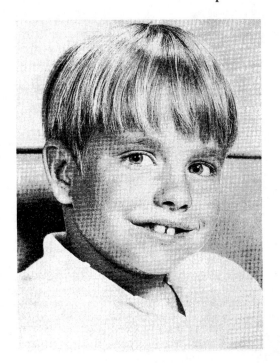

Buddy Foster as Mike Jones.

highest-rated episode in the series. It garnered a 33.4 audience share.

"Mayberry R.F.D."

Episode #241. Air date: 4-1-68. Writer: Bob Ross. Director: Peter Baldwin.

Sam Jones is awaiting the arrival of his old Italian army buddy, Mario Vinchenti, at the Mayberry train station. They haven't seen each other in over seven years. Mario is a farmer, and he's coming to America to help Sam on his farm. But when the train arrives, Sam is shocked to discover that Mario's father and his sister, Sophia, have come to help out and live on the farm as well.

From this point on, everything starts going wrong. First, Mrs. Fletcher, Sam's cook and housekeeper for over twelve years, leaves when Sophia starts to take over in the kitchen. Next, Papa Vinchenti proceeds to drive Sam's automatic, three-speed, model #D432X tractor right through Sam's barn. At this point, Sam is ready to tell the family to leave. In fact, he confides to Andy that the Vinchentis would be better off living in the large Italian farming community in Siler City.

Meanwhile, unbeknownst to Sam, the Mayberry Civic League, headed by Aunt Bee, is hon-

oring the Vinchenti family that evening. Andy takes Sam over to the Mayberry Town Hall, where they watch Aunt Bee and Mario make moving speeches about United States citizenship. Aunt Bee spots Sam and calls him up to the podium, where he reluctantly tells everyone in attendance that the Vinchenti family will help make his farm the best one in the entire state of North Carolina.

MEMORABLE SCENE. Aunt Bee and the Mayberry Civic League honoring the Vinchenti family by singing what they mistakenly believe is the Italian national anthem, "'O Sole Mio."

CAST NOTES. Regulars: **Andy Griffith, Frances Bavier, Aneta Corsaut, George Lindsey, Jack Dodson,** and **Hope Summers.**

Ken Berry makes his first appearance as Sam Jones. Berry was born on November 3, 1930, in Moline, Illinois. As a teenager in the 1940s, he toured for over a year with Horace Heidt's Youth Opportunity Caravan. He made his television debut on Arlene Francis's *Talent Patrol* in the mid-1950s. Shortly after that, he appeared on *The Ed Sullivan Show.* In the late 1950s, he landed several small roles in television comedy programs. In the next two decades he had regular roles in the following programs: *The Ann Sothern Show* (1960-1961) as Woody; *The Bob Newhart Show* (1962); *F-Troop* (1965-1967) as Captain Wilton Parmenter; and *Mayberry R.F.D.* (1968-1971) as Sam Jones. In 1972, he hosted his own variety series called *The Ken Berry Wow Show.* From 1983 to 1984, he appeared in the syndicated series *Mama's Family* as Vinton Harper. Berry has been in many specials and has made dozens of guest appearances on such television programs as *The Andy Williams Show, Apple Pie, Arthur Godfrey's Portable Electric Medicine Show, The Brady Bunch, The Carol Burnett Show, CBS: On the Air* (a 9½ hour 1978 special); *Combat, The Dick Van Dyke Show* (in two episodes as Rob's psychiatrist, Dr. Tony Daniels), *Dr. Kildare, Ellery Queen, Fantasy Island, The Glen Campbell Goodtime Hour, Gimme a Break, Hazel, Hennesy, Here's Lucy, The Jim Nabors Hour, The Life and Times of Grizzly Adams, Little House on the Prairie, Love American Style, The Love Boat, Medical Center, Mrs. G. Goes to College,* several Mitzi Gaynor specials, including *Mitzi and 100 Guys,* in which he was part of her Million Dollar Chorus, *No Time for Sergeants, Rowan and Martin's Laugh-In, Small Wonder,* and *Wendy and Me.* He has also appeared in several made-for-television movies, including *Wake Me When It's Over* (1969), *The Reluctant Heroes* (1971), *Every Man Needs One* (1972), *Letters from Three Lovers* (1973), *Fantasy Island* (1977), and *The Love Boat II* (1972). He has also graced the silver screen in such films as *Two for the Seesaw* (1962, with Shirley MacLaine), *Hello Down There* (a.k.a. *Sub-a-Dub-Dub*, 1969, with Tony Randall and a very young Richard Dreyfuss), *Herbie Rides Again* (1974, with Helen Hayes), *Mountain Man* (1976), and *The Cat from Outer Space* (1978). Berry appeared in the theatrical production *Lend Me a Tenor*. Those wishing to hear some of Berry's tenor singing should check out the album (or tape) "Ken Berry, R.F.D." Berry's voice is also featured on the children's animated video *Peter No-Tail*. In 1993, Berry appeared in *Alone Together* at the Conklin Dinner Theater in Goodfield, Illinois, for 10 weeks. In 1994, he teamed with Tim Conway and began touring in the play *Just for Laughs*. Berry emceed the 1974 Miss Teenage America Pageant, and appeared on the Fashion Awards special in 1975.

Buddy Foster appears as Sam Jones's son, Mike Jones. Buddy's sister is the Academy Award winning–actress Jodie Foster. Buddy Foster would continue portraying Mike Jones on *Mayberry, R.F.D.* until its end in 1971. Foster was born on July 12, 1957. Before being cast as Mike Jones, he was co-starring in 1967's *Hondo* as Johnny Dow. He made guest appearances on a few series, such as *Green Acres* and *Petticoat Junction*. In 1971, he lent his voice to an ABC animated movie, *The Point*, as the count's young son. Foster has appeared in movies, too, including *Angel in My Pocket* (1969, with Andy Griffith) and *Foxes* (1980, starring Jodie Foster).

Gabrielle Tinti stars as Mario Vinchenti. **Letitia Roman** appears as Sophia Vinchenti. **Bruna Della Santina** portrays Papa Vinchenti. **Almira Sessions** appears as Mrs. Fletcher.

EPISODE NOTES. 1. Howard Sprague and his mother both love Italian food. 2. Goober refers to his Ivy League jacket as "Ivory League." He also tells Mario and Sophia that Goober is an American name. Mario had referred to him as "Groober Pyle." 3. Sam Jones drives a light yellow Ford pickup truck. 4. Both Goober and Mike attempt to teach Papa Vinchenti how to play checkers. Mike also tries to teach Mario how to play baseball. 5. Mario and Sophia speak broken English, while Papa Vinchenti speaks none at all. 6. Sam's farm has been in his family for over 100 years. 7. Mario refers to North Carolina as "North California" during his speech to the Mayberry Civic League. 8. In her speech to the Mayberry Civic League, Aunt Bee relates the accomplishments of these two Italian heros: (1) In the field of transportation, Fiorella LaGuardia; and (2) in the field of sports, Rocky Graziano. She also mentions the high quality of Italian shoes. 9. A sign at the Mayberry train depot states that Mayberry's elevation is 671 feet above sea level, and the town's population is 5,360. (In previous episodes the population has been much less.

Episode 162 places it at "under 2,000," and 208 gives it as 1,800.) 10. Mr. Schwump appears at the Mayberry Civic League celebration. 11. This episode was filmed as episode 241 but aired as the final episode, number 249. Thus, as *The Andy Griffith Show* neared its end, this episode paved the way to the highly successful spinoff series, *Mayberry R.F.D.* The Vinchenti family was not in the new series.

"Goober Goes to an Auto Show"

Episode #242. Air date: 3-5-68. Writer: Joseph Bonaduce. Director: Lee Philips.

Aunt Bee is looking for a new car, so she, Andy, Opie, and Goober go to an auto show at the Raleigh Convention Center. Goober looks up Roy Swanson, a fellow he went to automobile trade school with 15 years earlier. They also worked together at a gas station in Raleigh before Roy was fired. Their friendship was quite competitive in the old days. Roy tells Goober that he currently holds the position of senior vice president in charge of engineering at Amalgamated Motors. Not to be outdone, Goober tells Roy that he owns a chain of service stations up and down the eastern coastline.

Goober offers to treat Roy and the Taylors to dinner at the Golden Palace, Raleigh's most expensive restaurant. (Since the meal will cost him a full week's pay, Andy agrees to pay Goober back for all the Taylors' meals at a later time.) Unfortunately, at dinner, Opie innocently reveals that Goober only owns and operates one station, and Roy proceeds to ridicule his old buddy.

On the next day, the Taylors and a dejected Goober prepare to head home. Andy stops to gas up and spots Roy Swanson working as a grease monkey. He brings this fact to Goober's attention, but Goober is a kind and considerate man and refuses to show up Roy. The pair quietly leave, with Goober's self-confidence restored.

CAST NOTES. Regulars: **Andy Griffith, Ronny Howard, Frances Bavier,** and **George Lindsey.**

Noam Pitlik stars as Roy Swanson. Pitlik appeared as Officer Swanhouser on *Sanford and Son* in 1972. He also portrayed Mr. Gianelli on *The Bob Newhart Show* from 1972 through 1973. He is best known, however, as the producer and director on numerous episodes of *Barney Miller*. In fact, he received an Emmy award as best director of a comedy series for his work on *Barney Miller* in 1976.

Patty Regan returns to the series. This time she portrays the frazzled manicurist. **Jack Good** appears as the foreign car salesman. **Freddy Roberto** portrays the waiter at the Golden Palace. **Don Sturdy**

appears as the counterboy who sells hot dogs at the convention. Sturdy is better known as Howard Hesseman, who starred as Dr. Johnny Fever on *WKRP in Cincinnati* from 1978 through 1982. He later starred as schoolteacher Charlie Moore on *Head of the Class*.

EPISODE NOTES. 1. Goober tells Andy that when he was in the service, he once let a guy have it for referring to him as a "hayseed." 2. Goober hires a boy named Norris to mind the service station while he is in Raleigh. Andy states that the Norris boy is not too bright. 3. Goober and the Taylors stay in suites 416 and 418 at the Commodore Hotel in Raleigh. The rooms cost $15.00 a day. In a minor goof, viewers can plainly see that Goober's suite is actually 421. 4. Andy refers to Goober as "a straw in the wind." 5. Goober gets a manicure in Raleigh to impress Roy Swanson and to prove that he doesn't have dirt and grease under his nails. 6. Roy Swanson's wife, the former Ruthie Matthews, once dated Goober. 7. Goober pumps around 80 gallons of gas per day at his service station. 8. Ernie Lewis was a classmate of Goober and Roy at trade school. He currently owns a gas station that pumps about 200 gallons of gas a day. Goober said that Ernie loved hot dogs. 9. At the Golden Palace, Aunt Bee orders lobster, Roy gets the roast beef, Andy gets a big steak, and Opie gets a small steak. Viewers do not get to see what Goober ate. Goober also orders a bottle of Silver Ribbon Champagne, imported from New York. It is the best champagne on the wine list. Goober doesn't know how to properly sample the champagne, and he has to be told by the waiter that champagne is wine. 10. At the end of the episode, Andy has bought a bottle of soda pop and has just taken his first sip when he sees Roy. After he points out Roy's actual occupation to Goober, Andy walks off, inexplicably leaving behind the full bottle of pop.

"Aunt Bee's Big Moment"

Episode #243. Air date 2-12-68. Writers: Dick Bensfield and Perry Grant. Director: Lee Philips.

In her youth, Helen Crump was the eighth-grade spelling champ in Kansas. Goober once won a pancake-eating contest at the local county fair by consuming 57 pancakes with butter and syrup. Howard once lived on a Caribbean island (see episode 235). Andy recalls that during his high school days, he was the fourth-string end on the football team, yet he once caught the winning touchdown pass against arch rival Mount Pilot. Andy's jubilant teammates carried him off the field after the game.

Aunt Bee listens to these highlights and comes to the conclusion that she has never achieved one big moment in her life. So, on a suggestion from Opie (and to the dismay of Andy), Aunt Bee begins taking flying lessons. Her instructor is a nice man named Mr. MacDonald who owns a operates MacDonald's Flight School at the Mayberry Airfield.

Aunt Bee progresses well, and after eleven lessons, her instructor believes she is ready to solo. She is nervous and tries to talk herself out of soloing, but after hearing some words of inspiration from Howard Sprague about how he has always admired Aunt Bee's self-assurance in times of trouble, she decides to give it her best shot. Aunt Bee solos perfectly and finally achieves her big moment in the sun.

CAST NOTES. Regulars: **Andy Griffith, Ronny Howard, Frances Bavier, Aneta Corsaut, George Lindsey, Jack Dodson,** and **Paul Hartman.**

John McLiam stars as Mr. MacDonald. The Canadian-born actor appeared on television as Parker on the western *The Men from Shiloh* from 1970 through 1971. He also portrayed Woody Daley on the television drama *Two Marriages* from 1983 through 1984.

EPISODE NOTES. 1. Helen tells Opie how to spell renaissance. 2. Hors d'oeuvres was the word Helen spelled to win the spelling championship in Kansas. 3. Goober's normal order of pancakes varies between 12 to 15 per sitting. 4. While under the dryer at the beauty parlor, Aunt Bee reads the magazine *Aviation Journal* while two other ladies read *Lady Beautiful* and *Home Decor*. 5. The Records Store in Mayberry is shown in this episode. 6. Emmett's highlight was landing a 361-pound marlin in St. Petersburg. 7. A demonstration flight at MacDonald's Flight School costs $5.00. 8. The number of the plane that Aunt Bee practices and solos in is N59558. 9. Andy, Opie, Helen, Howard, Goober, Emmett, and Mr. MacDonald are all on hand to witness Aunt Bee's solo flight. 10. Goober once had some auto parts air-mailed to him from Detroit. 11. Aunt Bee sings "Off We Go into the Wild Blue Yonder" after she begins her flying lessons.

"Helen's Past"

Episode #244. Air date: 2-19-68. Writer: Doug Tibbles. Director: Lee Philips.

While helping Helen search for a history outline that she needs for school, Andy happens upon an old newspaper clipping. The news photo shows Helen being arrested in her old hometown of

Kansas City. Unbeknownst to her, Andy takes the clipping with him and leaves it on his desk at the courthouse. When Andy is called away for a few minutes, Howard and Goober come in and read the clipping. When Andy returns, he swears Howard and Goober to secrecy until he can uncover the facts. Naturally, Goober immediately tells Ethel Pendleton, who happens to be the president of the P.T.A.

An inquisitive Andy telephones a lady named Miss Blanchard at the *Kansas City Chronicle* and asks her about the arrest. She reports that Helen was arraigned on a felony charge on August 3, 1959. Further investigation reveals that on August 4, Helen was charged with the following offenses: (1) carrying a .38 revolver; (2) dealing cards at an illegal gaming house; and (3) being in the company of Harry Brown, a known hoodlum.

Meanwhile, Mrs. Pendleton has called a special meeting of the Mayberry School Board to decide if Helen should be fired. At the meeting, Helen acknowledges the charges, but before she can elaborate, Andy walks in with an explanation. He discovered that at the time of her arrest, Helen was doing undercover work on organized crime, the subject of her college thesis. She was subsequently cleared of all charges by a court in Kansas City. Andy and all of the others apologize to Helen, and her good standing as a citizen and teacher in Mayberry remains intact. As Opie says at the conclusion of the episode, "Pa, why didn't you just ask Miss Crump?"

CAST NOTES. Regulars: **Andy Griffith, Ronny Howard, Frances Bavier, Aneta Corsaut, George Lindsey,** and **Jack Dodson.**

Ruth McDevitt appears as Ethel Pendleton. McDevitt was born Ruth Shoecraft in Coldwater, Michigan, on September 13, 1895. She died on May 27, 1976. She had several regular roles on television. On *A Woman to Remember* (1949) she played Thatcher. From 1953 to 1955 she was Mom Peepers on *Mr. Peepers*. She was Grandma Hanks on the 1966-1967 series *Pistols n' Petticoats*. She was featured on the 1970 summer series *Johnny Cash Presents the Everly Brothers Show*. From 1973 to 1975, she appeared as Jo Nelson on *All in the Family*. From 1974 to 1975, she appeared as advice-to-the-lovelorn columnist Emily Cowles on *Kolchak: The Night Stalker*. McDevitt has guest-starred in such series as *The Alfred Hitchcock Hour, The Cheerleaders, The Doctors, Mayberry R.F.D., My World...and Welcome to It, Nanny and the Professor, The New Andy Griffith Show* (as Mrs. Gossage), and *Room 222*. In the latter, she appeared in two moving episodes as schoolteacher Elizabeth Brown. (In one, she stirs up controversy when she teaches her students about

VD. In the other, she is diagnosed as being senile.) McDevitt has appeared in many television specials, including two in 1949. One was a production of *Arsenic and Old Lace*, in which she appeared as Martha Brewster. The other production was *Little Women*, in which she portrayed Kathryn March. Among her television movies are *In Search of America* (1971), *The Girl Most Likely To...* (1973), *Skyway to Death* (1974), *The Abduction of Sainte Anne* (1975), *My Father's House* (1975), *Man on the Outside* (1975), and *One of My Wives Is Missing* (1976). She also made many motion pictures, such as *The Parent Trap* (1961, with Brian Keith), *The Birds* (1963, directed by Alfred Hitchcock), *The Shakiest Gun in the West* (1968, with Don Knotts), *Angel in My Pocket* (1969, with Andy Griffith), *The Love God?* (1969, with Don Knotts), *Change of Habit* (1969, with Elvis Presley), *The Out-of-Towners* (1970, with Jack Lemmon), and *Homebodies* (1974, with Ian Wolfe).

Peter Hobbs returns to the series. He portrays Mr. Lockridge, the head of the School Board. In episode 217, "Big Brothers," Hobbs appeared as Mr. Tracy, the principal of the high school.

Connie Sawyer appears as Miss Blanchard. **Monty Magretts** returns to the series as Mrs. Crane. **Michael Freeman** appears as Hollis.

EPISODE NOTES. 1. Helen has an unnamed cat. 2. Maynard Myers was an old boyfriend of Helen back in Kansas City. She kept his old love letters and claims that he is currently married and has six children. 3. Helen is running late for her movie date with Andy because she has invited a friend named Jane Marcus to her house for dinner. 4. Helen needs the history outline because she is taking over Miss Foster's history class at school for two weeks. 5. During the episode, Wallace Crenshaw backs his car into Mr. Benson's vegetable stand. The two Mayberrians then proceed to get into a fight. 6. Goober collects $2.40 for the P.T.A. fund. 7. Judge Branson of Mount Pilot is a good friend of Andy's. 8. In order to make Helen feel comfortable, Aunt Bee admits that her great uncle was a cattle rustler, and Opie admits that he and Arnold once sneaked into the movie theater without paying. 9. Howard Sprague is a member of the Mayberry School Board. 10. Helen has a master's degree in journalism. 11. It is quite possible that the character of Mr. Lockridge was based on an outstanding member of the community in Mount Airy, North Carolina, named Vernon Lockridge.

"Emmett's Anniversary"

Episode #245. Air date: 2-26-68. Writers: Perry Grant and Richard Bensfield. Director: Lee Philips.

Tightfisted Emmett Clark decides to splurge and surprise his wife Martha by giving her a mink coat as a twenty-fifth anniversary present. She has had her heart set on a mink for many years. Flora tells Emmett that she has a friend in the fur business in Mount Pilot who will give him a 40 percent discount if she accompanies him to the store. Emmett informs Andy about the plan and tells Martha that he is going out that night to bowl with some of his pals. Unfortunately, Martha and Ethel Pendleton, on their way to watch a Greer Garson movie currently playing in town, spot Emmett picking Flora up at the Mayberry Diner. Martha believes that Emmett is stepping out on her. She confronts Andy, who is forced to tell her the truth. Needless to say, she is thrilled by the news.

At Bernie's Fur Shop in Mount Pilot, Emmett comes to the conclusion that, even with a 40 percent discount, a fur coat is simply out of his price range. He thanks Bernie, and he and Flora head back to Mayberry. He decides to buy Martha a simple bathrobe at Burford's Store in Mayberry. However, when he discovers from Andy that Martha knows about the trip to Mount Pilot, he rushes back to Bernie's and, with some reluctance, buys Martha a ranch mink coat. Now, Martha Clark is the happiest woman in the town of Mayberry.

MEMORABLE SCENE. Emmett getting caught by Martha, gloating about buying a mink coat, *after* he had bought the bathrobe.

CAST NOTES. Regulars: **Andy Griffith, Ronny Howard, George Lindsey,** and **Paul Hartman. Mary Lansing** returns as Martha Clark. **Ruth McDevitt** returns as Ethel Pendleton. After being absent since the sixth season, **Alberta Nelson** returns for her final appearance as Flora Mallerby. She is once again working as a waitress at the Mayberry Diner.

Ronnie Schell returns to the series. This time he portrays Bernie, the furrier. In episode 187, "The Foster Lady," Schell appeared as Jim Martin.

EPISODE NOTES. 1. Emmett originally plans to spend around $50.00 on Martha's present. Goober suggests he should consider buying her one of the following items: perfume, a smoked ham, a set of nylon tires, or a fox coat that goes around her neck and bites its tail. Andy suggests a purse or a black negligee. 2. Martha grows begonias and suffers from bursitis. 3. In an odd scene, Martha is shown drinking alcoholic beverages with Ethel Pendleton when she thinks Emmett is being unfaithful. 4. Aunt Bee is out of town during this episode, so Ethel Pendleton takes over the cooking and housekeeping chores at the Taylor household. 5. A lady named Dorothy works at the Mayberry Diner with Flora. 6. *Goodbye, Mr. Chips* is one of Martha and Ethel's favorite Greer Garson movies. 7. The best ranch mink that Bernie has for sale costs $1800.00, even with the 40 percent discount. It is similar to one that Princess Grace owns. Since Emmett and Flora arrive at Bernie's after normal working hours, Bernie models some of the furs, complete with a cigar in his mouth. 8. Ethel tells Andy to set up the table to play some dominoes after dinner. 9. Mount Pilot is said to be a thirty-minute drive from Mayberry.

"The Wedding"

Episode #246. Air date: 3-4-68. Writer: Joseph Bonaduce. Director: Lee Philips.

Howard is pleasantly surprised when his mother announces that she has accepted a marriage proposal from her beau of six months, George Watkins. After the wedding, the couple will reside in Mount Pilot, where George's business is located. Howard will continue to live in his mother's Mayberry home, but he will definitely be making some changes. He plans to turn the place into a bachelor pad.

After the wedding ceremony, Howard begins devoting much of his time to refurbishing his home. Andy, Emmett, and Goober are very curious to see just what Howard is doing, so they pay him a visit. Howard proudly displays his new decor, which includes a bearskin rug, a miniature gong, abstract paintings, a wooden Indian, colorful floor pillows, indirect lighting, and a beaded entrance. Howard says, "It's the real me!"

Howard invites Andy and Goober to his first bachelor party, which will be held on Saturday. He tells his friends to bring their dates. When Emmett exclaims that he and Martha will be there, Howard apologetically explains that this is a "singles only" bash.

Unfortunately, when Saturday rolls around, neither Howard nor Goober has been successful in finding a date. Imagine Andy and Helen's surprise when they discover that Helen is the only female there!

Howard does his best to be a good host. He offers his guests swiss cheese sandwiches and attempts to get some dialogue going. Next, he plays an album by a new group called the Silver Herringbones. It is a jazzy instrumental LP, and Howard encourages Andy and Helen to dance. Then Goober and Howard each take a turn cutting the rug with Helen. The three men dance with her repeatedly, until she nearly drops from sheer exhaustion.

Around 9:00 P.M., Andy is ready to leave. He

claims that Helen has to teach Sunday School in the morning. Goober wants to leave, too. The party has been a bore.

As the trio prepares to leave, Emmett makes a surprise appearance. He says he was in the area, waiting around to pick up Martha after her bridge game. A former finalist in the annual Harvest Ball, Emmett offers to show the group what dancing is all about. He then proceeds to trip the light fantastic, performing an amazing and hilarious dance routine. Everyone is delighted, and the evening ends on a good note.

MEMORABLE SCENE. Howard, Goober, and Emmett dancing, and Howard yelling, "Go, Man Go!" as Emmett does his routine.

CAST NOTES. Regulars: **Andy Griffith, Jack Dodson, Aneta Corsaut, George Lindsey,** and **Paul Hartman.**

Mabel Albertson makes her final appearance as Mrs. Sprague, Howard's overbearing mother. Her character's first name was never revealed.

Teri Garr appears briefly as a girl who rejects Goober. She makes an awful face at him at the filling station. Garr is well known to both television viewers and moviegoers. She made many commercials, selling everything from coffee to underwear, and she appeared on *Late Night with David Letterman* on many occasions. A veteran film actress, her most notable films include *Oh God!, Mr. Mom, Close Encounters of the Third Kind*, and *Tootsie.*

Iggie Wolfington portrays Mr. George Watkins.

EPISODE NOTES. 1. A few facts about George Watkins: (1) He proposed to Mrs. Sprague as they were eating rice pudding at Morelli's Restaurant. (2) He would prefer not to be called "Dad" by Howard. (3) His car's license plate number is the familiar GP-780. 2. Howard bought his abstract paintings from an out-of-the-way shop in Mount Pilot. The price of his art was in the $10 to $20 range. The shop also had paintings for $5 to $7, but these were regular prints of everyday items such as apples and clowns. 3. Offering up drinks, Howard asks his friends to "name their poison." He offers grapefruit juice, lemon-lime, and orange soda. But, if they prefer "the hard stuff," he has some apple cider that has started to turn. 4. The six-foot, three-inch tall Howard pays a visit to his recently wed mother in Mount Pilot. While he is there, he meets two nurses who agree to come to his next bash. One will be his date, the other will be Goober's. Unfortunately, they'll be bringing their mothers. 5. In his quest for a date, Goober is turned down by a girl named Jenny (she's engaged), a woman named Irene (she went into the operating room at 5:00 P.M.), a

female customer at his gas station (she gives him a dirty look), and Sally Marsh, whom he refers to as "the end of the line." Howard is rejected by Dorothy (who is visiting her folks), Marian (who is busy), and Shirley (who barely remembers him). Howard reminds Shirley that they met at a dance last fall at the lodge.

"Sam for Town Council"

Episode #247. Air date: 3-11-68. Writers: Dick Bensfield and Perry Grant. Director: Lee Philips.

Herb Bradshaw has resigned his post as the head of the Mayberry Town Council in order to take the job of head teller at the Raleigh Security Bank. Emmett Clark believes that he is the man to succeed Herb on the council. Andy, Howard, and Goober believe that Emmett lacks the proper experience to be a good councilman. They recall the time that Emmett was unsuccessful when he was put in charge of the "Patronize Your Local Merchant" campaign. In fact, Mayberry experienced one of its rare business slumps during this campaign.

Emmett is shocked when his friends endorse a somewhat reluctant candidate, Sam Jones. With the help of some coaxing by Andy, Howard, and Goober, Sam accepts the nomination, and the war is on. Emmett begins making campaign promises that will be impossible to keep, while Sam runs on a "No Favoritism" platform.

The race is nip-and-tuck, but on election day, Andy announces that he has received word from Mrs. Blair (the lady who tabulates the votes) that Sam has won by 405 votes. A gracious Emmett immediately leaves his campaign headquarters at the Fix-It Shop to congratulate Sam at his headquarters, the Taylor residence.

Sam's elation is short-lived however, when his constituents start asking for personal favors, which goes against everything his campaign stood for. First, Goober wants a stop sign by his gas station at the intersection of Main Street and Garden Road, in order to attract more customers. Next, Howard tells Sam that his county clerk's office needs to be redecorated. Also, Mr. Calvin, one of Sam's volunteer workers, requests some changes on Elm Street, where he resides. Even Aunt Bee asks Sam to allocate money to her garden club so the members will be able to attend a flower show in Raleigh.

Andy consoles Sam by telling him that any decisions he makes must be for the good of the town, not the individual. Andy also tells Sam that he believes that he will do the right thing. This little chat with Andy guides Sam in the right direction,

and he looks forward to being the head of the Mayberry Town Council.

CAST NOTES. Regulars: **Andy Griffith, Ronny
Howard, Frances Bavier, Aneta Corsaut, George
Lindsey, Jack Dodson,** and **Paul Hartman. Ken
Berry** returns as Sam Jones. For viewers who
remember the original run of *The Andy Griffith Show*
on CBS, in 1968, this episode was Berry's first
appearance on the series. Episodes are shown in
syndication as they were filmed, not as they were
originally broadcast. Thus, in syndication, Berry's
first appearance was in episode 241, "Mayberry
R.F.D."

Roy Engel returns to the series. This time he
appears as Mr. Perkins, though the cast credits
incorrectly list him as *Mrs.* Perkins. **Gil Lamb** is
listed in the credits for his appearance as Lou. However, in the two different copies of this episode we
had to review for this book, we never saw the character of Lou. **Don Sturdy** portrays Harry. **Penny
Kunard** appears as Mrs. Farley. **Dick Johnstone**
portrays Mr. Calvin. **Mary Lou Taylor** returns to
the series. She appears as Mrs. Barton. Taylor had
previously appeared in episode 212, "Barney Comes
to Mayberry."

EPISODE NOTES. 1. The "Mayberry Theme
Song" is played while Emmett is daydreaming about
becoming the head of the Mayberry Town Council. 2. Sam Jones is a military veteran. He earned a
sharpshooter's medal in the service. 3. Howard
Sprague is the person who originally suggests nominating Sam Jones. 4. Goober's campaign slogans for
Sam are "Fair and Square Sam," "Sam's the Best, to
Heck with the Rest," and "Tippecanoe and Sam,
Too." 5. Mrs. Farley complains to Emmett about
the moving of her son Evan's Cub Scout meeting
place from the school to the building behind the
firehouse. 6. Emmett greets a man named Harry on
Main Street. Harry is on his way to do some fishing
at Miller's Pond. 7. In an attempt to solicit votes for
Sam, Andy and Howard visit Mr. Perkins, and
Aunt Bee and Helen visit Mr. Calvin. Aunt Bee
promises the elderly Mr. Calvin that Helen will pick
him up and take him to the polls on election day.
This excites Mr. Calvin. 8. Goober and Sam visit
Mrs. Barton and her young daughter, Cindy.
Goober makes Sam kiss Cindy, who is eating a jelly
sandwich. 9. Emmett greets an unseen Mayberrian
named Mr. Linke. This could be an acknowledg-
ment to Andy Griffith's long-time friend, partner,
and manager, Richard O. Linke.

"Opie and Mike"

*Episode #248. Air date: 3-18-68. Writer: Doug
Tibbles. Director: Lee Philips.*

Sam Jones's eight-year-old son, Mike, is having
trouble at school with an older and bigger boy
named Edgar Watson. Fourteen-year-old Opie volunteers to help Mike deal with the situation. When
Opie rescues Mike from one of Edgar's attacks,
Opie suddenly becomes Mike's idol and constant
companion. They walk to and from school together,
play baseball and Chinese checkers, and generally
are inseparable.

Everything is fine until new neighbors move in
next door to the Taylors. One of the newcomers is
a pretty fourteen-year-old girl named Heather
Campbell. Heather tells Opie that she and her family have just moved from West Virginia. In no time
at all, Opie becomes so preoccupied with Heather,
that he no longer has any time at all for Mike.

In a funny scene, Sam makes a futile attempt to
explain human relationships to his son. However,
Mike remains "down in the dumps"—until he meets
Heather's eight-year-old sister, Claudia. They
immediately hit it off and quickly become good
friends.

MEMORABLE SCENE. Aunt Bee and Andy
spying on the Campbells as they are unloading their
belongings.

CAST NOTES. Regulars: **Andy Griffith, Ronny
Howard, Frances Bavier,** and **George Lindsey.
Ken Berry** returns as Sam Jones. **Buddy Foster**
returns as Mike Jones. In the original CBS broadcasts of *The Andy Griffith Show* in 1968, this episode,
"Opie and Mike," was the first one in which Buddy
appeared. In syndication, however, the episodes are
aired in the order in which they were filmed. Thus
Buddy's first appearance in syndication is episode
241, "Mayberry R.F.D."

Diane Quinn appears as Heather Campbell.
Kellie Flanagan portrays Claudia Campbell. Flanagan would later become a regular on *The Ghost and
Mrs. Muir,* appearing as Candace Muir from 1968
through 1970. **Russell Schulman** portrays the bully,
Edgar Watson. Television fans may remember
another occasion when young Schulman appeared
as a bully. In *The Brady Bunch* episode entitled "A
Fistful of Reasons," he portrayed Cindy Brady's
tormentor, Buddy Hinton.

EPISODE NOTES. 1. The Mayberry City
Council building is shown. Portraits of Abraham
Lincoln and George Washington adorn the walls of
the building. Goober offers Sam his portrait of John
Wayne to hang up next to them. Sam politely
declines the offer. 2. Mike imitates Opie by putting

his comb in his shirt pocket. 3. Opie gives Mike his old baseball mitt. 4. Goober says that corn on the cob is one of his favorite vegetables. He also says that fellow Mayberrian Old Joe Benson has a hard time eating corn on the cob because he's missing a front tooth. 5. Andy relates to Sam the events that occurred to Opie in episode 34, "Opie and the Bully." 6. L & B Movers are the company that transports the Campbells' belongings from West Virginia to Mayberry. 7. Opie and Heather Campbell are both in the eighth grade. 8. Opie takes Heather to the Mayberry Record Shop. Mike tags along. Opie buys two albums. Later, Opie, Heather, and a disenchanted Mike dance to the groovy sounds. Heather shows Opie a dance that she learned in West Virginia. Opie claims that he doesn't know any out-of-state dances. 9. Aunt Bee tells Andy that when Opie gets married, he can use Andy's mother and father's furniture that is currently in storage in the Taylors' attic. 10. Heather Campbell takes piano lessons. 11. Claudia Campbell arrives in Mayberry a few days after the rest of her family. She had been staying with her grandmother while her parents and sister were getting settled in.

"A Girl for Goober"

Episode #249. Air date: 3-25-68. Teleplay: Bruce Howard. Story by: Bob Ross. Director: Lee Philips.

Andy and Sam feel sorry for Goober. It seems that the lonely mechanic tags along every time Andy and Sam go out on double dates with their respective girlfriends, Helen and Doris. Goober tells his buddies that his "girlfriend," Juanita, the telephone operator, has been parking with Harold Fossett from 8:00 P.M. until midnight every night at Myers' Lake.

Andy and Sam want to help Goober and are pleased to discover that a company in Mount Pilot, called Scientific Introductions, is providing a new computer dating service in the Mayberry area. The head of the company is a pretty lady named Edith Gibson. Edith has a Ph.D. in psychology from State. For a trial run, she and her assistant, Mr. Franklin, have placed ads for the dating service in a few selected newspapers, including *The Mayberry Gazette*. Andy and Sam convince Goober to give the service a try.

Dr. Gibson uses herself as the first female applicant in order to test the program. Meanwhile, Goober misrepresents himself as he fills out the questionnaire that he hopes will match him up with a compatible date. For example, one of the questions is "How many books do you read per month?"

Goober's response is thirty. He doesn't bother to mention they are comic books. Also on the questionnaire, Goober claims to love sports and painting. He fails to mention that "painting" refers to the time he repainted Sam's barn.

Back at Scientific Introductions, Dr. Gibson is amazed to see that she and Goober apparently have the same interests. She telephones him, and they set up a 7:00 dinner date at Morelli's on the following evening. For the date, Goober borrows Andy's blue suit and Sam's cuff links. He also gets a funky haircut for $6.00 (including a can of hair spray) from Mayberry's new barber. He even buys a corsage for Edith. He also asks a reluctant Andy and Sam to tag along and sit at a nearby table at Morelli's, just in case the date goes sour.

When Edith finally arrives, the dinner date is awkward at first, when she discovers the truth about Goober's responses to the questionnaire. Surprisingly, the rest of the evening goes very well, once Goober relaxes. In fact, they become friends and start dating. Edith explains to her associate, Mr. Franklin, that sometimes opposites attract, and computers are only machines.

CAST NOTES. Regulars: **Andy Griffith, Ronny Howard, Aneta Corsaut,** and **George Lindsey. Ken Berry** returns as Sam Jones.

Nancy Malone stars as Dr. Edith Gibson. Malone starred in the television series *Naked City* as Libby from 1960 through 1963. She also appeared on television in *The Long Hot Summer* as Clara Varner from 1965 through 1966. She has also produced numerous television programs over the years. **Tod Andrews** portrays Mr. Franklin. Andrews had previously appeared in the series in episode 26, "The Inspector," as Inspector Ralph Case. **Maggie Peterson**, best known to fans of the series as Charlene Darling, makes her one and only appearance away from that role as Sam's girlfriend, Doris. **Richard Poston** appears as the waiter at Morelli's. **George Sawaya** and **Yvonne Shubert** portray a couple who are dining at Morelli's.

EPISODE NOTES. 1. Goober states that he is 33 years old. 2. The cost of the dating service is $5.00. 3. Dr. Gibson's telephone number is Mount Pilot — 4872. 4. Sam's girlfriend, Doris, plays the piano. 5. It took Edith Gibson three weeks to read *The Rise and Fall of the Roman Empire*. During the dinner date, Edith refers to the Greek philosopher Aristotle. This prompts Goober to check out and read a book about the writings of Aristotle. 6. Andy gives Opie some money to buy a turtleneck shirt at Weaver's Department Store. The shirt has been marked down from $2.50 to $1.85. 7. The song that the gang sings at the beginning and end of the episode is entitled, "You and I." 8. Dr. Gibson mentions the town of Toast as a possible test site for the dating service. The real town of Toast, North Carolina, is located just a few miles from Mount Airy. 9. This episode was the final one to be filmed, and it is the last episode seen in the syn-dication packages that are shown today. In the original run of *The Andy Griffith Show* on CBS in 1968, the final episode aired was episode 241, "Mayberry R.F.D."

THE CONTINUATION

This section summarizes the first episode of *Mayberry R.F.D.* It is, undoubtedly, the funniest of the series. Andy and Helen finally tie the knot, Barney returns to act as Andy's best man, and Aunt Bee makes a major decision. The entire series is very enjoyable, but this is the only episode to include many of the original cast members of *The Andy Griffith Show.*

"Andy and Helen Get Married"

Episode #1. Air date: 9-23-68. Writer John McGreevey. Director: Christian Nyby.

After years of dating steadily, Andy and Helen are about to tie the knot. Andy's friends throw him a nice bachelor party, capped off by a toast from Sam Jones.

Andy informs Sam that although he and Helen will return to live in Mayberry after a Florida honeymoon, Aunt Bee will be going away to live with her sister, Laura, in West Virginia. She has declined Andy and Helen's invitation to stay with them, saying that, as much as she loves Helen, two women in one household is one woman too many.

Sam is facing a minor domestic crisis himself. His housekeeper, Miss Jellico, has moved back to Fayetteville to deal with some family problems. He has placed an ad in the newspaper for help, but has yet to receive a response. His young son, Mike, suggests he should ask Aunt Bee to be their new housekeeper. It's a great idea, but unfortunately, Aunt Bee's plans are set.

Reverend Tucker officiates at Andy and Helen's wedding, and Barney Fife serves as Andy's best man. Helen's father, from Kansas, escorts her down the aisle. Opie sits with a weeping Aunt Bee. Barney provides some unintentional comic relief during the ceremony. First, he holds hands with Andy. Next, he clears his throat at a crucial point, drowning out the vows, and then proceeds to temporarily misplace the wedding ring. Finally, after Reverend Tucker completes the ceremony, Barney walks down the aisle with the happy couple, waving to his friends.

As the reception at the Taylors' house ends, Reverend Tucker unwittingly encourages Aunt Bee to stay in Mayberry and help out Sam and Mike.

The role of housekeeper is familiar to Aunt Bee. However, she has never lived on a farm. She is intimidated first by Irma, Sam's dairy cow, and then by the laying hens, as she tries to retrieve some eggs. On one particular day, a neighboring farmer runs his cattle down the road. Aunt Bee witnesses this and begins screaming, "Stampede!" All in all, Aunt Bee finds that farm living just isn't right for her. Regretfully, she tells Sam that she has decided to go ahead with her original plans.

Mike is especially sad to hear her decision. He shows Aunt Bee some photographs of his ancestors and tells her about the hardships they faced as they settled the land. Hearing these stories inspires the pioneering spirit in Aunt Bee. Deciding to face the challenge of farm life, she proudly retrieves an egg from the chicken coop.

Aunt Bee decides to stay and take care of Sam and Mike, the same way she took care of Andy and Opie for eight years. The stage is set for a successful three-year run and more tales from Mayberry.

MEMORABLE SCENE. Barney's wedding antics, and the revelation that he tagged along with Andy and Helen on their honeymoon to Florida.

CAST NOTES. The following actors appeared in this episode and would go on to have regular roles in *Mayberry R.F.D.*: **Ken Berry** as Sam Jones, **Buddy Foster** as Mike Jones, **Frances Bavier** as Aunt Bee Taylor (until 1970), **George Lindsey** as Goober Pyle, **Jack Dodson** as Howard Sprague, and **Paul Hartman** as Emmett Clark.

The remaining actors were guest stars in the new series, and for some, this would be their only appearance. A few, however, would come back for a few more episodes of *Mayberry R.F.D.* The actors are as follows: **Andy Griffith** appears as Sheriff Andy Taylor. He would return to make a few more appearances on the show, including for the baptism of his infant son in the episode "Andy's Baby." **Don Knotts** appears as Barney Fife. This was his only appearance in the series. **Ronny Howard** appears as Opie Taylor. This was his only appearance in the series. **Aneta Corsaut** appears as Helen Crump Taylor. She would appear one more time, in the episode "Andy's Baby." (By the way, the baby's name was Andrew Samuel Taylor, Jr.) **William Keene** returns as Reverend Tucker. He would also return to baptize Andy's son (called Samuel) in the episode, "Andy's Baby."

EPISODE NOTES. 1. Barney is noticeably absent from Andy's bachelor party. 2. Goober assumes the role of sheriff while Andy is on his honeymoon. Andy refused to allow him to wear a gun, but Goober wears a gun belt and holster. He uses the holster to hold his newest comic book. 3. In 1962, Howard Sprague and his mother took a memorable trip to Florida. They especially enjoyed the Wildlife Sanctuary near Orlando, where they watched the mating dance of the scarlet egrets. 4. During the honeymoon, Opie goes on a camping trip with the Hutterfield family. 5. Howard suggests that Andy take Helen to see the Great Dismal Swamp while in Florida. On *The Andy Griffith Show*, in episode 141, "Otis Sues the County," it is said that Mary Pleasance and Dixie Bell Edwards went to the Great Dismal Swamp to hunt black bear. 6. Barney wears his salt and pepper suit when he appears as Andy's best man. 7. Among the items Aunt Bee serves at the reception are shrimp, finger sandwiches, potato salad, cake, and punch. 8. The Jones family has owned their farm for over 100 years. Mike's great-great grandfather started the farm. His wife had never lived on a farm until she moved to Mayberry from Philadelphia. According to Sam, the woman never had fewer than 300 chickens, and she milked three cows every day. 9. Mike's great-grandmother was originally from Charlotte. She once shot a bear that had wandered into her yard. On another occasion, she talked a group of Indians out of burning down her farm. 10. Goober claims that it took him a year and a half before he felt at home in the eighth grade. 11. Andy sends a postcard from Florida to his friends. 12. Good old Mr. Schwump (complete with bad toupee) appears at Andy's bachelor party and at the wedding. 13. *Mayberry R.F.D.* was still popular when it was canceled in 1971. Fred Silverman, the president of CBS at that time, decided to do away with all "rural-oriented" programs, including *Green Acres, Petticoat Junction*, and *The Beverly Hillbillies*.

REUNION

In 1986, *The Andy Griffith Show* had been out of production for 18 years. Its continuation series, *Mayberry R.F.D.*, had been over for 15 years. Incredibly, America's love of Mayberry never waned. So, veteran writers Everett Greenbaum and Harvey Bullock, director Bob Sweeney, and many of the regulars from *The Andy Griffith Show* reunited to make one of the most popular television movies of 1986, *Return to Mayberry*.

"Return to Mayberry"

NBC TV Movie. Air date: 4-13-86. Writers: Harvey Bullock and Everett Greenbaum. Director: Bob Sweeney.

Twenty years have gone by since Andy and Helen left Mayberry. They have been living in Cleveland, where Andy has been serving as a U.S. postal inspector. Andy, knowing that back home a sheriff's election is drawing near, decides to return to Mayberry to win his old job back. In Mayberry, Sheriff Patterson has died, and Barney Fife has become the acting sheriff. Some years ago, Barney left his Raleigh job and returned home to become the sheriff's deputy.

Andy has planned his return. He contacted Howard Sprague before leaving for Mayberry so that the county clerk could file the necessary papers which will allow him to be put on the ballot. Andy will make the trip to Mayberry by car. Helen stays behind to take care of a few things but will join Andy in a few days.

Andy is a happy man. He is coming home to old friends, he is a virtual shoo-in to win his old job back, and most importantly, he is about to become a grandfather. Opie, publisher and editor of Mayberry's newspaper, *The County Courier Express*, is married to Eunice, and they are eagerly awaiting the birth of their first child. The couple lives in a large house in the Mayberry countryside.

As Andy nears Mayberry, he stops at one point to gaze out over Myers' Lake and remember the many happy hours he and Opie spent there.

As he pulls into town, his car begins acting up.

He pulls into the G&G Garage and is greeted by its owners and operators, Gomer and Goober Pyle. Andy tells them his car is lurching and says he believes the carburetor is the trouble. Unfortunately, the Pyle cousins do not have a spare one to replace Andy's, but they promise to order him one. Andy tinkers with his car, hoping to get by until the new carburetor arrives.

Goober and Gomer show Andy Barney's campaign poster, which says, "Vote Fife For Sheriff." Andy is surprised. He did not know Barney was going to run. After some good-natured ribbing from Goober and Gomer about becoming a grandfather, Andy drives into the heart of Mayberry...Main Street. He takes a good, long look. Some things have changed. The area is more modern than it used to look, and Main Street is now much wider, with a flagpole in the middle of it, splitting the street into two directions. Some things, though, never seem to change. The courthouse looks the same, and there are still a few town loafers about.

Opie's office is on Main Street, and Andy is very happy to see him. Opie has a mustache now, and when Andy asks him about it, Opie replies that Aunt Bee always said he had a short lip.

Andy is surprised to find Howard Sprague working for Opie. Howard is a part-time photographer for the paper. Howard confides to Andy that he is worried about losing his looks. His hair is now totally gray. Andy informs him that he could dye his hair using store-bought products. This idea interests Howard, who wants to look younger. You see, he fancies a woman named Rose, a librarian in nearby Mount Pilot.

Andy Griffith and writer Everett Greenbaum during the writing of the 1986 NBC TV-Movie, *Return to Mayberry.*

Andy informs Opie and Howard that he will be withdrawing from the sheriff's race. He doesn't want to compete against Barney. He says there haven't been too many high spots in Barney's life, and becoming sheriff just may be the lifelong lawman's moment in the sun. Andy wouldn't want to stand in Barney's way.

Next, Andy is shocked to discover that Otis Campbell has completely reformed himself. Howard says Otis stopped drinking years ago. Otis now drives his own ice cream truck. He stops when he sees Andy and leaves him holding a free sample.

Andy meets businessman Wally Butler when the young man drops by to see Opie about advertising in his paper. Wally bought what used to be known as the Shanghai Gardens Restaurant, one of Mayberry's finest eateries. He has refurbished the place and changed the menu to continental cuisine. He has also added on a 16-unit motel. The new name of the establishment is Butler's Pantry and Inn.

Unbeknownst to everyone but Wally and mountain wild man Ernest T. Bass, a controversy is about to erupt in Mayberry. Wally wants to draw tourists to Mayberry and get his business off to a good start. Inspired by "Nessie," the Loch Ness monster, Wally

has taken a pink rubber dragon head from an old Shanghai Gardens sign, and, by using machinery hidden in a shed at Myers' Stone quarry, he has rigged it to make it appear that there is a monster in Myers' Lake. Ernest T. runs the machinery for him and is also stealing numerous chickens and dogs from the area (and stowing them at the Darlings' mountain home). This is to make it appear that the monster has eaten them. Ernest T. also makes huge animal footprints around the lake. The mountain man is more than happy to help Butler out. Besides, Wally lets Ernest T. keep a discarded old frock that has "Wally Butler" embroidered on the lapel.

Back to the sane world for a moment…Andy is anxious to reunite with Barney. He finds him crooning a familiar love song on the courthouse phone. Clearly the deputy still stays in touch with Juanita. Barney is very happy to see Andy again, and he is looking and feeling well (though he does admit to a touch of bursitis in one shoulder). Barney gives credit to the weight room at the Y in Raleigh for his fitness.

Andy tells Barney that he is happy to see him running for sheriff. He also informs him that Thelma Lou is back in town and staying with her sister. Barney admits that he hasn't been in contact with her over the years, although it is clear he still has strong feelings for the woman he once described as "the cat's" and "the only girl I ever loved." He tries to mask his feelings by saying, "Women are like trolley cars. If you miss one, so what? There'll be another one along any minute." But Andy senses that Barney is still interested in Thelma Lou, and he makes a few deliberate misstatements to test his theory. Sure enough, Barney knows the facts about her past. Her marriage to wrecking crew foreman Gerald Whitfield ended in divorce after 16 months. Whitfield's yearly take-home pay was less than $14,500. Barney admits he plans to call on Thelma Lou soon, after he shaves his face and steams his suit.

Barney faces a tough opponent in the election. Ben Woods, who finished twelfth in his class, constantly drives around Mayberry and makes belittling remarks about Barney over his car's public address system. Barney fights back by issuing his campaign posters all over town. In fact, Otis's ice cream truck is covered with them.

Just as Andy and Barney begin to walk out of the courthouse, a rock whizzes past them and strikes the door. It's Ernest T. Bass, who welcomes Andy to town with one of his inimitable rhymes, which ends with, "Your hair was brown and now it's gray. Make that monster go away!" Barney, however, has little time to mess with Ernest T. He is on his way to an elementary school, where he will give a traffic safety seminar. He does so every other week.

Meanwhile, Andy heads to the cemetery to pay his respect to his beloved late Aunt Bee. There, in a moving moment, he remembers some of her loving words of advice.

While still at the cemetery, Andy runs into Thelma Lou, who had recently put a new headstone on her Uncle Ephraim's grave. She still carries a torch for Barney, and Andy informs her that Barney feels the same way about her.

Andy and Thelma Lou surprise Barney by paying him a visit immediately after his seminar. Thelma Lou and Barney embrace and quickly realize that time has not dealt a fatal blow to their relationship. They will get together for supper that evening.

Andy drives to Opie's house and is greeted by Eunice, who informs him she has recently gone into labor. She has already telephoned Opie, and he is on his way home. However, he is in such a hurry to get there, he plows into a tree near his home. Opie is okay, but his car is not. Andy loads the frantic couple into his car, and off they go. However, the car begins to lurch badly. Andy manages to get to the G & G Garage, but incredibly, Gomer tells

him there are no cars in running condition to be found on the premises. Eunice's contractions quickly intensify, and as Opie calls for an ambulance, Andy is forced, literally, to take matters into his own hands. He delivers his own grandson. Both Eunice and the baby are fine. Andy and Opie share a poignant moment before the ambulance arrives to whisk Eunice and the newborn to the hospital.

Barney arrives on the scene too late to do anything and is upset that he wasn't called to come handle the situation. He feels an added twinge of pain when Gomer and Goober refer to Andy as "Sheriff."

Later, Andy retreats to Opie's front porch, and a faint chorus of "Welcome Sweet Springtime" ("good o' 14A") can be heard, as if echoing sweet memories of years gone by. Barney soon joins Andy and apologizes for his quick temper. He explains that a quick temper is a curse of the Fifes.

The next morning, Andy, Barney, Gomer, and Goober go fishing at Myers' Lake. As Gomer is snapping a picture of Goober proudly displaying the fish he caught, he spots the monster in the lake. Barney soon notices the beastly footprints and decides to have a sign made prohibiting all fishing, swimming, and boating in the area.

Wally Butler summons Barney to his establishment and proceeds to make a generous contribution to Barney's campaign. Butler has arranged for a television crew from Siler City to be there. Channel 10 reporter Lloyd Fox interviews Barney about the monster reputed to be living in Myers' Lake. Ultimately, Barney frantically blurts out that the Mayberry monster is a very real concern. Opie knows that the notion of such a monster is ludicrous, but he is pressured into printing the story in his paper, along with Gomer's blurry photo of Goober, in which the alleged monster can be glimpsed.

Opie and Howard beg Andy to reconsider his stance about the election, because Barney is almost certain to lose. All of this publicity about the monster nonsense is making Barney look foolish. Andy refuses, but he does try to talk Barney into playing down the monster story. However, Otis fires Barney up again by reporting that he personally witnessed the monster rearing its ugly head. Meanwhile, Helen finally arrives (by bus) and is dismayed when she discovers that things have not worked out as she and Andy planned.

Andy, Helen, Barney, and Thelma Lou decide to dine together one evening at Butler's Pantry and Inn. The guys recall bringing the "fun girls" there one night, back when it was known as the Shanghai Gardens. Barney says the girls danced so close that his date (Skippy) actually bent his badge.

During a private moment, Thelma Lou confides to Helen that she isn't certain that Barney wants to pursue a serious relationship. Helen tells her that Andy said Barney plans to ask her to be his wife once he wins the election. Thelma Lou is ecstatic.

As he leaves the restaurant, Andy notices an old photo on the wall depicting the Shanghai Gardens sign. He sees the dragon head, and it gives him an idea. Andy is on the verge of unraveling the mystery of the monster in the lake. He recalls the line in Ernest T.'s poem about making that monster go away, and he strikes out to find the nutty mountain man. He goes to the home of Briscoe Darling and immediately notices the many chickens and dogs on the property. When he asks Briscoe about them, he is told that the extra dogs are just visiting his dogs and that the chickens merely followed Ernest T. home one night. Speaking of Ernest T., Andy does indeed find him there and manages to worm some information out of him. He discovers that the dragon will reappear at noon the following day. He also notices the "Wally Butler" label on Ernest T.'s frock, and that provides him with another piece of the puzzle. Eventually, an annoyed Ernest T. chases Andy away from the Darlings' home, tossing several items at his car in the process.

The next morning, a small crowd gathers at Myers' Lake to watch Barney and a local man named Dick attempt to capture the monster. From their speedboat, the men plan to lure the monster with a large frozen chicken. Then, they'll snare him in a volleyball net that Barney borrowed from Mayberry High School.

Andy brings Howard to the lake under the guise of having him take pictures of the capture. Actually, Andy hopes the capture that Howard documents will be of the culprits behind the scam. Andy uses binoculars to look out for Butler and Bass. He spies Ernest T. entering the machinery shed just before noon.

Meanwhile, Helen and Thelma Lou are having lunch at Butler's Pantry and Inn. Helen tells Wally that Andy is at Myers' Lake watching Barney attempt to capture the monster. A panic-stricken Wally speeds toward the lake, hoping to stop Ernest T. from operating the machinery in Andy's presence.

Andy sees Wally enter the shed just as the dragon's head has been put into motion. A startled Barney manages only to get himself all tangled up in the netting.

Andy rushes over to the machinery shed and catches the culprits red-handed. Butler brags that Andy cannot expose the ruse, less he make Barney look awfully foolish. However, as he has done so many times in the past, Andy finds a way to make Barney out as the hero. He makes it appear that Barney was aware of the deception the entire time

and was merely setting the culprits up. Barney is, of course, startled by this turn of events. Howard photographs the evidence while Andy has a word with the pranksters. Andy orders Ernest T. to return all of the stolen animals to their owners, and he advises Butler to throw himself on the mercy of Acting Sheriff Fife. He also asks Butler to try being honest for a change.

The day before the election, a big rally for Barney is taking place. Just before taking the podium, Barney inadvertently discovers that Andy had returned to Mayberry with the intention of running for sheriff. In a heartfelt address to the gathering, Barney surprises everyone by urging them to write in the name Andy Taylor at the ballot booth. The crowd welcomes the endorsement, and Thelma Lou consoles Barney by telling him that she loves him unconditionally.

Soon, Barney and Thelma Lou do something they should have done many years ago: They get married. Of course, Andy is in the wedding party as best man. Everyone, including the Darling family, gathers at the joyous wedding reception. Andy makes a toast in which he announces that Barney will again be his deputy but that Opie and family will be leaving Mayberry for "a big new job out of state." But, as Andy points out, he'll always have Mayberry with him. "No matter where life takes you," he says, "you always carry in your heart the memories of old times and old friends." He ends his toast, "To all of us…old friends!" The Darlings provide music, and everyone dances.

In the last moments of the film, Sheriff Andy Taylor and Deputy Barney Fife are shown respectfully lowering and removing the U.S. flag from the Main Street flagpole.

CAST NOTES. Appearing in this film are series regulars **Andy Griffith, Don Knotts, Ron Howard, Jim Nabors, George Lindsey, Hal Smith, Aneta Corsaut, Jack Dodson,** and **Betty Lynn. Howard Morris** is in fine form, returning as Ernest T. Bass. **Denver Pyle** returns as Briscoe Darling. **Rodney Dillard, Doug Dillard, Dean Webb,** and **Mitch Jayne** are back as the Darling boys. **Maggie Peterson Mancuso** returns as Charlene.

Richard Lineback portrays Wally Butler. **Karlene Crockett** appears as Eunice (Mrs. Opie) Taylor. **Rance Howard** appears as the preacher who marries Barney and Thelma Lou. Also appearing are **Allen Williams, Paul Wilson, Robert Broyles,** and **Karen Knotts** (Don Knotts's daughter).

EPISODE NOTES. 1. Andy's statement that he has been out of town for 20 years does not jibe with the facts in the real world. This film is set in 1986. Andy was still in Mayberry in 1968. 2. Although it is never specifically stated in this film, Andy and

Helen are married. They were wed on the first episode of *Mayberry R.F.D.* Barney served as Andy's best man. However, fans of *Mayberry R.F.D.* may wonder about the whereabouts of Andy and Helen's son, Samuel Taylor, who was born in the *Mayberry R.F.D.* episode entitled "Andy's Baby." 3. This episode repaired the damage done to Barney and Thelma Lou's relationship in episode 176, "The Return of Barney Fife." 4. Andy drives a Buick with an Ohio license. The plate number is 790-VTQ. 5. Barney accidentally calls reporter Lloyd Fox "Floyd," perhaps a nice acknowledgement of Howard McNear. 6. Gomer and Goober have a placard at their new garage that says, "Gas War — Low Prices" on one side. Barney's campaign poster adorns the other side. 7. Thelma Lou brought her two-tone car to the G & G Garage to be serviced. Gomer says it has a dry differential. He says that's because Thelma Lou is "just gas and go." 8. Opie worries because the baby is overdue. Andy tells him that first babies like to "lurk." 9. Working for the local paper, Howard Sprague covered the ribbon-cutting ceremony at the opening of the new Mayberry Solid Waste Station. 10. Two of Otis's flavors of the week are white chocolate bubble gum and dutch chocolate bubble gun. Some other ice cream treats he sells are Peanutty Pops, Sidewalk Gobble-Up, Italian Sludge, and Eskimo Cheese Whip. 11. Howard likes the modernization of Mayberry. He claims that soon it will be "the main stopping-off point between New York and Florida." 12. The car from which Ben Woods campaigns via speakers has the license plate number RAG-410. 13. Juanita's sister has reported that she is missing four chickens. Old man Sam Burrows is missing seven chickens, too. Virgil Prouty is missing six chickens and all of his hunting dogs. Each of these citizens lives out by Myers' Lake, and all are the victims of Ernest T. Bass. Mr. Bass takes pride in his work. He boasts that his daddy and granddaddy were two of the best "chicken thievders" in the state. 14. Thelma Lou's Uncle Ephraim was the first person in Mayberry to own a convertible. 15. Eunice refers to Andy as "Papa Taylor." 16. The G & G Garage has vending boxes for two newspapers: *The County Courier Express* and *The Raleigh Observer.* 17. Andy has delivered about a half-dozen babies in his lifetime. 18. During his traffic seminars for young children, Barney dresses up as a clown and calls himself Denny Doodlenut. 19. The Mayberry Manor Senior Citizens' Retirement Home is being built adjacent to the G & G Garage. 20. Barney refers to Gomer and Goober as "those cousins." 21. Thelma Lou's sister offers Barney some pistachio nuts while at Thelma Lou's for supper. 22. The Mayberry squad car's license plate now reads S-9437. 23. Howard

uses Cuban Sunset and Flamenco Brown dyes on his hair. The former turns his hair an awful shade of red, while the latter makes him look like a gypsy. Finally, he hits upon the right coloring agent, and he looks as young and as spiffy as ever. 24. Opie talks to a zoology professor because he wants to see if there is any possibility that a prehistoric-type monster could exist in Myers' Lake. The question caused the professor to laugh uproariously because Myers' Lake is too new. It is merely a flooded-out stone quarry. 25. Goober says there'll be no further pictures of him until he gets a gold tooth. 26. Barney puts up a sign at Myers' Lake that says, "Warning: Unidentified Large Predator. No Swimming, Boating, Fishing. B. Fife, Sheriff (Acting)." 27. While trying to butter Barney up, Wally Butler tells him, "I like the cut of your jib," and calls him "the people's bastion of defense." 28. A man named Richard Kelly painted the sign that is posted at Myers' Lake. He suffers from arthritis in two knuckles. It is not mere coincidence that Richard Kelly is also the name of the author of the first book on *The Andy Griffith Show.* 29. Andy picks up Helen at the Cardinal Trails Bus Stop in Mayberry. She arrives on the Macon bus. She tells Andy that the lease on their apartment in Cleveland expires in three weeks. 30. Opie gets (and later accepts) an offer to work for the *Binghamton Post,* a newspaper in New York. It's a bigger job with more responsibility and better pay. He asks Andy if he should take the job and leave Mayberry behind him. Andy reminds him of the baby birds Opie had to raise and eventually release (episode 101, "Opie the Birdman"). He advises Opie to "sleep on it." 31. The *Courier Express* headline under Goober's photo reads, "Is It Or Isn't It?" 32. A Mayberrian named Eddie Peterson drops depth charges into Myers' Lake, trying to rouse the monster. 33. Barney calls *The Freesboro Daily Record* to tell that newspaper about the monster. 34. A man named Ralph is part of the Channel 10 news crew. 35. Barney still keeps his bullet in his pocket. When he loads his gun, his "Manhunt" theme is played. 36. Barney attempts to shoot the monster while seated in Davis Tick's rowboat. 37. Barney wears his salt and pepper suit to supper at Butler's Pantry and Inn. There, he treats Andy, Helen, and Thelma Lou to supper one night. He says he'll just write it off as a business deduction. He says he always leaves a 10 percent tip because it's easy arithmetic. He pays by credit card and burns the carbons at his table (he does this so no one will get hold of the number). During this process, he accidentally starts a small fire in the candleholder. He douses it quickly and gets up to leave. In the background, another patron can be heard to say, "Just like old times!" 38. Thelma Lou remembers when Barney used to get frisky with her in the car. 39. After supper, Barney says he would like to "go to Ernie's Oasis and hoist a few Riunites." 40. Although Charlene Darling appears, her husband, Dud Wash, and child, Andelina, are not seen. Ernest T. Bass even mentions that he has pledged his troth to Charlene. Speaking of Ernest T., where is his beloved Romeena? 41. Charlene is Briscoe's third-born child. 42. Andy and the Darlings sing "Dooley." 43. Ernest T. dances to "Pig on a Piano." 44. Barney tried to enlist help snaring the monster from the Elbert boy. Unfortunately, the boy has "that fungus on his back." 45. Andy informs Wally Butler that the monster scam is a misdemeanor and that occupying the machinery shed is trespassing. 46. Barney discovers that Andy had filed for candidacy after he speaks to Howard Sprague. 47. The Mayberry High School cheerleaders do a special cheer for Barney at the rally, after which Barney makes the speech nominating Andy. 48. "The Mayberry Theme Song" is played after Barney's speech. 49. The Darlings come to Barney's wedding reception in their old truck (license plate number DAN-241). They bring chicken and dumplings. 50. Ernest T. calls Wally Butler "Mr. Hotel." 51. The Mayberry Feed and Grain Store is shown, as is Hubacher's Hardware Store. Apparently, Junior Hubacher or one of his three inmate brothers went straight! (Refer to the notes for episode 11, "Christmas Story.") 52. Ben Woods hands some campaign literature to a Mayberrian named Zeno. 53. According to Stephen J. Spignesi's book *Mayberry, My Hometown*, the movie's original script had Gomer singing "Because" at Barney and Thelma Lou's wedding. This and other material apparently ended up on the cutting room floor. 54. As he did in the series, Earle Hagen provides the music for this movie. He does his usual masterful job.

THE PEOPLE

REGULAR CAST

ANDY GRIFFITH

Andrew Samuel Griffith, son of Carl Lee and Geneva Nann Nunn Griffith, was born on June 1, 1926, in Mount Airy, North Carolina. By most accounts, despite growing up during the Great Depression, Andy had a happy childhood. His parents doted on their only child. Andy's mother was very protective of him. His father was a foreman at the Mount Airy Furniture Factory, and Andy sometimes joined him there when school was out. Andy was born with a birthmark on the back of his head. His mother called it a "strawberry patch" and claimed she had seen a strawberry patch just before he was born. The Griffith family worshipped at the Second Baptist Church in Mount Airy, and Andy's early social life revolved around the Baptist Young People's Union. Andy first sang before a gathering during his third-grade term at the Rockford Street Grammar School. He sang a couple of choruses of "Put on Your Old Gray Bonnet." Some of the kids teased him a bit. Some called him "Andy Pandy" and "Andy Gump," after two popular comic strip characters. He saw his first stage production when he and his parents traveled to nearby Winston-Salem to see *Carmen*. It made an impression on young Andy, who took to the stage himself at the age of 11, playing a farmer in a Christmas play at the Second Baptist Church.

Around the age of 14, Andy became interested in swing music. He especially enjoyed the movie *Birth of the Blues*, a 1941 film starring Bing Crosby and Mary Martin. Andy wanted to play an instrument, and he decided it should be the trombone. He began looking through the Spiegel Catalog, which had a trombone listed for $33.00. He took a job sweeping out Mount Airy High School after classes let out and began making payments of $6.00 a month to Spiegel. In 5 1/2 months, he had his trombone, a silver-plated tenor. However, he was at a loss as to how to play it. He knew that the

Grace Moravian Church had a brass band, so he introduced himself to the church's new preacher, Ed Mickey. Although Reverend Mickey did not know how to play the trombone, he told Andy he'd give him one free lesson a week. At age 16, Andy, along with his parents, became a member of Grace Moravian Church. After three years, Andy could sing well, read music, and play every instrument in the brass band, as well as the banjo and guitar. Andy may have been at his best, however, when he played the e-flat alto horn.

Eventually, Reverend Mickey was called away to serve another Moravian church elsewhere in North Carolina. Andy was acting as the new band leader until a new preacher and band leader could be found. Some church members would point at Andy and say, "There's our new preacher!" Andy liked the idea. In the summer of 1944, he enrolled at the University of North Carolina at Chapel Hill. He entered as a pre-divinity student, majoring in theology. He wasn't crazy about having to take certain classes, such as sociology and languages. He began to miss music. He sought, and obtained, permission from Bishop Pfohl, head of the Southern Province of the Moravian Church, to change his major to music. Soon he was playing the e-flat sousaphone in the college band, as well as singing in the Glee Club. Before long, he found himself drifting toward the drama department. He joined a group called the Carolina Playmakers. The Playmakers put on an annual operetta. Andy won the role of Don Alhambra del Bolero, the grand inquisitor, in *The Gondoliers*. His college newspaper gave him a rave review. From then on, Andy was in every musical. He thought opera would be his future.

One of his fellow Playmakers was Barbara Edwards. She, too, majored in music and was an accomplished singer, dancer, and actress. She and Andy graduated in June of 1949 and married just two months later.

Andy made his professional stage debut in Paul Green's *The Lost Colony*. This outdoor drama is

Andy Griffith stars as Sheriff Andy Taylor.

staged every summer on Roanoke Island in North Carolina, the site of the first English settlement in that state. It is based on the life of Sir Walter Raleigh. Andy appeared in *The Lost Colony* for several years, thrice winning the coveted role of Sir Walter Raleigh.

From 1949 to 1952, Andy held a job as music teacher at North Carolina's Goldsboro High School. Andy felt he was not doing well as a teacher. He was having a hard time handling the kids and was not enjoying the job. While Andy taught, his wife was teaching, too. Barbara was musical director at the Methodist and Episcopal churches in Goldsboro.

In the spring of 1952, the couple were studying singing under the guidance of Katherine Warren. One day, Ms. Warren was visited by a friend who happened to be a publicity agent en route to New York. Ms. Warren introduced the agent to Andy and Barbara, and the energetic couple impressed the man. He offered them a ride to New York, which they accepted. There, the agent set up an audition for the Griffiths at the Paper Mill Playhouse in Millburn, New Jersey. At the audition, Barbara sang, "In the Still of the Night," and Andy sang, "Dancing in the Dark." Unfortunately, both were turned down, and Andy heard someone utter a disparaging remark about his voice. It hurt him, but he quietly agreed that maybe he shouldn't showcase his singing. He decided to turn to humor. That fall, Andy took out his teacher's retirement pay ($300), and he and Barbara borrowed $1,000 and

purchased a used station wagon. They rented a house in Chapel Hill for $85.00 a month and took in a student boarder, who added $25.00 per month to their income. Andy and Barbara wrote a brochure about themselves, describing a song and comedy act. They prepared a list of every convention and public dinner held by civic organizations in the state of North Carolina for the next six months. They sent brochures to all of them, hoping that some of them had yet to hire entertainment. Slowly but surely, jobs offers trickled in, and the couple traveled by car to each and every job. Their usual fee was $60.00. Barbara sang operative arias and popular standards. Andy played his guitar as she performed interpretive dance. At one insurance convention, Andy delivered a monologue he had just made up. He called it, "What It Was, Was Football." Folks loved it, and Andy began getting offers for return engagements. A recording was put out by a small North Carolina record company, and Andy was dubbed "Deacon Andy Griffith." After one luncheon show, a representative from Capitol Records asked Andy to record the delightful monologue. He did, and the record sold well throughout the United States, but especially well in North Carolina. Andy and Barbara were then able to pay off all their debts and furnish their house as they wished.

At the end of 1953, the couple moved to New York in search of nightclub work. By 1954, Andy had met Richard O. Linke, who would become his manager and friend for well over three decades. In early 1954, Andy appeared on *The Ed Sullivan Show*. This was his first television appearance, and he was extremely nervous. He performed "What It Was, Was Football," but felt he didn't do well. So did Sullivan, apparently, as he wasn't asked back. Andy followed this up with a lackluster performance at the Blue Angel. He wrote other monologues, such as "Carmen" and "Hamlet." He also appeared on *The Tonight Show*, hosted by Steve Allen. It went very well, and Andy gives much credit to Mr. Allen, who brought him back many times.

One night, Andy sat in the audience at the Blue Angel and watched Burl Ives perform. Andy was awed by Ives's ability to capture his audience. He was determined to be as successful with his own act. He put songs back in his repertoire and went back on the road. It was in the southern and southwestern states that he regained his confidence and mastered the art of entertaining.

In 1955, Andy starred as Will Stockdale on television's *U.S. Steel Hour*. The production was "No Time for Sergeants." He played the same role on Broadway in the same year, winning both critical and popular acclaim. He won the coveted Theater World award for his work in the play, and was nominated for a Tony award as best actor. Andy appeared in almost all of the play's 345 performances.

In 1956, director Elia Kazan had the distinction of directing the first film in which Andy appeared, *A Face in the Crowd*. It was Andy's first serious dramatic role, and he was outstanding as Lonesome Rhodes, a homespun hobo turned major television entertainer. His character becomes absolutely mad with power, revealing him to be a two-faced evil monster. The film is justly considered a classic today. However, some critics were not so kind in 1956. The big newspaper critics generally gave it quite favorable reviews, but the box office wasn't great. Andy would later say that the experience of making his first film taught him virtually everything he knows about acting.

In 1958, he reprised the role of country bumpkin Private Will Stockdale in the movie version of *No Time for Sergeants*. Don Knotts, who had been in the previous incarnations with Andy, was also aboard for the film. It was a big hit. In 1958, the Broadway musical *Destry Rides Again* began at the Imperial Theater on April 23. Andy starred as pacifist Sheriff Tom Destry. Singer Jack Prince (who would later become Rafe Hollister on *The Andy Griffith Show*) appeared as Wash. Andy sang "Tomorrow Morning" and "Only Time Will Tell" as solos. He sang with Frenchy (Delores Gray) "Anyone Would Love You" and the reprise of "Once Knew a Fella." Andy and Jack combined their talents in "Ballad of the Gun." The play did fairly well, and Andy earned a second Tony nomination for his fine work. He was also honored by *Variety* in the category of best performance by a male lead in a musical.

It was Sheldon Leonard, then producer of *The Danny Thomas Show*, along with writer Arthur "Artie" Stander, who came up with the idea of creating a spinoff series about a small-town sheriff who was also the town's justice of the peace and newspaper editor. Through the William Morris Agency, they discovered that Andy Griffith had been searching for a suitable regular role on television. Mr. Leonard met with Andy, and they discussed the plot. Andy wasn't sure about it, but he liked Mr. Leonard. Andy, Leonard, and Richard O. Linke had many meetings, and the pilot was filmed (at Desilu Studios in Los Angeles) during Andy's January break from *Destry Rides Again*. The title was *Danny Meets Andy Griffith*. General Foods was first to jump on board to sponsor the ensuing series.

The Andy Griffith Show hit the airwaves on October 3, 1960. Andy, Ronny Howard, and Frances Bavier were the only actors in the pilot to appear as regulars in the series. *The Andy Griffith Show* was a big hit for CBS and was never out of the top 10 in the yearly Nielsen ratings. Buoyed by an excellent cast, superb writing, and topnotch directors, the series ran eight seasons (1960-1968). In its final season, it finally achieved the number one ranking among all programs. It was only the second series in television history to end its run while holding the rank of number one. (The other series was *I Love Lucy*.)

Andy and most of the cast have been quoted as saying that the years spent working on *The Andy Griffith Show* were among the best years of their lives. Andy participated in every aspect of the show, directly or indirectly. He worked very long hours and encouraged suggestions from cast and crew. Although uncredited, he wrote parts of many episodes and participated in countless rewrites. The wonderful production team, headed by Aaron Ruben and later by Bob Ross, worked just as hard. Don Knotts was almost as vital behind the scenes as he was before the camera. Everyone added something to create this fine series.

During the final season of *The Andy Griffith Show*, Ken Berry and Buddy Foster joined the cast. Ken portrayed farmer Sam Jones, who, like Andy Taylor was widowed with a young son (Foster, as Mike). They were brought in for the purpose of heading the spinoff series, *Mayberry R.F.D.* The pilot for the series aired, as part of *The Andy Griffith Show*, on April 1, 1968. On September 23, 1968, the first episode of the series hit the air. It was titled "Andy and Helen Get Married." Frances Bavier would continue as Aunt Bee, but now she would take care of Mike and his father. Other cast members stayed, too, most notably George Lindsey, Jack Dodson, and Paul Hartman. Andy appeared in a few episodes, and he and Richard O. Linke served as executive producers. The show was very successful. Unfortunately, rural-oriented programs fell victims to wholesale slaughter in 1971, in order to bring more realistic programming to a growing urban audience.

Andy had already moved on by then to star in another series, *Headmaster*, which ran from 1970 to 1971. Andy portrayed Headmaster Andy Thompson. Unfortunately, the show failed to gather an audience. He then quickly reincarnated his earlier hit into *The New Andy Griffith Show*. The series was set in Greenwood, North Carolina, and featured Andy as Mayor Andy Sawyer. Only a few episodes were produced, and only a few people tuned in. It didn't matter much anyway, as the anti-rural trend had made such shows obsolete. In 1973, Andy narrated a syndicated documentary series, *Great Roads of America*.

Andy turned his attention to made-for-television

Tennessee Ernie Ford, Danny Thomas and Andy Griffith singing their hearts out in Tennessee Ernie Ford's 1967 special.

movies and mini-series in the 1970s. He appeared in the following mini-series: *Washington: Behind Closed Doors* (1978) as former U.S. president Esker Scott Anderson; *Centennial* (1978), as Professor Lewis Vernor; *From Here to Eternity* (1979) as General Barney Slater; and *Roots: The Next Generation* (1979) as Commander Robert Munroe. In 1980, he appeared in four episodes of *The Yeagers* as Carroll Yeager, owner of a logging and mining company.

He was memorable in the following television movies: *The Strangers in 7A* (1972, with Ida Lupino), *Go Ask Alice* (1973, with William Shatner), *Savages* (1974, as Horton Maddock, a sadistic hunter), *Pray for the Wildcats* (1974, as the unscrupulous tycoon Sam Farragut; Angie Dickinson, William Shatner, and Robert Reed also star) *Winterkill* (1974, as Sheriff Sam McNeill), *Street Killing* (1976, as N.Y. Prosecuting Attorney Gus Brenner), *The Girl in the Empty Grave* (1977, as Police Chief Abel Marsh), *The Deadly Game* (1977, a sequel to *The Girl in the Empty Grave*), *Salvage* (1979, as Harry Broderick; this pilot film, directed by *Andy* alumnus Lee

Philips, spawned the short-lived series *Salvage I*, in which Andy also starred), *Murder in Texas* (1981, as wealthy oil man Ash Robinson; Andy earned an Emmy nomination for his work in this film, whose cast also included Farrah Fawcett, Sam Elliott, and Katherine Ross), *For Lovers Only* (1983), *The Demon Murder Case* (1983, with Kevin Bacon), *Murder in Coweta County* (1983, as a murderous businessman; this film, which also starred Johnny Cash, was directed by *Andy* director Gary Nelson), *Fatal Vision* (1984, with Karl Malden), *A Crime of Innocence* (1985, as a fanatical judge), *Diary of a Perfect Murder* (1986, as attorney Benjamin Matlock; this was the pilot for the long-running series *Matlock*), *Under the Influence* (1986, as an alcoholic family man; the film also features Season Hubley, Keanu Reeves, and William Schallert), and *Return to Mayberry* (1986, as Andy Taylor, past and future sheriff of Mayberry; this film reunited many cast members and was one of the highest rated television movies that season). In 1994, Andy appeared in *The Gift of Love*, co-starring Blair Brown, and in 1995 he starred in *Gramps*.

Andy has appeared on many specials. In 1965, he and two *Andy* regulars appeared on *The Andy Griffith-Don Knotts-Jim Nabors Show*. This special included material from their Las Vegas acts. The program was scripted by Aaron Ruben. Skits included Andy telling the story of two friends, Julius Caesar and Brutus; Andy Taylor revealing why he hired Barney Fife to be his deputy; and Andy, Jim, and Don attending a family picnic. Andy and Don sang "Friendship," and Jim sang, "Gomer Says Hey!" Other specials included *Adams of Eagle Lake* (1975, as Sam Adams), *The Andy Griffith Uptown Downtown Show* (1967), *The Andy Williams Special* (1962), *C.B.S.: On the Air* (1978 9 1/2 hour retrospective), *C.B.S.: Opening Night* (a one-hour program celebrating the network's line-up of shows), *Celebration: The American Spirit* (1976), *The Danny Thomas Special: City vs. Country* (1971), *Dinah—In Search of the Ideal Man* (in this 1973 program, Shore labels Andy as "Mr. Already Married"; Don Knotts was also a guest star), *The Don Knotts Nice Clean Decent Wholesome Hour* (1970), *The Don Knotts Show* (1967, featuring a skit in which Don is nervous about a big date and Andy tries to calm him, and one in which Andy recalls old times that are better left forgotten; Andy and Don sing "Give Me the Simple Life"), *The Don Knotts Special* (1967), *Friends and Nabors* (1966, in which Andy sang "La Triviata" and he and Tennessee Ernie Ford appeared as hillbillies facing an evening without television), *Frosty's Winter Wonderland* (a 1976 animated Rankin/Bass sequel to *Frosty the Snowman* in which Andy was the narrator and appeared in animated form; he sang "Frosty the Snowman" and "Winter Wonderland"), *Looking Back* (Andy co-wrote this 1969 special), *Mitzi and One Hundred Guys* (along with Don Knotts and Ken Berry, Andy was part of Mitzi's Million-Dollar Chorus in this 1975 program), *NBC Follies* (1973), *Six Characters in Search of an Author* (a 1976 PBS drama special in which Andy appeared as "Father"), *The Tennessee Ernie Ford Special* (1969, also featuring Danny Thomas, Diana Ross and the Supremes, the Dillards, and the Going Thing), *30 Years of Andy* (Andy appeared briefly in this reunion show aired by WTBS on October 3, 1990), *The Treasure Chest Murder* (a 1975 sequel to the *Adams of Eagle Lake* special), and *Tribute to Tennessee Ernie Ford* (1990 on TNN).

Griffith has made many guest appearances in other programs. These include *The Andy Williams Show* (1963; Andy sang "On Behalf of the Visiting Firemen" with the New Christy Minstrels and "Tomorrow Morning," a song from *Destry Rides Again*, with Andy Williams), *The Andy Williams Show* (1964; a salute to St. Patrick's Day), *Best of the West, The Bionic Woman, The Bob Hope Show* (1963),

The Charlie Rose Show (1993; this is a television talk show on PBS), *The David Frost Show* (1971; David interviews Andy, with friend and manager Richard O. Linke). *Day One* (1994; this ABC magazine show had a clip of Andy speaking about Ron Howard), *The Doris Day Show, Fantasy Island, Gomer Pyle, U.S.M.C.* (a 1966 episode entitled "Andy's Visit"), *Hawaii Five-O, Here's Lucy* (a 1973 episode entitled "Lucy and Andy Griffith"), *Hotel, Hour Magazine* (1986 interview), *The Jim Nabors Show* (the episode had a biblical theme: Andy relates his version of Daniel in the lion's den and plays the devil in search of his lost soul; Andy, Jim, and others sing a gospel medley, and Andy sings "Have a Little Talk with the Lord" and "Just a Closer Walk with Thee), *The Jud Strunk Show* (1972), *Late Night with David Letterman* (1986 interview), *The Love Boat, Person to Person* (1957), *Rowan and Martin's Laugh-In, Showbiz Today* (1986 interview), *The Tennessee Ernie Ford Show* (1967), and *Today* (1986 interview, appearing with Don Knotts and Jim Nabors). In 1995, he was interviewed on TNN's *A Phyllis George Special*.

Andy Griffith has somehow managed to squeeze in a few movies, too, including *A Face in the Crowd* (1957, with Lee Remick and Walter Matthau; Andy, making a very impressive debut, portrays Lonesome Rhodes), *No Time for Sergeants* (1958, with Don Knotts; Andy is outstanding as Will Stockdale), *Onionhead* (1958, with Walter Matthau; Andy stars as a ship's cook in the U.S. Coast Guard), *The Second Time Around* (1961, with Debbie Reynolds), *Angel in My Pocket* (Andy stars as the new minister of a troubled small-town church), *Hearts of the West* (1975, a tribute to the Old West, starring Jeff Bridges as an unlikely star of silent Western movies), and *Rustler's Rhapsody* (1985, a spoof of Westerns).

Andy has recorded many albums over the years. They range from hilarious comedic monologues to great gospel music. Here's a brief list of his recordings: "Andy and Cleopatra" (1964), "Andy Griffith: American Originals" (1992), "Andy Griffith: Just for Laughs" (1958), "Andy Griffith Shouts the Blues and Old Timey Songs" (1959), "Budd Schulberg's *A Face in the Crowd*" (soundtrack, 1957), "*No Time for Sergeants*" (soundtrack, 1958) "The Original Cast Album of *Destry Rides Again*" (1958), "Somebody Bigger Than You and I" (1972), and "This Here Andy Griffith" (1959). Fans of *The Andy Griffith Show* would also enjoy the 1961 Capitol Records release "Songs, Themes and Laughs from *The Andy Griffith Show*." This features Andy singing old favorites and Earle Hagen's wonderful music.

In 1983, Andy was stricken with Guillain-Barre Syndrome, a rare neurological disease that may result in paralysis of the legs, arms, face, and respiratory system. Andy waged a long and painful battle against the affliction. After months of intense physical therapy, he triumphed over the disease. He went on to star in the very successful series *Matlock*. In 1993, the series changed networks (from NBC to ABC) and production sites (from Hollywood to Wilmington, N.C.). *Matlock* concluded after 10 successful seasons.

Over the years, Andy has endorsed several products. You may recall his ads for Post cereal, such as Sugar Crisp and Grape-Nuts, or his long-running ads for AT&T and cracker ads for Ritz. Andy once owned Nag's Head Supermarket, located in Greensboro, North Carolina. In 1996 Griffith released a gospel album, *Precious Memories*. He also became the spokesman for Shoney's Restaurants.

HONORS AND AWARDS

Andy Griffith has been honored by many organizations. Here is a sampling: In 1956, he was nominated for a Tony award for best actor for the Broadway version of *No Time for Sergeants*. He lost to Ed Begley (*Inherit the Wind*). In 1959, Andy was nominated for a Grammy in the category of comedy (spoken word) for *Hamlet*. It lost to Shelley Berman's LP, "Inside Shelley Berman." In 1960, Andy received another Tony nomination for best actor in a musical for his work in *Destry Rides Again*. He lost to Jackie Gleason, who had starred in *Take Me Along*. In 1961, Andy was honored by his home state of North Carolina with the Tarheel award. In 1962, he received the Distinguished Salesman's award. In 1968, he was named Outstanding TV Personality of the Year by the Advertisers Club of Baltimore. In January of 1992, he was named the recipient of the Lifetime Achievement award by the National Association of TV Programming Executives. Ron Howard made the presentation. On October 3, 1992, Andy was inducted into the Academy of TV Arts and Sciences Hall of Fame (along with the legendary Sheldon Leonard). There to pay tribute to both men were Earle Hagen, Don Knotts, George Lindsey, and Aaron Ruben. In August of 1993, Andy was honored with the North Carolina Fine Arts award at Manteo's Waterside Theater by Governor Jim Hunt.

On March 23, 1990, the Museum of Broadcasting saluted Danny Thomas and Sheldon Leonard and the Cahuenga Studios legacy. Andy attended, as did Don Knotts, Aaron Ruben, Charles Stewart, and Bob Sweeney (among others).

Mr. Griffith wrote the foreword for Sheldon Leonard's 1995 autobiography, *And the Show Goes On*.

DON KNOTTS

Don Knotts was born, believe it or not, in Fidgety, West Virginia, on July 21, 1924. His parents, William Jesse and Elsie (Moore) Knotts, were farmers. When Donald Jesse Knotts was still an infant, his family moved to Morgantown, West Virginia, where they operated a boarding house. Don developed a ventriloquism act in his early teens and had a good sense of humor. He graduated from Morgantown High School in 1942. Later, he attended the University of Arizona, as well as the University of West Virginia (where he earned a B.A. degree and majored in speech). The army intruded, temporarily, on his college education. He served two years during WW II in the Special Service division. It was there that he teamed up with Red Ford and, later, Mickey Shaughnessy in an army revue called *Stars and Gripes*. It entertained the other soldiers.

After returning to school and finishing up, Don went to Pittsburgh with a nightclub act. He became a radio star as Windy Wails on *Bobby Benson's B-Bar-B Ranch*, a role he continued for about five years. He also appeared on *Experience Speaks*, *The Lanny Ross Show*, and *This is Nora Drake*, among others.

His first major television exposure came on *The Garry Moore Show*. He had perfected a nervous character by, in part, imitating an unfortunate fidgety speaker he had heard. In 1953, Don landed the role of Wilbur Peabody on the serial *Search for Tomorrow*. Wilbur was mute, due to shock. It seems his stepfather was molesting Rose, Wilbur's sister. Wilbur nearly killed the stepfather. By 1956, the storyline had run its course. In 1956, Don became a regular on *The Steve Allen Show*. Also in 1956, Don appeared on Broadway with Andy Griffith in *No Time for Sergeants*.

A few years later, after watching the 1960 pilot for *The Andy Griffith Show*, Don suggested that Sheriff Taylor could use a deputy. Andy agreed, and history was about to be made. Andy and Don made a great team. Don's Barney Fife was an especially big hit with fans and critics. He won three Emmy awards during this period as best supporting actor in a comedy series. He won in 1961, 1962, and 1963.

By 1965, Don was working on a lucrative deal with Universal Pictures. He believed that Andy was going to quit after the fifth season. However, Andy changed his mind and decided to stay. Don felt it was too late to back out of his deal with Universal. He returned for five special appearances over the remaining three seasons, winning two more Emmy awards, one in 1966 and the other in 1967. Don also appeared in the first episode of *Mayberry R.F.D.*

Don Knotts, assistant producer Billy Sands and writers Everett Greenbaum and Jim Fritzell on the set of the 1967 movie *The Reluctant Astronaut*.

("Andy and Helen Get Married") as Andy's best man. That was his last appearance as Barney Fife, until the 1986 telefilm *Return to Mayberry*, which reunited much of the cast.

In 1970, Don hosted *The Don Knotts Show*, a variety series that ended in 1971. He pursued movies, stage work, and specials over the next several years. In 1979, he joined the cast of *Three's Company*, a popular television series starring John Ritter, Suzanne Somers, and Joyce Dewitt. He portrayed landlord Ralph Furley. The series ended in 1984. In 1985, Don served as the sole host of a special, *The Andy Griffith Show 25th Anniversary Special*, which aired on WTBS. Like all *"Andy"*-related programs, this special was highly popular. Don Knotts has returned to appear on all the reunion programs, including appearances in Opryland in September of 1991. Those shows also featured George Lindsey, Betty Lynn, Hal Smith, and Jack Prince. On the November 29, 1988, episode of *Matlock*, entitled "The Lemon," Don re-teamed with the series's star, Andy Griffith. He portrayed

Les "Ace" Calhoun, retired king of plastics and new neighbor of attorney Ben Matlock. His character was seen only occasionally. (Interestingly, Les referred to Matlock as "Benj," as Barney often called Andy "Ange.")

Don has kept busy touring the country while appearing in such productions as *A Good Look at Bernie Kern, Mind with the Dirty Man*, and *Last of the Red Hot Lovers* with Barbara Eden. (Fans of *The Andy Griffith Show* series will not forget Eden's appearance in episode 48, "The Manicurist.") Don, in 1994, was touring quite successfully in a production of *Harvey*.

Over the years, Don has appeared on many television specials, including the memorable *Andy Griffith-Don Knotts-Jim Nabors Show*. This 1965 special had friendship as its theme. In one skit, Don described the flight of *Gemini* 12 as piloted by two unfriendly astronauts. In another sketch, Don appeared as Barney, and audiences learned why Andy hired him as deputy. In a third sketch, Don attended a family picnic with Andy and Jim Nabors.

Don and Andy sang "Friendship." Other specials include *Alan King's Final Warning* (1977), *Andy Griffith's Uptown-Downtown Show* (1967), *Bob Hope's All-Star Birthday Party, Bob Hope's Stand Up and Cheer for the National Football League's 60th Year, Burke's Law* (1994), *The Captain and Tennille in Hawaii* (1978), *The Comedy in America Report* (1976), *Dean Martin* (1960), *Dinah: In Search of the Ideal Man* (Dinah Shore chooses Don as her "super lover"; Andy Griffith also appears), *The Don Knotts Show* (1967, featuring one skit in which guest star Andy Griffith tries to calm Don before a big date, and another in which the duo recalls old times that are best forgotten; he and Andy also sing "Give Me the Simple Life"), *The Don Knotts Nice, Clean, Decent, Wholesome Hour* (1967, featuring Andy Williams, Juliet Prowse, and the singing group the Establishment. Skits included Don as a jittery ex-smoker lecturing to fellow quitters, Don trapped in an elevator with Ms. Prowse, trying to "play it cool," and Don in a pantomime sketch as a man trying to get service at a bank. This special was co-written by Don and features Andy Griffith as a special visitor), *The Don Knotts Special Variety Special* (1967), *Guess Who's Knott Coming to Dinner?* (Don was the narrator of this 1973 special), *Harry and Maggie* (a 1975 comedy special, with Don as Harry Kellogg), *Hats Off to America* (1972), *Joys!* (1976), *Looking Back, The Many Faces of Comedy, The National Love, Sex and Marriage Test* (a 1978 program hosted by Tom Snyder and Suzanne Somers), and *Texaco Presents: Bob Hope's Bicentennial Star-Spangled Spectacular* (Don made a cameo appearance in this 1976 salute to Uncle Sam).

Don has made appearances on many regular television programs, too, including *The Arthur Godfrey Show, The Bill Cosby Show, Bobby Benson, Bob Hope Chrysler Theater* (Don portrayed the Curly Kid in the episode entitled "The Reason Nobody Hardly Ever Seen a Fat Outlaw in the Old West Is as Follows"), *Fantasy Island, George Burns' Comedy Week* (a 1985 installment, "Disaster at Buzz Creek"), *The Girl with Something Extra* (a 1974 episode entitled "The Not So Good Samaritan," which also starred Arlene Golonka), *Glenn Ford's Summertime U.S.A., Hallmark Hall of Fame Presents: The Man Who Came to Dinner* (Don was Dr. Scott Bradley in this acclaimed 1972 special), *Here's Lucy* (a 1973 episode, "Lucy Goes on Her Last Blind Date"; Don portrays a country boy, misrepresenting himself as a Hollywood swinger), *Howdy Doody* (a few appearances in 1954 as Buffalo Bob's nervous friend, Tim Tremble), *Kenny Delmar's Schoolhouse, Las Vegas Palace of Stars, The Love Boat, Love That Bob, The Many Loves of Dobie Gillis, McHale's Navy, The Mouse Factory, The Muppet Show, The New Andy Griffith Show* (in

the first episode, as an unnamed old friend; he wore his old salt and pepper suit), *Newhart* (1990), *The Scooby Doo Show* (Don's animated image and voice was used in one episode of this cartoon series), *She's the Sheriff* (starring Suzanne Somers), *The Sonny and Cher Comedy Hour, Step by Step* (on the December 10, 1993, episode of this Suzanne Somers sitcom, Don portrayed Deputy Fief [pronounced feef], a character quite similar to Barney Fife; towards the end of the show, he even says, "My body is a weapon!" and adds, "I have to keep it finely tuned."), *Today* (1986 interview, along with Andy Griffith and Jim Nabors), *Vicki*, and *Wait 'Til Your Father Gets Home* (Don appears in cartoon form in the 1974 episode, "Don Knotts, the Beekeeper"). He starred in a 1988 pilot called *Mr. Moe's* as Mr. Moe, proprietor of a beauty shop. Hal Smith also appeared. Don Knotts also was in a 1979 pilot called *Piper's Pets*. He also regularly appeared on the syndicated 1987 series *What a Country!* as Principal F. Jerry "Bud" McPherson. During the taping of the September 23, 1993, edition of *Late Show with David Letterman*, Don was sitting in the audience. Dave began reading "The top 10 New York Mets excuses for losing over 100 games this season." During excuse #3, Don was shown drinking a Slurpee and getting a "brain freeze." After Dave read excuse #6, "Mistake to let Don Knotts bat clean-up," Don pretended to be offended and left the studio. He appeared in *I Love a Mystery*, aired on television in 1973 but made in 1967. He also narrated the 1974 television film *The Spooky Fog*.

On March 23, 1990, Don was among the crowd who saluted Danny Thomas and Sheldon Leonard in a retrospective on the Cahuenga Studios legacy. Don was also on hand for the October 30, 1990, WTBS special *30 Years of Andy: A Mayberry Reunion*. On October 3, 1992, Andy Griffith was inducted into the Academy of Television Arts and Sciences Hall of Fame. Don Knotts was there to pay tribute to his friend.

In films, Don also has an impressive resume, including *No Time for Sergeants* (1958, with Andy Griffith), *Wake Me When It's Over* (1960, with Dick Shawn and Ernie Kovacs), *The Last Time I Saw Archie* (1961, with Jack Webb), *Move Over Darling* (1963, with Doris Day), *It's a Mad, Mad, Mad, Mad World* (1963), *The Incredible Mr. Limpet* (1964, as Henry Limpet), *The Ghost and Mr. Chicken* (1966, Don stars as Luther: Written by Everett Greenbaum and Jim Fritzell and directed by Alan Rafkin, this funny film is chock full of such familiar faces as Hal Smith, Reta Shaw, Hope Summers and Jim Begg; throughout the film, an unseen person calls out "Atta Boy, Luther!"—the voice belongs to Greenbaum; Andy Griffith reportedly made some helpful suggestions on the set; Don even wears Barney's salt and pepper suit), *The Reluctant Astronaut* (1967, written by Everett Greenbaum and Jim Fritzell; Don stars as Roy Fleming and again wears Barney's salt and pepper suit), *The Shakiest Gun in the West* (1968, a remake of 1948's *Paleface*, directed by Alan Rafkin and written by Everett Greenbaum and Jim Fritzell), *The Love God?* (1969, with Maggie Peterson and Ruth McDevitt; this was the last film project directed by Nat Hiken, the creator of television's *Sgt. Bilko*), *Me and My Shadow* (1969), *How to Frame a Figg* (1971, directed by Alan Rafkin; once again, Don, who co-wrote the film with Edward J. Montagne, wears his salt and pepper suit), *The Apple Dumpling Gang* (1975, with Tim Conway), *No Deposit, No Return* (1976, with David Niven), *Gus* (1976, with Tim Conway and Ed Asner), *Herbie Goes to Monte Carlo* (1977), *Hot Lead and Cold Feet* (1978), *The Prizefighter* (1979, with Tim Conway), *The Apple Dumpling Gang Rides Again* (1979, with Tim Conway), *The Private Eyes* (1980, with Tim Conway and Bernard Fox), *Cannonball Run II* (1984, with Burt Reynolds, Jim Nabors, and George Lindsey), *Pinocchio and the Emperor of the Night* (1987, an animated film in which Don is the voice of a glow bug named Gee Willikers; voices of Ed Asner and Tom Bosley are also featured), and *Mule Feathers* (1989, as the voice of the mule). Check your local video stores' children's religious section for an animated film called *The Little Troll Prince — A Christmas Parody*. Don lent his voice to the project.

Don's older fans will recall his 1961 comedy album, "An Evening with Me," which features his great sportscaster and weatherman routines.

Thanks to some trickery, Don appears (actually, a clip from *Andy Griffith Show* episode 73, "Lawman Barney") in an Ad Council commercial reminding viewers to buckle up. He issues a ticket to crash dummies Vince and Larry. Incidentally, Jack Burns is the voice of Vince.

RONNY HOWARD

Ronny Howard was born on March 1, 1954, in Duncan, Oklahoma. His parents, Rance and Jean Howard, were actors, and their son quickly followed in their footsteps. He appeared in his first film, *Frontier Wagon*, at the age of 18 months. At the age of two, he performed with his parents in a stage production of *The Seven Year Itch* at Baltimore's Hilltop Theater. At four, Ronny appeared with his folks in the film *The Journey*, which was shot in Vienna.

Early television appearances for Ronny include *Dennis the Menace, Johnny Ringo, The June Allyson Show, Kraft Theater, The Many Loves of Dobie Gillis, The Red Skelton Show*, and *The Twilight Zone* (in an episode titled "Walking Distance," starring Gig Young as a man who tests the saying "You can't go home again"; Ronny appears as the Wilcox boy).

In 1959, Ronny did two teleplays for CBS. On *Playhouse 90*, he appeared in a story called "Black December," and on *G.E. Theater*, he played a boy named Barnaby Baxter in "Barnaby and Mr. O'Malley." Television producer Sheldon Leonard was watching *G.E. Theater* and was impressed with Ronny. He cast him as Opie Taylor in "Danny Meets Andy Griffith," a pilot airing on *The Danny Thomas Show*. (The name "Opie" was chosen because Andy Griffith and others involved with the creation of this pilot admired the music of famed clarinetist Opie Cates. Cates passed away on November 6, 1988.) The pilot did well, and the ensuing series, of course, became known as *The Andy Griffith Show*.

Everyone on the set was impressed with Ronny. He was very well behaved. His parents, usually his father, would accompany him on the set. Because Ronny was too young to read in 1960, Rance would read the scripts to his son. Yet Ronny's folks were determined that he would grow up with as normal a life as possible. He attended public schools, played baseball, and earned an allowance.

Ronny continued to act during breaks from *The Andy Griffith Show*. By the time the series ended in 1968, he had appeared in several television productions, including *The Big Valley, The Danny Kaye Show, The Danny Thomas Show, Dr. Kildare, The F.B.I., The Fugitive, G.E. Theater* (in the 1961 musical *Tippy Top*), *Gentle Ben* (in two 1967 episodes; his brother, Clint, co-starred in the series about a boy and his bear), *Gomer Pyle, U.S.M.C.* (a 1966 episode, "Opie Joins the Marines"), *Great Adventure, I Spy, The Monroes* (guest-starring with brother Clint), *Pete and Gladys, Route 66, The Virginian*, and *The Wonderful World of Disney* (in a 1967 production, "A Boy Called Nuthin'").

When *The Andy Griffith Show* ended production in 1968, Ronny continued guest-starring in other series. He appeared as Opie in the first episode of *Mayberry R.F.D.*, "Andy and Helen Get Married." He also appeared on *Daniel Boone, Gunsmoke, Headmaster* (a 1970 episode of Andy Griffith's short-lived series), *Lassie*, and *The New Breed*. In 1970, he appeared in his second feature for *The Wonderful World of Disney*, "Smoke."

Ron Howard attended John Burroughs High School in Burbank, California, and was a self-described sports nut. He played on his basketball team's B squad, and after nine months of foregoing

Ron and Clint Howard relax with Andy Griffith during a break in filming.

acting jobs, he was ready to return to his craft. Later, he would attend Los Angeles Valley College and study Cinema Arts at U.S.C.

He landed his second regular role (as Bob Smith) in a new television show called *The Smith Family*, starring Henry Fonda. The show never caught on, running only from 1971 to 1972. As the series was ending, Ron filmed an episode of *Love American Style*, titled "Love and the Happy Day." This episode, together with the nostalgic 1973 film hit *American Graffiti*, which featured Ron, created the right atmosphere for a new television series. *Happy Days* burst onto American television sets on January 15, 1974. Ron played all-American teenager Richie Cunningham. The show, set in Milwaukee, Wisconsin, in the 1950s, was a huge hit, and Ron Howard began another long series run.

Ron has been involved in made-for-television movies, including *Black Harvest* (a.k.a. *Locusts*, 1974; Ron portrays Danny Fletcher, a young navy pilot who is traumatized by an incident in flight school), *The Migrants* (1974; Ron portrays fruit picker Lyle Barlow in this powerful drama), *Huckleberry Finn* (1975; Ron had the title role, brother Clint appeared as Arch, Rance Howard was seen as Pap Finn, and Jean Howard was the widow Douglas), *Cotton Candy* (1978, Ron's television-movie debut as a director), *Act of Love* (1980; Ron portrays a man who ends his paralyzed brother's misery), *Skyward* (1980; Ron directed Bette Davis and also

co-wrote and co-produced, with Anson Williams, this uplifting story, which was followed by a television special sequel, *A Skyward Christmas*), *Leo and Loree* (1980; Ron served as executive producer), *Bitter Harvest* (1981; Ron plays Ned Devries, a distraught dairy farmer who is mysteriously losing his cattle, and Art Carney co-stars), *Fire on the Mountain* (1981), *Through the Magic Pyramid* (1981; Ron directed, co-wrote, and co-produced, with his father), and *When Your Lover Leaves* (1983; Ron was co-executive producer). Of course, Ron appeared as Opie in the 1986 television film *Return to Mayberry*.

Ron did return for a couple of appearances on *Happy Days*, including its special final episode in 1984. He even contributed his voice to the cartoon *Fonz and the Happy Days Gang* (1980-1982). On a retrospective special, aired on March 3, 1992, Ron reunited with other former *Happy Days* cast members. Likewise, Ron has taken part in a couple of the *Andy Griffith Show* get-togethers.

Ron's many guest appearances in other television programs and specials include *ABC's Silver Anniversary Special: 25 and Still the One* (1978), *Amanda Fallon* (a 1972 drama pilot, with Ron as Cory Merlino, a 14-year-old boy with bleeding ulcers), *The American Film Institute's Salute to Henry Fonda* (1978), *An All-Star Tribute to John Wayne* (1976), *The American Short Story Collection* (1976; Ron appeared with Amy Irving in the PBS teleplay, "I'm a Fool"), *Anson and Loree, The Arsenio Hall*

Show, Battle of the Network Stars (1976; Ron was on the ABC team), *Bob Hope Special: The Bob Hope Special, Bonanza* (1972, in the episode "The Initiation"; Ron starred as a drifter named Ted), *CBS This Morning* (1994 interview), *Challenge of the Network Stars* (1977; Again, Ron played for the ABC team), *Channel 99* (a 1988 NBC pilot), *The Charlie Rose Show* (1994 interview), *Day One* (1994 interview), *The Dinah Shore Show, The 11th Hour, Five Fingers, Hollywood on Hollywood* (Ron served as a host on this 1993 American Movie Classics special), *Homeward Bound* (a 1994 American Movie Classics production), *Insight* (1975), *Judd for the Defense, Lancer, Larry King Live* (1994 interview), *Late Night with Conan O'Brien, Late Night with David Letterman, Lassie, Later* (1993 interview show, hosted by Bob Costas), *Laverne and Shirley, Little Shots* (Ron produced and directed), *M*A*S*H* (a 1973 episode, "Sometimes You Hear the Bullet"), *The Olivia Newton-John Show, The Pat Sajak Show, Saturday Night Live* (Ron hosted, and participated in a parody of *The Andy Griffith Show*), *A Special Olivia Newton-John* (1976), *Texaco Presents: Bob Hope's Bicentennial Star Spangled Spectacular* (1976), *Today* (1994 interview), *The Tonight Show, 20/20* (1986 interview), *Variety's 1977: The Year in Entertainment*, and *The Waltons* (1974).

Ron's involvement with feature films, as already noted, began early. After *Frontier Wagon* (1956) and *The Journey* (1959), he went on to appear in *Five Minutes to Live* (1961; re-released in 1966 as *Door to Door Maniac*, the film starred Johnny Cash), *The Music Man* (1962, as Winthrop Paroo, young brother of Marian, the librarian, Shirley Jones), *The Courtship of Eddie's Father* (1963), *Village of the Giants* (1965, as "Genius," a boy who discovers a substance that enables life-forms to grow to gigantic proportions; remade in 1976 as *Food of the Gods*), *Happy Mother's Day...Love, George* (a.k.a. *Run, Stranger, Run*, 1973), *American Graffiti* (1973, as Steve Bollander), *The Spikes Gang* (1974, with Lee Marvin; Ron portrays a young and naive Texas farm boy), *The First Nudie Musical* (1976; Ron has one line, "Is this S. A. G.?"), *The Shootist* (1976, John Wayne's final film; Ron is Gillom Rogers), *Eat My Dust* (1976, as Hoover Niebold; the trailer for the film announced, "Ron Howard pops the clutch and tells the world to 'Eat My Dust!'"), and *More American Graffiti* (1979, again as Steve Bollander).

As a boy on the set of *The Andy Griffith Show*, Ron Howard used to tell people that he wanted to write, produce, and direct when he grew up. He pursued those ambitions from a young age; by 15, he was making short Super 8 films with his own camera, and ended up winning a national Kodak Film contest for one of those films. In 1976, Ron began working with film director Roger Corman,

who holds an unmatched reputation for churning out films at a breakneck pace on a shoestring budget. Under Corman, Ron co-wrote (with Rance Howard) and starred in his first directorial effort, *Grand Theft Auto* (1977). The film set a Corman company record for most camera set-ups (91), but it held fast to other Corman traditions, taking just under four weeks to complete on a $602,000 budget. It went on to gross over $15,000,000. With this evident flair for turning a profit, Ron would go on to become the second-most successful director in American film history, in terms of box-office receipts (the number one slot is held by Steven Spielberg).

By 1979, Ron, Clint, and Rance Howard had formed their own production company, Major H Productions. Today, Ron and partner Brian Glazer are co-chairs of Imagine Films Entertainment. Because Ron was able to realize his childhood dreams of writing, producing, and directing, movie audiences have been treated to many memorable features, including the following films directed by Ron: *Night Shift* (1982, in which Michael Keaton makes his film debut; Clint Howard appears), *Splash* (1984, starring Tom Hanks and Darryl Hannah; Howard Morris appears, as do Rance and Clint Howard), *Cocoon* (1985, starring Hume Cronyn, Jessica Tandy, Wilford Brimley, and Don Ameche, who won an Oscar for his remarkable supporting role; Rance and Clint also appear), *Gung Ho* (Ron was an executive producer; the film starred Michael Keaton), *Willow* (1988, a fantasy starring Val Kilmer), *Parenthood* (1989; Ron was also a writer on this film, which starred Steve Martin, Jason Robards, Mary Steenburgen, Dianne Wiest, Martha Plimpton, and Keanu Reeves, with appearance by Ron's father, brother, wife, daughter and secretary), *Backdraft* (1991, starring Kurt Russell, Robert DeNiro, and Donald Sutherland), *Far and Away* (1992; Ron earned a story credit for this one, a lush-looking film set in Ireland and starring Tom Cruise and Nicole Kidman, with an appearance by Hoke Howell), *The Paper* (1994, starring Michael Keaton; the veteran cast includes Jason Robards, Glenn Close, and Marisa Tomei (watch for several cameos), and *Apollo 13* starring two-time Oscar winner Tom Hanks and Oscar nominee (for *Forrest Gump*) Gary Sinise (1995). Imagine Films Entertainment also produced such fare as *Clean and Sober* (1988, starring Michael Keaton and Kathy Baker), *Vibes* (1988, starring Cyndi Lauper), *The 'Burbs* (1989, starring Tom Hanks), *Kindergarten Cop* (1990, starring Arnold Schwarzenegger), *Cry-Baby* (starring Ricki Lake), *Opportunity Knocks* (starring Dana Carvey), *Closet Land* (1991, starring Alan Richman and Madeline Stowe), and *Cop and a Half* (1993, starring Burt Reynolds).

Everyone's favorite aunt, Frances Bavier as Aunt Bee.

Ron married his high school sweetheart, Cheryl Alley, on June 7, 1975. The Howard family resides in Connecticut. Cheryl has had minor roles in all of the films Ron has directed.

FRANCES BAVIER

Frances Bavier was born December 14, 1902, in New York City, and died December 6, 1989 in Siler City, North Carolina, where she had spent the last years of her life.

Bavier was educated at Washington Irving High School, Columbia University, and the American Academy of Dramatic Arts, from which she graduated in 1925. She made her dramatic debut on Broadway in the play *The Poor Nut*, also in 1925. She continued performing on Broadway and in vaudeville until World War II broke out. Then, she toured Europe and the Pacific with the U.S.O.

She had two regular roles on television in the 1950s. Her first role was landlady Mrs. Amy Morgan on *It's a Great Life* from 1954 to 1956. From 1957 to 1958, she had the role of Nora on *The Eve Arden Show*. In 1959, she appeared on the pilot for *The Andy Griffith Show* as widow Henrietta Perkins. This led to her becoming Aunt Bee Taylor when *The Andy Griffith Show* began in 1960. Even when the series ended, she continued on as Aunt Bee in *Mayberry R.F.D.* until 1970. She worked very little after leaving the series, although she did do some commercial work. After settling in Siler City, she began operating her own antique shop, Aunt Bee's Antiques. She had a very large house in Siler city, which she shared with many cats. She was an extremely private person, perhaps a bit eccentric. However, everyone involved with *The Andy Griffith Show* certainly respected her work as an actress.

Bavier made guest appearances in several series in the 1950s and 1960s. They include *Alfred Hitchcock Presents, The Danny Thomas Show, Gomer Pyle, U.S.M.C.* (as Aunt Bee, in an episode titled "A Visit from Aunt Bee"), *The Lone Ranger* (in the episode "Sawtelle Saga End!"), and *Perry Mason* (as Louise Marlowe in "The Case of the Crimson Kiss"). One must believe that the highlight of her career was *The Andy Griffith Show*. She was awarded an Emmy in 1967 for her work as Aunt Bee. The category was outstanding performance by an actress in a supporting role in a comedy. Other than Don Knotts (winner of 5 Emmies) she was the only member of the cast so honored.

Here's a brief list of plays in which Bavier appeared: *Bitter Stream, Kiss and Tell, Native Son* (with Orson Welles), *On Borrowed Time, Point of No Return*, and *The Strings, My Lord, are False* (with Ruth Gordon).

She was as fine in dramatic roles as she was in comedic ones. Some of her films are available on videotape. Here's a listing of some of her movies: *The Lady Says No* (1951), *The Day the Earth Stood Still* (1951), *Bend of the River* (1952, with Jimmy Stewart and Rock Hudson), *Horizon's West* (1952, again with Rock Hudson), *The Stooge* (1952, with Dean Martin and Jerry Lewis), *The Man in the Attic* (1954, with Jack Palance), *A Nice Little Bank That Should Be Robbed* (1958, with Mickey Rooney), *It Started with a Kiss* (1959, with Glenn Ford), and *Benji* (1974, with Edgar Buchannon, who appeared on *The Andy Griffith Show* in episode 38, "Aunt Bee's Brief Encounter"). This was Bavier's last motion picture.

The voice heard as Aunt Bee's in the 1986 television movie *Return to Mayberry* was not Bavier's. She refused to be part of the project.

HOWARD McNEAR

Howard Terbell McNear was born January 27, 1905, in Los Angeles, Calfornia. McNear studied drama at the Marta Oatman School of Theater. In 1927, he joined the Savoy Players in San Diego, California, and worked in such stock productions as *Lightnin'*, *The Fall Guy*, and *White Cargo*. In 1935, he married Helen Spats, a successful model and beauty queen. In 1941, he entered World War II, joining an army corps that specialized in broadcasting. In 1944, he and his wife adopted a son, Christopher. Then McNear went back to the stage and to radio. From 1952 to 1961, he was the voice of Doc Adams on *Gunsmoke*. He was basically a dramatic actor on radio and television, until he played the recurring character of Mr. Hamish on television's *The George Gobel Show* in the early 1950s. After that, more comedic roles were offered to him. He appeared occasionally, as Wilbur Wilgus, on *The Donna Reed Show*, and as Plumber Cuspert Jansen on *The George Burns and Gracie Allen Show*. From 1956 to 1957, he was seen as Captain Sam Box on *The Brothers*. In 1960, he did a comedy pilot titled *Tom, Dick and Harry*. Also in 1960, he guest-starred on the variety special *The Many Sides of Mickey Rooney*. Then came his years on *The Andy Griffith Show*. He wasn't the first Floyd (Walter Baldwin holds that distinction) but he was the one audiences remember. In episode 13, "Mayberry Goes Hollywood," Mr. McNear appears as (Mayberry barber) Floyd Colby. The next mention of his surname has it as Lawson, and it remained Lawson throughout the run of the series.

McNear appeared on many programs in a variety of guest roles before and during the production of *The Andy Griffith Show*. Among these programs: *Bachelor Father*, *Dennis the Menace*, *George Sanders Mystery Theater*, *Gunsmoke*, *Have Gun, Will Travel*, *I Love Lucy* (In "Little Ricky Gets Stage Fright," he appears as Ricky's drum teacher, Mr. Crawford), *The Jack Benny Show*, *The Joey Bishop Show*, *Leave It to Beaver* (as a barber); *The Man Who Thought for Himself* (with Steve Allen), *The Many Loves of Dobie Gillis*, *Maverick*, *The People's Choice*, *Pete and Gladys*, *Peter Gunn*, *Please Don't Eat the Daisies*, *Private Secretary*, *The Real McCoys*, *Room for One More*, *Schlitz Playhouse of Stars*, *The Steve Allen Show*, *The Tall Man*, and *The Wide Country*. He also appeared in two memorable episodes of *The Twilight Zone*. (In "Hocus-Pocus and Frisby," he portrayed a man named Mitchell. This fun episode, which dealt with tall tales, starred Andy Devine. In "The Bard," he appeared as a man named Bramhoff. The episode starred a young Burt Reynolds.) McNear also lent his voice to the cartoon series *The Jetsons* (1962-1963).

McNear appeared in several movies, including *Escape from Fort Bravo* (1953, his debut film), *The Long Long Trailer* (1954, with Lucille Ball and Desi Arnaz), *Drums Across the River* (1954, with Audie Murphy), *Affair in Reno* (1956), *You Can't Run Away from It* (1956, with Jack Lemmon), *Bundle of Joy* (1956), *Bell, Book and Candle* (1958, with Jimmy Stewart), *Good Day for a Hanging* (1958), *The Big Circus* (1959), *Anatomy of a Murder* (1959, with Jimmy Stewart), *The Errand Boy* (1961, with Jerry Lewis), *Blue Hawaii* (1961, with Elvis Presley), *Follow That Dream* (1962, again with Elvis Presley), *The Wheeler Dealers* (1963, with James Garner), *Irma La Douce* (1963, starring Jack Lemmon and Shirley MacLaine), *Kiss Me Stupid* (1964, with Dean Martin), *Viva Las Vegas* (1964, with Elvis Presley), and *The Fortune Cookie* (1966, starring Jack Lemmon and Walter Matthau).

Long plagued by ill health, Howard McNear died on January 3, 1969.

HAL SMITH

The man who brought Otis Campbell to life was born Harold John Smith on August 24, 1916, in Petoskey, Michigan, and died on January 28, 1994. His parents were Jay and Emma Smith. He was preceded in death by Louise Curtis Smith, his wife of 45 years, and is survived by their son, Terry (born in 1950).

Hal Smith was raised in Wilmington, North Carolina; Suffolk, Virginia; and, finally Massena, New York (when the family settled there in 1924). At the age of 14, Hal became the vocalist for a local band, headed by Joe Callpari. Hal and his brother, Glen, had their own vaudeville act, called "Cough & Drop," and, later, "Trade & Mark." In high school, Hal joined up with Johnny Morrison's Krazy Kats as a full-time vocalist. After graduating from Massena High School, Hal bought the music for and owned his own band for a year and a half. They toured the area and were known as the Hal Smith Orchestra. Next, he began taking radio jobs as a singer, announcer, and commercial jingle writer. At WIBX in Utica, New York, he had an early morning radio show called "Yawn Patrol." He would sing, play the piano, and read the news. He worked for several radio stations in Buffalo, including WGR and WKBW. Writer Everett Greenbaum also worked at these stations early in his career. Hal performed in summer stock productions in Buffalo and also worked for radio station WSYR in Syracuse.

In 1943, Hal signed up to serve as an entertainer in the Special Services division for the U.S. military.

He had longed to be a cadet pilot, but he was 27 and had surpassed the maximum age limit. His wartime duties took him all over the world. He reached the rank of sergeant and became manager of the enlisted men's club at the Far East Air Force Headquarters.

Shortly after returning to Utica after the war, Hal moved to California to pursue his show business dreams. He worked for radio stations KIEV in Glendale and KFI in Hollywood. Soon, he was in movies; then came marriage, a baby, and television.

Smith enjoyed a lengthy and successful television career. Most everyone knows of his 1960-1967 role as Otis Campbell on *The Andy Griffith Show*, but he had regular roles before and after that series. Two early jobs for Hal were live daily programs on the West Coast: *Hearts and Flowers* and *Stop, Look and Listen*. From 1952 to 1955, he was Charlie, the neighbor, on the Joan Davis sitcom *I Married Joan*. He also had regular roles in *Jefferson Drum* and *Saints and Sinners*. After *Andy Griffith*, he was a regular on the 1970 series *Pat Paulsen's Half a Comedy Hour* and on *The Redd Foxx Comedy Hour* (1977-1978). He was also featured on the PBS children's series *Villa Alegre* from 1974 to 1979.

In 1967, he appeared, as Judge Grant, in a television pilot called *Sheriff Who?* It was written by Garry Marshall and directed by Jerry Paris. In 1988, Hal appeared with Don Knotts in the 1988 television pilot, *Mr. Moe's*.

Smith made numerous guest appearances over the years. Look for him in such series as *Adam-12* (as a drunk driver in two episodes), *The Addams Family*, *The Adventures of Ozzie and Harriet* (Smith appeared in 22 shows in one season, never playing the same character twice!), *Alcoa Theater*, *Alfred Hitchcock Presents*, *Bonanza*, *The Brady Bunch* (in his first appearance, an episode called "The Voice of Christmas," he was Santa Claus; in another episode, "The Winner," Hal was judging an ice cream eating contest as "The Kartoon King"), *Broken Arrow*, *Columbo*, *Death Valley Days*, *Dennis the Menace*, *Dog Tails from Howlywood* (a children's program), *The Donna Reed Show*, *The Doris Day Show*, *Ellery Queen*, *Fair Exchange*, *Gomer Pyle, U.S.M.C.*, *The Great Gildersleeve*, *Green Acres*, *Gunsmoke*, *Have Gun-Will Travel*, *Hazel*, *Here's Lucy*, *Lassie*, *Leave It to Beaver*, *Little House on the Prairie*, *The Loretta Young Show*, *Love, American Style*, *The Love Boat*, *The Lucy Show*, *The Man from U.N.C.L.E.*, *The Merv Griffin Show*, *My Favorite Martian*, *The Mod Squad*, *Night Court*, *The Odd Couple*, *Perry Mason*, *Petticoat Junction*, *The Red Skelton Show*, *Route 66*, *Santa Claus and Major Domo* (a children's program), *Smitty and the Keystone Kop*, *Space Patrol* (as Charlie the Chief), *The Streets of San Francisco*, *Tomb-*stone *Territory*, *The Tony Randall Show*, *Trails West*, *Union Pacific*, and *The Virginian*.

Perhaps it is not his face, but his voice that is most familiar to children. He has lent his vocalizations to dozens of cartoons and other children's programs. These include *Abbott and Costello*, *Augie Doggie*, *Davy and Goliath* (as Goliath, the dog), *Doctor Doolittle* (as Tom Stubbins), *Ducktales* (Flintheart Glumgold, Gyro, and Ludwig Von Drake), *Dumbo's Circus* (for Disney), *The Fantastic Four*, *The Flintstones* (as Dino and the original Barney), *Frankenstein Jr. and the Impossibles* (as Coleman), *Funny Company*, *Garfield* (several specials), *Help! It's the Hair Bear Bunch*, *Huckleberry Hound*, *Jabber Jaws*, *Jeannie*, *The Jetsons* (as J.P. Gotrockets), *Laurel and Hardy*, *The Little Mermaid*, *The Partridge Family*, *2200 A.D.*, *The Peter Potamus Show* (as Yippie, the dog), *Popeye*, *Quick Draw McGraw*, *The Roman Holidays* (as Mr. Tycoonius Gussbuss), *Saber Fighters* (as several characters in this Japanese-made program), *Scooby Doo, Where Are You?*, *Sinbad Jr.*, *The Smurfs* (as Sludge), *Space Angel*, *Speed Buggy*, *The Three Stooges*, *The Tom and Jerry/Grape Ape/Mumbly Show*, *Top Cat*, *Winnie the Pooh*, and *Yogi's Gang*. Mr. Smith also provided voice to Disney characters, including Goofy, Jiminy Cricket, and Owl, at various times. He was Owl in the 1970 animated special *Winnie the Pooh and the Honey Tree*. His voice can be heard on Disney's *101 Dalmatians* album and in some of Disney's talking toys. He gave voice to some characters in several Dr. Seuss specials, and he was also the voice of the Warner Bros. cartoon character Elmer Fudd before Mel Blanc took over. In 1991 he gave voice to Philippe the horse in *Beauty and the Beast*.

Others may recognize his work on ads for Apple Chips, Bell Telephone, Bisquick, Burger Chef, Claussen Pickles, the Dodge Aspen, Flintstone Vitamins, Frito Lay, Hickory Farms, Kellogg's (as Tony the Tiger, Jr.), Mattel, McDonald's (as a soft drink cup and as a McNugget), Pioneer Chicken (Hal was Pioneer Pete), Pioneer Electronics, Pizza Hut, 3M Company, Toyota, Western Airlines, and Westinghouse.

He also continued his work on radio, including the 1993 program *Morris Has a Cold*, and he had the very long-running role of John Avery Whitacre in *Adventures in Odyssey*.

His voice can be heard on Artist Lee James's "How to Draw" cassettes. Hal served as the narrator. Hal also lent his voice to countless film strips and educational recordings for McGraw-Hill, Disney, Time-Life, and many other companies. Many of these are still being seen and heard in schools across America.

Three television movies of note in which Smith

appeared, are *Getting Away From It All* (1972, with Larry Hagman and Barbara Feldon), *Return to Mayberry* (1986), and *Switched at Birth* (1991; he played a landlord). Smith also appears in country music star Alan Jackson's hit video *Don't Rock the Jukebox*.

Smith appeared in (or lent his voice to) several motion pictures, including *Stars Over Texas* (1946, his film debut), several *Ma and Pa Kettle* and *Francis* (the talking mule) films in the 1950s, *The Milkman* (1950, with Jimmy Durante), *You for Me* (1952, with Peter Lawford), *Walking My Baby Back Home* (1953, with Janet Leigh), *There's Always Tomorrow* (1956, with Barbara Stanwyck and Fred MacMurray), *Hot Car Girl* (1958), *The Apartment* (1960), *The Three Stooges Meet Hercules* (1962), *Son of Flubber* (1963), *The Miracle of Santa's White Reindeer* (1963), *Hey There, It's Yogi Bear!* (1964), *Dear Heart* (1965, with Glenn Ford), *The Great Race* (1965), *The Ugly Dachshund* (1966), *The Ghost and Mr. Chicken* (1966, with Don Knotts; Hal was a drunkard named Calvin Weems), *The Boy Who Stole the Elephant* (1969), *Archy and Mehitabel* (1969), *A Jellystone Christmas* (1969), *Santa and the Three Bears* (1970), *Shinbone Alley* (1971), *The $1,000,000 Duck* (1971), *Fantastic Planet* (1973), *Oklahoma Crude* (1973, with George C. Scott), *Mad Bull* (1977, with Alex Karras), *The Hazing* (1977), *Here Come the Littles* (1985), and *18 Again* (1988, with George Burns).

Smith was well-loved by those who knew him. He was always happy to perform for his fans, whether it meant doing voices or transforming himself into Otis. He did the latter at a four-day "Andy Fan Fest" at Opryland in 1991 and in a couple of the series get-togethers, such as the WTBS special *30 Years of Andy*, aired on October 3, 1990.

On February 13, 1988, the city of Nashville declared the day "Otis Campbell Day." In a fitting tribute, Hal was given the key to the county jail.

BETTY LYNN

Elizabeth Ann Theresa Lynn was born in Kansas City, Missouri. Her mother was a prominent opera singer throughout the Midwest. Her father, George Lynn, was an engineer for the Missouri Pacific Railroad. (President Franklin Delano Roosevelt once requested that Mr. Lynn guide him on the Midwest leg of a campaign tour.) At the age of five, Betty Lynn began taking dance lessons at the Kansas City Conservatory for Music. At age 14, she began taking small dramatic roles and soloist parts on local radio shows. She graduated from Southwest High School at 16. During her time at Kansas City Junior College, she sang at local supper clubs.

Soon, Lynn successfully auditioned for U.S.O. Camp Shows, Inc., but she could not be put under contract until she reached the age of 18. When she did, she was sent to New York, where she spent the next year or two touring and entertaining U.S. troops in American hospitals and in such exotic locals as Iran, Casablanca, India, and China. Eventually, she received a special commendation from the U.S. State Department and was named an (honorary) colonel in the American Legion.

Eventually, Lynn settled in New York City to begin a show business career. In 1946, she appeared in her first play, *Park Avenue*, which first toured in the northeastern states before running on Broadway. Some Hollywood studios beckoned, and she signed a movie deal with Twentieth Century–Fox. She was just 20 years old. In the ensuing years, she worked for many of the big movie studios, such as Universal, Warner Bros., RKO, and MGM.

Lynn's television career began in the late 1940s and prospered in the next two decades. She appeared on several anthology series, such as *Schlitz Playhouse of Stars*. Also, she continued appearing in plays (on the West Coast) such as *King of Hearts, Come Blow Your Horn, The Moon Is Blue,* and *Peg of My Heart*. Early television appearances include *The George Burns and Gracie Allen Show* and *Jane Wyman's Fireside Theater*. Prior to her role on *The Andy Griffith Show* (on which she portrayed Thelma Lou from 1960 to 1965) she was a regular on *The Ray Bolger Show*. Her character was named June. After 1965, she appeared frequently as Miss Lee, the secretary to Bill Davis (Brian Keith) on *Family Affair* (1966-1971). Towards the end of the 1950s, she appeared as Mrs. John (Viola) Slaughter in the western serial *Texas John Slaughter*, aired as part of *Walt Disney Presents*. She was also a regular on the 1976 series, *Gibbsville*. She has made guest appearances in many series, including *Benedict Arnold, Bronco, Cheyenne, The Egg and I* (a live show from N.Y.C.), *The Farmer's Daughter, The Freddy Martin Show, The Gale Storm Show, Little House on the Prairie, Markham, Matinee Theater, The Mod Squad, My Three Sons, Police Story, Rose, The Smith Family* (a 1971 episode reuniting her with Ron Howard), *The Smothers Brothers Comedy Hour, Sugarfoot, Wagon Train, Wells Fargo* and *The Word*. She had a regular role, as Ellen in the syndicated religious series *This Is the Life*. She has appeared, infrequently, as secretary to Ben Matlock (played by Andy Griffith) on *Matlock*. Lynn returned as Thelma Lou in the 1986 television film *Return to Mayberry*. She also appeared in the Disney television films *The Boy Who Stole the Elephant* and *Stranger of Strawberry Cove*.

Lynn has appeared in many motion pictures, including *Sitting Pretty* (1948, her debut film, for

A glamorous pose of Betty Lynn.

which she earned a Photoplay Gold Medal), *Apartment for Peggy* (1948, with William Holden), *June Bride* (1948, with Bette Davis), *Mother Is a Freshman* (1949), *Father Was a Fullback* (1949), *Cheaper By the Dozen* (1950, with Myrna Loy and Clifton Webb), *Take Care of My Little Girl* (1951), *Payment on Demand* (1951, with Bette Davis), *Many Roads to Cross* (1955), *Behind the High Wall* (1956), *Meet Me in Las Vegas* (1956), *Gun for a Coward* (1957), and *The Hangman* (1959).

Lynn has participated in several of the *Andy* reunion shows (including the October 30, 1990, WTBS special, *30 Years of Andy: A Mayberry Reunion*) and it is clear that she loved performing on the show. A note of interest: She acted as a celebrity judge at the fourth annual Jack Daniels World Invitation Bar-Be-Cue in Lynchburg, Tennessee, in 1992.

ANETA CORSAUT

Like her character Helen Crump, Aneta Corsaut is a native of Kansas. She was born in the city of Hutchinson on November 3, 1933, and passed away on November 6, 1995. She once told *TV Guide* that she was a true tomboy as a child. (In her youth,

she fractured her nose three times playing baseball.) She also stated that she always dreamed of becoming an actress.

Corsaut enrolled at Northwestern University, but left after her junior year. She held a variety of jobs, working as a dental assistant, a department store sales clerk, a model, and a market researcher. She studied acting under Lee Strasberg. Corsaut moved to California in 1960 and landed the role of Irma Howell on *Mrs. G. Goes to College* (a.k.a. *The Gertrude Berg Show*). The show lasted from 1961 to 1962. Jim Fritzell, a writer on this series, introduced her to Bob Sweeney, a noted director, and in 1964, Miss Corsaut became Miss Helen Crump on *The Andy Griffith Show*. The role lasted until 1968, when the series ended. She reprised the role of Helen Crump in the first episode of *Mayberry R.F.D.*, "Andy and Helen Get Married," and in the episode entitled "Andy's Baby." She also returned for the 1986 television movie *Return to Mayberry*.

From 1979 to 1982, Corsaut portrayed head nurse Bradley on *House Calls*. After Andy Griffith landed the role of "Matlock," he invited his former television wife to appear on the show. She made several appearances as Judge Cynthia Justin. As the judge, she got to chastise Ben Matlock from time to time.

Corsaut has appeared on several programs as a guest star. These include *Adam-12*, *Black Saddle*, *The Blue Knight*, *Bonanza* (in the episode "The Way of Aaron," she portrayed Rebecca Kaufman, an immigrant who strikes Adam's fancy), *Columbo* (as Nurse Morgan in "A Stitch in Crime"), *Crunch and Des*, *Death Valley Days*, *Dick Powell's Zane Grey Theatre*, *The Eleventh Hour*, *The Farmers Daughter*, *Full House* (a 1976 comedy pilot in which she portrayed Paulene Campbell), *Gunsmoke* (including a 1968 episode as a nun named Sister Ruth), *Harrigan and Son*, *The Imogene Coca Show* (an early television appearance, quite possibly her first), *Johnny Ringo*, *Kraft Television Theater*, *Marcus Welby, M.D.*, *Nanny and the Professor*, *Philco Playhouse*, *The Real McCoys*, *Robert Montgomery Presents*, *The Runaways*, *Sergeant Bilko*, and *Studio One*. She has also appeared on the daytime television dramas *General Hospital* and *Days of Our Lives*. In the latter, she portrayed Caroline Brady. It is interesting to note that Peggy McCay, the actress who portrayed Andy's old flame, Sharon Despain, in *Andy Griffith* episode 82, "Class Reunion," is currently portraying Caroline Brady on *Days of Our Lives*.

In 1974, Corsaut appeared in the television movie *Bad Ronald*. She appeared in very few feature films, but look for her co-starring with Steve McQueen in the 1958 hit *The Blob*.

Corsaut, who once toured Europe with the USO, was also an accomplished writer. In fact, she co-wrote some episodes of the 1970s television show, *Anna and the King* with former *Andy Griffith* writer Jim Fritzell. In the 1980s, she co-wrote *The Mystery Quiz Book* with Bob Wagner and Muff Singer.

JIM NABORS

James Thurston Nabors was born on June 12, 1932, in Sylacauga, Alabama. His father, Fred Canada Nabors, was a policeman. His mother, Mavis Pearl (Newman) Nabors, taught herself to play the piano by ear. As a child, Jim Nabors had problems with asthma, which limited the amount of time he could spend playing. He began to experiment with his voice, exploring his vocal range. Although he never took vocal lessons, he had a wonderful, rich voice. He also taught himself to play the ukulele, played the clarinet in his high school band, and sang in high school and college glee clubs too.

He earned a B.A. in business administration and got a job as a typist in the United Nations building in New York. While there, he auditioned, unsuccessfully, for a role in Broadway's *No Time for Sergeants*. When his asthma worsened, he moved to Chattanooga, Tennessee, where he worked as an assistant film editor for a television station. He began to sing on the station's local shows and was well received. Three years later, he moved to Los Angeles and got a job at NBC. He began doing odd jobs, such as stacking film cans, but then started editing film there. He worked nights at The Horn, a comedy club in Santa Monica, mostly doing Gomer-like monologues and throwing in a few operatic arias. Then his first break occurred. One evening, Bill Dana, then a head writer for *The Steve Allen Show*, watched Nabors' act. He booked him at ABC for a few appearances. Things were going well for Nabors, and he quit his job at NBC. However, Mr. Allen's show was canceled shortly afterward. So, it was back to The Horn. Nabors was working there for no pay in 1962 when he landed a four-month booking at the Purple Onion, a San Francisco nightclub. Eventually, in Santa Monica, Andy Griffith saw Nabors' act and came away impressed with the young entertainer. This was his second break. A few weeks later, Jim was hired to play gas station attendant Gomer Pyle on the 1963-1964 season of *The Andy Griffith Show*. His character was based on a simple-minded gas station attendant that Everett Greenbaum (an important writer for *Andy Griffith*) chanced upon one day. The name "Gomer" came from a writer named Gomer Cool, while "Pyle" came from Denver Pyle, who played Briscoe Darling on the series.

The one and only Gomer Pyle, Jim Nabors.

Around the time of his appearance on *The Andy Griffith Show*, Jim did a pilot about a minor-league baseball team, *Butterball Brown*, which also featured George Lindsey. It failed. Interestingly, Lindsey and Nabors were both up for the role of Gomer. Lindsey would later appear as Goober, Gomer's cousin.

Next, writer and producer Aaron Ruben created a series for Nabors placing him in the U.S. Marine Corps. The pilot aired on *The Andy Griffith Show* (episode 107, "Gomer Pyle, U.S.M.C."). The series proved to be very popular. Many of its scripts were written by such *Andy Griffith* alumni as Harvey Bullock, Ray Saffian Allen, and Jack and Iz Elinson. The program ran from 1964 to 1969. In the Marines, Gomer got to sing more often. In 1966, Nabors released his first record album, "Jim Nabors Sings." It quickly went gold. Between 1966 and 1972, Jim Nabors had 12 albums on the bestseller charts.

After his series ended, Nabors hosted his own variety program, *The Jim Nabors Hour*, from 1969 to 1971. He returned to television to take the role of "Fum" in the 1975-1976 Saturday morning show for kids called *Lost Saucer*. In 1978, he hosted his own syndicated talk show, *The Jim Nabors Show*. This show got him nominated for an Emmy award on the 1978 Daytime Emmy telecast. The category was best host or hostess in a talk, service or variety series. He lost to Phil Donahue of *Donahue*. In 1986, Jim appeared in a 1986 pilot for NBC called *Sylvan*

Jim joins Andy Griffith and Don Knotts in a 1965 music/variety special.

in Paradise. It didn't sell. In 1988, Jim made a pilot for a new series called *The Jim Nabors Show*. In the pilot, Jim was the owner of a feed and fertilizer store. The pilot, written by (*Andy* alumni) Art Baer and Ben Joelson, did not go to series.

Nabors appeared on many specials in the 1960s and 1970s. These include *An All-Star Party for Carol Burnett, An All-Star Salute to Mothers Day, And Debbie Makes Six* (this 1967 special had a skit with Jim as a soldier, and he also sang "Mame"), *The Andy Griffith-Don Knotts-Jim Nabors Special* (airing on October 7, 1965, this special was adapted from the trio's nightclub act and featured Nabors in a sketch in which he and his pals attend a family picnic; he also sang "Gomer Says Hey!" The trio later played Caesar's Palace in Las Vegas in the summer of 1968), *The Best Little Special in Texas, The Bob Hope Special* (1972), *Burt Reynolds' Late Show* (1973), *CBS: On the Air, Celebrity Daredevils, Friends and Nabors, Girlfriends and Nabors, Jim Nabors' Christmas in Hawaii, The Jim Nabors Show*, and *Mitzi and One Hundred Guys* (as part of entertainer Mitzi Gaynor's Million Dollar Chorus, along with Andy Griffith and Ken Berry). Nabors has also made several guest appearances on such programs as *Aloha, Paradise, The Carol Burnett Show* (Nabors was Burnett's good

luck charm and was present for the first episode of every season), *Easy Street, Funshine* (Nabors co-hosted, with Ruth Buzzi, this Saturday sneak peek at ABC's 1975 line-up), *The Glen Campbell Goodtime Hour* (in this appearance, Nabors sang "Vesti La Giubba" from *Pagliacci*, "If My Friends Could See Me Now," and, with Campbell, "There a Kind of Hush"; he also participated in a sketch with Pat Paulsen about a running feud and a skit about pesky insects), *The Love Boat, The Lucy Show* ("Lucy Gets Caught Up in the Draft"), *Mr. Smith Goes to Washington, The Redd Foxx Show, The Rookies* (a rare dramatic role in a 1973 episode), *The Sally Jessy Raphael Show* (a March 1990 appearance with George Lindsey), *Sesame Street* (in a 1971 episode, show 176, singing "The Alphabet Song"), *A Special Evening with Carol Burnett* (Burnett's last taping in 1978), *Today* (1986 interview, along with Andy Griffith and Don Knotts), and *Tom Snyder* (chatting with the CNBC host about his health and his involvement with the organ donation program).

In 1993, Nabors discovered his liver was dysfunctional, and he told Mary Hart on *Entertainment Tonight* that he was in need of a transplant. It was obvious that his health was deteriorating rapidly. He received his transplant just in time. In May of

1994, Nabors was once again singing "Back Home Again in Indiana" just prior to the start of The Indianapolis 500. He is a welcome tradition at the brickyards, having sung the song before most of the races in the past two decades. By the summer of 1994, Nabors was planning to continue touring, something he has done year after year.

Nabors has appeared in three movies starring his friend Burt Reynolds: *The Best Little Whorehouse in Texas* (1982), *Stroker Ace* (1983), and *Cannonball Run* (1984).

Some interesting notes regarding Nabors: (1) In the late 1960s, he had a dog named "Goober." (2) He has had (at least) 5 gold albums and 1 platinum album. Two of his LPs are "Very Special" and "The Special Warmth of Jim Nabors." (3) In 1964, he was voted "Most Promising Male Star" and was awarded the television "Champion" award by Quigley Publications. Quigley was an organization that polled U.S. television critics to determine its champions. (4) On January 31, 1991, Nabors was finally immortalized with a star on Hollywood's Walk of Fame. Today, he spends much of his time tending to his macadamia nut plantation in Hawaii.

George (Goober) Lindsey

GEORGE LINDSEY

George Lindsey was born in Jasper, Alabama, one December 18th during the depression years. Although he had a lot of acting experience to his credit when he joined the cast of *The Andy Griffith Show*, he was such a smash hit as Goober that the character has stuck to the actor like a shadow. Stereotyping tends to drastically reduce the number of roles an actor will be offered. Lindsey has good-naturedly accepted this fate and has loyally attended every function associated with *The Andy Griffith Show*.

Lindsey enjoyed a diversified career in the days before *The Andy Griffith Show*. He played football at Florence State College, which sometime later was renamed the University of North Alabama. (In 1992, the university bestowed upon him an honorary doctorate of humane letters.) He served three years in the U.S. Air Force and then taught American History at Hazel Green High School in Huntsville, Alabama. Lindsey also attended Hunter College in New York, studying drama at its American Theater Wing. A couple of years later, he had developed a comedy routine and was performing in small clubs in the Greenwich Village area. In 1961, he made his first big television appearance on *The Jack Paar Show*, although he had already appeared on such programs as *Playhouse 90*, *The Sid Caesar Show*, *To Tell the Truth*, and *Who Do You Trust?* He began acting on the stage, too, in such productions as *All-American* and *Wonderful Town*. He had previously auditioned to be Andy Griffith's understudy for *No Time for Sergeants*, but lost out. He later acted in two pilots, neither of which got off the ground. One was *My Fifteen Blocks* (for Sheldon Leonard) and the other was *Butterball Brown*, which also featured Jim Nabors.

He appeared in many guest roles before 1965, when he took the role of Goober on *The Andy Griffith Show*. He had almost gotten the role of Gomer, but then Jim Nabors was discovered. It was natural that Lindsey and Nabors, both natives of Alabama, be cast as cousins, but actually they only shared one episode (123, "The Fun Girls"). They were reunited in the 1986 television film *Return to Mayberry*.

Lindsey continued the role of Goober Pyle (strangely, he was referred to as "Goober Beasley" in one episode) to co-star with Ken Berry in *Mayberry R.F.D.*, until it ended in 1971. This was followed by nearly 20 years — still as Goober — on *Hee Haw*, the popular country music and comedy series. In 1978, he co-wrote and starred in a pilot called *Goober and the Trucker's Paradise*, in which the mechanic had become an owner of a truck stop cafe. In 1994, live productions of *Hee Haw* began at Opryland in Nashville, Tennessee. These shows feature George Lindsey, Grandpa Jones, Lulu Roman, and others from the television series.

Goober was and is a popular character. Once, cartoonist Leonard Starr used Lindsey's likeness as the subject of his *On Stage* cartoon strip. The character was called Claude Harper, and his goal was to make it on Broadway.

Some of the many television programs on which Lindsey has made guest appearances are *The Alfred Hitchcock Hour, Banacek, CHIPS, The Danny Thomas Special: City vs. Country, Celebrity Outdoors* (1993), *A Day in Court, Death Valley Days, Fantasy Island, Flo, The Glen Campbell Goodtime Hour, Gomer Pyle, U.S.M.C.* ("A Visit from Cousin Goober"), *The Great Adventure, Gunsmoke, The Jonathan Winters Show, The Johnny Cash Show, the Loretta Lynn Show, Love American Style, M*A*S*H,* (a 1978 episode, "Temporary Duty," as a boisterous surgeon who rubs everyone the wrong way), *The Merv Griffin Show, The Miss Teen America Pageant* (1992, as host), *The Miss USA Pageant* (1967, as a judge), *The Nashville Palace, The New Andy Griffith Show* (in the first episode, as Goober), *The Orange Blossom Special* (a 1973 special with Loretta Lynn), *Profiles in Courage, The Ray Stevens Show, The Real McCoys, The Rifleman, The Sally Jessy Raphael Show* (with Jim Nabors), *Take One* (starring Jonathan Winters), *Tattletales, Temple Houston, The Twilight Zone* (in a 1964 episode titled, "I Am the Night—Color Me Black," as a ruthless deputy named Pierce), *Voyage to the Bottom of the Sea,* and *The Woody Woodbury Show.* He was once part of a production company called Akorpios/Lindsey and Lovello.

As previously mentioned, George has taken part in the various *Andy Griffith* reunion shows, such as *30 Years of Andy: A Mayberry Reunion,* which aired on WTBS on October 3, 1990. In September of 1991, he and other cast members performed four big shows at Opryland before large audiences. Lindsey read his own poem, "What Mayberry Means to Me." On January 31, 1993, WTBS aired *Eight Great Hours of Andy.* George Lindsey was the vocal host.

Lindsey is a big part of the Nashville scene. Turn on the Nashville Network and odds are you'll catch him on such programs as *Crook and Chase.* He was on *Nashville Now* many times and has been in many TNN specials, such as a 1992 tribute to Minnie Pearl, *Salute to the Lady in the Hat.* On May 9, 1990, the city of Nashville declared the day to be Goober Pyle Day. Lindsey was presented with "the tire gauge to the city!" Lindsey was also Tennessee's 1993 spokesperson for the American Cancer Society's Great American Smokeout.

Lindsey and former co-star Jim Nabors also reigned over another "Music City," Branson, Missouri, when they performed *The Gomer and Goober Show.*

George Lindsey has raised millions of dollars for charity. One charity close to his heart is the Special Olympics, and he has also raised money for the Sarah Cannon (Minnie Pearl) Cancer Center. In 1972, he initiated an annual charity celebrity golf tournament. He also raises money for his alma mater, the University of North Alabama. He often makes unpublicized visits to hospitals to boost patients' morale. Fellow actor and friend Ernest Borgnine claims that Lindsey once saved his life by supporting him through a personal crisis.

Lindsey has appeared in several films, including *Ensign Pulver* (1964, with Walter Matthau and Jack Nicholson), *Snowball Express* (1972), *Charley and the Angel* (1973), *Treasure at Matecumbe* (1976), *Take This Job and Shove It* (1981, with Art Carney), *Going Ape!* (1981, with Tony Danza and Danny Devito), and *Cannonball Run II* (1984, with Burt Reynolds). He has given voice to animated characters in *The Aristocats* (1970), *Robin Hood* (1973), and *The Rescuers* (1977).

In 1973, George Lindsey was named alumnus of the year by the University of North Alabama. In 1983, he was inducted into the Alabama Hall of Fame. In 1986, he was also appointed ambassador of tourism for the state of Alabama.

He has performed in such theatrical productions as *Paint Your Wagon* and *Inherit the Wind.*

In September of 1993, he appeared on the Home Shopping Channel to help sell Mayberry Trading Cards. He has also appeared in television ads for Fluffo Mattresses. Lindsey was once a spokesperson for the Getty Oil Company and for Liberty Overalls. He also once owned a chain of steakhouses, which bore his name. George Lindsey International, with its headquarters in Little Rock, Arkansas, consisted of steakhouses, restaurants, lake chalets, and an insurance company.

He has recorded a few record albums, including: "George 'Goober' Lindsey Goes to Town" (a comedy LP issued in 1982); "Goober Sings!" (1968), and "96 Miles to Bakersfield" (1969).

Lindsey appeared in the Tammy Wynette-Dolly Parton-Loretta Lynn video "Silver Threads and Golden Needles" and as a detective in Aaron Tippin's video "Honky Tonk Superman."

In 1995, George released his autobiography, *Goober in a Nutshell.* It is a poignant, interesting, and funny account of his life. The book was co-written by two longtime "Andy" authors, Ken Beck and Jim Clark, and features a foreword by Ernest Borgnine.

JACK DODSON

The man who gave us Howard Sprague was born John Smeaton "Jack" Dodson, son of John and

Margaret, on May 16, 1931, in Pittsburgh. As a youngster, he loved the movies, especially those starring Spencer Tracy. He admitted that during his awkward adolescent years (he was 6'3" tall and weighed 130 pounds at one point) his interest in acting became a refuge for him. During his senior year in high school, he won the prestigious Hearst National Oratorical Contest. This led to his acceptance to Carnegie Tech (known today as Carnegie-Mellon University), where he majored in drama and graduated in 1953. Jack won the Freedom Foundation Gold Medal award for a speech he wrote in 1950. In 1956, he served as a clerk-typist in the U.S. Army after a cease-fire in Korea was declared. After serving for 18 months, he came to New York to look for work as an actor. He secured a job as a night clerk at the Statler Hotel and worked in off-Broadway plays such as *The Country Wife* (1957). He joined the Circle-in-the-Square Theater Group in Greenwich Village and performed in plays such as *The Balcony, Infancy, Our Town, The Quare Fellow,* and *Under Milkwood.* He also performed in Theodore Mann's production of *Six Characters in Search of an Author.* Many plays were performed at the José Quintero Playhouse. In 1964, director Quintero paired Mr. Dodson with well-known star Jason Robards, and the duo hit Broadway with *Hughie.* The show got good reviews. In 1965, *Hughie* was playing on the West Coast when Andy Griffith first saw Dodson's work. Andy liked what he saw and complimented Jack. Later, when Jack was looking for work in L.A., he mentioned to a possible employer that Griffith had admired his work. Griffith was consulted but unfortunately did not recall ever meeting Dodson. Later, Griffith's memory improved, and he contacted Jack offering him a guest role on *The Andy Griffith Show.* In episode 178, "Lost and Found," Jack guest-starred as insurance agent Ed Jenkins. Shortly afterwards, he would become Mayberry's county clerk, Howard Sprague. Dodson based Howard on some of his own traits, specifically, his nasal voice and allergies. Actually, Jack gave credit to producer Bob Ross for his guidance in helping to develop the character.

Dodson continued in the role of Howard Sprague on *Mayberry R.F.D.* until the series was canceled in 1971. He found a new series, working with Richard Crenna, in *All's Fair* (1976–1977). He portrayed Senator Wayne Joplin. His next regular role was as Monsignor Francis X. Barlow in *In the Beginning* (1978). He was Edgar "Truck" Morley in the 1980 series *Phyl and Mikhy.* In the mid-1980s, he was seen in three episodes of the award-winning drama *St. Elsewhere* as Judge Thornton Farnum. (Judge Farnum sat on the board of directors at St. Eligius Hospital. Unfortunately, the judge discov-

Mayberry's county clerk, Howard Sprague, portrayed by Jack Dodson.

ered he was dying of pancreatic cancer and has to be hospitalized there. In one bizarre moment, the ailing judge attempted to ring for a barber—*Floyd* the barber! Unfortunately, the chaplain answered instead. The judge complained, "Call Floyd! Undertakers give lousy haircuts!") Dodson also had the recurring role of a radio-television station manager on the 1992–1993 series *Homefront.*

Jack Dodson made guest appearances on a variety of programs, including *Barney Miller, Cagney and Lacey, Car 54, Where Are You?, The Defenders, The Defenders of the Sons of Liberty* (a 1992 pilot), *The Doris Day Show, Duet, The Fugitive, Great Performances, Happy Days* (as Ralph Malph's optometrist father), *Hawaii Five-O, It's Garry Shandling's Show* (on Showtime; the plot had Howard Sprague moving into Garry's condo building and spreading the Mayberry spirit), *Just the Ten of Us, L.A. Law, Lou Grant, The Lucy Show* ("Lucy, the Undercover Agent"), *Matlock, Maude, Mr. Belvedere, Mork and Mindy, The Naked City, The Nancy Walker Show, One Day at a Time, Peyton Place, Room 222, The Virginian,* and *Welcome Back Kotter.* He also appeared in two comedy specials worth mentioning: *Walkin' Walter* (1977, as Wendell Henderson) and *Snavely* (1978, as Mr. Bishop). The latter was created by the creators of the zany British series *Fawlty Towers,*

John Cleese and Connie Booth. Dodson also appeared in two 1975 television movies with Andy Griffith. First was *Adams of Eagle Lake*, followed by *The Treasure Chest Murder*. He also appeared in some feature films, including *Munsters, Go Home!* (1966), *Angel in My Pocket* (1969, with Andy Griffith), *The Getaway* (1972, with Steve McQueen), *Pat Garrett and Billy the Kid* (1973), *Thunderbolt and Lightfoot* (1974, starring Clint Eastwood), and *Something Wicked This Way Comes* (1983, with Jason Robards). He appeared in the 1990 cable television movie *A Climate for Killing*, which is available on videotape. He also appeared in *You Can't take It with You* on the premium channel Showtime.

You've no doubt seen or heard Dodson in commercials for such businesses as Starkist Tuna, Perkins' Restaurants, McDonalds, Polaroid, Aunt Jemima, Apple Computers, Disneyworld, Orkin Pest Control, the Mormon Church, Nabisco (Keebler Cookies), Publix Supermarkets, Texas Bank, Green's Ice Cream, Thrifty Drugs, and Campbell's Soups Home Cooking. The latter ads cast him as Stanley and features the voice of screen legend, Jimmy Stewart.

Jack Dodson's wife, Mary, whom he met at Carnegie Tech, has long been involved with the entertainment industry. One of her brothers is noted actor Fritz Weaver; another, Robert, is a prominent New York illustrator; and a third brother, Daniel is a writer and editor. Mary was once a designer on *The Perry Como Show* and was most recently working as an art director on *Murder She Wrote*. Jack and Mary's daughters are also active in show business. Amy designs costumes, and Christina is a writer and associate producer with the premium cable channel Showtime.

Jack Dodson died on September 16, 1994.

PAUL HARTMAN

The veteran comic actor, best known to baby boomers as Mayberry's fix-it man, Emmett Clark, was born on March 1, 1904, in San Francisco, California. As viewers of *The Andy Griffith Show* know, Emmett could "cut a rug" quite nicely. The fact is that Paul Hartman was an experienced professional dancer; he and his wife, Grace, had a comic dance routine in the 1930s. They were in several Broadway musical hits. Their work in *Angel in the Wings* earned both of them the coveted Antoinette Perry and Donaldson awards in 1948. Today, the Perry award is commonly called a "Tony." *Angel in the Wings* was broadcast on NBC's *Philco Television Playhouse* in 1948.

In 1949, Paul and Grace played themselves in their own television series, *The Hartmans*. From 1953 to 1955, Hartman portrayed Albie Morrison in *Pride of the Family*. Next, Hartman played Emmett Clark from 1967 to 1968 on *The Andy Griffith Show* and from 1969 to 1971 on *Mayberry R.F.D.* Paul Hartman made many guest appearances on a variety of programs throughout his career. His credits include: *Adventures in Paradise, The Adventures of Ozzie and Harriett, The Alfred Hitchcock Hour, Alfred Hitchcock Presents, Alfred of the Amazon* (a 1967 pilot), *Ben Casey, The Bing Crosby Show, Checkmate, The Defenders, Family Affair, For the People, The Greatest Show on Earth, Hansel and Gretel* (a special), *Have Gun…Will Travel, Hazel, The John Forsythe Show, Kraft Theater, The Legend of Jesse James, Love American Style, The Lucy Show* (a 1963 episode titled "Lucy Is a Soda Jerk"), *The Naked City, The New Andy Griffith Show* (first episode, as Emmett), *Occasional Wife, Of Thee I Sing* (an October 24, 1972, special), *Our Man Higgins, Our Town, Outlaws, Peter Loves Mary, Petrified Forest, Petticoat Junction, Studio One* (the 1954 production of *Twelve Angry Men*), *Thriller*, and *The Twilight Zone* (as a police sergeant in an episode titled "Back There," which originally aired in 1961. The plot involved a man who tried to change history by attempting to stop the inevitable assassination of President Abraham Lincoln).

Hartman appeared in many movies, most notably *Sunny* (1941, along with wife Grace and Ray Bolger), *Higher and Higher* (1943, with Frank Sinatra in Sinatra's first starring role), *Man on a Tightrope* (1953), *Inherit the Wind* (1960), *The Longest Day* (1962, with John Wayne and Henry Fonda), *The Thrill of It All* (1963, with Doris Day), *Inside Daisy Clover* (1965, with Natalie Wood and Robert Redford), *Luv* (1967, look for a young Harrison Ford), and *The Reluctant Astronaut* (1967, with Don Knotts).

Paul Hartman died at the age of 69 on October 2, 1973.

JACK BURNS

The actor who portrayed Deputy Warren Ferguson was born November 15, 1933, in Boston, Massachusetts. He began his career as a radio announcer and reporter in the 1950s. He teamed up with another young announcer, George Carlin, to do a humorous morning radio show for their Los Angeles listeners. Later, Carlin would move on to become a very popular and successful stand-up comedian. Burns found his way to Chicago and joined the famous Second City troupe, which is where he met Avery Schreiber in 1962. The duo formed a comedy act that would prove to be quite popular throughout the 1960s. They appeared on many variety programs of that era, including *The David Steinberg Show*, *Hollywood Palace*, and *The Roger Miller Show*. The team broke up around 1970, and Burns added writing and producing to his resume. He wrote for such programs as *The Flip Wilson Show*. In fact, Flip's character of Geraldine Jones was created by Jack Burns. Burns reunited, briefly, with Schreiber in 1972.

Burns had regular roles in *The Entertainers* (1964-1965, as himself) and *Our Place* (1967, with Avery Schreiber, a summer replacement for *The Smothers Brothers*). From 1969 to 1970, he was a regular on *The Smothers Brothers Show*. An episode of *The Partridge Family* served as a pilot for the spinoff series *Getting Together* (1971-1972). In this series, which featured singer Bobby Sherman and actor Wes Stern, Burns appeared as police officer Rudy Colcheck. Next Burns lent his voice to an animated character named Ralph in the prime-time cartoon series *Wait 'Til Your Father Gets Home* (1972-1974). In 1973, he and his old partner teamed again to star in their own show, *The Burns and Schreiber Comedy Hour*. In 1978, Jack starred in and produced the series *Bonkers!* From 1980 to 1982, he served as the announcer on the ABC variety series *Fridays*. He also served as the show's head writer.

Burns has appeared on many programs as a guest, including *The Dean Martin Show*, *The Glen Campbell Goodtime Hour*, *The Jack Paar Program*, *The Perry Como Valentine Special* (and other Como specials), *The Class of 1967*, *The Fabulous Funnies*, *Hee Haw*, *The Jud Strunk Show*, *Love, American Style*, *Nanny and the Professor*, *Operation Greasepaint*, *The Partridge Family*, *Saturday Night Live*, *That Was the Year That Was*, and *This Will Be the Year That Will Be*.

Burns's achievements as a writer include *The Burns and Schreiber Comedy Hour*, *The Flip Wilson Show* (and several Flip Wilson specials), *Hallmark Hall of Fame Presents: Peter Pan*, *The Harlem Globetrotters Popcorn Machine*, *John Ritter: Being of Sound Mind and Body*, *The Jud Strunk Show*, *The KopyCats*, *The Kraft Music Hall*, *The Melba Moore-Clifton Davis Show*, *Merry Christmas...With Love, Julie*, *The Muppet Show* (as head writer and producer), *The Paul Lynde Show* (as writing supervisor), *The Sandy Duncan Show*, *Tin Pan Alley Today*, *Variety*, *We've Got Each Other*, and *Zero Hour*. In 1973 Burns was one of seven writers for *The Burns and Schreiber Comedy Hour* to win a Writers Guild of America Award.

Burns produced much of the work in which he served as a writer. He produced *Bonkers!*, *Happy Days* (an hour-long variety series in 1970), *The Muppet Show*, *The Paul Lynde Comedy Hour*, *We've Got Each Other*, and a slew of Flip Wilson specials. For his work as producer on *The Muppet Show*, he was nominated for an Emmy in 1977 in the category of outstanding comedy, variety, or music series.

You may have heard Burns's unmistakable voice on television and radio ads, especially the "Buckle Up" series (the safety belt campaign). This long-running series of ads features talking crash dummies, Vince and Larry. Burns is the voice of Vince.

Burns appeared in the following movies: *Goldstein* (1965), *The Night They Raided Minsky's* (1968, with Jason Robards), and *The Muppet Movie* (1979, which Burns co-wrote).

HOPE SUMMERS

Hope Summers, who played Aunt Bee's friend and neighbor, Clara, was born in Mattoon, Illinois, in 1901. She received her education at Northwestern University's School of Speech. Later, she taught speech and diction at Northwestern. She also served as the head of the speech department at Bradley College in Peoria, Illinois, and taught private acting classes in Illinois and California.

In the early 1930s, Summers toured America with her one-woman show, *Backstage of Broadway*. Later, she operated two stock theater companies in Evanston, Illinois.

In 1950, she portrayed Mrs. Catherwood in the comedy series *Hawkins' Falls, Population 6,200*. From 1958 to 1963, she made frequent appearances as Hattie Denton on the popular series *The Rifleman*. From 1966 to 1967, she was Gigi on *The Pruitts of Southampton*. He last role as a regular was in *Another Day* (1978), in which she had the role of Olive Gardner. Summers also appeared in two comedy pilots. The first, *The Good Family*, aired in 1949. She portrayed Mrs. Call. In the other pilot, *The Flim-Flam Man* (1969), she guest-starred as Debbie Packard.

She made many guest appearances on other series, including *Alfred Hitchcock Presents*, *Banacek*, *The Beverly Hillbillies*, *Dennis the Menace*, *The Detective*, *The Dick Van Dyke Show* (in the 1965 episode "Odd But True," she portrays a lady who claims that her dog hasn't eaten a thing in five years), *Gomer Pyle, U.S.M.C.*, *Little House on the Prairie*, *Love on a Rooftop*, *M*A*S*H* (a 1973 episode, "The Trial of Henry Blake"), *Maverick*, *Mayberry R.F.D.*, *No Time for Sergeants*, *Petticoat Junction*, *That Girl*, *Wagon Train*, and *Welcome Back Kotter*. Summers appeared as Emily Boylan in the 1974 television film *Death Sentence*.

Her feature film credits include *Storm Fear* (1955, her debut), *Zero Hour* (1957), *The Return of Dracula* (1958; the television title is *The Curse of Dracula*), *I Want To Live!* (1958, with Susan Hayward), *Hound-Dog Man* (1959), *Inherit the Wind* (1960), *The Children's Hour* (1961), *Parrish* (1961), *Homicidal* (1961), *Claudelle Inglish* (1961), *The Couch* (1962), *Rome Adventure* (1962), *Spencer's Mountain* (1963, from the creator of *The Waltons*, Earl Hamner), *One Man's Way* (1964), *The Hallelujah Trail* (1965, with Burt Lancaster), *The Ghost and Mr. Chicken* (1966, with Don Knotts), *Rosemary's Baby* (1968, as a devil worshipper), *The Shakiest Gun in the West* (1968, again with Don Knotts), *Five Card Stud* (1968, with Dean Martin), *The Learning Tree* (1969), *Get to Know Your Rabbit* (1972, directed by Brian DePalma), *Where Does It Hurt?* (1972, starring Peter Sellers), *Ace Eli and Rodger of the Skies* (1973, with Cliff Robertson, story by Steven Spielberg), *Charley Varrick* (1973, with Walter Matthau), and *Foul Play* (1978, with Chevy Chase).

Hope Summers died on July 22, 1979.

DENVER PYLE

Denver Pyle, the actor who portrayed mountain man Briscoe Darling, was born May 11, 1920, in Bethune, Colorado. Denver Pyle has enjoyed a long television career. In the early 1950s, he appeared on such programs as *The Roy Rogers Show*, *The Gene Autry Show* and *You Are There*. He appeared in the following series as a regular: *The Life and Legend of Wyatt Earp*, as Ben Thompson (1955-1956); *Code 3*, as Sgt. Murchison (1957); *Tammy*, as Grandpa Mordecai Tarleton (1965-1966); *The Doris Day Show*, as Buck Webb (he also directed several episodes); *Karen*, as Dale Busch (1975 pilot only); *The Life and Times of Grizzly Adams*, as Mad Jack (1977-1978); and *The Dukes of Hazzard*, as Uncle Jesse Duke (1979-1985). Pyle also directed several episodes of this last series.

Pyle has appeared in scores of television programs. A sample of his guest-starring credits follows: *The Adventures of Jim Bowie*, *The Adventures of Superman*, *Annie Oakley*, *Barnaby Jones*, *Ben Casey*, *Bonanza*, *Broken Arrow*, *The Californians*, *Cannon*, *Channing*, *Checkmate*, *Cheyenne*, *The Cisco Kid*, *Court of Last Resort*, *Dallas*, *Death Valley Days*, *The Deputy*, *The Detectives*, *The Dick Van Dyke Show*, *Dirty Sally* (he also wrote and directed some of the episodes), *The Dukes* (1983, voice only), *The Family Holvak*, *Fury*, *Gomer Pyle, U.S.M.C.* (as a tomato farmer in "The Price of Tomatoes"), *Great Adven-*

ture, *Gunsmoke*, *Have Gun…Will Travel*, *Here Come the Brides*, *High Chaparral*, *Hondo*, *Hopalong Cassidy*, *Hotel de Paree*, *How the West Was Won*, *Kung Fu*, *L.A. Law* (as 82-year-old testosterone patch patient Harold Nordoff in 1994), *Law of the Plainsman*, *Lassie*, *The Lieutenant*, *The Lone Ranger*, *The Love Boat*, *The Man from Blackhawk*, *Medic*, *Mr. Novak*, *Murder, She Wrote*, *National Velvet*, *The New Perry Mason*, *Overland Trail*, *Perry Mason* (in the last episode of the original series, "Final Fade-Out," as Jackson Sidemark; the villain was former *American Bandstand* host Dick Clark), *Petrocelli*, *Public Defender*, *Ramar of the Jungle*, *Rawhide*, *The Real McCoys*, *Rescue 8*, *The Restless Gun*, *The Rifleman*, *Route 66*, *Slattery's People*, *Stagecoach West*, *The Streets of San Francisco*, *The Suzanne Somers Show*, *Tales of the Texas Rangers*, *Temple Houston*, *The Tall Man*, *The Texan*, *The Twilight Zone*, *Two Faces West*, *Wagon Train*, *The Waltons*, *Wild Bill Hickok*, and *The Wonderful World of Disney*. He has also appeared in several specials, such as *Dean Martin's Celebrity Roast of Dan Haggerty*; a 1976 PBS drama special for *Hollywood Television Theater* entitled *The Last of Mrs. Lincoln* (Pyle portrayed Senator Austin); and *When the West Was Fun: A Western Reunion*.

Pyle has appeared in several television movies, including *Hitched* (1973), *Sidekicks* (1974), *Murder or Mercy* (1974), *Mrs. R — Death Among Friends* (1975), and *Return to Mayberry* (1986, as Briscoe Darling). He has also appeared in many major motion pictures, including: *The Flying Saucer* (1950), *To Hell and Back* (1955, with Audie Murphy), *Jet Pilot* (1957, with John Wayne), *Good Day for a Hanging* (1958), *The Left-Handed Gun* (1958, with Paul Newman), *Cast a Long Shadow* (1959), *The Horse Soldiers* (1959), *The Alamo* (1960, with John Wayne), *The Man Who Shot Liberty Valance* (1962, with Jimmy Stewart and John Wayne), *Cheyenne Autumn* (1964, directed by John Ford), *Mail Order Bride* (1964), *Shenendoah* (1965, with Jimmy Stewart), *Mara of the Wilderness* (1965), *Bonnie and Clyde* (1967, with Warren Beatty), *Tammy and the Millionaire* (1967, a compilation of four of the television series episodes), *Five Card Stud* (1968, with Dean Martin and Robert Mitchum), *Something Big* (1971), *The Legend of Hillbilly John* (1973), *Hawmps!* (1976), *Winterhawk* (1976), *Welcome to L.A.* (1977), *Return from Witch Mountain* (1978), and *Maverick* (1994).

Pyle was inducted into the Western Walk of the Stars in Newhall, California, in 1991. He has hosted "The Big Bass Classic," an annual fishing tournament at Pat Mayse Lake in Paris, Texas, since 1988.

Incidentally, *Andy Griffith Show* writers Everett Greenbaum and Jim Fritzell used Denver's surname to give Gomer Pyle a last name.

THE DILLARDS

Brothers Doug and Rodney Dillard, along with Mitch Jayne and Dean Webb, played the Darling boys. As viewers know, they weren't too talkative, but they had no trouble belting out such tunes as "Ebo Walker," "Boil Them Cabbage Down," and "Dooley."

In the early to mid–1960s, this foursome constituted the Dillards, a bluegrass band, whose repertoire ranged from folk to gospel. Andy Griffith, a musician himself, enjoyed the band's music, and so they were transformed into the Darling boys. Singer Maggie Peterson and actor Denver Pyle completed the television family.

Doug and Rodney were the founders of what would become the Dillards. They spent their early years just south of Salem, Missouri. They recorded their first single, an instrumental called "Banjo in the Hollow," in St. Louis in 1958. After Jayne and Webb joined, the band moved to California and signed a record deal with Elektra. As the Dillards, they released "Back Porch Bluegrass" (1963, their debut LP, which included a version of "Duelin' Banjos"), "Live…Almost!" (1964, a live LP that highlighted their down-home humor), "Pickin' and Fiddlin'" (1965, featuring fiddler Byron Berline; that year, the Dillards toured with the Byrds), "Wheatstraw Suite" (1968; by this time, Doug had left the Dillards and was replaced by banjo player Herb Pederson), "Copperfields" (1970), "Roots and Branches" (1972; Herb Pederson was replaced by Billy Ray Latham), "Tribute to the American Duck" (1973), "Glitter Grass from the Nashwood Hollyville Strings" (1975), "The Dillards vs. the Incredible L.A. Time Machine" (1977), "Decade Waltz" (1979), and "Homecoming and Family Reunion" (1981, featuring Homer "Pop" Dillard and John Hartford). After leaving the Dillards in the late 1960s, Doug Dillard, with his own band, released "Banjo Album" (1972), "Jackrabbit" (1980), "What's That?" (1986), and "Heartbreak Hotel" (1988). Rodney Dillard released "Rodney Dillard at Silver Dollar City" in 1985. A full-length video, "A Night in the Ozarks" was released in 1989. It featured the Dillards, the Doug Dillard Band, and family and friends. In 1990, the Dillards released "Let It Fly," and in 1992, they released "Take Me Along for the Ride." A 29-song collection, "There Is a Time," features songs from the years 1963 through 1970. Another collection is entitled "Glitter Grass and Permanent Wave."

Both the Dillards and the Doug Dillard Band have been nominated for Grammy awards.

The Doug Dillard Band is the official band of the annual "Mayberry Days" festival, held annually in Mount Airy, North Carolina, since 1990.

The Andy Griffith Show was not the Dillards' only television experience. In 1969, the Dillards, along with Danny Thomas, Andy Griffith, the Going Thing, and Diana Ross and the Supremes appeared on *The Tennessee Ernie Ford Special.* In 1977, the Dillards appeared on the PBS program *An Evening of Bluegrass.* They also appeared on *Real People.* Doug, Rodney, Homer "Pop" Dillard, and family and friends (including John Hartford) reunited when Homer was honored by his hometown, Dixon, Tennessee. This aired on PBS in 1992 as *Precious Memories.*

Doug Dillard's banjo music can be heard in several motion pictures, including *Bonnie and Clyde* (1967), *The Rose* (1979), and *Popeye* (1980). Doug has appeared in an ad for Visa.

Rodney Dillard serves as music director for Patch Entertainment and is a music executive at the Jim Stafford Theater in Branson, Missouri. He is at work developing projects for television, music recordings, animation, radio, and movies. He also serves as director of development at the International Bluegrass Music Museum, located in Owensboro, Kentucky.

Mitch Jayne is also involved with the bluegrass museum. An accomplished writer, he contributes to many publications on a regular basis. He wrote a novel called *Old Fish Hawk* which was recently released in audio cassette form. He is working on a sequel to this novel. A movie version of the book was produced in 1981 and is available on video. Moviemakers are planning on turning another of Jayne's novels, *Hiram,* into a film. Look for his LPs, "Stories from Home," volumes one and two.

Dean Webb has recovered from heart surgery in March of 1994.

MAGGIE PETERSON

Margaret Ann Peterson, who played Charlene Darling, was born in Greeley, Colorado. Among this actress and singer's television roles: She was Susie, the waitress on *The Bill Dana Show,* from 1963 to 1965. After *The Andy Griffith Show,* she guest-starred in an episode of *Mayberry R.F.D.* ("Howard, the Dream Spinner") as waitress Edna Pritchard. She appeared in two episodes of *Green Acres.* (In "Eb Returns," she is Eb's girlfriend, Cynthia Appleby. She returned a couple of seasons later, in "The Picnic," as a girl named Linda.) On February 21, 1967, she was a guest on the special *Andy Griffith's Uptown-Downtown Show.* She also appeared in a 1969 comedy pilot, *Doc*, as Amy Fillmore. In the 1986 television movie *Return to Mayberry*, she returned as Charlene Darling, billed as Maggie Peterson Mancuso. In 1989, she was on TNN's *Nashville Now* with the entire Darling clan. Rerun watchers may also catch her appearances in such programs as *Growing Pains*, *The Nasty Boys*, and *Perry Mason*. She also appeared in the 1994 Stephen King miniseries *The Stand*.

Among her films are two from 1969 with connections to *The Andy Griffith Show*: *Angel in My Pocket*, starring Andy Griffith, and *The Love God?* starring Don Knotts. In recent years, she has appeared in such films as *Rain Man* (1988, with Dustin Hoffman and Tom Cruise), *Honey, I Shrunk the Kids* (1992, with Rick Moranis), and *Honeymoon in Vegas* (1992, with James Caan and Nicholas Cage).

Peterson has appeared in over 100 national television commercials and has worked as a location scout and coordinator for the Nevada Motion Picture Division.

HOWARD MORRIS

Howard Morris—actor, director, writer, and producer, and the man who gave life to Ernest T. Bass—was born September 4, 1919, in New York City. Morris was educated at New York University and spent four years in the U.S. Army. He began acting on the Broadway stage in the 1940s, appearing in such productions as *Hamlet*, *Call Me Mister*, *Finian's Rainbow*, *John Loves Mary*, and *Gentlemen Prefer Blondes*. His stage appearances led to television roles and, soon, to *The Admiral Broadway Review*, which turned into *Your Show of Shows*, starring Sid Caesar, Carl Reiner, and Imogene Coca. Morris was an integral part of the show, which ran from 1951 to 1954. This led to another regular role, again with Sid Caesar, as Fred Brewster in *Caesar's Hour*. The series ran from 1954 to 1957, after which Morris served as a regular panelist on the program *Pantomime Quiz* in 1958. A few years later, Aaron Ruben, then the producer of *The Andy Griffith Show* (and a former writer on *Caesar's Hour*), asked him to portray Ernest T. Bass. As Ernest T., Howard Morris was featured in only a handful of episodes. He also directed several episodes of *The Andy Griffith Show*. (For information on his accomplishments as a director, please refer to the Directors section found elsewhere in this book.)

Morris has lent his voice to several animated series. These include *Alvin and the Chipmunks*, *Archie* (as Jughead Jones), *The Atom Ant/Secret Squirrel Show* (1965-1968, as Atom Ant), *The Famous Adventures of Mr. Magoo* (various voices, 1964-1965), *The Flintstones* (as Weirdly Gruesome, in the Gruesomes episode), *Garfield and Friends*, *The Jetsons* (various voices, 1962-1963), *King Features Trilogy* (1963, voices of Snuffy Smith and Beetle Bailey), *The Magilla Gorilla Show* (as Mr. Peebles and Mush Mouse), *Mission Magic* (as the voice of students Harvey and Socks), *My Favorite Martians*, *The Peter Potamus Show* (as Breezly, the polar bear), *Scooby-Doo*, *The Secret Lives of Waldo Kitty* (1975-1976, as Waldo, the day-dreaming cat), and more. In the 1970 animated special *Winnie the Pooh and the Honey Tree*, he was the voice of Gopher.

Morris has guest-starred in many series and specials, including *Alfred Hitchcock Presents*, *The Bang-Shang Lola Palooza Show*, *The Bob Newhart Show*, *The Chun King Chow Mein Hour*, *The Danny Kaye Show*, *Love, American Style* (also wrote some segments), *The Many Faces of Comedy*, *Murder She Wrote*, *The Sid Caesar, Imogene Coca, Carl Reiner, and Howard Morris Special* (this special won the Emmy for outstanding variety program during the 1966-67 Emmy telecast), *The Sid Caesar Special* (1960); *Twelfth Night*, *The Twilight Zone*, and *Variety: The World of Show Biz*. In an episode of *The Dick Van Dyke Show* entitled "The Masterpiece," Howard Morris appears as Mr. Holdecker, an art appraiser. (This is the episode where Rob and company accidentally bid on a painting.) Morris also appeared in two television reunion movies. First was *The Munster's Revenge* (1981, reuniting him with Sid Caesar, who also made a guest appearance), and then *Return to Mayberry* (1986).

Morris has returned for the *Andy Griffith Show* television specials, such as the 3-hour WTBS special *30 Years of Andy: A Mayberry Reunion* and Opryland gatherings. He continues to make appearances at "Andy Griffith" conventions and smaller shows. He has appeared, or lent his voice, in many commercials. In ads for Quantas Airlines, he was the voice of the cuddly koala who whined, "I *hate* Quantas." He was also the voice of the Hamburglar in ads for McDonalds Restaurants.

Morris has starred in many movies, including *Boys Night Out* (1962), *40 Pounds of Trouble* (1963, with Tony Curtis), *The Nutty Professor* (1963, with Jerry Lewis), *Mr. Magoo in Sherwood Forest* (1964, animated), *Fluffy* (1965), *Way... Way Out* (1966, with Jerry Lewis), *Alice of Wonderland in Paris* (1966), *The Big Mouth* (1967, with Jerry Lewis), *Mr. Magoo's Holiday Festival* (1970, animated), *Ten from Your Show of Shows* (1973, a video of several skits from the classic comedy), *High Anxiety* (1977, directed by Mel Brooks), *History of the World, Part 1* (1981, directed by Mel Brooks), *Portrait of a Showgirl* (1982, with Tony Curtis), *Splash* (1984, directed by

Ron Howard; Morris was Dr. Zidell), *End of the Line* (1988, with Mary Steenburgen), *Transylvania Twist* (1990), and *Life Stinks* (1991, directed by Mel Brooks).

On November 22, 1986, Howard Morris was honored by the city of Nashville, Tennessee. The day was declared Ernest T. Bass Day, and Mayor Richard Fulton presented Morris with "the rock to the city."

In 1994, Morris appeared on HBO's *Comic Relief*, along with his *Your Show of Show* co-stars.

ELINOR DONAHUE

The actress who played Ellie May Walker was born in Tacoma, Washington. She took tap lessons when she was just 16 months old and was singing on radio at two years. By the time she was 5 years old, she was appearing in her first movie, *Mr. Big*.

She has obviously had a lengthy career, especially in television. She's had several regular roles in series television, including *Father Know Best*, as Betty "Princess" Anderson (1954-1960); *Many Happy Returns*, as Joan Randall (1964-1965); *The Odd Couple*, as Miriam Welby (1972-1974); *Mulligan's Stew*, as Jane Mulligan (1977); *Please Stand By*, as Carol Lambert (1978-1979); *Doctor's Private Lives*, as Mona Wise (a 1978, 4-episode medical series); *The New Adventures of Beans Baxter*, as Susan Baxter (1987-1988); *Get a Life*, as Gladys Peterson (1990-1992, on the Fox Network); and *Coach*, as Lorraine, girlfriend of Luther (Jerry Van Dyke) (1992-1993). She has also had roles in other series on Fox, including *Herman's Head* and the animated series *Eek the Cat* (she lent her voice). Donahue portrayed an evil nurse during the 1984-1985 season of *Days of Our Lives*. In 1978, she appeared as Major Oberlin in a drama pilot called *Aeromeds*.

Donahue has made many guest appearances on television too, on such programs as *Alcoa Goodyear Theater*, *The Battle of the Network Stars* (1977, for NBC), *Condominium*, *Crossroads*, *Dennis the Menace*, *Dick Clark's Good Ol' Days: From Bobby Sox to Bikinis* (a 1977 NBC special), *The Father Knows Best Reunion* and *The Father Knows Best Christmas Reunion* (both 1977 specials, reuniting the original cast, Robert Young, Jane Wyatt, Elinor Donahue, Billy Gray, and Lauren Chapin), *The Flying Nun*, *Ford Television Theater*, *General Electric Theater*, *The*

Andy's first girlfriend on the show was Ellie Walker, portrayed by Elinor Donahue.

Grady Nutt Show, *Miss Teen USA Pageant* (as a celebrity judge), *Mork and Mindy*, *Newhart*, *Occasional Wife*, *The Rookies*, *Schlitz Playhouse*, *Sign On*, *Star Trek* (as Nancy Hedford in the episode entitled "Metamorphosis"), *Sweepstake$*, and *U.S. Steel Hour*. She has appeared in a few television movies, such as *In Name Only* (1969), *Gidget Gets Married* (1972), and *High School USA* (1983).

As stated before, her film career began with *Mr. Big* (1942). She has also appeared in *The Unfinished Dance* (1947, with Danny Thomas), *Three Daring Daughters* (1948), *Her First Romance* (1951), *Love Is Better Than Ever* (1952, with Elizabeth Taylor), *Girl's Town* (a.k.a. as *The Innocent and the Damned*, 1959, with Mamie Van Doren, Mel Torme, and Paul Anka), *Going Berserk* (1983, with John Candy), *Pretty Woman* (1990, with Julia Roberts; Donahue portrayed a fashion consultant), and *Freddy's Dead-The Final Nightmare* (1991).

One last interesting note on Elinor Donahue: She was once a candidate for the role of Laura Petrie on *The Dick Van Dyke Show*.

PRODUCERS
AND DIRECTORS

SHELDON LEONARD

Sheldon Leonard was creator and executive producer for all eight seasons of *The Andy Griffith Show*. He directed episodes 1, "The New Housekeeper," and 162, "The Bazaar."

Leonard was born Sheldon Leonard Bershad on February 22, 1907, in New York City. After receiving his formal education at Syracuse University, he became involved with acting in stage productions. He later went on to appear in nearly 150 feature films, usually as a gangster or some type of "heavy." Leonard's best-known work as a film actor includes *Another Thin Man* (1939, with William Powell and Myrna Loy), *Tortilla Flat* (1942, with Spencer Tracy), *Lucky Jordan* (1942, with Alan Ladd), *Hit the Ice* (1943, with Abbott and Costello), *To Have and Have Not* (1944, with Humphrey Bogart), *It's a Wonderful Life* (1946, with James Stewart), *Sinbad the Sailor* (1947, with Douglas Fairbanks, Jr.), *Come Fill the Cup* (1951, with James Cagney), *Here Come the Nelsons* (1952; the movie that inspired the television show *The Adventures of Ozzie and Harriet*), *Money from Home* (1953, with Dean Martin and Jerry Lewis), *Guys and Dolls* (1955, with Marlon Brando and Frank Sinatra), *Pocketful of Miracles* (1961, with Bette Davis), and *The Brinks Job* (1978, with Peter Falk).

Over the years, Leonard has made countless guest appearances on television shows and specials, including *Burke's Law*, *The Burns and Allen Show*, *Cheers* (Leonard earned an Emmy nomination for this appearance), *The Colgate Comedy Hour*, *The Damon Runyon Theater*, *The Danny Thomas Show*, and an episode of *The Dick Van Dyke Show* entitled "Big Max Calvada." (In this episode, Leonard plays Max Calvada, a mobster, who hires Rob, Sally, and

Buddy to write a comedy routine for his non-talented nephew, an aspiring stand-up comedian. Calvada was the name of the production company that produced *The Dick Van Dyke Show*. The "CA" stands for Carl Reiner, the "L" for Sheldon Leonard, the "VA" for Dick Van Dyke, and the "DA" for Danny Thomas.) Leonard appeared on *The Bob Hope Show* in 1954. In 1965, he appeared with his friend Danny Thomas in an NBC special, *The Wonderful World of Burlesque I*. In 1967, he and Danny Thomas worked together once again on an NBC special. This one was called *Danny Thomas: The Road to Lebanon*. It was a spoof on the Bob Hope and Bing Crosby "Road" movies. Leonard also appeared on "The Duke," an episode of *Gomer Pyle, U.S.M.C.*, an episode of *I Love Lucy* ("Sales Resistance"), *I Married Joan*, two episodes of *I Spy*, *It's Always Sunday* (a pilot episode aired on *Screen Director's Playhouse*), *The Joey Bishop Show*, *The Lucy Show* ("Lucy Meets Sheldon Leonard"), *Later with Bob Costas* (a two-part interview in 1993), *Matlock* (reuniting him with Andy Griffith), *Murder, She Wrote*, *My World...and Welcome to It*, *Sanford and Son*, and the 1950s anthology series, *Your Jeweler's Showcase*. In 1987, Leonard made a brief appearance on a special episode of *This Is Your Life*, hosted by Ralph Edwards. This particular show honored Dick Van Dyke.

In the mid-1960s, Leonard lent his voice to Linus in the animated children's series, *Linus the Lionhearted*. In 1975, he returned to television to star in the CBS series *Big Eddie*. He portrayed an ex-gambler and promoter named Eddie Smith.

In 1978, Leonard appeared in and served as the executive producer of a television movie called *Top Secret*. Bill Cosby co-starred in this vehicle. Also in 1978, Leonard appeared with Dennis Weaver in a television movie entitled *The Islander*. He also made a brief appearance on *30 Years of Andy: A May-berry Reunion*, which aired on WTBS on October 3, 1990.

Even with such a noteworthy acting career, Sheldon Leonard is most widely recognized for his work as a television producer and director. In those roles he made tremendous contributions to television shows such as *Aces Up*, *The Danny Thomas Show* (a.k.a. *Make Room for Daddy*), *The Dick Van Dyke Show*. The 1961 pilot episode of *The Joey Bishop Show* (known as "Everything Happens to Me"), *Jeff's Collie*, *The Jimmy Durante Show*, *My World...and Welcome to It*, and the pilot episode of *Singles*.

As a producer or executive producer only, Leonard's credits include *Accidental Family*, *The Bill Dana Show*, *The Don Rickles Show*, *Gomer Pyle, U.S.M.C.*, *Good Morning World*, *I Spy*, *Mayberry R.F.D.*, *My Fifteen Blocks* (a pilot), *My Friend Tony*, and *Shirley's World*.

As a television director only, Leonard's resume includes *It's Always Jan*, the pilot episode and the reunion show of *Make More Room for Daddy*, *My Favorite Martian*, and *The Real McCoys*. Leonard also directed the first episode of *The Dick Van Dyke Show*. (The episode was aired on October 3, 1961, and was entitled "The Sick Boy and the Sitter.") In 1965, Leonard produced, directed, and wrote the pilot episode of *Patrick Stone*. It was aired on CBS.

Leonard's involvement with *The Andy Griffith Show*, according to an interview in the book *The Andy Griffith Show* by Richard Kelly, began when an idea and an available actor appeared on the horizon at the same time. While Leonard was producing *The Danny Thomas Show*, one of the show's writers Arthur (Artie) Stander, thought of a storyline in which the central character would be the sheriff, justice of the peace, and editor of a newspaper in a small town. At this time, Leonard was notified by the William Morris Agency of the availability of a young actor named Andy Griffith. Leonard believed Andy would fit the bill, because of his interest in working on television and because of his rural upbringing. He successfully negotiated a deal with Griffith and Griffith's business manager, Richard O. Linke, then asked Artie Stander to write the episode.

Once *The Andy Griffith Show* got rolling, Sheldon Leonard, Andy Griffith and Aaron Ruben were the principals involved with inventing the stories on the show. Once a storyline was set, Leonard would personally assign it to the pool of writers who worked on *The Andy Griffith Show*. Any subsequent changes were handled by Sheldon, Andy, and Aaron Ruben.

The creator and executive producer of *The Andy Griffith Show*, Sheldon Leonard.

Sheldon Leonard has been nominated for numerous Emmy awards as an actor, director, and producer. He has won many Emmies for his work on *The Danny Thomas Show*, *The Dick Van Dyke Show*, and *My World...and Welcome to It*. He was nominated four times for "Television Director of the Year" by the Directors Guild of America. He also served as the secretary of the Directors Guild of America for ten years. Finally, Leonard has been the recipient of the prestigious Sylvania and Aldrich awards for his contributions to television and the field of entertainment.

On March 23, 1990, Sheldon Leonard and Danny Thomas were saluted by the Museum of Broadcasting. The event was referred to as "The Cahuenga Studios Legacy." In attendance were many people from *The Andy Griffith Show*, including Andy Griffith, Don Knotts, Aaron Ruben, Bob Sweeney, Ronald Jacobs, and Charles Stewart. On April 18, 1990, the Museum of Broadcasting hosted "A Seminar with Sheldon Leonard."

On October 3, 1992, Sheldon Leonard and Andy Griffith, along with Ted Turner (a great fan of *The Andy Griffith Show*), Bill Cosby, Dinah Shore, and Ted Koppel, were inducted into the Television Academy Hall of Fame. Milton Berle was the host at the festivities.

In 1995, Leonard's autobiography, *And the Show Goes On*, was published. The book features a Foreword by Andy Griffith.

In his interview with Richard Kelly, Leonard muses on the staying power of *The Andy Griffith Show* and states, "I think *The Andy Griffith Show* maintained a higher level of quality than almost any other show I can think of. I think it received less recognition for that level of quality than almost any show I can think of, because its rural nature tended to downgrade it when it came time for handing out awards of recognition. But an inspection of the show will prove to any discriminating operator in our area of entertainment that the story construction, the performance, the direction, the editing, and the scoring were of a quality that has seldom been equaled."

AARON RUBEN

Aaron Ruben produced seasons 1, 2, 3, 4, and 5 of *The Andy Griffith Show*. He wrote the seven following episodes: 68, "Barney Mends A Broken Heart"; 71, "Floyd, the Gay Deceiver"; 73, "Lawman Barney"; 92, "A Wife for Andy"; 107, "Gomer Pyle, U.S.M.C." (also directed); 123, "Fun Girls"; and 240, "Barney Hosts a Summit Meeting." Mr. Ruben also directed 132, "Opie Loves Helen."

In Richard Kelly's book *The Andy Griffith Show*, Aaron Ruben is credited with creating both of Mayberry's "unseen" characters, Barney's waitress girlfriend, Juanita Beasley, and the infamous telephone operator, Sarah.

Ruben was heavily involved with the entire process of taking an idea for the show and ultimately developing the dialogue into a working script. In the early years, Andy Griffith, Sheldon Leonard, and Aaron Ruben comprised the team that gave final approval on all script submissions. This is one of the main reasons why *The Andy Griffith Show* always maintained such a high level of quality.

Prior to working on *The Andy Griffith Show*, Aaron Ruben wrote for numerous radio personalities in the 1940s, including George Burns and Gracie Allen, Henry Morgan, and Fred Allen. In the 1950s, he wrote for such television stars as Sam Levenson, Danny Thomas, Milton Berle, and Sid Caesar.

Ruben's contributions to television have been plentiful. For example, as a writer, he worked on such television shows and specials as the 1965 CBS special *The Andy Griffith-Don Knotts-Jim Nabors Show*, *Caesar's Hour*, *Garry Moore's Daytime Show*, The

Milton Berle Show (a.k.a. *The Buick-Berle Show*), and Milton Berle's legendary *Texaco Star Theatre*.

As a television director, Ruben's credits include *Headmaster* (with Andy Griffith), *The Phil Silvers Pontiac Special: Keep in Step* (1959, CBS), and *You'll Never Get Rich* (a.k.a. *Sergeant Bilko*), also starring Phil Silvers.

Following the fifth season of *The Andy Griffith Show*, Ruben left to create and serve as executive and line producer of its spinoff series, *Gomer Pyle, U.S.M.C.* This show was a huge success for six full seasons.

Ruben produced and wrote for many other popular television shows and specials throughout the years, including the 1967 CBS special *Andy Griffith's Uptown-Downtown Show*, *Charo and the Sergeant*, the 1967 CBS special presentation *The Don Knotts Special*, *Grandpa Max*, *Great Day*, *Jackie and Darlene*, *The New Andy Griffith Show* (also directed), *Piper's Pets*, *Sanford and Son*, *The Stockard Channing Show*, *Teachers Only* (starring Lynn Redgrave and created by Ruben), *Trouble with Richard* (with Dick Van Dyke), and *Wendy Hooper-U.S. Army*.

Other television shows that Ruben served as either writer or producer include the following: *C.P.O. Sharkey* (also created by Ruben), *The McLean Stevenson Show*, *The Phil Silvers Show*, *The Rag Business*, and *Too Close for Comfort*.

On the big screen, Aaron Ruben wrote and produced the 1969 feature film *The Comic*, starring Dick Van Dyke and directed by Carl Reiner.

BOB ROSS

Bob Ross was the producer of seasons 6, 7, and 8 on *The Andy Griffith Show*. He succeeded the only other person to produce the show, Aaron Ruben. Ross was also the script consultant for most of the episodes during the last four seasons. He wrote or co-wrote the following eight episodes: 131, "Barney's Physical"; 132, "Opie Loves Helen"; 141, "Otis Sues the County"; 149, "If I Had a Quarter Million"; 159, "Banjo-Playing Deputy"; 175, "Otis the Artist" (with Fred Freeman and Lawrence J. Cohen); 241, "Mayberry R.F.D."; and 249 "A Girl for Goober" (with Bruce Howard).

Following *The Andy Griffith Show*, Ross was credited as the creator of its spinoff series, *Mayberry R.F.D.* In fact, he produced the show and was the script consultant on the majority of episodes. Bob Ross and David Evans co-wrote the teleplay for the *Mayberry R.F.D.* episode "Goober's New Gas Station." (In this one, Goober builds his new gas station over ground occupied by the remains of a

Pickin' and grinnin' Mayberry style (left to right: Everett Greenbaum, Andy Griffith and director Bob Sweeney).

dinosaur. Howard Sprague, a noted historian, attempts to excavate the area without Goober's permission.)

In 1966, Ross wrote the screenplay for the feature film *Three on a Couch*, starring Jerry Lewis and Janet Leigh.

Prior to becoming involved with *The Andy Griffith Show*, Ross wrote for many successful television shows, including *The Amos and Andy Show*, *Ichabod and Me*, and *Leave It to Beaver*.

BOB SWEENEY

Bob Sweeney directed 80 episodes of *The Andy Griffith Show*, numbers 11, 12, 13, 14, 15, 16, 20, 21, 22, 23, 24, 25, 26, 27, 28, 29, 30, 31, 32, 33, 34, 35, 36, 37, 38, 39, 40, 41, 42, 43, 44, 45, 46, 47, 48, 49, 50, 51, 52, 53, 54, 55, 56, 57, 58, 59, 60, 61, 62, 63, 64, 65, 66, 67, 68, 69, 70, 71, 72, 73, 74, 75, 76, 77, 78, 79, 80, 81, 84, 85, 86, 87, 88, 89, 90, 91, 92, 93, 94, and 95. The most prolific director on *The Andy*

Griffith Show, he was born on October 14, 1918, in San Francisco, California. Upon graduating from San Francisco State College, he became a radio announcer. He later starred on radio dramas, and in the late 1940s, he formed a comedy team with Hal March. (In later years, March went on to host such game shows as *The $64,000 Question*.) Television appearances came next, and Sweeney appeared on a 1951 variety show called *Summer in the City*. He also appeared in the 1954 CBS *Shower of Stars* production of *A Christmas Carol*. He portrayed Bob Cratchit, while Fredric March starred as Ebenezer Scrooge and Basil Rathbone appeared as Jacob Marley.

During the 1950s, Sweeney appeared as Dangle on *The Life of Riley*. He was Harry Morton on *The George Burns and Gracie Allen Show* and Gilmore Cobb on *My Favorite Husband*. Sweeney went on to co-star with Gale Gordon and Howard McNear on *The Brothers*. He was also Oliver Munsey on *Our Miss Brooks*. In 1959, Bob Sweeney received the title role in *Fibber McGee and Molly*. Among his guest-starring roles on television, Sweeney lists *Alfred Hitchcock Presents* and *The Rifleman*. In the movies, Bob Sweeney's acting credits include *It Grows on Trees* (1952, with Irene Dunn), *Mister Scoutmaster* (1952, with Clifton Webb), *The Last Hurrah* (1958, directed by John Ford and starring Spencer Tracy), *Toby Tyler* (1960, a Walt Disney production), *Moon Pilot* (1962, another Disney production), *Son of Flubber* (1963, Disney's sequel to *The Absent Minded Professor*), *Marnie* (1964, directed by Alfred Hitchcock and starring Sean Connery), *How to Succeed in Business Without Really Trying* (1967, with Robert Morse), and *Trying* (1976).

As a television director, Bob Sweeney's credits include *Aloha Paradise*, *At Ease*, the 1990 version of *The Bradys*, *Bring 'Em Back Alive*, *The Courtship of Eddie's Father*, *Crazy Like a Fox*, *The Dukes of Hazzard*, *Dynasty*, *Fantasy Island*, *Finder of Lost Loves*, *Flamingo Road*, *Goodnight Beantown*, *Hogan's Heroes*, *Just Our Luck*, *Love and Marriage*, *The Love Boat*, a reunion with Andy Griffith on *Matlock*, *Oh, Nurse!*, *Private Benjamin*, *The Scarecrow and Mrs. King*, *Simon and Simon*, *The Six O'Clock Follies*, *Strike Force*, *That Girl*, and *Trapper John, M.D.*

As a producer and director, Sweeney's credits include *The Andros Targets*, *The Doris Day Show*, *Hawaii Five-O*, *Hey Teacher*, and *Spencer's Pilots*.

As solely a television producer, Sweeney's credits include *Alone at Last*, *The Baileys of Balboa*, *Ethel Is an Elephant*, and *The Patty Duke Show*. He also served as the executive producer on the 1975 television movie *Dead Man on the Run*. In 1986, Sweeney directed the hit television movie *Return to Mayberry*.

Sweeney, along with William Finnegan, formed a production company, Sweeney/Finnegan Productions. The company produced numerous television shows and movies.

In 1987, Sweeney directed the television movie *If It's Tuesday, It Still Must Be Belgium*.

Bob Sweeney passed away on June 7, 1992.

In the 1970-71 season, Sweeney was nominated for an Emmy for outstanding directorial achievement in drama, single program of a continuing series, for *Hawaii Five-O*. (He lost to Daryl Duke for *The Bold Ones*.) In the 1972-73 season, he was nominated for an Emmy for outstanding drama series, for *Hawaii Five-O*. Nominated along with executive producer Leonard Freeman and co-producer William Finnegan. (He lost to the producers of *The Waltons*.) And in the 1982-83 season, Sweeney was nominated for an Emmy for outstanding directing in a comedy series, for *The Love Boat*. (He lost to James Burrows, for *Cheers*.)

LEE PHILIPS

Lee Philips directed 60 episodes of *The Andy Griffith Show*, numbers 173, 174, 180, 181, 190, 191, 192, 193, 194, 195, 196, 197, 198, 199, 200, 201, 202, 203, 204, 205, 206, 207, 208, 209, 210, 211, 212, 213, 214, 215, 216, 217, 218, 219, 220, 221, 222, 223, 224, 225, 226, 227, 228, 229, 230, 234, 235, 236, 237, 238, 239, 240, 242, 243, 244, 245, 246, 247, 248, and 249. Only Bob Sweeney directed more episodes.

Philips was born in Brooklyn, New York, on January 10, 1927. He began his professional life as an actor and quickly established himself in television. He had the starring role in the 1959 television version of *The Further Adventures of Ellery Queen*. He also appeared in the television drama *Marty* and in the *Studio One* version of *Twelve Angry Men*.

Philips has made numerous guest appearances on television shows throughout the years. Among these are a pilot episode called "Satan's Waitin'" (1964), three episodes of *Alfred Hitchcock Presents*, *Perry Mason*, *The Fugitive*, *The Outer Limits*, *Surfside 6*, and the mini-series *QB VII*. He also appeared in two episodes of *The Twilight Zone* ("Passage on the Lady Anne" and "Queen of the Nile"). On *The Dick Van Dyke Show*, Philips appeared as Drew Patton in "The Man from Emperor." (In this episode, Rob Petrie is offered a job as a humorist for Mr. Patton's men's magazine.)

Philips' credits as a film actor include *Peyton Place* (1957, with Lana Turner), *Middle of the Night* (1959, with Kim Novak), *Tess of the Storm Country*

(1960), *Psychomania* (1963), and *The Lollipop Cover* (1965).

As a television director, Lee Philips' credits include *The American Girls, Bracken's World, Crazy Times, The Donna Reed Show, Dynasty, The Ghost and Mrs. Muir, Gidget, Going Places* (a pilot series), *Inspector Perez, Kung Fu, Lottery, Love, American Style, Love on a Rooftop, The Man and the City, Medical Center, My World...and Welcome to It*, a reunion with Andy Griffith on *The New Andy Griffith Show, Of Men of Women, The Partridge Family, The Practice, Riding High* (a pilot series), *Room 222, Salvage I* (another reunion with Andy Griffith), *The Survivors*, and numerous episodes of *The Waltons*, including the 1982 special *A Wedding on Walton's Mountain*. He also directed four episodes of *The Dick Van Dyke Show*, including "Your Sweet Home Is My Home" (in which Rob recalls when he and his best friend, Jerry Helper, try to buy the same house), and "The Ugliest Dog in the World" (in which Rob and Laura try to find a good home for an ugly pooch). Philips also has to his credit the direction of two episodes of *M*A*S*H*. They are "Yankee Doodle Doctor," (in which the doctors of the 4077th rebel against the making of a propaganda film about the war) and "Love and Marriage (in which Hawkeye and Trapper try to unite a soldier with his pregnant wife and attempt to stop another soldier from marrying a Korean prostitute).

Lee Philips has directed many television movies. His resume includes *Getting Away From it All* (1972, with Larry Hagman), *The Girl Most Likely To...* (1972, written by Joan Rivers), *The Stranger Within* (1974, with Barbara Eden), *The Red Badge of Courage* (1974, with Richard Thomas), *Sweet Hostage* (1975, with Martin Sheen), *Louis Armstrong-Chicago Style* (1976, with Ben Vereen; Philips also co-produced), *Wanted: The Sundance Woman* (a.k.a. *Mrs. Sundance Rides Again*, 1976), *The Spell* (1977, with Lee Grant), *The War Between the Tates* (1977, with Elizabeth Ashley), *Special Olympics* (a.k.a. *A Special Kind of Love*, 1978, with Charles Durning), *The Comedy Company* (1978, with Jack Albertson), *Salvage* (1979; this was the pilot episode for the Andy Griffith series *Salvage I*), *Valentine* (1979, with Mary Martin), *Hardhat and Legs* (1980), *On the Right Track* (1981, with Gary Coleman), *Mae West* (1982, with Ann Jillian), *Games Mother Never Taught You* (1983, with Loretta Swit), *Samson and Delilah* (1984), *Space* (1985, a mini-series with an all-star cast), *Barnum* (1987, starring Burt Lancaster), *Windmills of the Gods* (1988), and *Blind Vengeance* (1990).

Philips has twice been Emmy-nominated: in the 1972-73 season, for outstanding directorial achievement in drama, a single program of a series with continuing characters and or theme, for *The Waltons* (lost to Jerry Thorpe, for *Kung Fu*), and in the 1981-82 season, for outstanding directing in a limited series or special, for *Mae West* (lost to Marvin Chomsky, for *Inside the Third Reich*).

ALAN RAFKIN

Alan Rafkin directed 27 episodes of *The Andy Griffith Show*, numbers 133, 134, 147, 148, 149, 165, 166, 167, 168, 169, 170, 171, 172, 175, 176, 177, 178, 179, 182, 183, 184, 185, 186, 187, 188, 189, and 231.

Alan Rafkin's directorial credits include *Alice, Another April, Bewitched* (including the Christmas episode, "A Vision of Sugar Plums"), *Blansky's Beauties, The Bob Newhart Show, The Cara Williams Show, Charles in Charge, Coach, The Courtship of Eddie's Father, Daddy's Girl, The Donna Reed Show, Get Smart, The Girl with Something Extra, The Good Guys, The Governor and J.J., Hanging In, Harry's Battles, Here We Go Again, I Dream of Jeannie, It's Garry Shandling's Show, The Jeff Foxworthy Show, Laverne and Shirley, Living in Paradise, Love, American Style, The Love Boat, The Mary Tyler Moore Show, My Favorite Martian, My World...and Welcome to It, The Nancy Walker Show, The Odd Couple, The Partridge Family, Paul Sand In Friends and Lovers, Rhoda, Room 222, Sanford and Son, That's My Mama, The Tim Conway Show, What's Happening!!*, and *A Year at the Top*.

Rafkin directed three episodes of *The Dick Van Dyke Show*. They are "My Husband Is Not a Drunk" (in which Rob unintentionally falls under a posthypnotic suggestion that renders him hopelessly drunk every time a bell rings), "Pink Pills and Purple Parents" (in which Rob recalls Laura's disastrous first meeting with his parents), and "The Death of the Party" (in which Rob tries to muster up the strength to make it through Laura's family reunion, even though he's suffering from the flu).

Rafkin also directed two memorable episodes of *M*A*S*H*: "The General's Practitioner" (in which Hawkeye gets upset when he is assigned to be the personal physician of a certain general), and "Lieutenant Radar O'Reilly" (in which Radar wins a promotion in a poker game).

Rafkin directed the pilot episodes for four proposed television series: *Handle with Care, Legs, Local 306*, and *Stick Around*. He was the producer and director on *Me and the Chimp, One Day at a Time, The Super, Viva Valdez*, and *We Got It Made*. He also directed the 1975 television movie *Let's Switch*, starring Barbara Eden and Barbara Feldon.

Rafkin's feature films as a director include *Ski*

Party (1965, with Frankie Avalon), *The Ghost and Mr. Chicken* (1966, with Don Knotts), *The Ride to Hangman's Tree* (1967, with Jack Lord), *Nobody's Perfect* (1968, with Doug McClure), *The Shakiest Gun in the West* (1968, again with Don Knotts), *Angel in My Pocket* (1969, with Andy Griffith), and *How to Frame a Figg* (1971, once again with Don Knotts).

Rafkin has had a number of Emmy nominations. In the 1970-71 season, he was nominated for an Emmy for outstanding directorial achievement in comedy for a single program of a continuing series, for *The Mary Tyler Moore Show*. (He lost to Jay Sandrich, also of *The Mary Tyler Moore Show*). In the 1976-77 season, he was nominated for outstanding directing in a comedy series, single episode, for *M*A*S*H*. (He lost to Alan Alda, also for *M*A*S*H*.*) In the 1981-82 season, Rafkin won an Emmy for outstanding directing in a comedy series, for *One Day at a Time* (the episode "Barbara's Crisis"). In the 1987-88 season, he was again Emmy-nominated for outstanding director in a comedy series, this time for *It's Garry Shandling's Show*. (He lost to Gregory Hoblit for *Hooperman*.)

COBY RUSKIN

Coby Ruskin directed 18 episodes of *The Andy Griffith Show*, numbers 111, 112, 117, 123, 124, 125, 126, 127, 135, 136, 150, 151, 152, 153, 156, 157, 158, and 159.

Ruskin has directed many television favorites throughout the years, particularly in the 1950s and 1960s. His list of directorial credits on television includes *The Bill Cosby Show*, *The Bob Newhart Show*, *The Doris Day Show*, *George Gobel Presents*, numerous episodes of *Gomer Pyle, U.S.M.C.*, *Here's Lucy*, *Julia*, *Love, American Style*, *The Paul Lynde Show*, and *When Things Were Rotten*.

Ruskin also directed two memorable episodes of *The Dick Van Dyke Show*: "Don't Trip Over That Mountain" (in which Rob tries to hide from Laura the fact that he sprained his entire body during a skiing trip) and "The Secret Life of Buddy and Sally" (in which Rob believes that his co-writers are having an affair, while actually, they are leaving every weekend to practice new comedy material at an out-of-the-way nightclub).

Ruskin produced and directed three television shows: *The All-Star Revue*, *Sammy Kaye's Music from Manhattan*, and *So You Want to Lead a Band?* He also produced an early television variety show, *Star of the Family* from 1950 through 1952.

In 1960, Ruskin directed the variety special *Just Polly and Me*, starring Polly Bergen and Phil Sil-

vers. He also produced and directed the 1962 special *The All-Star Comedy Show*, hosted by Johnny Carson.

In 1967, Ruskin directed the pilot episode for a suggested NBC series of the popular comic strip *Li'l Abner*. It was written by *Li'l Abner*'s creator, Al Capp, but the series was never picked up by the network.

DON WEIS

Don Weis, who directed 9 episodes of *The Andy Griffith Show* (numbers 2, 3, 4, 5, 6, 7, 8, 9, and 10), was born on May 13, 1922, in Milwaukee, Wisconsin. He started his long career in the film industry as a messenger boy at Warner Bros. after studying film at the University of Southern California. After a hitch in World War II, he became a script consultant and dialogue director before becoming a film director in the early 1950s. Weis was the dialogue director on such films as *Body and Soul* (1947), *The Red Pony* (1949), *Champion* (1949), *Home of the Brave* (1949), and *The Men* (1950).

Weis's long list of television credits includes *Alfred Hitchcock Presents*, *The Andros Targets*, *The Barbary Coast*, *Baretta*, *Batman*, *The Bob Hope Chrysler Theater*, *Bring 'Em Back Alive*, *Bronk*, *Burke's Law*, *Cagney and Lacey*, *Casablanca*, *Charlie's Angels*, *Checkmate*, *Chips*, *Code Red*, *The Courtship of Eddie's Father*, *Dear Phoebe*, *Delta House*, *The Dooley Brothers*, *Fireside Theater*, *Flamingo Road*, *Flo's Place*, *Happy Days*, *Hard Knocks*, *Harry O*, *Hawaii Five-O*, *Hill Street Blues*, *Ironside*, *It Takes a Thief*, *The Jack Benny Program*, *Kingston: Confidential*, *Lollipop Louie*, *Lottery*, *The Love Boat*, *The Magician*, *Mannix*, *Matt Helm*, *McKeever and the Colonel*, *The Millionaire*, *Murphy's Law*, *The Night Stalker*, *Off We Go*, *Papa Said No*, *Paris 7000*, *The Patty Duke Show*, *Perry Mason*, *Petrocelli*, *Planet of the Apes*, *Quick and Quiet*, *Remington Steele*, *Riddle at 24000*, *Roll Out!*, *The San Pedro Beach Bums*, *Schlitz Playhouse of Stars*, *Secrets of the Old Bailey*, *The Six O'Clock Follies*, *Skip Taylor*, *Spencer's Pilots*, *Starsky and Hutch*, *The Survivors*, *T.J. Hooker*, *The Virginian*, and *Wagon Train*.

Weis directed one episode of *The Twilight Zone* ("Steel"). He also directed 16 episodes of *M*A*S*H*, including "Dear Dad...Three" (in which Henry Blake watches a home movie of his daughter's birthday party that he couldn't attend), "Iron Guts Kelly" (in which a general dies of a heart attack while making whoopee with Hot Lips), and "Big Mac" (in which General MacArthur makes an unforgettable visit to the 4077th).

Weis also directed Carl Reiner's original pilot episode of *The Dick Van Dyke Show*. It was called

"Head of the Family" and aired on CBS's *Comedy Spot* anthology series on July 19, 1960. Carl Reiner starred as Rob Sturdy. (In the actual series, Dick Van Dyke replaced Reiner, and his last name was changed to Petrie, because Reiner thought the original name sounded too much like "Rob's dirty.")

Weis also produced and directed numerous episodes of *Fantasy Island*.

Don Weis has directed some television movies, including *The Longest Hundred Miles* (1967), *Now You See It, Now You Don't* (1968), *The Night Stalker: Two Tales of Terror* (1974), *The Millionaire* (1978, an updated version of the 1950s television show), and *The Munster's Revenge* (1981, with many original cast members, plus Howard Morris).

Weis's feature film directing credits include *Bannerline* (1951), *It's a Big Country* (1952; Weis was one of seven directors), *Just This Once, You for Me* (1952, with Janet Leigh and Peter Lawford), *Remains to Be Seen* (1953, with Van Johnson and June Allyson), *I Love Melvin* (1953, with Donald O'Connor and Debbie Reynolds), *A Slight Case of Larceny* (1953, with Mickey Rooney), *The Affairs of Dobie Gillis* (1953, with Debbie Reynolds), *Half a Hero* (1953, with Red Skelton), *Ride the High Iron* (1956, with Raymond Burr), *Catch Me If You Can* (1957), *Deadlock* (1957, originally made for television), *Mr. Pharaoh and His Cleopatra* (1959, made in Cuba and not released in the United States), *The Gene Krupa Story* (1959, with Sal Mineo), *Critic's Choice* (1963, with Bob Hope and Lucille Ball), *Looking for Love* (1964, featuring Johnny Carson's only film appearance), *Pajama Party* (1964), *Billie* (1965, with Patty Duke; Weis also produced this one), *The Ghost in the Invisible Bikini* (1966), *The King's Pirate* (1967), *Did You Hear the One About the Traveling Saleslady?* (1968, with Phyllis Diller), and *Zero to Sixty* (1978).

Weis has been honored with two awards from the Directors Guild of America, first in 1955 for *The Little Guy*, which aired on *Fireside Theater*, and then in 1957 for *The Lonely Wizard*, which aired on the *Schlitz Playhouse of Stars*.

RICHARD CRENNA

Richard (Dick) Crenna, who directed eight episodes of *The Andy Griffith Show* (numbers 99, 100, 101, 105, 106, 108, 109, and 110), may be the best known of all the directors who worked on *The Andy Griffith Show*. Many remember his portrayal of Luke McCoy from 1957 through 1963 on *The Real McCoys*, with Walter Brennan.

Richard Crenna was born on November 30,

Well-known actor and director, Richard Crenna, directed eight episodes of the *Andy Griffith Show*.

1926, in Los Angeles, and few remember that he started in the entertainment arena at a young age. As a teenager in the 1940s, he had starring roles on radio programs such as *Boy Scouts Jamboree*, *Burns and Allen*, *A Date with Judy*, *The Great Gildersleeve*, *The Hardy Family*, and *Our Miss Brooks*. When *Our Miss Brooks* moved to television in 1952, Crenna had his first starring role in the new medium as a problem student named Walter Denton. Eve Arden starred as his schoolteacher, Connie Brooks. Crenna stayed with this program through the 1955 season and later went on to other television roles. In 1964 and 1965, he appeared in *Slattery's People* as James Slattery, a lawyer and minority leader in his community. In 1976 and 1977, he starred with Bernadette Peters in *All's Fair*, appearing as a political columnist named Richard Barrington. In 1981, he hosted a television magazine show called *Look At Us*. In 1982 and 1983, Crenna starred with Patty Duke Astin in *It Takes Two*. In this one he appeared as Doctor Sam Quinn, a surgeon.

Throughout the years, Crenna has appeared on numerous television shows and specials, including *ABC's Silver Anniversary Celebration: 25 and Still the One*, *CBS on the Air* (as co-host for this 9 1/2-hour retrospective aired in 1978), the mini-series *Centennial* (as the misguided Colonel Frank Skimmerhorn), *Cheyenne, Conflicts, The Deputy, Father Knows Best, Frontier, The Hollywood Squares, I Love Lucy* (an episode entitled "Young Fans," in which he portrayed Arthur Morton), the pilot episode of *Joshua's World, The Kraft Suspense Theater,* a CBS variety special called *The Lily Tomlin Show, London and Davis in New York, Matinee Theater, Medic, The Millionaire, Musical Comedy Tonight, The People's Choice Awards* (as a co-host), *Plaza Suite* (a 1987 ABC special), *Pros and Cons, Sally,* and *Silent Service.* He also appeared on the 1974 PBS drama *Double Solitaire,* which was aired on *Hollywood TV Theater.* In 1994, Crenna appeared on the ABC show *World of Discovery.* He narrated an episode of this series entitled "Chasing India's Monsoon." He also appeared in and narrated an Audubon Society video entitled *Wood Stark Barometer of the Everglades.*

Richard Crenna has appeared in numerous television movies since the early 1970s. His credits are many and include *Thief* (1971), *Footsteps* (a.k.a. *Nice Guys Finish Last,* 1972), *Double Indemnity* (1973), *Nightmare* (1974), *Honky Tonk* (1974), *Shootout in a One-Dog Town* (1974), *A Girl Named Sooner* (1975, with Lee Remick), *The War Between the Tates* (1977), *A Fire in the Sky* (1978), *Devil Dog: The Hound from Hell* (1978), *First You Cry* (1978, with Mary Tyler Moore), *Mayflower: The Pilgrim's Adventure* (1979, with Anthony Hopkins), *Fugitive Family* (1980), *The Order of Bill Carney* (1981), *The Day the Bubble Burst* (1982), *Passions* (1984, with Joanne Woodward), *Doubletake* (1985), *The Rape of Richard Beck* (1985, with Meredith Baxter Birney), *On Wings of Eagles* (1986, with Burt Lancaster), *The High Price of Passion* (1986), *A Case of Deadly Force* (1986), *Police Story: The Freeway Killings* (1987), *Kids Like These* (1987, with Tyne Daly), *Internal Affairs* (1988), *Stuck with Each Other* (1989, with Tyne Daly), *The Case of the Hillside Stranglers* (a.k.a. *The Hillside Stranglers,* 1989), *After the Shock* (1990, made for cable television), *Montana* (1990, made for cable television), *Murder in Black and White* (1990), *Murder Times Seven* (1990), *The Last Flight Out* (1990, with James Earl Jones), *And the Sea Will Tell* (1991), *The Intruders* (1992, made for cable television), *The Forget-Me-Not Murders* (1994), and *Jonathan Stone: Threat of Innocence* (1994).

Crenna has also appeared in many feature films, including *Red Skies of Montana* (1952), *The Pride of St. Louis* (1952), *It Grows on Trees* (1952), *Our Miss Brooks* (1956, a feature film with the original television cast), *Over-Exposed* (1956), *John Goldfarb, Please Come Home* (1965), *Made in Paris* (1966, with Ann-Margaret), *The Sand Pebbles* (1966, with Steve McQueen), *Wait Until Dark* (1967, with Audrey Hepburn), *Star!* (1968, with Julie Andrews), *Midas*

Run (1969, with Fred Astaire), *Marooned* (1969, with Gregory Peck), *Red Sky at Morning* (1970), *Catlow* (1971, with Yul Brynner), *Doctor's Wives* (1971, with Dyan Cannon), *The Deserter* (a.k.a. *Ride to Glory,* 1971), *Dirty Money* (1972, made in France), *Jonathan Livingston Seagull* (1972, voice only), *The Man Called Noon* (1973), *Breakheart Pass* (1976, with Charles Bronson), *The Evil* (1978), *Wild Horse Hank* (1979), *Hard Ride to Rantan* (1979, made in Canada), *Deathship* (1980), *Stone Cold Dead* (1980, made in Canada) *Body Heat* (1981, with William Hurt and Kathleen Turner), *First Blood* (1982, with Sylvester Stallone), *Table for Five* (1983, with Jon Voight), *The Flamingo Kid* (1984, with Matt Dillon), *Summer Rental* (1985, with John Candy), *Rambo: First Blood II* (1985, with Sylvester Stallone), *50 Years of Action* (1986, narrator), *Rambo III* (1988, with Sylvester Stallone), *Leviathan* (1989), and *Hot Shots! Part Deux* (1993).

As a television director, Richard Crenna's credits include *Allison Sydney Harrison, Cap'n Ahab, The Cheerleaders, Grandpa Goes to Washington, The Hoyt Axton Show, Lou Grant, Marie, No time for Sergeants, The Real McCoys, Rosetti and Ryan, Turnabout,* and *Wendy and Me.* Crenna directed the 1979 television movie *Better Late than Never,* starring Harold Gould and Strother Martin.

Crenna produced the short-lived television series *Make Room for Granddaddy.* This show aired on ABC in 1970 and 1971 and starred many of the original cast members of *The Danny Thomas Show* (a.k.a. *Make Room for Daddy*), including Danny Thomas, Marjorie Lord, Rusty Hamer, and Angela Cartwright.

In the 1965-66 season, Crenna was nominated for an Emmy for outstanding continued performance by an actor in a leading role in a dramatic series, for *Slattery's People.* He lost to Bill Cosby for *I Spy,* but nearly twenty years later, in the 1984-85 season, he won an Emmy for outstanding lead actor in a limited series or special, for the ABC television movie *The Rape of Richard Beck.*

HOWARD MORRIS

Howard Morris, familiar to viewers of *The Andy Griffith Show* as Ernest T. Bass, directed eight episodes of the show (numbers 128, 129, 130, 131, 139, 140, 141, and 142). Morris has a distinguished career as both actor and director. His acting credits are listed in the "Starring Cast" section of this book.

Besides directing countless television commercials, for which he has won Clio and Andy awards for excellence in advertising direction, Howard Morris has directed episodes of the following television shows and specials: *The ABC Afternoon Playbreak Special* ("Oh, Baby, Baby, Baby"), *Aloha Paradise*, *The Beatrice Arthur Special*, *Bewitched*, *Gomer Pyle, U.S.M.C.*, *The Good Life* (a pilot for a series), *The Good Old Days*, *Hogan's Heroes*, *Laverne and Shirley*, *Love, American Style*, *The Love Boat*, *The Mighty Orbots*, *One Day at a Time*, *The Patty Duke Show*, *Please Don't Eat the Daisies*, *Private Benjamin*, and *Turbo-Teen*.

Morris directed five episodes of *The Dick Van Dyke Show*, including "The Ballad of Betty Lou" (in which Rob and Jerry buy a sailboat), "Scratch My Car and Die" (in which Rob buys a new sports car called a Tarantula and goes bonkers when it gets scratched), and "A Friendly Game of Cards" (in which Rob gets caught playing poker with a marked deck).

Morris directed the pilot episode for *Get Smart*. The episode was entitled "Mr. Big" and was the only *Get Smart* episode that was filmed in black and white. It was also the only episode from this series that Howard Morris directed.

As a television producer, Morris produced both versions of *The Corner Bar*. This show was aired on ABC during the 1972 and 1973 seasons.

On December 4, 1973, Howard Morris produced and appeared in the ABC special *The Many Faces of Comedy*. Don Knotts also appeared in this special.

Morris has also directed some feature films, including *Who's Minding The Mint?* (1967, with Milton Berle), *With Six You Get Eggroll* (1968, with Doris Day), *Don't Drink The Water* (1969, with Jackie Gleason), and *Goin' Coconuts* (1978, with Donny and Marie Osmond).

Howard Morris has won the Clio award for direction in advertising more than a dozen times. Two of his commercials, one for Kellogg's and one for McDonald's, were voted into the Clio Hall of Fame.

JEFFREY HAYDEN

In addition to directing 8 episodes of *The Andy Griffith Show* (numbers 102, 103, 104, 118, 119, 120, 121, and 122), Jeffrey Hayden has compiled an impressive list of television shows that he has either directed or produced during his career. His television directorial credits include *Alias Smith and Jones*, *The Chocolate Solder*, *The Curse of Dracula*, *Dennis the Menace*, *The Dick Powell Show*, *The Donna Reed Show*, *Emerald Point, N.A.S.*, *From Here to Eternity*, *Hawaiian Heat*, *The Incredible Hulk*, *Ironside*, *Jessica*

Novak, *Julie Farr, M.D.*, *Knight Rider*, *Lady in the Dark*, *Lassie*, *Leave It to Beaver*, *The Loretta Young Theater*, *Love, American Style*, *Magnum, P.I.*, *Mannix*, *The Mississippi*, *Mr. Merlin*, *No Time for Sergeants*, *Omnibus*, *Palmerstown U.S.A.*, *The Philco-Goodyear Playhouse*, *Please Don't Eat the Daisies*, *The Powers of Matthew Star*, *Quincy, M.E.*, *Route 66*, *The Runaways*, *77 Sunset Strip*, *Shane*, *Space Academy*, *Surfside 6*, and *That Girl*. Hayden also directed two episodes of the camp classic *Batman*. They are "The Puzzles Are Coming" and "The Duo Is Slumming." The shows were aired on December 21 and 22, 1966, and starred Maurice Evans as the Puzzler.

As a television producer, Hayden's credits include *The Billy Beane Show*, *How the West Was Won*, and *Santa Barbara*.

Hayden directed the 1957 feature film *The Vintage*, starring Mel Ferrer. He acted in the 1956 Bob Hope movie *That Certain Feeling*.

PETER BALDWIN

Peter Baldwin, who directed 7 episodes of *The Andy Griffith Show* (numbers 143, 144, 145, 163, 232, 233, and 241), has directed some of the best-loved television situation comedies of all time. His directorial credits include *Alone At Last*, *Benson*, *The Bob Newhart Show*, *Carter Country*, *C.P.O. Sharkey*, *Chico and the Man*, *Dinah and Her New Best Friends*, *The Doris Day Show*, *The Duck Factory*, *Goodnight Beantown*, *Gossip*, *Gun Shy*, *Joe and Sons*, *The Living End*, *Love, American Style*, *The Lovebirds*, nine episodes of *The Mary Tyler Moore Show*, *The Michelle Lee Show*, *Newhart*, *9 to 5*, *One in a Million*, *One of the Boys*, *Out of the Blue*, *The Partridge Family*, *Please Don't Eat the Daisies*, *Sanford and Son*, *Space Force*, *Teachers Only*, *13 Queens Boulevard*, *Too Close for Comfort*, *Wonderworks*, and *Zorro and Son*.

Peter Baldwin directed two episodes of *The Dick Van Dyke Show*: "A Vigilante Ripped My Sport Coat" (in which Jerry Helper forms an early version of a neighborhood watch group), and "It Wouldn't Hurt Them to Give Us a Raise" (in which Rob attempts to get a salary increase for Buddy and Sally).

Baldwin also directed seven episodes of *The Brady Bunch*, including "Quarterback Sneak" (in which Marcia's new boyfriend tries to steal Greg's football play book), "Marcia Gets Creamed" (in which Marcia is the afternoon manager at Haskell's Ice Cream Hut and is forced to fire her brother Peter), and "Out of This World" (in which real-life astronaut James McDivitt visits the Bradys). Baldwin went on to direct some episodes of *The Brady*

Brides, two Brady Bunch television movies, and a few episodes of the 1990 hour-long series called *The Bradys*.

Baldwin directed some episodes of the Emmy award–winning series *The Wonder Years*. A couple of these are "She, My Friend and I" (in which Kevin Arnold gets jealous when his best friend, Paul, goes out on a date with his girl, Winnie Cooper) and "Our Miss White" (in which Kevin falls for his beautiful English teacher).

Baldwin directed the pilot episodes for *Hollywood High* and *Making It*. He also directed the 1977 comedy special *Great Day*.

Peter Baldwin has acted on television and in the movies over the years, particularly in the 1950s and 1960s.

Baldwin's directing credits for television movies include *The Brady Girls Get Married* (1981, the pilot episode for the *Brady Brides* series), *The Harlem Globetrotters on Gilligan's Island* (1981, the third "Gilligan" reunion movie), *Lots of Luck* (1985, a Disney Network movie, starring Martin Mull and Annette Funicello), and *A Very Brady Christmas* (1988).

In the 1971-72 season, Baldwin was nominated for an Emmy for outstanding achievement in comedy, for *The Mary Tyler Moore Show*. (He lost to John Rich, for *All in the Family*.) He won an Emmy in the 1988-89 season for outstanding directing in a comedy series, for *The Wonder Years* (the episode "Our Miss White"). In the 1990-91 season, he was again nominated for an Emmy for outstanding directing in a comedy series, for *The Wonder Years*. (He lost to James Burrows, for *Cheers*.)

EARL BELLAMY

Earl Bellamy, who directed 7 episodes of *The Andy Griffith Show* (numbers 96, 97, 98, 113, 114, 115, and 116), was born on March 11, 1917, in Minneapolis, Minnesota. He was educated at City College in Los Angeles.

Bellamy has directed many shows that rate among the best situation comedies and dramas in the history of the medium. It would take a small book to list all of his credits, but an abbreviated list includes *The Adventures of Rin Tin Tin, Alcoa Premiere, Alfred Hitchcock Presents, Arrest and Trial, Bachelor Father, Chips, Code Red, The Crusaders, Daniel Boone, The Desilu Playhouse, The Donna Reed Show, Fantasy Island, The F.B.I., The First Hundred Years, Future Cop, Get Smart, Getaway Car, I Spy, Isis, A Knight in Shining Armour, Laramie, Laredo, Lassie, Leave It to Beaver, The Lone Ranger, M Squad, Matt Helm, McHale's Navy, Medical Center,*

The Mod Squad, The Monroes, The Munsters, My Friend Tony, My Three Sons, O'Connor's Ocean, The Partners, The Partridge Family, Perry Mason, The Quest, Rawhide, Schlitz Playhouse, The San Pedro Beach Bums, Science Fiction Theater, Sergeant Preston of the Yukon, Sheriff of Cochise, The Sixth Sense, Solders of Fortune, Starsky and Hutch, Stranded, S.W.A.T., Tales of Wells Fargo, Tarzan, To Rome with Love, Trapper John, M.D., The Virginian, Wagon Train, and *Young Dan'l Boone*.

Bellamy directed an episode of *The Brady Bunch* entitled "The Big Bet" (in which Bobby beats Greg in a chin-up contest and Greg must do everything Bobby asks of him for one full week). He directed two episodes of *M*A*S*H*: "Love Story" (in which Hawkeye and Trapper John attempt the cultural improvement of Radar, who has a crush on a sophisticated nurse), and "Ceasefire" (in which the inhabitants of the 4077th start to close-up shop when rumors of a ceasefire are running rampant). Bellamy also directed and wrote numerous episodes of the popular Robert Wagner and Stephanie Powers series, *Hart to Hart*.

Earl Bellamy has directed many television movies. They include *The Pigeon* (1969, with Sammy Davis, Jr.; Bellamy also produced this television movie), *The Trackers* (1971, again, with Sammy Davis, Jr., as well as Mayberry alumna Julie Adams), *The Desperate Mission* (1971), *Flood!* (1976, produced by Irwin Allen and starring Robert Culp), *Fire!* (1977, produced by Irwin Allen and starring Ernest Borgnine), *Desperate Women* (1978, starring Susan St. James), *The Castaways of Gilligan's Island* (1979, the second "Gilligan" reunion movie), and *Valentine Magic on Love Island* (1980).

In feature films, Bellamy's directorial credits include *Seminole Uprising* (1955), *Blackjack Ketchum, Desperado* (1956), *Toughest Gun in Tombstone* (1958), *Stagecoach to Dancer's Rock* (1962; Bellamy also produced this movie), *Fluffy* (1965, with Howard Morris), *Gunpoint* (1966, starring Audie Murphy), *Munster, Go Home* (1966, featuring the original television cast), *Three Guns for Texas* (1968, a movie comprised of three episodes of *Laredo*; Bellamy directed the segment entitled "No Bugle-One Drum"), *Backtrack* (1969, an elongated 1965 episode of *The Virginian*, released theatrically), *Sidecar Racers* (1975, filmed in Australia and starring Ben Murphy), *Seven Alone* (1975), *Walking Tall, Part II* (1975, sequel to *Walking Tall*, featuring Bo Svenson), *Against a Crooked Sky* (1975, with Richard Boone), *Sidewinder 1* (1977, a motorcycle racing flick with Marjoe Gortner), and *Speedtrap* (1977, with Tyne Daly).

In the 1966-67 season, Bellamy was nominated for an Emmy for outstanding directorial achievement in comedy, for *I Spy*. He lost to James Frawley, for *The Monkees*, but 1967 was still a good year for Bellamy. It was the year he won the prestigious Directors Guild of America award for his work on *I Spy*.

GENE REYNOLDS

Gene Reynolds directed episodes 17, 18, and 19 of *The Andy Griffith Show*. However, he is best known as the co-creator, co-producer, director, and writer of *M*A*S*H*.* Reynolds has had an extensive career in television as a director, producer, and writer. As a television director, his credits include the following: *Alfred Hitchcock Presents, Bliss, Captain Nice, The Cara Williams Show, The Duck Factory, F-Troop, The Farmer's Daughter, The Fitzpatricks, Gidget, Hogan's Heroes, Leave It to Beaver, Mr. Roberts, The Munsters, My Three Sons, Room for One More, 77 Sunset Strip, Swingin' Together, Wanted: Dead or Alive,* and *Wendy and Me.*

Reynolds co-wrote 11 episodes of *M*A*S*H* and directed 24. Among those he directed are the pilot episode, which aired on CBS on September 17, 1972. (Hawkeye and Trapper try to raise enough money to send their Korean houseboy to a college in America), "Dear Dad" (Hawkeye writes the first of many letters home to his dad describing the war), "Adam's Ribs" (Hawkeye orders 40 pounds of ribs from his favorite restaurant in Chicago), "Welcome to Korea" (Trapper John leaves and is replaced by B.J. Hunnicut), "Change of Command" (Colonel Sherman Potter takes over the 4077th), "Out of Sight, Out of Mind" (Hawkeye is temporarily blinded in an accident), "Margaret's Marriage" (Frank Burns cracks up when Margaret marries Donald Penobscott), and the Emmy award–winning episode "O.R." (heavy fighting brings in an endless stream of casualties).

As a television director and producer, Reynolds' resume includes *The Ghost and Mrs. Muir, If I Loved You, Am I Trapped Forever?, Karen, People Like Us, Roll Out!, Room 222* and *Southern Fried.*

As a television producer only, Reynolds' credits include a 1967 CBS pilot called *Alfred of the Amazon.* Reynolds was the co-producer of this comedy, which starred Wally Cox, Paul Hartman, and Allan Melvin. He was the executive producer on the 1972 CBS series *Anna and the King.* This production starred Yul Brynner, who reprised his stage and movie role. Reynolds went on to direct, produce, and write numerous episodes of the highly successful series *Lou Grant.*

Television movies that Gene Reynolds has directed include *In Defense of Kids* (1983, with Sam

Waterston), *Doing Life* (a.k.a. *Truth or Die*, 1986, with Tony Danza), and *The Whereabouts of Jenny* (1991, a reunion with *M*A*S*H** star Mike Farrell).

Reynolds has appeared as an actor in a few shows, including *I Love Lucy* and *Captain Nice.*

Gene Reynolds has been nominated for several Emmy awards as a producer, director, and writer. For *M*A*S*H*,* he garnered a total of 12 nominations and won 3 times for the following:

• 1973-74 season: With co-producer Larry Gelbart, for outstanding comedy series.

• 1974-75 season: Outstanding directing in a comedy series, for the episode "O.R."

• 1975-76 season: Outstanding directing in a comedy series, for the episode "Welcome to Korea."

Reynolds also received 6 Emmy award nominations for his work on *Lou Grant,* and he has won the prestigious Directors Guild of America Award on three occasions for the following shows:

• 1972 — Best direction in a comedy series, for *M*A*S*H*.*

• 1973 — Best direction in a comedy series, for *M*A*S*H*,* for the episode "Deal Me Out."

• 1978 — Best direction in a dramatic series, for *Lou Grant,* for the episode "Prisoner."

THEODORE J. FLICKER

Given his name, Theodore J. Flicker, who directed episodes 146, 154, and 155 of *The Andy Griffith Show,* was evidently born to work in the film industry. In fact, Flicker's directorial credits merit him a special place in the entertainment field. On television, his credits include *Ann in Blue, Banyon, Here We Go Again, The Man from U.N.C.L.E., Rod Serling's Night Gallery, The Rogues,* and *The Streets of San Francisco.*

On *The Dick Van Dyke Show,* Flicker directed two memorable episodes: "A Show of Hands" (in which Rob and Laura attend a prestigious awards banquet wearing white gloves, having accidentally dyed their hands black while working on a costume for Ritchie), and "100 Terrible Hours" (in which Rob recalls the time when he was an unknown disc jockey and he attempted to stay on the air for 100 consecutive hours).

As a writer and director, Flicker worked on the popular series *Banacek,* starring the future leader of *The A-Team,* George Peppard.

On August 22, 1974, Flicker directed, produced, and co-wrote *The Life and Times of Barney Miller.* This was the original pilot episode for the hit show, *Barney Miller.* It was aired on ABC's summer anthology series, *Just for Laughs.* In this episode,

Abby Dalton, not Barbara Barrie, portrayed Barney's wife. The actual series began five months later, and Flicker co-wrote the first episode with Danny Arnold. It was called "Ramon." Theodore J. Flicker and Danny Arnold would go on to receive credit as the co-creators of *Barney Miller*.

Flicker occasionally made an acting appearance in a movie, including *The Chocolate Licorice Store* (1961, with Beau Bridges). He has directed numerous television movies, including *Playmates* (1972, with Alan Alda), *Guess Who's Sleeping in My Bed?* (1973), *Just a Little Inconvenience* (1977; Flicker also produced and co-wrote this movie), *The Last of the Good Guys* (1978; Flicker co-wrote this movie), and *Where the Ladies Go* (1980).

Features directed by Flicker include *The Troublemaker* (1964; an independent movie that Flicker wrote and appeared in), *The President's Analyst* (1967, with James Coburn; Flicker wrote the screenplay), *Up in the Cellar* (a.k.a. *Three in the Cellar*, 1970; Flicker wrote the screenplay), *Jacob Two-Two Meets the Hooded Fang* (1979; Flicker wrote the screenplay), and *Soggy Bottom USA* (1984, with Don Johnson). Flicker also wrote the screenplay for Elvis Presley's movie *Spinout* in 1966.

LARRY DOBKIN

Lawrence (Larry) Dobkin directed two episodes of *The Andy Griffith Show*, numbers 160 and 161. He has had quite a successful and busy career as an actor, director, and producer on television and in the movies. On television, Dobkin appeared in a pilot episode in 1958 called *The Lady Died at Midnight*. In 1959, he appeared with comic genius Ernie Kovacs in a pilot episode entitled *I Was a Bloodhound*. He also appeared with Bob Cummings in another proposed series. This pilot episode was aired in 1963 and was entitled *The Last of the Private Eyes*. Dobkin was a regular on *Mr. Adams and Eve* in 1957 and 1958. The series starred the real-life husband and wife team of Howard Duff and Ida Lupino. Ironically, Larry Dobkin appeared as a director on this sitcom.

Probably Dobkin's most famous television role was on the great crime drama *The Untouchables*. He made recurring appearances as underworld crime boss "Dutch" Schultz. During the 1950s, Dobkin appeared in seven of the twelve segments of the acclaimed religious series *The Living Christ*. As recently as 1994, Dobkin was still appearing in small roles on television, including a recurring role as Judge Saul Edelstein on *L.A. Law* and an appearance on *Melrose Place*.

Throughout the years, Larry Dobkin has appeared in guest roles on countless television shows, including *The Adventures of Superman*, *The Big Valley*, CBS *Playhouse*, *Empire*, *The Hawaiian Eye*, two episodes of *I Love Lucy* ("Equal Rights" and "Ricky and Fred Are TV Fans"), *James Garner as Bret Maverick*, *Klondike*, *The Kraft Mystery Theater*, *Mission: Impossible*, *Night Court*, *O'Hara U.S. Treasury*, *Rawhide*, *The Roaring 20s*, *Studio '57*, *The Tab Hunter Show*, *Trackdown*, and *Wagon Train*. He also appeared in the 1990 television movie *Curiosity Kills* and the 1994 made-for-cable movie *Roswell*.

Dobkin's feature film acting credits include *The Day The Earth Stood Still* (1951), *Red Skies of Montana* (1952), *Tokyo After Dark* (1959, *The Gene Krupa Story* (1959), *The Cabinet of Caligari* (1962, a remake of the 1919 film *The Cabinet of Dr. Caligari*), *Geronimo* (a.k.a. *Apache Nation*, 1962), *Johnny Yuma* (1966), *Patton* (1970, starring George C. Scott), *Mysteries Beyond Earth* (1976, as narrator), *In Search of Historic Jesus* (1980), and *Beastmaster 2: Through the Portal of Time* (1991).

As a television director, Dobkin's resume include *Adams of Eagle Lake* (with Andy Griffith), *Barnaby Jones*, *The Big Valley*, *Brenda Starr, Reporter*, *Burke's Law*, *Cannon*, *Caribe*, *Charlie's Angels*, *Concrete Cowboys*, *The Detectives*, *Doctor Kildare*, *The Donna Reed Show*, *Dynasty*, *Emergency!*, *Ensign O'Toole*, *The Fall Guy*, *Fantasy Island*, *The Fitzpatricks*, *Freebie and the Bean*, *The Fugitive*, *Gilligan's Island*, *Intertect*, *The Invaders*, *Manhunter*, *Maverick*, *Movin' On*, *Mr. Roberts*, *The Munsters*, *My Living Doll*, *Nashville 99*, *N.Y.P.D.*, *The Rat Patrol*, *The Rifleman*, *77 Sunset Strip*, *Strike Force*, *Tarzan*, *The Treasure Chest Murder* (a continuation of the *Adams of Eagle Lake* saga, with Andy Griffith), *Vega$*, *The Waltons*, a Waltons television special called *The Children's Carol*, *What Really Happened to the Class of '65?*, and *The Wild Wild West*. Dobkin also directed one episode of the classic series *Star Trek*. The episode was entitled "Charlie X" and featured Robert Walker, Jr., in the title role.

As a television producer, Larry Dobkin's credits include *O'Hara, United States Treasury*, with David Janssen, and *Temple Houston*, with Jeffrey Hunter.

On the big screen, Dobkin co-directed the 1970 feature film *Tarzan's Deadly Silence* with Robert L. Friend. This movie was actually a two-part episode taken from the *Tarzan* television show starring Ron Ely. Dobkin also directed the 1972 film, *Sixteen*, a.k.a. *Like a Crow on a June Bug*, starring Mercedes McCambridge.

Dobkin's career also includes screenwriting. Among his writing credits is the 1976 television movie *The Life and Times of Grizzly Adams*, which spawned the successful hit television show starring Dan Haggerty and Denver Pyle.

In the 1967-68 season, Dobkin was nominated for an Emmy for outstanding performance by an actor in a supporting role in a drama, for the *CBS Playhouse* episode of *Do Not Go Gentle Into That Good Night*. (He lost to Milburn Stone, for his portrayal of "Doc" on *Gunsmoke*.)

GENE NELSON

Director of episodes 137 and 138 of *The Andy Griffith Show*, Gene Nelson was born Gene Berg in Seattle, Washington, on March 20, 1920. In his youth, he was a member of Sonja Henie's Hollywood Ice Revue. Later on, Gene appeared in numerous musicals and dramas as a stage actor. His credits include *It Happens on Ice* and *Lend Me an Ear*.

Nelson has appeared in many movies over the years, including *This is The Army* (1943, with Ronald Reagan), *I Wonder Who's Kissing Her Now* (1947), *Gentleman's Agreement* (1947, with Gregory Peck), *Apartment for Peggy* (1948, with William Holden), *The Daughter of Rosie O'Grady* (1950), *Tea For Two* (1950, with Doris Day), *West Point Story* (1950, with James Cagney), *Lullaby of Broadway* (1951, again with Doris Day), *Starlift* (1951), *Painting the Clouds with Sunshine* (1951), *She's Working Her Way Through College* (1952), *She's Back on Broadway* (1953), *Three Sailors and a Girl* (1953), *So This Is Paris* (1954, with Tony Curtis), *Crimewave* (1954), *Oklahoma* (1955, with Gordon McRae and Shirley Jones), *The Atomic Man* (1956), *The Way Out* (1956), *20,000 Eyes* (1961), *The Purple Hills* (1961, co-written by a young Jack Nicholson), *Thunder Island* (1963), and *S.O.B.* (1981, with Julie Andrews).

On television, Gene Nelson has appeared on numerous shows and specials, including *The Kaiser Aluminum Hour, Best of Broadway, Tom, Dick and Harry* (a 1960 pilot episode), *Shangri-La* (a 1960 NBC special), *Married Alive* (a 1970 NBC special), *Bat Masterson, Burke's Law, Ironside, Maverick, The Rifleman*, and *The Wackiest Ship in the Army*.

In the 1970s, Nelson returned to the Broadway stage. He starred in *Good News with Alice Faye, Music Music*, and *Follies*. He was nominated for a Tony award for *Follies*. (He lost to Larry Blyden for the revival of *A Funny Thing Happened on the Way to the Forum*.)

As a television director, Nelson has left his mark on such shows as *The Bad News Bears, Burke's Law, The Cara Williams Show, Dan August, The Donna Reed Show, Fantasy Island, The Farmer's Daughter, The F.B.I., The Felony Squad, Get Christie Love!, Gilligan's Island, Hawaii Five-O, I and Claude, I Dream of Jeannie, The Iron Horse, Lancer, Laredo, The Letters, McNaughton's Daughter, The Mod Squad, The New Operation Petticoat, The Pruitts of Southhampton, Quincy, M.E., The Rookies, Salvage I* (with Andy Griffith), *The San Pedro Beach Bums, Shirley, Twelve O'Clock High*, and *Where's Everett*. Nelson also directed one episode of *Star Trek*, "the Gamesters of Triskelion" (in which the crew of the Enterprise is transferred to a planet where they are held as captives and forced to fight in an arena for the enjoyment of their captors).

Nelson's television movie directorial credits include *Wake Me When the War Is Over* (1969, with Ken Berry; Nelson also co-produced), and *The Letters* (1973, co-directed with Paul Krasny and starring John Forsythe). His feature films include *Hand of Death* (1962), *Hootenanny Hoot* (1963, with Johnny Cash), *Kissin' Cousins* (1964, with Elvis Presley; Nelson also co-wrote the screenplay), *Your Cheatin' Heart* (1964, starring George Hamilton as Hank Williams), *Harum Scarum* (1965, with Elvis Presley), and *The Cool Ones* (1967, with Roddy McDowell).

In 1989 and 1990, Nelson was a professor of theatre arts at San Francisco State University's School of Creative Arts.

CHARLES IRVING

Charles Irving made the most of his two directorial assignments in *The Andy Griffith Show*. His two episodes, 82, "Class Reunion," and 83, "Rafe Hollister Sings," are two of the most highly regarded in the series' eight-year run.

As a television actor, Charles Irving is known for his role as Admiral Vincent Beckett on *The Wackiest Ship in the Army*. He remained in this role from 1965 through 1966. He also appeared on such shows as *Bewitched, Bonanza*, and *The Hathaways, Our Man Higgins*, and he had a recurring role as a judge on *Perry Mason*.

In the movies, Irving appeared with Andy Griffith in the 1957 Elia Kazan movie *A Face in the Crowd*, and with Mamie Van Doren in *Three Nuts in Search of a Bolt* (1964). He appeared in Robert Altman's 1968 space movie, *Countdown*, and also in 1968, he appeared with the singing group the Monkees in the cult favorite *Head*. This movie was co-written by Jack Nicholson. Irving also appeared with Christopher George in the 1968 film *Project X*.

Irving holds the distinction of being the first of many directors and producers of the long-running daytime drama *Search for Tomorrow*, which ran for 35 years.

As a television producer, Charles Irving was in

charge of *Kitty Foyle, The Secret Jury*, and *That Wonderful Guy*. The latter was a 1950 romantic comedy starring a then-unknown actor by the name of Jack Lemmon.

Irving also produced a 1959 pilot episode for a proposed television series called *The Happy Time*. It was never picked up by the networks.

GARY NELSON

Although he directed only one episode of *The Andy Griffith Show* (episode 164, "Malcolm at the Crossroads"), Gary Nelson has had a very productive career behind the camera. Gary Nelson's television credits include *Ace, Adam's Rib, Bracken's World, Call Holme, The Cop and the Kid, Crazy Like a Fox, Faraday and Company, The Farmer's Daughter, F-Troop, Get Smart, The Ghost and Mrs. Muir*, seven episodes of the cult classic *Gilligan's Island, Gomer Pyle, U.S.M.C., The Good Guys, Have Gun-Will Travel, Hawaii Five-O, The Hero, Hunter, McClain's Law, McMillan and Wife, The Mod Squad, Nanny and the Professor, The Outer Limits, The Partners, The Patty Duke Show, Please Don't Eat the Daisies, Police Story, Seven Brides for Seven Brothers, Shane*, and *Toma*. He directed two of Mickey Spillane's Mike Hammer television films, *More Than Murder* and *Murder Me, Murder You*. He also directed the widely acclaimed television mini-series *Washington: Behind Closed Doors*. Andy Griffith appeared in this production.

Nelson produced and directed *The Boys in Blue* and *Revenge of the Gray Gang* on television.

Other television movies directed by Gary Nelson include *The Girl on the Late, Late Show* (1974), *Medical Story* (1975, with Beau Bridges), *Panache* (1976), *To Kill a Cop* (1978, with Louis Gossett, Jr.), *The Pride of Jesse Hallam* (1981, with Johnny Cash), *For Love and Honor* (1983), *Murder in Coweta County* (1983, with Andy Griffith as a murderer), *The Baron and the Kid* (1984), *Shooter* (1988), *Get Smart Again* (1989, featuring most of the original cast of the television show *Get Smart*), *The Lookalike* (1990), and *The Revolver* (1992).

In feature films, Gary Nelson's directorial credits include *Molly and Lawless John* (1972, with Vera Miles and Sam Elliott), *Santee* (1973, with Glenn Ford), *Freaky Friday* (1977, with Jodie Foster), *The Black Hole* (1979, with Anthony Perkins), *Jimmy the Kid* (1983, with Gary Coleman), and *Allan Quartermain and the Lost City of Gold* (1987, featuring Sharon Stone.

In the 1977-78 season, Nelson was nominated for an Emmy for outstanding directing in a drama series, for *Washington: Behind Closed Doors*. (He lost to Marvin J. Chomsky for *Holocaust*.)

WRITERS

JIM FRITZELL AND EVERETT GREENBAUM

Think about your ten favorite episodes of *The Andy Griffith Show*. Chances are your list includes a few of the 29 gems written by Jim Fritzell and Everett Greenbaum: episodes 29, 65, 67, 72, 74, 77, 78, 80, 82, 84, 88, 90, 93, 94, 96, 97, 99, 104, 105, 106, 112, 113, 116, 118, 121, 125, 129, 133, and 139. Among the characters this team brought to the show are Ernest T. Bass, the Darlings, and Gomer Pyle. Clearly, they were influential in creating *The Andy Griffith Show* as it is remembered today.

Everett Greenbaum was born on December 20, 1919, in Buffalo, New York. He is one of four children of Alexander and Rose Greenbaum. His father owned a motor tire company and hoped Everett would work in his business. Unfortunately, young Everett didn't like the smell of tires. He could have gone into the candy business, too. His maternal grandfather, David Goldenberg, was known as "the Candy King." Goldenberg's Peanut Chews are still popular in the northeastern states. But Everett was not interested in sales. His first love was airplanes. He was fascinated by them and used to ride his bicycle to a nearby airfield. He even managed to coax a few pilots into letting him ride with them.

After high school, Greenbaum attended M.I.T. Next came a job at Bell Aircraft before Greenbaum enrolled in a civil pilot training program during World War II. Soon he was flying solo and even instructing would-be pilots in Maryland. After Japan bombed Pearl Harbor, Greenbaum served the U.S. Navy as a flight instructor in Peru, Indiana, and Oahu, Hawaii. In Oahu, he wrote a one-act play for a Navy writing contest and won third prize. He made up his mind to make his living as a writer.

Back in New York after the war, he couldn't find work, despite the fact that a job at the motor tire store was left open for him. He decided to go to Paris, where he used his G.I. Bill privileges to study arts and writing at the Sorbonne. After a year, with finances dwindling, he returned to Buffalo. He wrote an account of his learning to glide in Paris, which was published in an aviation magazine. That led to radio interviews and a job as a humorous disc jockey at WKBW radio. He wrote his own material and had his own live Sunday night show called *Greenbaum's Gallery*.

When his radio program was canceled due to weakening ratings, Everett had to look elsewhere for work. He took a job at Macy's Department Store, selling toy jumping frogs. Then, in 1952, he got a break. The William Morris Agency got him a two-week writing assignment on NBC's hit sitcom *Mr. Peepers*. He was paired with a fellow named Jim Fritzell, who co-created and wrote for the series. Fritzell had previously written for *Our Miss Brooks*. Obviously, the assignment lasted longer than two weeks. The two young writers worked on this show from 1952 through 1955 before heading out on their own. They were nominated for an Emmy award for their work in 1954, and they won the prestigious George Peabody award. (Greenbaum also became friends with *Mr. Peepers* star Wally Cox, and many years later, in 1972, Simon & Schuster published a children's book Cox and Greenbaum wrote together, *The Tenth Life of Osiris Oakes*. Unfortunately, Wally Cox died the following year.)

When *Mr. Peepers* ended, Greenbaum went west to Hollywood to write for *The George Gobel Show*. Fritzell was in Hollywood, too, writing for *Mr. Adams and Eve*. Fritzell called Greenbaum for help on a troublesome script, and soon the men teamed up to write for five years on *The Real McCoys*. Like *Mr. Peepers*, the show was a success.

Jim Fritzell was born on February 22, 1920, in San Francisco, California. He was born to parents of Scandinavian descent. While his writing partner was interested in aviation, literature, and music, Fritzell enjoyed more down-to-earth pleasures, such as watching sports events, playing poker, drinking, and smoking. Their differences complemented each

Everett Greenbaum (on phone) working with Jim Fritzell on an episode of *The Andy Griffith Show*.

other's writing style. Fritzell seemed especially attuned to the dialogue of the blue collar man.

In 1961, Fritzell and Greenbaum were hired to write for *The Andy Griffith Show*. Among their scripts are some of the best episodes in the series. They wrote such classics as "Convicts-At-Large," "Man in a Hurry," "Class Reunion," "The Darlings Are Coming," "Dogs, Dogs, Dogs," "Barney's Sidecar," and "My Fair Ernest T. Bass."

After 1964, their attention turned to the big screen. The team collaborated on some half-dozen motion pictures, including *Good Neighbor Sam*

(1964, with Jack Lemmon), *The Ghost and Mr. Chicken* (1966, with Don Knotts — that's Greenbaum's voice you hear yelling, "Atta Boy, Luther!" in the film), *The Reluctant Astronaut* (1967, with Don Knotts), *Did You Hear the One About the Traveling Saleslady?* (1968, co-written with John Fenton Murray), *The Shakiest Gun in the West* (1968, with Don Knotts), and *Angel in My Pocket* (1969, starring Andy Griffith).

In the early 1970s, Larry Gelbart created the television series *M*A*S*H**, which was based on the hit book and movie of the same name. He hired

Fritzell and Greenbaum to write over a five-year period. They wrote (or co-wrote) 24 episodes, many of them among the series' most memorable. For example, they penned "The General Flipped at Dawn," which featured Harry Morgan as a lunatic general. (He would return in another Fritzell and Greenbaum episode, "Change of Command," which added him to the regular cast as Colonel Sherman Potter.) Fritzell and Greenbaum also wrote "Abyssinia, Henry," which remains the most controversial episode of the long-running series. The plot had beloved Colonel Henry Blake being helicoptered away from the 4077th, towards home. Shockingly, his chopper was shot down over the Sea of Japan, leaving no survivors. CBS and Twentieth Century–Fox were flooded with a torrent of angry calls and letters from viewers who had wanted a happy ending, but critics praised the show for its daring and realistic resolution.

Among other important episodes scripted by Fritzell and Greenbaum were "Welcome to Korea," an hour-long episode in which a new surgeon at the 4077th, B. J. Hunnicut was introduced to replace the departing Trapper John MacIntyre; "Margaret's Marriage," in which the ill-fated marriage of Major Houlihan to Donald Penabscot drives Frank Burns crazy and he goes A.W.O.L.; and "Fade In-Fade Out," another hour-long episode, in which the 4077th makes room for a new and pompous surgeon, Major Charles Emerson Winchester.

After ending their work with *M*A*S*H**, Fritzell and Greenbaum wrote for the short-lived series *The McLean Stevenson Show*. They had just finished writing two television pilots, *Heaven on Earth* for NBC and *Semi-Tough* for ABC, when Fritzell suffered a massive coronary. He died on March 9, 1979. Although shocked and saddened by the loss of his partner and friend, Greenbaum teamed with another friend and former *Andy Griffith Show* writer, Harvey Bullock, to write the award-winning *A Mouse, a Mystery and Me*, a live action and animated feature. He also wrote on the *M*A*S*H** sequels, *W*A*L*T*E*R* (a pilot starring Gary "Radar" Burghoff) and *AfterM*A*S*H**, which starred Harry Morgan, William Christopher, and Jamie Farr, as their *M*A*S*H** characters, working at a U.S. veterans' hospital. Greenbaum also wrote for *How to Marry a Millionaire, Lou Grant*, and *United States*.

Here's a brief listing of other Fritzell and Greenbaum collaborations on television: *The Girl with Something Extra, Make Room for Daddy, Mrs. G. Goes to College* (which featured Aneta Corsaut), *The Odd Couple* (including an episode featuring Hal Smith, entitled "Surprise! Surprise!"), *Stripe Playhouse* (a 1958 pilot), *Gomer Pyle, U.S.M.C.* (only one episode, "The Rumor"), and *Sybil* (a 1965 pilot).

In 1954, Fritzell and Greenbaum together received an Emmy nomination for best written comedy material, for *Mr. Peepers*. (They lost to the writers of *The George Gobel Show*.) In 1955, Greenbaum was one of four writers nominated for best comedy writing, for *The George Gobel Show*. (He and his co-writers lost to the writers of *The Phil Silvers Show*.)

Although the partners never won an Emmy, they won the following Writers Guild of America (W.G.A.) awards: 1963, best television comedy variety episode, for *The Andy Griffith Show* ("Barney's First Car"); 1975 (with co-writer Larry Gelbart), best comedic episode for *M*A*S*H** ("Welcome to Korea"); and 1976, the W.G.A. Laurel award, honoring the duo's outstanding career achievements. Fritzell and Greenbaum were also nominated for a W.G.A. award for "Fade In-Fade Out," a 1978 *M*A*S*H** episode.

Everett Greenbaum still contributes to television, but mostly as an actor. He has appeared in *Love and War*, an early episode of *The New Andy Griffith Show*, in which he warbled a line from the Glen Campbell hit "Wichita Lineman!"; and in David Lynch's *On the Air*. He appears on *Matlock* on occasion, usually as Judge Lawrence Katz. He has also written dialogue for some *Matlock* episodes.

Greenbaum does commercial endorsements for such companies as AT&T, Hallmark, Pepsi-Cola, Subaru, Stanley Tools, Pizza Hut, and United Airlines.

Along with Harvey Bullock, Greenbaum penned the excellent 1986 television movie *Return to Mayberry*.

His autobiography, published in 1973, is *The Goldenberg Who Couldn't Dance*.

JACK ELINSON AND CHARLES STEWART

With 29 episodes to their credit, Jack Elinson and Charles Stewart tie with Jim Fritzell and Everett Greenbaum as the most prolific writing team on *The Andy Griffith Show*. Episodes by Elinson and Stewart, from "The New Housekeeper" to "Andy on Trial," set the tone for the series. They wrote episodes 1, 2, 3, 6, 12, 14, 15, 17, 20, 22, 24, 26, 31, 32, 33, 35, 36, 37, 39, 45, 46, 48, 49, 52, 53, 55, 56, 59, and 61. Jack Elinson also wrote one episode with Iz Elinson, 187, "The Foster Lady." He wrote four episodes without a partner. They are 160, "Aunt Bee, the Swinger"; 172, "The Cannon"; 179, "Wyatt Earp Rides Again"; and 180, "Aunt Bee Learns to Drive."

Elinson and Stewart wrote for such series as *Hey, Jeannie, Joe's World* (also co-produced), *The Real McCoys*, and *The Danny Thomas Show* (also co-produced).

In 1960, they were honored with a Writers Guild Award for their outstanding writing on "The Manhunt," an episode of *The Andy Griffith Show*. They were nominated for an Emmy in 1961 for their work on *The Danny Thomas Show*. The category was outstanding writing achievement in comedy. (They lost to the writers of *The Red Skelton Show*.)

Jack Elinson has written for or produced such programs as *The Academy*, *The Academy II*, *A.k.a. Pablo*, *The All-Star Revue*, *Arnie*, *Danny Thomas Looks at Yesterday, Today and Tomorrow* (a 1970 special), *The Danny Thomas TV Family Reunion* (a 1965 special), *The Doris Day Show*, *The Duke*, *The Facts of Life*, *Full Speed Anywhere* (a 1960 pilot); *Good Times*, *Jo's Cousin*, *Make More Room for Daddy*, *Make Room for Granddaddy*, *My Hero*, *One Day at a Time*, *The Parkers*, *P.O.P.*, and *Texaco Star Theater*. He also wrote for and produced the 1983 television movie *The Facts of Life Goes to Paris*.

Charles Stewart, who has acted in such programs as *Little Vic* and *Picture Window*, served as a producer and script consultant on *Mayberry R.F.D.* during its last season. He also wrote for the series. He wrote for or produced such programs as *Adams of Eagle Lake*, *All in the Family* (with co-writer Ben Starr), *Chico and the Man* (with Michael L. Morris), *The Don Knotts Show*, *The Joey Bishop Show*, *Love, American Style*, *O.K. Crackerby*, *Petticoat Junction*, and *Three's Company*. Stewart also co-produced the 1975 special *The Treasure Chest Murder*.

HARVEY BULLOCK AND RAY SAFFIAN ALLEN

This team of writers and producers wrote five episodes of *The Andy Griffith Show*: 60, "The Bookie Barber"; 66, "Mr. McBeevee"; 69, "Andy and the New Mayor"; 70, "The Cow Thief"; and 75, "The Bed Jacket." Bullock wrote 26 episodes by himself: 40, 43, 50, 57, 58, 79, 81, 83, 85, 89, 91, 95, 98, 101, 109, 110, 114, 115, 119, 124, 127, 130, 138, 153, 164, and 177. Along with Everett Greenbaum, Harvey Bullock co-wrote the 1986 television reunion movie, *Return to Mayberry*.

Harvey Reade Bullock, Jr., was born on June 4, 1921, in Oxford, North Carolina. His family moved to Binghamton, New York, when he was very young. He returned to his home state to attend Duke University, where he majored in English.

After serving in the Naval Reserves in World War II, he began writing for audience participation programs. In 1949, he started writing comedy for the popular radio program *Breakfast with Burrows*, starring Abe Burrows. This is where he began writing with Ray Saffian Allen (born Morris Saffian), a partnership that would last until Allen's death in 1981. They also wrote for Robert Q. Lewis on both his radio and daily television shows.

Harvey Bullock also worked behind the scenes on Dave Garroway's *Today* show. During this assignment, he met and married Betty Jane Folker, who was the producer of the fashion segments on the *Today* show. They have three daughters, Kerry, Diana, and Courtney and one son, Andy — named after Andy Griffith.

Later, Bullock and Allen worked together on the NBC television special *Salute to Baseball*. They wrote a sketch which starred Gertrude Berg. That work won them the Random House award. Next, they traveled to London, and in 1958, they wrote for the British television series *Dick and the Duchess*, which starred Patrick O'Neal and Hazel Court. Bullock and Allen wrote all 26 episodes of the series. While Allen stayed in England to produce other programs, Bullock returned to New York and began writing for Johnny Carson's *Who Do You Trust?* and for *The Charley Weaver Show*.

The team reunited in 1961, in California. Bullock and Allen sold a pilot, *McKeever and the Colonel*, to NBC. It then became a series.

When Ray Allen went back to London, Bullock became acquainted with Sheldon Leonard, the creator and executive producer of *The Andy Griffith Show* while writing an episode of *The Real McCoys*. Sheldon put Harvey in touch with Aaron Ruben, the producer of *The Andy Griffith Show*, and this relationship paved the way for his involvement in the series.

In the ensuing years, as a team, Bullock and Allen also wrote for or produced other programs, such as *Alice*, *Big John, Little John*, *The Bill Dana Show*, *The Danny Thomas Show*, *The Dick Van Dyke Show*, *The Doris Day Show*, *The Flintstones*, *From a Bird's Eye View*, *Gomer Pyle, U.S.M.C.*, *Hogan's Heroes*, *I Spy*, *The Jetsons*, *The Jim Nabors Show*, *The Joey Bishop Show*, *Love, American Style*, *The Love Boat*, *Man in the Middle* (a pilot), *MacDuff, the Talking Dog* (1976), *Monster Squad*, *Mr. Terrific*, *My World...and Welcome to It*, *Papa and Me* (1976), *The Red Hand Gang* (1977-1978 series), *Top Cat*, *Wait 'Til Your Father Gets Home*, and *The Wonderful World of Burlesque II*.

They joined Hanna-Barbera Productions as executives in charge of program development. While there, they created two pilot episodes which aired as segments of *Love, American Style*. One, *Love and the Private Eye*, never made it to series. The other, *Love and the Old-Fashioned Father*, did. This animated *All in the Family*–style pilot, was renamed *Wait 'Til Your Father Gets Home*.

In 1975, Bullock and Allen, along with William D'Angelo, formed a production company, D'Angelo/Bullock/Allen Productions. The company focused on shows for children. One of their specials, *Papa and Me*, earned them an Emmy award in 1976.

After dissolving the company, Bullock and Allen joined Aaron Spelling Productions in 1978. They served as writers and producers for *The Love Boat*. After Allen's death, Bullock continued at the company as a creative consultant.

Harvey Bullock and Jim Parker were two of the creators of *Flo*, the short-lived spinoff from *Alice*.

Bullock's solo efforts as a writer include: *The Ann Sothern Show, Bachelor Father, Cavalcade of Sports, Cyrano* (a 1974 ABC Afterschool Special), *The Many Loves of Dobie Gillis, Medic, The Pinky Lee Show*, and *The Walter Winchell Show*. He wrote and produced the play *The Hill*, which became a movie in 1965. The star of the film was Sean Connery. In the early 1980s, Bullock produced an animated movie, *Asterix the Legionary*, for French television.

Harvey Bullock and Ray Allen wrote six motion pictures during the 1960s: *Honeymoon Hotel* (1964), *Girl Happy* (1965, starring Elvis Presley), *The Man Called Flintstone* (1966), *Who's Minding the Mint?* (1967, with Milton Berle), *With Six You Get Egg Roll* (1968), *Don't Drink the Water* (1969), and the Donny and Marie Osmond movie *Goin' Coconuts* (1978). The last four movies in the list above were directed by Bullock and Allen's old friend from *The Andy Griffith Show*, Howard Morris.

In recent years, Harvey Bullock has written television commercials for Zenith and Molson Beer, and a few television shows in England. He has also written two books on dieting, *The Fat Book* and *How to Cheat on Your Diet*.

When Hurricane Andrew struck the U.S., Bullock built and auctioned off birdhouses (in honor of episode 101, "Opie the Birdman") to raise money for the American Red Cross. This humanitarian effort raised over $1,200.

BILL IDELSON AND SAM BOBRICK

This duo wrote 19 episodes of *The Andy Griffith Show*: 117, 122, 126, 128, 135, 140, 143, 144, 152, 156, 166, 167, 171, 173, 176, 184, 185, 198, and 211.

Bill Idelson (sometimes listed in credits as William or Billy) began as a radio performer. In the 1930s and 1940s, he was a regular on the radio series *Vic and Sade*. On television, in 1949, he was a regular on two dramatic series: *Mixed Doubles*, as Bill Abbott, and *One Man's Family*, as Cliff Barbour. Most television viewers will recognize him as Herman Glimsher, the mother-dominated boyfriend of Sally Rogers on *The Dick Van Dyke Show*. He also appeared as a bellboy in one episode, and he wrote or co-wrote three episodes of this series, including "Uncle George," which featured Denver Pyle.

Idelson and Bobrick wrote together on such series as *Bewitched, Get Smart*, and *The Hero*.

Idelson's first script sale resulted in a spooky episode of *The Twilight Zone*, "Long Distance Call," which deals with a young boy who contacts his dead grandmother on a toy telephone. This was the last episode of the series to be videotaped.

Idelson has written for such series as *Barefoot in the Park, Beanes of Boston, The Betty White Show, The Bob Newhart Show* (also served as a producer), *Fish, The Ghost and Mrs. Muir, Guess Who's Coming to Dinner?* (a 1975 special), *Love, American Style, M*A*S*H*, and *The Odd Couple*. He and Harvey Miller were script consultants on the latter series. Idelson also produced *Anna and the King* and *The Montefuscos*.

As an actor, Idelson has worked in several series, notably *Leave It to Beaver, My Favorite Martian*, and *Happy Days* (on the latter, he appeared as Fonzie's psychiatrist). His voice was put to use in two animated specials: *Fred and Barney Meet the Shmoo* and *The New Shmoo*.

Idelson, who has also worked as a real estate agent, has written for such films as *The Crawling Hand* (1963). He also wrote a book, *Writing for Dough*, in which he gives advice to aspiring writers.

Idelson was nominated for an Emmy, along with two other producers, for *Love, American Style* in 1971.

Sam Bobrick has written for such series as *The Late Summer Early Fall Bert Convy Show* (he also produced this comedy series), *The Paul Lynde Show, The Smothers Brothers Comedy Hour*, and *The Tim Conway Comedy Hour* (also co-produced). He co-wrote and co-produced the comedy pilot *This Week in Nemtin* and has written for other pilots and specials, including *Eddie and Herbert* (1977), *How to Survive the 70s and Maybe Even Bump Into Happiness, Singles*, and *Quick and Quiet*. He created the syndicated comedy series *Saved by the Bell*, which proved to be quite popular with teenagers in the 1990s.

Among the movies he has written are *Norman...Is That You?* (1976, with Redd Foxx), *The Last*

Remake of Beau Geste (1977, directed by, co-written by, and starring Marty Feldman), and *Jimmy the Kid* (1982, starring Gary Coleman).

In 1968, Mr. Bobrick and ten other writers were nominated for an Emmy for writing *The Smothers Brothers Comedy Hour*. (They lost to the writing team of *Rowan and Martin's Laugh-In*.) Also in 1968, Bobrick was one of five writers honored with a Writers Guild of America Award for best comedy special, *Alan King's Wonderful World of Aggravation*.

Idelson and Bobrick's writing on *The Andy Griffith Show* earned them their first Writers Guild of America Award, for their 1964 episode, "The Shoplifters." In 1968, they won their second Writers Guild of America Award for co-writing (with Norman Paul) "Viva Smart," an episode of the popular spy spoof, *Get Smart*.

DAVID ADLER

David Adler's real name is Frank Tarloff, and he wrote nine memorable episodes of *The Andy Griffith Show*, numbers 7, 8, 11, 16, 18, 23, 27, 34, and 51.

Tarloff was blacklisted in the 1950s as an accused Communist sympathizer. Fortunately, he managed to survive this ugly period in America's past.

Tarloff holds the distinction of being the first person, other than creator Carl Reiner, to write an episode of *The Dick Van Dyke Show*. He went on to write other episodes, including "The Curious Thing About Women." (The plot revolved around Laura's inability to resist opening her husband's mail. When a big package arrives for Rob, she tries, in vain, to curb her nosiness. She loses the battle, and ends up causing the box's contents—a rubber raft—to inflate in the living room.) He also wrote for *M*A*S*H** and *My World...and Welcome to It*.

In 1975, Frank Tarloff served as executive story consultant on Sheldon Leonard's series *Big Eddie*. He also worked as story consultant and story editor, on the long-running series *The Jeffersons*.

In 1964, Tarloff and co-screenwriter Peter Stone received Academy awards for best screenplay, for the delightful motion picture *Father Goose* starring Cary Grant and Leslie Caron. Tarloff wrote the 1967 film *A Guide for the Married Man* as well as its 1978 sequel, *A Guide for the Married Woman*. He also co-wrote the 1970 movie *Once You Kiss a Stranger*, which starred Paul Burke and Carol Lynley.

Frank Tarloff is the father of Erik Tarloff, who wrote several episodes of *M*A*S*H** and *All in the Family*. Erik was nominated for an Emmy for an episode of the latter, "Edith's Crisis of Faith, Part II." (He lost to other *All in the Family* writers, who wrote "Cousin Liz.")

FRED FREEMAN AND LAWRENCE J. COHEN

This productive pair wrote nine episodes of *The Andy Griffith Show*: 137, 145, 147, 151, 158, 165, 168, 169, and 175. They also wrote and produced many television pilots and projects, including *After George, Calling Dr. Storm, Empire, Fog, Inside O.U.T., The Shameful Secrets of Hastings Corners*, and *Stick Around*. They wrote for such series as *Apple Pie, Bewitched* (including the Halloween episode, "Trick or Treat"), *The Dick Van Dyke Show, Gilligan's Island* (including the first episode, "Two on a Raft," and "Wrongway Feldman," starring Hans Conried), *The Good Life, The Pruitts of Southhampton*, and *Struck by Lightning*. In the 1990s, the two were serving as executive producers of the hit series *Empty Nest*.

They wrote or produced the following motion pictures: *Start the Revolution Without Me* (1970, with Gene Wilder and Donald Sutherland), *S* (1974), *The Big Bus* (1976), *Delirious* (1991, with John Candy), and *Two Times Two*.

Without his partner, Freeman wrote for *Jackie Gleason and His American Scene Magazine*. Working without Freeman, Cohen wrote for the popular series *Branded*, starring Chuck Connors. He has also written for *Columbo, The Defenders, Kraft Television Theater*, and *The Mask of Marcella* (a pilot).

Cohen also wrote or co-wrote *I Deal in Danger* (1966, starring Robert Goulet; this was a feature version of the series *Blue Light*), and *Return of the Seven* (1966, with Yul Brynner; this was the first sequel to the 1960 hit *The Magnificent Seven*).

BEN GERSHMAN AND LEO SOLOMON

Together, Ben Gershman and Leo Solomon wrote eight episodes of *The Andy Griffith Show*: 21, 25, 28, 30, 38, 44, 47, and 54.

Other than their work on this series, Gershman and Solomon worked together infrequently. They did hook up to write an episode of *The Dick Van Dyke Show* "One Angry Man" (in which Rob, while serving jury duty, finds himself distracted by a beautiful blonde defendant).

Ben Gershman, working solo, wrote for such

series as *It's About Time*, *Leave It to Beaver*, and *Please Don't Eat the Daisies*. He worked with another partner, Bill Freedman, who, along with Henry Sharp, wrote one episode of *The Andy Griffith Show*: 76, "Barney and the Governor." Gershman and Freedman wrote for such series as *The Addams Family*, *The Patty Duke Show*, and *Run, Buddy, Run*. They also wrote several episodes of *The Brady Bunch*, including "The Drop-Out" (in which Greg is visited by pitching legend Don Drysdale).

Leo Solomon wrote for *The Alan Young Show* (1950-1953); wrote for and produced the series *Leave It to Larry*; and wrote the 1946 film *The Dark Horse*.

JOHN WHEDON

Writer of eight episodes of *The Andy Griffith Show* (86, 87, 100, 102, 103, 108, 111, and 120), John Whedon has also written for such programs as *The Alcoa Hour*, *The Dick Van Dyke Show*, *The Donna Reed Show*, *Kraft Television Theater*, *Leave It to Beaver*, *Room 222*, and *Walt Disney's Wonderful World of Color* (*Kilroy*, a four-part special).

Along with co-writer George Roy Hill, Whedon was nominated for an Emmy in 1956 for best teleplay writing (one hour or more), for *A Night to Remember*, which aired on *Kraft Television Theater*. (It lost to Rod Serling's *Requiem for a Heavyweight*, which aired on *Playhouse 90*.) His writing has earned him such awards as the Christopher, the Sylvania, and a Writers Guild of America award.

Whedon has written for other media. His films include two 1974 movies, *The Bear and I* and *The Island at the Top of the World*. He has written such plays as *Life's Too Short*, *Li'l Darlin'*, and *Texas*. He has also been published in magazines such as *Colliers*, *Cosmopolitan*, *Harpers*, and *The New Yorker*. In fact, he was once on the editorial staff of *The New Yorker*.

ART BAER AND BEN JOELSON

This longtime partnership wrote seven episodes of *The Andy Griffith Show*: 136, 150, 154, 161, 162, 170, and 182. These men also co-produced such programs as *The Cop and the Kid*, *It's Your Move* (a game show), *Madhouse 90*, and *Picture This* (a game show). They produced and wrote for the series *Glitter* and *The Love Boat*. They wrote such series and specials as *Alice*, *The Ann Sothern Show*, *Arnie*, *The Carol Burnett Show*, *The Garry Moore Show*, *Get Smart*, *Good Times*, *The Jeffersons*, *The Jim Nabors Hour*, *The Odd Couple* (including the episode "The Big Mouth," starring Howard Cosell), *The Partridge Family*, and several Victor Borge specials. They wrote one special episode for *The Dick Van Dyke Show*, entitled "Buddy Sorrell-Man and Boy." (In this touching episode, Buddy begins acting mysteriously. It is finally revealed that he has been studying for his Bar Mitzvah. Sheldon Golomb also appears in the episode.)

Ben Joelson also wrote for *Happy Days*. Art Baer produced the game show *Make a Face*.

In 1972, Joelson and Baer won an Emmy (along with eight other writers) for best writing for a variety or music program, for their work on *The Carol Burnett Show*.

MICHAEL L. MORRIS AND SEAMAN JACOBS

Together, these two men penned seven episodes of *The Andy Griffith Show* (214, 216, 218, 221, 228, 230, and 231); yet otherwise they have worked alone or with other writers.

Michael Morris has written for such programs as *All in the Family*, *The Cara Williams Show*, *The Flying Nun*, *The Goldbergs*, *Good Times*, *It's About Time*, *Jack and the Beanstalk* (a fantasy special), *McHale's Navy*, *Nanny and the Professor*, *Perry Mason*, and *Second Chance*. He wrote and directed *Please Don't Eat the Daisies*. He co-wrote and co-produced the comedy pilot *We'll Take Manhattan*, and he served as a producer on *Chico and the Man*. He wrote several episodes of two very popular sitcoms, *Bewitched* and *The Brady Bunch*. For *Bewitched*, among other episodes, he wrote "Samantha and the Beanstalk," the episode that introduced the new Darrin (Dick Sargent). He also wrote the final episode, "Serena's Youth Pill." For *The Brady Bunch*, he wrote many memorable episodes, including "The Private Ear" (in which Peter eavesdrops on his family), "Jan's Aunt Jenny" (in which Jan worries that she'll grow up to look like her homely Aunt Jenny), "Bobby's Hero" (in which Bobby idolizes the legend of Jesse James), and "My Brother's Keeper" (in which Bobby saves Peter from bodily harm, so Peter agrees to be his slave for life).

Michael Morris has also written for the big screen, including *For Love or Money* (1963, starring Kirk Douglas), and *Wild and Wonderful* (1964, starring Tony Curtis).

Much of Seaman Jacobs' work has been done

with the accomplished Fred S. Fox. Together, they, along with other writers, have written for over 30 Bob Hope specials and for several George Burns specials, including *George Burns' One Man Show*, for which they were nominated for an Emmy in 1977. The Writers Guild of America honored them with an award for the same program, in the category of best variety special. They've written for such regular programs as *Family Affair*, *The Jeffersons*, *The Lucy Show*, *The Mothers-in-Law*, *What's Happening?*, and *Alice* (including the episode, "Oh, George Burns!" in which the aged comedian pays a visit to Mel's Diner and Vera, the waitress, believes he really *is* God. By the way, Fox and Jacobs co-wrote the 1980 film, *Oh, God! Book II*.)

Jacobs has written many episodes without a partner. They include episodes for the following programs: *The Addams Family* (including the first episode), *The Addams Family Goes to Court*, *Bachelor Father*, *Bringing Up Buddy*, *The CBS Newcomers*, *F-Troop*, *Here's Lucy*, *How to Marry a Millionaire*, *The Johnny Carson Show*, *The Love Boat*, *Maude*, *Monty Hall's Variety Hour*, *Mr. Roberts*, *My Favorite Martian*, *No Time for Sergeants*, *Run, Buddy, Run*, *Sigmund and the Sea Monsters*, and *The Tim Conway Comedy Hour*.

With writer Si Rose, Jacobs wrote the 1963 film, *It Happened at the World's Fair*, starring Elvis Presley and a bratty young Kurt Russell.

DICK BENSFIELD AND PERRY GRANT

This teaming was quite productive. They have over 1,000 television episodes to their credit, including seven from *The Andy Griffith Show*: 224, 227, 234, 235, 243, 245, and 247. Perry Grant has said that the idea for episode 235, "Howard's New Life," came to him in a dream about being on an island.

Among the many series for which this talented duo has written for are *The Adventures of Ozzie and Harriett*, *Big Daddy* (a 1973 pilot), *The Girl with Something Extra*, *Good Times*, *Happy Days*, *I Dream of Jeannie*, *The Jeffersons*, *Love, American Style*, *The Lucy Show*, *Maude*, *Mayberry R.F.D.*, *The Odd Couple*, *The Partridge Family* including the final episode, "..._ _ _... (SOS)", *Popi*, and *Three for the Road*. They wrote and produced *Another Man's Shoes*, *Hello Larry*, and *One Day at a Time*. They also produced *T.L.C.* and, more recently, the Marla Gibbs series *227*.

FRED S. FOX AND IZ ELINSON

During their brief partnership, Fred Fox and Iz Elinson wrote two episodes of *The Andy Griffith Show*: 42, "The Clubmen," and 63, "Deputy Otis."

Outside of this series, these men worked together only sparingly. They wrote for *The Ann Sothern Show*, *F-Troop*, *The Lucy Show*, *The Many Loves of Dobie Gillis*, *My Favorite Martian*, *My Sister Eileen*, *Run, Buddy, Run*, and *Wonder Bug*.

Fox spent much of his time writing with another *Andy Griffith* writer, Seaman Jacobs. (For information about this partnership, please look at the listing for Michael L. Morris and Seaman Jacobs.) Among Fox's other efforts are *Bungle Alley*, *The CBS Newcomers*, *Give My Regards to Broadway*, *Here's Lucy*, *Hey, Jeannie*, *The Love Boat*, *The Man from Everywhere* (a 1961 pilot), *The Tim Conway Hour*, and *Where's Raymond?* As an actor, he appeared, with Ron Howard, on *Happy Days*, in the episode, "Stolen Memories."

Fox wrote five solo episodes of *The Andy Griffith Show*: 191, "The Barbershop Quartet"; 200, "Politics Begins at Home"; 205, "Don't Miss a Good Bet"; 208, "The Statue"; and 217, "Big Brother." Fox served as a script consultant on *The Andy Griffith Show*, as did Bob Ross.

Iz Elinson teamed with Jack Elinson for one episode of the series, 187, "The Foster Lady." Iz Elinson has also written for *Bewitched*.

JIM PARKER AND ARNOLD MARGOLIN

This successful team wrote five episodes of *The Andy Griffith Show*: 192, "The Lodge"; 193, "The Darling Fortune"; 203, "Only a Rose"; 204, "Otis the Deputy"; and 210, "Floyd's Barbershop."

Together, Parker and Margolin have written for several television projects, including *Harry and Maggie* (a 1975 comedy special starring Don Knotts as Harry Kellogg and Eve Arden as Maggie Sturdivant), *The Krofft Super Show*, *Love, American Style* (they also served as executive producers), *Mr. Terrific*, *My Mother the Car*, *The Orphan and the Dude*, and *The Smothers Brothers Show*. They produced the 1970 pilot *The Boys* and the 1973 pilot *Going Places*.

Love, American Style was nominated for Emmies in 1970 and 1971 in the category of best comedy series. This was during Parker and Margolin's tenure as the show's executive producers.

Among the motion pictures they have written together are *Star Spangled Girl* (1971) and *Snowball Express* (1972, for Disney, starring Dean Jones).

Jim Parker was one of the creators of *Flo*, a short-lived *Alice* spinoff. He also co-produced the critically acclaimed but controversial series *Love, Sidney*, starring Tony Randall. The series was Emmy-nominated for best comedy series in 1982. Jim Parker wrote the 1977 pilot *Handle with Care*, and he co-wrote *The Osmond Brothers Special* (1978).

Arnold Margolin wrote and produced such projects as *The Dooley Brothers*, *He & She*, *The McLean Stevenson Show*, and *Private Benjamin*. He directed and produced the 1977 pilot *Walkin' Walter*, and served as a director for the series *That's My Mama*. He wrote the 1975 film *Russian Roulette*, which starred George Segal.

Along with another writer, Margolin won an Emmy (for outstanding achievement in music, lyrics and special material) for his work on *Love, American Style* in 1970.

RICHARD M. POWELL

Richard Powell wrote the following four episodes of *The Andy Griffith Show*: 142, "Three Wishes for Opie"; 146, "The Lucky Letter"; 148, "Barney Runs for Sheriff"; and 155, "The Arrest of the Fun Girls."

Powell has written for a variety of programs, including *All That Glitters* (also served as script consultant to this 1977 series), *Apple Pie*, *Baby, I'm Back!*", *The Baileys of Balboa*, *Big Eddie*, *The Cheap Detective*, *The Farmer's Daughter*, *Hee Haw*, *The Lucille Ball Comedy Hour*, *The Mary Tyler Moore Show*, and *M*A*S*H**.

Among the films Powell has written for are *My Gun is Quick* (1957, with Whitney Blake), *The Young Philadelphians* (1959, starring Paul Newman), *Follow That Dream* (1962, starring Elvis Presley), and *Wild and Wonderful* (1964, with Tony Curtis).

From 1965 to 1967, Powell served as a member of the Writers Guild of America Council. From 1967 to 1969, he was president of the Writers Guild of America's television and radio branch.

JOHN L. GREENE AND PAUL DAVID

These two men wrote three episodes of *The Andy Griffith Show*: 178, "Lost and Found"; 188, "The Battle of Mayberry"; and 196, "Goober Makes

History." Apart from *Andy Griffith*, they wrote together on such series as *Bewitched* and *My Favorite Martian*. Two memorable episodes they wrote for the former are "Speak the Truth" (in which the folks at McMahon and Tate are under a "truth" spell) and "Disappearing Samantha" (which features a pre–Dr. Bombay Bernard Fox as Osgood Rightmire).

John L. Greene wrote several episodes of *Bewitched*, some alone and some with other writers. He co-wrote the episode "Samantha and Darrin in Mexico City," which was the last episode with Dick York as Darrin.

Greene wrote for and produced the *Blondie* television series. He also wrote for *I Dream of Jeannie*, *My Friend Irma*, *No Time for Sergeants*, and *Screen Directors Playhouse*. With Phil Shuken, he wrote the film, *Plunderers of Painted Flats* (1959). He also wrote *The Private Navy of Sgt. O'Farrell* (1968, starring Bob Hope and Phyllis Diller).

Paul David's credits include writing for *Mr. Lucky*, *One Step Beyond*, and *Wagon Train*.

BENEDICT FREEDMAN AND JOHN FENTON MURRAY

Freedman and Murray, in their two episodes of *The Andy Griffith Show* showcased the town itself: 13, "Mayberry Goes Hollywood" and 19, "Mayberry on Record."

Freedman and Murray had previously written movies together, including *The Atomic Kid* (1954, starring Mickey Rooney), *Jaguar* (1956, starring Sabu), and *Everything's Ducky* (1961, starring Mickey Rooney and Buddy Hackett).

Freedman wrote for the television series *My Favorite Martian* and also wrote the 1949 movie *Mrs. Mike*, starring Dick Powell. The film was based on his novel of the same name.

John Fenton Murray wrote for such programs as *The Brady Bunch* (including the Christmas episode, "The Voice of Christmas," (in which Carol loses her voice just days before her scheduled Christmas solo at church and little Cindy turns to Santa Claus — played by Hal "Otis Campbell" Smith — for help), *The Ghost and Mrs. Muir*, *Gilligan's Island*, *Good Times*, *Love, American Style*, *McHale's Navy*, *The New Show*, *Operation Petticoat*, *Pandora and Friend* (a 1951 pilot), and *Sigmund and the Sea Monsters*. Murray directed episodes of *The Dennis O'Keefe Show* and *Gilligan's Island*.

Murray has written for several films, too, including *Sabu and the Magic Ring* (1957, originated as two television pilots), *It's Only Money* (1962, starring Jerry Lewis), *The Man from the Diners Club* (1963, starring Danny Kaye; look for Harry Dean Stanton as a beatnik), *Man's Favorite Sport* (1964, with Rock Hudson), *McHale's Navy Joins the Air Force* (1965, with Tim Conway), *Did You Hear the One About the Traveling Saleslady?* (1965, starring Phyllis Diller, co-written by Everett Greenbaum and Jim Fritzell), *Pufnstuf* (1970, based on the children's television series *H.R. Pufnstuf*), and *Arnold* (1973, with Stella Stevens).

STAN DREBEN AND HOWARD MERRILL

Together, these two wrote two episodes of *The Andy Griffith Show*: 186, "Goober's Replacement," and 189, "A Singer in Town." They also wrote for *F-Troop* and *Get Smart*.

Dreben teamed with Sid Mandel to write one episode of *The Andy Griffith Show*, 202, "Opie Finds a Baby." Mandel has written for such series as *Camp Runamuck* and *Gilligan's Island* (including the episode "Our Vines Have Tender Apes," which had an ape man paying a visit to the castaways' island).

Dreben has written for such television projects as *All My Darling Daughters* (a 1975 television film, co-written by Robert Presnell, Jr.), *The Beautiful Phyllis Diller Show*, *The Facts of Life*, *Funny You Should Ask* (a game show, which he also produced), *Johnny Carson Presents The Sun City Scandals*, *Letters to Laugh-In*, *Love, American Style*, *McHale's Navy*, *The Milton Berle Special*, *Pat Boone in Hollywood*, *The Paul Lynde Show*, *The Paul Winchell and Jerry Mahoney Show*, *Take My Advice*, *You're Only Young Twice*, and *Your Funny, Funny Films*.

Merrill has written for such series as *The Love Boat*, *Mrs. G. Goes to College*, and *The Dick Van Dyke Show* (including "All About Eavesdropping," in which a toy allows Rob and Laura to listen in on their neighbors' conversations).

BUDD GROSSMAN

This former World War II weatherman authored two episodes of *The Andy Griffith Show*: 190, "Opie's Girlfriend, and 206, "Dinner at Eight." He has written for several other programs, including *Almost American* (also produced), *Danny and the Mermaid*, *Dennis the Menace*, *Diff'rent Strokes* (also produced), *The Doris Day Show*, *The Farmer's Daughter*, *Full House* (a 1976 pilot), *Get Smart*, *Gilligan's Island*

(several episodes, including "Will the Real Mr. Howell Please Stand Up?" in which Thurston Howell discovers he has an evil twin, "Allergy Time," in which the Skipper is, apparently, allergic to Gilligan, and "Man with a Net," in which Lord Beasley (John McGiver) comes to the island in pursuit of the elusive pussycat swallowtail butterfly), *It's About Time*, *Maude*, *The Paul Lynde Show*, *Run, Buddy, Run*, *Small Wonder* (also served as creative consultant), *Three's a Crowd*, and *Three's Company* (also produced).

Among the films to his credit are *Going Steady* (1958) and *Bachelor Flat* (1962, with Terry-Thomas and Tuesday Weld). He also produced a play called *Bachelor Flat* and wrote a book entitled *Something for the Birds*.

RON FRIEDMAN AND PAT McCORMICK

These very experienced writers teamed up to write two episodes of *The Andy Griffith Show*: 199, "Mind Over Matter" and 219, "Goober's Contest." Together these two have written for such programs as *The Danny Kaye Show*, *The Dick Van Dyke Special*, *Get Smart*, *The Jonathan Winters Show*, and *Lucy in London*. Friedman, along with others from the writing team of *The Danny Kaye Show*, won a Writers Guild of America award in the category of outstanding writing in a comedy or variety series.

Both men have had long writing careers. Friedman has written for such projects as *Ace Crawford, Private Eye*, *All in the Family*, *All's Fair*, *Bewitched*, *The Changing Scene*, *Dick Van Dyke Meets Bill Cosby*, *The Fall Guy*, *Fantasy Island*, *The Ghost and Mrs. Muir*, *G.I. Joe*, *Gilligan's Island*, *Harper Valley*, *Home Cookin'* (a 1975 special), *I Dream of Jeannie*, *Love, American Style*, *Love on a Rooftop*, *Me and the Chimp*, *Murder Can Hurt You*, *My Favorite Martian*, *The Odd Couple*, *The Partridge Family* (including "A Partridge by Any Other Name," in which Danny mistakenly believes he is adopted — an episode originally pulled from the syndication package due to its "sensitive" nature), *A Real American Hero*, *The San Pedro Beach bums*, *Say Uncle* (a 1978 pilot, which he also co-produced), *Strike Force*, *This Is My Mama*, *Ver-r-ry Interesting*, and *Wonder Woman*. Friedman also wrote the 1977 film, *Record City*, which had a cast of comic actors such as Leonard Barr and Ed Begley, Jr.

Pat McCormick, born on July 17, 1934, is famous both as a writer and as an actor. He has written for such programs as *Bette Midler: Ol' Red*

Hair Is Back (he was one of six writers nominated for an Emmy for this special), *The Bob Newhart Show, Comedy News II, A Couple of Dons, The Cracker Brothers* (also appeared), *The Danny Thomas Special, The Don Rickles Show* (also appeared), *The Funny Side, Get Smart, Hello, Columbus, Goodbye America, Johnny Carson Discovers the Cypress Gardens, The Jonathan Winters Special: Wild Winters Night* (co-written by Phil Shuken), *Kraft Music Hall, The Many Sides of Don Rickles, The Marty Feldman Comedy Machine, The Merv Griffin Show, The New Bill Cosby Show, Pan Alley Today, The Red Skelton Show, Shaughnessy* (also starred, as Eddie Shaughnessy, in this 1976 pilot), *The Tonight Show with Johnny Carson*, and *Zero Hour*. He has written for other talents such as Phyllis Diller and Jack Paar, and has served as producer for some programs shown on *The ABC Afterschool Special.*

McCormick has acted in such programs as *The Bay City Movement Company, Crosswits* (a game show), *The Gong Show, Gun Shy, How Do I Kill a Thief-Let Me Count the Ways, The Mike Douglas Show, The Pat Boone Show*, and *We Dare You*. He appeared in the 1984 telefilm *The Jerk, Too*, meant as a sequel to the 1979 film, *The Jerk*.

McCormick has also appeared on some premium channels in such programs as *Likely Stories* (Volume 3), which is available on video under the same title. He was also host of *Best Chest in the West*, an adult-oriented program, featuring buxom women and celebrities such as Dick Shawn, Avery Schreiber, and Carol Wayne. This, too, is available on tape.

McCormick has been quite active in movies, too, including writing the narration for *Oh, Dad, Poor Dad, Momma's Hung You in the Closet And I'm Feeling So Sad* (1967). He also wrote for, and acted in, *Under the Rainbow* (1981), which claimed to be an accounting of the activities of the midget actors who portrayed the munchkins in the 1939 classic film *The Wizard of Oz*. Other films as an actor include *Buffalo Bill and the Indians, Or, Sitting Bull's History Lesson* (1976, starring Paul Newman), *The Shaggy D.A.* (1976), *Smokey and the Bandit* (1977, with Burt Reynolds), *A Wedding* (1978), *Hot Stuff* (1978), *Scavenger Hunt* (1979), *The Gong Show Movie* (1980), *Smokey and the Bandit II* (1980, sequel to the 1977 hit), *History of the World, Part I* (1981, directed by Mel Brooks), *Rooster* (1982, a television movie reuniting him with his *Smokey and the Bandit* partner, singer and songwriter Paul Williams), *Smokey and the Bandit III* (second, and, one hopes, last sequel to the 1977 hit), *Doin' Time* (1985), *Bombs Away* (1986), *Rented Lips* (1987, written and produced by Martin Mull), and *Scrooged* (1988, starring Bill Murray).

McCormick can also be seen in a video by country music star Reba McIntyre, "Take It Back." Pat is seen as Judge McCormick, wailing away on a saxophone.

In 1980, the writing team from *The Tonight Show Starring Johnny Carson*, which included Pat McCormick, won an Emmy for that series's eighteenth anniversary show. In 1981, the Writers Guild of America honored Mr. McCormick, and several other writers, for the award for the best variety special, for *All Commercials*.

ROBERT C. DENNIS AND EARL BARRET

These two worked together to write two episodes of *The Andy Griffith Show*: 222, "Howard's Main Event," and 238, "The Church Benefactors." They also teamed up to write episodes for two tongue-in-cheek series, *Batman* and *Get Smart*.

Dennis wrote more than two dozen episodes of *Alfred Hitchcock Presents* and was also a regular writer on the classic courtroom series *Perry Mason*. He wrote for several other series, including *Dragnet, Mission: Impossible*, and *The Outer Limits* (including the episode "I, Robot," starring a pre-*Star Trek* Leonard Nimoy. He also wrote for the 1978 limited series *The Return of Captain Nemo*.

Dennis has written for movies, too, including *Danger Has Two Faces* and *My World Dies Screaming!* He also wrote for *Crime Against Joe* (1956), *The Man Is Armed* (1956), *Revolt at Fort Laramie* (1952), and *McGuire, Go Home!* (1966) (video titles: *A Date with Death* or *The High Bright Sun*).

Barret's body of work includes the following television credits: *Bewitched, The Bob Newhart Show, Family Business* (also produced), *The Girl with Something Extra, I Spy, Poor Devil* (a 1973 pilot), *Popi, The Sandy Duncan Show* (also produced), *The San Pedro Beach Bums* (also produced), *Viva Valdez* (also story consultant), *Welcome Back Kotter, The Wild Wild West*, and *Windows, Doors and Keyholes*. He co-created, wrote for, produced, and directed the Ted Knight series *Too Close for Comfort*. Barret co-wrote, with Arne Sultan, the 1974 television film *It Couldn't Happen to a Nicer Guy.*

JAMES L. BROOKS

James L. Brooks has two *Andy Griffith Show* episodes to his credit: 236, "Emmett's Brother-in-Law," and 237, "The Mayberry Chef."

Brooks has created or helped to create many popular programs on television. Among these are *The Associates, The Mary Tyler Moore Show, Paul Sand in Friends and Lovers, Rhoda, Room 222,* and *Taxi.* He produced all of these except for *Room 222,* and he wrote for all but for *The Associates.* He also wrote, and served as executive producer for, *Lou Grant.* He produced *The Tracey Ullman Show* and the 1990s animated hit *The Simpsons.* He served as executive consultant on *Taxi* and co-wrote its acclaimed first episode, "Like Father, Like Daughter." In 1994, he was acting as executive consultant for a new series, *Phenom.*

Brooks wrote the first episode of *Room 222,* "Richie's Story." He co-wrote a handful of *The Mary Tyler Moore Show* episodes, including the first episode, "Love Is All Around," in which Mary Richards is hired as associate producer of the 6 o'clock news at WJM TV, as well as the series finale, "The Last Show," in which everyone at the station is fired...that is, everyone except incompetent Ted Baxter. Among other programs Mr. Brooks has written for are *Going Places* (a 1973 pilot), *My Friend Tony, My Three Sons,* and *The New Lorenzo Music Show.* He co-wrote and co-produced the 1978 television movie *Cindy,* which featured a retelling of "Cinderella" using an all-black cast. He wrote the screenplay for the 1979 film *Starting Over,* which starred Burt Reynolds and Candice Bergman.

Brooks has also acted. He was in two of Albert Brooks' films, *Real Life* (1979), and *Modern Romance* (1981).

Brooks hit the jackpot in his film directing debut with the powerful *Terms of Endearment* (1983). This film netted him an Oscar for best director and for best screenplay — adapted (from Larry McMurtry's novel). The film also won the Oscar for best picture. Two of its stars, Shirley MacLaine and Jack Nicholson, took home Oscars for their performances. The film was also produced by Brooks.

Brooks continued working in feature films. In 1987, he produced, directed, and wrote the acclaimed film *Broadcast News,* which featured William Hurt, Holly Hunter, and Albert Brooks. In 1993, he produced, directed, and wrote the comedy *I'll Do Anything,* starring Nick Nolte, Albert Brooks, Julie Kavner, and Tracey Ullman.

Brooks has been nominated for over 30 Emmy awards, and has won more than a dozen, for such shows as *Lou Grant, The Mary Tyler Moore Show, Rhoda, The Simpsons, Taxi,* and *The Tracey Ullman Show.*

PAUL HENNING

Born September 16, 1911, in Independence, Missouri, this former drugstore soda jerk used to serve President Harry S. Truman. He served *The Andy Griffith Show* by writing episode 41, "Crime-Free Mayberry."

Henning began his career in the 1930s, writing for such radio programs as *Burns and Allen, Fibber McGee and Molly,* and *The Rudy Vallee Show.* Moving on to television, he created, wrote, and produced *The Bob Cummings Show* in 1955. It ran for many years and was also known as *Love That Bob.* It is likely, however, that Henning will forever be known as the man who created and produced *The Beverly Hillbillies.* He also directed some episodes.

Henning produced *Green Acres,* and its sister show, *Petticoat Junction.* He also co-wrote and co-produced the 1981 television special *The Return of the Beverly Hillbillies.* He served as executive producer of *Carol,* a 1967 spinoff pilot from *Green Acres.*

Henning produced other programs as well, including *The Alan Young Show, The All-Star Revue, The RCA Victor Show, The Secret World of Kids* (also wrote), and *Where's Raymond* (also wrote).

Henning was nominated for an Emmy for his writing on *The Bob Cummings Show* in 1959. It was for the episode, "Grandpa Clobbers the Air Force." He was nominated again in 1963 for writing for *The Beverly Hillbillies.*

Henning wrote the 1961 film *Lover Come Back,* which starred Doris Day and Rock Hudson and was nominated for the best picture Oscar. He also wrote the 1964 film, *Bedtime Story,* starring Marlon Brando and David Niven. The film was remade in 1988 as *Dirty Rotten Scoundrels,* with Michael Caine and Steve Martin as its stars.

Henning's daughter, Mary Kaye Henning, was the voice of Jethrine Bodine on *The Beverly Hillbillies.* She is better known for portraying Betty Jo Bradley on *Petticoat Junction.*

PHILLIP SHUKEN AND JOHNNY GREENE

This teaming produced a fine script for *The Andy Griffith Show,* episode 62, "Cousin Virgil." Shuken and Greene also wrote for television's *Screen Directors Playhouse* and the 1959 film *Plunderers of Painted Flats.*

Shuken has written for such programs as *Calamity Jane, The Jonathan Winters Show: Wild Winters Night* (co-written by Pat McCormick), and *Shindig.* He also wrote for *Mr. Ed.* In fact, in 1958 he co-wrote a pilot for *Mr. Ed* called *The Wonderful World of Wilbur Pope.* It never aired. However, he did co-write the first episode of *Mr. Ed,* "The First Meeting." It aired on January 5, 1961.

Among the films Shuken has written for are *Doctor, You've Got to be Kidding* (1967, with Sandra Dee), and *Speedway* (1968, starring Elvis Presley).

For more on Greene's career, see the listing "John L. Greene and Paul David," found elsewhere in this section.

BILL FREEDMAN AND HENRY SHARP

This team's lone contribution to *The Andy Griffith Show* was the memorable episode 76, "Barney and the Governor." Otherwise, the two did not work together. Both Freedman and Sharp wrote for *The Addams Family*, but they did so alone or with other writers.

Freedman has done much of his work with Ben Gershman. For their screen credits, please look at the material found under the heading "Ben Gershman and Leo Solomon" found elsewhere in this section.

Among the shows for which Freedman has written are *The Brady Bunch* and *Gilligan's Island*. On the former, two of the most memorable he wrote were "Kitty Karry-All Is Missing" (in which Tiger, the Brady's dog, secretly steals Cindy's favorite doll) and "The Possible Dream" (in which Cindy gives away Marcia's diary).

Freedman was honored with a Tony nomination for co-writing the 1969 play *Hadrian VII*. It lost to the writers of *The Great White Hope*.

Henry Sharp has written for such series as *The Ann Sothern Show*, *The Donna Reed Show*, *The Man from U.N.C.L.E.*, *Mission: Impossible*, and *The Wild Wild West*, for which he also served as story consultant. He wrote many episodes of *The Addams Family*, including "Cousin Itt Visits the Addams Family" (which featured the debut of the family's hirsuite Cousin Itt).

LAURENCE MARKS

Marks wrote episode 163, "Andy's Rival," for *The Andy Griffith Show*. However, he is perhaps best known for his work with the critically acclaimed series *M*A*S*H*. He wrote or co-wrote 28 episodes and served as a creative consultant.

Among the many memorable *M*A*S*H* episodes Marks wrote are "Yankee Doodle Doctor" (in which the 4077th is approached by the Army to appear in a propaganda film, and Hawkeye rebels and makes his own hilarious and poignant film),

"Adam's Ribs" (in which Hawkeye craves barbecued spare ribs so badly, he orders some flown in from Chicago), "O.R." (set entirely in the operating room, with surgeons facing heavy casualties; there is no laugh track for this gritty episode), "Five O'Clock Charlie" (a North Korean pilot persists in trying to bomb a dummy ammunitions dumpsite but always misses), and "The Trial of Henry Blake" (in which Henry undergoes a military hearing to determine if he is competent).

In 1974, the Writers Guild of America nominated Marks for two writing awards for two *M*A*S*H* episodes, "Carry On Hawkeye" and "The Incubator." That same year, he and Larry Gelbart won a Writers Guild of America award for "O.R." In 1976, the Writers Guild again nominated Marks, this time for his solo effort on yet another *M*A*S*H* episode, "Big Mac."

Marks has written for many other series and specials, including *Dean Martin's Celebrity Roast*, *Dick Clark's World of Talent*, *The Donna Reed Show*, *The Doris Day Show*, *Hogan's Heroes*, *I Was a Bloodhound* (a 1959 pilot), *Johnny Cash and Friends*, *Love, American Style*, *McHale's Navy*, *My World...and Welcome to It*, *Pat Paulsen's Half a Comedy Hour*, *The Paul Lynde Show*, *Perry Mason*, *Phil Silvers Arrow Show*, *Phyllis*, and *Tony Orlando and Dawn*.

Marks co-produced the 1975-1976 series *Doc*, served as executive producer for the 1976 pilot *Making It*; and developed and co-produced the 1976 pilot *You're Just Like Your Father*. He wrote the 1946 movie *One Way to Love* and co-wrote the 1989 film *BullsEye*.

PAUL WAYNE

Paul Wayne wrote episode 174, "The Church Organ," for *The Andy Griffith Show*. He has had a long history of writing for comedy programs and specials. His resume includes *All in the Family* (including "Archie Eats and Runs," in which Archie believes he may have consumed poison mushrooms), *Benson*, *Bewitched*, *Doc* (also produced), *The Flying Nun*, *The Ghost and Mrs. Muir*, *The Ken Berry Wow Show*, *The Leslie Uggams Show*, *Love, American Style*, *Love and Learn* (also produced), *My World...and Welcome to It*, *Pat Paulsen's Half a Comedy Hour*, *The Sonny and Cher Comedy Hour*, *The Smothers Brothers Comedy Hour*, *The Smothers Brothers Organic Prime Time Space Ride*, *Three's Company* (also served as story consultant), and *Van Dyke and Company*. He wrote the 1967 film *King's Pirate*, which was directed by Don Weis. It was a remake of *Against All Flags* (1952).

For the 1968-1969 season, Wayne was nominated for an Emmy as part of the ten-member writing team of *The Smothers Brothers Comedy Hour*. For 1971-1972 and 1973-1974, he was nominated as part of a nine-member writing team for *The Sonny and Cher Comedy Hour*. For the 1976-1977 season, he was nominated as part of the 14-member writing team for *Van Dyke and Company*.

BEN STARR

Starr, who wrote episode 181, "Look Paw, I'm Dancing" for *The Andy Griffith Show*, enjoyed a productive career both before and after this series. Among his credits are *All in the Family* (he co-wrote many episodes, including "Birth of the Baby, Part II," in which Gloria gives birth to Joey Stivic, and "Archie's Dog Day Afternoon," in which Archie accidentally runs over Barney Hefner's dog), *Almost American, Bachelor Father, Bob Hope in Joys, The Brady Bunch* (including the episodes "The Personality Kid," in which Peter believes he has no personality, and "Dough Re Mi," in which Peter's changing voice threatens a planned recording session until the Brady kids come up with the song "Time to Change"), *The Dick Powell Show, Diff'rent Strokes* (also produced), *The Facts of Life* (including the pilot episode), *I Married Joan, Mission Magic* (1973-1974 cartoon series), *Mork and Mindy, Mr. Ed, My Favorite Martian, My Favorite Martians* (animated), *My Sister Hank* (1972 pilot), *The Paul Lynde Show, Perry Mason, Silver Spoons,* and *Tom, Dick and Harry* (a 1960 pilot, which he also produced).

Among the films written by Ben Starr are *Texas Across the River* (1966, with Dean Martin), *Our Man Flint* (1966, with James Coburn), *The Pad, and How to Use It* (1966, with Julie Sommars), *The Spirit Is Willing* (1967, with Sid Caesar), *The Busy Body* (1967, featuring Richard Pryor's debut), and *How to Commit Marriage* (1969, with Bob Hope).

Starr has also written many original plays for Spanish production.

RAY BRENNER AND BARRY E. BLITZER

This team's contribution to *The Andy Griffith Show* was episode 201, "A New Doctor in Town." Elsewhere, they have written together on such shows as *Get Smart, The Jimmie Rodgers Show,* and *McHale's Navy*.

Brenner has written for such series as *Charlie's Angels, Code Red, Enos, Here We Go Again, Instant Family, Kojak, Love, American Style, My Three Sons, Nurse,* and *Trapper John, M.D.*

Blitzer's writing credits include *The Ann Sothern Show, Arnie, Goober and the Ghost Chasers* (animated), *Hot L Baltimore, The Jetsons, The Love Boat, McKeever and the Colonel, Partridge Family: 2200 A.D.* (animated), *The Paul Lynde Show, The Phil Silvers Show, The Rich Little Show* (two specials by this name), *Too Many Sergeants* (a 1963 pilot), *Trauma Center,* and *When Things Were Rotten*.

LEO AND PAULINE TOWNSEND

The Townsends wrote one episode for *The Andy Griffith Show*, 215, "Opie's Piano Lesson." Pauline Townsend was the only female to write for this series.

Leo and Pauline Townsend wrote together on such series as *Batman, Bewitched, Gidget,* and *My Three Sons*. Leo Townsend also wrote without Pauline on *Bewitched* (including "Sam's Witchcraft Blows a Fuse," in which an exotic drink has a bizarre effect on Samantha), *The Man from U.N.C.L.E., Maverick* (several episodes), *Perry Mason,* and *Wagon Train*.

Leo Townsend has written for many motion pictures, including *It Started with Eve* (1941, remade in 1964 as *I'd Rather Be Rich*), *Seven Sweethearts* (1942), *The Amazing Mrs. Holliday* (1943), *Chip Off the Old Block* (1944), *Can't Help Singing* (1944), *Night and Day* (1946, with Cary Grant), *That Way with Women* (1947), *Port of New York* (1949, Yul Brynner's debut), *Southside I—1000* (1950), *One Big Affair* (1952), *Dangerous Crossing* (1953), *Vice Squad* (1953, with Edward G. Robinson), *Vicki* (1953), *A Life in the Balance* (1955), *White Feather* (1955), *Running Wild* (1955), *Flight to Hong Kong* (1956), *Four Boys and a Gun* (1957), *The Shadow on the Window* (1958, with Jerry Mathers), *Fraulein* (1958), *Bikini Beach* (1964, with Frankie Avalon and Annette Funicello in the third beach party film), *I'd Rather Be Rich* (1964, remake of the 1941 film *It Started with Eve*), *Beach Blanket Bingo* (1965, with Frankie Avalon and Annette Funicello in the fifth beach party film), *How to Stuff a Wild Bikini* (1965, with Annette Funicello in the sixth beach party film), and *Fireball 500* (1966, with Frankie Avalon and Annette Funicello in a film about racing).

BRUCE HOWARD

Bruce Howard wrote the teleplay for episode 249, "A Girl for Goober," with the story credit going to Bob Ross.

Howard has written for many series, including *Alice*, *The Brady Bunch* (several episodes, including "the Not-So-Rose-Colored Glasses," in which Jan is told she must wear her eyeglasses and her disobedience leads to tragic results), *The Dukes of Hazzard*, *Far Out Space Nuts*, *The Flying Nun*, *Gilligan's Island* (including "Smile, You're on Mars Camera," in which a NASA space probe camera lands on the island), *I Dream of Jeannie* (Howard even appeared as a drunk in one of the episodes he wrote), *It's About Time*, *The Jeffersons*, *Love, American Style*, *The Lucy Show*, *McHale's Navy*, *The Mothers-in-Law*, *My Favorite Martian*, *The Red Skelton Show*, *Too Close for Comfort*, and *What's Happening!*

Howard co-wrote the 1963 film *King Kong vs. Godzilla*.

OTHER WRITERS

Gus Adrian and David Evans, episode 134, "Man in the Middle."

Ronald Axe and Les Roberts, episode 209, "Aunt Bee's Restaurant." Ronald Axe also wrote episode 194, "Aunt Bee's Crowning Glory," and has written for such programs as *Get Smart*, *The Hero*, and *The Mothers-in-Law*.

Kent Wilson, episode 223, "Aunt Bee the Juror," and episode 239, "Opie's Drugstore Job."

Richard Morgan, episode 157, "Opie Flunks Arithmetic," which marked the last regular appearance of Barney Fife. Morgan also wrote for the classic western series *Bonanza*.

Roland MacLane, episode 183, "The Gypsies." Maclane has written for such series as *Gilligan's Island* (several episodes, including "The Court-Martial," in which the castaways attempt to recreate the shipwreck which stranded them), *How To Marry a Millionaire*, *Dennis the Menace*, and *Leave It to Beaver*.

Douglas (Doug) Tibbles, five episodes: 213, "Helen the Authoress"; 220, "Opie's First Love"; 229, "Opie's Group"; 244, "Helen's Past"; and 248, "Opie and Mike." Tibbles also wrote for *Bewitched*, *The Doris Day Show* (also directed), *Love, American Style*, *The Munsters*, *My Three Sons*, *Raquel* (a 1970 special starring Raquel Welch), and *Room 222*.

Joseph Bonaduce, five episodes, all of which aired during the final season of *The Andy Griffith Show*: 225, "Opie Steps Up in Class"; 226, "Andy's Trip to Raleigh"; 233, "Howard and Millie"; 242, "Goober Goes to an Auto Show"; and 246, "The Wedding." Bonaduce has written for *Apple's Way*, *California Fever* (also produced), *The Dick Van Dyke Show*, *The Ghost and Mrs. Muir*, *Joe's World*, *Little House on the Prairie*, *Love, American Style* (also produced), and *Me and the Chimp*. He is the father of Danny Bonaduce, who starred as Danny Partridge on *The Partridge Family*.

Arthur Stander, the pilot episode, "Danny Meets Andy Griffith," and four series episodes: 4, "Runaway Kid"; 5, "Opie's Charity"; "9, "Andy the Matchmaker"; and 10, "Stranger in Town." Stander has also written for such programs as *The Danny Thomas Show* (including "Everything Happens to Me," a 1961 pilot for Joey Bishop), *I Married Joan*, *It's Always Jan* (also produced), and *Mrs. G. Goes to College*.

Sid Morse, five episodes: 64, "Opie's Rival"; 195, "The Ball Game" (teleplay only, story from Rance Howard); 197, "The Senior Play"; 207, "Andy's Old Girlfriend"; and 212, "Barney Comes to Mayberry." Morse's television writing credits include *Battle of the Planets*, *The Clue Club* (story editor for this 1976-1977 animated series), *Davy Crockett on the Mississippi* (a 1976 animated film), *Isis*, *Jeannie* (animated series), *The Love Boat*, and *The Patty Duke Show*. He co-wrote the 1983 television film *The Love Boat*.

Jack Raymond, episode 232, "Suppose Andy Gets Sick." Among the other series for which Raymond has written are *The Addams Family*, *The Dick Van Dyke Show* (including the episode "A Word a Day," in which Rob and Laura are alarmed when young Ritchie begins swearing), *The Farmer's Daughter*, *Gilligan's Island*, *The NBC Follies* (a special), *Please Don't Eat the Daisies*, *Sigmund and the Sea Monsters*, and *The Smothers Brothers Show*.

THE MAN BEHIND THE MUSIC: EARLE HAGEN

The man responsible for the music, including the theme song, on *The Andy Griffith Show* was born in Chicago, Illinois, on July 9, 1919. After moving to Los Angeles, Hagen graduated from Hollywood High School in 1937. During his career, Hagen played the trombone in both Benny Goodman's and Tommy Dorsey's bands. After a 3½ year stint in the Air Force, he began working on musical arrangements with Frank Sinatra's conductor, Axel Stordahl. Hagen worked on arrangements for Sinatra on the popular radio show *Hit Parade*. While working on this show, he was also arranging for such noted singers as Dick Haymes, Tony Martin, and Helen Forrest.

In 1946, Hagen was hired as the musical arranger for the movie company Twentieth Century–Fox. He worked on numerous Betty Grable movies and for such stars as Marilyn Monroe, Dan Dailey, and Mitzi Gaynor.

Before leaving Fox, Hagen struck up what was to be a lifelong friendship with fellow composer and arranger Herbert Spencer. The pair hooked up with the William Morris Agency, who landed them jobs with two new television shows that soon became very popular, *The Danny Thomas Show* and *The Ray Bolger Show*. Through Danny Thomas's production company, Hagen did the musical score for two pilot episodes that also became big hits, *The Real McCoys* and *The Life and Legend of Wyatt Earp*.

In 1960, Earle Hagen and Herbert Spencer were given the assignment of writing the theme song for a new series, *The Andy Griffith Show*. Hagen describes the creation of the famous theme song:

"As you know, the pilot for *The Andy Griffith Show* was an episode of *The Danny Thomas Show*. The sponsor's agents bought the show that night.

That gave me the off-season to come up with a theme. I wrote a lot of themes, but none of them was right. One morning I had the idea of a simple piece of music that someone could whistle. I wrote it in about an hour. I then hired a small recording studio for that night. I called my drummer (Alvin Stoller), guitarist (Vito Mumulo), and bass player (Manny Stein), and delegated the finger-snaps to my eleven-year-old son, Deane. ...I recorded the theme to main title length—58 seconds—that night and whistled it myself. The next morning I called Sheldon Leonard at his home and told him that I had a demo that I wanted him to hear. He listened to it and said, 'That's great. I'll shoot it next week with Andy and Ronny walking alongside Myers' Lake with a couple of fishing rods over their shoulders,' and that was that."

The only difference between the demo and the actual theme viewers have heard through the years is that, because of the Musician's Union rules, Deane Hagen's finger-snapping was replaced by Earle's and a few other musicians. Even today, Earle Hagen is often asked to whistle the famous theme song.

A few years later, lyrics (never sung on the show) were added to the theme song by actor Everett Sloane (see episode 46, "The Keeper of the Flame"). Thus *The Andy Griffith Show* theme song became known as "The Fishin' Hole."

In 1986, Earle Hagen returned to do all of the musical chores (including whistling the theme song) on the television movie *Return to Mayberry*. This project was his last professional job before retiring from the entertainment field. To this day, Hagen remains good friends with his fishing buddy Sheldon Leonard.

On a 1961 Capitol Records album entitled "Songs, Themes and Laughs from The Andy Griffith Show," Hagen conducts a full orchestra on many tunes that are familiar to fans of the series, including instrumental and vocal versions of "The Fishin' Hole, "Jack, the Giant Killer," "Flop Eared Mule," "Ellie's Theme," "Sourwood Mountain," Barney's theme, which is called "The Manhunt," "Aunt Bee," "The New River Train," "Cindy," "Barney's Hoe Down," and "The Mayberry March," which later became the theme song for the spinoff series, *Mayberry R.F.D.* Roland White and the Country Boys, who appeared on the series during the first season, also appear on this album. Some of the songs on this album may also be heard on the 1992 record "Andy Griffith: American Originals."

Hagen's career in television music included involvement with many shows, either as music director, composer of the theme song, or the source of musical material heard on the show. His television credits include *Accidental Family*, the pilot episode of *Along the Barbary Coast* (aired on *The Barbara Stanwyck Theater*), *The Bill Dana Show*, *Concrete Cowboys*, *The Danny Thomas Hour* (an anthology series), *The Danny Thomas Show* (a.k.a. *Make Room for Daddy*), *The Danny Thomas Special*, *The Dick Van Dyke Show* (including the theme song), *The Dick Van Dyke Special*, *Doc Elliott*, *The Don Rickles Show*, *The Dukes of Hazzard*, *Eight Is Enough*, *Everything Happens to Me* (the pilot episode of *The Joey Bishop Show*, aired on *The Danny Thomas Show*), *Gomer Pyle U.S.M.C.* (including the theme song), *The Guns of Will Sonnett*, *I Spy*, *It's Always Jan*, *The Joey Bishop Show*, three pilot episodes for a proposed series entitled *Josephine Little, Love and Marriage*, *M*A*S*H*, *Make More Room for Daddy*, *Make Room for Granddaddy*, *Mary Hartman, Mary Hartman*, *Mayberry R.F.D.*, *Mickey Spillane's Mike Hammer*, *The Mod Squad*, the pilot episode of *The Monk*, *My Friend Tony*, *Nashville 99*, *The New Adventures of Perry Mason*, *The New Andy Griffith Show*, *The New People*, *Rango*, *The Royal Follies of 1933* (a 1967 music special), *That Girl*, *Where's Raymond*, and *Young Dan'l Boone*. All in all, Earle Hagen contributed in some capacity to more than 3000 television episodes.

Hagen has also contributed his music to some television movies, including *Having Babies* (1976), *True Grit* (1978, with Warren Oates repeating John Wayne's feature film role of Rooster Cogburn), *I Take These Men* (1983), and *Mickey Spillane's Murder Me, Murder You* (1983). In feature films, Hagen's credits include *Call Me Mister* (1951, with Betty Grable and Danny Thomas), *With a Song In My Heart* (1952, with Susan Hayward), *Call Me Madam* (1953, with Ethel Merman and Donald O'Connor), *Man on a Tightrope* (1953, with Fredric March), *Spring Reunion* (1957, with Betty Hutton and Dana Andrews), *The Man Who Understood Women* (1959, with Henry Fonda and Leslie Caron), and *The New Interns* (1964, with Dean Jones).

In 1990, Earle Hagen wrote a book entitled *Scoring for Films*. He also taught a ten-week workshop from the material within this textbook.

In 1968, Earle Hagen won an Emmy in the category of outstanding achievement in musical composition, for his work on *I Spy*.

APPENDIX:
COLLECTING
MEMORIES OF
MAYBERRY

On the surface it seems odd that the majority of Mayberry memorabilia was produced and sold after *The Andy Griffith Show* ceased production in 1968. However, during the series' original run, many of the viewers were children, with little purchasing power. Not until this generation grew up did *Andy Griffith Show* items become a hot commodity, as baby boomers with money to spend began to seek items of nostalgic value. Mayberry-related items actually produced during the series' original run proved scarce, since the show's producers (unlike television executives of today) did not concentrate their energy on saturating the market with items related to the series. Then, in 1989, Viacom Enterprises, the owners of *The Andy Griffith Show*, decided to open the doors with a new licensing agreement that allowed the production and sale of Mayberry memorabilia. Thus far, both Viacom and the general public should be pleased with results.

Anyone interested in buying collectibles produced during the original run of *The Andy Griffith Show* should be prepared to spend some money, because many of these items are over thirty years old and some were not produced in mass quantities. The following is a list of some items issued when the series ran on CBS from 1960 through 1968. Please be advised that the values listed (as of spring 1996) are simply a guide for items in excellent to mint condition. Also, it must be noted that we are not authorities in the memorabilia industry, so prices will vary.

(1) Issues of *TV Guide* depicting characters from *The Andy Griffith Show*: **Week of January 28 — Feb-**ruary **3, 1961,** features Andy Griffith and Ronny Howard. Since this is the first *TV Guide* produced featuring *The Andy Griffith Show*, the price range is $50 to $75. **Week of May 12 — May 18, 1962,** depicts Don Knotts. Price range is $20 to $30. **Week of May 11 — May 17, 1963,** features a laughing trio of Ronny Howard, Don Knotts, and Andy Griffith. Price range is $20 to $30. **Week of March 21 — March 27, 1964,** depicts a laughing trio of Jim Nabors, Andy Griffith, and Don Knotts. Price range is $20 to $30. **Week of April 24 — April 30, 1965,** features Andy Griffith. Price range is $15 to $20. **Week of June 4 — June 10, 1966,** features Andy Griffith sitting in a chair with his guitar. Price range is $15 to $20. **Week of May 20 — May 26, 1967,** depicts Andy Griffith and Aneta Corsaut. Price range is $15 to $20. **Week of July 13 — July 19, 1968,** features a cartoon-like photo of Andy Griffith, Jim Nabors and Don Knotts. Price range is $15 to $20.

(2) From 1960 through 1968, many cities across the country issued Sunday television supplements that depicted the characters of *The Andy Griffith Show* on their covers. The cost of these hard-to-find collectibles ranges from $20 to $40. Many of these feature rare photos and original art work.

(3) The 1961 Capitol Records album "Songs, Themes and Laughs from the Andy Griffith Show." This record was produced by Tom Morgan, and all of the music was conducted by Earle Hagen. The songs on the album are "The Andy Griffith Theme," "Jack, The Giant Killer," "Flop Eared Mule," "Ellie's Theme," "Sourwood Mountain," "The Manhunt," "The Fishin' Hole," "Aunt Bee," "The

New River Train," "Mayberry March," "Cindy," and "Barney's Hoe Down." The price range on this very enjoyable piece of memorabilia is $75 to $125.

(4) In the early 1960s, two coloring books were issued by the Saalfield Artcraft Company: *Ronny Howard of the Andy Griffith Show: Pictures to Color* (which features a cartoon picture of Opie drinking a soda, with small pictures of Andy, Barney and Aunt Bee in the background) and *The Andy Griffith Show Coloring Book* (which features a cartoon picture of Opie holding a baseball bat with Andy and Barney in the background). These coloring books are very rare and command premium prices (if you can locate them). Be prepared to pay over $100.00 for each.

(5) In 1961 and 1962, Dell Comic Books issued two comic books featuring *The Andy Griffith Show*. Like the coloring books, these comics are extremely difficult to locate today, and the price range is at least equal to that of the coloring books. The first one, dated Jan.—Mar., 1961, features Andy and Opie on the cover. The second one is dated Apr.—June, 1962, and depicts Andy, Opie, and Aunt Bee on the cover. It also has a small picture of Andy and Barney at the courthouse in the lower right hand corner.

(6) A black-and-white, 7 x 9" autographed photo of Andy Griffith and Ronny Howard as Andy and Opie Taylor was issued in the early 1960s. The price range is approximately $50 to $75.

(7) A writing tablet issued in the early 1960s has a picture of Andy and Opie on the cover. It is rather odd that Andy has a large owl perched on his right shoulder. Price range is $40 to $50.

(8) In the early 1960s, one of the sponsors of the show, Post Cereals, featured Andy Griffith on the back of its Corn Flakes and Grape Nuts cereal boxes. These hard-to-find cereal boxes cost between $50 and $75 today.

In recent years, promotional items from the show have occasionally slipped into the market. One item in particular is a rerun promotional folder sent to television stations. The price for this rare item can run into the $100 range.

Today, there are two main sources for all kinds of items related to *The Andy Griffith Show*. The top source is the Mayberry Collection. This company is owned and operated by two long-time fans of *The Andy Griffith Show*, Mendy Abrahamson and Greg Akers, and is licensed by Mayberry Enterprises. The catalog is updated as new collectibles are added. Among the items in the Mayberry Collection are Mayberry Union High varsity jackets (these beautiful jackets are identical to the ones worn by the cast members on the February 1993 CBS reunion special), all types of t-shirts, sweat shirts,

and golf shirts, assorted caps, Barney boxer shorts, Aunt Bee's apron, and a khaki sheriff shirt. Also available are badges, patches, coffee mugs of your favorite characters, ceramic pie trivets, pennants, posters, postcards, clocks, watches, key chains, books, license plate holders, and the list goes on.

The Mayberry Collection catalog has many video tapes that are currently on the market. These videos were produced by the leading manufacturer of all Mayberry tapes, United American Video Corporation of Charlotte, North Carolina. UAV strives to maintain a high quality of video and tries to preserve the entire episode, including the opening and closing scenes, which are routinely lost in most syndication packages available on television today. Some of the tapes are single episodes, while others contain three, four, five, and even ten episodes. All of them are reasonably priced. The multi-episode tapes contain shows featuring a particular character or theme, such as "Barney the Love God," "Opie's Misadventures," "Floyd's Hair-Raising Adventures," and "Mayberry Music." There are numerous "Best Of" tapes, featuring Ernest T., the Darlings, Andy, Barney, Goober, Gomer, and others.

For a catalog or information, call the Mayberry Collection at 1-800-933-2357, or write Mendy Abrahamson and Greg Akers at Hometown TV, Inc., 10016 International Blvd., Cincinnati, Ohio 45246-4839. They also have catalogs for *Gilligan's Island* and *The Beverly Hillbillies*.

The other main source for locating souvenirs of *The Andy Griffith Show* by mail is *The Bullet*, which is the official newsletter of the Andy Griffith Show Rerun Watchers Club. This newsletter began in 1982 and is issued quarterly by Jim Clark. It contains numerous stories on the cast and crew, information about fan clubs, and interviews. Within *The Bullet* is a shopper's guide that has many items for sale, such as Series I, II and III of the Pacific Cards set (described later in this section); licensed t-shirts, by UAV Corporation and Talking Toys, including the popular "Pink Floyd (The Barber) Deep Purple" shirt; many musical recordings; books; officially licensed Mayberry caps; and finally, numerous episodes on video tape. If you would like to join The Andy Griffith Show Rerun Watchers Club and receive *The Bullet*, send a check ($8.00 per year) to TAGSRWC, 9 Music Square South, Suite 146, Nashville, Tennessee 37203-3203.

In July of 1994, a new newsletter on *The Andy Griffith Show* appeared on the scene. This one is called *The Mayberry Times* and contains stories and interviews about the show. It also has two sections, "The Collectors Corner" and "Scoby's Trading Post," in which collectibles are discussed and numerous items, including original record albums by stars of the series, are available. The newsletter is published by Mike Creech, and a yearly subscription costs $6.00. Write to The Mayberry Times, 7762 East Co. Rd. 150 South, Plainfield, Indiana 46168.

In the mid 1980s, a newsletter called *The Mayberry Gazette* was published by John Meroney. This publication also sold photos, shirts, bumper stickers, and other memorabilia from the show. Unfortunately, the newsletter ceased publication at the end of 1991.

In late 1991, Mayberry Enterprises issued an *Andy Griffith Show* calendar for 1992. One of these calendars today is worth around $20.00.

In 1990, Hallmark Greeting Cards issued a few Father's Day cards featuring color photos of Andy and Opie. These cards are rather difficult to locate today. We have seen them at antique and curio shops for $10.00 to $20.00 each.

In 1990, McCalla/Lacking Products released an assortment of licensed lollipops that were available in many stores through 1993. The flavorful suckers were produced in Hickory, North Carolina, which is not too far from Andy Griffith's birthplace, Mount Airy, North Carolina. The lollipops had Mayberry-related names such as "Andy's Big Orange," "Nip It Lemon," "Otis' Pina Colada," "Opie's Bubblegum," "Gomer's Goll-ay Grape," "Floyd's Barber Cherry," "Aunt Bee's Blueberry," "Barney's Hot Cinnamon," "Andy's Outstanding Orange," "Raspberry Shazam!," "Thelma Lou's Tutti Fruiti," "Mayberry Watermelon," and "Ernest T.'s Sour Apple."

In 1992, All-Star Bobbins issued two extremely nice bobbin' head dolls of Sheriff Andy Taylor and Deputy Barney Fife by sculptor J.D. Bentley. These dolls were available through TAGSRWC's newsletter, *The Bullet*, as late as 1993. The cost was $35.00 for each bobbin' head. Since that time, the dolls have become more difficult to locate, so be prepared to pay a higher price today.

Speaking of figurines, in 1991, Mayberry's Homestead, which is located in Andy Griffith's hometown of Mount Airy, North Carolina, released three figurines. They are "Andy Goin' Fishin'," "Opie Goin' Fishin'," and "Aunt Bee Crocheting." each of these figurines is handcrafted in a mold taken from a wood and clay sculpture by folk artist Sandy Spillman and then painted by hand. The figurines were available through *The Bullet*, and they were $36.00 to $38.00 each. If you are able to locate them today, they will command a considerably higher price.

In 1992, the Hamilton Collection released the first collector's plates in honor of *The Andy Griffith*

Show. These collectibles are issued every six to eight weeks and cost $32.18 each, which includes shipping and handling. The plates are issued exclusively through the Hamilton Collection, and the artwork is done by Robert Tannenbaum. Each plate features a character from the show or honors a single episode. Eight plates have been issued thus far: "Sheriff Andy Taylor," "A Startling Conclusion," "Mayberry Sing-Along," "Aunt Bee's Kitchen," "An Explosive Situation," "Surprise! Surprise!," "Meeting Aunt Bee," and "Opie's Big Catch."

In 1990, Pacific Trading Cards issued a 110-card set of *The Andy Griffith Show*. This set was put together with great care and utilized a mixture of black-and-white and color photos from the show and from behind the scenes. The 1990 set is known as Series I and was well received by the public. In 1991, Pacific released Series II and III of the set, both containing 110 cards, making the entire collection a 330-card set. Today, these cards may be purchased through many sport card outlets (including Pacific Trading Cards) for a reasonable fee. The usual cost for Series I in mint condition is around $15.00, while Series II and III can be found for $10.00 per set.

In 1990, Ernst, Inc., located at 148 South Vinewood Street in Escondido, California 92029, issued the first one of their commemorative Mayberry mugs. It featured Andy and Opie at the fishing hole and was entitled "Fishin with Pa." In 1992, Ernest, Inc., issued a second mug. This one featured Andy and Barney at the courthouse. Both mugs are made of porcelain and stand 5 inches tall and are 3 1/2 inches in diameter. They were sold from 1990 through 1993 in *The Bullet* but have since been discontinued. The price for each mug in 1992 was $22.50. Prices for the mugs today will be higher.

In conjunction with the above-mentioned mugs, Ernst, Inc., also issued the same two pictures on plaques that were suitable for hanging on the wall. The 9 inch x 7 inch ceramic plaques feature the same outstanding full-color artwork as the mugs. They are framed in solid hardwood. The costs for these plaques in 1992 was $27.00. As with the mugs, if you are able to find them today, the price will be considerably higher.

In 1994, Hawthorne Architectural Register, from Niles, Illinois, released a lighted porcelain sculpture of the Mayberry Courthouse. This hand-painted sculpture is 4 3/4 inches tall and costs approximately $40.00. Other items are available.

Several books about *The Andy Griffith Show* are currently available at your local bookstore or directly from the publishers. Each book approaches the series from a different angle and contains unique information, so it is worthwhile and enjoyable to peruse them all.

The first book, written by Dr. Richard Kelly, is *The Andy Griffith Show*, published by John F. Blair, Publisher. Since its first appearance in 1981, the book has been revised and expanded. This is the definitive book on the creation of the series, and a great behind-the-scenes look at the production of the show is also included. The book includes, in its entirety, the script for an unfilmed episode entitled "The Wandering Minstrel," written by Harvey Bullock and Ray Saffian Allen.

In 1985, St. Martin's Press published *The Andy Griffith Show Book* by Jim Clark (the editor of *The Bullet*, the official newsletter of the Andy Griffith Show Rerun Watchers Club) and Ken Beck. This book takes the reader into the real world of Mayberry, and includes photos, trivia tests, and other interesting features.

The third entry is called *Mayberry, My Hometown*. Written by Stephen J. Spignesi and published in 1987 by Popular Culture, Inc., this large book comprises a complete A — Z encyclopedia on Mayberry. It also has some great interviews with cast members and some useful charts on the different characters and seasons.

Next up is the extremely popular *Aunt Bee's Mayberry Cookbook*. This one was also written by Ken Beck and Jim Clark and was published in 1991 by Rutledge Hill Press. This book contains over 300 Aunt Bee–style recipes. What makes this cookbook extra special is that about 40 of the recipes were provided by cast and crew members of the series.

In 1993, Ken Beck and Jim Clark released a companion to the cookbook entitled *Postcards from Aunt Bee's Mayberry Cookbook*, also published by Rutledge Hill Press. In this volume, 30 of the recipes from the cookbook are reproduced on detachable postcards. Each of the postcards features a photo of one of the cast members, plus the recipe.

Also in 1993, the Summit Group published *Barney Fife's Guide to Life, Love and Self-Defense* by Len and John Oszustowicz. This 165-page, hardcover book contains advice on living, from the lips of Bernard P. Fife.

In 1994, Lee Pfeiffer's *The Official Andy Griffith Show Scrapbook* was published by Citadel Press. This book is loaded with photos, interviews, an episode guide, and numerous stories about cast members. It is an easy-to-read and interesting book.

The second book released in 1994 was *Inside Mayberry: The Andy Griffith Show Handbook*. This informative book is written by Dan Harrison and Bill Habeeb and published by HarperPerennial. The book is loaded with trivia from the series. There are also interviews with cast members and writers, who discuss the behind-the-scenes happenings during the production of the show.

BIBLIOGRAPHY

BOOKS

Andrews, Bart. *The I Love Lucy Book.* Garden City, N.Y.: Doubleday, 1985.

Beck, Ken, and Jim Clark. *The Andy Griffith Show Book.* New York: St. Martin's, 1985.

_____. *Aunt Bee's Mayberry Cookbook.* Nashville: Rutledge Hill, 1991.

_____. *Postcards from Aunt Bee's Mayberry Cookbook.* Nashville: Rutledge Hill, 1993.

Brooks, Tim. *The Complete Directory to Prime Time TV Stars, 1946–Present.* New York: Ballantine, 1987.

_____, and Earle Marsh. *The Complete Directory to Prime Time Network TV Shows, 1946–Present,* 4th ed. New York: Ballantine, 1988. First published in 1979.

Castleman, Harry, and Walter J. Podriziak. *Harry and Wally's Favorite TV Shows.* New York: Prentice Hall, 1989.

Cox, Stephen. *The Beverly Hillbillies.* Chicago: Contemporary, 1988.

_____. *The Munsters: Television's First Family of Fright.* Chicago: Contemporary, 1989.

_____. *The Hooterville Handbook: A Viewer's Guide to Green Acres.* New York: St. Martin's, 1993.

David, Nina. *Who's Who in TV: 1974-1975.* Phoenix, Ariz.: Oryx, 1976.

Dawidziak, Mark. *From the Columbo Phile: A Casebook.* New York: Mysterious, 1988-1989.

Eisner, Joel. *The Official Batman Batbook.* Chicago: Contemporary, 1986.

_____, and David Krinsky. *Television Comedy Series: An Episode Guide to 153 Sitcoms in Syndication.* Jefferson, N.C.: McFarland, 1984.

Grant, Lee, with Jean Carson. *More Than Just a Fun Girl from Mt. Pilot: The Jean Carson Story.* Memphis: Koren and Koren, 1994.

Green, Joey. *The Unofficial Gilligan's Island Handbook.* New York: Warner, 1988.

_____. *The Get Smart Handbook.* New York: Collier, 1993.

_____. *The Partridge Family Album: The Official Guide to America's Grooviest Television Family.* New York: HarperPerennial, 1994.

Gross, Edward. *Growing Up in the Sixties: The Wonder Years.* Las Vegas, Nevada: Pioneer, 1990.

Hake, Ted. *Hake's Guide to TV Collectibles: An Illustrated Price Guide.* Rapnor, Pa.: Wallace-Homestead, 1990.

Harrison, Dan, and Bill Habeeb. *Inside Mayberry: The Andy Griffith Show Handbook.* New York: HarperPerennial, 1994.

Katz, Ephraim. *The Film Encyclopedia.* New York: Perigee, 1979.

Kelleher, Brian, and Diana Merrill. *The Perry Mason TV Show Book.* New York: St. Martin's, 1987.

Kelly, Richard. *The Andy Griffith Show,* 4th ed. Winston-Salem, N.C.: John F. Blair, 1984. First published in 1981.

McCrohan, Donna. *The Life and Times of Maxwell Smart.* New York: St. Martin's, 1988.

McNeil, Alex. *Total Television,* 3d ed. New York: Penguin, 1991. First published in 1980.

Nalven, Nancy. *The Famous Mr. Ed.* New York: Warner, 1991.

Oszustowicz, Len, and John Oszustowicz. *Barney Fife's Guide to Life, Love and Self-Defense.* Fort Worth, Texas: Summit Group, 1993.

O'Neil, Thomas. *The Emmy's.* New York: Penguin, 1992.

Parish, James Robert, and Vincent Terrace. *The Complete Actors' Television Credits, 1948-1988, Volume I: Actors,* 2d ed. Metuchen, N.J.: Scarecrow, 1989.

Pfeiffer, Lee. *The Official Andy Griffith Show Scrapbook.* New York: Citadel, 1994.

Pilato, Herbie J. *The Bewitched Book.* New York: Dell, 1992.

Robertson, Ed. *Maverick: Legend of the West.* Beverly Hills, Calif.: Pomegranate, 1994.

Sackett, Susan. *Prime Time Hits.* New York: Billboard, 1993.

Schow, David J., and Jeffrey Frentzen. *The Outer Limits: The Official Companion.* New York: Ace Science Fiction, 1986.

Shapiro, Melany. *Bonanza: The Unofficial Story of the Ponderosa*. Las Vegas, Nevada: Pioneer, 1993.
Spignesi, Stephen J. *Mayberry, My Hometown*. Ann Arbor, Mich.: Popular Culture, Ink, 1987.
Terrace, Vincent. *Encyclopedia of Television: Series, Pilots and Specials*. *Volumes I and III*. New York: New York Zoetrope, 1986.
Van Hise, James. *The Addams Family Revealed: An Unauthorized Look at America's Spookiest Family*. Las Vegas, Nevada: Pioneer, 1991.
Waldron, Vince. *Classic Sitcoms*. New York: Macmillan, 1987.
Weissman, Ginny, and Coyne Steven Sanders. *The Dick Van Dyke Show*. New York: St. Martin's, 1983.
White, Patrick J. *The Complete Mission Impossible Dossier*. New York: Avon, 1991.
Williams, Barry, with Chris Kreski. *Growing Up Brady: I Was a Teenage Greg*. New York: HarperPerennial, 1992.
Zicree, Marc Scott. *The Twilight Zone Companion*. New York: Bantam, 1982.

ARTICLES

TV Guide

1/28/61. Edson, Lee. "Andy Griffith: Cornball with a Steel-Trap Mind" (first of two parts).
5/12/62. Gehman, Richard. "TV Guide Interviews Don Knotts: A Mouse of a Different Color."
5/11/63. "The Andy Griffith Show Has H.A.Q."
3/21/64. "Jim Nabors: The Sylacauga Flash."
4/24/65. Dern, Marian. "Andy Griffith Ponders His Future."
6/4/66. Condon, Maurice. "Andy Griffith: He Never Left Home."
10/8/66. Fox, William Price, Jr. "That Jim Nabors Assignment."
5/20/67. Raddatz, Leslie. "Aneta Corsaut's Cluttered Life."
10/21/67. Hobson, Dick. "Fright Has Paid Off for Don Knotts."
7/13/68. Lewis, Richard Warren. "The Wondrous Andy Griffith TV Machine" (first of two parts).
3/15/69. Durslag, Melvin. "Ken Berry, Who Took Over Mayberry."
10/24/70. Raddatz, Leslie. "Look Who's a Star! Don Knotts!"
1/9/71. Davidson, Bill. "Andy Griffith's $3,500,000 Misunderstanding."

Other Periodicals

Bakke, Dave. "One Hundred Reasons to Love Andy." *The State Journal—Register, Heartland Magazine*. September 20, 1991.
Clark, Jim. *The Bullet: Official Newsletter of the Andy Griffith Show Rerun Watchers Club*. 1987-1994.
Creech, Mike. *The Mayberry Times*. 1994.
Meroney, John. *The Mayberry Gazette*. 1989-1991.

Other Sources

"Andy Griffith/American Originals." Audio cassette (C4 0777 7 98476 4 8) released by Capitol Records, a subsidiary of Capitol-EMI Music, Hollywood, California, 1992.
"A Great Place: Mount Airy and Surry County, North Carolina." Informational brochure issued by the town of Mount Airy, North Carolina, 1993.
"The Mayberry Confidential: Official Newsletter of Mayberry Days." Published by the Mayberry Surry Arts Council, 1991-1993.
"Second Annual Mayberry Squad Car Rendezvous." Publicity brochure issued by Wally's Service, 10870 Circle Hill Road, Bradford, Ohio, 1994.
"Songs, Themes and Laughs from the Andy Griffith Show." Record album (T 1611) released by Capitol Records, Los Angeles, California, 1961.
"Songs of the Civil War." Audio cassette (CT 48607) released by Sony Music Music Entertainment/Columbia Records, New York, N.Y., 1991.
"The Surry Arts Council Presents: Mayberry Days." Publicity brochure issued by the town of Mount Airy, North Carolina, 1994.

INDEX OF NAMES